# Constitution-Making under UN Auspices

# Constitution-Making under UN Auspices

*Fostering Dependency in Sovereign Lands*

Vijayashri Sripati

OXFORD
UNIVERSITY PRESS

OXFORD
UNIVERSITY PRESS

Oxford University Press is a department of the University of Oxford. It furthers the University's objective of excellence in research, scholarship, and education by publishing worldwide. Oxford is a registered trademark of Oxford University Press in the UK and in certain other countries.

Published in India by
Oxford University Press
22 Workspace, 2nd Floor, 1/22 Asaf Ali Road, New Delhi 110 002, India



First Edition published in 2020



ISBN-13 (print edition): 978-0-19-949802-4
ISBN-10 (print edition): 0-19-949802-4

ISBN-13 (eBook): 978-0-19-909836-1
ISBN-10 (eBook) 0-19-909836-0

Typeset in Dante MT Std 10.5/13
by The Graphics Solution, New Delhi 110 092
Printed in India by Rakmo Press, New Delhi 110 020

*Pithru Devo Bhava*
(Father equals God)
I dedicate this book to
my dearest grandfather, Sripati Sarangapani,
from whom I inherited my passion
for learning, writing, public speaking, and public service
and to my dearest late father, Sripati Rammohan Rao
who selflessly nurtured my passions

# Contents

# A Note on all the Tables

All tables are compiled by the author. However, since UNCA sires ITA and I use Ralph Wilde's Method to fit UNCA into Wilde's Family (i.e., my Framework), his book *International Territorial Administration: How Trusteeship and the Civilizing Mission Never Went Away* (2008) became an inevitable source for Foreign Territorial Administration, FTA/International Territorial Administration, ITA.

Tables 1.2 to 1.4 have the same source: Guidance Note of the Secretary-General: United Nations Assistance to Constitution-making Processes (2009) and other relevant documents.

Tables 3.1 and 9.1 use the following common acronyms: WL Constitution = the Western Liberal constitution; LON = League of Nations; T = Trusteeship; CM = Civilizing mission; MM = Modernizing mission; FM = Free markets; ROL = Rule of Law; SOC = Standards of Civilization; WR = Women's Rights; and PILP = Public International Law and Policy; and GG = Good Governance. Next, in both tables, the terms Western liberal constitution's internationalized making and internationalized constitution-making are used interchangeably. Finally regarding these two tables' sources, for the 'standards of civilization' see Gerrit Gong, *The standard of civilization in international society of states* (OUP, 1984). Vijayashri Sripati, the author, offers all the remaining insights.

# Tables and Figures

## Tables

## Figures

# Foreword

I am delighted to write this foreword for Vijayashri Sripati, who has long been an ardent and conscientious advocate for human rights. A constitution is the highest legal expression of a state's vision and identity, and therefore it seems implausible that international organizations would regularly sculpt a state's own constitution. But in this enlightening book, Sripati proves that this implausibility is in fact true. She explores United Nations Constitutional Assistance (UNCA), a 1949 colonial trusteeship programme through which the UN internationalized the Western liberal constitutions. UNCA's rise after 1989 was *the most significant development of that era*, rendering UNCA the world's key restructuring mechanism. As Sripati shows, its championing of the Western liberal constitution strongly shaped developments in all other sectors within UNCA client states, from the political, juridical, and electoral, to the parliamentary and the security-related. Despite Sripati's strong evidence for this phenomenon, international law and constitutional law scholars have unwittingly missed UNCA for the reason that UNCA spans both their subjects and areas that overlap two fields often end up attended by neither. Now, UNCA falls within then ascent but fast-growing sub-field of international law known as international constitutional law. It is a discipline pioneered by among others, two scholars I know and respect. They are the late Louis Henkin and Wiktor Osiatynski.

Sripati outlines a novel constitutional approach to the history of international law: She conceptualizes the Western liberal constitution's internationalization by foreign states and pre-1945 international organizations as a "policy institution" or established practice. She deftly shows how UNCA has served to create within developing states constitutional regimes that have the effect of throwing open their resources for multinational corporations or what she calls the transnational capitalist class.

It is undeniable but also deplorable that globalization re-shapes developing states' *constitutional and legal* systems along Western lines, thus facilitating the entry of these global corporations. Because of their vast resources, these companies undertake several activities and perform functions which have serious repercussions and impinge upon the human rights of Third World people. Therein lies the enduring consequences that global restructuring poses for them, especially in relation to economic and social rights. This is a valid point well elaborated by Sripati in Chapters 5–7.

To my mind, there cannot be a fair process of globalization unless it is accompanied by an effective Rule of Law structure. The quintessential principle of Rule of Law is the protection and promotion of human rights and human dignity of all human beings irrespective of religion, caste, sex or colour.

Without an equitable global order Third World peoples will be unable to freely exercise their right to pursue their all-round development. Sripati's pioneering book will not only inform and provoke but motivate remedial action. It is an outstanding study and fills a major and important gap in the relevant discourses. It is a must read for all who value human rights and work for their meaningful enforcement.

Soli J. Sorabjee
Former Attorney General for India (1998–2004)
Member, UN Sub-Commission on Promotion &
Protection of Human Rights (1998–2006)
23 January 2019

# Preface

This book on United Nations Constitutional Assistance (UNCA) is a milestone in my academic life, which has been fuelled by inspiration. From 1949 till the present, the UN has assisted colonies and/or states, in response to their supposed incapacities, to adopt the Western liberal constitution. The vehicle for this activity is UNCA, which falls within international constitutional law (ICL), a fast-growing but still nascent sub-field of international law. This volume is the first full account of UNCA and its colonial origins, from its birth in 1949 to the present day. Although it is rooted in my 2010 doctoral dissertation, it is a wholly new work, written from 2013 to 2017. My interest in the field, in fact, dates from when I was 14.

In a nutshell, this work shines a light on an underexamined, indeed consistently overlooked, phenomenon in the post-colonial age: the activities of UNCA. Through the vehicle of constitution-making, UNCA has promoted the adoption of Western-style economic, political, and juridical values and institutions in the politically weak and economically poor regions of the world. Whatever the motivations for these activities, their effect has been to establish in these states many neocolonial concepts and characteristics. The irony of course is that UNCA-recipients-states are all sovereign nations, and the legal device that is continuing these colonial concepts and characteristics is none other than constitutions—the basic charters of states' independence.

But why did a 14-year-old become enthralled by this unlikely field? Quite simply, it was at that age that civics and international human rights fell in love with me. The civics school curriculum covered the Indian Constitution, and I learned about international human rights through a high-school programme sponsored by the Indian Federation of United Nations Associations. These two subjects found me, enchanted me, and chased me wherever I went. They still do. At 15, at the Mock

UN Session, I donned an *odni* (veil) and played the female version of then-Afghan president Babrak Karmal, passionately *supporting* Soviet intervention in Afghanistan! At 17, I published my first article advocating the inclusion of international human rights in the civics curriculum ('World Problems in School Curriculum', *The Hindu*, India's national English daily, 28 November 1983). Like the star of Bethlehem, these subjects have guided me for the last 35 years.

This book is a karmic manifestation of my childhood passion for constitutions. Thinking about the genesis of the book, as well as the five UNCA-related factors described subsequently, has helped me to appreciate the contributions of those I thank here and in my acknowledgements. These individuals and organizations are karmic in that they helped me in varied ways to realize my childhood dream. I find it joyful to thank them, and I can do so only in spiritual terms. I consider the five factors discussed subsequently karmic as well, and therefore also frame them in spiritual terms. In this way, this preface provides a spiritual context for the acknowledgements section.

Four allied Indian spiritual concepts resonate with me. The first, *Budhi karma anusari*, posits that one's passion foretells one's destiny, for the Universe is waiting to conspire with you to manifest your desires. The second, *Satya meva Vijaya-te*, reminds us that manifesting one's desires requires remaining inspired, for 'truth alone will triumph'. The third spiritual concept, *Karma yogi*, encourages us to pursue our passions yet remain 'detached' from the 'fruits' of our karma (actions), leaving it to the Universe to decide the outcome. The fourth, *Vasudeva kutumbakam*, considers the whole Universe as one family, since we all are divinely connected.

Equally inspirational to me is a vibrant story from the Mahabharata, the famous Indian Sanskrit epic. The tale unfolds in the ancient Indian city of Hastinapur where there lived a renowned *acharya* (teacher) named Dronacharya, who taught archery only to the royals. In the forest, overlooking the opulent marble palace, lived Ekalavya—a *shudra* (lower-caste Hindu). Ekalavya longed to learn archery. But as an 'untouchable' he was shunned. Undeterred, he sculpted Dronacharya's bust out of clay, mounting it in front of his thatched hut. He worshipped it daily before practising archery. (Note: Hindus practice idol worship, and equate teachers to God—Gurudev.) Years sped by. One day, Dronacharya and King Dhritharashtra happened to witness

Ekalavya's martial prowess and were astounded. In robe and crown, the King stepped down from his throne and asked Ekalavya: Who is your teacher? 'There he is!' said Ekalavya, pointing to Dronacharya.

The five UNCA-related circumstances discussed below shaped my quest for learning along the lines of Ekalavya. Indeed, like Ekalavya, I taught myself a subject, keeping in the forefront of my mind the great teachers of my field, using them for both guidance and inspiration.

First, during the 1990s, I was unable to learn in a comprehensive way how Western constitutional law and international law intersected. The field that we now know as 'international constitutional law' or 'global constitutionalism' did not exist. Second, as a result, I was compelled to pursue my interests through three graduate programmes, one each in the United States, United Kingdom, and Canada over a 16-year period (1990–2006). Third, as we will see, these programmes, too, did not fully help. International constitutional law still eluded me. Why?

Point four offers the answer. From the 1990s to the 2000s, American constitutional law and public international law (including human rights) that historically ally, evolved academically speaking, in parallel ways. (To some extent they still do not intersect). Consequently, few American scholars realized how their own constitutions were integral to international law. Conversely, most international law scholars overlooked the constitutional dimension of such post-1989 developments as the rule of law, peace-building, and UN territorial administration, ITA. Happily however, during the 1990s a few American constitutional scholars, such as Dick Howard and the late Louis Henkin, and visiting scholars, such as Upendra Baxi, Rett Ludwikowski, and the late Wiktor Osiatyński, taught courses in constitutionalism and human rights, including their comparative dimension.

These pioneers enabled students like me to explore the intersections between constitutional law and international law. (Tellingly, their courses were small seminars rather than main curriculum offerings.)

I learned about those intersections in two stages: first, in the mid-1990s and then in the mid-2000s.

In 1990, on a scholarship from the Rotary Foundation (United States) I took my first LL.M., in international human rights, at American University's Washington College of Law, WCL. Four years later, this same school opened to me the wonders of international constitutional law. I audited for a few weeks Professor Baxi's thought-provoking 'Comparative Constitutionalism' course, which focused on the internationalization of the Western liberal constitution by foreign states.

In 2001, I heard about Professor Osiatyński and his signature course on constitutionalism and human rights. I contacted him at the University of Chicago Law School, where he was then teaching his course. (He had offered his course at Central European University, CEU since 1995, and at other universities, including Harvard and Stanford.) Wiktor kindly couriered me his course materials, and his student, Ilya Shapiro, emailed me his class notes. Wiktor encouraged me to keep in touch, and in touch I kept, with Wiktor virtually 'adopting' me as his student. In 2003, armed with his materials, I enrolled at the University of Alberta Faculty of Law, determined to formulate a doctoral proposal in my dream subject.

My determination paid off. Guided by Wiktor (from Warsaw), I arrived at UNCA, which is the Western liberal constitution's internationalization by the UN! (Nothing much, other than a 1970 book on UNCA's birth, existed then.) In this way, in 2006, I finally began my doctoral studies in international constitutional law at Osgoode Hall Law School in Toronto.

UNCA is an international constitutional law topic par excellence. The increasing globalization of the 2000s (that entails the Western liberal constitution's internationalization) facilitated this theme's exploration. Baxi and Wiktor are the two scholars who helped me to so arrive at UNCA.

But the story hardly ends there. The Sripati elders, particularly my father, long drilled into me that quality research hinges on the questions one asks and the method one uses to answer them. Analysing UNCA requires a method that recognizes the Western liberal constitution's *salience*. In 2008, the 'policy institution—purposive analysis' method designed by international law scholar Ralph Wilde (see *International territorial administration: How trusteeship and the civilizing mission never went away*, 2008) enabled me to do just that. Herein lie Baxi's, Osiatyński's and Wilde's karmic roles.

Fifth, although UNCA projects mushroomed after 1989, the UN had long shrouded UNCA's use under confusing terms such as 'electoral assistance'. Given this, when I commenced my doctoral studies on post-1989 UNCA, I was both relying on fragmentary sources and virtually creating new knowledge. But as the maxim goes, 'The power of an idea whose time has come is really the power of the Spirit at work.' Happily, the UN made UNCA public in 2009. Relying on the UN's 2009 UNCA Guidance Note, I completed my dissertation on time in 2010. But I had merely touched upon UNCA. I was determined to continue these explorations; I wanted to place UNCA at the centre stage. Happily again, the Universe cooperated; after 2012, UNCA documents became increasingly available. Seizing the opportunity, in 2013 I began the four-year task of writing of this book. Wiktor's advice, materials, encouragement, and his signature CEU course, which I delightedly audited in the fall of 2007, made this book possible. (Similarly, in the fall of 2016, I visited Yale Law School only to meet Justice Dieter Grimm who readily understood why UNCA has remained uncharted. He sympathized with my predicament, and kindly advised me on how best to proceed with my book.)

Indeed, what Dronacharya was to Ekalavya, Professors Baxi and Wiktor, and Ralph's book, are to me. I, an Indian Hindu, pursuing my childhood passion, eventually found teachers from all backgrounds to help me: an Indian Hindu, a British Christian, and a Polish Catholic, who in turn learned how those subjects were connected from his American guru Louis Henkin.

Dearest *Gurudevas* Baxi, Osiatyñski, and Wilde: How might I best pay you my tribute? I believe I can pay it forward; do what you did for me: selflessly help others manifest their karmic dreams. With profound gratitude from me and my late father, affectionately, your karmic student.

# Acknowledgements

In the spiritual world, everything happens for a purpose. There are no coincidences. I gratefully acknowledge the generosity of the Rotary Foundation, United States; the Foreign and Commonwealth office of the British Government; the Danish International Development Agency; The Alberta Law Foundation, Edmonton, Canada; Osgoode Hall Law School, Toronto, and its Jack and Mae Nathanson Centre on Transitional Human Rights, Crime and Security Studies; and the Social Sciences Humanities and Research Council (SSHRC), Canada.

These organizations are karmic in that they sent me to institutions where scholars who would help me realize my destiny showed up. For example, with the British Chevening Scholarship I went to the University of Hull (1995–6) where I studied international environmental law and therefore connected in 1998 with Armin Rosencranz, an environmental law professor whose unalloyed friendship and superb advice have since been critical for all my successes including this book's publication. Hull is also where I began my conversations about constitutionalism with political theorists, Noel Sullivan and Bikhu Parekh, whose crisp counsel over the years has been hugely beneficial in writing this book.

Similarly, SSHRC made my scholarship tenable only in Canada and, so, tied me to Toronto (Osgoode Hall) where I met visiting professor Jim Tully whose seminal work became one of the building blocks for this book while my dissertation supervisor, Obiora Okafor, recognized that I was pursuing my 'calling'. Also being in Toronto helped me meet three scholars at University of Toronto (UOT)—Robert O. Matthews, Peter Russell, and David Cameron—all of whom selflessly supported what Professor Russell referred to as my 'pioneering study'. In 2006, UNCA was an unknown peace-building activity, and Professor Matthews' fall 2006 UOT peace-building course enabled me to establish this point. Through the good offices of one of his former students, Neçla Tsirgi, he also helped me secure a crucial in-house UN document. Professor Russell lent his constitution-making expertise to my doctoral committee, and the SSHRC connected me with the world-class University of Toronto which became my home for post-doctoral research under Professor Cameron. (Despite the valuable support the aforementioned scholars lent, let me add that the 'civilizing mission' theme of this book is entirely my own.)

Sometimes, my karmic destiny unfolded in an unexpected way: I chose some scholars who ended up choosing me. For example, in 2005, due to his hectic schedule, Yash Ghai declined my invitation to visit the University of Alberta to enchant us with a talk on constitution-making. But then he graciously invited me to speak at his constitution-making workshop at Wisconsin Law School, where I met a host of karmic friends: Said Arjomand, Guido Galli, Makau Mutua, Muna Ndulo, Boaventura de Sousa Santos, Alexei Troicheva, and Crawford Young. A special thanks to all for their sound advice.

Guido Galli and Ramaswamy Sudarshan recommended a few United Nations officials who in turn connected me to many other UN officials, UN experts, activists, and stakeholders. Among the officials are: Brian Atwood, Bakhodir Burkhanov, Peter Barwick, Jamal Benomar, Gabriel Dava, Mario Buil-Merce, Surya Dhungel, Filippo Di-Capegra, Nicholas Haysom, Robert Husbands, Josse M. Jassi, Sakuntala Kagardimar, Fred Mwanthagere, Cristiano Papile, Frederick Rohorua, Thusitha Pilapitiya, Robert Pulver, Bertrand Ramcharan, Alvaro Rodriguez, Charmaine Rodriguez, Roland Rich, Francois Simard, John M. Tuhaika, and Mohammad Bilal Waqad. The experts and activists include: Abdullah Abdhullah, Louis Aucoin, Michelle Brandt, Jill Cottrell, Justice L. Chikopa, Wazma Frogh, Shalmali Guttal, Malalai Joya, Kåra Lode, Hashim Kamali, Grant Kippen, Gianni Magazzeni, William Malley, Anthony Regan, Katy Le Roy, Barnett Rubin, Andras Sajo, Amos Sawyer, Seema Samar, Susanne Schmeidl, and Amin Tarzi. Special thanks to you all. This book may be a critique of the United Nations Constitutional Assistance but not a critique of your honesty and professionalism.

At David Kennedy's invitation, I spent 2007–8 at the European Law Research Institute at Harvard Law School, where I had productive conversations with him, Duncan Kennedy, Noah Feldman, Peter Wallenstein, and Swanee Hunt. Thanks to all.

The Universe has great organizing intelligence. It *sends* you the guidance you need. For example: The topic of Bretton Woods Institutions and constitutional design is severely under-researched. Two years before commencing my doctoral studies, I received a karmic gift from Warsaw: Wiktor's glittering Christmas card and a book containing Issa Shivji's chapter on the aforementioned theme. Another example: Although writing a book on UNCA required a comprehensive UNCA inventory that was non-existent in 2010, my 2012 publication provided a UNCA inventory for 1989–2011. But what about before 1989? Again, the Universe responded. In 2012, Carsten Stahn and Henning Melber invited me to contribute to their book about UN Secretary General Dag Hammarskjöld. My chapter on why and how Hammarskjöld pioneered UNCA in Congo (1960) helped me fill in those pre-1989 blanks.

I thank these scholars for generously assisting me with particular enquiries: William Bain, Simon Chesterman, Davide Rodogno (Crete), Mark Mazower, John McLaren and James Phillips (Chapters 2–3); Daniel Bradlow and Craig Murphy (Chapter 5); Alex Thier and Amalendu Misra (Afghanistan); and the late Saubhagya Shah (Nepal, Chapter 6). A special thanks to noted historian Paul Halliday who read Chapters 2–3 and provided acute insights.

For providing me opportunities to present and discuss my ideas, I thank the event organizers at the Academic Council on the United Nations System (ACUNS); American Society of International Law—International Organizations Interest Group; International Association of Constitutional Law; International Law Association; Albany Law School, State University of New York; Central European University; Harvard University; Osgoode Hall Law School; York University; University of British Columbia; University of Toronto; The Harriet Tubman Institute, York University; and the School of Oriental and African Studies (SOAS), University of London.

The following scholars kindly discussed my ideas with me: Tony Anghie, Nathanial Berman, David Chandler, Christine Chinkin, Rajeev Dhawan, Martin Doonbros, Jan Erik-Lane, Jeremy Farrell, Trevor Farrow, Gregory Fox, James Gathii, David Grewal, Joanna Harrington, Martii Koskiennemi, Sari Kouvo, Bert Lockwood, Rett Ludwikowski, Susan Marks, Aziz Rana, Linda Reif, Manoj Kumar Sinha, Jim Tully, David Claire Williams, Justices Dieter Grimm, Sujata Manohar, and M.N. Venkatchaliah; and the late Gisbert Flanz, Gerry Gall, and Louis

Henkin (international constitutional law) and Dennis Davis, Gerrit Gong, Gus van Harten, Scott Newton, M. Sornarajah, Louis Pauly, Moin Yahya, and Robert Wai (international political economy). A huge thanks. Justice Grimm mentioned Anne Peters as one of the few contemporary experts in international constitutional law. I am determined to stay inspired so that the Universe connects me with her!

Over the years, I have received moral support from: O.P. Vaish and Sudarshan Aggarwal, and professors Jaffer Hussain, A. Jayagovind, Sam Bernsen, David Chandler, Moin Yahya, Wayne Renke, Craig Scott, and Trevor Farrow. I offer my profound gratitude.

Thanks also to the library staffs at the University of Alberta, Harvard University, the University of Toronto and the *Bibliothèque nationale de* France. I am particularly grateful to Kim Wilson and Shelley Brown (UOA), Graham Bradshaw (UOT), Nathan Wolfe (UOT) and Rebecca Melhem (France).

I also thank my students at Osgoode Hall Law School and the University of Toronto for feedback and ideas.

Francis Flaherty's *The Elements of Story: Field Notes on Nonfiction Writing* (2009) guided me in writing this book. I am truly blessed to have received Professor Flaherty's and Joe Shaw's editorial support. I thank the anonymous reviewers of this book for supporting its publication and providing helpful appraisals. Dr Vipan Chandra, Emeritus Professor of History and Asian Studies, Wheaton College, United States, helped me with choosing the book's title. Kulsum Zakir, Frank Flaherty and Alexei Troicheva helped me choose my jacket cover design. A special thanks to the commissioning, editorial, production, and design teams at Oxford University Press for their support.

My dearest late father created a scholarly and spiritual environment at home for which I can never fully thank him. I express immense gratitude to him and Leela Sripati (my mother), Bhanushri, Rajyashri, Pranay, Kaila Padma, and Arantxa for their unalloyed love and support. When I was growing up, my father's brother, the late Dr Sripati Chandrasekhar (name listed in this order: family name, given name), a scholar-statesman, deeply inspired me. I regret that I was unable to ask him, a master of manifesting destiny, to bless this book with a foreword. (Relatedly, many thanks to President Daniel Johnson of the University of Toledo for showing me my uncle's archives, the 'Chandrasekhar Collections', at his school's Ward M. Canaday Center.) But as usual, the Universe stepped in, providing this book with the blessings of Soli J. Sorabjee, an internationally acclaimed constitutional human rights expert and former UN Special Envoy. A special thanks to Sorabjee for graciously agreeing to write the foreword. What more can I ask for!

I am also indebted to A.V. Achar, Jaya and Janakiram, Raman Kaur, Frank Luce, Paul Livingston, the P.V. Raju family, Paul and Balbir Randhawa, Sambasiva Rao, Vikramaditya and Neeraja Reddy, Randy Schmidt, and Vikram Shah.

Despite my passion, I have at times become fatigued. Thanks to scholar Louis Pauly (Toronto), among others, for reminding me to 'persist'. Moreover, there have been numerous occasions when the right talk/book/scholar has appeared and I experienced a vigorous enthusiasm rising within me. This reinvigoration has prompted my students and many scholars—from Morton Krajeum (Denmark) and Joanna Harrington (Alberta), and Peter Russell (Toronto) to David Kennedy (Brown University) and Robert Wai, and Bruce Ryder (Osgoode)—to good-naturedly ask me why I am so passionate. My answer has remained constant: I am simply following my childhood dream, heeding my own inner *dharma* (higher purpose), and reacting spontaneously to karmic manifestations with gratitude. And so, at Brown University, I thanked David for inviting Duncan Kennedy, who enthralled us all on constitution-making and who, I said, spoke on this topic just for me! I now say that Baxi came to Washington College of Law just for me, and so did Jim to Osgoode. And that David (Chandler) and—Professors Gong, Shivji, and Stephen Gill who I have never met—wrote on political economy just for me. 'Just for me'—I could say it on and on and on.

I know that the same divine energy that nurtures me animates others as well. I believe and hope that this book will help fulfill others' destinies, just as they have helped to fulfill mine.

With profound gratitude to my dear karmic Guru-devas, colleagues, and friends. *Namaste!*

# Abbreviations

| | |
|---|---|
| ADB | Asian Development Bank |
| AfrDB | African Development Bank |
| CCA | Common Country Assessment |
| CPA | Coalition Provisional Authority |
| FAO | Food and Agriculture Organization of the United Nations |
| GAL | Global Administrative Law |
| ICL | International Constitutional Law |
| ITA | International Territorial Administration |
| IMF | International Monetary Fund |
| League Covenant | Covenant of the League of Nations, Versailles, 28 June 1919 |
| OHCHR | Office of the High Commissioner for Human Rights |
| ONUC | United Nations Operation in the Congo |
| PCNA | Post-Conflict Needs Assessment |
| PDA | Peace and Development Adviser |
| PFM | Public Financial Management |
| PRSP | Poverty Reduction Strategy Paper |
| ROL | Rule of Law |
| RECO | Restoration of Constitutional Order |
| SAP | Structural Adjustment Programme |
| SFRY | Socialist Federal Republic of Yugoslavia |
| SRSG | Special Representative of the Secretary General |
| UNAMA | United Nations Assistance Mission in Afghanistan |
| UNAMIR | UN Assistance Mission for Rwanda |
| UN Charter | Charter of the United Nations, San Francisco, 26 June 1945 |
| UNCA | United Nations Constitutional Assistance |

| | |
|---|---|
| UNCEA | United Nations Constitutional Electoral Assistance |
| UNDAF | United Nations Development Assistance Framework |
| UNDESA | United Nations Department of Economic and Social Affairs |
| UNDP | United Nations Development Programme |
| UNDPA | United Nations Department of Political Affairs |
| UN DPKO | United Nations Department of Peacekeeping Operations |
| UNESCO | United Nations Educational, Scientific and Cultural Organization |
| UN GAOR | United Nations, General Assembly, Official Records |
| UNRC | United Nations Resident Coordinator |
| UNSGR | United Nations Secretary General |
| UN SCOR | United Nations, Security Council, Official Records |
| UNHCR | Office of the United Nations High Commissioner for Human Rights |
| UNIFEM | United Nations Development Fund for Women |
| UNMIK | The United Nations Interim Mission in Kosovo |
| UNOSOM II | UN Operation in Somalia |
| UNOWA | United Nations Office in West Africa |

# PART I

1

# United Nations Constitutional Assistance

## A Significant but Uncharted Field

### 1.0 Introduction

*Bombay, India, February 1928*

Simon, go back! Simon, go back! Chanting this slogan, a crowd of Indian students waving black flags, women draped in white sarees, and men sporting black turbans, thronged toward *Rawalpindi*, the steamer that had just arrived. Helmeted police grimly guarded the dock. As soon as Sir John Simon, the Chairman of the Simon Commission (Commission) and his fellow British commissioners stepped out of the steamer, they were whisked off to the Viceroy's lodge.

The British Prime Minister, Sir Stanley Baldwin, having rejected self-rule for Indians, had tasked the Commission with designing their (colonial) constitution. An all-white body, the Commission had no Indian. Therefore, all through India, the nation's long imprisoned soul was manifesting itself in the courage of ordinary men and women who demanded independence: the right to sculpt their own constitution.[1]

[1] India gained independence in 1947. *See* "Indian riots mark arrival of Simon," *N. Y. Times*, 3 February 1928, at 1. *See* Ministry of Information and Broadcasting, Government of India, Lajpat Rai, *Available at*: www.youtube.com/watch?v=-cJtrZSWsM0.

Much time has passed since the 1920s, when colonial/internationalized constitution-making or colonial/international trusteeship was the norm for developing countries. In 1960, the United Nations General Assembly (UNGA) rejected internationalized constitution-making.[2] (That is, all colonies acquired an absolute right to independence: to sculpt constitutions of their choice without international assistance.) Yet today, the United Nations (UN) tutors the nationals (hereinafter local actors) of developing states in making a constitution and sculpting its content.[3] Why? This book is the first to pose this question. This book is the first comprehensive attempt to describe and analyse United Nations Constitutional Assistance (UNCA) (1949–2019), a sizeable but uncharted phenomenon of global governance. Indeed, from 1949 till now, the UN has assisted developing countries, in response to their perceived incapacities, to adopt as their *highest law*, the Western liberal constitution (hereafter WL Constitution).[4] This is UNCA. Therefore, the aforementioned question can be reframed as: How does the UN explain promoting the WL Constitution in sovereign states?

In doing so, this book reveals the deeper implications behind internationalizing constitution-making in over 40 poor, sovereign states. Consider these UNCA statistics:

1949: Libya & Eritrea (colonies)
*(Independent) Least Developed Countries [LDCs]*
*& two territorial units* (Unit):
1960: Congo
1989–2019: Afghanistan, Angola, Bhutan, Burundi, Bolivia, Cambodia, Central African Republic, Colombia, Côte d'Ivoire, Democratic Republic of Congo (DRC), East-Timor (Unit), El Salvador, Egypt, Guatemala, Guinea, Guinea-Bissau, Haiti, Iraq, Kenya, Kosovo (Unit), Kyrgyzstan, Liberia, Libya, Madagascar, Malawi, Maldives, Mali, Mozambique, Nauru, Nepal, Papua New Guinea, Rwanda, Solomon Islands, Sierra

[2] *See* G.A. Res. 1514 (XV), U.N. Doc. A/1514 (1960); this resolution is reproduced in part, on page 19.

[3] *See* UN, United Nations Assistance to Constitution-Making Processes Guidance Note (2009). Hereafter and until Chapter 10 I will refer to this document as UNCA Guidance Note (2009). I have used the terms third world states and developing states interchangeably.

[4] Id. Adrian Pelt, *Libyan Independence and the United Nations—A Case of Planned Decolonization* (Yale University Press, 1970).

Leone, Somalia, Sudan, Southern Sudan, Syria, The Gambia, Tunisia, Yemen, Zambia, and Zimbabwe (listed in alphabetical order).[5]

The UN empowered itself to offer constitutional assistance to produce in each state the WL Constitution,[6] which:

- was central to colonial trusteeship: a key eighteenth century international 'standard of civilization', (hereafter Civilized Standard), that protected property rights;
- was therefore, imposed ostensibly to promote four (market-oriented) Civilized Standards, namely the rule of law, free markets, good governance, and civilized social practices; [7] and
- as the state's 'supreme law' enshrines the legislature, executive, and judiciary; and provides the basis for territorial administration (for example, law-making).

Given the aforementioned three bullet points, UNCA is the WL Constitution's internationalized making by the UN. The Constitution so made, gives rise to, and guides UN territorial administration (ITA) (for example, internationalized law-making by the UN.) *In the remainder of this book, the word 'Constitution' with capital C means the Western Liberal Constitution.*

Indeed, UNCA covers two subjects which historically ally, but academically speaking, evolved in North America during the 1990s (when UNCA rose), in parallel ways: Western/US Constitutional law and public international law (including human rights) (hereafter Point X.) It helps to see Figure 1.8. In fact, UNCA falls within public international law and/or its fast-growing but still nascent sub-field: international constitutional law (ICL), also known as 'global constitutionalism'.[8]

[5] Vijayashri Sripati, *UN Constitutional Assistance projects in comprehensive peace missions: An inventory 1989-2011* 19 (1) Int'l Peacekeeping 93 (2012).

[6] *See* UN, UN Approach to Rule of Law Assistance 4–5 (undated). Dieter Grimm, *Types of Constitutions, in* the Oxford Handbook of Comparative Constitutional Law 98, 116 (Andras Sajo ed., Oxford University Press, 2012).

[7] *See* Gerrit Gong, *Standards of 'civilization' in International Society* 1–15 ( Clarendon Press: Oxford University Press, 1984); Martii Koskiennemi, *Gentle Civilizer of Nations* (Cambridge University Press, 2001).

[8] *See The Constitutionalization of International Law* (Anne Peters, ed., Oxford University Press, 2011); Vidya Kumar, *Towards a Constitutionalism of the Wretched,* (Völkerrechtsblog, 27 July 2017).

The aforementioned two subjects still evolve separately. As Professor Stephen Gill suggests, the increasing global restructuring in the post-Cold War era, particularly from the 2000s, which essentially entails the Constitution's internationalization, has made it imperative to note why they intersect.[9] My book attempts to do that.

In the post-1989 era, poor developing states, both conflict-torn, and stable, aided by the UN, adopt the Constitution to secure debt-relief. Regarding the post-1989 era, the UN says, it promotes the Constitution because it is universal, builds peace, prevents conflict, promotes development (understood as market-oriented poverty reduction), and good governance, and so, democracy.[10] In fact, the Bretton Woods Institutions' (BWIs') key members of the UN Family, invisibly drive UNCA (see Chapters 5–6). Indeed, UN peace-building/UN state-building/ UN transitional governance[11] and global restructuring, all entail the Constitution's internationalization, which UNCA achieves. However, international law scholars, *for no fault of theirs*, and owing to point X overlooked this. So, for example, UNCA-ITA projects were conceptualized as ITA only (*see* section 1.3). This book attempts to fill this gap in the discourse.

In so doing, the book aims to steer the international law discourse in a more inclusive and conceptually, the right direction. It seeks to demonstrate that analysing relevant international developments requires starting, not from the peripheral activity (internationalized law making, ITA), but from the parent one: the Constitution's making, which UNCA is. Further, it seeks to explain why the Constitution is being internationalized. In this way, my book offers an ICL analysis, and seeks to start a dialogue (Dialogue) between constitutional law scholars and their public international law and international political economy counterparts. My book underscores the importance of third world states' constitutional events, moments, and documents to international law analysis. Happily, this ICL analysis is now being called for. So too, is the Dialogue.[12] Broadly, this study shows that the political control and

[9] *See* Stephen Gill, *New constitutionalism, democratization, and global political economy*, 10 (1) Pacifica Review: Peace, Security, & Global Change 23 (1999).

[10] *See* UN, *supra* note 6.

[11] *See* Emmanuel de Groof, *International law and transitional governance* 9. (Emmanuel de Groof *et al* eds., Routledge, 2018) (Terms of reference for contributors [forthcoming]).

[12] Id.

domination that typified third world states' constitution-making when they were colonies, continues in this post-colonial era.

The absence of prior scholarly attention significantly shaped the questions I asked, the method I embraced, the themes I highlighted, and the format, categories, and content I selected, for analysing the UNCA projects undertaken between 1949 and 2019. For this pioneering study, I ask: Why has the UN empowered itself to offer constitutional assistance in this post-colonial era? In my answer, I concentrate on how the UN officially, in its own words, explains the purposes of, justifications for, and assumptions behind, its constitutional assistance activities. This close look at the UN's official explanations (ostensible purposes) is 'purposive analysis' (*see* section 1.7). According to Justice Aharon Barrack, 'purposive analysis is analysis of the text, not psychoanalysis of its author.'[13]

My broad argument is: UNCA, which was conceived as colonial trusteeship in 1949, to produce the Constitution, and was, for that reason rejected in 1960, continues to play that role now, in *sovereign* states. Hence, its child, ITA (by the UN), acts as trusteeship. In particular, I argue that UNCA adds a new Civilized Standard: transparent, inclusive, and participatory constitution-making. This study is not ideologically inspired. It is motivated by my long fascination with the Constitution whose salience I underscore. This is done by exploring historical and contemporary sources, the constitution's intersection with international law, including human rights and political economy.

Although scholars have resisted drawing a colonial analogy to ITA by the UN,[14] and by extension, UNCA—the UN disagrees with them. Consider:

> The UN should recognize that constitution-making is a sovereign national process, and that to be successful, the process must be nationally owned and led. The UN should be particularly sensitive to the need to provide advice and options without causing national actors to fear that UN assistance could lead to a foreign imposed constitution–United Nations.[15]

[13] Aharon Barack, *Purposive Interpretation in Law – translated from the Hebrew by Sari Bashi* 110 (Princeton University Press, 2005).

[14] *See* e.g., Ralph Wilde, *International Territorial Administration: How Trusteeship and the Civilizing Mission Never Went Away* 612 (Oxford University Press, 2008).

[15] *See* UN *supra* note 3.

> Recent years have seen an increased focus by the United Nations on questions of the rule of law in conflict and post-conflict societies, yielding important lessons for our future activities. ... Our operations have helped national actors vet and select national police, judges and prosecutors, draft new constitutions, revise legislation, educate the public, develop human rights commissions .... Unfortunately, the international community has not always provided assistance that is appropriate to the country context. Too often, the emphasis has been on foreign experts, foreign models and foreign-conceived solutions .... (UN Secretary-General.)[16]

Indeed, this book explores how a particular constitutional model, though designed by and for powerful Western states, is produced in poor and politically weak states by the UN. I am not suggesting that the general populations of powerful states are somehow the beneficiaries of these arrangements. I also do not mean to suggest that these arrangements are consciously motivated by the desire to exploit Third World resources. Rather, I explore how powerful Western states create within developing states constitutional regimes that have the effect of throwing open the latter's resources for the transnational capitalist class (TCC),[17] that is, the banks, investors, corporations, and geopolitical/imperialist strategists.[18] This effect is clear from both the UN Family's official documents that are cited and, secondarily, from the fact that the TCC and conservative economists like Friedrich A. von Hayek and Milton Friedman comprise those most in favour of UNCA-produced arrangements.[19] Nevertheless, it is true that the underlying motivation

[16] Report of the Secretary-General, *The rule of law and transitional justice in conflict and post-conflict societies* ¶12 UN Doc., S/2004/616 (23 August 2004) (The UN long shrouded UNCA under the term 'rule of law' – see *infra* table 9, Chapter 6). *Note:* I am in no way implying that scholars serving as foreign experts are acting in colonial ways.

[17] I respectfully borrow Professor B. S. Chimni's phrase. *See* B. S. Chimni, *International institutions today: An imperial global state in the making* 15 EJIL 1–16 (2004).

[18] *See* e.g., World Bank, *World Development Report – Attacking poverty, 2000/2001* 129 (2000) .

[19] *See* e.g., F.A. Hayek, *The Road to Serfdom* (University of Chicago Press, 1995); World Bank, *World Development Report 1997: The State in a Changing World* (World Bank, 1997) (promoting the Western liberal constitution); Table 6.3,

for these arrangements may be the factors other than or in addition to conscious resource exploitation, such as Cold War concerns, a belief in the legitimacy of international institutions, and so on.

The ostensible reason is the perceived incapacity of these poor states to make a sound constitution, and the assumption that once made, this constitution will erase bad governance, allow proper use of their resources, modernize them, and strengthen their weakened (national) sovereignty.[20] This idea of creating within developing states a constitutional environment that is not inimical to the West, but officially explaining it as being intended to modernize[21] the former —is reminiscent of the imperial civilizing mission.[22] So too, is the idea of 'strengthening sovereignty' by making their governance 'civilized', or 'good'.[23]

This argument is framed by using:

- a concept and research method that were developed by Ralph Wilde: Policy Institution and Purposive Analysis,[24] (*hereafter* Wilde's Method, see section 1.7);
- a framework that was developed by Wilde: Wilde's Family — described in the following paragraph; and
- the Third World Approaches to International Law (TWAIL) theoretical perspectives (*see* section 1.8). Suffice it to note here that TWAIL is a historically located intellectual movement that assails the West's

---

Ch. 6; Milton Freidman's ideas inspired and shaped the UN family's post-1989 constitutional and legal assistance projects. On this point, see Javier Couso, *Constructing Privatopia: The Role of Constitutional Law in Chile's Radical Neoliberal Experiment, in* The Politics of Legality in a Neoliberal Age 88 (Ben Golder & Daniel McLoughlin, eds., Routledge, 2018).

[20] Report of the Secretary-General, *Prevention of Armed Conflict* at 3, U.N. Doc. A/55/985 – S/2001/574 (7 June 2001).

[21] Id.

[22] *See* Jim Tully, *Modern constitutional democracy and imperialism* 46 (3) Osgoode Hall L. School J. 461, 465 (2008)

[23] Antony Anghie, *The evolution of international law: Colonial and post-colonial realities* 27 (5) Third World Q. 739, 740 (2006)

[24] Wilde, *supra* note 14 at 36–38. His book won the 2009 ASIL merit certificate.

use of international norms and institutions to subordinate developing countries.

Wilde devoted his international law/ICL work to ITA, which recognizes ITA's Western liberal constitutional parentage. Accordingly, Wilde defines territorial administration as covering only legislative, executive, and judicial activities.[25] However, Wilde's analysis excludes constitution-making, including internationalized constitution-making, and UNCA. In fact, UNCA was made public only in 2009; a year after Wilde's book was released. ITA is not governance by local actors. Indeed, when international organizations (IOs) displace local actors to conduct territorial administration, so defined, they perform ITA. Using his own Method, Wilde conceptualizes ITA as a 'Policy Institution': an 'institution' or 'established practice' that is put toward four common ostensible ends: free markets, the rule of law, good governance, and civilized practices/women's rights (Civilized Standards). In fact, these goals are essentially those of the Constitution's. Wilde does this using the TWAIL theoretical perspective.[26] On this basis, he frames a family of ITA or 'international trusteeship' Policy Institutions (hereafter Wilde's Family):

(1) Post-Renaissance (exploitation) colonialism practiced by European imperial powers;
(2A) 'Protection' (activity occurring in 'protectorates') (that is, ITA by the League of Nations) (an inter-war period IO);
(2B) ITA projects since 1945, that is, ITA by the UN;
(3)–(4) State-conducted administration of Mandated and UN Trust Territories;
(5) Representative Bodies; and
(6) Occupation[27]

Wilde's Family is obviously based on, and reflects the conceptual ties binding the Constitution with territory and territorial administration, elaborated below (see section 1.1). Wilde concludes that the two allied

[25] Id. at 22.
[26] Id.
[27] Id.

eighteenth century policies—'trusteeship and the civilizing mission, never went away'.[28]

For my book, which is the first to explore UNCA–ITA's parent, Wilde's Method and Wilde's Family made appropriate analytical choices. Accordingly, I conceptualize UNCA (the Constitution's internationalized making by the UN) as a Policy Institution: an 'established practice' that is key to achieving four common ostensible ends / Civilized Standards: rule of law, good governance, free markets, and civilized practices / women's rights.

This enables me to analyze UNCA, both non-chronologically and chronologically, and as I will show below, admit it into Wilde's Family, joining it with its off-spring: ITA by the UN. I trace UNCA's historical origins non-chronologically, (*that is,* through Wilde's Family): for instance, to the Constitution's making by foreign states and / or an inter-war IO (for example, the League of Nations) (see Ch. 3). This enables me to arrive at its (Constitution) promotion by a post-World War II IO, the UN, in this way: In Chapter 4, I arrange my Chapter 3 findings about the Constitution's internationalization during the early twentieth century, that is, from 1919 (the Treaty of Versailles) to 1952, chronologically. This reveals that the Constitution's use increased during this period and brings me to its first-time promotion by the UN in 1949: UNCA. I chronologically examine UNCA in Chapters 4 to 6. It helps to see Table 1.1 (see page 13).

Indeed, as we will see, in the post-Cold War era, the UN and the BWIs first universalized the Constitution, and then co-conceptualized it as a Rule of Law (ROL) or development (understood as market-oriented poverty reduction) strategy. UNCA was revived to enable conflict-torn and stable debtor states to produce this constitution, in return for debt-relief.

In fact, the Constitution heads Wilde's Family. I show that it sires each of Wilde's six ITA institutions. On this basis, I conclude that international trusteeship comprises the Constitution's making and ITA, working together to achieve four common ostensible ends (Civilized Standards): the rule of law, free markets, good governance, and civilized social practices / women's rights. In fact, the Constitution is key to achieving the Civilized Standards. So, Wilde's Family members must be reframed to admit their respective parents: the Constitution's making,

[28] Id. at book title.

particularly as a way to pursue trusteeship goals. For instance, in this way, I join UNCA projects with their off-springs: post-1945 ITA projects. At this initial stage, it helps to look at Table 9.1, which illustrates Wilde's Family, fully reframed.

This section, particularly the aforementioned six paragraphs, clarify that this book, from start to the end focuses on one constitution that is the state's 'supreme law'—the Constitution—and its internationalization to achieve four *ostensible ends*: free markets, rule of law, good governance, and civilized customs/women's rights. This analysis is non-chronological, and is conducted through Wilde's Family, which reflects the conceptual ties binding the Constitution with territorial administration. The Constitution's internationalization to promote these four ends rose during 1919–1952. I have analysed chronologically, the Constitution's internationalization by the UN alone (1949–2019). This analysis is historically and conceptually grounded, whether it is chronological or non-chronological, and regardless of the internationalizing actor involved. What makes it so are the chosen constitution's nature, the chosen method, and the chosen framework.

This book offers the first comprehensive analysis of UNCA projects, with and without its child ITA, from 1949 to 2019. As already noted, UNCA was essentially conceived by powerful Western states with a view to create, in non-Western states, a constitutional environment that is not inimical to the West. Accordingly, at its birth, UNCA comprised these activities: drafting assistance, knowledge-based support (provision of experts and constitutional and human rights materials), and fiscally-oriented constitutional advice. Of these, one activity was critical: the International Monetary Fund (IMF) officials' expert guidance.[29] Such displacement and/or tutoring of non-Western peoples was ostensibly undertaken in response to their perceived incapacity, and above all, to civilize/modernize them.[30]

UNCA's activities during its early run (1949–52; 1960–4) and in the post-1989 era, suggest that there has been no change in its key actors (for example, IMF), no change in its ostensible ends and purposes, and

[29] *See* Pelt, *supra* note 34 at 580.

[30] *See* Ronald Bruce, St. John, *Libya and the United States: Two Centuries of Strife* 8 (University of Pennsylvania Press, 2002).

TABLE 1.1 United Nations Constitutional Assistance Statistics

| | | |
|---|---|---|
| UNCA time frame: 1945–52, 1960–4, 1989–2019<br>Total no. of UNCA-recipients: 47 (2 colonies; 42 sovereign states, & 3 territorial units)<br>*This statistics excludes constitutional assistance provided by the UN Trusteeship Council and 'UN decolonization' projects, except the project in East-Timor<br>FTA: Foreign Territorial Administration<br>ITA: International Territorial Administration | | |
| First project | Libya, 1949–52: UNCA-(partial ITA) & FTA | |
| UNCA and ITA/FTA rejected in 1960 by the UN General Assembly<br>UNCA and ITA revived in 1960: 1st project in an independent state: Congo (1960); UNCA-(partial) ITA | | |
| | UNCA: 6 features | |
| 1. | The same country may receive UNCA at two different periods (e.g., Libya) | |
| 2. | The 1964–88 period witnessed no UNCA project for the Cold War split the world into two ideological blocs | |
| 3. | UNCA projects mushroomed from 1989 | |
| 4. | Total no. of post-1989 UNCA-ITA/FTA projects: 5.<br>(i) UNCA-(partial) ITA: Cambodia (1993); (ii) UNCA-(plenary) ITA: Somalia (1992–3); (iii) UNCA-plenary ITA: Kosovo (1999) & (iv) UNCA-plenary ITA: East-Timor (1999); (v) UNCA-FTA: Iraq | |
| 5. | UNCA-(plenary) ITA's use in sovereign states, ended in 1993. Thereafter, UNCA-(plenary)ITA was used only in territorial units: Kosovo & East-Timor | |
| 6. | Majority of post-1989 projects are: UNCA (without ITA) | |
| **UNCA's treatment in this book** | | **BOOK PART, CHAPTER** |
| UNCA - Historical Background | | I, 1–4 |
| Libya | | I, 4 |
| Eritrea | | I, 4 |
| Congo | | I, 4 |
| UNCA's rise 1989–2019 | | II, 5–10 |
| UNCA projects, with and without ITA/FTA | | II, 6 |

*Source*: Author (based on Wilde, 2008).

no change in its activities.[31] In fact, as we will see, international constitutional assistance dates back to 1856, when France and Great Britain, with a view to promote the Constitution, co-drafted 'barbaric' Turkey's monetary laws, ostensibly to civilize its economy and make it sovereign (see Chapter 3). Indeed, although UNCA activities have expanded since the 1990s, their financial orientation has remained a constant.[32] Above all, the same justification animates their use: developing countries' governance incapacities. The same ostensible purposes are put forth for their use: to modernize these states (in line with the West's preferred standards) and to strengthen their sovereignty,[33] supposedly weakened by their bad self-governance. How can this be? For it doesn't make sense to frame sovereignty in terms of capacity for adopting the Constitution. This book explores how sovereign developing states came to be locked in as UNCA-recipient-states.

Answering my first-order international constitutional law question (Question) as to why the UN offers UNCA in sovereign developing states, entails establishing the UN's ostensible 'purposes' and 'justifications' for displacing these states' local actors from and/or tutoring them in sculpting their own constitutions. This makes these states' constitutional events (Events) that is, the contexts for their constitution-making, utterly critical, and the logical starting point for answering the Question. Here lies my chosen Policy Institution concept's merit, which calls for establishing those very aspects (for example, purposes and justifications) and thereby acknowledges the Events' importance. (I will revisit this point in section 1.3.)

Answering this Question has taken up my whole book. This means that other important subsidiary questions, such as the critical empirical ones, of exactly how UNCA has operated on the ground, and whether its purposes (for example, promotion of free markets and anti-corruption) have been met, go largely unexplored. Again, in order to properly and fully assess those purposes (for example, free markets), requires starting from the UN's justifications, that is, knowing why those ends are being promoted in the first place, and how the UN itself explains their

31 *See* Sripati, *supra* note 5 at appendix.

32 *See* UN, *supra* note 6 at 6.

33 *See* UN, *supra* note 20.

promotion. This non-doctrinaire study strives to supply the foundation for these future inquiries.

'Simple but shocking, no one has, as yet, asked why the UN displaces Third World peoples from making their constitution,' said Dr. (Professor) Trevor Farrow, an expert on globalization, who commented on my paper on UNCA at a workshop in 2010. Indeed, the normative question as to why the UN is intervening in independent developing states' constitution-making, is important for four reasons. First, this question is important in its own right. For Great Britain could only deny self-rule for Indians in 1928, and for Libyans in 1943, because then, and in fact until 1960, self-determination was merely a political principle. And so, colonial peoples lacked an absolute right to self-determination. Consider these two factual details:

- In 1943, the Second World War's victorious powers (Powers), overriding the Libyans' demand for independence, mandated the UN in 1949, to help Libya sculpt the Constitution so that it might transit to independence.[34]

Again, in 1960, the UN General Assembly (UNGA) declared that:

- All peoples have the right to self-determination.
- Inadequacy of political, economic, social or educational preparedness should never serve as a pretext for delaying independence.[35]

The 1960 anti-colonial resolution (reproduced above, in part), supposedly rejected colonially imposed constitutions and the FTAs they undergirded.[36] Accordingly, it also rejected the internationalization of constitution-making and territorial administration. In fact, the UN Trusteeship Council has been shuttered since 1994.

There is a second reason for asking why UNCA is being used in this post-colonial era: to evaluate the legitimacy of the UN's idea of displacing local actors from, or tutoring them in constitution-making. For

[34] *See* Adrian Pelt, *Libyan Independence and the United Nations—A Case of Planned Decolonization* (Yale University Press, 1970).

[35] *See* G.A. Res. 1514 (XV), U.N. Doc. A/1514 (1960).

[36] For FTA see Wilde, *supra* note 14 at 373.

the UN itself concedes that today, 'constitution-making is a sovereign national process', and so, the default (constitution-making) method is one, that is 'nationally-owned and led' without leading to a 'foreign-imposed constitution'.[37] This recalls international law professor Christine Chinkin's advice that since the UN Charter nowhere mentions constitutional assistance, she would like to see my work answer this question: 'Can local actors respond in this way to an offer of UNCA: Thank you Ms. UN official. But no thank you. We are able and willing to write our constitution without international assistance.'[38]

The third factor, addressing the accountability of UNCA projects, a normative issue, makes it important to question for what purposes those projects are being mounted. (Only then can one ask whether those purposes have been met). Fourth, and finally, so do these intertwined issues about UNCA projects: their challenges and solutions for their improvement.[39]

How specifically did UNCA's unspecified nature affect my approach? As already noted, one way UNCA has remained uncharted until now is because American constitutional law and international law evolved in parallel ways during the 1990s. As a result, international law scholars missed the Constitution's salience. Next, and for the same reason, although they rightly associated the BWIs' rule of law assistance with promoting economic liberalization, they failed to note that such assistance was a logical corollary of its (Constitution's) internationalization. Given this, my answer is, UNCA's unspecified nature affected my approach in three ways. It spurred me to ask a first-order type of question set out on page 3. Second, construct a glossary of terms relevant to this subject, showing the terms used by the Security Council for constitutions, constitution-making, and UNCA: 1960, 1989–2009 because they are presumably unfamiliar to many. This second and simpler example comes in Table 6.4, Chapter 6. Third, I devote the following four sections to presenting only so much background information as is essential to showing how and/or why the Constitution:

[37] UN, *supra* note 3 at 4.

[38] Professor C. Chinkin, personal communication, University of Toronto Law School, January 2009.

[39] For accountability re: ITA see *Wilde, supra* note 14 at 9.

- historically protects property rights, and gave rise to the powerful technique of 'constitutionalization' (*see* section 1.1);
- requires that all other laws such as commercial (in the territorial unit to which it applies) comply with it, and makes the BWIs' rule of law assistance *legislative* in nature, and UNCA its parent (see section 1.1.1);
- relates conceptually to territorial administration, and so, makes UNCA ITA's parent (see section 1.2); and
- was internationalized after 1989, to promote economic liberalization, privatization and so on, ostensibly to build peace, (where relevant, create states), speed development–understood as market-oriented poverty reduction, prevent conflict, and promote good governance (*see* section 1.3).

This backdrop will enable me to thematically review the literature, and establish that, despite UNCA's salience, it has been overlooked.

## 1.1 The Origins of the Western Liberal Constitution

To understand UNCA-ITA's parent-child ties requires considering how and why, *territory* and *jurisdiction*—two Western legal concepts—tie up with a third, a constitution. These three concepts are known as the 'legal trinity'. In Europe, the modern concept of the territorial state as the basic form for political organization first appeared during the Renaissance (1300–1700).[40] What then emerged as a 'technology' of (territorial) jurisdiction was this: 'legal writing that is hierarchically, in its most superior form: the "Constitution".'[41] In fact, it was during the Renaissance that 'the term "constitution" received the conceptual content it still has today, meaning a set of institutions that limit the exercise of State power.'[42] It was only the concept of the state that was new and not the concept of constitutionalism (that is, ideas of limited government and the rule of law). For, as Erik-Lane states, 'one may speak of constitutions without any reference to the state.'[43]

[40] Jan Erik-Lane, *Constitutions and Political Theory* 40 (Manchester University Press, 1996).

[41] Patrick Glenn, *Cosmopolitan State* 69 (Oxford University Press, 2012)

[42] *See* Erik-Lane, *supra* note 40 at 40

[43] *Id.* at 15–16

The new concept of the territorial state separated constitutionalism's modern version (with its characteristic ideas of limited government and the rule of law), from its medieval one. Still, for its development, the new concept of the state required the concepts of medieval constitutionalism, which of course had to be 'reformulated to fit to the new context'.[44] Herein come Baron de Montesquieu and John Locke.[45] These two thinkers, prominent among the founders of liberal political philosophy, the philosophy of individual rights and limited government, rendered the classical formulations of modern constitutionalism, the doctrine of limited government.[46] To do so, both these philosophers 'placed themselves in a fictitious state of nature'.[47] They each approached this idea (modern constitutionalism) very differently.[48] However, both of them drew the same conclusions: 'the necessity of [basing] the modern state on the rule of law and a separation of powers or a constitutional set-up.'[49]

Locke set out premises ('constitutionalist conclusions'),[50] which shaped and help to theorize the North American and French revolutions.[51] Those conclusions or ideas took the shape of a constitution that protects equality, independence, and property.[52] In fact, the United States constitution, a prototype of the Western liberal constitution, though not drafted by Locke, is undoubtedly based on his philosophy. Indeed, so are all the Western political systems.[53] To sum up, European constitutionalist tradition was long animated with this question: What type of institutions can produce 'good government'?[54] Such institutions included the adherence to an explicitly framed written constitution.[55]

[44] *Id.* at 36.

[45] *Id.*

[46] *Id.*

[47] Grimm, *supra* note 6 at 98, 116.

[48] *Id.*

[49] Erik-Lane, *supra* note 40 at 37.

[50] Id.

[51] Grimm, *supra* note 6 at 117

[52] Erik-Lane, *supra* note 40 at 36.

[53] Id.

[54] Id.

[55] Id. Note: I am not suggesting that Western constitutional history consists of only Locke's and Montesquieu's ideas.

*Constitutional supremacy and constitutionalization of property rights*

The constitution became the territorial state's legal foundation. Accordingly, the Constitution:

1) was the highest, that is, the state's 'supreme' law[56]; –
2) enshrines
   a) the legislature, judiciary, and executive and
   b) property rights.

Feature 1) gave rise to the concept of 'constitutional supremacy' and the allied technique of 'constitutionalization'. For the purpose of the present discussion, constitutional supremacy and constitutionalization will be explained regarding 2) b) property rights. To 'constitutionalize' property rights means to define and write them into the actual document: the state's supreme law. The rights are formally incorporated within the text of the constitution to limit the capacity of the legislature and/or executive to supersede them through their own unilateral actions, including by revising them like an ordinary law. In this way, constitutionalization provides the best and most lasting assurance that the future laws, policies, and decisions of the state will work to proactively advance property rights and/or any other rights. Revision of property rights would only be possible through a distinct procedure (constitutional amendment), and difficult to achieve.

### 1.1.1 UN Constitutional Assistance and the Bretton Woods Institutions' 'Rule of Law' (Legislative) Assistance Work Toward Common Ends

Owing to features 1) and 2) a), the Constitution provided a framework for the conduct of territorial administration and formation of government, and subordinates laws in all areas, such as torts, crime, labour, and commerce, within the territorial unit to which it applied. In short, feature 1) required that all other laws in a state, governed by the Constitution needed to comply with it. Owing to features 1) (and its

[56] Id. at 21.

advantages), and 2) a, in the post-Cold War era, the UN and the BWIs co-prescribed for developing states a constitution that is 'supreme', and 'constitutionalizes' an independent judiciary and property rights, (the BWIs' conditionalities) and guarantees of women's rights (see section 1.3).[57] Accordingly, the World Bank stated:

> ..., several countries have started privatization efforts. In this process, some have already amended their constitution to make provision for private property rights. Others have not yet changed their constitution to this effect, but, nevertheless, proceeded with the privatization effort. In the context of World Bank operations, an effort is being made to address these issues.
>
> ....There are, for instances, countries whose constitution forbids private ownership of the means of production. In the context of private sector development projects, the Bank seeks to aid the country in ensuring that the project is based on a sound legal premise.[58]

As per the World Bank's guidelines:

> Key institutions need to be empowered to operate autonomously from government. These include the *central bank*, ... and a range of oversight bodies. These institutions should be provided with full constitutional underwriting to do their job without interference ....[59] On this point, see Figures 1.6 and 5.3.

It is only the UN that offers 'constitutional assistance': It helps developing states draft their constitutions to constitutionalize just those conditionalities and guarantees.[60] For political reasons, the BWIs only offer legislative assistance: They help developing states fashion laws that comply with the Constitution. Accordingly, the BWIs state:

> Create a Proper legal and/or Regulatory Framework
>
> The fiscal operations in any country are anchored in two main legal sources: the *constitution* and tax and budget *laws*. .... In several post-conflict countries, the IMF's Legal Department (LEG) provided substantial

[57] *See* UN, *supra* note 6 .

[58] World Bank, *Governance and Development* 32–33 (World Bank, 1992).

[59] *See* Commonwealth Secretariat, "Guidelines for Public Financial Management Reform" vii (Commonwealth Secretariat, undated)

[60] *See e.g.*, UN Women, Guidance Note: Women's Human Rights and National Constitutions 5 (New York, 2012).

assistance in drafting these laws (Afghanistan, Liberia, Mozambique, Rwanda, and Timor-L'este.) [61]

> As regards the coherence of rules, when disbursements for a Bank financed project are conditional on the enactment or modification of certain laws, it is essential that the country both enact and implement these laws. .... A decree should not be at variance with legislation.[62]

Meanwhile, the increasing globalization has caused a mission creep:

> The Bank is providing advice to ... countries (in country dialogues) on defining a legal and constitutional framework – World Bank.[63]

In any event, the BWIs' assistance is essentially *legislative* in nature and therefore works with UNCA toward common goals: privatization, and so on. Figure 1.1 illustrates UNCA and the rule of law assistance's ties.

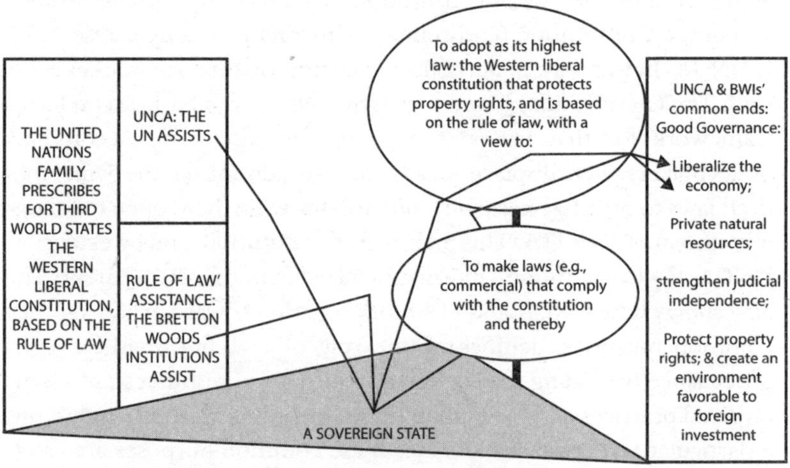


FIGURE 1.1 United Nations Constitutional Assistance (UNCA) and the BWIs' rule of law assistance work together toward good governance
*Sources*: UN, *Guidance Note of the Secretary-General: UN Approach to Rule of Law Assistance* (2009); World Bank, *Legal and Judicial Reform: Strategic Directions* 37 (2003).

[61] IMF, Rebuilding Fiscal Institutions in Post-Conflict Countries 15 (IMF, 2004) [emphasis added].

[62] *See* World Bank, *supra* note 58 at 32.

[63] World Bank, *Reforming public institutions and strengthening governance – A World Bank strategy* 127 (The World Bank Group, 2000).

## 1.2 UNCA Sires and Works with International Territorial Administration (ITA) towards Common Ends

Point 1) is also how and why the Constitution emerged as a 'technology' of jurisdiction, working symbiotically with territory, lending a distinct political character to a given territorial unit, and conferring a distinct 'status' (including statehood) on a given territorial Unit. Accordingly, conceptually, the Constitution and its making tie up with territorial administration (legislative, executive, and judicial activities), and establish jurisdiction.

The Constitution's internationalized law making led to internationalized territorial administration. The following UNCA-(plenary) ITA example best illustrates UNCA and ITA's parent-child relationship.[64] Here, UN policymakers displace the relevant territorial unit's local actors from the activity of constitution-making, with a view to promulgating the Constitution (enshrining the market economy clause). This is UNCA. In this way, policymakers constitutionalize the market economy. The Constitution, so produced (by UNCA), establishes a preferred framework for that Unit's (territorial) administration. Accordingly, policymakers then displace local actors to administer the Unit: they draft laws to privatize natural resources, throwing them open to foreign investment. This is ITA. This makes the Constitution, and by extension, UNCA (the Constitution's internationalized making), ITA's parent. This also shows how UNCA and ITA work together toward achieving their common purposes: democracy, the rule of law, free markets, good governance (including the exploitation of natural resources), modern/civilized practices and/or human rights, including women's rights, and a particular territorial status. Since these common purposes are essentially those of the Constitution, UNCA is committed to achieving them.

The relationship (mentioned in the above paragraph), holds good in UNCA–partial/plenary-ITA projects, where ITA (UN's law-making) may

[64] This model mirrors UNCA in Kosovo where the UN assumed complete de facto governmental power. Determining the legality of this concentration of power lies outside the scope of my enquiry. Figure 1.3 mirrors the UNCA-(partial) ITA model in Congo and Cambodia and UNCA-(plenary) ITA model in Somalia and East-Timor. Note: In Somalia and East-Timor, the UN began plenary ITA (i.e., to first administer/make laws) in ways consistent with the impending Constitution, which it helped produce.

have begun before the Constitution is made. Here, as the Constitution is the highest law of the land, it and by extension, UNCA governs ITA. Figures 1.2–1.3 illustrate UNCA's salience vis-à-vis plenary, and partial ITA respectively.

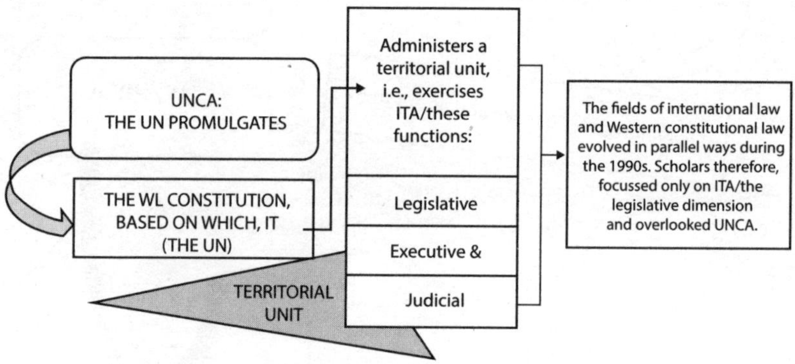


FIGURE 1.2. United Nations Constitutional Assistance Sires International Territorial Administration (ITA)
*Note*: This figure reflects the UNCA-plenary-ITA model mounted in Kosovo

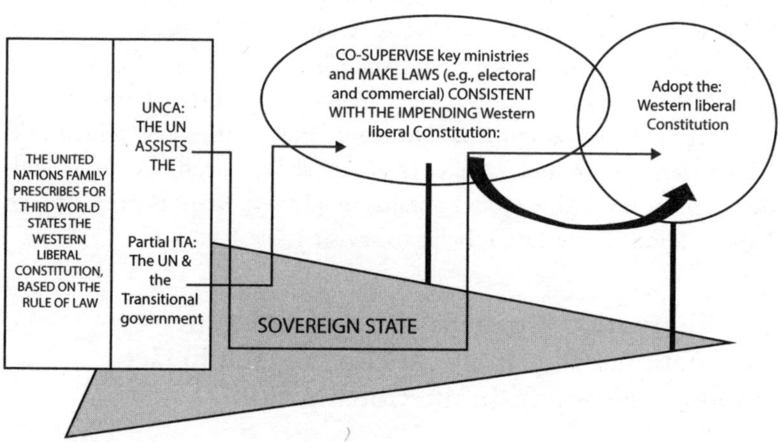


FIGURE 1.3 The Western liberal Constitution / UNCA guides and governs partial international territorial administration
*Note*: This figure reflects the UNCA-(partial)-ITA model, mounted in Congo and Cambodia

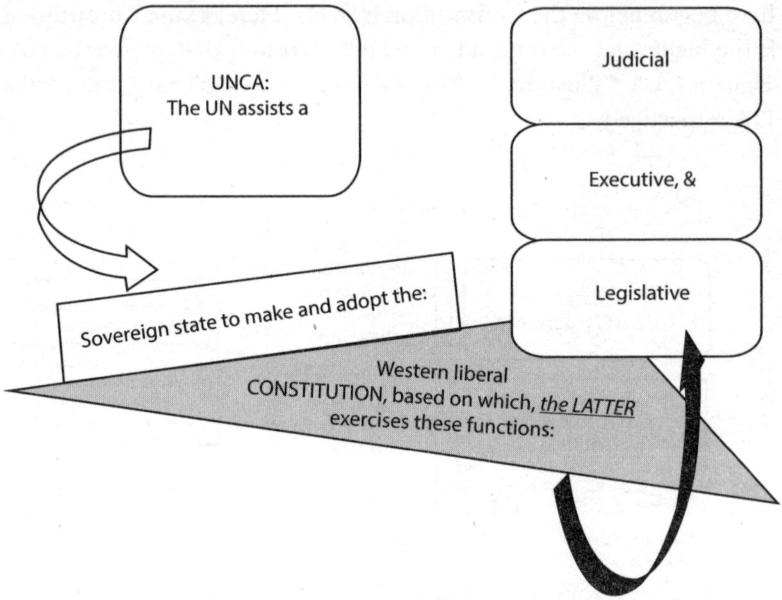


FIGURE 1.4 UNCA (without ITA): The Western liberal Constitution guides the sovereign state's territorial administration

Finally, this salience of the Constitution (and by extension, UNCA) holds well, even where only UNCA (without ITA) operates in sovereign states. For here, a sovereign state in adopting the Constitution with UNCA locks in the Western liberal constitutional framework. As a result, even though it is that state, and not the UN, which self-administers (for example, makes laws), those laws need to comply with the Constitution. This model obtains in all the post-1993 projects (see Table 1.1 and Figure 1.4). It helps to revisit Table 1.1.

## 1.3 International Law Analysis of Relevant International Developments Lies in, and in fact, *Requires* Starting from the Constitution

### Thematic Review: Setting the Backdrop

I start from 1989 for two reasons. First, UNCA projects mushroomed only after 1989. Whatever little scholarship exists about the

Constitution's internationalized making by the UN, takes 1989 as the starting point. Second, hardly anyone noticed the first UNCA project in 1960, in a sovereign state, (in newly decolonized Congo), that the late Dag Hammarskjöld, the second UN Secretary-General pioneered during the Cold War (discussed further below in this section). Hammarskjöld called UNCA International Executive Rule.

According to the UN, super-power rivalries, in Angola and elsewhere, fueled some of the decade's longest and most deadly conflicts in the late 1980s.[65] Indeed, by 1996, 14 of the 53 countries in Africa were afflicted by armed conflicts. These conflicts ended when the Soviet Union collapsed, coupled with UN intervention.[66]

Powerful western states—and the financial institutions they backed – traced this havoc to these sovereign states' 'bad governance'.[67] They alleged that governance was bad when leaders rigged elections, the military trafficked children, and weak central banks kowtowed to corrupt leaders and endorsed their budget deficits. This type of governance, said the West, triggered conflict and threatened world peace and security. In particular, the West traced these states' bad governance to their 'deficient' constitutions.[68]

As the Soviet Union began to crumble, a confident assumption developed among powerful Western states about the need to bring the blessings of democracy to the new states. The thinking went like this: The Soviet Union's demise spelt the triumph of capitalism, liberal democracy, and market-oriented policies. To encourage the gradual evolution of liberal market democracy in developing countries and the former Soviet satellite states, 'the democratic creed must be evangelized.'[69] Indeed, evangelization is what the West engaged in. Western scholars and policymakers used the end

[65] *See* Report of the Secretary-General, *The causes of conflict and the promotion of durable peace and sustainable development in Africa*, ¶10 U.N. Doc., A/52/871-S/1998/318 (13 April 1998)

[66] Id. at ¶4

[67] *See* e.g., World Bank, *Sub-Saharan Africa – From Crisis to Sustainable Growth* 60 (November 1989).

[68] UN, *An Agenda for Peace*, ¶59 U.N. Doc. A/47/277-S/24111 (June 17, 1992)

[69] *See e.g.*, Joshua Muravchik, *Endowing Democracy*, *N. Y. Times*, June 18, 1984 (Op-Ed).

of the Cold War to espouse the universality of capitalism, human rights (economic rights), and liberal market democracy.[70] The liberal human rights narrative articulated a particular vision for these states: liberal Western (market) democracy, underpinned by a constitution (as epitomized by that of the United States).[71] What is more, this narrative recommended a process of external legitimation for promoting that vision.[72]

Is this narrative new? No, as we will see in chapters 2–5. However, what was rejected in 1990 was the Cold War era's peace, security, and development architecture (hereinafter Architecture).[73] That Architecture comprised two parallel sets of institutions. One set addressed poverty and development; the other addressed peace and security.[74]

The new Architecture reflected the international community's 'holistic' approach to, and collective role in tackling poverty, security, and development.[75] For, as the UN suggests, 'the international community, freed from the super-power rivalries, was eager to exercise its newly acquired capacity for collective decision-making.'[76] Henceforth, UN functionaries, the UN Secretariat (and all its wings), the Security Council, and the UN Agencies —including the UN Development Programme (UNDP) and the BWIs—would jointly lend their hands to assisting these states in improving governance along international standards, and so reduce poverty, prevent conflict, and promote peace, security, and sustainable development.[77] (Tellingly, the UN Secretary-General's top-level Executive Committee on 'Peace and Security'

[70] *See e.g.*, Louis Henkin, *A Post-Cold War Human Rights Agenda* 19 Yale J. of Int'l L. 249 (1994).

[71] *See* Anne-Marie Slaughter, *The Liberal Agenda for Peace: International Relations Theory and the Future of the United Nations* 4 Trans. L. & Contemp. Problems 377, 396 (1994).

[72] Id.

[73] *See* Necla Tsirgi, "Peacebuilding as the link between security and development: Is the window of opportunity closing?" 1 (International Peace Academy, 2003).

[74] Id.

[75] *See* UN, *supra* note 20 at 1–2.

[76] *See* UN, *supra* note 65 at ¶10.

[77] Id. at ¶ 71–103.

comprised the BWIs' officials).[78] Accordingly, the UN was positioned to build these states' capacity to create an appropriate constitution in response to their perceived incapacity. And so, in the mid-1990s, the UN declared:

> The ... mandates entrusted to the United Nations now often include both the restoration of democracy and the protection of human rights. United Nations departments, agencies and programmes have been called upon to help States draft constitutions ....[79]

Three allied concepts, coined in the wake of the Cold War, internationalized the Constitution: peace-building, conflict prevention, and good governance. (Here is how and why the Constitution appeared on the international radar.) The UN first defined peace-building in 1992, as an 'action to solidify peace and avoid relapse into conflict'.[80] Indeed, peace-building covered everything, including disarming armed groups, fighting corruption, designing market economies, promoting foreign investment, and holding free and fair elections, thereby following the model of the Constitution.[81] For post-conflict states, these peace-building goals were a given, says a former top-level UN official:[82] 'The triumph of liberal democracy and market-oriented economic policies since the fall of the Berlin Wall clearly affected the search for solutions, both theoretical and practical.'[83]

Indeed, as we will see, the Constitution's making was key to achieving most, if not all, of the peace-building goals. In fact, the UN stressed that it had an obligation to respond to the supposedly 'new requirement' of helping states transform their 'deficient national structures' by sculpting new constitutions.[84] In 1996, the UN described its constitutional assistance this way:

78 *See* UN, *supra* note 20 at ¶106.

79 UN, *An Agenda for Democratization* 2 (1996).

80 *See* UN, *supra* 68 at ¶21.

81 Id. at ¶55. *See Report of the Secretary-General on Peace-Building in the Immediate Aftermath of Conflict*, UN Doc. A/63/881-S/2009/304 (11 June 2009).

82 Graciana del Castillo, *Rebuilding War-torn States: The Challenge of Post-conflict Economic Reconstruction* 25 (Oxford University Press, 2009).

83 Id. (emphasis added).

84 UN, *supra* note 68 at ¶55 & –59 (quote).

> United Nations departments, agencies and programmes have been called upon to help States draft constitutions, create independent systems for the administration of justice....[85]

During this time (the mid-1990s), the UN broadened the peace-building concept, stating that it falls within conflict prevention. Conflict was defined broadly to include:[86]

> [t]he deep-rooted socio-economic, cultural environmental, institutional and other structural causes that often underlie its immediate political symptoms.[87]

As in peace-building, here too, the UN's role was to support national conflict-prevention efforts and assist in building national capacity in this regard.[88] UNCA was labelled a key conflict-prevention activity.[89]

Given the broad way in which conflict was defined, improving governance to promote development acquired a preventive hue:

> Development assistance can facilitate the creation of opportunities and the political, economic, and social spaces within which indigenous actors can ... develop and use the resources necessary to build a peaceful ... society. ...
>
> An essential aspect of conflict prevention is the strengthening of the rule of law, and within that, the protection of women's human rights achieved through a focus on gender equality in constitutional reform.[90]

Indeed, Kofi Annan, the UN Secretary-General, considered the promotion of human security and human development key to preventing conflict.[91] Hence, making an appropriate constitution, (that is, the Constitution) to remedy bad governance became a key development activity.[92]

[85] See UN, *supra* note 79 at 2.

[86] *See* UN, *supra* note 20 at ¶106.

[87] Id. at 2.

[88] Id.

[89] *See Report of the Secretary-General, Progress Report on the Prevention of Armed Conflict*, UN Doc. A/60/891 35, 39–40 (18 July 2006) .

[90] *See* UN, *supra* note 20 at ¶99 and 132.

[91] *See* UN, *supra* note 65 at ¶2.

[92] *See* UN, *supra* note 20 at Recommendation 18.

According to the UN, for developing states to build peace, prevent conflict, and achieve sustainable development, they need to establish good governance.[93] What are good governance's cornerstones? They include: respect for the rule of law and human rights; strong judicial and public financial institutions (for example, an independent central bank); participatory and democratic decision-making; and good natural resource and public sector management.[94] How might developing states create these basic elements? The UN says they need to do adopt a constitution that:

a) Is the highest/ supreme law of the land;
b) Is based on the rule of law;
c) embodies the principle of 'separation of powers';
d) enshrines core, court-policed civil and political rights and,
e) anchors among other independent bodies, the judiciary, a central bank, an electoral commission, an anti-corruption commission, and a National Human Rights Institution (inclusive list).[95]

Clearly, these features (a–e) suggest that the UN Family promotes the Constitution. (It helps to note that democratic governance, an allied UN concept, shares the same core elements with good governance.)[96]

Accordingly, starting from the 1990s, both the UN and the BWIs offered yet another allied activity (rule of law assistance), for the same ostensible purposes.[97] The BWIs subsumed the Constitution under the rule of law label, and so, assisted states in making (or reforming) laws, to promote the market economy, economic liberalization, privatization of natural resources, and so on.[98] This is precisely why, in the post-Cold War era, the term 'rule of law' (or rule of law promotion) in the peace-

93 *See* UN, *supra* note 65 at ¶71. Note: The UN Family (which comprises the BWIs) embraces a common definition of good governance.

94 Id. at ¶77–78.

95 *See* UN *supra* note 6 at 3–5.

96 *See* UN, *supra* note 65 at ¶77–78.

97 *See* UN, *supra 6 at* 3–5.

98 Id. at 1; *Memorandum from James D. Wolfensohn to the Board, Management, and Staff of the World Bank Group* (January 21, 1999).

building/conflict prevention/development assistance contexts, equaled the BWIs' pursuance of neo-liberal economic policies.[99] Section 1.1.1 explains why the BWIs' ROL assistance was a logical corollary of the Constitution's internationalization. Throughout this book, the term rule of law is used in the sense that the BWIs use it: economic liberalization.

Before turning to consider the Constitution's internationalized making in the developing world, one may recall from section 1.0, that as an activity, constitutional assistance was in the UN's repertoire. It was readily available in 1990. In the post-Cold War era, it was simply revived in independent states to produce the Constitution. It was explained as a: peace-building, conflict-prevention, and market-oriented development (poverty-reduction) activity.

Given this, during 1989–2019, the UN began to mediate between warring parties, nudging and assisting them in concluding peace agreements—most of which mandated among other things, the Constitution's making— to prevent conflict and build peace.[100] This means, first, peace processes and peace-making assumed constitutional dimensions.[101] Second, and accordingly, UN peacemaking equates with the Constitution's internationalized making. So, UNCA included peace-making.[102] Third, 'power-sharing,' the UN's oft-prescribed solution for ethnic conflicts, is consonant with the Constitution. In fact, power-sharing arrangements (governments of national unity) are mandated to adopt this Constitution during the 'transition period' (see chapter 6). Finally, and therefore, the UN's post-Cold War's peace operations grew multidimensional.[103] Authorized by the Security Council, they used UNCA to make the Constitution mandated by relevant peace agreements. They were manned by experts in topics including security, human rights, fiscal decentralization, and natural resource management.[104]

[99] Vera Gowland-Debbas & Vassilis Pergantis, *Rule of Law, in* Peacebuilding: A Lexicon 320, 329 (Vincent Chetail, ed., Oxford University Press, 2009).

[100] *See* Sripati, *supra* note 5

[101] *See* UN, *supra* note 3 at 2.

[102] Id.

[103] Id.

[104] Id.

Earlier in this chapter, we noted the UN's bold (mid-1990s') declaration about its constitutional assistance. Almost a decade later, it declared:

> The UN worked tirelessly around the globe throughout the year to prevent and resolve conflicts and to consolidate peace. ... My envoys used their good offices in seeking peace agreements .... Peacekeepers ... were working ...to help war-torn countries write constitutions, ... strengthen human rights and the rule of law.[105]

As for stable states, the UNDP helped them to formulate and implement poverty reduction strategy papers (hereinafter conditionalities) or national development frameworks which mandated the Constitution/good governance. In this way, the UNDP melded constitutional assistance with development assistance. And UNCA served to enable stable states to adopt the Constitution, as a way of implementing their conditionalities/frameworks.

In these ways, 'post-conflict' and development assistance became the two contexts for UNCA's use in the post-colonial and post-Cold War era. Conversely, this was how, and why, the internationalization of constitution-making came to be revived in sovereign states.

Figure 1.5 captures the two contexts for UNCA's use. Figures 1.1 and 1.6 intertwine for they both illustrate the Constitution's salience. Figure 1.1 shows how UNCA and the BWIs' rule of law assistance work together toward common goals. Figure 1.6 builds on this relationship, showing UNCA's salience vis-à-vis the UN, and the BWIs' rule of law assistance, and the UN's assistance in electoral, judicial, and security sectors, for instance.

This section reveals that the Constitution is being internationalized because it is key to achieving privatization and so on, viz. the BWIs' ends (see Figures 1.1, 1.5, 1.6, and 5.3). Given the Constitution's status as a conditionality, its internationalization is integral to post-1989 allied fields of study: UN rule of law promotion, UN peace-building, and UN state-building: Power-sharing (sub-field). The Constitution is integral to two additional Fields: Globalization / Global Restructuring and 'Law

105 *Report of the Secretary-General on the Work of the Organization*, Supplement No. 1, UN Doc. (A/60/1) (2005) [emphasis added].

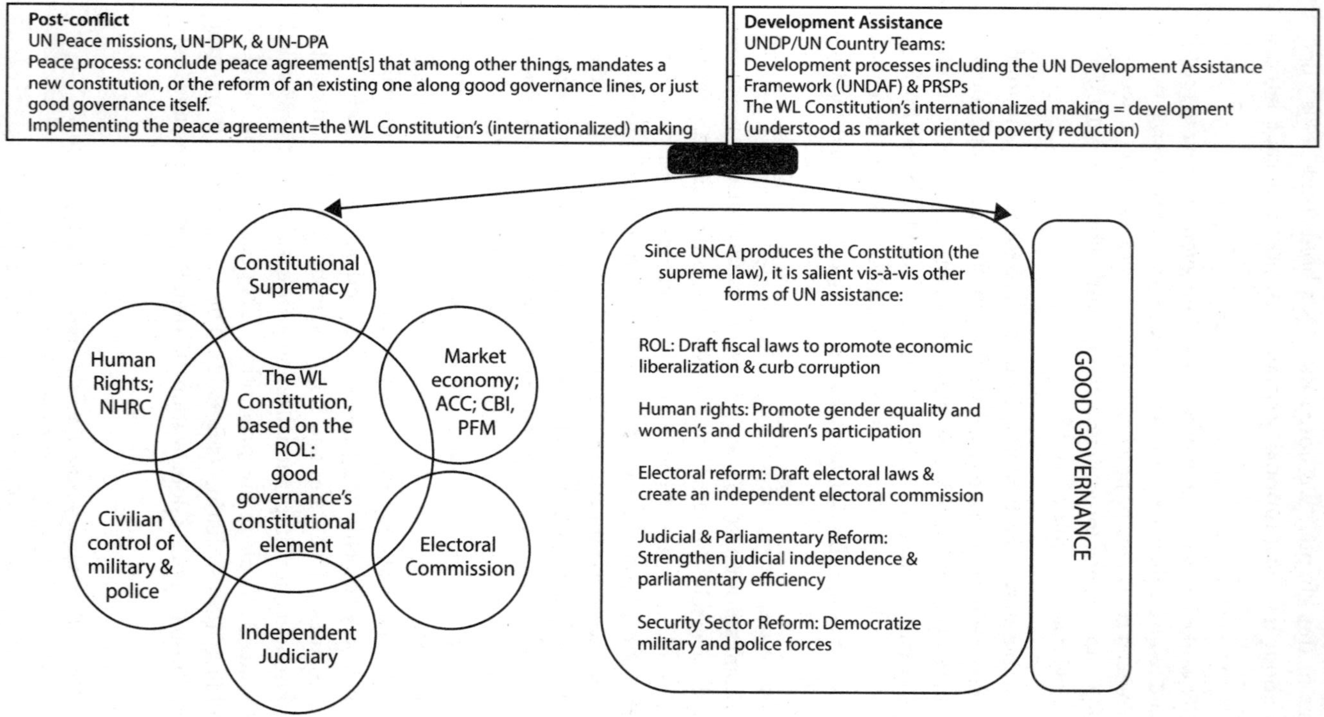


FIGURE 1.5 The post-1989 era: United Nations Constitutional Assistance operates in two contexts: post-conflict and development assistance

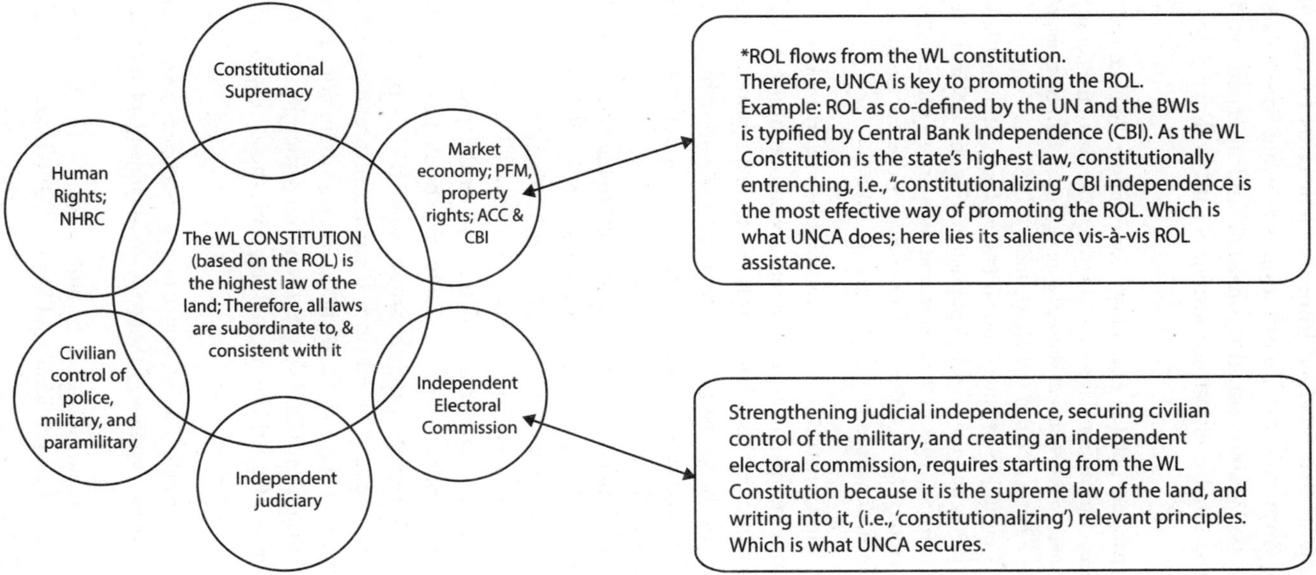


FIGURE 1.6 Nations Constitutional Assistance's salience vis-à-vis international assistance in other sectors

*Source: Example: World Bank, *World Development Report* Ch. 3 (1997).

BWI=Bretton Woods Institutions; ACC = Anti-corruption commission; CBI = Central Bank independence; NHRC= National Human Rights Commission; PFM = Public Financial Management

and Development'[106] that emerged from the debt crisis of the 1980s (see Chapter 5). Given this, the Constitution is relevant to scholars of these two subjects: Western constitutional law and international law (including international political economy). As the following review will reveal,

1. A few international political economists (for example, Stephen Gill) *and* (Western) constitutional law scholars who write about the *Constitution's relevance to international political economy,* missed only its *internationalization by the UN (that is, UNCA)*; and
2. The parallel evolution of international law and constitutional law during the 1990s, and the terms co-popularized by the UN and the BWIs (for example, rule of law; electoral assistance), successfully drew international law scholars' attention away from the Constitution's co-internationalization *by the UN and the BWIs.*

In any event, the Constitution's overlooking has been innocent, all through. In these circumstances, five allied caveats obtained, which I will offer as I go along, in this section itself. First, throughout this book I, an avid explorer of the Constitution's internationalization by the UN, have no immediate international law conversationalist in the aforementioned Fields and sub-fields.

Why has UNCA eluded academic exploration? In particular, why has no one questioned UNCA's revival? Indeed, the UN itself has received scant scholarly attention. For instance, Edward Neuman and Roland Rich's lament, made in 2004, still holds true today: 'The role of the UN –the embodiment of international society– in the promotion of democracy remains understudied.'[107] Only one book has done that in the last decade. Although it rightly argues that the UN promotes a Western market democracy based on a textual interpretation of the very UN documents, I have cited in the aforesaid discussion, it does not base its conclusion on UNCA's use mentioned therein. Rather, it proceeds to group the Constitution's making with those very activities

[106] *See* e.g., Kerry Rittich, *The Future of Law and Development: Second Generation Reforms and the Incorporation of the Social*, 26 Michigan J. of Int'l L. 199 (2005) (focusing on judicial reform).

[107] Edward Neuman and Roland Rich, *Introduction, in* The UN Role in Promoting Democracy: Between Ideals and Reality 3, 3 (Edward Neuman & Roland Rich, eds. 2004).

that it sustains (for example, judicial reform) under 'rule of law'. It, instead, arrives at this twisted conclusion: 'UN's democracy assistance: Governance + electoral assistance.'[108] Thus, UNCA has been ignored. Evidence for this is plentiful.[109] So has the Constitution's making in the context of development assistance.

Given this, in the thematic review that follows, I will briefly consider just six books on peace-building, state-building, the rule of law, ITA, and state-formation, and two extant articles on UNCA proper, to show what has been foregrounded. As we will see, even an article on UNCA proper ignores UNCA. Regarding state-formation, I consider a book and a review essay authored by Guy Sinclair, because they both examine the role of Hammarskjöld's International Executive Rule, IER/UNCA, in modeling developing states along Western lines. In conclusion, I will offer four more reasons for why the scholarship has evolved in this way, and discuss how my previous scholarship helped fill some of the gaps in the literature, and how those gaps have shaped this book.

*UNCA / The Constitution's internationalized making is ignored, but what it promotes, receives attention*

Of the following three peace-building books, the first two are reference works, (an inventory and a lexicon), and the third is Roland Paris' award-winning scholarly book. It is worth noting at the outset that the UN provides no official, comprehensive UNCA inventory. Given this, to analyse UNCA requires knowing in which states the Security Council has mandated its use. The 2015 Oxford Handbook on peacekeeping operations covers the period 1948-2013 (hereafter Oxford Handbook). It aims to provide a 'historical overview of the missions' mandates

[108] Kirsten Haack, *The UN Democracy Agenda—A Conceptual History* (Manchester University Press, 2011).

[109] *See e.g., Building Sustainable Peace: Timing and Sequencing of Post-Conflict Reconstruction and Peacebuilding* (Armin Langer and Graham K. Brown, eds., Oxford University Press, 2016); James Dobbins and Seth G. Jones, *The UN's Role in Nation-Building: From the Congo to Iraq* (Rand Corporation, 2005); Gregory Fox, *Democratization, in* The UN Security Council from the Cold War to the 21$^{st}$ Century 6984 (David M. Malone, ed., Lynne Rienner Publishers, 2004); Richard Caplan, *International Governance of War-Torn Territories: Rule and Reconstruction* (Oxford University Press, 2005) (overlooking the Constitution).

and strengths and achievements'.[110] It recognizes that after the Cold War ended, UN peacekeeping missions broadened to include 'peace-building' ones, with this broad set of goals: governance, rule of law, civilian police, and economic development.[111] Yet UNCA is filtered out from each mission's mandate. Instead, each mission's analysis covers only these components: elections, rule of law, civilian police, civil administration, human rights, economic reconstruction, and refugee repatriation.[112] In this way, the Constitution's making receives short shrift. It finds brief mention only in the discussions about Namibia and Burundi.[113]

This inventory has thus left a huge gap. So too has another inventory provided by an article.[114] Both add nothing to our knowledge about whether a post-conflict situation involved the making of a new constitution, or the revising of an existing one. Ascertaining this aspect is very challenging, because the Security Council's early resolutions use other terms for constitutions, constitution-making, and UNCA (see Chapter 6, Table 6.4).

When a whole set of activities is hidden, other important aspects, such as the interaction between the various dimensions of peace operations and peace-building activities and their goals are also cloaked. So, Paul Diehl and D. Druckman's analysis of the sequencing of peace-building activities (in the Oxford Handbook) is unhelpful, because it omits that key, pre-elections activity: the adoption of the (new) Constitution or constitutional reform along good governance lines.[115] Indeed, starting from the early 1990s, policymakers pushed Third World states to constitutionalize democratic electoral systems, in an effort to prevent intra-state ethnic conflicts that the exclusionary political processes of

[110] *The Oxford Handbook of United Nations Peacekeeping Operations* 8 (Joachim A. Koops *et al*, eds, Oxford University Press, 2015).

[111] Id. at 30.

[112] Id. at 617–628.

[113] Id. at 301, 735.

[114] Volker C. Franke and Andrea Warnecke, *Building Peace: An Inventory of UN Peace Missions since the End of the Cold War* 16 Int'l Peacekeeping 407 (2009) (overlooking Constitution-making despite noting its salience to peace-building).

[115] Paul F. Diehl and Daniel Druckman, *Evaluating Peace Operations, in* UN Peacekeeping Operations, *supra* note 110 at 93–108.

the late 1980s–early 1990s had reportedly triggered. Thus, although Diehl and Druckman identify rule of law, elections, and democratization as key peace-building goals, the constitution-making activity undertaken to achieve them escapes attention. So does constitution-making's centrality to peace-building. As a result, Diehl and Druckman render peace-building very narrowly, as Figure 5.2 in their chapter indicates.[116] I have modified that figure and reproduced it, indicating where the Constitution's making fits in, and to which peace-building goals it relates.

The UNCA-ignoring trend continues with the *Peacebuilding Lexicon*, a 2009 Oxford publication edited by Vincent Chetail.[117] It is instructive to reproduce all of Chetail's 26 entries here, although I have switched their original order for my readers' convenience. I have italicized and numbered only those items most relevant to UNCA: *(1) capacity-building, (2) free and fair elections, (3) rule of law, (4) peace operations, (5) peace process, (6) private sector, (7) security sector reform, (8) state-building, (9) transitional administration, (10) transitional justice, (11) responsibility to protect, (12) Disarmament, Demobilization and Rehabilitation, (13) human security, (14) international crimes, (15) democratic governance*, conflict economies, civil-military interface, civil society, conflict transformation, local ownership, mine action, non-state actors, reconciliation, recovery, reparation, and return and reintegration.

At first glance, we can see what this publication does, in light of my points in 1.1–1.2. Indeed, Chetail's book foregrounds what the Constitution sustains: the rule of law. Therefore, noting this chapter's contents will be useful. That co-authored chapter affirms that the rule of law's promotion, spearheaded by the BWIs, became widely associated with promoting the market economy, achieving economic liberalization, and creating a safe legal environment for foreign investment.[118] Accordingly, the BWIs' rule of law assistance comprises commercial law-making or law-reform activities.[119] The authors point out that pursuing extensive

[116] Id. at 106 (Figure 5.2:). *See* Sean McFate, "The link between DDR and SSR in conflict-affected countries" (2010).

[117] Vincent Chetail, *Peace-building: A Lexicon* (Oxford University Press, 2009).

[118] Vera Gowland & Pergantis, *Rule of Law, in* Peacebuilding: A Lexicon, *supra* note 97 at 320, 329.

[119] Id. at 329.

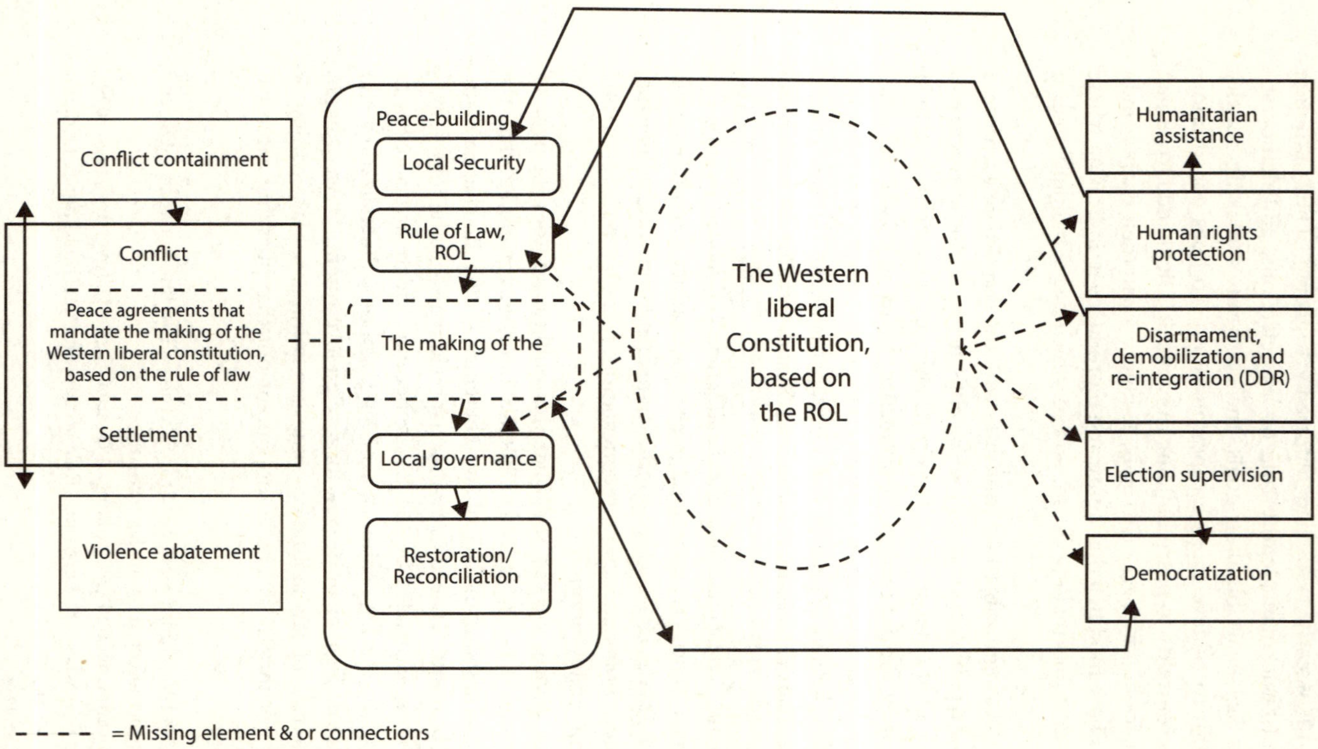


FIGURE 1.7 'Core goals, new missions and peacebuilding' – Missing jigsaw

*Note*: Disarmament, demobilization and re-integration (DDR) falls within security sector reform.

Reprinted with permission from Paul F. Diehl & Daniel Druckman, *Evaluating the Effectiveness of Peace Operations: Addressing the Challenges in* The Oxford Handbook of United Nations Peacekeeping Operations (Joachim A. Koops *et al*, eds., OUP, 2015).

privatization (for instance, of natural resources) in a peace-building context, imperils the right to self-determination.[120] Regrettably, they stop at that. They neglect to mention that key activity essential to promoting the rule of law, namely the adoption of the Constitution (see section 1.2), an aspect that Figures 1.1 and 1.6 illustrate, using an example offered by the World Bank itself. And so does the capacity-building chapter, which only covers assistance offered to build states' capacity to promote the rule of law.[121]

The Constitution's wholesale bypass, begun in the capacity-building chapter, continues through the fifteen chapters listed above, completing a full circle in its homeland: the democratic governance chapter.[122] This last, Chapter 15, affirms that democratic governance and good governance share the same criteria.[123] Instead of pointing to the Constitution, it states that promoting democratic governance includes constitution-making.[124] This chapter thus erroneously implies, and so contradicts the rule of law chapter, that post-conflict states are free to fashion a constitution of their choice (see Chapters 5–6). In light of section 1.3's discussion, this chapter even contradicts the UN, which explicitly recommends and promotes a particular constitutional model for and in developing states.

Overall, this 385 page book devotes only eight lines to the most salient peace-building activity: the Constitution's making. In tune with the aforesaid publications' approach, Chetail's work recognizes and foregrounds peace-building's politico-economic dimension. But it ignores its constitutional dimension.

So too, do Paris and Dominik Zaum's books on peace-building and state-building respectively. With a view to analysing how 14 UN peace missions (1989–99) built peace, Paris underscores the BWIs' underlying powerful role and focuses on the UN's economic liberalization and electoral assistance activities. On this basis, he concludes that the Western liberal ideology guides UN peace-building.[125] Meanwhile, in 2003,

120 Id.

121 *See* id. at 34, 39 (Capacity-building).

122 *See* id. at 105–21 (Democratic Governance).

123 Id. at 107.

124 Id. at 110.

125 Roland Paris, *At War's End: Building Peace after Civil Conflict* (Cambridge University Press, 2003)

Michael Pugh, editor-in-chief of *International Peacekeeping*, commended Paris for this breakthrough (offering this insight).[126] Before turning to Zaum, it helps to note that Paris previously analogized peace-building-minus-the-Constitution's-making to the colonial civilizing mission.[127] Zaum, with a view to considering how three Territorial Units (Kosovo, East-Timor, and Bosnia) morphed into 'States', focuses only on their internationally imposed responsibilities for promoting democracy, rule-of-law (economic liberalization), and human rights. Zaum asserts that these responsibilities constitute a 'standard of civilization',[128] which international administrations use, both to justify denying these Units the right to self-governance, and to serve as a blueprint for their activities.[129]

## Post-1989 Rule of Law Assistance's Parent Goes Unrecognized: UNCA

What about Stephen Humphrey's doctrinaire study of the rule of law as a Western concept? Logically, it briefly covers post-1989 rule of law promotion and finds colonial continuities therein.[130] Humphrey skips rule of law promotion's parent: the Constitution's internationalized making by the UN.

## Works on ITA

*Technically appraising constitution-making and missing ITA's parent: UNCA/ the Constitution's making*

Works on ITA evidence the second way in which UNCA escapes attention. They do so in two ways, the first of which Carsten Stahn's book illustrates (discussed in this para). Stahn's book devotes 10 pages to describing and technically appraising internationalized

[126] Id. at back cover ("Few studies in peacebuilding merit the description 'breakthrough.' This is one of them.").

[127] Roland Paris, *International Peacebuilding and the 'Mission Civilisatrice'* 28 Rev. of Int'l Studies 637–656 (2002) (overlooking a key Civilized Standard: the Constitution).

[128] Dominic Zaum, *The Sovereignty Paradox* (Oxford University Press, 2007).

[129] Id. at 114.

[130] *See* Stephen Humphreys, *Theatre of the Rule of Law – Transnational Legal Intervention in Theory and Practice* 109–122 (Cambridge University Press, 2010).

constitution-making, but overlooks the actors that internationalize constitution-making, namely the UN and the BWIs, and the context for such internationalization; and the model they promote, namely the Constitution.[131] Stahn fails to note that the UN was able to administer Kosovo, Congo, and East-Timor because the Constitution was internationalized there. Consequently, UNCA-ITA projects in these and other relevant territorial units are identified as ITA only.

Meanwhile, tellingly, once again, the IMF affirms my point: the Constitution's salience: It provides the basis for, and guides and governs ITA (for instance, law-making or law-reform). For example, take the IMF's submission that it co-commenced (with the UN), ITA (law-making) in East-Timor, guided all along by the latter's (East-Timor's) impending [2002] Constitution:

> The foundations of a market-based economy were implicitly set during the UNTAET period and have since been confirmed in the articles of the constitution. This enabled the Government to embark in 2005, on a model of economic growth … an open approach to trade and investment, and … good governance.[132]

Again, this innocent lack of attention to constitutional matters leads Stahn to conclude, (based on Lakhder Brahimi's misleading statement) that the UN left a 'light-foot print' in Afghanistan,[133] thereby implying that Afghans were free to choose their own constitutional model (see chapter 6). As a result, Stahn simultaneously shrouds the Constitution's salience which is precisely why it is being internationalized via UNCA and, thereby contradicts the UN itself. Nonetheless, Stahn suggests that we must interrogate constitution-making's internationalization because it violates the 1960 anti-colonial resolution.[134] I do precisely that.

*'Purposive simplification' implicitly distorts the purposes for internationalizing the Constitution, that is, using UNCA and so, ITA*

[131] Carsten Stahn, *The Law and Practice of International Territorial Administration: Versailles to Iraq and Beyond* 707729 (Cambridge University Press, 2008). (Erroneously positing that the practice of international administration shapes constitution-making when conceptually and factually, it is just the reverse). Id. at 708.

[132] IMF Country Report No. 05/247 para 14.3 (July 2005); For East-Timor's constitutional provisions see *infra* Table 6.3.

[133] Id.

[134] *See* id. at 707.

A second way that ITA works have indirectly distorted our understanding of UNCA is through what Ralph Wilde calls 'purposive simplification'.[135] That is, how commentators who have chosen to affix the 'post-conflict' label to ITA projects, particularly the well-known ones in Kosovo and East-Timor, thereby imply that ITA:

1. is always used in the post-conflict context;
2. that it is necessarily concerned with addressing the consequences of conflict; and so administration by international actors is introduced to fill the administrative vacuum and 'reconstruct.'[136]

Wilde has invalidated the aforementioned implications.[137] In so implying, commentators are implicitly explaining the Constitution's purposes simplistically. Thus, they mislead. I join Wilde in invalidating these implications by showing that UNCA-ITA projects in Congo (see Chapter 4), and Kosovo and East-Timor (see Chapter 6), were in fact mounted in the wake of conflict. However, in all three territorial units, the UN displaced local actors from the allied activities of constitution-making and territorial administration (that is, law-making), in response to their perceived inability and/or unwillingness to constitutionalize the market economy and other conditionalities. In short, the three UNCA-ITA projects were conceived to fill an internationally created vacuum.

## Works Bypassing Internationalized Constitutional Moments

Sinclair's Essay (about a book devoted to Hammarskjöld), and his own 2017 book on state-formation, and Charles Call, an international relations scholar's policy paper on UNCA, illustrate the third way that UNCA has been overlooked.[138] Regarding his Essay, it helps to note that Sinclair's comments about my chapter on UNCA—which makes these three points—alone are relevant: (1) Hammarskjöld pioneered UNCA/International Executive Rule (IER), in Congo; at his behest, the UN

135 *See* Wilde, *supra* note 14 at 12.

136 Id.

137 Id.

138 G. Sinclair, *The international civil servant in theory and practice: Law, morality and expertise* 26 EJIL 747–766 (2015).

Operation in Congo, though deployed to repel Belgium's invasion, abandoned its neutrality to pursue his capitalist vision, which clashed with that held by Patrice Lumumba, Congo's socialist Prime Minister; and (2) UN experts displaced local Congolese to draft Congo's Constitution and laws (for example, mining) to promote free markets.[139]

Regarding this chapter, Sinclair states: 'Sripati examines the practice of (UN) constitutional assistance, tracing its origins to the Congo peacekeeping operation.'[140] Yet, in conclusion, Sinclair laments that the book under review neglects to 'discuss Hammarskjöld's *signal* contribution to the evolution of UN technical assistance' [IER], which according to him, Hammarskjöld took still further in Congo, this way:

> By inserting senior experts with de facto policy and decision-making responsibility into governmental ministries, Hammarskjöld … effectively placed much of the Congo under UN administration.[141]

In this way, Sinclair refers to Hammarskjöld's IER, minus its constitutional context.

Moving onto his own book, what might Sinclair examine, with a view to establish that IOs shaped post-colonial states on a broadly Western model? Indeed, he considers none other than Hammarskjöld's IER in Congo, and the BWIs' conditionalities, but of course, minus their constitutional contexts.[142] But, then again, Sinclair notes UNCA's emergence as a post-1989 UN activity, in fact, citing to my article, 'United Nations Constitutional Assistance Projects in Comprehensive Peace Missions: An Inventory 1989–2011' (hereafter UNCA inventory) published in 2012.[143] How might Sinclair conclude? Interestingly, he states: IOs' interventions resonate of imperialism.[144]

[139] *See* V. Sripati, *Hammarskjöld and International Executive Rule: A Third World Perspective on International Law*, in Peace diplomacy, global justice and international agency: Rethinking human security and ethics in the spirit of Dag Hammarskjöld 477–507 (Carsten Stahn and Henning Melber, eds., Cambridge University Press, 2015).

[140] Sinclair, *supra* note 137 at 751.

[141] Id. at 763.

[142] G. Sinclair, *To Reform the world: International Organizations and the Making of Modern States* (Oxford University Press, 2017).

[143] Id. at 4.

[144] Id. at 1, 13.

Given section 1.1–1.3's revelations, what conceptual confusions do Sinclair's works create and reflect? Which of them can we trace to the 1990s' parallel evolution of international law and constitutional law, which I call Point X? Indeed, the answer is: all of them. In fact, Point X is why, Sinclair missed the Constitution, which is central to the territorial State, a Western paradigm. Conceptually (i) examining IOs' role in modelling post-colonial states, along Western lines, requires starting from the latter's constitutional events; (ii) Hammarskjöld brought in UN experts (in ways that Sinclair himself notes), who sculpted the Constitution (for example., of UNCA) and revised Congo's mining laws to meet the Constitution (for example., of ITA), to divert the Congo engine from the socialist track; (iii) Hammarskjöld's IER equals UNCA, and its use in 1960 is 'signal' because then, Congo enjoyed the right to create its own constitution, and laws below it, without international assistance; and (iv) the 1999 conditionalities are significant because they launch the Constitution, which UNCA produces. My chapter in the book devoted to Hammarskjöld, and my UNCA inventory discussed points i–iii, and iv respectively, both contributions whose salience to state-formation, Sinclair misses.

Next comes Call's work which considers how the UN has dealt with cases of unconstitutional changes of government in Kenya, Guinea, Kyrgyzstan, and Madagascar.[145] Regrettably, Call fails to discuss the key way in which the UN restored constitutional order. For instance, regarding Guinea, Call mentions that the UN helped broker the crucial Ougadougou Accord of January 15, 2010, which would guide Guinea's return to constitutional order.[146] But in his discussion, he omits the Accord's key provision –good governance, including that which provides its constitutional dimension: the Constitution. Therefore, he leapfrogs straight to the UN's assistance in the electoral and security sectors to show how the UN helped to restore constitutional order.[147] Alas, in this way, owing to point X, Call and many other scholars have omitted what is central (Constitution-making), and foregrounded what is peripheral (elections). Here, it is worth revealing at this early stage, some of my key findings regarding Guinea:

[145] Charles T. Call, "UN Mediation and the Politics of Transition after Constitutional Crises" (International Peace Institute, February 2012).

[146] Id. at 16.

[147] Id.

> First, when Guinea's constitutional order broke down, the UN and the BWIs stepped in to restore order: they pushed Guinean authorities to implement good economic governance. Guinea, a poor, debt-ridden state, complied.
>
> Second, accordingly, the conflicting parties signed the *Ougadougou* Accord (2010), wherein they pledged to abide by the "good governance" principles in restoring constitutional order.
>
> Third, accordingly, the 150-member National Transition Council (NTC), led by Hajah Serah Diallo, a well-known trade union leader, sculpted with UNCA, a new Constitution, which was promulgated in May 2010 (see chapter 6).

Indeed, UNCA equals the promotion of the market economy, privatization, anti-corruption, and so on (see Table 6.3), key purposes that Call's analysis obscures. Accordingly, (and as I will discuss in Chapter 6), in Guinea and elsewhere, the UN has interpreted the breakdown of constitutional order (in the wake of conflict) in economic terms, and therefore, has set market-oriented criteria for its restoration. This makes Call's focus on the UN's electoral assistance, and security sector reforms, misplaced. The internationally supported security sector reforms that he alludes to require for their full implementation a Constitution (*see* Figure 1.6).

## UNCA's Use is Questioned but its Use to Produce the Constitution (A Conditionality) Remains Unknown

Ratuva's field-work based article is welcome, for it reveals how UNCA works in practice, in Nauru.[148] (Although Ratuva is understandably unaware of UNCA's birth and post-1989 rise to produce the Constitution, he is the first to join me in questioning UNCA's use, which I discuss in chapter 10.) According to Ratuva, while there was consensus that the Government of Nauru had to speed up constitutional (fiscal) reforms, differences arose about what the reforms had to be, and how they were to be implemented. Those differences, says Ratuva, arose because two major development discourses obtained:

148 *See* Steve Ratuva, *The gap between global thinking and local living: Dilemmas of constitutional reform in Nauru* 120 (3) J. of Polynesian Society 241–268 (2011).

> on one hand, the global discourse represented by UNDP and its 'international best practice' aphorism; on the other hand, the local Nauru community and its ways of knowing, shaped by years of colonial control and cultural degradation.[149]

Accordingly, experts hired by the UNDP offered policy advice, designed public consultation programs, and drafted Nauru's constitution along good governance lines.[150] In this way, 'consent was manufactured', says Ratuva, but there was 'little, if any, explicit provision for improving community livelihood', an issue that the local Nauruans reportedly raised with him.[151] In conclusion, Ratuva laments that:

> the basic assumption [driving UNCA] is that Nauru people, like anyone else, needed to conform to the *universal* UNDP reform principles, rather than the other way around....[152]

It helps to note here that, those Reforms flowed from the Asian Development Bank's PRSPs, which the Nauru government had consented to implement, only to secure debt-relief. Accordingly, those differences eventually became irrelevant, and the above rationale underpins UNCA (see Chapter 6). Meanwhile, some who do not know that the Constitution is a conditionality, argue that international assistance stems from local actors' demands for accountable governance. Ratuva's findings, coupled with mine (see Chapters 5–6) affirm the UN's own admission (see pages 8–9), reiterate and so invalidate that claim.

Given section 1.1–1.3's revelations and the aforesaid review, how might we say, have point X and the UN and the BWIs' frameworks (for example, rule of law), distorted the discourse? Indeed, while point X triggered the Constitution-ignoring trend, the frameworks effectively turned international law scholars' attention toward law-making, a peripheral activity. Consider. The aforesaid first eight international law works ignore the Constitution, including its parentage of rule of law and ITA. They instead, focus on what it underpins (the Western state), gives rise to (ITA, that is, legislative activity), promotes (ROL), and

[149] Id. at 241.
[150] Id. at 253.
[151] Id. at 248.
[152] Id. at 247.

enables (state-formation, holding free and fair elections and/or achieving economic liberalization). In these ways, scholars focussed on, and built the post-1989 international developments' *legislative* dimension. This, in turn, triggered numerous writings on the Security Council's law-making role, (instead of its role in promoting the Constitution by mandating UNCA).[153]

*Why is international constitutional law (ICL) analysis important? 'To appraise the legitimacy of international interventions'*

What other effects might the Constitution-ignoring-trend have produced? Indeed, that trend created a knowledge-gap about the Constitution's internationalization that in turn, diminished its salience, and made constitutional issues to appear inconsequential. Accordingly, a 2018 book on Transitional Governance/UN Peace-building persists in conceptualizing UNCA-ITA as plenary ITA only, and adds to the confusion by considering "plenary ITA Kosovo Style" as the UN's most intrusive form of intervention.[154] We know where ITA arises from and what enabled the UN to achieve its ambitious post-Cold War agenda in Kosovo: the Constitution. However, two encouraging aspects regarding ICL analysis deserve mention. First is that, this very 2018 book, in addition to calling for an ICL analysis, reminds its international law audience that 'constitutional moments' and 'the period preceding and succeeding them deserves an analysis in its own right'[155] (see section 1.0).

The second is that, ICL was endorsed, almost a decade ago, by the American Society of International Law's 2009 Merit Prize Award Committee. Indeed, this Committee, which most probably consisted of international law scholars, affirmed that international law analysis of relevant developments requires starting from, and taking into account, constitutional and legislative issues. This Committee found Wilde's analysis of ITA, with its Western liberal constitutional parentage (see a. and b. below), 'critical to appraising the legitimacy of international interventions'.[156] The

[153] *See e.g., The Security Council as Global Legislator* (Vesselin Popovski and Trudy Fraser, eds, Routledge, 2014).

[154] See Groof, *supra* note 11; Groof's email dated February 16, 2018 to author (on file). The editors have since noted their error.

[155] Id. (quoting Justice Albie Sachs).

[156] *See* "Dr. Ralph Wilde awarded prestigious international law book prize," University College London, 30 March 2009 press release (on file).

Committee therefore commended Wilde's 'policy institution' concept and 'purposive analysis' method,[157] whereby Wilde and I analyse:

a. the context in which the UN tutors post-colonial people in creating the Constitution (for example, of UNCA)—and *other laws below the Constitution* (for example, of ITA),[158] and
b. the UN's ostensible purposes for so tutoring them in order that they adopt as their highest law the Constitution (for example, of UNCA), –and ensure all other laws comply with it (for example, of ITA).[159]

Put negatively, the Committee did not downgrade Wilde's coverage of legislative activities (that spring from the Constitution) and his consideration of IOs' purposes (for example, his Chapter 6 and my Chapter 7) for internationalizing those activities. Accordingly, the Committee did not say that Wilde's book has no analysis and no theory. My point is the same. Presenting the facts is often an essential part of analysis; it most certainly does not preclude analysis. Indeed, the Committee underscored that, starting from developing states' constitutional and legislative moments, and considering why they are internationalized, is enduringly important to international law analysis (for example., my Chapters 4–9). Here is the second reason, why I chose Wilde's research method: It recognizes the Constitution's salience and enables me to offer an ICL analysis and appraise the legitimacy of internationalized constitution-making by the UN.

Here lies my second caveat. In so focusing on the relevant international developments' *legislative* dimension, scholars have implicitly acknowledged its parent constitutional dimension. Which is precisely what my international constitutional law (ICL) analysis offers, and here our arguments unite! (I will revisit this point in section 1.8). For instance, international relations expert Tony Lang suggests that the global constitutionalism discourse views the Constitution as its epitome.[160] Although

157 Id.

158 *See* my Chapters 4–6; Wilde's Chapters 2; 4–5.

159 *See* my Chapters 7–10; Wilde's Chapters 6–8.

160 Tony Lang, *Constitutionalism and the Law: Evaluating the Security Council, in* The Security Council as Global Legislator 12 (Popovski, V. and T. Fraser, eds., Routledge, 2014).

this strongly suggests that discourse should start with the Council's Constitution-promoting role that has not happened.[161] Nevertheless, this book makes that case.

Next, Editor-in-Chief Pugh, who commended Paris in 2003 for revealing peace-building's Western liberal ideology, published in 2011 my UNCA inventory, which reveals what lends peace-building that ideology. How might the UN achieve economic liberalization (identified by Paris as its key peace-building goal)? By helping post-conflict states adopt what it prescribes: the Constitution that the BWIs clearly suggest (see sections 1.1.1–1.2) and Figure 5.3 and Chapters 5 and 6 offer as evidence. Put more directly, helping post-conflict states constitutionalize relevant rights, in ways noted in section 1.2, my Chapter 6 and Table 6.3 provide additional evidence. Consider how might the Units fulfill the three Civilized Standards, including rule of law (identified by Zaum) to become States? Again, why do Paris, Humphreys and Sinclair find colonial continuities in UN peace-building, post-1989 UN-rule of law assistance and the UN's-state-formation-role respectively? These two questions have the same answer. Indeed, the Constitution produced by UNCA is a key Civilized Standard that underpins the State. Finally, Ratuva's field-based study confirms my argument that is based on the UN's official explanations.

How then did I arrive at UNCA? As noted in the preface, my childhood passion to learn about constitutions and international human rights, (in this order) led me to UNCA. Since I was schooled in a former British colony, this passion meant being intuitively conversant with the legal trinity, and so, wanting to learn about the Constitution—and how it intersects with international human rights. Two scholars helped me to arrive at UNCA.[162]

Eminent constitutional law scholars such as Baxi, Henkin, Ran Hirschl, Howard, Ludwikowski, Osiatynski, and Stephen Gill, a political economist, apparently missed post-1989 UNCA. However, they perceptively saw in the BWIs' rule of law assistance to promote economic liberalization, a *legislative* assistance required by the *Constitution*'s promotion. For instance, Baxi alludes to this point in his 2015 critique

[161] Id.

[162] *See* Vijayashri Sripati, *To My Karmic Guru-Dev with Gratitude: Prof. Wiktor Osiatyñski, Feb. 1945-April 2017, Obituary* 39 (4) Hum. R. Q. 1033 (November 2017).

of the post-1989's global rule of law, regime, where he cites my UNCA inventory.[163] In Chapter 5 of this book, my findings that debtor-states aided by the UN constitutionalize the BWIs' conditionalities (for example, judicial independence) would hardly surprise Baxi, Gill, Gerrit Gong, and Hirschl.

As a result, when I began to explore UNCA, I found UN documents that shrouded the Constitution (by using other terms for 'constitution' and constitution-making), and commentary that ignored it. I gradually realized that UNCA-ITA projects were erroneously cast as ITA only. However, that was not enough. I still had to find the missing piece in the jigsaw puzzle. Here lies the third caveat. Given the Constitution's famed feature (property rights),[164] and my own previous findings about how the BWIs' conditionalities were re-shaping Indian (Western liberal) constitutionalism along neo-liberal lines,[165] I turned to the international political economy discourse. There, I found the non-UNCA writings of distinguished scholars like Baxi, Yash Ghai, Stephen Gill, Issa Shivji, Gerrit Gong, Hirschl, and Jim Tully. Put differently, this small group of non-UNCA scholars recognized the Constitution's *politico-economic* significance and focused on the Constitution's internationalization. For this reason, they logically became my immediate conversationalists and helped me find the jigsaw piece. Gill, Shivji, and Gong focused on the BWIs, and helped me to connect the BWIs' purposes with those of UNCA's. Indeed, in virtually all instances, IMF documents provided me with key details about these states' constitution-making, including their time-lines.

[163] *See e.g.*, Upendra Baxi, *Remaking progressive global governance: Some reflections with reference to the judiciary and the rule of law, in* Critical Perspectives on the Crisis of Global Governance: Reimagining the Future 162, 163 (Stephen Gill, ed., Palgrave Macmillan, 2015)

[164] I refer to the *capitalist private property rights*. *See generally* Gary D. Libecap, *Property rights in American Economic History*, in The Oxford Handbook of American Economic History (Louis P. Cain et al eds., OUP, 2018).

[165] *See*, e.g., Vijayashri Sripati, *India's National Human Rights Commission: A Shackled Commission?* 18 (1) Boston J. of Int'l L. 1-46 (Spring 2000) (establishing that India established a Western-style human rights commission by executive decree and without parliamentary deliberations only to meet the IMF's conditionalities.)

Gill's following observations resonated with me:

> Constitutional revision is a feature of the 1990s. Specifically, this involves initiatives to politically lock in neoliberal reforms. These initiatives serve to secure investor freedom and property rights for transnational enterprises. Yet students of international political economy have paid surprisingly little attention to the constitutional aspects of global restructuring.[166]
>
> Note: In line 2, Gill is obviously referring to the technique of constitutionalization, discussed in § 1.2`.

I took Gill's call seriously, and I engage with Shivji and Gong elsewhere in this book. Shivji showed me why, and how, international financial institutions influenced constitutional design – another under-researched area – in Africa from the 1960s to the late 1980s.[167] Tellingly, after Shivji's 2001 piece, the next short piece on the BWIs' promotion of the Constitution (by J. Couso) appeared.[168] This book starts from 1949, and my submissions dovetail with Shivji's and Couso's. Finally, Gong and Tully's works introduced me to the international "standards of civilization"[169] in the eighteenth century, and Western liberal constitutional democracy's (and by extension, the Constitution's) imperial role respectively. Gong, Tully, and Baxi (see *section* 1.8) thus offered me innovative ways of viewing the West's interventions to remedy developing states' governance.

In conclusion, I suggest that scholars can hardly be faulted for ignoring the Constitution's internationalization. On the contrary, the literature has so developed in this way, for four intertwined reasons. First, during the 1990s, fewer scholars had expertise in international constitutional law and avoided this subject.[170] Second, international

[166] Gill, *supra* note 9 at 23.

[167] Issa Shivji, *Three Generations of Constitutions and Constitution-making in Africa: An Overview of Social and Economic Context and Assessment*, in Constitutionalism in Transition: Africa and Eastern Europe, International Conference on Comparative Constitutionalism, Warsaw, Poland, May 17–20, 2001, 74–92 (M.S. Rosen, ed., Helsinki Foundation for Human Rights, 2003).

[168] *See* Couso, *supra* note 19.

[169] Gong, *supra* note 22.

[170] Contemporary scholars writing on ICL and/or aware of its existence, include Professors Baxi, David Kennedy Jed Kronke, Vlad Perju, and Ann Peters (listed in alphabetical order).

law scholars failed to see the making of the Constitution in the rule of law promotion. These factors explain why Chetail's Peace-building Lexicon was so formatted. Meanwhile, even if scholars did notice the Constitution's influence, and its promotion by the UN, hardly anyone questioned the UN's commitment to produce it in independent states.

Third, as a result, much of the peace-building literature (including what little exists about constitution-making) offers a technocratic appraisal of the projects, where the focus is on whether they have met their goals, and how to improve them. Here, it is useful to note that excellent scholarship coalesced around constitution-drafting (as a technical activity), federalism, power-sharing, and decentralization. These are topics on which many leading Constitutional law scholars—including Baxi, David Cameron (political scientist), Rajeev Dhawan, David Claire Williams, Jill Cottrell, Yash Ghai, Christina Murray, Muna Ndulo, Peter Russell, and Cheryl Saunders –advised constitution-makers across the globe.[171] Still, UNCA escaped attention.[172] In fact, some of these UN experts and others have themselves drawn from my UNCA inventory.[173] For not all constitutional law scholars including comparatists focus on international political economy issues.

A caveat is due here. Professors Ghai and Baxi are two senior scholars who have long noted the Constitution's politico-economic significance for colonial powers and the BWIs.[174] For instance, Ghai notes that Fiji adopted a new Constitution in 1997 to implement the BWIs' conditionalities.[175] I start from where he ends. Meanwhile and understandably, their respective students (for example, Shivji and Celine Tan, see section 1.8) also focussed on the BWIs, thus making not only their own

[171] *See* e.g., Cheryl Saunders, *Constitution-building in the Pacific in 2015, in* Annual Review of Constitution-Building Processes 31-45 (IDEA, 2016) (overlooking UNCA *and* the BWIs' role); Works in *infra* note 173.

[172] Id.

[173] *See* e.g., Christina Murray, *International institutions, constitutions and gender, in,* Constitutions and Gender 107, 112 (Helen Irving, ed., Edward Elgar Publishing, 2017); Tom Ginsburg, *Constitutional advice and transnational legal order* UC 2 Irvine J. of Int'l, Transnat'l & Compl. L 19 (2017).

[174] *See* Upendra Baxi, *The Future of Human Rights* (Oxford University Press, 2002).

[175] *See* e.g., Yash Ghai and Jill Cottrell, *The Role of Constitution-Building Processes in Democratization* (IDEA, 2004).

*non-UNCA* writings but also, their students' useful for my analysis. Since this is the first work to explore UNCA, I have chosen to unfold its story gradually. Chapter 5 will reveal why fiscal federalism and so on, acquired importance, and conversely, a demand for expertise in them grew.

Finally, ITA, rule of law, UN peacemaking, and state-formation have evolved into huge stand-alone topics. And so, just as it took me a whole book to explore UNCA, ITA, ROL, and UN peacemaking scholars were perhaps similarly constrained. For instance, although UN peacemaking equates with the Constitution's making, Jeremy Levitt's analysis of peacemaking and power-sharing in Liberia, Guinea-Bissau, and Sierra Leone misses this aspect. However, Levitt provides constitutional details leading up to UNCA's use, information otherwise hard to find and valuable.[176] (My findings dovetail with Levitt's, showing that the BWIs shape transitional governments' power-sharing's responsibilities; see Chapter 6.)

## A Lone Voice in the Field

This brings me to my fourth caveat. In the post-1989 era, scholars of international law, international political economy and constitutional law scholars rarely conversed with each other. This pattern is suggested by the title of a forthcoming peace-building book: *Investment and human rights: charting the elusive intersection.*[177] It helps to look at Figure 1.8. As a result of this lack of cross-communication, the constitutional dimensions of the following post-1989 fields and sub-fields remained un-sketched: international trusteeship; UN peace-building; UN state-building; UN peacemaking; UN rule of law promotion; ITA; global restructuring; and law and development.[178] My unique pursuit, exploring how the Constitution intersects with international law, helps to fill in those missing dimensions. Here lies my contribution.

Indeed, virtually nothing existed when I began my research in 2006. Therefore, I initially defined the steps in an internationalized constitution-making process, based on fragmentary sources.

[176] *See e.g.*, Jeremy Levitt, *Illegal Peace in Africa: An Inquiry into the Legality of Power Sharing with Warlords, Rebels and Junta* (CUP, 2012).

[177] *See* text of *infra* note 187.

[178] *See* Rittich, *supra* note 106.

My earlier publication, the first to explore UNCA, questioned its revival in sovereign states. I established UNCA's use, outside the context of implementing decolonization, in two aspects: post-conflict and development assistance. In the process, I uncovered hidden UNCA projects in many post-conflict as well as stable states such as the DRC, Bhutan, Rwanda, Malawi, Maldives, Zambia, Côte d'Ivoire, and Zimbabwe.[179] The UNDP's 2014 constitutional assistance guidance note cites my work.[180]

To spur a discussion about UNCA requires revealing its revival and mushrooming in the post-1989 era, in independent states. I did just that in 2012. At David Chandler's invitation, I contributed a chapter on UNCA to his edited handbook on State-Building.[181] I also published the first inventory of UNCA projects in comprehensive peace missions from 1989–2011, concentrating on the making of new constitutions. I showed that for this purpose, from 1989–2011, the Security Council had mandated UNCA in 14 states.[182] This book builds on my previous publications to offer the first comprehensive inventory of UNCA projects from 1949–2019. As in my previous publications, here too, the UNCA projects will be so described as to counter the limitations discussed in 1.3. In tracing the events that have led to UNCA's use, it will identify the BWIs' role and conditions, besides recognizing the UN Security Council's promotion of UNCA. (Indeed, in most cases, the Security Council itself calls for the BWIs' participation in laying good governance's cornerstone.) Finally, it will map out all the UNCA activities, identifying UNCA's process-based and content-based activities (see section 1.6), and tabulate the constitutional commonalities produced by UNCA. This will make evident how the UN helped shape both the constitution-making process and the constitutional content.

Meanwhile, few noticed UNCA's revival, that is, first used in an independent state, during the Cold War, in Congo. Still fewer know that

[179] *See The UN's Role in Post-conflict Constitution-Making Processes: TWAIL insights* 10 Int'l Community L. Rev. 411–420 (2008).

[180] UNDP, Constitutional Support Guidance Note 2 (2014).

[181] Vijayashri Sripati, *UNCA in State-building*, in The Routledge Handbook of International State-building 143 (David Chandler and Timothy D. Sisk, eds., Routledge, 2013).

[182] Sripati, *supra* note 5.

UNCA was revived by the late Dag Hammarskjöld. At the invitation of Carsten Stahn and Henning Melber, I contributed a chapter on just this topic to their edited book, dedicated to this former UN Secretary-General.[183] At their behest, I analyzed UNCA's revival, using the TWAIL theoretical framework. I made three points, of which the first two occur on page 31, and the third is presented here: Hammarskjöld revived UNCA as International Executive Rule ostensibly, in response to Congo, a newly decolonized country's supposed governance incapacities and to promote free markets there.[184] Indeed, as this book will demonstrate, at a deeper level, UNCA's revival is the story of internationalizing the Third World's constitution-making to advance the interests, not of the new countries but those of powerful Western states. Most recently, Steven Ratuva and Emmanuel de Groof invited me to contribute a chapter on UNCA to their edited books on ethnic conflict and transitional governance, respectively. De Groof's book, an outcome of a state-building conference, recognizes that peace-building/transitional governance is a topic requiring an ICL analysis, and calls upon his contributors to provide just that.[185]

To conclude, I have authored all the peer-reviewed work that exists on UNCA as a distinct theme. I trust that I have created a sturdy foundation that others will build upon.[186] Meanwhile, now that UN peace-building has been talked about for 30 years, stand-alone case studies (for example, are Afghanistan; Colombia; Bolivia and neoliberalism) are coming out, which have still not noticed the Constitution's promotion by the UN, despite its centrality to peace-building/neoliberalism.[187] But the case studies affirm my findings.[188] For instance, they argue that the UN's neoliberal policies have favored foreign investors to the detriment of

[183] Sripati, *supra* note 138.

[184] Id.

[185] Groof, *supra* note 11.

[186] Id. *The UN's Constitutional Assistance: New Additions to The 'Standard of Civilization'?* ASIL Int'l Org. Interest Group Rev. 26–28 (Fall 2009); *UN Constitutional Assistance: A Mechanism for Implementing International Law and Public Policy?* ASIL Int'l Org. Group Rev. 24–26 (2010).

[187] *See* e.g., *Neoliberal Legality: Understanding the Role of Law in the Neoliberal Project* (Honor Brabazon, ed., Routledge, 2016).

[188] Id. at Chapters 1, 7–8.

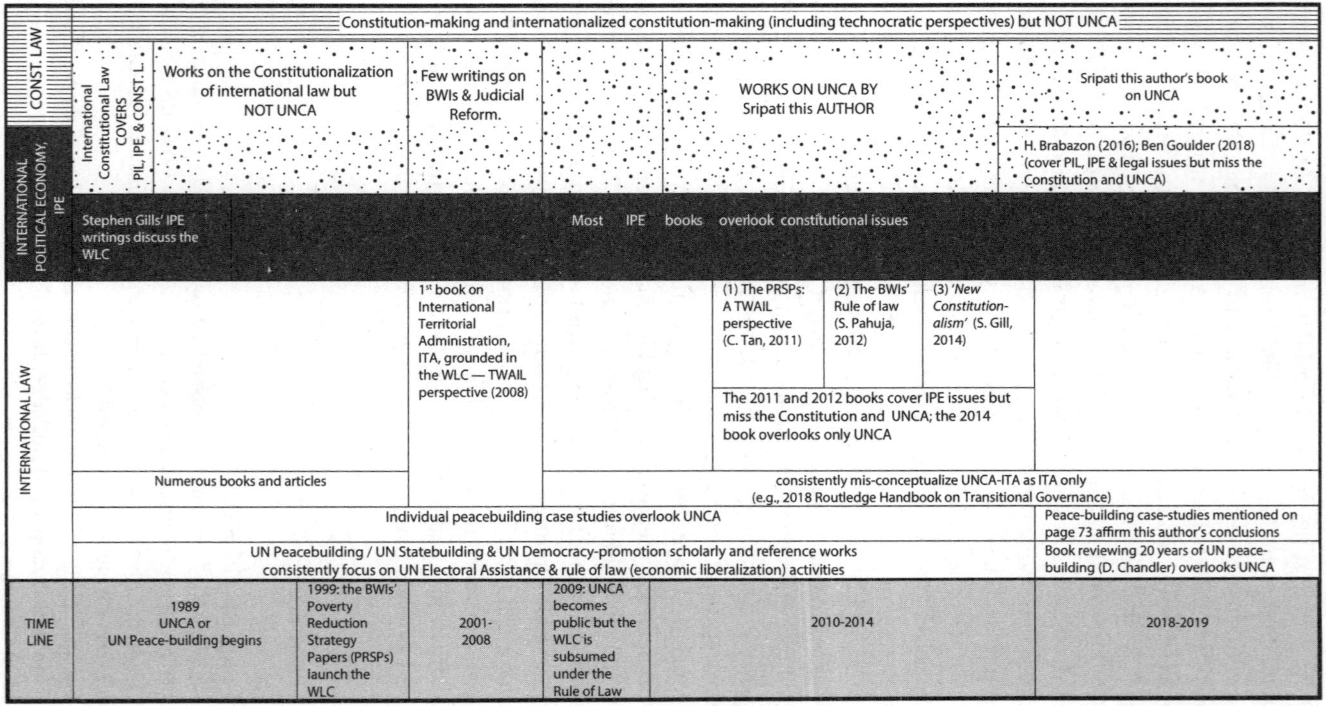


FIGURE 1.8 1989–2019: UNCA an international constitutional law topic, remains uncharted: Public international law, including international political economy and constitution law discourses run parallel

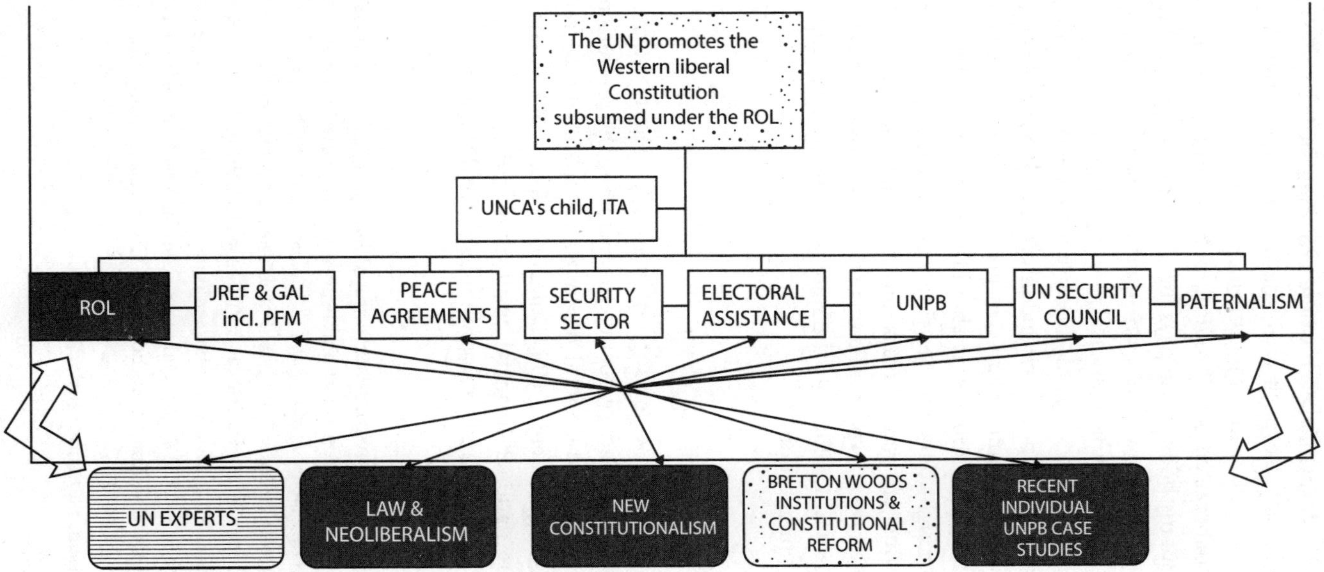


FIGURE 1.9 State of the discourse after my book's publication
Acronyms: UNPB=UN Peacebuilding, JRef=Judicial Reform, GAL=Global Administrative Law and incl.=including

local interests.[189] Meanwhile, even where exploring the law's role in the neoliberal project is the explicit goal, the "supreme law," the Western liberal *Constitution, fails to receive full attention.*[190] For instance, Brabazon asserts that neoliberalism is a "juridical, political and economic" phenomenon.[191] But my book which pays full attention to the Constitution reveals that neoliberalism *is first,* an international constitutional law phenomenon, and *only then*, a juridical one, as is argued.[192]

Here comes my final caveat. My book may be the magnet that pulls together relevant international law and international political economy strands, thus weaving a fuller picture of post-1989 developments. I will revisit this point in section 1.8. It should turn the international law discourse in the right direction, starting a conversation long-overdue, between policymakers and scholars, and between constitutional law scholars and their counterparts in international law and political economy. Figures 1.8 and 1.9 illustrate the state of the discourse, before and after my book's publication.

## 1.4 Sources

My sources comprise a wide range of materials. The UN materials cover: Primary and secondary documents including the resolutions of the Security Council and General Assembly, reports of the Secretary-General, peace agreements, UN Guidance Notes and documents from such international financial institutions [IFIs] as the World Bank, the IMF, the African Development Bank [AfrDB], and the Asian

[189] *See e.g.*, Id; Daria Davitti, *Investment and human rights in armed conflict: Charting an elusive intersection* (Hart Publishers, 2019) (forthcoming); Andrei Gomez-Suarez *et al*, *Foreign Investors and the Colombian Peace Process*, 18 Int'l L. Rev. 223, 232 (2016); Christine Schwöbel-Patel, *The market and marketing culture of International Criminal Law,* in Critical Approaches to Criminal law (C. Schwöbel, ed., Routledge, 2014); *New Constitutionalism and World* Order (Stephen Gill and Claire Cutler, eds, CUP, 2012). Helena A. García, *Neoliberalism as a form of Authoritarian Constitutionalism*, in Authoritarian Constitutionalism (eds, Helena A. Garcia, *et al.*, eds, 2019).

[190] *See* Brabazon, *supra* note 185 at 3.

[191] *Id.*

[192] *Id.*

Development Bank [ADB]. As "members of the UN family"[193] as well as financiers of post-conflict reconstruction and development aid, the BWIs have deeply influenced UNCA, and for that reason their reports, factsheets, and policy papers (and letters of intent submitted to them by states) form a significant part of my sources. The UNDP, UN Environment Programme [UNEP], UN Women (hitherto, UNIFEM), Office of the High Commissioner for Human Rights [OHCHR], UN Office on Drugs and Crimes (UNODC), and UN Children's Emergency Fund [UNICEF] perform key UNCA functions. I therefore, draw from these agencies' slides, primers, reports, websites, newsletters, job postings, policy papers, and guidance notes. Reports and other documents shared with me by UN officials, and posted on the websites of peace operations, the Department of Political Affairs [DPA], the Department of Peacekeeping Operations [DPKO], and the UN Department of Economic and Social Affairs [UNDESA] come next.[194] Secondary commentary from the fields of law, history, economics, and political science and the constitutions of UNCA-recipients states and other member states complete the list.

From 2006 to 2014, I conducted qualitative interviews and informal conversations with a sample of politicians, UN officials, and other stakeholders involved in some of the relevant constitution-making processes. These interviews have supplemented, expanded upon, or clarified data drawn from the previously mentioned literature.

## 1.5 The Subject Matter: UN Constitutional Assistance

Defining UNCA requires starting from the Constitution. According to the UN:

1. At the center of the ROL Framework [Framework] sits a 'constitution that as the highest law of the land':

    a) Incorporates internationally recognized human rights and fundamental freedoms as set out in international treaties (for example, life, liberty, property, dignity, and gender equality) and provides for their applicability in domestic law, and

[193] *See* "United Nations Structure and Organization." *Available at:* www.un.org/en/aboutun/structure.

[194] *See* UN, *supra* note 3, ¶D.

b) Establishes effective and justiciable remedies at law for violations; ...
c) Defines and limits the power of government and its various branches and the people; ...
d) Enshrines and empowers an independent and impartial judiciary; effective oversight institutions or mechanisms (for example, anti-corruption bodies, national human rights institutions consistent with the Paris Principles).[195]

The UN clarifies that the constitution defined in 1 above, must be based on the ROL, which is so defined:

> A principle of governance in which all persons, institutions and entities, public and private, including the state itself, are accountable to laws that are publicly promulgated, equally enforced and independently adjudicated, and which are consistent with international human rights norms and standards. It requires as well measures to ensure adherence to the principles of supremacy of the law, equality before the law, accountability to the law, fairness in the application of the law, separation of powers, participation in decision-making, legal certainty, avoidance of arbitrariness, and procedural and legal transparency.[196]

The UN obviously recommends and promotes a written constitution. My book is concerned with UNCA's use in enabling states adopt the (written) constitution as defined in this section, or in reforming their existing constitutions along the lines set out in the Framework. Whether the constitution is obeyed or implemented, lies outside the scope of my enquiry. I am concerned with the bare document (and its provisions), that the UN helps to produce.

## 1.6 The UN Defines the Constitution's Making

How does the UN enable a state or a territorial unit's local actors make, and adopt the Constitution, defined in section 1.5? Before proceeding, it is useful to note three points. First, as previously noted in section 1.0, I use "local actors" to refer to "nationals" (of a state or territorial unit)—the term used by the UN.[197] Second, local actors covers those nationals who, owing to conflict, reside outside their respective countries (for

[195] *See* UN, *supra* note 6 at 2, 3.
[196] Id.
[197] *See* UN, *supra* note 3 at 5.

example, Afghan refugees in Pakistan). (The UN too, uses nationals in this broad sense). Third, for operational purposes, the UN discusses UNCA under two broad headings: (1) Constitution-making *process*; and (2) Constitutional *content*.[198] Given this, to consider UNCA's definition requires knowing the steps in a constitution-making process, and the creation of constitutional content.

According to the UN, a constitution-making process and creating constitutional content comprise the following steps (inclusive list) respectively:[199]

Constitution-making process: Steps

1) High level negotiations between the relevant stakeholders that ends in the adoption of an agreement or agreements that outline the constitution-making's process;
2) Public information campaign;
3) Public consultation process (consulting all local actors, particularly, women and children);
4) Creation of a representative body, either through election (for example, Constituent assembly) and/or a democratic selection process (for example, the creation of the *Loya Jirga* in Afghanistan);
5) Adoption of the constitution; and
6) Or holding of a referendum, which would then involve
    a. the conduct of a public information cum civic education campaign; followed by the
    b. followed by the adoption of or rejection of a constitution at the referendum

Crafting constitutional content: Steps

1) High level negotiations among the relevant stakeholders that ends in the adoption of a peace agreement or agreements, outlining the content of the constitution
2) Creation of the constitutional drafting body
3) Sculpting the initial draft (of the constitution, that is, the bare document)
4) Collecting, collating, and channeling public input to the drafting body;
5) Channeling public input and/or that of experts and/or that of gender/child audit to the drafting body

198 Id.
199 Id.

6) Redraft after receiving input (from public and other channels mentioned in point 5)
7) Make relevant amendments to the document after the debate
8) Adoption of the constitution (either with or without a referendum)

The UN posits that the aforesaid steps (regarding process and content), and the corresponding UNCA activities (mapped out in the tables below), render constitution-making 'transparent, inclusive and participatory'.[200]

## UNCA Activities

The UN 'assists' local actors in conducting the constitution-making process and creating constitutional content, whose steps are listed in section 1.6. The UN either displaces local actors and/or tutors them in carrying out the steps, relating to process and content, outlined in sections 1.6. Accordingly, the UN discusses UNCA in terms of process-related and content-related activities, mapped out below.[201]

## UNCA Actors

According to the UN, providing UNCA mapped out in section 1.6, and Tables 1.2–1.3, entails drawing upon a 'combination of expertise that resides across various departments and agencies, as well as outside the UN System'[202] (see Table 1.4).

## UNCA's Salience

In conclusion, four points about UNCA's salience deserve mention.

First, the steps in the constitution-making process indicate that elections, (whether to a constituent assembly, or any other representative constituent body) are key milestones. Accordingly, electoral assistance is integral to UNCA (*see* Table 1.2). However, it is very important to note that, not all UN electoral assistance projects involve the making of a constitution or the reform of an existing one. Put simply, not all

[200] Id.
[201] Id. at 4–6.
[202] Id. at 4.

TABLE 1.2 United Nations Constitutional Assistance: Process related activities

| | | Activities (inclusive list) |
|---|---|---|
| Constitution-making process | Political and Strategic support | Directly participate in mediation talks;<br>Conduct extensive consultations with all key stakeholders, national governments, rebel movements, tribal leaders, the civil society, and regional actors<br>Provide input about international human rights and humanitarian law standards and the relevant state's financial obligations;<br>Draft or participate in the drafting of all necessary documents, including constitutions & peace agreements;<br>Strategic assistance on determining the selection process for the constituent bodies/representative forum (elections of various kinds or a representative nomination process)<br>Draft rules of procedure for the drafting body and the representative forum<br>Political facilitation on key contentious issues (both substantive and procedural) |
| | Constitutional (electoral) assistance | Conduct or supervise constituent assembly elections/constitutional referendum<br>Prepare electoral budgets; conduct voter registration |
| | | Provide policy and legal advice regarding the electoral system;<br>Elaborate the electoral system in the constitution;<br>Draft electoral laws, rules, and regulations;<br>Draft electoral laws and regulations disallowing political parties from involving children in demonstrations; |

| | | |
|---|---|---|
| | | Child Protection Teams hold meeting with political leaders & groups to share information on the rights of children and the responsibilities of political parties towards children |
| | | Tutor women in the legal aspects of elections; strengthen their public speaking and media-interaction skills |
| | | Register voters, determine the voting eligibility of refugees and Internally displaced persons (IDPs), & print and distribute copies of draft constitution |
| | Public consultation & Public education campaign | Develop and disseminate public education posters, materials, and booklets<br>Hire focus groups, coin questionnaires, hold village meetings, and create websites to seek public input, particularly from children, women, and youth; where relevant conduct broad public consultations in refugee camps outside the state territory;<br>Broadcast weekly bilingual radio programmes, stage theatre plays, host weekly press conferences, publish election magazines/newsletters & distribute fliers and posters; Collaborate with Civil Society Organizations (CSOs) to develop civic education programmes |
| | Logistic support | Develop electoral budgets, coordinate donor support, and create & manage a trust fund |

*Source*: UN, Guidance Note of the Secretary-General: United Nations Assistance to Constitution-making Processes (2009) and allied relevant UN documents.
*Note*: Common source for Tables 1.2–1.4.

TABLE 1.3 United Nations Constitutional Assistance: Content-related activities

| Activities (inclusive list) | | | |
|---|---|---|---|
| Constitutional content | Knowledge-based support | Political and strategic support | Directly participate in mediation talks<br>Conduct extensive consultations with all key stakeholders, national governments, rebel movements, tribal leaders, the civil society, and regional actors<br>Provide input about human rights standards and the relevant state's financial obligations<br>Draft or participate in the drafting of all necessary documents, including peace agreements<br>Drafting bodies/representative forum: Strategic assistance on designing the selection process and drafting rules of procedure;<br>Political facilitation on key contentious issues (both substantive and procedural) |
| | | Drafting assistance | Formulate final adoption procedures (e.g., qualified majority in the representative forum, referendum)<br>Draft or participate in the drafting of all necessary documents, including constitutional provisions relating to women, children, indigenous groups, Anti-Corruption Commissions, and Central Banks);<br>Review previous constitutions and compile articles that may be included in the new draft constitution |

| | | | |
|---|---|---|---|
| | | Expert guidance | Provide a library of state-of-the art materials and access to online materials Sponsor talks by IMF experts and conduct lectures, study tours and seminars for the drafting body's members Provide expert guidance on constitutional matters (e.g., power-sharing, natural resource governance, fiscal decentralization, international human rights, rules on acquisition and loss of nationality, judicial independence, and NHRIs)<br>Secure states' ratification of international treaties and assist them in completing their legal obligations under various treaties |
| | | Gender/ Child Audit | Facilitate links with OHCHR/ UNICEF/UNHCHR/UN Women to initiate dialogue and obtain comments on the constitution's drafts<br>Audit the draft constitutional provisions relating to women, children, minorities, and refugees, and good governance, (inclusive list)<br>Promote public outreach initiatives that will foster dialogue and debate among the wider population, on procedures, structure and content of the constitution |

| | | | |
|---|---|---|---|
| | | Monitor Constituent Assemblies (CAs) | Create space for an informed debate on constitutional issues with particular reference to international norms and comparative best practice; Inform the CA members about the need to comply with commitments made in the relevant peace agreements and/ or their states' development strategies |
| | | Logistic support | Establish a Secretariat for the constitutional committee; provide necessary office and Information Technology equipment; train officials |

TABLE 1.4 United Nations Constitutional Assistance Actors

| **The Rule of Law Unit, UN Secretariat** | |
|---|---|
| UN Secretary-General, Special representatives of the Secretary-General | Office of the High Commissioner for Human Rights (OHCHR) |
| Security Council | United Nation's Children Emergency Fund (UNICEF) |
| Department of Political Affairs (DPA)/ | UN Development Fund for Women (UNIFEM) (now, UN Women) |
| Department of Peacekeeping operations (DPK) | United Nations High Commissioner for Refugees (UNHCR) |
| United Nations Development Programme (UNDP), UN Resident Coordinators (UNRCs) | UN Department of Public Information |
| UN Department of Development and Social Affairs, (UNDESA) | The International Financial Institutions |
| UN-Office of Legal Affairs | External actors |

UN electoral assistance includes UNCA. A key way the UN shrouded UNCA, was to use the term electoral assistance to cover for it. Since my book is the first to explore UNCA, for my readers and future researchers' benefit, I distinguish between UN constitutional electoral assistance (UNCEA) and UN electoral assistance. Throughout this book, I focus on, and am concerned only with UNCEA, which covers creating an independent electoral commission that is essential for organizing presidential/parliamentary elections (*see* Angola, Chapter 6), and so, sequence-wise, precedes UN electoral assistance.

Second, when does UNCA start and end? As the UN itself, clearly indicates, UNCA begins at the negotiating stage, and ends when a new constitution is adopted or an existing constitution has been reformed along stated lines (see section 1.6).[203] Where the state is a conflict-torn, and/or post-conflict one, the negotiations, among warring parties typically occur in the context of an internationalized peace process (with constitutional dimensions). In the case of a stable state, the stakeholders' negotiations occur, for instance in the context of implementing the Millennium Development Goals (MDGs) via a new constitution, or reforming an existing one (for example., development assistance context). Importantly, in both instances, the negotiations cover the state's implementation of the Conditionalities. In some instances, UNCA may continue even after the adoption of a new constitution, when that constitution is subjected to a review, as occurred in Iraq.[204]

Finally, the UN affirms that:

> UNCA will usually not be limited to high-level political facilitation or technical legal expertise. ... Assistance may include, but is not limited to, the following [activities] (depending on the country context).[205] (The activities listed in this quote find mention in Tables 1.2–1.3).

## 1.7 Methodology

As previously noted, this book examines the purposes served by UNCA through Wilde's Method (Ralph Wilde's concept of 'policy institution' and purposive analysis method).[206]

203 Id. at 10.

204 UNAMI *Fact Sheet* (10 August 2007).

205 UN, *supra* note 3 at 5.

206 *See* Wilde, *supra* note 14 at 36. Therefore, Wilde's clarifications on his stance on the 'policy institution' concept pertain equally to my study.

According to Wilde, Policy institution' combines an "institution" ("established practice") with a focus on "policy"', that is, the purposes for which the practice is associated or 'the ends to which the practice is put'.[207] Thus, under Wilde's Method, policy *implementation* and not policy definition or formulation receives focal attention.[208] Further, the word 'institution' in Wilde's 'policy institution' stands for a more common meaning of the term as is set out in the Oxford Dictionary: '...established law, custom, usage, practice, organization, or other element in the political or social life of a people'.[209] Wilde clarifies that although 'institution' in his 'policy institution' lacks normative value, his adoption of a more common meaning of the term 'institution' is, "without prejudice to the question of whether any normativity persists."[210]

What does purposive analysis do? According to Wilde, 'purposive analysis', analyses:

> ... the official explanations given for the projects, evaluating the projects on their own terms to establish what purposes they are ostensibly set up to serve.
>
> ... the objective is not to suggest the 'real' reasons for the projects, in terms of causation and rationality, and the effect that these projects necessarily have. Rather, it is to identify a justificatory framework to explain how the projects are understood in international policy discourse. Although the purposes to be considered may not have 'caused' the projects, nor have actually been the 'real' motivations for introducing the projects, nor been realized in practice, they are nonetheless, the purposes with which the projects are associated in international policy discourse .... The justificatory structure has a significance in its own right, independent of any validity it may enjoy in terms of causation, motivation, and effect.[211]

According to Justice Aharon Barack, the essence of purposive analysis is just what Wilde underscores in the above passage: It is "analysis of the text, not psychoanalysis of its author."[212] I embrace Wilde's

[207] Id. at 37.

[208] Id.

[209] Id. at 36, fn. 99.

[210] Id.

[211] Id. at 39 [emphasis added].

[212] *See* Barack, *supra* note 13.

Method, as so explained, for my enquiry about the purposes served by the Constitution's internationalization by states and/or IOs (including the UN).

## 1.8 Theoretical Perspectives: Third World Approaches to International Law (TWAIL)

The TWAIL perspective provides an effective means for understanding why in this post-colonial era, poor, debtor, *sovereign* Third World states are either displaced from, or tutored in the activities of constitution-making. This is so, even though TWAIL scholars have overlooked UNCA, for more or less the same reasons, as their mainstream counterparts in international law. Still, TWAILERS such as Tony Anghie, Upendra Baxi, B.S. Chimni, Sundhya Pahuja, Celine Tan, and Ralph Wilde, (listed in alphabetical order), have provided valuable insights that illuminate some aspects surrounding UNCA.

Barring Baxi, the remainder TWAILERS are noted international law scholars who focussed on international law topics of their choice: Colonialism (Anghie); FTA/ITA (Wilde); the UN's neoliberal agenda (Chimni); and the BWIs' conditionalities: PRSPs (Tan) and rule of law (Pahuja) which as previously noted, have become huge stand-alone ones whose constitutional dimension (Dimension), they therefore, legitimately overlooked. (Regarding ITA, as previously noted, Wilde has rightly recognized its constitutional parentage.) But, that is the Dimension I provide, only because I am fascinated with the Constitution and its intersection with international law. Accordingly, I undertake an ICL analysis, which reveals that it: sires FTA; is central to colonialism/international trusteeship; is key to achieving the BWIs' neoliberal policies which is precisely why they are internationalizing it, after 1989, as a development strategy, subsumed under the 'rule of law' label; and from 1999, as a market-oriented poverty reduction strategy by the PRSPs. For this reason, my argument unites with these international law scholars' as well, and with whom I will engage with at appropriate places, throughout this book, starting from this section. It helps to revisit Figures 1.8–1.9.

I will start with noting TWAIL's principal tenets here. Indeed, Maria Santos who has surveyed TWAIL literature, has very lucidly summarized them as follows.[213] I make additions (see italicized points) to them at appropriate places, based on the insights that I offer in the following chapters.

1. The current era of globalization is bearing witness, and contributing to the growing south-north divide.
2. This growing divide has fortified the claim of the northern, Western or first world states to power over the southern, eastern or third world states.
3. International law is the main tool for propagating and reinforcing this hegemonic claim (see point 4A for one way, in which it does).
4. The Western world maintains its power through the construction of the rest of the world as its inferior 'other' (*see point 4A* for one way, in which it does).

4A. *The Western World revived international trusteeship in response to the Third World's supposed incapacities: assisting them in response to perceived challenges, with the way they conduct their constitution-making, and what they write into their content. In this way, the Western world constructs the Third World as the inferior "other," and so, controls the latter. Indeed, legitimizing arguments rooted in international law have made UNCA, (with and without ITA), normatively acceptable.*

5. This hegemonic status dates back to the era of colonialism, when Western states occupied and exploited erstwhile uncharted territories mainly for economic gain; Point 6A affirms this.
6. Such economic gain translated into political and social domination at both the domestic and international levels, which are carried over to the present in multifarious ways (known as neocolonialism).

6A. *Colonial powers imposed the Constitution to establish jurisdiction over the uncharted territories, to exploit their resources and administer them. For this reason, and in this way, constitution-making in the Third World was internationalized to secure economic gain and political domination.*

7. The present neo-colonial status of the third world is manifested in various forms, ranging from political patronage and economic manipulation to discriminatory and racist government policies.

213 Maria Deanna Santos, *Human Rights and Migrant Domestic Work: A Comparative Analysis of the Socio-legal Status of Filipina Migrant Domestic Workers in Canada and Hong Kong* 47–48 (Martinus Nijhoff Publishers, 2005).

8. *One key manifestation of the third world sovereign states' neocolonial status is that despite their independence/rejection of international trusteeship, they have consented to UNCA: adopting a constitution that was designed by, and for the West's (transnational interests) benefit.*
9. The continuing subordination of the formerly colonized states makes the practical application of concepts such as sovereignty, territoriality, and human rights highly problematic. Indeed, point 9A affirms this.

9A. *The UN promotes sovereignty's colonial notion, that is, graded sovereignty, thereby rendering this concept's application highly problematic. For instance, it ostensibly explains reviving UNCA/international trusteeship to "strengthen" Third World states' supposedly eroded sovereignty.*

10. The various international law norms and other related factors, which contribute to this unjust world order, must be revisited, unpacked, questioned, and reformed. This book does precisely that.

As a prelude to the next chapter, where I consider the origins of internationalized constitution-making, I engage with Upendra Baxi and Celine Tan here. Indeed, Baxi states that:

> Constitutionalism is not unique to the West or the North, only it has been made to appear so; All legal cultures have their own distinct conceptions of constitutionalism, a fact under-valued by dominant traditions of discourse.[214]

In fact, colonial powers used this very rationale to justify imposing the Constitution, whose property rights were key to exploiting the Third World's resources for furthering their own colonial economic interests. This means that the Constitution's imposition by foreign states and/or IOs, can also be framed as the internationalization of (domestic) economic decision-making.

Indeed, Tan has framed PRSPs in just these ways.[215] Besides this author, Tan is one of the few international law scholars to have noted that, PRSPs mandate constitutional reforms:

[214] For the quote see Comparative Constitutionalism Course Syllabus, Global Law School Program, 1999, New York University; Baxi, *Constitutionalism as a Site of State Formative Practices* 21 Cardozo J. of L. 1184 (2000) (expanding on the quote).

[215] *See* Celine Tan, *Governance through Development: Poverty Reduction Strategies, International Law, and the Disciplining of Third World States* 3 (Routledge, 2011).

> PRSPs have led to in varying degrees, the reconfiguration of the political landscape in PRSP countries, as legal and political institutions, (legislatures, *constitutions,* regional and local governments), and relationships between the executive and the legislature, between state and civil society, are reorganized to conform with the operational dictates of the new architecture of aid.[216]

However, Tan fails to connect the Constitution (explicitly integral to international law since the eighteenth century) with its launching pad, the PRSPs. She nonetheless, rightly situates the PRSPs within post-colonial international law, by tracing their origins to colonialism, that is, international law's historical context. Building on Baxi and Anghie, Tan argues that international law has long created, and rested on the 'dynamic of difference' between the West ('civilized'), and the Third World ('barbaric').[217] Moreover, through their conditionalities, the BWIs coerce Third World states, helping to model and rebuild them along preferred lines. And indeed, the imperial character of international law has both, facilitated and legitimized the PRSPs' interventions (*see* above quote).[218]

I concur wholeheartedly with Tan. I assert: PRSPs reconfigure debtor states' political landscapes along good governance lines in this way: they launch the Constitution.

## 1.9 Book outline

This book has two Parts. Part I (Chapters 1–4) provides UNCA's historical background, and Part II (Chapters 5–10) sets UNCA's post-1989 rise, center-stage. After establishing that UNCA has seldom been studied before, this first chapter has analysed the particulars of its operations.

Chapters 2 and 3 introduce UNCA's colonial origins. Chapter 1 establishes that the Constitution provides a framework for the conduct of territorial administration. Accordingly, its internationalized making sired foreign/international territorial administration. Given this, Chapter 2 provides the historical context in which these conceptual ties were forged.

[216] Id. at 169
[217] Id. at 1—52.
[218] Id.

Chapter 3 traces UNCA's origins through Ralph Wilde's Family of FTA institutions:

- (1) Post-Renaissance (exploitation) colonialism practiced by European imperial powers;
- (2A) 'Protection' (activity occurring in 'protectorates') (that is, ITA by the League of Nations - League);
- (2B) ITA projects since 1945, that is, ITA by the UN. (I consider this institution, starting from chapter 4);
- (3)–(4) State-conducted administration of Mandated and UN Trust Territories;
- (5) Representative Bodies; and
- (6) Occupation 'including so-called belligerent occupation'.[219]

Chapter 3 thus, follows a 'cross-project'[220] focus of analysis, rather than a chronological one. Specifically, I ask whether these institutions "operate in a practical manner in a common fashion, and also manifest important policy connections" regarding their ostensible policies, and purposes/ends.[221] Chapters 7 and 9 ask this same question about UNCA, and make the same sequence of moves to answer it.

In my answer, I show that (1) the Constitution's making is common to all these FTA institutions. Indeed, in each FTA institution, the relevant colonial power (Foreign Power, FP) imposed the Constitution, a Civilized Standard, that is central to trusteeship to achieve these four trusteeship goals or Civilized Standards: (a) free markets; (b) the rule of law; (c) good governance; and (d) civilized social practices. The Constitution provided the framework for (foreign) territorial administration which means, each of Wilde's FTA institutions is undergirded in a colonially imposed constitution—the Constitution. Put simply, Wilde's Family is based on, and results from constitutions siring and working together with FTA/ITA. On this basis, Chapter 3 concludes that international trusteeship comprises the Constitution's (internationalized) making and FTA. So, Wilde's 'Family of FTA Policy Institutions' must be reframed to include the parent policy institution: the Constitution's internationalized making, particularly as a way to pursue trusteeship goals, that is,

219 *See* Wilde, *supra* note 14 at 297.

220 Id.

221 Id. at 45.

set perceived civilized standards. Table 9.1 illustrates Wilde's family so reframed.

Chapter 4 introduces UNCA's birth as international trusteeship in 1945, and its use in Libya in 1949, tracing its origins *chronologically*. To arrive at UNCA's birth, (drawing partially from chapter 3), I trace the rise, rejection (in 1960), and revival of international trusteeship during the twentieth century. (I start conceptualizing UNCA as a 'Policy Institution' from this chapter.) In 1960, the self-determination principle morphed into an absolute right for colonies. Therefore, colonially imposed constitutions and their off-springs, foreign-state or IO-run territorial administrations (FTA/ITA), were automatically rejected. Nonetheless, UNCA and ITA were revived, but only for the limited purpose of realizing the right of self-determination. Put simply, UNCA was used to implement decolonization.

This juncture, the end of UNCA's historical background, brings us to July 1960, when far from fading, UNCA was revived again, but this time in a sovereign state (the newly decolonized Congo). Chapter 4 analyses UNCA in Congo, showing how it sired and guided ITA there. This juncture, the end of Part 1, brings us to 1990, when UNCA projects, far from ending, began to mushroom in the world of sovereign states.

Chapter 5 analyses the Constitution's re-appearance in the post-Cold War era as part of establishing UNCA as an 'institution'. It helps to note that the Constitution's internationalization in the Third World can also be framed as the internationalization of economic decision-making there. Given this, Chapter 5 considers the milestones marking the internationalization of economic decision-making in the Third World during the Cold War (1950–91), and after Cold War (1991–99). (I have started from 1950 for clarity and continuity instead of starting from 1989.) This chapter's analysis reveals that this 'established practic'" (internationalized economic decision-making) culminated with the Constitution's promotion through two similar, consecutive but differently named conditionalities from 1983–99 and from 1999 till the present day. In order to be launched in 1999, the BWIs first conceptualized it as a rule of law or development (understood as market-oriented poverty reduction) or poverty reduction (so understood) strategy. This chapter aims to offer a macro view of developments, and so, it will cover those milestones in the proportion to which they concern the Constitution's internationalization in 1999. To that end, it will elaborate on the 1999 milestone:

the BWIs' Conditionality/Poverty Reduction Strategy Papers (PRSPs): which prescribed a ROL or development (so understood) strategy to secure debt-relief: the Constitution.

Having so traced the Constitution's internationalization to the BWIs' Conditionalities, Chapter 5 shows how UNCA serves to produce that very constitution and thereby constitutionalize the BWIs' lending conditions/standards: free markets, anti-corruption measures, and so on. The Constitution is thus, promoted in both "post-conflict," and stable, but debtor LDCs. But what underpins its making is not the eighteenth century's 'civilized'/'uncivilized' paradigm, but a newer universal language of development, deployed by powerful western states: The developed countries vs. LDCs' framework.

I argue that the broad way in which the UN defined 'conflict prevention' extended the Constitution, (a Conditionality), to the sphere of development, so understood. As a result, the UNDP was empowered to meld constitutional assistance with development assistance, ostensibly to erase bad economic governance in LDCs, and thereby reduce their poverty and speed their (market-oriented) development. In this way, Chapter 5 analyzes and establishes the two contexts, in which the Constitution is produced: post-conflict and development assistance. Next, it explores how the UNDP frames its constitutional assistance in terms of implementing Public International law and Policy goals (hereinafter Law & Policy goals). The question of how UNCA's use in the post-conflict context promotes Law and Policy goals is postponed to Chapter 8. Chapter 5 concludes by showing how, although UNCA mushroomed after 1989, it was made public only in 2009, and so, normalized and consequently institutionalized.

With the factors that extended UNCA into sovereign states in hand, Chapter 6 proceeds to show that UNCA fulfills Wilde's criteria for an 'established practice', and so, can be considered manifestations of a parent "institution." This Chapter therefore catalogues the remainder UNCA projects (1989–2019), prefacing and ending their analytical description with four Tables, Table 6.1, 6.2, 6.3, 6.4, respectively. The first two connect the implementation of the Conditionalities with the Constitution's (internationalized) making. The third identifies the consequent constitutional commonalities in PRSP/UNCA-recipients-states. The UNCA projects are described in the same order that they appear in Tables 6.1–6.2 and in a way that counters the drawbacks previously mentioned (*see* section 1.8). This comprehensive inventory, which also underscores the BWIs' role, offers details never before put together, thus benefiting those who wish to explore individual UNCA projects in-depth. This chapter completes UNCA's conceptualization as a 'parent institution' which began in Chapter 4.

Chapter 7 establishes UNCA as a 'Policy Institution'. Chapter 7 therefore considers the explanations or justifications put forth by the UN for UNCA's use in all territorial units, including independent states. Drawing partially on Chapters 4 and 6, this chapter demonstrates that UNCA ostensibly serves to raise the quality of local governance consonant with its (and ITA's) wide range of standards, including free markets, and women's rights. Importantly, it argues that UNCA was conceived in response to perceived challenges about the conduct of the constitution-making process by local actors, and the types of content created by them. On this basis, UNCA projects are classified collectively on a purposive level, thus establishing UNCA as a parent 'Policy Institution'. (Note: I postpone considering until Chapter 9, whether UNCA, in so promoting the ends outlined in this and the previous chapter, pursues two allied policies: trusteeship and the civilizing mission).

Chapter 8 considers how the UN explains the standards promoted by UNCA that Chapter 7 outlines, in terms of implementing Law and Policy goals. This Chapter reveals that until 1993, UNCA-ITA projects were mounted ostensibly to serve as a dispute prevention and settlement mechanism, with a view to promote peace and security through the promotion of the rule of law, free markets, good governance, and modern practices to strengthen women's emancipation. After 1993, only UNCA (without ITA) served explicitly as a 'conflict preventive' measure to promote peace and security. In both periods, (when UNCA-ITA and only UNCA were used), it was the Constitution that implemented these aspects of Law & Policy.

So far, my analysis has shown that colonially imposed constitutions, and the foreign territorial administrations they undergird are parent-child policy institutions. (This relationship can be framed as internationalized constitution-making tied with foreign territorial administrations.) So are UNCA (or internationalized constitution-making) and ITA, which work toward common purposes and ends.

Drawing on the analyses in Chapters 2–4 and 7–8, Chapter 9 establishes the continuation of international trusteeship in sovereign states:

UNCA. This chapter answers the question, left unanswered in Chapter 7: Does UNCA, in promoting the purposes and Law and Policy ends, outlined in Chapters 7-8, pursue two allied policies: trusteeship and the civilizing mission? In answering this question, I fully conceptualize UNCA as a 'Policy Institution'. It establishes that the Constitution (which the UN and the BWIs co-conceptualized as a development strategy), symbolizes financial modernity. This is precisely why the UN ostensibly helps sovereign Third World states, in response to their supposed incapacities, to produce this very constitution, and promote its Law and Policy ends, (outlined in chapters 7–8). In short, UNCA ostensibly serves to 'modernize' these states, and thereby 'strengthen' their sovereignty, supposedly weakened by their bad self-governance. In this way, this book shows that UNCA-ITA, and only UNCA, operate in a practical manner in a common fashion, and also manifest important 'purposive connections'. For these reasons, UNCA with and without ITA, fulfills Wilde's Policy Institution criteria.

Based on these commonalities and continuities, I will establish that the institutions I reframed in Chapter 2, (see list in paragraph three from top), and 2B) UNCA-ITA, and 2C) only UNCA (1993–2018), 'act in the same fashion in an elemental sense':[222] Indeed, all of Wilde's reframed institutions 'are of a piece'.[223] In fact, the Constitution heads Wilde's Family. Its internationalized making, (whether by foreign states and/or IOs including the League/the UN), constitutes Wilde's Family's *Parent* Policy Institution. On this basis, I reframe Wilde's Family, one last time, to admit UNCA-ITA and only UNCA. I specifically argue that the Constitution's internationalization represents a continuation of external domination and control in constitution-making in the Third World. I modify Table 3.1 (see Chapter 3) and reproduce it here, illustrating Wilde's fully reframed family with UNCA-ITA and only UNCA admitted therein.

I conclude the UNCA (international trusteeship) story in Chapter 10, considering how UNCA's revival in sovereign states escaped the colonial tag. This chapter will show that the UN has invoked ideas rooted in international law to legitimize UNCA's revival. It will foreground some aspects of UNCA, missed by the legitimizing discourse, to reveal its and

[222] Id. at 312.
[223] Id.

therefore, ITA's colonial continuities. It will show why UNCA's revival in sovereign states entails deeper implications, and so merits attention: it promotes therein a Constitution that is conceptually a state's highest law. In this way, I will close on the same theme with which I began this book: UNCA's salience.

As the first exploration of UNCA, this book establishes the purposes of UNCA projects, engaging with the purpose or standards to which they have ostensibly been put, without addressing the question of whether UNCA projects have managed to meet those purposes or ends. Finally, this first exploration of UNCA does not encompass many of the complex legal issues raised by the activity, such as accountability.

2

# The Western Liberal Constitution's Internationalized Making Sires Foreign Territorial Administration

## The Historical Context

### 2.0 Introduction

This chapter and the next one establish the historical background of UNCA, which as we know, equates to the WL constitution's (hereinafter, Constitution is spelt with a capital C) internationalized making.[1]

This chapter establishes that Post-Renaissance European colonialism (1700–1960) (as defined by Wilde, see section 2.2) (hereafter Colonialism)[2] can be conceptualized as the Constitution's internationalization (for example, by Western colonial powers) siring and working with FTA (its child) toward common goals. Indeed, small wonder

[1] I will use these terms interchangeably: colonial Constitution-making, Constitution's making, Constitution's internationalized making, and internationalized Constitution-making (in Chapters 2 to 4)

[2] *See* Ralph Wilde, *International Territorial Administration: How Trusteeship and the Civilizing Mission Never Went Away*, 301–306 (Oxford University Press, 2009).

that Jim Tully calls Colonialism, 'constitutional imperialization'.[3] In this way, this chapter sets the stage for tracing UNCA's origins non-chronologically (in the next chapter) through Ralph Wilde's Family of international trusteeship Foreign Territorial Administration (FTA) policy institutions (hereafter Wilde's Family), of which Colonialism is the first:

1. Post-Renaissance European colonialism (1700–1960)
2. International Territorial Administration (ITA)
   A) 'Protection'—ITA by the League of Nations
   B) ITA by the UN ('ITA projects since 1945')
3. State-conducted administration under the Mandate System of the League of Nations;
4. State-conducted administration under the United Nations Trusteeship System;
5. Representative bodies; and
6. Occupation (including 'belligerent occupation') (conducted by foreign states).[4]

FTA refers to foreign state-conducted territorial administration, whereas ITA refers to an IO conducted territorial administration. The term foreign territorial administration includes ITA. (I will discuss Wilde's definition of territorial administration in Chapter 3.)

I trace UNCA's origins through Wilde's Family for two reasons. The first reason is as already noted, colonial constitution-making sires FTA, and therefore UNCA sires ITA (see chapter 1). The second reason is because this book's overarching goal is to conceptualize UNCA as a 'Policy Institution' (using Ralph Wilde's concept and method: the 'Policy Institution-Purposive Analysis'[5]), which I will finally admit into Wilde's Family.

I undertake analysis at two levels: first, outer and second, inner. At the first level, which is in this shorter chapter, I establish that Colonialism

3 Jim Tully, *Constitutional Democracy and Imperialism* 46 (3) Osgoode Hall L. School J. 461, 482 (2008).

4 *See* Wilde, *supra* note 1 at 49–50, 289–311. The terms colonial trusteeship and international trusteeship are used interchangeably.

5 Id. at 36–42 (methodological framework).

provided the context in which the Constitution sired FTA. I show that in the eighteenth century, the Constitution emerged as a Civilized Standard under international law.[6] Conceptually, Western colonial powers—foreign states and / or IOs—imposed the Constitution in the Third World, to establish jurisdiction and administer the territories. Hereafter, I will refer to Western colonial powers as Foreign Powers (FPs). In this way, colonial constitution-making worked symbiotically with FTA, its child, toward these common ends / Civilized Standards: free markets, rule of law, good governance, and civilized practices and common policies: trusteeship and civilizing mission.[7] In the process, I suggest how and why, the rest of Wilde's Family of FTA 'Policy Institutions' (*see* FTA institutions listed above, in points 2–6) were born, and operate (historically and conceptually) in the way they do.

This sets the stage for Chapter 3: Wilde's FTA international trusteeship institutions. Here, I will undertake the second (inner) level of analysis, which is not chronological, but rather utilizes a 'cross-project focus on policies'.[8] I will use Wilde's Method to analyse Wilde's Family. I will show that the relevant FPs imposed the Constitution, and in so doing, created each of Wilde's FTA institutions. The Foreign Powers imposed the Constitution to promote these common ends: free markets, rule of law, good governance, and civilized practices. They did so ostensibly to civilize the Third World, and in response to its perceived incapacities. In this way, the FPs pursued or fulfilled the trusteeship policy. This is how colonial constitution-making worked symbiotically with each of its children (Wilde's FTA institutions) in pursuit of common policies (for example, trusteeship) and toward common ends (Civilized Standards), such as the rule of law. This is precisely why the Constitution undergirds each of Wilde's FTA institutions.

In this way, I will establish that Wilde's Family rests on, and reflects the conceptual relations I established in this chapter. Indeed, Wilde's Family comprises two symbiotic parent-child Policy Institutions: the Constitution's internationalized making and FTA. In fact, the Constitution heads Wilde's Family. On this basis, I will argue that

[6] Gerrit Gong, *Standards of Civilization in International Society* (Oxford University Press, 1984); Tully, *supra* note 2 at 461, 465.

[7] *See* Wilde, *supra* note 3 at 317-341 (analyzing FTA's ends).

[8] Wilde's phrase. Id. at 363.

Wilde's Family must be reframed to admit its parent colonial trusteeship Policy Institution: the Constitution's internationalized making. Table 3.1 captures the Constitution's salient cum symbiotic role vis-à-vis Wilde's Family.

## 2.1 Tracing the Internationalization of Constitution-Making in the Third World

Which entities, when, and for what purposes imposed the Constitution over the Third World, and thereby *internationalized* constitution-making there? Here, Patrick Glenn reminds us that:

> the political circumstances of empire rendered it more likely for the notion of a written Constitution, [defined as 'the most hierarchically superior form of Western legal writing'] to be adapted outside Europe than within Europe.[9]

Again, Stuart Elden helps us to connect the dots between the (Western liberal) Constitution and territory, and colonization. He reminds us that questions of colonization and conquest all have territorial elements[10] and that 'territory is dependent on a number of techniques and on the law'.[11] Indeed, colonization means appropriation, taking possession, and includes extending jurisdiction over new territories and new peoples.[12] The constitution, so defined, was just the measure necessary to realize these and other essential processes of colonization.[13]

Given this, and for reasons already noted in the introduction, to answer the question just posed: 'Which entities, when, and for what purposes internationalized constitution-making in the Third World?' I consider constitution-making during Colonialism (1700–1960). Before proceeding, it is useful to note these points.

[9] Patrick Glenn, *Cosmopolitan State* 69 (OUP, 2011)

[10] Stuart Elden, *Land, Terrain, territory*, Progress in Human Geography 34 (6) 799, 809, 813 (2010).

[11] Id. at 809.

[12] *See* Diane Erika Kirkby, *Colonial Systems of Law*, in Encyclopedia of Western Colonialism since 1450 703, 705 (Thomas Benjamin, ed. ABC-CLIO, 2007).

[13] Id. at 706 (quoting Christopher Tomlin).

- In defining and describing colonialism in the following section, I reveal how it offered the context in which the conceptual relations mentioned in the introduction were forged. To state this is not to define or explain colonial Constitution-making once and for all; rather, my point is only to underscore that the Constitution's internationalized making sires FTA. Therefore, I will use broad brush strokes to sketch the historical practice that reflects these relations.

The next three bullet points intertwine.

- Constitutions were imposed to assert jurisdiction, not sovereignty. Indeed, non-Western peoples were deemed 'barbaric', uncivilized and so, not fully or properly sovereign.[14] On this basis, 'European states, used sovereignty then conveniently available as an institution for taking legal possession of foreign territories in an orderly fashion.'[15]
- As I will show, although the Constitution was imposed to exploit non-Western peoples and their resources, within and outside the Third World, such imposition was however, ostensibly undertaken to 'civilize' them, and thereby, make them sovereign.[16]
- This reveals a paradox: Constitutional democracy has an imperial lineage. It was evolving in Europe and North America at the precise historic moment when non-Western peoples in North America and the Third World were being colonized. Given this, tracing the Constitution's imposition in the Third World requires noting that good government meant authoritarian government—not, the promotion of democracy.

## 2.2 Defining Post-Renaissance European Colonialism (1700-1960)

I embrace Ralph Wilde's definition of post-Renaissance European colonialism (hereafter colonialism):

[14] Antony Anghie, *The Evolution of International Law: Colonial and Post-colonial Realities* 27 (5) Third W. Q 739, 740 (2006).

[15] Robert Jackson, *Sovereignty – Evolution of an Idea* 73 (Cambridge University Press, 2007). This means, sovereignty followed in the wake of jurisdiction. Id.

[16] *See* Gong, *supra* note 5; Tully, *supra* note 5 at 461, 465.

> The practice and ideology of a particular historical manifestation practiced by the European powers after the Renaissance, often represented as 'imperial', 'modern', or 'capitalist' colonialism.[17]
>
> Colonialism involves some kind of direct administrative control exercised over the colonial territory by the imperial state, even if power was exercised through local representatives and officials to a significant degree: the key point in such cases is that the officials in question are themselves understood to be under the direct control of the colonial authority, for example through appointment and removal and/or being subject to overall imperial law and policy.[18]

It should be noted that Wilde adopts 'a narrower frame of reference'[19] regarding colonialism. For as he explains, regarding colonialism, he covers 'only those representations of particular manifestations' that compare with ITA, as he has defined it.[20] According to Wilde, ITA is where an IO displaces the local actors of a territorial unit to administer that Unit, and 'administration' covers all three types of activities: legislative, executive, and judicial.[21] Having so defined Colonialism (see the two aforesaid passages in this section), Wilde proceeds to describe some of the activities it involved:

> The varied character of 'colonialism' includes, of course, the nature of the activity performed; during this period the activity is usually represented as having ranged from staking a claim over territory without introducing any substantive presence, to informal control exercised by corporate entities such as the East India Companies, to direct administrative presence by European states exercised on top of local structures of governance, to more intrusive and extensive administrative conduct.[22]

17 Wilde, *supra* note 3 at 302. According to Wilde:

> The term colonialism is, of course, a site of contestation and used in various different ways beyond the simple meaning of 'implanting … settlements on distant territory.' Id. at 301 ….
>
> One main way the term colonialism is used is to stand for the practice… Id. at 301.
>
> For the remainder of this quote see the text attached to this footnote.

18 Id. at 303.

19 Id. at 302.

20 Id.

21 Id. at 32–36.

22 Id. at 302–303.

> Differences of degree in this regard are commonly understood to have subsisted across and within individual manifestations of colonialism over time.[23]

What does Wilde says regarding the ends of colonialism so defined? According to him:

> For present purposes, colonization, or colonialism as settlement, *is excluded* from consideration when it was the exclusive or primary purpose associated with a particular case.
>
> This (Wilde's) study, then, is concerned with what is commonly called 'exploitation' or 'domination' as opposed to 'settlement' colonialism. The term 'exploitation' is used to suggest that the purposes associated with colonialism were either directly exploitative (e.g. the plunder of natural resources) or smokescreens for exploitation (e.g., the civilizing mission).[24]

In offering this definition of colonialism (reproduced earlier in this section, 2.2), and describing the varied activities it involved, Wilde makes clear that he does not treat and/or represent Colonialism during 1700–1960 as being of a single epoch.[25] In embracing Wilde's definition, I don't either. Indeed, this period holds a complex past, that runs over some crucial distinctions and developments, that help us see, how significantly thought and practice changed, in the eighteenth and nineteenth centuries. My own analysis—with its emphasis on the later part of this period implicitly demonstrates this. As underscored in Chapter 1, I will focus only on those purposes or ends (pursued by exploitation colonialism) that Wilde does: free markets, the rule of law, good governance, and civilized practices. Indeed, as we will see, these purposes are essentially those of the Constitution, to achieve which, it was imposed. This is precisely why, it was indispensable to Colonialism, as defined by Wilde.

For the sake of continuity, I will briefly note the varied practices during Renaissance, (that is, between 1450 and 1700), which we might anachronistically call 'Constitution-making' in relation to empire. As already noted, in North America, the idea of a written Constitution was in vogue since the 1600s.[26] Various European powers, including

[23] Id. at 303

[24] Id. at 314.

[25] Id. at 302.

[26] Glenn, *supra* note 8 at 69.

England, France, Portugal, and Spain, acquired extensive territorial (colonial) possessions from the sixteenth to the mid-twentieth century.[27] 'Colonization means appropriation, taking possession,' and entailed the following processes for whose realization, law/Constitutions were salient (the list is inclusive):

Authorizing colonial ventures,
Recording the facts of occupation,
Establishing order,
Introducing and extending legal control,
Extending jurisdiction,
Binding commerce to territory,
Creating new relationships between the colonizers and the colonized, and
Formalizing the legal difference in legal categories.[28]

(However, I hasten to add that in some instances, possession was avoided in the interest of other forms of control).[29]

Consider the act taken by the British Government in 1578, to promote colonial enterprise: Queen Elizabeth granted the Royal Charter to Sir Humphrey Gilbert.[30] Again, the 1606 Royal Charter created and provided the Virginia Company with a license to found a colony in the Americas.[31] Most likely drafted by Sir Edward Coke, the 1606 Charter extolled conquest as a means of converting heathens to Christianity.[32] Written charters served to record the facts of occupation, and 'create jurisdiction in bounded space'.[33]

[27] European colonialism shifted to Asia and Africa in the first quarter of the nineteenth century, that is, after Spain's defeat in the war against Napoleon. This coincided with the first wave of independence in Latin America.

[28] Kirkby, *supra* note 11 at 706–707.

[29] On this point, see Laurie Benton & Richard Ross, *Legal Pluralism and Empires, 1500-1850* (New York University Press, 2013).

[30] Arthur Mills, *Colonial Constitutions: An Outline of Constitutional History and Existing Government of the Dependencies* xxxii (J. Murray, 1856).

[31] Aziz Rana, *The Two Faces of American Freedom* 31 (Harvard University Press, 2010).

[32] Id.

[33] Shannaugh Dorsett, *Mapping Territories*, in Jurisprudence of Jurisdiction 136, 146 'quote' (Shaun Mc Veigh ed., Routledge, 2004); Roger D. Congleton, *Perfecting Parliament – Constitutional Reform, Liberalism, and the Rise of Western Democracy* 217 (Cambridge University Press, 2010).

Constitutions' salience did not end with this. When trade and commercial interests replaced Christianity as a rationale for overseas territorial conquest, possession, and expansion, a need arose for binding, predictable, and enforceable rules and regulations. Now, colonialists powerfully wielded assertions about ethnic and religious superiority to justify the elimination of the natives, and the appropriation of their lands in the Americas.[34] As regards land appropriation, the key proponent was the famed English theorist, John Locke, who drafted the Fundamental Constitution of Carolina (1669) that protected the rights of property owners.[35] So did the other initial American state constitutions.[36]

Constitutions were imposed to colonize Asia and Africa as well. For instance, Martin Wright writes:

> The Dependent Empire illustrates how in constitutional development the stage of judicial power precedes the stage of legislative power. Early or undeveloped constitutions are concerned with organizing jurisdiction rather than with establishing legislative and executive organs; ....[37]

Before 1880, European states had colonized only some parts of Africa. By 1909, however, they claimed to have control of almost the entire continent—except Ethiopia.

The later constitutions, such as the Government of India Act, 1909 (hereafter the Minto-Morley Act) and the Government of India Act, 1919 (the Montague-Chelmsford Act), created legislative and executive organs.[38] Enacted by the Imperial (British) Parliament, the Minto-Morley and Montague-Chelmsford Acts were then known as 'colonial constitutions'.[39] They both are still known as 'colonial constitutions'.[40] They were so categorized to differentiate them from the 'imperial constitution' of the imperial power, Great Britain.[41]

[34] Rana, *supra* note 30 at 12, 24, and 30–31.

[35] Id. at 34.

[36] Paul Finkelman, *Encyclopedia of American Civil Liberties* 475 (Routledge, 2006).

[37] *See* Martin Wright, *Colonial Constitutions 1947*, 55 (Clarendon Press, 1952).

[38] *See* Bipan Chandra, *India's Struggle for Independence 1857-1947* 84, 141–142 (Penguin books, 1989).

[39] Mills, *supra* note 29 at xi.

[40] Chandra, *supra* note 37 at 142.

[41] Mills, *supra* note 29 at 19.

Constitutions were no less important in inaugurating jurisdiction, and introducing administration for the other European/Foreign Powers. French colonial policy mandated that the arrangements for colonies must differ from those of the mainland (metropole).[42] Toward this end, some jurists recommended crafting 'colonial constitutions'.[43] In practice, 'special laws' enacted by Parliament placed French colonies under a 'distinct and special *régime*'.[44] Overall, the French achieved colonial subordination through a combination of different legal techniques, including decrees.[45]

As for the Portuguese, they first drew up all the laws meant for their colonies in Portugal and then 'shipped them out like wine or wool'.[46] Indeed, unlike British colonies that reflected legal pluralism, Portuguese colonies illustrate 'a pattern of complete metropolitan domination'.[47] So, colonial administration in 'Mozambique was completely dominated by Portuguese laws, Portuguese legal officers and Portuguese legal thinking'.[48] Belgium, Germany, and the United States emerged as colonial powers (Foreign Powers) only during the late nineteenth and early twentieth centuries.

As I will show in Chapter 3, European powers treated the Ottoman Empire as well, as an area of imperial exploitation. Therefore, they imposed Western-oriented constitutional reforms there, but ostensibly, to civilize Ottomans.[49]

Meanwhile, the Minto-Morley Act (and the colonial constitutions that replaced it) left unchanged the character of British rule: undemocratic, foreign, and exploitative; It did not allow Indians to significantly

[42] Stephen H. Roberts, *History of French Colonial Policy 1870-1925* 154 (Archon Books, 1963).

[43] Id.

[44] Id.

[45] Id.

[46] *See* Upendra Baxi, *Postcolonial Legality, in* A Companion to Postcolonial Studies 540, 542 (Henry Schwartz & Sangeeta Ray, eds., Blackwell Publishers, 2005) (quoting Albie Sachs).

[47] Id.

[48] Id.

[49] *See* Davide Rodogno, *Against Massacre – Humanitarian Interventions in the Ottoman Empire, 1815-1914: The Emergence of a European Concept and Practice* 36–62 (Princeton University Press, 2012) .

participate in their country's administration.[50] However, this was not true of all colonial constitutions; some of them allowed representative government.[51] Indeed, in terms of their institutions, British colonies differed from one another, and also from the colonies of other FPs.[52]

Constitutions were even critical for building empires, which though territorially constituted, lacked elaborate colonial governments, as in Siam (now Thailand) and China (for example, the port city of Shanghai: 1854–1943) (*see* Chapter 3). Those Constitutions created Western courts to protect Western people and Western commercial interests.[53] Significantly, law so used, categorized civilizations into Western and Non-western.[54]

All of this suggests that conceptually, FPs (Western states) imposed Constitutions on territorial units within, and outside the Third World to achieve their (territorial) goals: to establish jurisdiction there, with a view to exploit their resources and administer them (*see* Chapter 3). Constitutions provided the legal framework for introducing territorial administration: legislative, judicial, and executive activities, the very activities that Wilde collectively calls territorial administration, and which I shall discuss in Chapter 3. Conversely, this symbiotic reliance on constitutions to achieve territorial goals brings us to those goals espoused by FPs in the nineteenth century: the legally binding Civilized Standards.

## 2.3 The Civilizing Mission and Trusteeship Policies

The nineteenth century was the period when Europe's domination over the rest of the world reached its zenith. Ironically, this was the time when most political philosophers began to defend the principles of universalism and equality. One way of reconciling colonialism with those

50 Chandra, *supra* note 37 at 142.

51 Mills, *supra* note 29, at Chapter 1.

52 *See* id. at Chapters 1–3.

53 Anthony Webster, *Gentlemen capitalists—British Imperialism in South East Asia 1770-1890* 150–162 (Tauris Academic Studies, 1998); William Johnston, *The Shanghai problem* 45–98 and 128–159 (Hyperion Press, 1937).

54 Turan Kayaoglu, *Legal Imperialism: Sovereignty and Extraterritoriality in Japan, the Ottoman Empire and, China* 9 (Cambridge University Press, 2011).

apparently opposed principles was to argue for the civilizing mission and trusteeship policies. The 'civilizing mission argument suggested that a temporary period of tutelage was necessary in order for "uncivilized" societies to advance to the point where they were capable of sustaining states with Civilized Standards.'[55]

Trusteeship, the second policy, stems from the British concept of 'trust'.[56] (As Wilde notes, 'it became associated with certain, but by no means, all forms of colonialism in the period under evaluation').[57] Based on the Civilized Standards, trusteeship is a sub-species of the civilizing mission. Accordingly, trusteeship pursues a common goal: Civilized Standards.[58] So, it has at its heart, a key Civilized Standard: the Constitution.

Trusteeship arose in part, to position colonial rule along ethical and humanitarian lines. The call for trusteeship was invoked to replace the earlier forms of state, or mercantile colonialism, and stem the exploitation associated with trading companies such as the East India Company.[59] As we will see in Chapter 3, the trusteeship policy was internationalized. Put crudely, the argument that internationalized trusteeship went something like this: 'Non-Western peoples are 'uncivilized'; therefore, their societies lack civilized features, their governance is bad, and their sovereignty is absent or wanting.'[60] 'All of this invites the colonial guardian to 'civilize' them, that is, provide governance in tune with Civilized Standards (hereafter civilized governance), and sometimes also 'tutelage' to remedy governance, and thereby transform these societies into civilized, that is, sovereign states.'[61]

[55] Margaret Kohn, *Colonialism, in* Stanford Encyclopedia of Colonialism (2012), *available at:* http://plato.stanford.edu/entries/colonialism/.

[56] *See* Wilde, *supra* note 3 at 318.

[57] Id. at 317

[58] Id.

[59] Id. at 321.

[60] *See* Ralph Wilde, *Foreign Territorial Administration and International Trusteeship over People: Colonialism, Occupation, the Mandates and Trusteeship Arrangements, and International Territorial Administration, in* Research Handbook on International Conflict and Security Law Jus ad Bellum, Jus in Bello and Jus post Bellum 548, 549 (Nigel White & Christian Henderson, eds., Edward Elgar Publishing, 2013).

[61] Id.

Gerrit Gong's ground-breaking work tells us the story about the Civilized Standards. But before I turn to consider Gong's valuable insights, these clarifications by Jürgen Osterhammel are instructive:

> The universal character of British civilization mirrored the global reach of its empire, but it also reflected a greater identification with two normative practices whose operational radius was theoretically unlimited: international law and the free market.
>
> *Law and the Standard of Civilization*
>
> Market economy, law, and religion were the three pillars supporting the British civilizing mission, the most effective of its kind. In the French case –though not so emphatically anywhere else – assimilation to the high culture of the colonial power added a further dimension. Particular civilizing initiatives differed not only from country to country but also according to their time frame, principal agencies, local conditions, and the degree of the perceived cultural gap.[62]

Evidencing Osterhammel's last point, in the late nineteenth century, in addition to Great Britain and France, other FPs—notably, Belgium, for instance, ostensibly promoted a Civilized Standard: the abolition of the slave trade.[63] Indeed, Leopold II colonized Congo solely for its rubber and minerals. Yet, his declaration to abolish the slave trade there, made him the British Abolitionist Society's 'poster boy'.[64]

## The International Law's Civilized Standards

The Civilized Standards arose from the eighteenth century. As Gong reveals, before that time, there was only the international society of European states (Society), governed by the 'law of Christian nations' (Christian Law).[65] Christian Law was also known as the public law of Europe.[66] Thus, a global international society wherein countries of the world operated as equal members did not exist.[67]

[62] Jurgen Osterhammel, *The Transformation of the World: A Global History of the Nineteenth Century* 831 (Princeton University Press, 2014) [emphasis added].

[63] John Ayoade & A. Akinsanya, *Nigeria's Critical Election, 2011* 18 (Routledge, 2013).

[64] Id.

[65] Gong, *supra* note 5 at 5.

[66] Id.

[67] Id. at 10.

The Civilized Standards underpinned this inequality. Gong defines them as 'expressions of the assumptions, tacit and explicit, used to distinguish those that belong to a particular society from those that do not'.[68] The Civilized Standards doctrine distinguished the so-called civilized, that is, sovereign states, from those that were 'uncivilized', not properly sovereign.[69] (As mentioned in Chapter 1, the United Nations puts forth 'strengthening sovereignty' of the Third World states, as an ostensible purpose for pushing UNCA.) The Civilized Standards doctrine was used by European powers as a justification for expanding into and colonizing non-European societies and their peoples.[70] Put simply, it was used to deny colonized peoples sovereignty, and thereby deny them the protections of international law.[71] Tony Anghie, who builds on Gong's work, shows that colonialism was based on these culturally and racially constructed Civilized Standards—and was thus, integral to international law.[72]

Meanwhile, by the end of the nineteenth century, the Society had broadened with the membership of a non-European power: the United States.[73] Comprising 'self-proclaimed civilized states',[74] the Society announced its 'universalistic aspirations'.[75] However, subsequently, the Civilized Standards morphed into 'legal principles,'—because the Society changed its earlier stance—and bestowed them with a juridical character.[76] Consequently, they (Civilized Standards ) served to determine states' membership into or exclusion from civilized society.[77] By the turn of the twentieth century, the Christian Law was redefined as the 'law of civilized nations', that is, public international law.[78] Under public international law, a civilized state was one that fulfilled the following requirements:

[68] Id. at 3.

[69] Id.

[70] Gong, *supra* note 5 at 3–21.

[71] Id.

[72] *See* Antony Anghie, *Imperialism, Sovereignty and the Making of International Law* (Cambridge University Press, 2005).

[73] Gong, *supra* note 5 at 5; Tully, *supra* note 5.

[74] Gong, id. at 3, 4.

[75] Id. at 5.

[76] Id. at 5.

[77] Id.

[78] Id.

> Guarantees basic rights, i.e., life, dignity, and property; freedom of travel, commerce, and religion, especially that of foreign nationals; has an organized political bureaucracy with some efficiency in running the state machinery; maintains a domestic system of courts, codes, and published laws which guarantee legal justice for all within its jurisdiction, foreigners and native citizens alike; by and large conforms to the accepted norms and practices of the civilized international society (*Sati* – the practice of a Hindu widow immolating herself on the pyre of her husband –polygamy and slavery were considered uncivilized and therefore, unacceptable).[79]

### 2.3.1 The Western Liberal Constitution Tops the Civilized Standards

What Civilized Standard underpinned the 'civilized' state? As noted at the outset, it was the Constitution.[80] Constitutional supremacy is the Constitution's defining and well-known feature. As mentioned in the previous chapter, so is the right to property, which—as we saw there, defines the civilized state as well.

In 1895, only European states and the United States met the Civilized Standard: the Constitution. Therefore, they alone were deemed sovereign under international law.[81] In fact, constitutional democracy was gradually evolving and spreading in Europe and North America at the same time that it was being denied in the Third World. Indeed, the Constitution was imposed to exploit the so-called uncivilized Third World peoples and their resources.[82] This is precisely why they were displaced from the symbiotic activities of constitution-making, and territorial administration, that is, denied sovereignty, self-determination, and the protections of international law.[83] However, such constitutional imposition was ostensibly undertaken to *civilize* them.[84]

European powers labelled non-Western constitutions, which lacked the Constitution's features, as ancient, 'uncivilized', 'customary', or

[79] Id. at 14–15.

[80] Tully, *supra* note 5 at 465.

[81] Id. at 483–484.

[82] Id. at 481–482.

[83] Id. Wilde, *supra* note 3 at 301–305 (making this point only about FTA).

[84] *See* Tully, *supra* note 2 at 48—482.

'something less than law'.[85] On this basis, they declared non-Western constitutions 'to be no constitutions at all',[86] and what is more:

> This elision was then applied to virtually all non-European legal orders by the nineteenth century authors of modern international law.[87]

As Tully reminds us, 'any persisting legal order, whether customary or formal, *is* a constitution in the Aristotelian or ancient sense.'[88] So then, the West's approach to non-Western constitutions went something like this: 'to find constitutional/legal systems only when one recognizes them, instead of the reverse'.[89] This meant delegitimizing those constitutional/legal systems which did not fit the Western mold. The Bretton Woods Institutions have adopted this circular type of reasoning with a view to promote the rule of law,[90] –which, as we saw in Chapter 1, subsumes the Constitution.

As already noted, all this reveals a paradox: Constitutional democracy was evolving in Europe at the precise historic moment when non-Western peoples in North America, and the Third World were being colonized. Indeed, distinguished historians and legal scholars including David Armitage, Upendra Baxi, Yash Ghai, John McLaren, Issa Shivji, and Jim Tully have long exposed liberal theory's imperial lineage.[91]

[85] Id. at 466. "Something less than law" are Shannaugh Dorsett's words. Id. at Dorsett & Mc Veigh, *Jurisdiction, supra note* 84 at 104.

[86] Tully, *supra* note 2 at 466

[87] Id.

[88] Id.

[89] Sundhya Pahuja, *Decolonizing International Law—Development, Economic Growth and the Politics of Universality* 193 (Cambridge University Press, 2011).

[90] Id. at 193–202.

[91] Listed in alphabetical order: *See* David Armitage, *The Ideological Origins of the British Empire* (Cambridge University Press, 2000); Upendra Baxi, *Constitutionalism As a Site of Formative Practices* 21 Cardozo L. Rev. 1183 (2000); Yash Ghai, *A Journey around Constitutions Reflecting on Contemporary Constitutions*, 122 S. Afr. L. J. 804, 808 (2005); John McLaren, *The Uses of the Rule of Law in British Colonial Societies in the Nineteenth Century, in* Dorsett & Hunter, *supra* note 8 at 71–91; Rodogno, *supra* note 48 at 25–26; Shivji, *Constitution-making in Africa: An Overview and Assessment in Social and Economic Context, in* Constitutionalism in transition: Africa and Eastern Europe 74, 75 (Mihaela Serban Rosen eds., Helsinki Foundation of Human Rights, 2003); Tully, *supra* note 2 at 467.

Given this, tracing the Constitution in the Third World requires looking for its legal prototypes there, in ways they, and others have noted:

- Imperial law and *lex mercatoria* regimes are imposed to coercively open colonies to trade and privatize resources and labour;
- Colonial constitutions lacked a bill of rights to allow the courts to de-recognize any overriding constitutional principles;
- Separation of powers between executive and judiciary occurs, but more as a design for efficient rule, than as a mechanism for superior protection of peoples' rights against bad governance;
- The rule of law was relied on,
    - o 'but, less for political legitimacy and more to support the market, albeit a highly administered market;' and
    - o to secure economic dominance and disallow judicial independence so that judges remain loyal to the colonial regime (governors), and act as close advisors to them (the executive);
- 'Good government' means authoritarian government–not, democracy promotion;
- Colonial policing equals using violence to maintain white racial and economic dominance.[92]

And so, imposing the Constitution over a colony to *civilize* it, thereby manufacturing its sovereignty, went something like this:

*British colonial rule in India: Dec. 1600-Aug. 1947*

- The British arrive as traders in 1600; Until 1858, the East India Company using 'the crude tools of plunder and mercantilism' controls India; In 1858, 'a more disguised and complex mechanism of free trade and foreign investment is introduced, ostensibly to ensure good government:' Crown rule, where an all-powerful Governor-General, aided by a powerless Legislative Council, meets on an average, for only twenty-five days in a year, till 1892;

[92] Eight sources (listed in the order in which the ideas are presented): Tully, *supra* note 2 at 482; Baxi, Postcolonial legality, in Schwartz & Ray, *supra* note 45 at 540, 541 (Point 3); McLaren, *The Uses of the Rule of Law in British Colonial Societies in the Nineteenth Century, in* Dorsett & Hunter, *supra* note 12 at 71, 72–73; Yash Ghai, *A Journey Around Constitutions Reflecting on Contemporary Constitutions*, 122 S. Afr. L. J. 804, 808 (2005) (bullet points 2 & 4); Rodogno, *supra note* 48 at 23-24; Thomas Martin, *Violence and Colonial Order—Police, Workers and Protest in the European Colonial Empires, 1918–1940* 12–13 (CUP, 2013).

- In 1872, the British draft and impose the Indian Contract Act to introduce 'that thing called the market;'
- India becomes a supplier of cotton and spices to the (British) metropolis, a market for the metropolitan manufacturers, and a field for the investment of British capital; the policy of free trade ruins India's handicraft industries and 'foreign capital investment creates vested interests which demand security for investors';
- Lord William Bentinck abolishes *Sati* in 1829 'to save brown women from brown men';
- Only in 1909 is a lone Indian male, S.P. Sinha, included into the Viceroy's Executive Council;
- Finally, in 1946, the British allow Indians to sculpt their own constitution but only through a constituent assembly that is elected, based on the invidious 'communal representation' system (and not adult franchise).[93]

Thus, creating civilized states essentially entailed the promotion of four Civilized Standards: free markets, the rule of law, 'good governance', (which includes the exploitation of natural resources), and the promotion of civilized customs. Conceptually, FP imposed the Constitution to promote the Civilized Standards: to achieve their territorial goals.

(As previously noted), starting from the inter-war period, IOs joined foreign states in imposing the Constitution. Conceptually, they did so because they were entrusted with the administration of territories, (previously held by Germany and Turkey, —the defeated powers). The League of Nations' (hereafter referred to as the League) Mandates System embodied the international trusteeship concept.[94] The Mandates System inaugurated the era of 'enlightened colonialism' or

[93] Sources (listed in the order in which the ideas appear): Chandra, *supra note* 50 at 92, 113, and 317 (1989); Ritu Birla, *Law as Economy: Convention, Corporation, Currency* 1 UC Irvine L. Rev. 1015, 1022 (2011); Chandra, *supra note* 50 at 95; Saving brown women from brown men is Gayatri C. Spivak's well-known quote; John F. Riddick, *The History of British India: A Chronology* 94 (Greenwood publishing group, 2006); Vijayashri Sripati, *Comparing Constitutionalism in India and South Africa from a Human Rights Perspective* 16 Tulane J. of Int'l L. 1, 22 (2008).

[94] *See* Article 22, The Versailles Treaty, June 28, 1919 *at:* Avalon Project, Yale University.

'development' (as we now know it).[95] Development meant: developing the Third World for the West's benefit.[96] This is precisely why the defeated powers' territories (Mandate territories) were denied independence so that they could function essentially as colonies (resource banks).[97] Again, they were ostensibly denied independence because they were deemed to be lacking the Civilized Standards. And so, some type of "tutelage" was deemed necessary.[98] Accordingly, the Constitution was imposed to civilize their governance through foreign administration and promote their development. "Development" was equated with Civilized Standards.

The mandate territories were divided into three classes (A, B, and C), based on their degree of advancement or backwardness.[99] For instance, as I will show in the next chapter, the Constitution was imposed by IOs (the Permanent Mandates Commission) in the form of market-oriented standards – and by foreign states (for example, Great Britain) to simultaneously develop (exploit) and democratize Iraq, an A-class territory because it was provisionally recognized as independent.[100]

## 2.4 Conclusion

In summary, during both eras of colonialism, that is, exploitative colonialism (before the inter-war period) and 'enlightened colonialism' (the inter-war period), foreign states imposed Constitutions to administer territories. IOs also imposed Constitutions to administer territories, but starting from the inter-war period. Both these entities required the Constitution to promote the Civilized Standards. In so doing, they pursued the civilizing mission and engaged in colonial trusteeship, thus reflecting political paternalism.

95 *See* Anghie, *supra* note 71 at 185.

96 Id.

97 Id. at 156–62.

98 Id.

99 Id.

100 *See* Phebe Marr, *The modern history of Iraq* 29–46 (Longman, 1985).

3

# Internationalizing the Western Liberal Constitution

## To Settle Disputes and Civilize

### 3.0 Introduction

This chapter traces UN Constitutional Assistance's (UNCA) historical origins non-chronologically through Wilde's Family of international Trusteeship Foreign Territorial Administration (FTA) Policy Institutions (Wilde's Family). In this way, I establish that Wilde's Family is based on the symbiotic ties binding the Constitution with FTA, underscored in Chapter 2. My chief argument here is that, what heads Wilde's Family is a key Civilized Standard[1] that is central to Trusteeship: the Constitution. Its internationalized making has sired each of Wilde's FTA institutions who therefore, act as Trusteeship. (In this way, I will reveal the entities, other than the United Nations [UN], which have imposed the Constitution.) I therefore, concur with Wilde that international Trusteeship comprises FTA/International Territorial Administration (ITA)[2] and its parent: the Constitution's making, which work symbiotically. On this basis, I argue that Wilde's Family must

[1] *See* Gerrit Gong, *The 'Standard of Civilization' in International Society of States* 1–15 (Oxford University Press, 1984).

[2] Ralph Wilde, *International Territorial Administration: How Trusteeship and the Civilizing Mission Never Went Away* 312 (Oxford University Press, 2008).

be reframed to admit the Constitution's making: the Family's parent 'Policy Institution'.[3]

On a broader level, my analysis shows that historically, Constitution-making (and so, territorial administration) have been internationalized to achieve:

1) Strategic advantage: to lend a distinct political character to, and thereby confer a distinct 'status' on a given territorial Unit, as a means to settle disputes between states/entities vying for that Unit.
2) Exploitation: To exploit a Unit and/or Third World state's territorial resources.
3) Carry out such exploitation, ostensibly to civilize Third World states: promote free markets, the rule of law, good governance (including natural resources' exploitation), and civilized practices aimed at emancipating women.

Herein comes the Constitution,

- which was, for reasons noted in Chapter 1, indispensable to achieving purposes (1)–(3) and
- whose imposition by Foreign Powers (FPs) (Western states and IOs) is what *first internationalized* Constitution-making and *subsequently* territorial administration.

Before proceeding, it helps to note that in the present chapter I will only consider ITA during the inter-war period, that is, by the League of Nations (LON). I will consider ITA by the UN in Chapter 4 because that is where I will introduce its parent, UNCA. In Chapter 4, I will analyse UNCA–ITA: the UN's making of the Constitution and the UN's administering of a territorial unit in tune with the Constitution.

How will this chapter establish that Wilde's Family reflects the Constitution-making's ties with FTA, underscored in Chapter 2? I will develop my answer in sections 3.1–3.4. To set the stage, section 3.1 will consider Wilde's definition of territorial administration and show the

[3] I will use the terms colonial constitution-making, Constitution's making, Constitution's internationalized making, and internationalized constitution-making interchangeably.

two steps that he took to conceptualize his family. Starting from section 3.2, I will take the same two steps as Wilde. First, I will sketch the contours of Wilde's institutions, foregrounding an activity that each FP engaged in: the Constitution's making. Since Constitution-making varied under each FP, I am not concerned with its form, unless it is relevant. Rather, I stress only on the principles of domination and control that underpinned it. Section 3.2.7 will show that, to use Wilde's phrase, his (Wilde's) institutions are 'analogous': each of them 'operates in the same fashion' 'in an elemental sense'. Indeed, each FP imposed the Constitution to establish jurisdiction and carry on FTA. In this way, this chapter will establish that the Constitution's making is an 'institution' or 'established practice'. This means that, Wilde's Family comprises two institutions: the Constitution's internationalized making and FTA.

In Section 3.3, I establish that Wilde's reframed analogous institutions are symbiotic 'Policy Institutions'. I take the policies pursued by, and ends achieved by the FP, under each of Wilde's FTA institutions. I will show how the Constitution's making, the activity engaged in by each of the FPs, contributed to achieving those policies (for example, Trusteeship) and ends/Civilized Standards (for example, free markets). Indeed, as we will see, the Constitution was indispensable in this regard.

In summary, this chapter establishes a salient feature of colonial Constitution-making: it is internationalized. The Constitution's making is a parent Policy Institution: It is an 'institution' or established practice that provides the framework and legal basis for introducing FTA, another Policy Institution, and so works symbiotically with its child, FTA, toward common ostensible policies and ends/purposes. Table 3.1 illustrates that Wilde's Family comprises the Constitution's internationalized making and FTA, thus underscoring the Constitution's salient and symbiotic role.

## 3.1 Tracing UNCA's Origins through Ralph Wilde's Family of Foreign Territorial Administration 'Policy Institutions'

According to Wilde,

> Territorial administration is a formally-constituted, locally-based management structure operating with respect to a particular

TABLE 3.1 Ralph Wilde's reframed Family of International Trusteeship 'Policy Institutions': The Western Liberal Constitution's Internationalized Making *and* Foreign Territorial Administration

| The Western liberal constitution, an 18th century 'standard of civilization' heads Wilde's reframed Family of International Trusteeship Policy Institutions | | | | | | | | | | |
|---|---|---|---|---|---|---|---|---|---|---|
| FOREIGN STATES AND/OR INTERNATIONAL ORGANIZATIONS IMPOSE OR PROMOTE THE WL CONSTITUTION TO ESTABLISH JURISDICTION/ CREATE FTA/ITA | Wilde's FTA institutions stem from the Western liberal Constitution | | Wilde's Family opened to: admit / identify the parent institution: the Western Liberal Constitution's International-ized making (WLCM) | The parent-offspring institutions work toward common policies & ends | | | | | | Wilde's Family reframed to comprise two international trusteeship Policy Institutions: Internationalized constitution-making & FTA/ ITA |
| | | | | Two common allied policies | | Four allied ends | | | | |
| | | | | T | CM/ MM | 'Standards of civilization' (SOC)/ Public International Law & Policy (PILP) Goals | | | | |
| | | | | T | CM/ MM | FM | GG | ROL | CC/ WR | |
| | 1. | European Colonialism, 1700-1960 | √ | T | CM | SOC | SOC | SOC | SOC | Internationalized constitution-making FTA/ITA |
| | 2A. | Protection - ITA by the League of Nations [LON] (interwar period) | √ | T | CM | SOC | SOC | SOC | SOC | Internationalized constitution-making & ITA |

| | | | | | | | | | | |
|---|---|---|---|---|---|---|---|---|---|---|
| FOREIGN STATES AND/OR INTERNATIONAL ORGANIZATIONS IMPOSE OR PROMOTE THE WL CONSTITUTION TO ESTABLISH JURISDICTION/CREATE FTA/ITA | 2B. | ITA by the UN (post- 1945 projects) | I will | complete these blank columns in | | | | | | |
| | Post-1993: Plenary ITA's use in sovereign states ends but continues only in territorial units | | 2C. UNCA (without plenary ITA) (1993-2018) | Table 9.1, Ch. 9 | | | | | | |
| | 3. | State-conducted administration under the LON | √ | T | CM | SOC | SOC | SOC | SOC | Internationalized constitution-making & FTA |
| | 4. | State-conducted administration under the UN Trusteeship System | √ | T | CM | SOC | SOC | SOC | SOC | Internationalized constitution-making & FTA |
| | 5. | Representative Bodies | √ | T | CM | SOC | SOC | SOC | SOC | Internationalized constitution-making & FTA |
| | 6. | Occupation | √ | T | CM | CM &/or MM | SOC &/or PILP | SOC &/or PILP | SOC &/or PILP | Internationalized constitution-making, FTA & UNCA |

> territorial unit, whether a state, a sub-state unit or a non-state territorial entity[4]....
>
> And the identity of the actor conducting the aforesaid activity is a foreign state or group of foreign states or an international organization.[5]
>
> Situations of partial administration, (for example, a territorial programme concerned with certain matters such as food distribution) should be covered as a well as plenary administration (for instance, a territorial government)....[6]
>
> The meaning of the word 'administration' in 'territorial administration' is, broad. All three types of activity (legislative, executive and judicial) potentially fall within the word administration as it is used here.[7]

FTA refers to foreign-state conducted territorial administration, whereas ITA refers to an IO-conducted territorial administration. However, the term 'foreign territorial administration' includes ITA.[8]

Furthermore, according to Wilde, the activity of FTA is understood:

> [i]n terms of a distinction as between the spatial identities of the administering actor, on the one hand, and the administered entity, on the other.[9]

Before proceeding, it helps to note the basics:

- In Wilde's Family, foreign territorial *administrators* displaced local actors to engage in three types of activities: legislative, executive, and judicial. Wilde calls these activities (foreign) 'territorial administration'.[10]
- The foreign territorial administrators comprise foreign states and/or IOs.
- As the earlier discussion suggests, foreign territorial administrators displaced local actors to first impose constitutions or engage in Constitution-making (see Chapter 2). Given this, the acronym, FTA, can refer to both the foreign territorial *administrators* and to the activities they engage in. To avoid confusion, I will, as I did in Chapter 2, use this shorter form: Foreign Power (FP).

[4] Wilde, *supra* note 2 at 21.

[5] Id. at 25.

[6] Id. at 22.

[7] Id.

[8] Id. at 343.

[9] Id. at 303.

It also helps to briefly revisit Wilde's Method and see how he used it in creating his Family.

### 3.1.1 Revisiting Wilde's Method

According to Wilde:

> The term 'policy institution' is adopted as shorthand for this teleological enquiry, combining an 'institution' as an 'established practice' with a focus on 'policy' in the sense of the ends to which the practice is put.[11]
>
> Purposive analysis means analyzing an institution's ostensible ends or purposes.[12]

To sum it up, 'purposive interpretation is analysis of the text, not psychoanalysis of its author.'[13]

Wilde takes two steps to conceptualize his FTA institutions as a Family. First, he sketches the contours of each of his FTA institutions to establish that they all are analogous 'institutions': 'they all operate in the same fashion' in 'an elemental sense'.[14] In each of Wilde's FTA institutions: The relevant FP/FPs 1) administered a distinct territorial unit; 2) in doing so, each FP displaced local actors/nationals from the activity of territorial administration, ostensibly in response to local actors' perceived governance incapacities and to provide civilized governance.[15] In this way, he establishes that FTA is an 'institution' (established practice).[16]

Second, Wilde connects his FTA institutions' common activity, that is, territorial administration (legislative, executive, and judicial activities) with common *ostensible* policies (Trusteeship and the civilizing mission) and resultant ostensible purposes or ends: (i) Civilized Standards: free markets, rule of law, good governance, and civilized practices and

[10] Id. at 22 (definition of territorial administration).

[11] Id. at 37.

[12] Id. at 36–37.

[13] *See* Aharon Barak, *Purposive Interpretation in Law—Translated from the Hebrew by Sari Bashi* 110 (Princeton University Press, 2005).

[14] *See* Wilde, *supra* note 2 at 312.

[15] Id. at 289–312.

[16] Id. at 312–343.

(ii) territorial status and strategic advantage.[17] This way, Wilde shows 'purposive commonality' between all the institutions.[18] On this basis, he conceptualizes them collectively as a 'Family of colonial Trusteeship FTA Policy Institutions'.[19]

Regarding the ends listed in (i) and (ii), the following should be noted.

1) First, Wilde has arrived at them by looking for parallels between ITA (by the UN) and the rest of his FTA institutions/ 'established practices' 'in the broadest sense';[20]
2) Second, and this is very important, Wilde has identified these ends: rule of law, free markets, good governance and civilized practices because they bear comparison with these international law and policy purposes associated with ITA (by the UN): free markets, rule of law, good governance, and women's rights, respectively.[21]
3) Third, Wilde concedes that not all of his FTA institutions were associated with all the policies considered in (i) and (ii). To varying degrees, 'each FTA institution was heterogeneous across its individual manifestations, in terms of the purposes with which it was associated';[22]
4) Fourth, an exception to point three is state administration under the Mandate and Trusteeship institution, because it was associated with a particular objective. But even here, a variation arose between the different classes of Mandate territories and between these territories and the UN Trust territories. This variation arose regarding 'the nature of the perceived problem being addressed,' and 'the way state administration was understood to address `it.'[23]

[17] Id. at 343–363.

[18] Id. For the phrase "purposive commonality" *see* id., at 38.

[19] Id.

[20] Id. at 351.

[21] Id. at 313.

[22] Id. at 313.

[23] Id.

## 3.2 Analogous Institutions: Common Activity—The Constitution's Internationalized Making

### 3.2.1. Post-Renaissance European Colonialism

For the sake of continuity, I start my analysis with Colonialism.[24] As we saw in Chapter 2, Colonialism (as defined by Wilde) reflected and resulted from:

1) colonial Constitution-making working symbiotically with foreign territorial administration; and
2) the Constitution's symbiotic use:
   a) to create jurisdiction and introduce territorial administration (legislative, executive, and judicial activities); and
   b) to legally demarcate the spatial identities of the FP (the colonial power) from that of the administered entity (colony).

To be accurate, Wilde's conceptualization of Colonialism as FTA must show that colonial Constitution-making gives rise to and works with FTA toward common goals. Indeed, Wilde implicitly affirms those ties in these ways. First, FTA as defined by Wilde excludes Constitution-making (as an activity).[25] Second, Wilde affirms that the colonial constitution creates and underpins FTA when he proffers British colonialism as an example of FTA, describing it as:

> a model of supervision exercised over government institutions operated by local officials, on the basis of a distinct 'legal personality, *constitution*, laws'.[26]

Third, and finally, having affirmed that the colonial constitution undergirds FTA, that is, the latter flows from the former, Wilde implicitly points to the colonial constitution's role in separating the spatial identities of the administering actor from that of the administered entity in this way. He states that, as an activity, FTA is:

[24] Wilde's FTA institutions appear in this order: Protection, Colonialism, The Mandate and Trusteeship Systems, Representative bodies, and Occupation. Id at xxii.

[25] Id. at 21.

[26] Id. at 304.

> understood in terms of a distinction between the spatial identities of the administering actor, on the one hand, from the administered entity, on the other.[27]

Meanwhile, Wilde concedes that as a feature, separateness did not typify French and Portuguese colonialism, where an 'aspiration may have existed to assimilate the colony (territory) and its people politically and culturally into the Metropolitan State'.[28] He notes that 'more subtle distinctions, including those of a legal and administrative nature operated between the metropolis and the colony', which diluted the assimilationist idea in practice.[29] For instance, the reader can be reminded that Portugal devised the assimilationist idea only to evade the UN's scrutiny in the 1960s, when the latter was empowered to decolonize—to help colonies realize their newly acquired right to independence.[30]

To round off the discussion about colonial Constitution-making's centrality to colonialism (begun in Chapter 2), I focus on Belgium. Belgium's King Leopold set out to colonize Congo, which as we now know, was not yet colonized during the 1870s. To exploit Congo's ivory and rubber, Leopold first created the International African Association (IAA), an exploitative commercial enterprise.[31] Next, he hired Travers Twiss, an English lawyer to draft a constitution for Congo.[32] The Constitution drafted by Twiss, named the new state as 'L'Afrique Equatoriale'.[33] 'It contained the legislative, judicial, and bureaucratic offices that were to be expected in an era of metropolitan and colonial political reform.'[34] 'It empowered the King to suspend laws and officers

27 Id. at 303.

28 Id. at 304.

29 Id.

30 *See* Malyn Newitt, *Portugal in Africa – The Last Hundred Years* 199 (C. Hurst, 1981).

31 Michael A. Rutz, *King Leopold's Congo: A Short History with Documents* 8–9 (Hackett Publishing Company, Inc., 2018).

32 *See* Andrew Fitzmaurice, *The Justification of King Leopold II's Congo Enterprise by Sir Travers Twiss, in* Law and Politics in British Colonial Thought: Transpositions of Empire 109, 118 (Shannaugh Dorsett & Ian Hunter, eds., 2010).

33 Id. at 118.

34 Id.

of the state *a sa discretion*.'[35] In this way, Leopold and the IAA were able to forcibly introduce Leopold's (Belgian) administration there, by taking the Constitutional route.[36] Thus, was born the Congo Free State (Congo) (1885–1909).[37]

As mentioned in Chapter 1, colonialism was outlawed by international law in 1960. Until then, wherever it existed, colonial powers prioritized developing constitutional colonial orders so that they could develop substantive colonial law governing crime, commerce, and property.[38] Based on my analysis in this section as well as Chapter 2, I conclude with these submissions.

1) Conceptually, European colonialism as defined by Wilde and set out in section 3.2 involves a) foreign states' imposition of their constitutions or 'special laws' (that is, colonial Constitution-making) to assert jurisdiction and introduce territorial administration (as defined by Wilde), and thus, achieve their territorial goals. On this basis, I argue that Wilde has accurately conceptualized European colonialism as FTA.
2) The Constitution's salience: Since laws may be used to achieve the Civilized Standards, Wilde is correct to proffer these ends as those met by FPs engaging in FTA. As we have seen, the Constitution is the highest law of the land. So, it governs substantive law in all areas including crime, labor, and commerce—three areas which cover the Civilized Standards. Herein lies the Constitution's indispensability in promoting the Civilized Standards.
3a) The colonial constitution lies at the heart of colonialism, conceptualized as foreign territorial administration; b) Colonial Constitution-making was typically internationalized: It excluded the local actors in the territorial unit. Instead, the constitution was imposed by a foreign actor or actors. On this basis, I argue that colonialism is analogous to two symbiotic institutions: colonial/internationalized Constitution-making and FTA.

[35] Id.

[36] Id.

[37] Id. The name Congo Free State was a euphemism given King Leopold II's atrocities –that are far too well known.

[38] *See* Michael W. Doyle, *Empires* 356 (Cornell University Press, 1986); Martin Wright, *Colonial Constitutions 1947*, 18–22 (Clarendon Press, 1952). I am in no way suggesting that constitutional imposition ended after 1960.

### 3.2.2 'Protection'—International Territorial Administration by the League of Nations

'Protection' includes administration of a distinct territorial unit by a state and/or an IO.[39] The Free City of Danzig, administered by the LON from 1920 to 1939, is widely proffered as an example of a 'true' protectorate.[40]

Danzig, a formerly German *Hansa* city, sits on the edge of the Baltic Sea. In 1920, Danzig was a sophisticated shipping and commercial center, with a Corridor to the Baltic Sea, covering some 6,290 square miles.[41] After the First World War, the defeated power, Germany was compelled to renounce all rights and title over Danzig, in favor of the Principal Allied and Associated Powers.[42] Meanwhile, Poland sought to incorporate Danzig,[43] because it lacked a port and access to the sea.[44] However, the Germans who comprised 380,000 of Danzig's total population of 400,000 sought sovereignty or full autonomy.[45]

To address this dispute between Poles and Germans, the victorious powers decided to transform Danzig into an independent city ('free city') within the customs zone of Poland.[46] Accordingly, the Treaty of Versailles (Treaty) empowered the LON to draft and guarantee Danzig's constitution.[47] The Treaty expressly stipulated that Danzig's constitution be made by Danzig's duly appointed representatives '*in*

[39] Wilde, *supra* note 2 at 302. Here, the relevant unit is considered to be "a distinct juridical entity from the 'protecting' state (or IO), despite the exercise of control by the latter over it." Id.

[40] Id.

[41] *See* J.B. Mason, *The Danzig Dilemma: A Study in Peace-Making by Compromise* 10 and 11 (Stanford University Press, 1939).

[42] Id. at 61, 323 (reproducing Art. 100, Treaty of Versailles).

[43] Id. at 4.

[44] Id. Poland was re-established because and after the First World War. Id.

[45] Id. at 45.

[46] Id. Although the constitution was still in its provisional form when Danzig was constituted a Free City on 15 November 1920, it served as "the de facto foundation for the government of the Free City." It came into force on 11 August 1920. Mason, id. at 68, 286 & 323.

[47] Id. at 323 (reproducing Art. 100–102, Treaty of Versailles, 1919).

*agreement* with a High Commissioner to be appointed by the League of Nations'.[48] The constitution could only be amended with the LON's approval.[49] Once, it was so finalized, it was placed under the LON's guarantee.[50] Since the constitution conferred free city status on Danzig, guaranteeing the constitution counted as protecting Danzig's status. Thus, the League Commissioner enjoyed constituent powers only to protect and guarantee Danzig's free city status.

### 3.2.3 State-conducted Administration under the Mandates System of the League of Nations

As previously noted, under the Mandates System, the mandatory powers and the Permanent Mandates Commission (PMC) engaged in Constitution-making (*see* Chapter 2). Here, I will elaborate on this aspect.

Class A territories, whose provisional independence was recognized, comprised the former Turkish provinces of Iraq, Syria, Lebanon, and Palestine (including modern Jordan and Israel). The Mandates of Iraq, Syria, and Palestine were entrusted to Britain.[51]

Sir Percy Cox assumed responsibilities as Britain's high commissioner in Iraq in October 1920. Ostensibly to prepare Iraq for independence, Faisal, a British ally, was handpicked and placed on the throne allowing him to accede to the throne on the condition that his government would be 'constitutional, representative and democratic'.[52] Faysal's government was also required to be 'limited by law'.[53] To control Iraq, Cox next proposed expressing the mandatory relationship through a treaty (the Anglo-Iraq Treaty, February 1922) that continued the tutelary aspects in new ways.[54] The Treaty, designed to run for 20 years,

[48] Id.

[49] Id. at 64.

[50] Id. at 300.

[51] Nikshoy C. Chatterji, *Muddle of the Middle East* Chapter 13, 392–412, 361–391 (Abhinav Publications, 1973) (Volume I).

[52] Nathan Brown, *Constitutionalism, Authoritarianism, and Imperialism in Iraq* 53 Drake L. Rev. 923, 925 (2005).

[53] Phebe Marr, *The Modern History of Iraq* 36 (Longman, 1985).

[54] Id. at 38.

incorporated the open-door policy.[55] It mandated the king 1) to follow British advice on all matters relating to fiscal policy and affecting British interests; and 2) to appoint British officials at the head of eighteen Iraqi ministries and as government supervisors and inspectors.[56] In this way, far from abrogating the mandate, the Treaty prolonged Iraq's tutelage for 20 years, that is, until February 1944, even after it gained independence in 1932.[57]

Next, the British drafted a Western-style constitution for Iraq, which mandated Britain's High Commissioner in Iraq to uphold the Treaty.[58] The Treaty and Iraq's constitution interlinked in these ways. Finally, Iraq's Constituent Assembly—pressured by Cox—approved both these documents in 1924.[59]

Turning to Palestine, under Article 2 of the Palestine Mandate, the mandatory power was only required to create such conditions 'as will secure the establishment of the Jewish national home ... and the development of self-governing institutions...'.[60] Accordingly, Great Britain imposed a colonial constitution spelling out the government's structure, but without providing a representative government and individual rights.[61] Thus, was laid a basis for developing criminal, commercial (including copyright), and administrative law.[62] For instance, Great Britain established the Palestine Broadcasting Service to implement the colonial copyright law.[63]

By contrast, the Mandate for Syria and Lebanon explicitly empowered the Mandatory power to frame an organic law for these

[55] Id.

[56] Id.

[57] Id.

[58] Id. at 38–39.

[59] Id. at 45.

[60] *See* the Palestine Mandate, Yale Law School, The Avalon Project, *at:* http://avalon.law.yale.edu/20th_century/palmanda.asp.

[61] *See* Robert H. Eisenman, *Islamic Law in Palestine and Israel: A History of the Survival of Tanzimat and Sharia in the British Mandate and the Jewish State*, 78–82 (Brill, 1978).

[62] *See* e.g., Michael D. Birnhack, *Colonial Copyright: Intellectual Property in Mandate Palestine* 20 (Oxford University Press, 2011).

[63] Id. at 20, 101–102.

countries.[64] Tanganyika, Togoland, Cameroon, and Ruand-Urundi were placed under a Class B mandate.[65] The relevant colonial powers imposed colonial constitutions to administer their respective Mandate territories.[66]

Class C territories comprised South-West Africa (now Namibia, assigned to South Africa), New Guinea (assigned to Australia), West Samoa (now Samoa, assigned to New Zealand), and Nauru (assigned to Australia, with Great Britain and New Zealand). These territories, deemed the most backward, were therefore, regarded as 'best administered under the laws of the Mandatory as integral portions of its territory'.[67] As a result, here too, the Mandatory power engaged in Constitution-making. For instance, to administer West Samoa, New Zealand enacted its constitution, which remained in force until 1962 when West Samoa became independent.[68]

### *3.2.3.1 The Permanent Mandates Commission: Market-oriented Legal Standard-Setting: A Precursor to UNCA –See Chapter 5*

Development meant throwing open the mandate territories' resources and markets and making the natives economically beneficial for the benefit of the colonial powers.[69] Given this, the PMC supervised the mandatory powers, and advised the League Council on the territories'

[64] *See* Chatterji, *supra* note 51 at 400. It was only in mid-1930 that, France imposed a constitution on Syria. Id. at 405–406.

[65] *See* Peter A. Dumbuya, *Tanganyika under International Mandate, 1919-1946* 41–48 (University Press of America, 1995).

[66] Great Britain imposed this constitution: The Tanganyika Order-in-Council on 22 July 1920. Id. at 104.

[67] *See* Article 22, Covenant of the League of Nations.

[68] *See* J.W. Davidson, *Samoa mo Samoa – The emergence of the independent state of Western Samoa* 100 (Cambridge University Press, 1967). New Zealand passed the "Samoa Constitution Order" (Order), which came into force on 1 May 1920. The Samoa Act 1921 (re-enacting, with minor amendments, the contents of the Order) served as Samoa's constitution until its independence in 1962. Id. at 100-101.

[69] *See* Anghie, *Sovereignty, Imperialism, and the Making of International Law* 147–176 (Cambridge University Press, 2005).

progress and development.[70] The PMC approached its administrative functions legalistically, in ways described below.[71]

First, the PMC, a specialist body, regulated every aspect of the native's life. To stay abreast of the developments within the territories, it called for and received mountains of information on varied issues.[72]

Second, after analysing the information so received, the PMC coined useful principles and market-oriented standards. For instance, having kept track of how labor policies were faring in the different Mandate territories, it coined appropriate standards to ensure that the natives' labor and colonial revenue were both maximized.[73]

Third, the PMC created a rule of law regime to protect property rights and secure the exploitation of the Mandate Territories' resources. Since the colonial powers considered the Mandate territories' resources as the international community property, they set the terms for exploiting those resources. It fell to the PMC to create appropriate legal regulations to establish that regime of 'unequal exchange'.[74]

To sum up, under the Mandates System, the mandatory powers and the PMC imposed constitutions and legally oriented standards respectively to achieve common territorial goals. I argue that the legal assistance, so inaugurated by the PMC, is the precursor of today's international rule of law/constitutional assistance.

#### *3.2.3.2 Imposing the Constitution to Create Sovereignty: A Precursor to the UN's "Strengthening Sovereignty" Argument –see Chapter 9*

As mentioned earlier, European states denied Third World peoples (in mandate territories) independence because they were deemed uncivilized, and so, lacking in sovereignty. Put simply, Third World peoples were considered to be less sovereign or not sovereign—and so, not really states (see Chapter 2).[75] Herein comes the sovereignty-creating

[70] Id. at 123.

[71] Id.

[72] Id. at 182, 184, 164

[73] Id.

[74] Id. at 157–160, 161 (quote).

[75] Antony Anghie, *The evolution of international law: Colonial and postcolonial realities* 27 (5) Third World Quarterly 739, 740 (2006).

project (Project), which as Antony Anghie suggests began in the inter-war period, and in which both FPs and IOs engaged.[76] In fact, IOs (for example, the PMC) were conceived for this very purpose.[77]

This Project supported the idea of graded sovereignty.[78]

> [It] assumed that sovereignty existed in something like a linear continuum, and every society could be placed at some point along this continuum based on its approximation to the ideal of the European nation-state.[79]

In fact, this is precisely why mandate territories were classified into A, B, and C mandates, based on their degree of politico-economic advancement.[80] With the aim of morphing Mandate Territories into states, this Project created the requisite politico-economic and socio-cultural environment therein.[81] Towards this end, the Mandates System devised a technology: 'standard-setting'.[82]

Anghie suggests, this Project harmed Third World peoples because it entrapped them, in an exploitative system, in these ways:

The government created in mandate territories functioned to:

a. integrate their economies with that of the metropolitan power, to the natives' disadvantage,[83] and so, 'economic progress' equalled 'the furtherance of a system of economic inequalities specific to colonialism',[84]
b. transfer sovereignty to the natives (where relevant—for example, Iraq), but simultaneously entrapped them in new systems of subordination and control; and so,
c. Caused the 'economization of government'/'sovereignty'.[85]

76 *See* Antony Anghie, *Colonialism and the birth of international institutions: Sovereignty, economy, and the Mandate System of the League of Nations* 34 NYU J. of Int'l L & P 513 (2002).

77 Id. at 514.

78 Id. at 570.

79 Id.

80 Id.

81 Id. at 515.

82 Id.

83 Id. at 609.

84 Id. at 603.

85 Id. at 581.

I concur. I suggest, herein comes the Constitution, which for reasons noted earlier, was integral to the Project. First, as the highest law of the land, the Constitution offered a blue print for governance / territorial administration. This was why it was used to create, and in fact, underpinned functioning states. Second, to exploit the mandate territories' resources to their advantage, the colonial powers required an appropriate system of political economy (market economy). The Constitution provided them just that. This is precisely why the PMC imposed the Constitution, in ways described in this section.

Third, by imposing the Constitution and displacing local actors from territorial administration (law-making), the FPs transferred only sovereignty to the mandate peoples, but retained the powers of controlling the political economy. Take Great Britain, which though freed Iraq, drafted and imposed its (Iraq's) Western-style constitution (the Constitution) and headed key ministries with its officials. In this way, Great Britain transferred sovereignty to the Iraqis, but, simultaneously drained them off their economic power. Fourth, it is the Constitution's imposition that led to what Tony calls the 'economization of government / sovereignty'.

So then, manufacturing Third World sovereignty, which equaled securing the Third World's exploitation, suggests why Constitution-making there (the Third World), was internationalized. Again, exploiting the Third World (that is, ostensibly manufacturing Third World sovereignty) is another way of understanding the Mandates System, which I have conceptualized here, as the Constitution's internationalized making siring, and working with FTA toward common Trusteeship goals.

### 3.2.4 State-Conducted Administration under the United Nations Trusteeship System

The UN Trusteeship System (System) was established in 1945. As its name suggests, it was an international regime of tutelage that replaced the inter-war period's Mandates System,[86] and so, provided for the administration of former mandated territories and the former colonies of the defeated powers (called Trust Territories) by one or more states,

[86] Eleven Trust Territories were created and seven states were designated as administering authorities.

or the organization itself.[87] Conceptually, this is why those foreign states imposed constitutions on Trust Territories.

Overall, the foreign states and the UN Trusteeship Council were tasked with:

> Promoting the political, economic, social, and educational advancement of the inhabitants of the trust territories and their progressive development towards self-government or independence as may be appropriate to the particular circumstances of each territory and its peoples....[88]

This meant that the relevant foreign states acted as colonial guardians. They were obliged to provide civilized governance in the Trust Territories, to propel them towards self-government, or independence. Tanganyika may be used as an example. Its Trusteeship Agreement mandated Britain to create 'peace, order, good government'.[89] According to Peter A. Dumbuya, after 1945, Britain imposed such constitutional developments in Tanganyika as were meant for achieving self-government and independence.[90] Indeed, by the late 1960s:

> British rule had come to an end in eastern and southern Africa ... in a welter of Constitution-making. Teams of lawyers in the Colonial Office in Whitehall and in the territories, themselves toiled over ever more complex drafts. At the apogee of the process, the pace of constitutional change was rapid with independence coming in quick succession to Tanganyika (1961) ....[91]

The UN System enshrined the principles of the sacred trust, of international accountability, the non-permanent nature of trust, and

[87] The powers that had administered mandates on behalf of the LON were to conclude agreements with the UN and administer the same territories that were still dependent.

[88] *See* Chapter XII, UN Charter (1945).

[89] *See Text of Trusteeship Agreement as Approved by the General Assembly of the United Nations,* New York (13 December, 1946) (transforming Tanganyika's status from a mandate into a Trust territory). For quotes see Art. 6 & 76.

[90] *See* Dumbuya, *supra* note 65 at 262.

[91] John Hatchard *et al, Comparative Constitutionalism and Good Governance in the Commonwealth: An Eastern and Southern African Perspective* 15 (Cambridge University Press, 2004).

ensuring that colonial administration worked for the benefit of the trust territories and the international community at large.[92]

As for the UN Trusteeship Council (UNTC), it offered constitutional assistance as part of supervising the foreign states' administration of Trust Territories. The UNTC gently coaxed colonial powers to set target dates for the Trust Territories' independence, deputed UN Visiting Missions (Missions) to obtain reports on Trust Territories, informed political activists of the dates of these Missions' arrival, sought for and considered details about Trust Territories' prospective constitutions, and arranged to provide local actors with constitutional advisers.[93] For example, in 1962, the UNTC supporting Nauru's formal requests for self-government, deputed a four-member UN Mission to Nauru, urging Australia to set a realistic target date for its independence.[94] These UNCA activities constituted 'good Trusteeship practice'.

### 3.2.5 Representative Bodies

'Representative bodies' (Bodies) comprise the fifth FTA institution in Wilde's family. Wilde divides those Bodies into four broad categories, the first of which is most relevant for the purpose of this study,[95] and which covers the exercise of plenary or partial administrative prerogatives in various disputed territories, including: Cracow (1815–46), Shanghai (1854–1943), Crete (1897–1909), Albania (1913–14), and Tangier (1923–57).[96]

From the nineteenth to the mid-twentieth century, European colonial powers (Powers) such as Austria-Hungary, Russia, Great Britain, France, and Italy and the United States jointly installed bodies (comprising their representatives) to administer territories marked out for imperial exploitation. The Powers worked in concert and through their representatives. As we shall see, those Bodies imposed the Constitution

[92] Charmian Toussaint, *The Trusteeship system of the United Nations* 14 (Greenwood Press, 1976).

[93] Davidson, *supra* note 68 at 352 and 354.

[94] *See* e.g., Katy le Roy, "Nauru Constitutional Review: Background and Discussion Paper" 3 (UNDP, June 2006).

[95] *See* Wilde, *supra* note 2 at 307. For categories 2-4 see *infra* note 157.

[96] Id.

over Cracow, Shanghai, Crete, Albania, and Tangier to commercially exploit these territories' resources and 'civilize' their inhabitants.

### *3.2.5.1 Cracow*

Cracow is located in what is now Southern Poland. This city houses architectural splendours including the stunning Wawel Castle, a UNESCO World Heritage Site. The statesmen at the Congress of Vienna decided to internationalize Cracow to defuse the competing claims of Austria, Russia, and Prussia (the Three Powers) over it.[97]

An Internationalized, Imposed Constitution Established FTA Accordingly, the Three Powers had Cracow's constitution drafted by a Commission.[98] They then had Cracow's constitution added to the Treaty of 3 May 1815 (Treaty), which established 'Cracow with a surrounding area of 1,000 square kilometers and a population of 95,000 as a free city.'[99] The Treaty in turn was inserted textually in the General Act of the Congress of Vienna:[100] 'Ambiguously enough, (as per this Treaty), Cracow was to be "free, independent, and neutral" and yet, "under the protection of the three Powers".[101] Cracow's constitution came into effect in 1818. Under Cracow's Constitution, a Board of Delegates (comprising the three Residents of Austria, Prussia, and Russia) appointed the City's President and approved all his executive decisions. The City

[97] *See* Harold Nicolson, *The Congress of Vienna: A Study in Allied Unity: 1812-22* 179 (Constable, London, 2001). The Congress of Vienna assembly attended and represented only by European governments, began in September 1814 and completed its "Final Act" in June 1815. It redrew the political map of Europe after the Napoleonic Wars. Id. at 198–209.

[98] *See* Norman Davies, *God's Playground: A History of Poland* 246 (Oxford University Press, 1985) (Volume II: 1795 to the present).

[99] Id. at 179.

[100] *See Additional Treaty between Austria, Prussia, and Russia respecting Cracow,* 3 May 1815, Vienna, at: Hein online, World Treaty Library, accessed on August 25, 2016. The constitution of Cracow is contained in the annex to this Treaty, which in turn is "annexed to the Final Act (General Treaty) of the Congress of Vienna of June 9, 1815, as Act III (64 Parry 453)." Id.

[101] Davies, *supra* note 98 at 246. The constitution provided "all the forms of a liberal parliamentary system." Id. at 246

President held office for three years. The Constitution conferred on Cracow's citizens explicit guarantees of civic and personal liberty, and incorporated the principle of Free Trade.[102] In 1846, Austria and Russia awarded Cracow to Galicia.[103]

### *3.2.5.2 Shanghai*

Shanghai, a port city is situated on China's east coast. In 1842, China concluded the first of the 'unequal treaties', allowing British merchants to trade at five treaty ports including Shanghai.[104]

A CONSTITUTION CREATES FTA In 1845, the British established jurisdiction in Shanghai via a Constitution: the Land Regulations (1845) (Constitution).[105] This Constitution paved the way for combining Britain's settlement, with that of the United States in 1863, to form the International Settlement.[106] The Constitution's two provisions enabled the Western powers to secure exclusive concessions, and create the Shanghai Municipal Council (SMC).[107] And so, by the early twentieth century, Shanghai became:

> The permanent residence of an increasing number of Westerners, the center for trade and commerce, the home station of the Western gunboats, ..., all protected as semi-autonomous units with their own tax and legal-judicial systems;[108] and bound to a fixed and low ad valorem tariff that granted the Western powers immunity from direct taxation

[102] Id. at 246, 247.

[103] Id. at 247–249. Cracow was finally united with Poland when the latter gained independence in November 1918.

[104] *See* Gerrit Gong, *China's Entry into International Society, in* The Expansion of International Society 171–183 (Hedley Bull & Adam Watson, eds., OUP, 1984).

[105] William C. Johnston, *The Shanghai Problem* 13–14 (Hyperion Press, 1937).

[106] Id.

[107] Id. at 14. Jurgen Osterhammel, *Britain and China, 1842–1914, in* The Oxford History of the British Empire: Volume III: The Nineteenth Century 140, 151 (Andrew Porter and Wm Roger Louis, eds, Oxford University Press, 1999) (stating that Regulation XX provided a framework for the Municipal Council).

[108] Gong, *China & international society*, in Bull & Watson, *supra* note 104 at 177.

by China;[109] and, was administered by a foreign, 'exclusive and undemocratic' government (the SMC);[110] and possessed 'International Mixed Courts' which operated to control Chinese finance and large parts of the economy.[111]

Extraterritoriality, the principle governing the International Settlement, was abrogated in 1943.

A COMMON INTERNATIONAL CONTEXT FOR CRETE AND ALBANIA The same consortium of European Powers (Powers)—Austria-Hungary, Russia, Great Britain, France, and Italy—decided the fates of Crete and Albania (a Balkan state). The Powers did so, as part of resolving the 'Eastern Question': the Ottoman Empire's decline (including the revolt of the Cretan Christians and Albanian peoples there), and the successor states.[112]

The Powers considered the Ottoman State as barbarous and unsafe for Christian minorities.[113] So, as part of resolving the Eastern Question, they subordinated and tutored the Ottoman State, intervening in its internal affairs[114] ostensibly to promote 'good government'.[115] (However, as previously mentioned, that should not be confused with democracy-promotion.) The settlements concluded after the Crimean War at the Congress of Paris (1856), and the Congress of Berlin (1878)[116] evidence such interventions. I will discuss the settlements in the appropriate place. The Ottoman Sultan, financially ruined because of the Crimean war (1854–56), consented to introduce economic liberalization and so on, in return for being admitted into the Family of civilized

109 Id.

110 Osterhammel, in Porter and Louis, *supra* note 104 at 151.

111 Id.

112 *See* Barbara Jeravich, *Ottoman Empire, the Great Powers and the Straits Question, 1870-87* 186-187 (Indiana University Press, 1973).

113 *See* Davide Rodogno, *Against Massacre – Humanitarian Interventions in the Ottoman Empire, 1815-1914 – The Emergence of a European Concept and International Practice* 23–63 (Princeton University Press, 2012).

114 Id. at 24.

115 Id. at 26.

116 Stephen D. Krasner, Sovereignty: *Organized Hypocrisy* 85–86 (Cambridge University Press, 1999). The Congress of Berlin (1878) was held to resolve the 'Eastern Question' and stem Russia's rise in the region. Id.

nations. Accordingly, a month after the Sultan issued the February 1856 Reform Edict, (co-drafted by France and Britain), the Ottoman Empire was admitted into the Family of civilized nations.[117]

### *3.2.5.3 Crete*

Crete is the largest island in Greece. It had a mixed population of Muslims and Christians, and remained within the Ottoman Empire from 1669–1908. In the nineteenth century, Christian Cretans, instigated and supported by Greece, revolted against the Ottoman Empire, demanding union with Greece.[118]

To understand the events from 1897 requires starting from 1878, when to secure the good administration of the Turkish Empire, the Treaty of Berlin (1878) placed the 'constitution [of Crete] under the auspices of the international law of Europe'.[119] This 'gave the constitution an international character'.[120] Crete's constitution, drafted by the British Consul Sandwith, was promulgated on 21 November 1878.[121] Christian Cretans revolted twice, first in 1895 on the ground that Crete's governor had violated the 1878 Constitution, (which protected Christians), and again, in 1896.[122] In an effort to return Crete to constitutional order, the Powers' Ambassadors imposed a constitution in 1896 and 1897, which sired two foreign governments from 1896–7, and 1897–9, respectively.[123]

INTERNATIONAL TRUSTEESHIP CONTINUES (1899–1909) From 1899 to 1909, the Powers imposed a new status on Crete: 'full autonomy, subject

[117] Rodogno, *supra* note 113 at Ch. 2. Mehrdad Kia, *The Ottoman Empire* (Greenwood Press, 2008).

[118] Id. at 118.

[119] Id. at 213.

[120] Id.

[121] Id.

[122] Id. at 212–216.

[123] Id. The 1896 constitution called for a Christian Governor (approved by the Powers) for Crete, and reforming the judiciary and the *germanderie* (security sector). Id. at 214. The second foreign government (1897–99), an international military administration comprised the Powers' consuls in Crete who acted in concert, and with the approval of their respective ambassadors. Id. at 217.

to Ottoman suzerainty, but *de facto* under their Trusteeship'.[124] Deputed as Crete's high commissioner, Prince George of Greece, appointed a 15-member constitution-drafting committee, and allowed only one official language: Greek.[125] Eleftherios Venizelos drafted Crete's new constitution. Hostile to Muslims, it came into force on 8 February 1899.[126] In this way, from 1856 to 1909, Cretans (in the Ottoman Empire) lived under various constitutions (imposed by Powers). Eventually, Crete joined Greece in 1913.

### *3.2.5.4 Albania*

Turkey was roundly defeated in the first Balkan War (1912–13).[127] The Powers decided Albania's fate as part of imposing a settlement on the Balkan War's belligerents. For this purpose, the Powers convened the Ambassadors' Conference (Conference) in London (December 1912–August 1913).[128] Headed by the British foreign secretary, Sir Edward Grey, the Conference decided that Albania was to be a neutral, independent, constitutional monarchy, but subject to great power guarantee.[129] To protect the rights of Christian minorities, the Conference decided to head Albania with a Christian prince.[130] Meanwhile, although Albanians

[124] Id. at 220–223.

[125] Id. at 222.

[126] Id. at 223. Paschalis M. Kitromilides, *Eleftherios Venizelos: The Trials of Statesmanship* 68 (Edinburgh University Press, 2006).

[127] The Balkan Wars (1912–13) were two successive conflicts that deprived the Ottoman Empire of almost all its remaining territory in Europe. In the First Balkan War, the Balkan League (Serbia, Bulgaria, Greece, and Montenegro) defeated the Ottoman Empire. Under the Treaty of London (13 May 1913), Turkey relinquished her title to Crete, and under the Treaty of Bucharest signed with Greece, Turkey ratified Greece's annexation of Crete.

[128] Nicola Guy, *The Birth of Albania, Ethnic nationalism, the Great Powers of World War I and the Emergence of Albanian Independence* 39–41 48–53, 66 (I. B. Tauris, 2012).

[129] Id. at 37, 48–49, 66–69. By the Treaty of London (30 May 1913), the Ottoman Empire was forced to cede almost all of its remaining European territory including Albania. And the Ambassadors' Conference concluded in August 1913. Id. at 37.

[130] Id. at 49, 68–69.

had declared independence and set up a provisional government, the Powers refused to recognize it.[131]

THE INTERNATIONAL CONTROL COMMISSION DRAFTS ALBANIA'S CONSTITUTION AND ADMINISTERS THIS NEW STATE Instead, the Powers established an International Control Commission (ICC) to administer Albania.[132] The Powers chose as the head of the state, Lutheran German Prince William of Weid (Prince), a 35-year-old captain in the German army, and nephew of the Queen of Romania.[133] They did so, to prepare this predominantly Muslim, so-called 'newest nation in Europe' for a permanent regime.[134] The ICC was to govern Albania until the arrival of the Prince, and thereafter, transfer authority to, and assist him in administering the new state for 10 years.[135] The ICC comprised representatives of the six great powers, together with only one Albanian, Mufid bey Libohova.[136] Having arrived in Albania in October 1913, the ICC promulgated Albania's constitution on 10 April, 1914.[137] To further control Albania, Austria (as early as September 1913), sought to gain exclusive rights in the Albanian Bank.[138] The ICC's reign ended in August 1914.[139]

#### *3.2.5.5 Tangier*

Morocco is in the northwest corner of Africa. Therefore, Morocco connects and controls the commercial sea trade between Europe, Africa, Asia and the Far East.[140]

[131] Id. at 33, 71.

[132] Id. at 66–68.

[133] Id. at 69.

[134] Id. at 63.

[135] Id. at 66.

[136] Id. at 66, 67.

[137] Id. at 67, 72. The Prince would appoint ministers who were responsible to him. Id.

[138] Id. at 77.

[139] Id. at 83. When the First World War broke out, "one by one, the great powers withdrew their representatives" sitting in the ICC and Prince William left Albania on 3rd September. Id.

[140] Graham Stuart, *The International City of Tangier* 1 (Stanford University Press, 1955).

Tangier is Morocco's northern-most port city. It is therefore not surprising that the three great naval powers of that time (that is, 1920s), France, Spain, and Great Britain vied for Morocco and Tangier.[141] By the nineteenth century, Tangier, had become Morocco's main center of foreign activity, and was inhabited predominantly by Muslims and non-Europeans.[142] At the turn of the twentieth century, in addition to France, Spain, Great Britain, Italy and the United States vigorously sought to internationalize Tangier to protect their trading interests.[143] By 1912, having become a French protectorate, technically, Morocco, and by extension, Tangier, its port city, came under French control.[144] However, to appease Spain, France consented to specifically exempt the zone of Tangier from French control.[145]

WESTERN POWERS IMPOSE A CONSTITUTION AND AN INTERNATIONAL GOVERNMENT Eventually, France, Spain, and Great Britain, as part of a compromise they had agreed to, decided to internationalize Tangier. Accordingly, on 25 October 1923, a conference comprising these colonial powers' representatives drew up Tangier's constitution (the Statute of the Tangier Zone), inserting it in the Convention Regarding the Organization of the Statute of the Tangier Zone (18 December 1923).[146] The constitution came into effect in 1925.[147] It rendered Tangier a neutral zone,[148] enshrined the open door policy, and provided for an international administration: an international assembly (law-making body), and a Committee of Control (Committee).[149] The Committee, comprising the Powers' consuls, was empowered with implementing

141 Id. at 1–20

142 Id.

143 Id. at 79.

144 Id. at 53. "The Treaty of Protectorate, 30 Mach 1912 gave France full rights to establish the reforms considered necessary, to preserve order, and to direct its foreign affairs" Id.

145 Id. at 53, 54.

146 Id. at 85 and 201–216 (reproducing the Statute).

147 Id. at 85 (This Convention became binding on 14 May 1924, when the Three Powers deposited their ratifications).

148 Id. at 202 (Art 3 - neutrality).

149 Id. at 85–87.

the constitution, including the observance of the 'regime of economic equality', (the open door policy).[150]

### 3.2.6 Occupation, Including the So-called 'Belligerent Occupation'

Occupation, the last institution in Wilde's family, is defined under international law as:

> [t]he territorial control by a state or group of states over territory, the title to which is not vested in the state or states concerned.[151]

As far as the role of the occupier as a trustee is concerned, Sir Arnold Wilson's comments of 1932 are instructive:

> ... enemy territories in the occupation of the armed forces of another country constitute in the language of article 22 of the League of Nations Covenant) a sacred trust, which must be administered as a whole in the interests of both the inhabitants and of the legitimate sovereign or the duly constituted successor in title.[152]

In many instances, since administering occupied territories required a legal framework, occupying powers made constitutions for them.[153] The most well-known examples include the Constitutions imposed by Allied occupation forces in both Germany and Japan.[154]

### 3.2.7 Commonalities

The question is whether Wilde's institutions are analogous: Do they 'operate in the same fashion in an elemental sense'? If so, is the Constitution's internationalized making an 'institution' or 'established

150 Id.

151 Wilde, *supra* note 2 at 308.

152 Id. at 322 (quoting Wilson)

153 The question of whether it is legitimate for an occupying power to reform the existing constitutional and legal order within an occupied territory lies beyond the scope of this book.

154 Werner Heun, *The Constitution of Germany – A Contextual Analysis* Ch. 2 (Hart Publishers, 2011); Dale Hellegers, *We the Japanese People: World War II and the Origins of the Japanese Constitution* (Stanford University Press, 2002).

practice'? My analysis in the previous section 3.2, suggests that the answers to both these questions are positive.

To recap the points, First, in each of Wilde's institutions, the FP is either a foreign state, a group of foreign states, or a collectivity of foreign state representatives and/or an IO.

Second, conceptually each of these FPs imposes a constitution (that is, engages in Constitution-making) to achieve its territorial goals: to establish jurisdiction and to introduce administration. What varieties of practices might we safely call 'constitutional' in relation to empire? Indeed, as both Jan-Erik-Lane and Patrice Glenn suggest, it was during Renaissance that the 'term constitution understood as hierarchically, the most superior form of legal writing' emerged as a 'technology' of territorial jurisdiction. The constitution did so, because the Renaissance was when, the concept of a territorially bounded state, started to emerge. This is why, historians assert that more generally, the varieties of practices that we might safely call Constitution-making in relation to empire are those from the eighteenth century. For instance, Professor Paul Halliday states that 'Constitution and its cognates were not generally used to describe these practices before the eighteenth century.'[155] Finally, Professor Jim Tully, who has analysed the Constitution's imperial role, calls post-Renaissance European colonialism 'constitutional imperialization'.

This brings us to the activity that was carried out during 1700–1960, which created each of Wilde's FTA institutions: the Constitution's imposition[156] in the ways described in Chapter 2. First, I conceptualize this, as (internationalized) Constitution-making. As the insights in the above paragraph suggest, this is correct. It is worth noting that in my discussion about the pre-eighteenth century era (1300–1700), I resisted using later, including our own definitions of constitution. For, I noted that colonial powers imagined politico-legal order in different ways. In this regard, I identified an array of instruments that were used,

155 Prof. Paul Halliday, Julian Bishko Professor of history and law, University of Virginia, USA, email dated 27 June 2016.

156 Wilde's four other FTAs: Representative Bodies, protection, state-conducted administration under the LON and the UN Trusteeship System operated during 1815-1960, and so fall within Colonial, i.e., from the post-eighteenth century era.

or imposed as 'constitutions' to establish jurisdiction: codes, charters, instructions and 'undeveloped constitutions'.'

Second, Constitution-making varied under each FP. As noted earlier, I am not concerned with its form, unless it is relevant. Rather, I stress only the principles of domination and control that underpinned it.

Third, as regards, the Mandates System, I have noted that in addition to the mandatory powers (foreign states), the PMC (an IO) engages in a rudimentary form of Constitution-making in this way: it sets legally oriented market-standards.

Fourth, in each of Wilde's institutions, the imposed constitution enables the FP to administer—either partially or in full—the relevant discrete territorial unit.

Fifth, regarding the fifth institution in Wilde's family: Representative bodies, only the first category engages directly in Constitution-making, and whereas, the remaining three categories, do so only tangentially. The remaining three categories comprise bodies which guaranteed the internationalization of rivers, held plebiscites, and implemented population exchanges (exchange of minorities) respectively.[157] As legal issues, conceptually, these three topics fall within constitutional law.[158] For instance, the Constitution governs territories. This makes rivers a constitutional topic because a riparian state's control of its fluvial

[157] Wilde, *supra* note 2 at 307. Categories 2–4 comprise:

- Waterway commissions such as the International Danube Commission, begun 1856), which exercised various administrative powers over their respective waterways;
- International commissions created by the Treaty of Versailles to hold plebiscites in certain territories, and
- Mixed commissions, including that created in 1923, to support and facilitate the compulsory exchange of Turkish and Greek minority populations between Greece and Turkey. Id

[158] *See* Angeliki Ziaha, *Muslims and Muslim education in Greece, in*, Islamic Education in Europe 141, 156 (Ednan Asian, ed., Böhlau Verlag Wien, 2009). The Lausanne Treaty (Treaty) mandated population exchanges between Greece and Turkey, and so, provided the legal framework for the rights of minorities. Accordingly, Greece had to revise its constitution and laws on a par with the Treaty. Id. Plebiscite is a constitutional topic because it refers to all types of popular votes bearing on a public issue or policy.

territory equates with its control of its own territory.[159] River Danube flows through 10 countries. To internationalize Danube, each of the Contracting powers to the Treaty of Paris (1856), consented to constitutionalize (international) principles that were designed to regulate the navigation of rivers, separating or traversing different states.[160]

On this basis, I argue that Wilde's Family comprises parent and child 'institutions', (established practices), respectively: (1) the Constitution's internationalized making and (2) FTA. In fact, Wilde noted the insights set out in point two. This is precisely why in conceptualizing colonialism as FTA, he wisely limited his scope to the post-Renaissance era. Again, those historical aspects explain why he considers as colonialism only those 'representations of particular manifestations that compare with territorial administration', (defined as only legislative, judicial, and executive activities), and flowing from the Western liberal constitution. In short, Wilde has woven his definition of Colonialism, using those very historical and conceptual strands that tie the Constitution with territorial administration. This is why his Family rests on a solid foundation, and reflects those symbiotic relations.

Indeed, European colonialism, protection (ITA by the LON), state-conducted administration under the Mandates System of the LON and the UN Trusteeship System, the Representative Bodies, and Occupation (including belligerent occupation), all mirror the Constitution's symbiotic working with FTA.

In summary, in Wilde's Family, the relevant FP engages symbiotically in two of the same types of activities: Constitution-making and territorial administration. So, Wilde's Family comprises two symbiotic institutions: the Constitution's internationalized making and FTA. Conceptually, colonial Constitution-making provides a legal blue print (the Constitution) from which flows FTA. Consequently, and conversely, each of Wilde's FTA institutions is rooted in the Constitution.

I suggest that it is possible to distinguish between Wilde's institutions, based on the identity of the constitution-imposing actor. First, in European colonialism and under the Mandates and Trusteeship Systems, foreign states imposed constitutions. Second, IOs also engaged

[159] J. Chamberlain, *Regime of the International Rivers: Danube and Rhine* 5 (P.S. King & Son, 1923).

[160] Id. at 47.

in internationalized Constitution-making. The LON engaged directly in making Danzig's constitution. Whereas the PMC, which approached its administrative and supervisory tasks legalistically, came to set legal and market-oriented standards. In this way, the PMC promoted the market-oriented Constitution. In the post-1945 era, the UNTC offered constitutional assistance, and thus, engaged tangentially in Constitution-making. Third, in Representative Bodies, we have representatives of foreign states crafting and imposing constitutions. Finally, in occupation, we have a foreign state (a victorious power) imposing a constitution, as occurred in Japan and West Germany.

I now turn to consider whether the Constitution's internationalized making is a 'Policy Institution'. For this purpose, I take the policies pursued by, and ends achieved by the FP, under each of Wilde's FTA institutions. I consider how the Constitution's making, the activity engaged in by each of the FPs, contributed to achieving those policies and ends. I start with considering the Trusteeship policy (briefly introduced in chapter 2), which is based on the Civilized Standards.

## 3.3 Analogous 'Policy Institutions'

### 3.3.1 First Common Policy: Trusteeship

Why did the FPs in Wilde's institutions, displace local actors from sculpting their constitutions, and administering their territories?[161] I will fully answer this question in the following section. The FPs did so, in the pursuit of Trusteeship. Which requires considering when and why this concept (Trusteeship) first originated, was legalized and internationalized, and thus, came to define each of Wilde's institutions.

The concept of trust was first articulated in 1783 by Edmund Burke, while opposing the harsh governmental regime instituted by the East India Company in India:

> All political power which is set over men and … all privilege claimed or exercised in exclusion of them, being wholly artificial, and for so much a derogation from the natural quality of mankind at large, ought to be some way or other exercised ultimately for their benefit. If this is true

[161] *See* Wilde, *supra* note 2 at 317–364 (analyzing FTA's Trusteeship role).

with regard to every species of political domination, and every description of commercial privilege, none of which can be original, self-derived rights, or grants for mere private benefit of the holders, then such rights, or privileges, or whatever you choose to call them, are all, in the strictest sense, *a trust.*[162]

### *'International Trusteeship'*[163] *Equals to the Constitution's Internationalized Making and Foreign Territorial Administration*

After 1783, Trusteeship was legalized and internationalized in the General Act of the Berlin Conference of 1884–5, the LON's Covenant, and the UN Charter, as will be illustrated below:

Article 6, Chapter I of the General Act
Colonial powers in Africa were bound to:
... watch over the preservation of the native tribes, and to care for the improvement of the conditions of their moral and material well-being, and to help in suppressing slavery, and especially the slave trade.[164]

Article 22 of the Covenant of the League of Nations:

To those colonies and territories which as a consequence of the late war have ceased to be under the sovereignty of the States which formerly governed them and which are inhabited by peoples not yet able to stand by themselves under the strenuous conditions of the modern world, there should be applied the principle that the well-being and development of such peoples form a sacred trust of civilization and

[162] E. Burke, *Speech on Fox's India Bill, 1 December 1783, reproduced in* The Writings and Speeches of Edmund Burke, vol. V: India: Madras and Bombay 1774-1785 378, 385 (P. Langford, ed., Clarendon Press, 1785); *see* Frank O'Gorman, *Edmund Burke: His Political Philosophy - Volume II* 49-75 (Geraint Parry, ed., Routledge, 1973) (discussing Burke's views on the British constitution); Morton J. Frisch, *Edmund Burke and the American Constitution* 17 Interpretation—A J. of Pol. Philosophy 59–68 (Fall 1989).

[163] For this Ralph Wilde's phrase, see Wilde, *supra* note 2 at 356.

[164] General Act of the Conference respecting (1) Freedom of Trade in the Basin of the Congo; (2) the Slave Trade; (3) Neutrality of the Territories in the Basin of the Congo; (4) Navigation of the Congo; (5) Navigation of the Niger; and (6) Rules for Future Occupation on the Coast of the African Continent, signed at Berlin, 26 February 1885, 165 CTS 485 (*hereafter* 'Berlin Conference General Act'), Chapter I, Art. VI.

> that securities for the performance of this trust should be embodied in this Covenant.[165]

UN Charter, Chapter XI: Declaration regarding non-self-governing territories:

> Members of the United Nations which have or assume responsibilities for the administration of territories whose peoples have not yet attained a full measure of self-government recognize the principle that the interests of the inhabitants of these territories are paramount, and accept as a sacred trust the obligation to promote to the utmost, within the system of international peace and security established by the present Charter, the well-being of the inhabitants of those territories.[166]

While the concept of trust was implicitly embraced by the Berlin Conference Act, it was formally adopted as the basis for the Mandate and UN Trusteeship systems.

At the start of this section, this question was posed: 'Why did each of the FPs in Wilde's FTA institutions, displace local actors from sculpting their constitutions and administering their territories?' Before proceeding, it helps to recall that Trusteeship is based on the Civilized Standards, of which the Constitution is a key one. Now to answer that question, I suggest that the FPs displaced local actors from the symbiotic activities of Constitution-making and territorial administration ostensibly to remedy governance at par with Civilized Standards (discussed further below in section 3.3.4). Toward this end, the FPs imposed the Constitution (previously considered in section 3.2), and thereby introduced their (that is, foreign) territorial administration, FTA. In this way, the FPs pursued 'international Trusteeship' which therefore, comprises the Constitution's internationalized making and FTA.

Throughout this section, I will concentrate on (colonial Constitution-making), that is, the Constitution's Trusteeship role. Which as the parent, therefore, guides all aspects of FTA/ITA's Trusteeship role. This is a conceptual reason that I will hereafter not repeat. Here comes Wilde who explicitly concentrates only on the Trusteeship role of FTA/

165 *See* Covenant of the LON, *at:* avalon.law.yale.edu/20th_century/leagcov.asp.

166 *See* UN Charter (1945).

ITA but whose Western liberal constitutional parentage, he implicitly acknowledges.[167] Given this, expectedly, our submissions meld, explicitly and implicitly. I concur with all of his submissions, and will engage with some of them as I go along. In conclusion, I will underscore the Constitution's salience vis-à-vis its child's Trusteeship role.

*Foreign Powers internationalize the Constitution to achieve two objectives*

The Constitution's making, a key Trusteeship activity had two objectives. First, FPs imposed it to care for the ward and thereby provide 'good governance' or 'civilized governance'. Second, since the Constitution provides a framework for carrying on territorial administration, it provided a framework for carrying on tutelage. That is, it enabled FPs to tutor local actors (the wards) in self-administration so that they may eventually learn to govern themselves.[168] Next, in so imposing the Constitution, the FPs fulfilled two obligations: 1) to fill a governmental 'gap'; and 2) to provide civilized governance.[169] (It should be noted that here, Constitution-making includes setting and imposing legally-and-market-oriented standards, as undertaken by the PMC.)

Take the Congo, where as previously discussed, Leopold II imposed the Constitution to assert jurisdiction and introduce his (that is, Belgian/foreign) administration. How might we frame Leopold II's actions in terms of colonial Trusteeship? He was ostensibly filling the Congo's supposed governmental vacuum and providing 'civilized governance', allegedly in response to perceived local incapacities for governance. Again, take the internationalized constitutions (and the FTA) imposed over Crete. Indeed, the Powers did so, ostensibly to fill a void with 'good government': to protect minorities, promote property rights; and thus, civilize the Ottoman Empire.

What type of a remedy did the FPs' Trusteeship offer? As the examples considered in section 3.2.1 suggests (for example, Congo), the FPs wholly displaced local actors from the allied activities of Constitution-making and territorial administration.

167 *See* Wilde, *supra* note 2 at 317–364 (analyzing FTA's Trusteeship role).

168 *See* Bipan Chandra, *India's Struggle for Independence 1857-1947* 142 (Penguin Books, 1989); Leslie William White & W.D. Hussey, *Government in Great Britain: The Empire, and the Commonwealth* 228 (quote); 225–245 (Cambridge University Press, 1961).

169 *See* White & Hussey, *supra* note 168 at 228.

*The Constitution's ameliorative use*

In the modern age, nationally made and owned constitutions symbolize independence and sovereignty. Given this, where the FPs did not envisage independence for, and pursued ameliorative goals regarding a colony, they imposed the Constitution (and thereby FTA) for an indefinite period. Accordingly, this arrangement led to no statement, (either explicit or implicit) about granting independence to the people, even at some future date.[170] So, here tutelage was not a goal.

We see colonial Constitution-making and FTA's (aforementioned) ameliorative use in the early twentieth century in India. The then Secretary of State for India, Lord Morley, asserted in the British parliament that self-government, as demanded by India's nationalist leaders, was not suitable for India. Morley famously declared:

> If it could be said that this chapter of constitutional reforms leads directly or necessarily up to the establishment of a Parliamentary system in India, I for, one, would have nothing at all to do with it.[171]

Accordingly, in 1909 a colonial Constitution (the Minto-Morley Act) was imposed, which left executive authority firmly in the hands of the viceroy and the provincial governors, all of whom were British officials.[172] We see the palliative model's use even in the 'C' class Mandate territories such as South-West Africa (later Namibia) and West Samoa.

*The Constitution provides a framework for tutelage*

Moreover, the discourse of colonial ideology became open to ideas about the possibility for progressive development in local capacities. These ideas entered the discourse first in the late nineteenth century, when policymakers proposed—as their ostensible goals—remedying governance and enhancing local actors' capacities through tutelage.[173] Consider these provisions of the Berlin Conference Act and Article 73 of the UN Charter:

> Article 6 of Chapter I of the Berlin Conference Act:
>
> All the Powers exercising sovereign rights or influence in the aforesaid territories bind themselves to watch over the preservation of the

170 *Id.* at 225–233; Wilde, *supra* note 2 at 317–364.

171 Chandra, *supra* note 168 at 142.

172 Id.

173 Wilde *supra* note 2 at 336.

> native tribes, and to care for the improvement of the conditions of their moral and material well-being, and to help in suppressing slavery, and especially the slave trade. They shall, without distinction of creed or nation, protect and favor all religious, scientific or charitable institutions and undertakings created and organized for the above ends, or which aim at instructing the natives and bringing home to them the blessings of civilization.[174]

Article 73 of the UN Charter requires colonial states 'to promote … the well-being of the inhabitants'

> a. to ensure … their political, economic, social, and educational advancement …
>
> […]
>
> b. [and] to develop self-government, take due account of the political aspirations of the peoples and to assist them in the progressive development of their free political institutions, according to the particular circumstances of each territory and its peoples and their varying stages of advancement.[175]

Significantly, these quotes about local actors' capacities contain this idea as well: to adjust their self-administration (which as we know, flows from Constitution-making) according to such capacity. Might this spell an end to the imposition of constitutions, and the introduction of self-rule and nationally driven Constitution-making? As previously noted, no. Indeed, tutelage meant the continuance of imposed colonial constitutions, but allowing natives to participate in rudimentary law-making. That is making laws lower than the Constitution, which is supreme.

Once again, British colonial rule in India offers a rich insight. Almost a decade after the imposition of the 1909 colonial Constitution, Sir Edwin Samuel Montague, the then Secretary of State for the Government of India, called for 'gradual development of free institutions in India with a view to ultimate self-government'.[176] His statement (which was subsequently modified in the Montague Declaration, 1919) called for:

> Increasing association of Indians in every branch of the administration, and the gradual development of self-governing institutions, with a view

[174] *See* General Act of the Conference of Berlin Concerning the Congo, February 26, 1885 *reprinted in* 3 (1) AJIL Suppl. 7, 12 (January 1909).

[175] *See* UN Charter (1945).

[176] *See* Chandra, *supra* note 168 at 168.

> to achieve the progressive realization of responsible government in India as an integral part of the British Empire.[177]

Accordingly, the Montague –Chelmsford Reforms introduced a bicameral legislature at both the federal and provincial levels. Meanwhile, instead of adult franchise, a communal electorate (a ploy to divide and rule the Indian populace), and voting rights based on property and educational qualifications were introduced.[178] This of course equated with the usual way the Constitution played out in the Third World (*see* Chapter 2). Indians so elected, were now eligible for advising the Governor only on relatively unimportant topics, such as museums, libraries, education, and local self-government.[179]

Understandably, a decade later, colonial/internationalized Constitution-making still reigned supreme. In 1928, the British appointed an all-White Commission, headed by Sir John Simon, to decide the next batch of constitutional reforms for Indians.[180] Put simply, Indians were deemed unfit for self-administration, and hence, were denied the right to sculpt their own constitution.

Tutelage was also framed as 'indirect rule', as in Tanganyika (see section 3.2.4). There, native Chiefs exercised customary law-making powers at the local level, subject of course to the overarching colonial constitution. 'Indirect rule' and its allied concept, the dual mandate, were coined by the famed colonial expert, Frederick Lugard. Consider:

> [t]he British Empire ... has only one mission for liberty and self-development .... [which] can be best secured to the native population by leaving them free to manage their own affairs through their own rulers, proportionately to their degree of advancement, under the guidance of the British staff, and subject to the law and policy of the administration.[181]

177 Id.

178 Id.

179 Id. *See also* White & Hussey, *supra* note 169 at 231 (emphasizing the concentration of power in Governors); J G. Kamoche, *Imperial Trusteeship and Political Evolution in Kenya, 1923-1963 – A Study of the Official views and the Road to Decolonization* xiii (University Press of America, 1981).

180 Chandra, *supra* note 168 at 260.

181 F.J. D. Lugard, *Dual Mandate in British Tropical Africa* 94 (Blackwood, 1922).

> Europe is in Africa for the mutual benefit of her own industrial classes and of the native races in their progress to a higher plane; the benefit can be made reciprocal, and it is the aim of civilized administration to fulfil this dual mandate.[182]

*Toward ending the Constitution's internationalization*

Logically, ending colonialism required entertaining the idea of conferring on local actors, the right to sculpt their own constitutions so that they may administer their territories in tune with them. Put differently, ending colonialism required rejecting first, the idea of denying local actors their right to sculpt their constitutions (and the consequent idea of displacing them from territorial administration). This stage would culminate in what Robert Jackson calls, 'evolutionary decolonization'.[183]

*Post-World Wars I and II's policymakers deploy the Constitution to achieve their varied goals*

However, before the aforesaid idea (of ending the Constitution's use or ending colonialism appeared), powerful states disagreed about whether colonies should be granted full independence, or allowed self-administration, subject to an overarching colonial constitutional order.[184] For example, the UN Charter's provisions concerning Non-Self-Governing Territories contained these phrases: self-government or independence.[185] Meanwhile, William Bain, another leading scholar on colonial Trusteeship, tells us how and why those differences of opinion arose:

> American skepticism of empire transformed Trusteeship from a justification of empire as it was in the British tradition, into an alternative to empire that was expressed concretely in the form of the League of Nations mandates system and the United Nations Trusteeship system....[186]

This means, as I will show, international policymakers used the League's Covenant and the UN Charter (see the provisions concerning

182 Neta C. Crawford, *How Previous Ideas Affect Later Ideas, in* The Oxford Handbook of Contextual Political Analysis, Volume 5 270 (Robert E. Goodin *et al*, eds., OUP, 2006).

183 *See* Wilde, *supra* note 2 at 337 (quoting Jackson).

184 Id.

185 *See* UN Charter, Art. 73 (b).

186 William Bain, *Between Anarchy and Society: Trusteeship and the Obligations of Power* 21 (Oxford University Press, 2003).

Non-Self-Governing Territories) to internationalize the Constitution in different ways, with a view to allow tutelage and achieve progress. Accordingly, the Covenant explicitly referred to issues of progressive improvement, and tasked the mandate powers and the PMC with developing the natives, and preparing (relevant mandate territories) for independence. So did the UN Charter.[187]

The Covenant sets the following three criteria for introducing the Constitution, all of which therefore, applied to FTA.[188] One was the development level:

> [t]he character of the mandate must differ according to the stage of the development of the people, the geographic situation of the territory, its economic conditions and other similar circumstances.[189]

Based on the three aforesaid criteria, the Covenant split the Mandated territories into three classes: 'A', 'B', and 'C'. The people of 'A' class Mandated territories were deemed to have:

> ... reached a stage of development where their existence as independent nations can be provisionally recognized subject to the rendering of administrative advice and assistance by the Mandatory until such time as they are able to stand alone.[190]

This meant that, people of 'A' class territories had to live under an imposed constitution, until such time 'as they are able to stand alone'. Once they were deemed fit to do so, as occurred in 1920 in Iraq, they would be granted independence.

Regarding 'B' class territories, the Mandatory power was tasked with imposing constitutions for an indefinite period and therefore, offering plenary administration, without any cut-off date.[191] Turning to the last, that is, the 'C' class of mandated territories, the colonial constitution's imposition and the creation of plenary foreign territorial administration rested not only on the level of development but, on these factors as well:

187 *See* UN Charter, Chapter XII, art. 76 (b).

188 Wilde, *supra* note 2 at 339.

189 *See* League Covenant, Art. 22.

190 *Id.*

191 Id.

> … the sparseness of their population, or their small size, or their remoteness from the centers of civilization, or their geographical contiguity to the territory of the Mandatory, and other circumstances …[192]

Taken together, one can see the Mandates System's arrangements pertaining to Class 'A', 'B', and 'C' class territories build on the Trusteeship concept, developed in the earlier colonial context (see sections 3.0–3.3 and Chapter 2): Accordingly, each arrangement achieved its goals via the Constitution, basing its imposition, ostensibly on the relevant peoples' developmental level. However, different policies underlay the Constitution's use. For the 'A' class mandated territories, the developmental level is the criterion, both for imposing it and ending its imposition (that is, allowing popular sovereignty). In the 'B' class territories, the same criterion, that is, the developmental level, is a factor for introducing the Constitution and therefore, FTA. The arrangement in 'C' class territories, resembles certain forms of colonialism, where the territory's small size (and not the level of development), is put forth as a reason for the idea of imposing the Constitution and therefore, FTA[193]—for an indefinite duration.

What about the UN's Trusteeship System? Like the Mandates System, the Charter does not set out when Trusteeship arrangements terminate. The UN's Trusteeship model differs from, and supplements the Mandate System's formula in that, it prescribes two objectives for imposing the Constitution: 1) to provide a blue print for governance until local actors develop self-governance capacities and; 2) to improve governance and thus, raise developmental levels.[194] That is, the same ostensible factors—a poor developmental level and improving that situation—apply for displacing local actors from the activities of Constitution-making and so, territorial administration. Tanganyika is a good example (see section 3.2.4). Under this Model, the Constitution was imposed to fill the governmental vacuum and build capacity, as well as improving developmental levels and governance. And once these goals are achieved, its imposition ends. Hence, so too, ends FTA.

192 *Id.*

193 *See* Wilde, *supra* note 2 at 343.

194 See UN Charter 1945, art. 76, 86 (a) & 88.

In occupation Trusteeship, constitutions are imposed for a temporary period, ostensibly to fill a governmental vacuum. Here is why, occupation Trusteeship is temporary, and its goals are not to improve governance. What about 'transformative' occupation, which on its termination is expected to manifest some benchmarks for improvement?[195] Here, the Constitution's making enjoys a key role, for it is used, both, to create government and to transform governance. As previously discussed, the Allied Powers imposed the Constitution in West Germany and Japan, to establish a Federal order in the former, and transform the latter into a market economy. To sum up, the Constitution's making is integral to occupation Trusteeship, transformative or otherwise. FTA roles flow from this.[196]

In the aforesaid ways, two Trusteeship models obtained, each of which relied on the Constitution. The first model lacked independence as an end-goal (for example, certain forms of colonial Trusteeship, 'C' class Mandated territories) and so, required the indefinite use of the Constitution and therefore, FTA. The second model came with the suggestion of self-administration, and so, required the Constitution whose use with FTA[197] rested:

a) implicitly on development improvements (for example, 'B' class Mandated territories); and
b) explicitly on development improvements, ('A' class Mandated territories, all Trust territories and colonies under the UN Charter, and 'transformatory' occupations), and
c) not necessarily on development improvements (non-'transformatory' occupations).

The second model acquires a tutoring dimension for the Constitution throws up a possibility for local actors enjoying some law-making powers at the local level (for example, indirect rule).

### 3.3.1.1 *The Constitution Guides FTA/ITA's Trusteeship Roles*

To conclude, the afore-discussed arrangements showcase how the Constitution was progressively internationalized to achieve common

[195] Id. Adam Roberts, *Transformative Military Occupation: Applying the Laws of War and Human Rights* 100 AJIL 580, 601-604 (2006).

[196] *See* Wilde, *supra* note 2 at 343.

[197] Id.

Trusteeship goals—discussed in section 3.3.4: 'Civilized Standards'. The Constitution governed FTA/ITA's Trusteeship roles in six ways. 1) Ideas by powerful Western states' about Third World peoples' Constitution-making capacities governed their plans for imposing the Constitution. 2) The Constitution's indefinite use spelt the same for FTA. 3) An end in the Constitution's use, foretold the end of FTA. 4) The Constitution constituted the 'imperial commercial system'[198] and provided a formal framework for politico-economic activity, whereby local actors could gain practice in making laws that meet it (that is, undertake FTA/ITA). This means that international tutelage rested on powerful Western states' ideas first, about Third World's Constitution-making incapacities, and next about their administration capacities. 5) The Constitution and its child, FTA/ITA pursued common Trusteeship ends: promoting good governance or civilized governance. 6) The Constitution enabled FTA/ITA to fill a governmental gap and thereby also provide civilized governance.

### 3.3.2 Common Policy-roles

#### *The Constitution's Internationalized Making and Foreign Territorial Administration Play Common Policy-roles*

Based on my analysis in the previous section, I submit that Constitution-making and FTA share several features.

First, the Constitution was conceived as a remedial governance tool.[199] The FPs imposed the Constitution to raise the quality of governance on a par with preferred standards: free markets, rule of law, good governance (including natural resources' exploitation), and civilized practices (discussed in detail in section 3.4). The Constitution provided a framework for foreign territorial administration (FTA) and confers status on a given territorial unit (territorial status). (Law-making [FTA] serves to further that status, so conferred).[200] In this way, both colonial Constitution-making and its child, FTA were conceived in response to, what Wilde too, considers and calls a 'governance problem'. Here is

[198] P. Burroughs, '*David Fieldhouse and the Business of Empire* 26 J. of Imperial & Commonwealth Hist. 6, 12 (1998)

[199] *See infra* Chapter 7, Table 7.1: UNCA-ITA play symbiotic policy roles.

[200] Wilde, *supra* note 2 at 207.

why, this parent and child share common ends. In fact, FTA's ends are simply those of its parent, the Constitution.

Second, common ends bring us to common policy roles. I approach colonial Constitution-making negatively to arrive at its and its child, FTA's policy roles. So then, what is not colonial Constitution-making? Indeed, this activity is the opposite of what we today in the post-colonial era consider to be its default model:

> Constitution-making is a sovereign national process, which to be legitimate and successful, must be nationally-owned and led –United Nations.[201]

It follows from this that the default model of territorial administration is:

> the conduct of territorial administration by actors whose spatial identity, as 'local,' corresponds to that of the territorial unit and its population[202] –Wilde.

Why were local actors displaced from the symbiotic activities? FPs imposed the Constitution because:

- it was supposed to be superior, civilized, and universal and fit to replace indigenous constitutions which were deemed defective, inferior—and indeed, no constitutions at all.[203]

In imposing the Constitution, the FPs:

> lent governance a preferred political character/ political orientation: introduced a legal order wherein the constitution as the supreme law enshrines the legislature, executive and judiciary and guides their activities (foreign territorial administration).

Following from the point made in the above para, I argue that, where the FP perceived a vacuum, it first produced the Constitution as a blue print for introducing, and carrying on FTA. (In this way, colonial Constitution-making enabled FTA to fill the vacuum.) Again,

201 *See* UN, UNCA Guidance Note 1 (2009).

202 Wilde, *supra* note 3 at 21.

203 *See* Jim Tully, *Modern Constitutional Democracy and Imperialism* Osgoode H. L. J. 46 (3) 461, 468 (2008).

where the FP aims to promote good governance, it first produces the Constitution. This way, it sets the stage for introducing and orienting FTA along Civilized Standards. Herein lie the allied policy roles of colonial Constitution-making and FTA: they both substitute what we today, in the post-colonial era consider to be their default method, and normal model respectively.

Third, point two suggests that the same notions underpinned the displacement of local actors from the activities of Constitution-making, and territorial administration. Conversely the same ostensible purposes were put forth for internationalizing these two symbiotic activities. For instance, I suggest, where and because FPs ostensibly embraced a proactive approach, they first internationalized Constitution-making with a view to introduce FTA. (I will revisit this point in Chapter 7.) Wilde is therefore right to state that, in introducing FTA, FPs were understood to be acting proactively.

Fourth, this brings us to the remedial roles envisaged for colonial Constitution-making and FTA. My first and second submissions suggest that, that remedy began with, and comprised colonial Constitution-making.

Fifth, under the palliative model, FPs step into the shoes of a territorial unit's local actors to draft a Constitution, and so provide a functioning administrative system. Thus, where and because colonial Constitution-making is conceived to be exclusively palliative, so is FTA.

Finally, FPs imposed the Constitution to exploit the colonies' resources, and so on. Indeed, FPs denied Third World peoples the right to sculpt their constitutions, and engage in self-governance only to fill their own (FPs) needs, and based on their (FPs) notions about the Third World's supposed incapacities. Which means, there was no need for internationalizing either Constitution-making or territorial administration in the Third World. Indeed, FPs internationalized these symbiotic activities only to fill a need they created.

With this, I end the discussion on Trusteeship, the first ostensible policy toward which the FPs in each of Wilde's FTA institutions, put their Constitution-making. (Previously, in section 3.2, I established that Wilde's FTA institutions are analogous institutions. I then, commenced considering whether internationalized Constitution-making is a 'policy institution' to which I devote the remainder of this section 3.3.) I therefore, turn to consider how the Constitution-making engaged in, by each of the FPs in Wilde's Family achieved:

1) The second allied policy (that is, the civilizing mission) and
2) common ostensible ends:
   (i) Territorial status outcomes and strategic advantage; and
   (ii) Civilized StandardsCivilized Standards (free markets, the rule of law, good governance, and civilized practices)

## 3.3.3. Common Ostensible Ends

### *3.3.3.1. Territorial Status Outcomes and Strategic Advantage*

Wilde rightly suggests that FPs used FTA institutions to achieve territorial status and strategic advantage.[204] As we have seen, conceptually, the Constitution lends political character to territory and territorial governance. On this basis, I posit that colonial Constitution-making was key to achieving these goals.

Drawing from my discussion in section 3.2., I argue that appropriate constitutions enabled the FPs to confer their preferred status, for instance, on Crete, Danzig, Cracow, Tangier, and Albania. Indeed, this is precisely why the LON and relevant Representative bodies were empowered to sculpt and "guarantee" constitutions.

Constitutions secured political, economic, and territorial advantages for the great powers in Iraq, Morocco, Tangier, Albania, and Shanghai. For instance, the Constitution (and the property rights protected by it) enabled France to secure access to Morocco's minerals and bring Morocco (which surpassed the other northern gateways—Algeria, Tunisia, and Tripolitania), under its political control. The open door provisions in the Anglo-Iraq treaty (protected by Iraq's constitution) benefited Great Britain and the United States economically. Great Britain and the United States benefited from the open door provisions in Tangier's constitution as well. Finally, the 'mini-constitution' (Land Regulations) (and the rule of law promoted by it) imposed over Shanghai enabled the United States and the United Kingdom to control Chinese finances.

Again, the Constitution enabled metropolitan states to pry open their colonies' economies and secure access to their raw materials and markets, thus gaining an economic advantage. It was to control Albania that the relevant Powers imposed a constitution: they imposed protections for minorities, and their preferred economic policies.

[204] Id. at 207.

Finally, one key way in which victorious states, after both the World Wars, gained prestige was to impose constitutions over defeated states and colonies, previously held by the defeated powers. West Germany and Japan demonstrate how constitutions enabled victorious powers to bring these vanquished states under their influence and control.

*International constitutional standards in the twentieth century*

By the inter-war period, the Concert of Powers had internationalized a standard for civilized governance: constitutional protection for minorities.[205] Internationalized Constitution-making secured this protection for Poles in Danzig, Christians in Albania, and Christian Cretans in the Ottoman Empire.

## 3.3.4. Second Common Policy: Civilizing Mission

Wilde suggests that in each of his FTA institutions, the relevant FP/FPs introduced (foreign) territorial administration to pursue these four Civilized Standards:

(I)-(II) Free markets & the rule of law: 'open-door' policy, preserving law and order and creating law in land, crime, and property.

(III) Good governance: exploitation of natural resources, promoting education and health (through prevention of alcohol consumption), sanitation, infrastructure projects (railways & public buildings); preserving security and order; eradicating human suffering, promoting individual rights (for example, freedom of conscience and religion)

(IV) Abolition of 'barbaric' practices such as Sati, polygamy, and slavery/promotion of Civilized Standards.[206]

I concur with Wilde's above analysis.

### *3.3.4.1 Civilized Standards*

Before proceeding, it is useful to note two points about the aforementioned ends, or four Civilized Standards. First, since laws may be used to achieve them, Wilde is correct to proffer these ends as those met

[205] *See* Mark Mazower, *The Strange Triumph of Human Rights, 1933–1950* 47 (2) The Historical Journal 379, 385 (2004).

[206] *See* Wilde, *supra* note 2 at 317–343.

by FPs engaging in FTA. (If we may recall, Wilde defines territorial administration as including law-making, but not Constitution-making.) Technically, a more accurate picture about their promotion requires noting that, as the highest law of the land, the Constitution 'is needed', to develop substantive law in crime, labor, property, and commerce, areas that cover the four Civilized Standards.[207] This is why, it is indispensable to achieving the four Civilized Standards (listed in I–IV).

Second, as previously noted, the Constitution protects property rights—its defining feature. Put simply, the Constitution is market-oriented. Accordingly, its imposition equates with these four Civilized Standards, which as we will see, are market-oriented: free markets, rule of law, good governance, and the abolition of barbaric practices. For instance, the rule of law promoted by the Constitution had a market orientation. With this caveat, I turn to considering the use of colonial Constitution-making by FPs to achieve common ends: The Civilized Standards.

European colonial powers vied for overseas markets to sell their manufactured goods such as cloth, guns, and implements. To achieve this end, they required rules and regulations that would pry open the colonies to their traders, bind parties, and protect their merchants from competition. The Constitution (based on the rule of law) provided a legal framework that allowed them to do just this.[208]

Colonialists initially argued that the free markets policy benefited both their economies and the colonies. This 'open door policy' was the external feature of the dual mandate, enabling all states, not just the colonial states, to benefit from the colonies. It formed the basis of the unequal treaties (see Shanghai international settlement, section 3.2.5.2). It was set out in various provisions contained in the Berlin General Act,

[207] This was true, not only of Britain. For instance, Portugal created a colonial legislative framework to guide the day to day administration of its colonies and coin other laws such as labor laws. Portugal set up a centralized structure in 1930. See Newitt, *Portugal in Africa*, *supra* note 30 at 100.

[208] *See* e.g., Doyle, *supra* note 38; Chandra, *supra* note 168 at 91–101; Gong, China's entry into international society, in Bull & Watson, *supra* note 104 at 176-179; Joel Benin, *Workers and Peasants in the Modern Middle East* Chapter 2 (CUP, 2001); Stephen Humphreys, *Theatre of the Rule of Law – Transnational legal Intervention in Theory and Practice* 113-114 (Cambridge University Press, 2010).

the League Covenant, and the UN Charter.[209] Tangier's constitution contained the open door provision to benefit Great Britain, and the United States economically. Again, Iraq's constitution guaranteed the Anglo-Iraq treaty and its open door provision, so that both Great Britain and the United States could control and exploit Iraq's oil.

However, after the Berlin Conference (1884–5), markets emerged as a civilizing tool.[210] For instance, in India, after 1880 the British introduced laws relating to trusts, companies, income tax, future trading, negotiable instruments, charitable endowments, and government securities.[211] The British ostensibly unleashed this torrent of laws to achieve India's 'moral and material improvement'.[212] And in Angola and Mozambique, Portugal's aim was to:

> … integrate the Africans with Portuguese society, making them Catholic, Portuguese in culture, and part of a wage-earning, market-oriented economy. This process was described as 'civilizing.'[213]

That markets performed a civilizing role, suggests that barbarity had an economic orientation. For instance, the British imposed the 1924 colonial copyright law to 'civilize' Palestinian culture on a par with the imperial view of culture in these ways: it protected property rights.[214]

Rule of law promotion meant creating substantive laws in land, labour, and crime.[215] Good examples are the PMC's creation of legally oriented standards concerning labor in the mandate territories, and the internationally dictated, and supervised police reforms in Crete, Morocco, and Tangier. Again, the Indian Penal Code, drafted by Lord Macaulay, was applied in East Africa and British Sudan between 1899

[209] *See* Art. 76 (d), UN Charter (1945), Chapters I, III, & IV, *The General Act of Berlin* (1885).

[210] *See* Anghie, *supra* note 69 at 90.

[211] *See* Ritu Birla, *Law as Economy: Convention, Corporation, Currency* 1 UC Irvine L. Rev. 1015, 1022, 1023 (2011).

[212] Id. at 1023.

[213] *See* Newitt, *supra* note 30 at 100; Lawrence W. Henderson, *Angola: Five Centuries of Conflict* 134 (Cornell University Press, 1979).

[214] Birnhack, *supra* note 62 at 20, 101–102.

[215] *See* Anghie, *supra* note 69 at 157; Humphreys, *supra* note 207 at 109-121; 116-121.

and 1907.[216] The 1877 Gold Coast Criminal Procedure Ordinance, sculpted by D. F. Chalmers, served as a model for all subsequent procedure codes.[217] This Ordinance drew from the rules and procedures crafted for Fiji and Hong Kong.[218] These colonial criminal techniques were directed at protecting colonial interests, particularly those of settlers and employers.[219]

Good governance was an elastic concept. In colonies acquired through conquest, the Constitution installed authoritarian governments, where all-powerful Governors presided over powerless advisory councils.[220] This model, rather than elected assemblies, was ostensibly adopted in response to the natives' perceived political backwardness.[221]

Good governance was also market-oriented. Therefore, its rhetoric emphasized courts, railways, natural resources' exploitation, and preventing crime and preserving law and order in racially ordered colonial workplaces: that which secured white economic dominance.[222] Good examples are Shanghai's mini-constitution, which promoted property rights, and the French-built Dakar-Saint Louis line that created and connected new markets for importing goods and channeling palm oil, groundnuts, and other agricultural products.[223] Similarly, during the inter-war period, coal, iron, and steel (export staples) were being extracted on an industrial scale.[224] Therefore, good governance then, meant reconfiguring the colonial constitution to provide legal and police protection for new vital locations that produced huge revenue: oil installations, mining compounds.[225]

[216] Humphreys, *supra* note 207 at 118, n.31

[217] Id.

[218] Id.

[219] Id. at 118.

[220] Peter Burroughs, *Imperial Institutions and the Government of Empire, in,* Oxford History of British Empire, *supra* note 107 at 170, 173.

[221] Id.

[222] Alice L. Conklin, *A Mission to Civilize: The Republican Idea of Empire in France and West Africa, 1895-1930* Chapter 2 (Stanford University Press, 1997).

[223] Id. at 58.

[224] *See* Martin Thomas, *Violence and Colonial Order: Police, Workers and Protest in the European Colonial Empires, 1918-1941* 1-13 (Cambridge University Press, 2015).

[225] Id. at 12–13.

The Constitution protected minorities: Christians in Crete and Albania, the Poles in the Free City of Danzig, and Jews, and the settler Italian community in Libya.[226]

In India, the British imposed the colonial Constitution to use laws, courts, and police to end *Sati*.[227] However in Siam, where the British lacked elaborate government, they used threats and legal assistance to promote Civilized Standards. For example, the British threatened to abrogate Siamese sovereignty for practicing polygamy, which they represented as indicating Siamese men's inability to provide good governance. (The British argued that Western men's self-controlled sexual behaviour created good governance.) Finally, with Britain's legal assistance, Siam amended its civil code (the marriage provisions).[228]

The slogan 'Commerce, Christianity and Civilization' suggests that a broader politico-economic dynamic animated the drive to end barbaric customs.[229] For instance, those evangelists who preached the gospel at temples, markets, and street corners in India, to convert Hindu women (and so, save them from Sati), also championed laissez faire capitalism.[230] Commerce was coupled with civilization, beyond India as well. The British outlawed *Pharaonic* circumcision (genital cutting), a Sudanese practice, only because it reduced Sudan, the colony's profitability.[231] Again in West Africa, the French colonialists saw in modern hygiene, and railroad construction great civilizing potential, only because they were understood to bring prosperity to the French. For instance, the French stressed hygiene to stem the spread of what most threatened Europeans, and hampered trade: malaria. (Whereas sleeping sickness, a disease that destroyed African populations was ignored.)[232]

[226] *See* Rodogno, *supra* note 113 at 36–37 (protection of Cretan Christians); Benin, *supra* note 207 at 47.

[227] *See* Lata Mani, *Contentious Traditions: The Debate on Sati in Colonial India* 86 (University of California Press, 1998).

[228] *See* Leslie A. Jeffrey, *Sex and borders – Gender, National Identity, and Prostitution Policy in Thailand* 3, 5-10 (UBC Press, 2003).

[229] Mani, *supra* note 226 at 2–5.

[230] Id. at 83-86; Kumari Jayawardene, *The White Woman's Other Burden – White Women and South Asia during British Colonial Rule* 23, 25 (Routledge, 1995).

[231] Janice Boddy, *Civilizing Women: British Crusades in Colonial Sudan* xxvi-xxvii, 3–5, Chapters 5–6 (Princeton University Press, 2007).

[232] Conklin, *supra* note 221 at 68.

Only those customs with a Christian orientation were deemed civilized. For instance, the Great Powers equaled Islam with the evils of political and social decadence: slavery, polygamy, despotism, and corruption. Eradicating these evils lay behind the reforms dictated for Crete and the Ottoman Empire.[233] Again, under Portuguese colonialism, Africans had to embrace Christianity to leapfrog into the 'civilized' category.

All of this shows that, a common thread strung all four standards together.

Finally, in the early twentieth century, FPs crafted international human rights treaties to promote Civilized Standards. For instance, the social conventions on trafficking provided international society's gender standards.[234] Siam, with a view to succeed in gaining entry into the international society of civilized states, signed the 1904 International Agreement for the Suppression of the White Slave Traffic, which focused on the protection of women and girls.[235] Securing the ratification of international human rights and anti-corruption treaties is a key UNCA activity (see Chapter 1, Table 1.3). Which means, in many ways, this activity is part of the same civilizing narrative.

Before concluding, it is worth asking: in promoting the Civilized Standards, did the Enlightenment colonizers learn nothing at all from their colonies? Yes, they did learn.[236] Consider how Mahatma Gandhi's ideas about 'duties' and *Satyagraha* (truth-force) shaped the 1948 Universal Declaration's content, and inspired a peaceful civil rights movement in the U.S. (a post-1945 colonial power) respectively.[237]

[233] *See Rodogno, supra note* 113 at 42–44.

[234] *See* Jeffrey, *supra* note 227 at 12.

[235] Id.

[236] For examples vis-à-vis settler colonialism, see Lauren Benton, *A Search for Sovereignty: Law and Geography in European Empires, 1400–1900* (Cambridge University Press, 2010).

[237] *See* Mary Ann Glendon, *A World Made New: Eleanor Roosevelt and the Universal Declaration of Human Rights* Ch.5 (Random House, 2001); The Martin Luther King, Jr. Institute, *at:* https://kinginstitute.stanford.edu/encyclopedia/gandhi-mohandas-k.

## 3.4 Wilde's Family Reframed to Admit the Constitution's Internationalized Making: A *Parent* 'Policy Institution'

To conclude, I have shown that the Constitution lies at the heart of colonial Trusteeship. Indeed, the relevant FPs imposed it to promote the Civilized Standards, and thereby, fulfill the Trusteeship and civilizing mission policies. (FTA by itself, would ill suffice in this regard.) On this basis, I argue that Wilde's family must be reframed to include the Constitution's internationalized making, and thereby, join respective parent institutions with their children: Wilde's FTA institutions. Wilde's family thus, comprises two sets of parent-child, colonial Trusteeship policy institutions: the Constitution's internationalized-making and FTA.

## 3.5 Conclusion

This chapter explored UNCA's historical origins *non-chronologically*. It reveals that the UN's predecessors—a different set of actors: states, groups of state representatives, and an inter-war period's IO (including the Permanent Mandates Commission) have internationalized the Constitution by displacing local actors in the Third World, with a view to achieving four ends: free markets, the rule of law, good governance (including natural resources' exploitation), and Civilized Standards, aimed at emancipating women. The next chapter addresses how and why this specific constitution came to be internationalized in 1949: by the UN.

# 4

# The Western Liberal Constitution's Internationalized Making

## Rise, Rejection, and Revival

### 4.0 Introduction

This chapter introduces the Constitution's internationalized making by the UN: United Nations Constitutional Assistance (UNCA). I situate and contextualize UNCA's birth as colonial/international trusteeship in 1945, and its use for Libya in 1949,[1] its rejection in 1960, and its subsequent revival in independent states, starting with newly decolonized Congo in 1960. In 1945, self-determination mentioned in the UN Charter was a mere political principle; it morphed into an absolute right for all colonies, only in 1960. Here is why, UNCA was rejected that year. Given this, to arrive at UNCA's birth in Libya, I chronologically trace international trusteeship's evolution during the twentieth century. That is, I will frame the Constitution's making working with its off-spring Foreign Territorial Administration (FTA) or ITA, toward common goals, during the twentieth century, in a chronological order. Therefore,

[1] *See* Adrian Pelt, *Libyan Independence and the United Nations – A Case of Planned Decolonization* (Yale University Press, 1970). For UN General Assembly Resolution 289 (IV) (1949), see id. at 891.

where relevant, I will draw from my previous analysis in Chapters 2 and 3.[2] I will show that colonial Constitution-making evolved with its child, FTA/ITA, through three phases over the twentieth century:

1. The rise in the Constitution's making, culminating with UNCA's birth: UNCA's use by the UN Trusteeship Council, (UNTC) in 1945, and UNCA's use outside the UNTC's context in 1949;
2. The rejection of internationalized Constitution-making in 1960, because all colonies acquired an absolute right to self-determination, and

2a) UNCA's subsequent, paradoxical use with ITA for one last time, and purpose: to realize self-determination/ implement decolonization; and

3. The revival of UNCA (with and without ITA), outside the context of promoting decolonization in *sovereign* states in 1960—and increasingly so, after 1989.

Indeed, as is expected, each of the aforesaid three phases (*see* Table 4.1 below) corresponds with those three through which, as per Wilde, FTA/ITA evolved.[3] As we will see, during each phase, FTA/ITA required the Constitution, its parent, to achieve the Civilized Standards and other territorial goals.

Table 4.1 Internationalized constitution-making and Foreign Territorial Administration evolve symbiotically, over the twentieth century

| **Phases** | **Colonial/ internationalized making internationalized making** | **Foreign territorial administration, (FTA)/ International** |
|---|---|---|
| First phase: From 1919 (the Treaty of Versailles) to 1952 | The rise of the Western liberal Constitution's making | Rise in FTA |

(*Cont'd*)

[2] *Hereinafter,* unless mentioned, "previous analysis" refers to that of Chapter 3's.

[3] *See* Ralph Wilde, *International Territorial Administration: How Trusteeship and the Civilizing Mission Never Went Away* 364 (2008).

TABLE 4.1 (*Cont'd*)

| Phases | Colonial/ internationalized making internationalized making | Foreign territorial administration, (FTA)/ International |
|---|---|---|
| | Foreign states and international organizations (IOs) impose the WL Constitution to achieve their territorial cum trusteeship goals. 1949: UNCA was used to enable Libya transit to independence | Colonially imposed constitutions give rise to FTA |
| Second phase starts from 1960 (the post- World War II-self-determination entitlement) when all colonies acquired an absolute right to be independent | The WL Constitution's making rejected | FTA/ITA rejected |
| | Paradoxically, UNCA works with, or without ITA to realize self-determination: The UN assists former colonies to replace their colonial constitutions with new constitutions, and thereby transit to independence. | ITA is used somewhat paradoxically, for realizing self-determination/ implementing decolonization |
| Third phase covers UNCA's use, with and without ITA, outside the context of implementing decolonization (1960, 1989-2017) | The revival of UNCA: the WL Constitution's internationalized making by the UN | ITA by the UN revived |
| | 1960, Post-1989: UNCA is revived in sovereign states; the UN displaces Third World peoples from, and/or tutors them in, constitution-making, to produce the WL Constitution, ostensibly to: 1) fill a gap in | The WL Constitution so produced provides a framework for legislative, judicial, and executive activities. The UN displaces Third World peoples from |

TABLE 4.1 (*Cont'd*)

| **Phases** | **Colonial/ internationalized making internationalized making** | **Foreign territorial administration, (FTA)/ International** |
|---|---|---|
| | governance and/or 2) address supposed deficiencies in the quality of governance. In these ways, UNCA works with, or without ITA to address governance problems, and toward common ends. From 1993 to 2019, UNCA worked without ITA, in sovereign states, ostensibly to address governance problems 1 and 2). | undertaking, and/ or tutors them in these activities, to ensure they are consistent with the WL Constitution. The UN does so, ostensibly to fill a perceived gap in governance and/ or address supposed deficiencies in the quality of governance. |

## 4.1 The First Phase: The Rise of the Constitution's Making— From the Treaty of Versailles (1919) to UNCA's Birth (1949–52)

In this section, I will consider the trusteeship models (hereinafter Model) that were internationalized during this period. Before proceeding to consider the relevant Models, it is useful to keep five points in mind. First, my purpose is not to evaluate each Model. Rather, my purpose is to consider how each Model made use of or internationalized the Constitution. As noted in Chapter 1, UNCA, including its colonial past remains uncharted. I therefore, engage with William Bains who has explored internationalized trusteeship in general (but minus its constitutional dimension), and Ralph Wilde and James C. Hales, experts on FTA/ITA and its trusteeship role and the Mandates System respectively.[4] Since the Constitution—FTA/ITA's parent—is central to trusteeship, my comments unite with all three scholars.

[4] William Bain, *Between Anarchy and Society: Trusteeship and the Obligations of Power* (Oxford University Press, 2003) [Bain, Trusteeship]; Wilde, *supra*

Second, although 1919 is my starting point, I first briefly consider how the Berlin Conference of 1884–5 (Conference), internationalized colonial Constitution-making.[5] For the major European powers negotiated and formalized claims to territory in Africa at this Conference, and the Conference was thus, an important international attempt to regulate colonialism.

Third, colonial Constitution-making essentially meant constitutional *imposition*. And the Constitution's imposition essentially meant the imposition of free markets, the rule of law, good governance (including natural resources exploitation), and civilized social practices rooted in Christianity.

Fourth, starting from the mid-1930s, the definition of good governance expanded. From denoting 'simple financial solvency and self-reliance, through conceptions of trusteeship ..., the term finally lent itself to the extraordinary commitment to social engineering and constitutional change'.[6] Therefore, by the 1940s, the Constitution again became important. For it was key to creating 'good governance': to create a legal system rooted in common law and property rights, and the concept of individual, not group rights.[7] (As we will see in the next chapter, this totality of socio-economic change later came to be known as Westernization, and then, modernization.)[8]

The Atlantic Charter (1941) implicitly embraced the good governance principle.[9] By 1945, when the UN was created, the two victorious

---

note 3; James C. Hales, *The Creation and Application of the Mandates System* 25 Transactions of the Grotius Society 185 (1939); James C. Hales, *The Reform and Extension of the Mandate System – A Study in International Colonial Supervision* 26 Transactions of the Grotius Society 153 (1940) [Hales, *Colonial supervision*].

5 The Berlin Conference concluded with all the participants signing and ratifying a General Act of 1885 (*hereinafter* Berlin General Act (1885). In the late nineteenth century, colonial powers, no longer satisfied with their existing territorial possessions, sought to acquire additional areas which resulted in the "scramble for Africa").

6 *See* Vernon Hewitt, *A cautionary tale: Colonial and post-colonial conceptions of good government and democratisation in Africa*, 44 (1) Commonwealth & Comp. Politics 41, 45 (2006).

7 Id. at 47.

8 Id.

9 Id. at 49

Western powers, the United States (US) and the United Kingdom (UK), subsumed development (as understood during the inter-war period), under state-driven 'good governance'.[10] The Bretton Woods Institutions (BWIs) embraced that notion.[11] (As we saw in Chapter 2, the notion of development that was inaugurated during the inter-war period meant preparing the Third World to exist for the West's benefit.) In fact, post-war conceptions of international development and industrialization were the 'direct legatees of Britain's state-based project of socio-economic engineering'.[12]

Fifth, – this is seemingly obvious – the Constitution's making *rose* at the very time that (or rather, because) people of the Third World countries were being denied self-determination.

According to William Bain, the Berlin Conference 'effectively internationalized *the idea* of trusteeship'.[13] When the signatory powers to the Berlin Conference General Act (Berlin Act, 1885) agreed to improve the conditions of the natives, they undertook an obligation to enable natives to achieve a sophisticated politico-social order.[14] The Berlin Act 1885 reoriented the Constitution's use and by extension, that of its off-spring FTA[15] toward humanitarian goals. Significantly, this international law obligation rested on an assumption that the natives were unable to govern themselves.[16] King Leopold II, who sculpted a constitution to create the Congo Free State (CFS),[17] certainly fulfilled this obligation under international law.

[10] Vernon Hewitt, *Empire, International Development and the Concept of Good Government, in* Development and Colonialism 30, 33 (Mark Duffield and Vernon Hewitt, eds. 2009).

[11] Id.

[12] Id. at 35–36.

[13] Bain, *supra* note 4 at 63.

[14] Id.

[15] Wilde, *supra* note 3 at 366 (Whereas the Berlin General Act introduced the trusteeship idea as a means of "reorienting existing arrangements").

[16] Id.

[17] *See* Andrew Fitzmaurice, *The Justification of King Leopold II's Congo Enterprise by Sir Travers Twiss, in* Law and Politics in British Colonial Thought: Transpositions of Empire, 109, 118 (Shannaugh Dorsett & Ian Hunter eds., Palgrave Macmillan, 2010).

Before moving on to consider later trusteeship models, it is useful to recall from Chapter 3 who the trustees were under the Berlin trusteeship model. The answer is the foreign states. They imposed the Constitution, based on which –they administered their colonies.[18] But was their Constitution-making regulated? No. Why? It is because the Berlin Act 1885 lacked such a mechanism.

The Treaty of Versailles departed from the Berlin Act of 1885, for it institutionalized the Constitution's imposition (trusteeship) whereas the latter merely reoriented the Constitution's making toward trusteeship goals. Versailles: a) expressly mandated the Constitution's imposition and b) empowered IOs and the victorious foreign states or powers (hereinafter FPs) to impose the Constitution. Here is how, –Versailles inaugurated ITA and substituted one form of FTA with another.[19] For, under the Mandates System, victorious FPs denied independence to territories (previously administered by the First World War's defeated powers) and instead imposed the Constitution in ways noted in the previous chapter. So, under Versailles, the trustees were: the League (the 'internationalized trustee' to use Wilde's words) and the FPs, who acted as the League's 'agents' (Wilde's word) to achieve the four Civilized Standards: rule of law, free markets, good governance, and civilized social practices.

The above paragraph suggests that the Berlin and Versailles trusteeship models promoted trusteeship in different ways. This raises a question about whether those models monitored the conduct of colonial Constitution-making, and if so, how. According to Hales, in 'perfect trusteeship', protecting the ward's rights is prioritized.[20] Which means, Constitution-making powers must be so exercised, as to develop mandate territories into a valuable asset, by the time the inhabitants are ready to administer them.[21] On this basis, Hales argues that:

> Under the Berlin arrangement, the colony is administered under the guidance of the Mother Country without appeal against any abuse existing in the administration other than remedies provided by the colony's constitution.[22]

18 Wilde, *supra* note 3 at 204.

19 Id. at 366

20 Hales, Colonial Supervision, *supra* note 4 at 184.

21 Id.

22 Hales, *supra* note 4 at 204.

Whereas the Mandates System provided greater protection to the native than the Berlin Model, because:

> … the idea overshadowing the whole administration is the idea of international supervision by certain institutions, in the working of which the Mandatory Power will only have one vote among many. As a result, the natives' interests are more fully protected, white settlers are prevented from exploiting the natural resources of the territory to their sole advantage, and all States members of the League of Nations are given an equal voice in this supervision, with a view to maintaining the trust.[23]

What about the United Nations' trusteeship Model? First, the UN Model resembled that of Versailles in that, here too, the FPs (the victorious powers) imposed the Constitution to administer the defeated powers' territories. Who was the trustee now? On whose behalf were the constitution-imposing actors acting, considering that the UN Charter contains no equivalent of this phrase 'on behalf of'? Drawing from my previous analysis, I suggest that under the UN model, first, a foreign state imposed the Constitution to introduce and conduct FTA.[24] Here, these symbiotic internationalized activities were geared toward an explicit goal: self-government or independence whose achievement, the UN Trusteeship Council (*see* Chapter 3) monitored in two ways.[25] First, by supervising colonial Constitution-making in trust territories.[26] Second, article 73 of the UN Charter brought all other colonial territories (known as Non-Self-Governing Territories or NSGTs) under the legal trusteeship umbrella.[27] Under article 73, relevant Member States

[23] Id. at 204.

[24] Wilde, *supra* note 3 at 338.

[25] UN Charter (1945), art. 76.

[26] *See* Art. 87, UN Charter. *See* Charmaine Edwards Toussaint, *The Trusteeship System of the United Nations* (1956). The UNTC considers reports submitted by the administering authorities (Foreign Powers), accepts and examines petitions from the inhabitants, and deputes Missions to visit the Trust Territories. Id. at 256. The UN Model improved on the Versailles' Model in that under the latter, the League relied only on annual reports and petitions. Id.

[27] Id. at 229–247. Article 73 (e) elaborates the way in which, Members responsible for the administration of non-self-governing territories are required to promote that 'well-being,' and requires them, to submit regular information to the Secretary-General about non-self-governing territories, not under the UN Trusteeship System. Id.

accepted as a 'sacred trust' the obligation to promote the well-being of NSGTs' inhabitants. To further strengthen the UN's authority over NSGTs' political developments, Member States were required to update the UN about the NSGTs' constitutional position.[28]

Here comes Peter Lyon who suggests that it was only in the twentieth century, and with the creation of the UN trusteeship model, that the international community rounded off its efforts 'to institutionalize trusteeship as a system of international surveillance and accountability'.[29] I suggest that the checks placed on colonial Constitution-making, (mentioned in the above para), must figure in Lyon's system of international surveillance and accountability.

My previous analysis shows that the Constitution remained equally important, for another reason, in the first half of the twentieth century. For instance, the Representative Bodies and the League of Nations were empowered to impose constitutions in territories marked out for imperial exploitation: Cracow, Tangier, Albania, and Shanghai. Tangier and Saar offer excellent examples. The Constitution (*see* art. 7) imposed over Tangier secured the open door policy.[30] Saar's Constitution (and its rule of law regime) drafted by the Anglo-Americans in the Committee of Three enabled the League to administer Saar and exploit its natural resources.[31]

This brings us to the first phase's last segment, 1945–52, when again, the Constitution proved vital for colonial trusteeship, though in its new avatar: in developed states. Indeed, two Foreign Powers, the

[28] Id. at 243–244.

[29] Wilde, *supra* note 3 at 369; Peter Lyon, *The rise and fall and possible revival of international trusteeship* 31 (1) J. of Commonwealth and Comp. Politics 96, 98 (1993).

[30] Penny M. Sonenburg, *Open Door Policy*, in Colonialism: An International, Social, Cultural, and Political Encyclopedia - Volume 1 440-441 (Melvin E. Page, ed., ABC-CLIO, 2003). Under the 'open door' policy, the colonial powers' (U.K. and U.S.) saw in some territorial units, "not so much an opportunity for empire per se but rather a chance to expand economically and commercially." Id. Under this policy, a colonial power that controlled any given territorial unit was required to keep it 'open' to all nations (remaining colonial powers).

[31] Frank M. Russell, *The Saar: Battleground and Pawn*, 23 (Stanford University Press, 1951) (discussing the Constitution's imposition); For ITA in Saar see Wilde, *supra note* 3 at 111–114.

Allied Powers, and the Allied Control Council of Berlin, imposed the Constitution with a view to administer two developed states: Japan and Germany respectively. Here, the Constitution (and its child, FTA[32]) were imposed, not in response to perceived local incapacities but to achieve three goals: a) to address deficiencies in governance caused by the Second World War's large-scale destruction, b) to fill an administrative vacuum, and c) to transform governance (deemed bad given its political orientation). Conceptually, the Constitution was indispensable to achieving these three goals. For instance, it alone could provide governance a distinct, that is, preferred political character and thereby erase its supposed badness. The Second World War's end also saw proposals for direct UN trusteeship.[33] As we will see in the following section, that idea never blossomed. Instead, there was UNCA and only partial ITA (by the UN).

### 4.1.1 1949: UNCA is Born

To understand the first UNCA project (1949–52) in Libya, a former Italian colony in 1943, requires noting three points. First, this colony was not granted independence in 1944 because then, self-determination existed only as a political principle. Next, Libyans were deemed to be disunited. Further, they were viewed as 'irrational, depraved, childlike, or simply different when compared to Westerners, who were deemed to be rational, virtuous, mature, and normal'.[34] Third, US strategic interests trumped Libyans' demand for outright independence.

Libya (comprising Cyrenaica, Tripolitania, and Fezzan) was colonized by Italy from 1911–43.[35] Right from the start, Italy crushed the Libyans' political freedoms and national unity. This colonization was pursued

[32] Id.

[33] Id. at 371–372.

[34] Ronald Bruce St John, *Libya and the United States: Two Centuries of Strife* 8 (University of Pennsylvania Press, 2002); Benjamin Rivlin, *Unity and Nationalism in Libya* 3 Middle East Journal 31, 37 (January 1949) (positing that the 8 million odd Libyans were unsophisticated and inarticulate).

[35] *See* Anna Baldinetti, *The Origins of the Libyan Nation—Colonial Legacy, Exile and the Emergence of a New Nation-State* 27 (Routledge, 2010).

ostensibly to 'civilize' the supposedly barbaric Libyans.[36] After Italy (the defeated power) surrendered in 1943, Cyrenaica and Tripolitania fell under British military administration and sparsely populated Fezzan fell to France.[37]

Here come the strategic interests. As early as 1945, it became increasingly evident to American policymakers that, if Washington was to project power in the post-World War II era, economic aid and political interference alone would ill suffice.[38] Rather, Washington had to establish its military presence. There was a growing appreciation that revitalizing the base at Mallaha in Tripolitania, (also known as Wheelus Field), would give the US a bomber, tanker-refueling, and recon-fighter base.[39] The Wheelus Field was demobilized in 1947. Revitalizing it would position the US close enough to targets in the Soviet Union.[40] Accordingly, by the summer of 1948, the US had begun plans to develop Wheelus Field into a major American air-base.[41] For their fruition, these military plans required preventing the UN's trusteeship, because a Trust Territory can never be used for military purposes. For this reason, in July 1948, the US abandoned its earlier proposals of UN Trusteeship for Libya.[42]

Meanwhile, the Councils' Commission of Investigation (Commission) which had just returned from Libya a month before (that is, June 1948) quickly concluded that Libya was wholly unprepared for independence.[43] (The Commission did so, despite the fact that Libyans had voiced their desire for complete and immediate independence from foreign rule.)[44]

When September 1948 arrived, the Allied Powers' had not yet resolved the Libyan question. Accordingly, as per the Treaty of Peace

[36] Id. at 27

[37] *See* Pelt, *supra* note 1 at 33–35.

[38] *See* St. John, *supra* note 34 at 40

[39] *See* Robert Looney, *Handbook of US-Middle East Relations: Formative Factors and Regional Perspectives* 262 (Routledge, 2009).

[40] Id.

[41] *See* St John, *supra* note 34 at 44, 49, 54–55.

[42] Id. at 51.

[43] Id. at 49.

[44] Id; John Oakes, *The History of Gaddafi's Pariah State* 45 (History Press, 2011).

with Italy, it fell to the UN General Assembly to resolve the Libyan question.[45] (Here, it helps to note that as a result, the fate of Eritrea, another Italian colony was left unresolved and so, gave rise to the second UN trusteeship project: UNCA).[46] However, what is important for this discussion is, noting why Eritreans were denied immediate independence and/or placed under international trusteeship: Like Libyans, they too, were deemed politically 'backward' and 'divided'.[47]

The UNGA began discussions in April 1949.[48] When proposals for British and French trusteeship were vetoed, 'some agreement on independence for Libya became a foregone conclusion.'[49] Finally, owing to the US and UK's insistence, the UNGA mandated independence for Libya, after a two-year trusteeship period: UNCA-FTA, 1949–52.[50]

### *4.1.1.1 UNCA-FTA in Libya (1949–52)*

Towards this end, the UNGA empowered the UN Commissioner to 'co-administer' Libya (with the existing Foreign Powers),[51] and assist the Libyans to determine and enact a constitution.[52] A Council comprising representatives from the victorious powers was to assist the UN Commissioner.[53] Although Libyans were ostensibly allowed to shape

[45] *See* St. John supra note 34 at 45 and Oakes, supra note 44 at 45

[46] *See* G.N. Trevaskis, *Eritrea - A Colony in Transition: 1941–52* 102 (Oxford University Press, 1960).

[47] Id. at 114. At different times, Eritrea was "pushed to the brink of partition, union with Ethiopia, independence, and even Italian trusteeship." Id. at 102. Finally, the UNGA set a transition period which ended on 15 September 1952, , tasked the UK to organize an Eritrean government during the Transition and the UN with drafting the Constitution in response to the Eritreans' supposed knowledge-gap about constitutional issues (e.g., federation). The UN Commissioner, Sr. Anze Matienz drafted Eritrea's Constitution. Id. at 81–121.

[48] *See* St. John, *supra* note 34 at 51.

[49] Id. at 52.

[50] *See* Pelt, *supra* note 1 at ¶ 10, 892 (reproducing G.A. Res. 289 (IV), 21 November 1949).

[51] Id. at 891, ¶4.

[52] Id. at ¶3–4.

[53] Id. at ¶4–5.

their constitutional future, their colonial past, their current subjection to foreign military administrations, and the Cold War politics, scarcely equipped them to do that.[54] For instance, in 1950 most Libyans were undecided, and divided on constitutional matters such as: a unitary versus a federal state, and elective versus selective procedures.[55] However, Libyans pushed by the Council's US representative,[56] quickly adopted a constitutional federal monarchy.[57] Furthermore, US officials strove 'to secure an early date for independence with a provisional agreement for strategic facilities in place, prior to independence, to minimize discussion and criticism in the UNGA, of US policy towards Libya'.[58] Great Britain, which underwrote this poor country's budget, secured its own (British) interests in other ways.

What process-related and content-related standards did the UN Commissioner, Adrian Pelt promote? As one of his first tasks, Pelt inducted an Italian (minorities' representative), into his Council.[59] Although Libyans were ostensibly elbowed out, in an effort to democratize their Constitution-making process, eventually, for political reasons, the constitution-adopting body, the National Assembly (later self-styled as NALC), instead of being elected, was composed of only sixty selected members.[60]

Work on drafting the Libyan constitution began on 4 December 1950.[61] Pelt prepared a model for guiding the NACL's Working Group in drafting the constitution's Chapter II ('Rights of the people').[62] (Drafting assistance has today become a core UNCA activity.) Pelt provided the Working Group with copies of the Iraqi Constitution (drafted by British lawyers), Minorities Treaties, ancillary to the Peace Treaty

54 *See 1950 Yearbook of the UN* 168–169 (UN, 1950).

55 Baldinetti, *supra* note 35 at 140.

56 *See* Majid Khadduri, *Modern Libya: A Study in Political Development 1908-2007* 113–115, 123–131 (John Hopkins Press, 1963).

57 *See* St John, *supra* note 34 at 53.

58 Id.

59 *See* Pelt, *supra* note 1 at 537, and 335–350 (discussion on minorities).

60 Id.

61 Id. at 509.

62 Id. at 512–513.

of Versailles, and the Universal Declaration of Human Rights.[63] These activities secured protections for women and Libyan minorities (Italians and Jews).[64] They were ostensibly undertaken to ensure Libya's constitution met the then international standards.

As noted in section 4.1, when the UN was born, good governance had expanded to mean state-driven socio-economic change, conducive to Western interests. Accordingly, the UNGA tasked Pelt with promoting Libya's socio-economic development.[65] Given this, what had this poor, destitute country got to offer to the West (apart from airfields)? Only markets and underground water. Indeed, Pelt consulted with IMF economists on how best to manage this natural resource.[66] Next, having consulted with IMF economists on how to pump in public and private foreign investment, Pelt drafted the constitution's fiscal provisions.[67] Indeed, Pelt says, the NACL members became more 'budget minded', thanks to the advice provided by IMF experts.[68] According to Pelt, 'Chapter IX of the constitution (Federal budgetary & Financial Administration) is almost entirely based on proposals formed by UN financial experts….'[69] Pelt next arranged foreign aid and budget support.[70] Finally, since Italy had disallowed a free Libyan press, the UN educated the Libyan public in this way: 'For the first time [in their history], Libyans heard the draft constitution read aloud to them.'[71]

The NACL adopted the Constitution in October 1951, after discussing the draft for one month.[72] On 25 December, Libya formally proclaimed its independence. Of course, before this date arrived, the US and Great Britain had consolidated their political and economic interests. For instance, the US State Department-drafted agreement that secured the Wheelus Field as a military base, hurt Libyan interests—but of course,

[63] Id. at Chapter 7, 536 (constitution-making details).
[64] Id at 537–542
[65] Id. at 892, ¶9.
[66] Id. at 687, 690.
[67] Id. at 687.
[68] Id. at 522.
[69] Id. at 575.
[70] Id. at 663.
[71] Id. at 635.
[72] Id. at 821.

it protected US interests.[73] As for the British, in March 1951, they handpicked six ministers who formed a token representative government.[74]

In summary, UNCA was conceived to assist a poor colony, declared by the World Bank as a Least Developed Country (LDC),[75] and faced with an adverse balance of payments crisis, to transit to independence. (Indeed, as we will see in the next chapter, since Libya, virtually all UNCA-recipients-states have been LDCs.) Right from the start, Libyans were denied independence because they were deemed politically backward and disunited. If Libya 'started down the road to independence', it was only because the foreign powers 'with the most interest in its future, failed to agree on what that future should be'.[76] Again, even when independence became inevitable, the Allied Powers stipulated trusteeship (FTA-UNCA) to secure their interests, but ostensibly to make Libya's internal governance good.

Policymakers stipulated that since the UN lacked manpower and materials, it would only co-administer Libya. However, UNCA was conceived because it was said to entail only tapping into the UN's pre-existing combination of expertise (for example, the IMF). (This argument holds good even today).[77] Overall, UNCA-ITA was based on the UN's neutrality, and was deployed in response to the Libyans' supposed incapacity. UNCA was used to civilize Libya by promoting western-style democracy based on the rule of law, free markets, and human rights (including the rights of minorities).

The year 1952 marked the end of the first phase of the Constitution's making or internationalized trusteeship.

As we can see, from the Berlin Conference to 1952, various trusteeship models were internationalized. Put differently, the Constitution's making moved through several different internationalized models. For

[73] *See* St John, *supra* note 34 at 65, 61–66.

[74] *See* Baldinetti, *supra* note 35 at 141. The provincial governments in Tripolitania and Fezzan were formed in the same way and to which the British and French military governments transferred powers. Id. The UK concluded a 20-year treaty of friendship and alliance with Libya on 29 July 1953, whereby it received extensive extraterritorial and jurisdictional rights in return for financial aid.

[75] *See* St John, *supra* note 34 at 16.

[76] Id. at 56

[77] *See* UNCA Guidance Note 2 (2009)

instance, the model used in the immediate post-Second World War era, utilized the Constitution for non-colonial contexts (in Japan and Germany). Under each trusteeship Model, the Constitution's making was constant. Under each Model, it sired and enabled FTA to achieve its trusteeship goals: the four Civilized Standards. To conclude, under each model, the Constitution's making enjoyed pride of place. For, it lies at the heart of international trusteeship.

I now take the reader to 1960 when international law rejected colonial Constitution-making and FTA. I will provide only, as much information about self-determination's evolution into a right, (a vast topic), as is essential to knowing why we must question UNCA's revival in sovereign states.

## 4.2 The Second Phase: The Rejection of Internationalized Constitution-making, Including UNCA

Self-determination has two dimensions: external and internal. In its external dimension, it refers to a territory's external, that is, international status. So, as a legal right, self-determination's exercise can lead to independence, free association, integration, or any other status freely chosen by a people.[78] The right to internal self-determination refers to peoples' rights within states.

The idea of self-determination evolved through three eras. The first era ran from the nineteenth century until 1945. During this phase, self-determination was a purely political principle that connoted some sort of autonomy for ethnic or national groups (for example, Albania—chapter 3).[79] It did not mean statehood.[80] The self-determination idea entered the second phase with the UN's establishment. As previously noted, this political principle which finds mention in Article 1 (2) and 55 in the UN Charter, clearly applies to states—not to people or groups. In

[78] *See infra* point 7.

[79] *See* Patricia Carley, "Self-Determination: Sovereignty, Territorial Integrity, and the Right to Secession: Report from a roundtable held in conjunction with the US Department of State's Policy Planning Staff" 3 (March 1996).

[80] Id.

the third phase, self-determination morphed into an absolute right for colonies. It is this phase with which, I am concerned.

### 4.2.1 The UN General Assembly Elaborates on Self-determination

To the UNGA goes the credit of morphing self-determination, a political *principle*, into a *right*. Within the UNGA, developed countries who had gained independence, and socialist countries led by the Soviet Union emerged as the strongest voice for dismantling colonialism. The UNGA laid down political standards regarding self-determination, 'couched in legal terminology'.[81] The UNGA did so in three important resolutions: 1) Resolution 1514 (XV) passed on 14 December 1960 (Declaration on the Granting of Independence to Colonial Peoples)[82] (hereafter 1514 (1960)); 2) Resolution 1541 (XV) passed on 15 December 1960[83]; and 3) Resolution 2625 (XXV), passed on 24 October 1970.[84] The third resolution supplemented the first two resolutions in some respects.[85]

*The International Right to Self-determination after 1960*

The aforesaid three resolutions were vital in developing the content of the international right to self-determination and its implementation, which may be summarized as follows:

1) Self-determination referred only to decolonization;
2) Self-determination was now considered an absolute right—though again, for colonies only: 'Not all peoples had the right of self-determination, but only all colonies had the right to be independent;'
3) Consequently, colonially imposed constitutions and the foreign territorial administrations they underpinned stood automatically repudiated; So too was the internationalization of these two symbiotic activities: Constitution-making and territorial administration;

[81] Antonio Cassese, *Self-determination of Peoples: A Legal Reappraisal* 68 (quote) & 70 (Cambridge University Press, 1999).

[82] Id. (I am not suggesting that other resolutions are unimportant).

[83] Id.

[84] Id.

[85] Id. at 71.

4) The right to self-determination only concerned external self-determination; this right was conceived in part to reject the notion of trusteeship and so, applied to a 'paradigmatic class of entities': Mandated territories, Trust territories and colonies;
5) Self-determination applied only to territories, and so, the territorial integrity of existing states and most colonial territories was assumed;
6) Self-determination is not synonymous with state independence, and may be achieved through other freely chosen political structures;[86]
7) 1541 (XV) (December 1960) recognized the UN's right to supervise constitutional evolution in the NSGTs;
8) New decolonization-implementing agency: Resolution 1654 (XV) (27 November 1961) established the Special Committee, endowing it with broad terms of reference to implement decolonization;[87]and
9) 1970: 'Universal right to self-determination:' The Declaration on Friendly Relations attributed to all peoples—not merely the inhabitants of colonies—the right freely to determine, without external interference, their political status; it reiterated the duty to end the continued conduct of FTA anchored in the colonially imposed constitution, which it posited was a 'crime'.[88]

Meanwhile, prior to the 1970 Declaration, the International Covenant on Civil and Political Rights (ICCPR, 1966) articulated the right to self-determination.[89] So, this right applied not only to colonial 'peopls', but applied to people anywhere, whether in a politically independent state, or a dependent territory. In 1973, the Assembly declared that 'attempts to suppress struggles against colonial domination' violated the UN Charter and, specifically, constituted a 'threat to international peace and security'.[90]

[86] Id.

[87] Yassin El-Ahouty, *The United Nations and Decolonization: The Role of Afro-Asia* 214-216 (Martinus Nijhoff, 1971).

[88] Sources: For 2) quote see Carley, Self-Determination, *supra* note 79 at 3–4; 3–4: 4) Wilde, *supra* note 3 at 364; Cassesse, Self-Determination, *supra* note 81 at 72–73.

[89] *See* Art. 1, International Covenant on Civil and Political Rights, *at*: http://www.ohchr.org/en/professionalinterest/pages/ccpr.aspx.

[90] *See* G.A. Res. 3103, U.N. GAOR 2197th Sess., 2 U.N. Doc. A/Res/3103 (1973).

The self-determination entitlement rejected outright all of Wilde's six FTA institutions, and the colonial constitutions supporting them.[91] The self-determination entitlement demolished the validity of using political and economic backwardness, (the developmental criteria) to impose a FTA, grounded in a colonial constitution. Consequently, as Wilde posits, 'no new foreign territorial administration projects were conceived.'[92] I posit that after 1960 this meant, as a logical corollary to the self-determination entitlement, that no colonial constitution could be imposed to establish foreign territorial administration, and so colonize a state.[93]

### 4.2.2 Revisiting the Symbiotic Relationship between Constitutions and Territories: The Constitution Confers Territorial Status

As a result of this *a priori* rejection of FTA, girded by a colonial constitution, the Foreign Powers were now obliged to pursue two new territorial goals: 1) Decolonization; and 2) a new status for their colonies: independence. This recalls the point I previously made about the symbiotic relationship between constitutions and territories. The Constitution confers a particular politico-legal character to territorial governance. Therefore, it is adopted to confer territorial status. In fact, as we saw in Chapter 2, this is precisely why and how Foreign Powers (before 1960) colonized overseas territories: they imposed colonial constitutions.

Given this, the Foreign Powers were, in the wake of the self-determination entitlement, required to implement decolonization. They were required to dismantle the existing colonial constitutions, and allow the colonized to freely sculpt and adopt new ones.[94] In taking these steps, the Foreign Powers were addressing as before (that

91 *See* Wilde, *supra* note 3 at 373.

92 Id. at 380.

93 I am not suggesting that the practice of imposing constitutions ended. As the next section will reveal, the relevant FP did not create foreign territorial administration, but put in place a model that Figure 1.4 partly illustrates.

94 Even where the colony opted for association with an independent state or integration into an independent state, it was incumbent on the Foreign Power to amend the colonial constitution to reflect this change of status.

is, during colonial rule) 'a governance problem'.[95] Understandably, Wilde, an ITA expert, also makes the aforesaid points.[96] In so doing, Wilde affirms that constitutions provide the framework for territorial administration. Put simply, they work symbiotically with territories, and territorial administration.

#### 4.2.2.1 *Remaining Role for UNCA: Implementing Decolonization*

This brings us to consider the task of dismantling FTA institutions girded by colonial constitutions. When the decolonization juggernaut began to roll, there were no ITA projects. (For, ITA projects mounted during the inter-war period had ended.)[97] Only FTA projects girded by colonial constitutions (for example, colonialism and trusteeship arrangements) existed.

Meanwhile, the actual task of dismantling these FTA projects entailed many problems. First, the legacy of colonialism had stunted the colonized (Third World) peoples' innate self-governing capabilities. Second, colonial powers were still in control of their colonies. To offer just one example: UN policymakers considered it inappropriate for New Zealand, the Foreign Power in control of West Samoa, to organize the referendum that would determine whether its administration continued. Accordingly, Western Samoans voted for independence in a 1961 UN-supervised plebiscite, sculpted a new constitution aided by a UN expert, and emerged independent on 1 January 1962.[98]

In this way, new UNCA-ITA projects were conceived, but only to realize self-determination or implement decolonization. I join Wilde in calling these projects 'UN decolonization' projects. Consequently, Constitution-making and territorial administration were again internationalized. Such internationalization was rightly deemed legitimate,

[95] Wilde, *supra* note 3 at 377.

[96] Id. at 376.

[97] The Saar was assimilated into Germany in 1935; Germany's invasion of Poland in 1939 ended Danzig's Free City status, and the arrangement for an administrative role for the new United Nations in the Free Territory of Trieste, remained unimplemented.

[98] *See* Guy Powles, *Constitution-making in Western Samoa,* The New Zealand J. 106–109 (20 March 1962).

because its objective was decolonization.[99] (It is useful to note that since for all practical purposes, colonial powers were still in control, the UN had little control over the actual content of former colonies' 'independence' constitutions.)

## 4.3 The Third Phase: UNCA's Revival in 1960 (The Post-Colonial Era)

However, as we shall see, the 1960 self-determination entitlement scarcely ended the treatment of people of the Third World as child-like.

### 4.3.1 Dag Hammarskjöld Pioneers International Executive Rule: Revives UN Constitutional Assistance[100]

The story of UNCA's Third Phase is the story of the Constitution's internationalization in *sovereign* Third World states. This political project was powered by the US and the UN.

'International executive rule' (IER), pioneered by Dag Hammarskjöld, the second UN Secretary-General (UNSG) to manage decolonization in 1960, offers the starting point. Hammarskjöld's liberal economic thinking (commitment to free markets) shaped IER practices,[101] including UNCA, ITA, and peace-keeping. Indeed, herein lies the key to understanding how UNCA was used to promote the Constitution (economic

[99] Wilde, *supra* note 3 at 376 (making this same point but, regarding only the re-internationalization of territorial administration).

[100] Some material in this section was originally published in Peace Diplomacy, Global Justice and International Agency: Rethinking Human Security and Ethics in the Spirit of Dag Hammarskjöld edited by Carsten Stahn & Henning Melber, and has been reproduced by permission of Cambridge University Press.

[101] *See* Ann Orford, *Hammarskjöd, Economic Thinking and the United Nations, in* Peace Diplomacy, Global Justice and International Agency: Rethinking Human Security and Ethics in the Spirit of Dag Hammarskjöld 156, 156–189 (Carsten Stahn & Henning Melber, eds, Cambridge University Press, 2015) (exploring how Hammarskjöld's liberal economic thinking shaped his international executive practices); Vijayashri Sripati, *Hammarskjöld and International Executive Rule: A Third World Perspective on International Law, in* Peace & Diplomacy, id, at 477–507.

liberalization), first in 1960, in Congo, a poor newly decolonized state, and subsequently, after 1989, in poor, debtor, sovereign, independent states. Indeed, as this book will demonstrate, at a deeper level, UNCA's third phase is the story of the Third World's transformation into first, western liberal constitutional market democracies, and after 1989, into *neo-liberal* ones.

Hammarskjöld espoused liberal economics as a means for development.[102] Orford suggests that, from the American perspective, Hammarskjöld's liberal economic orthodoxy may have well supported his candidature for the UNSG's post.[103] Indeed, as Orford notes, 'all through his term as UNSG, Hammarskjöld remained closely allied with a US administration that was shaped by an increasingly strident anti-communism, and by an emergent liberal (if not yet neoliberal) economics.'[104]

According to Hammarskjöld, a state is rooted in, and legitimized by economic freedom.[105] Hammarskjöld therefore, sought to create the requisite conditions to secure economic freedom in Third World states, many of which were then, still, shackled by colonial chains.[106] He pioneered UNCA as a form of international executive rule to promote that freedom in the Third World.[107]

Hammarskjöld assumed office in 1959, a time when the clanging of African states tugging at their colonial chains, reverberated across the globe. Hammarskjöld perceived decolonization as throwing up many challenges. Finding Africa potentially a vortex for Cold War politics, he placed 'maintaining order' and 'protecting life' in Africa, topmost among the UN's responsibilities.[108] Was the UN suited to fulfill these responsibilities? Yes, said, Hammarskjöld. According to Hammarskjöld, the UN's independence, neutrality, and impartiality made it so.[109] Hammarskjöld argued that achieving these responsibilities required a

102 Orford, *supra* note 101, at 174.

103 Id.

104 Id.

105 Id.

106 Id.

107 *See* Sripati, *supra* note 101 at 477–507.

108 Id. at 484.

109 Id.

dynamism that 'conference approach', then being followed by the UN, lacked.[110] Why? The conference approach said Hammarskjöld, was glacial because it stemmed from UNGA's time-consuming deliberations, and doctrinal elaborations.[111]

However, IER practices offered new prospects and injected much needed dynamism into the world body.[112] For after all, IER practices flow from operationally oriented documents such as Primers, Guidance Notes, Best Practices, instruction manuals, and Security Council mandates.[113] In fact, Hammarskjöld considered these texts, fit to guide the UN in its future operations as well.[114] Using IER, the UN could insert its neutral presence to fill the political vacuum caused, for instance, by a temporary crisis of authority within a territory.[115] (As we will see in this book's second part, IER practices, popularized by UNSG Kofi Annan mushroomed during his (Annan's) term.)

Congo passed from King Leopold II's genocidal regime to Belgian colonial rule in 1908.[116] In 1959, Belgium announced June 30 as the date of independence.[117] Before departing, Belgium imposed the *Loi Fondamentale* (a constitution), which duplicated the Belgian constitution.[118] The constitution divided power at two levels for a total of four: the Head of State (titular head) and the Prime Minister, exercising actual powers; the Senate and the Chamber of Representatives; and the central government and the provinces.[119]

The parliamentary elections of May 1960 resulted in a coalition government, patched together with Prime Minister Lumumba and President Kasavubu as its head.[120] Colonel Mobutu Sese Seko headed the force *republique* that soon turned into the national army.[121] When

110 Id.
111 Id.
112 Id.
113 Id. at 484.
114 Id. at 484–485.
115 Id. at 485.
116 Id.
117 Id.
118 Id. at 485–486.
119 Id. at 486.
120 Id.
121 Id.

Congo became independent, most Congolese lacked experience in self-rule, signs of a conflict flaring up over jurisdiction loomed large, and Belgium continued to control Congo's economy. Indeed, the foreign minority (representing only 1 per cent of the population) controlled 95 per cent of the assets, 88 per cent of private savings, and 82 per cent of all the firms.[122]

Given this, Belgium invaded Congo on 10 July 1960, because Lumumba agreed to increase the army's wages.[123] Belgium entered Congo from Katanga, the mineral rich province. A day later Katanga attempted to secede. Belgium airbrushed its invasion with the ostensible purpose of protecting European lives in Congo. Katanga's attempted secession loosened the (central) government's military and politico-economic pillars.[124]

Therefore, on 12 July 1960, Lumumba and Kasavubu jointly sought the UN's military assistance to protect Congo's territorial integrity from Belgium's aggression.[125] 'Avoiding any legal characterization of the situation in the Congo', Hammarskjöld concluded that the presence of Belgian troops threatened international peace.[126] These circumstances sparked the Security Council-mandated peace operation for the Congo in July 1960: the UN Operation in Congo (ONUC). According to the UN:

> The initial mandate of ONUC was to ensure the withdrawal of Belgian forces from the Republic of the Congo, to assist the Government in maintaining law and order and to provide technical assistance.[127]

#### 4.3.1.1 *An Internationally Created Governmental Vacuum*

Hammarskjöld did not support Lumumba in regaining control over Congo, because he saw the Katangese secession as an internal matter that lay beyond the UN's jurisdiction. What displeased Hammarskjöld

122 Orford, *supra* note 101, at 178.

123 Sripati, *supra* note 101 at 486.

124 Id.

125 Id. at 486.

126 Orford, *supra* note 112 at 174.

127 *See* ONUC, http://www.un.org/en/peacekeeping/missions/past/onuc.htm.

most was Lumumba's socialist leanings, as evidenced by his request for Soviet assistance in tamping down the Katangese insurgency.[128] This was why, relations between Congo's central government and the UN first soured.

Against this backdrop, two consequential events occurred in succession: a constitutional crisis and governmental collapse. On 5 September 1960, Kasavubu announced that he was dismissing Lumumba. However, Lumumba refused to step down. For, he had received his cabinet and the Parliament's overwhelming support.[129] We might question, which actor Hammarskjöld considered to enjoy lawful authority in the Congo. Framed negatively, the answer is that Hammarskjöld refused to recognize Lumumba's government.[130]

According to Hammarskjöld, in making decisions about emergency action, ONUC's representatives:

> [h]ad to act on their own responsibility, within their general mandate, to meet the emergency, which they were facing.[131]

Meanwhile, on 14 September 1960, Colonel Sese Seko Mobutu announced on the airwaves that he was 'neutralizing' the entire government until December 1960, and that he would be calling in 'technicians' to run the country.[132] On 29 September 1960, Joseph Kasavubu installed by constitutional decree, a Council of Commissioners (Council).[133] Now ONUC staff collaborated with Mobutu's Council of Commissioners-General, the *de facto* authorities to run the government.[134] Meanwhile, gradually, ONUC staff also helped unite the conflicting groups.[135] In this way, ONUC pushed the parliament to reconvene in isolation at

[128] Sripati, *supra* note 101 at 486; Jean O. Tshonda, *in*, Peace & Diplomacy, *supra* note 101 at 249–252.

[129] Sripati, *supra* note 101 at 487.

[130] Id.

[131] Orford, *supra* note 101 at 184.

[132] Jean O. Tshonda, *in* Peace & Diplomacy, *supra* note 101 at 240, 251. *See* also infra note 134.

[133] Id. The UN General Assembly recognized President Kasavabu's government. Id. at 252.

[134] *1964 Yearbook of the UN* 7-12 (UN, 1965).

[135] *See* Crawford Young, *Politics in the Congo: Decolonization and Independence* 337 (Princeton University Press, 1960).

Lovanium University in July 1961. However, not all groups attended.[136] Nonetheless, the parliament consented to a government led by Cyrille Adoula as Lumumba's successor.[137] With this, the UN helped to restore the constitutional order that had begun to collapse on 5 September 1960.[138]

Thus, Hammarskjöld refused to recognize the authority of a duly elected prime minister (Lumumba) and a sitting parliament. Hammarskjöld dismissed Lumumba's government with its socialist leanings in this way: 'a clumsy, inadequate government that does not do the proper thing.'[139] (As the details in the next paragraph suggest, Hammarskjöld's indictment of Lumumba's government sprang from his economic thinking.) Furthermore, when the constitutional crisis peaked in September 1960, just a little over two months after the Congo had gained its independence, Hammarksjöld made this statement before the Security Council:

> Members will have gathered from the report that … the financial situation is one of bankruptcy. …. They [Congolese] seem to believe that the independence of the Republic of the Congo, … means independence also in a substantive sense of the word which is unreal. A government without financial means … ties its fate to that of the donors. Or it may depend on the United Nations, … and so remain free. These are the hard facts which should be remembered when the relations of the United Nations with the central government are discussed.[140]

### *4.3.1.2 The Impending Constitution Guides ITA by the UN*

Having spelt out Congo's dire situation, Hammarskjöld set out to chart this poor nation's future in tune with his vision of decolonization. With a view to hook Congo to the world economy, ONUC undertook the largest programme of technical assistance for any country in the history of the world organization.[141] Six hundred UN (foreign) experts worked

136 Id.
137 Id.
138 Id.
139 Orford, International Authority & R2P, *supra* note 112 at 86.
140 Id. at 85–86.
141 *1964 Yearbook of the UN* 7 (UN, 1965).

at various governmental levels (for example, the Office of the Prime Minister) in 47 fields, of which the following four are relevant for this discussion: finance and economics, mining and natural resources, public administration, and judicature.[142]

These experts: collaborated with the IMF and prepared the monetary reform plan, helped Congo join the IMF; established credit controls and budgetary measures to further fiscal stability; manned Congo's judiciary; drafted several important statutes, including one for the creation of a Supreme Court and; drafted a mining code that removed state controls on foreign exchange, a step, that as we will see, is critical to morphing a 'socialist state' into a 'more capitalist one', and so, undertaken by the World Bank—see its statement attached to footnote 61, Chapter 5 ); and advised the government on judicial, police, and prison reform (a precursor to post-1989 UN security sector reform along neoliberal lines).[143]

Indeed, ONUC's aforementioned partial-ITA project recalls and falls within Wilde's second international trusteeship Policy Institution: 'ITA projects since 1945'. (Note: I will join UNCA with its off-springs 'ITA projects since 1945' in Chapter 9.)

#### *4.3.1.3 United Nations Constitutional Assistance (UNCA)*

Sadly, Hammarskjöld died in a mysterious air-crash in 1961. Following which, U Thant, his successor, both at the UN and ONUC, continued his (Hammarskjöld's) (aforementioned) IER/ITA activities which culminated with UNCA. Consider:

> A complete revision of the legal code was undertaken, and assistance was given in the drawing up of a new constitution to replace the *Loi Fondamentale* in 1964 – United Nations.[144]

That drafting assistance came from T.O. Elias, ONUC's lead expert.[145] Congo's 1964 Constitution replicated Elias' draft constitution.[146] How might this arrangement have come about? Indeed, Thant confronted Congo with a 'U Thant Package Plan' whose 'specific proposals were

[142] Id. at 10.
[143] Id. at 10–13.
[144] Id. at 11.
[145] *See* Young, *supra* note 135 at 344.
[146] Id. at 344 & 531

not negotiable'.[147] Two specific proposals were the provision for a federal constitution prepared by UN experts, and a threat of heaping economic sanctions on Katanga, if it rejected the Thant Plan. The Thant Plan triumphed.[148] Accordingly, by January 1963, Moïse Tshombe, the Katangese leader had announced he was jettisoning his secessionist plans.

Figure 1.4 captures Congo's situation where the UN commenced internationalized law-making activities (for example, of ITA) before the Constitution was made, but of course this impending constitution guided ITA activities.

In this way, UNCA-ITA was revived to switch the Congo-engine's rails, diverting it from the socialist destination, chosen by its elected leader (Lumumba), toward one determined by an international civil servant, Hammarskjöld: Western liberal market democracy. Which means that, although UNCA-ITA did materialize after conflict, contrary to the 'purposive simplification', (discussed in Chapter 1), it was used not to fill a governmental vacuum (caused by violence) and/or mitigate the post-conflict situation.

## 4.4 Conclusion

This Chapter traced UNCA's rise, rejection, and revival in a sovereign state. It showed that a Third World sovereign state's Constitution-making was internationalized again, and for the same purposes that had led to such internationalization, prior to independence. In introducing the first three UNCA projects in Libya, Eritrea, and Congo, (outside the context of the UN Trusteeship Council), this chapter took the first step toward conceptualizing UNCA as an 'established practice'/ 'institution'. I will complete conceptualizing UNCA as an 'institution', and Policy Institution in chapters 6, and 9 respectively. As part of establishing UNCA as an 'institution', the next chapter shifts the focus to the Constitution, exploring how and why it came to be internationalized by the UN, in the post-Cold War era.

[147] Id. at 342.

[148] Id. at 340–42.

# PART II

# 5

# The Western Liberal Constitution's Rise post 1989

## United Nations Constitutional Assistance

## 5.0 Introduction

This chapter focuses on the rise of UNCA post-1989. (It elaborates on some of the issues covered in Chapter 1.) It, therefore, concentrates on the Constitution's post-1989 return as a prelude to considering its internationalized making by the United Nations (UN) from 1989–2019 in Chapter 6. This chapter asks and answers this question: Why did the UN internationalize the Constitution, a former 'standard of civilization' (Civilized Standard) in the post-1989 era? It does so, based on the UN's official explanations. According to the UN, a constitution made without international assistance is the default method.[1] However, since the Least Developed Countries (LDCs) possess weak governance capacities, the UN assists them, with their consent, to make a constitution that is universal: the Western liberal Constitution, based on the rule of law (as defined by the UN).[2] Indeed, the Constitution, says the UN, promotes free markets, the rule of law, good governance (including natural resources exploitation), and women's rights. In this way, it promotes

[1] UN Constitutional Assistance Guidance Note 2 (2009).

[2] UN Approach to Rule of Law Assistance 1–4 (2009).

democracy, prevents conflict, builds peace, reduces poverty, and so, speeds development.[3]

I argue that the UN's explanations are far too simplistic, conceal more than they reveal, and are indeed ahistorical. Moreover, they echo an imperial past. I suggest that what underpins this Civilized Standard's making today, is not the 'civilized'/'uncivilized' paradigm, but a newer one, based on the universal language of development: the developed countries'/LDCs' paradigm (Paradigm). The Bretton Woods Institutions (BWIs), backed by powerful Western states, framed this Paradigm to promote their conditionality and achieve the latter's interests: the Constitution (defined in Chapter 1, section 1.5). Indeed, as we will see, the BWIs have been promoting this constitution from 1983 till the present day, through two similar, consecutive, but differently named conditionalities: Structural Adjustment Programmes (SAPs) (1983–99) and Poverty Reduction Strategy Papers (PRSPs) (1999–Present).[4] Overall, their aim has been to 'create a market-friendly, lean, decentralized, customer-oriented, managerial, and democratic state'.[5]

As regards to the post-1989 era, the BWIs who cannot for political reasons promote a constitution, used the Soviet Union's demise to

[3] Report of the Secretary-General, *Progress Report on the Prevention of Armed Conflict*, U.N. Doc. A/60/891 (July 18, 2006).

[4] World Bank, *World Development Report 1997: The State in a Changing World* (World Bank, 1997) (promoting the Western liberal constitution) [*Hereafter* 1997 *World Development Report*]; World Bank, *Structural and Sectoral Adjustment, World Bank Experience 1980–1992* (World Bank, 1995); *Aid and Reform in Africa - Lessons from Ten Case Studies* (S. Devarajan, *et al.* eds., The World Bank, 2001). With a view to internationalize the Constitution, the BWIs proposed constitutional, legal, and institutional changes covering (1) Public financial management (2) Privatization and (3) land, labour, and credit markets. In this way, they sought to achieve both sets of their reforms (first and second generation). For the 1983–1998 era see Emmanuel Akpa, *The World Bank and the State of Structural Adjustment, in* Seminar in Helsinki, Finland, 27.3.1998: KEPA's Reports-27 5–11 (Service Center for Development Cooperation, Finland, 1998) [*Hereafter* KEPA's Reports]; Section 5.3 offers sources regarding the post-1999 era. However, the Constitution's internationalization lagged because one-fourth of SAP-implementing states experienced war or civil strife during the late eighties.

[5] Economic Commission for Africa (ECA), *Public Sector Management Reforms in Africa* 1 (2001).

promote the Constitution (their conditionality), artfully subsumed under the 'rule of law' rubric.[6] To promote or internationalize the Constitution, the UN Family (including the BWIs) first universalized it, subsuming it under the 'rule of law' rubric then conceptualized the 'rule of law' as a development (understood as 'market-oriented poverty reduction') strategy[7]; and finally, fitted it into the UN peace, security, and development system (hereinafter UN System), ostensibly as a tool to prevent conflict, build peace, and speed development (so understood). Here is why, UNCA was revived in the post-Cold War era. The UN assisted sovereign, conflict-torn, and stable LDCs, to adopt the Constitution in return for debt-relief. In this way, UNCA came to operate in two contexts: post-conflict and development assistance.

I will, therefore argue that these states are once again entrapped in an imperial relationship, although this time they are ostensibly sovereign. In fact, UNCA starts from where the inter-war period's international constitutional assistance ends (*see* Chapter 3). Therefore, the BWIs and the UN (and its constitutional assistance) are the Mandate System's contemporary successors. (As we might expect, commentators have noted colonial continuities in the post-1989 rule of law promotion as well, *see* Chapter 1.)

Given the insights set out in the above paragraphs, these two allied strands have so far shaped the skeletal good governance story (Story): the internationalization of development,[8] and the internationalization of the rule of law[9] (that subsumes the Constitution). Figure 5. 1 illustrates that narrative. As already noted in Chapter 1, the Story is essentially about the internationalization of the Constitution—an aspect that has remained shrouded for reasons, noted there. Indeed, as this narration ends, I show that at its heart, this Story is about the Constitution's internationalization and by extension, the internationalization of Constitution-making. Consequently, as Figure 5.2 illustrates, the

[6] *See* World Bank, *Legal and judicial reform: Strategic directions* 37-38, 75 (World Bank, 2003).

[7] Id.

[8] *See generally* Antony Anghie, *Sovereignty, Imperialism and the Making of International Law* (Cambridge University Press, 2005),

[9] *See generally* Sundhya Pahuja, *Decolonizing International Law: Development, Economic Growth, and the Politics of Universality* (Cambridge University Press, 2011).

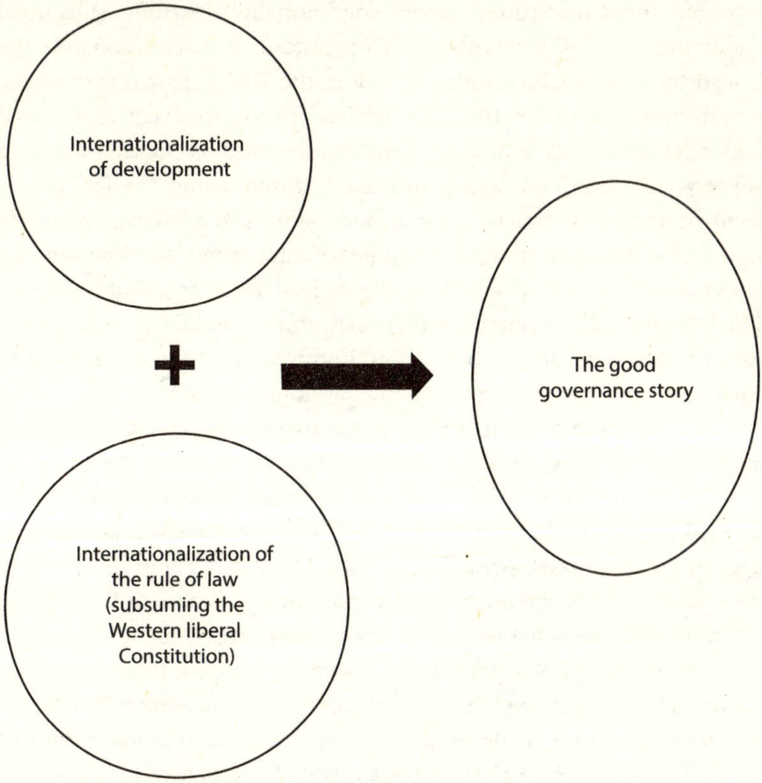


FIGURE 5.1 The good governance story: The internationalization of development and the internationalization of the rule of law that subsumes the Western liberal Constitution.

Constitution shapes the UN peace, security, and development system (System). Figures 5.1 and 5.2 depict how the good governance story has played out so far, and an alternate way of viewing and understanding it.

Before proceeding, it helps to:

- recall from Chapter 1 that the Constitution's internationalization can also be framed or understood as: the internationalization of (national) economic decision-making in the Third World—be it of colonies, or sovereign states; and
- note that Chapter 4 began to establish UNCA as an 'institution' ('established practice'), and so, described the first three UNCA projects

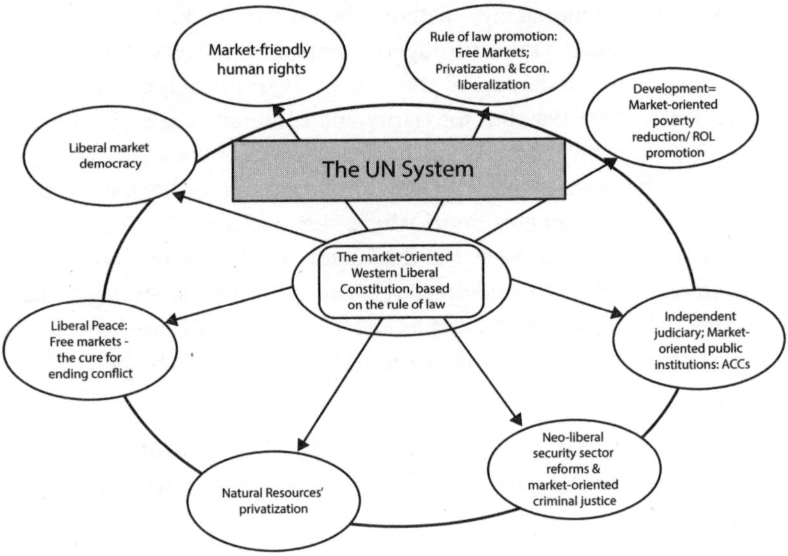


FIGURE 5.2. The Western liberal constitution shapes the UN peace, security and development system in a market-oriented constitutional dimension

(1949–52 and 1960–4); and that Chapter 6 will complete that conceptualization by analyzing the remainder of the UNCA projects (1989–2019).

Given the aforementioned bullet points, and that this chapter follows Chapter 4, and precedes Chapter 6, I will answer the question posed in section 5.0 (that is, discuss the Constitution's post-1989 internationalization as a ROL/development strategy) in this way. I will trace foreign powers' (FPs) (Western colonial powers and IOs) internationalization of economic decision-making in the Third World, during the Cold War (and decolonization) (1945–91) and after the Cold War (1991–9) for four ostensible ends: rule of law, free markets, good governance (including natural resources exploitation), and women's rights. In this way, I will show that this 'established practice' (internationalized economic decision-making) culminated with the Constitution's internationalization in 1999, as a development understood as market-oriented poverty reduction strategy.

My analysis, framed in tune with Ralph Wilde's Method, will foreground an activity and its ostensible purposes—internationalized economic decision-making—without focusing on its forms, unless they are relevant. Rather, I stress throughout, only the principles of domination and control that underpinned this activity. (Chronologically speaking, I should start from 1989 but for clarity and continuity's sake, I start from 1950. However, I will not repeat Chapter 4's points but build on them.) My aim is to offer a macro view of developments, and so, I will cover those milestones in the proportion to which, they concern the Constitution's internationalization in 1999. For this reason, I will elaborate on the 1999 milestone: the BWIs' Conditionality/Poverty Reduction Strategy Papers (PRSPs): which prescribed a development (understood as market-oriented poverty reduction) strategy, the Constitution to secure debt-relief.

## 5.1 Tracing the Internationalization of Economic Decision-Making in The Third World: Key Milestones (1950–99)

Why and how was economic decision-making in the Third World in the post-World War II era internationalized? Here, Vernon Hewitt's perceptive comments about that era are instructive:

> As a project, international development can be defined as a product of empire, a universal language of 'improvement' and civilization acted out through a series of complex processes…
>
> Post-war conceptions of international development and industrialization were the direct legatees of Britain's state-based project of socio-economic engineering. … Although the political endgame of Rostow was not spelt out, it was evident that the post-take-off phase merely substituted conceited views on English exceptionalism with American views on their own constitution and its universal relevance.[10]

### 5.1.1 Toward the Creation of the 'Least Development Countries' Category in 1971

In Chapter 3, we saw that the Mandates System had conceptualized non-European peoples' backwardness in economic terms. Continuing

[10] Vernon Hewitt, *Empire, International Development and the Concept of Good Government, in* Empire, Development & Colonialism – The Past in the Present 30, 32 (quote) (Mark Duffield & Vernon Hewitt, eds., James Currey, 2009).

on this theme (*see* aforementioned quote), the post-World War II thinking created a broader and universal sounding Paradigm: "developed"/ 'least developed countries' Paradigm (Paradigm). Under this Paradigm, FPs led by the US would internationalize economic decision-making in Third World states, ostensibly to alleviate their poverty and thereby develop and modernize them. Indeed, as we will see, the UN's creation of the LDC category in 1971, itself reflected, and resulted from the internationalization of economic decision-making in the Third World. Put differently, newly decolonized states who failed under, and because of imposed constitutions were to become LDCs. Activities so introduced to 'develop' the Third World gave rise to what we now know as 'development assistance'. (Note: True, the Cold War's ideological split offered not one but roughly two basic models/'universal' blue-prints of development. Nonetheless, consensus had it that development, understood as modernization, was both necessary and inescapable.[11]) Although all UNCA-recipients-states fall within the Third World, I use the LDC category in this section, to provide some degree of coherence, since most of the documents that illuminate UNCA frame its use with reference to the LDCs.

*1950-1971*

The international community's decision to make 'poverty reduction' in the Third World (subsequently known as LDCs) an international development goal, and authorize the BWIs to achieve this goal in ways noted in this paragraph, first internationalized decision-making in the Third World.[12] First, by 1950, underdevelopment became a domain of intervention, which in turn propelled poverty reduction onto the international agenda. Second was the decision to attach conditions to the International Monetary Fund's (IMF) lending and increase its surveillance powers. Third was the creation in 1960 of a body explicitly tasked with assisting states: the International Development Agency (IDA).[13] These events gradually extended the reach of BWIs in the Third World in a 'spatial, conceptual,

[11] *See* Richard Jolly *et al, UN Contributions to Development Thinking and Practice* (Indiana University Press, 2004).

[12] Id.

[13] Pahuja, *supra* note 9 at 161.

and juridical sense'[14] 1961 heralded the BWIs' dominant role in Third World states, for this year marked the start of the UN Development Decade (1961–71) when the international spotlight shone on them.[15]

Mention of the year 1960 calls to mind, the right to self-determination discussed in Chapter 4. Given this, did the Third Word not resist the internationalization of its economic decision-making? Yes, it did, but unsuccessfully. During the 1950s to1960s, states/colonies framed their quest for self-determination in terms of defining what their constitutions would be, and sculpting them without international assistance—in order that they might exercise permanent sovereignty over their natural resources (PSNR).[16] However, the PSNR battle ended with a victory for Foreign Investors (FIs).[17] How and why?

For, FPs cast LDCs' national/constitutional issues (for example, PSNR) as 'economic' or 'development' ones that required international regulation.[18] The US, an exporter of capital, took the lead, framing issues raised by the claim to PSNR (for example, natural resource governance [NRG]) as international economic developmental issues, insisting that its (foreign) investors receive protection from an internationally regulated standard, all of which brought NRG within the BWIs' legitimate remit.[19] (Note: The presence of newly decolonized states in the UN General Assembly did not end the Western domination of the BWIs.)

Meanwhile, the BWIs who had refused to respond to the PSNR debate, ostensibly because PSNR was a political issue, nonetheless, framed foreign investment as a non-political/technical issue that required international regulation.[20] For instance, during 1962–66, the World Bank framed foreign investment as essentially a technical issue that was integral to development. As a result, the International Centre for Settlement of Investment Disputes (ICSID) was created at the Bank

[14] Id.

[15] *See* UNGA Res. No. 1710 (XVI), pmbl ¶2 U.N. GAOR, 1084th Sess., U.N. Doc. A/Res/1710 (19 December 1961).

[16] *See* UNGA Res. No. 2625 (XXV), UN GAOR, 25th Session, U.N. Doc. A/Res/2625 (26 October 1970).

[17] Pahuja, *supra* note 9 at Chapter 4.

[18] Id. at 107–114.

[19] Id.

[20] Id at 161–163.

with a view to encourage arbitration in tune with international standards.[21] In this way, the Bank set the stage for compelling borrower-states to adopt the Constitution (and consistent laws) to foster export-oriented economies and trade liberalization, based on the idea that international private capital is essential to the development process.[22]

Economic decision-making in the Third World was internationalized in two other, allied ways. First, before exiting their colonies, the FPs imposed constitutions which failed the masses (Masses) who consequently came to 'live under disadvantaged economies'.[23] (Congo's case discussed in Chapter 4 is a good example.) Second, this triggered further international intervention in the Third World; the LDC category was created in 1971 to provide 'special support' to just those Masses in 23 states.[24]

I list here 16 of those states, which were to become debtor states in the post-Cold War era, and thus, implement the BWIs' conditionalities with UNCA: Mali, Haiti, Sudan, Nepal, Yemen, Bhutan, The Gambia, Guinea, Malawi, Maldives, Rwanda, Burundi, Somalia, Tanzania, Afghanistan, and Central African Republic. My aim is to offer a macro view of developments, rather than a detailed analysis of individual countries. So, I will frame my analysis first, in terms of African states, because ten of the aforesaid LDCs were, as we will see further below, the first to draw the BWIs' attention (*see* section 5.3). Second, and last, I will focus on five LDCs from Middle East and North Africa (MENA) states, for they were to become UNCA-recipients-states in the wake of the 2010 Jasmine Revolution.

#### *5.1.1.1 Least Developed Countries: Newly Decolonized States Who Failed under and because of Imposed Constitutions*

AFRICA Ten of those African states had thrown off the colonial yoke by about 1963. They had liberal Western constitutions thrust upon

[21] Id.

[22] Id. at 166

[23] *See* UNDESA, *Policy Note* v (Aug. 2010) (quote); UNCTAD, "Beyond Conventional Wisdom in Development Policy: An Intellectual History of UNCTAD 1964–2004" (UN, 2004).

[24] *See* UN-OHRLLS, *The Least Developed Countries—Things to know, Things to do* 20-21 (UN, 2011).

them by the departing colonial powers, which had enshrined property rights to protect vested interests: settler communities and indigenous propertied (agrarian) classes.[25] These liberal constitutions failed their masses because they were superimposed over a colonial order: an executive vested with wide discretionary powers.[26] Furthermore, they were manipulated by national elites, who as the local agents of metropolitan capital, had a vested interest in the status quo.[27] Sucked into the arms race because of the Cold War, these national elites squandered national wealth by stacking up arms instead of ameliorating the plight of the poor.[28]

For these reasons, Malawi, Uganda, Tanzania and other countries appeared on the UN radar in 1971. These states were found to be 'lagging further and further behind, and in some cases moving backwards'.[29] From whose perspective were these states found to be lagging? The answer is: from the Western perspective of modernization and 'law-and-development' paradigms, the 1970s' two reigning intellectual currents in the West. These approaches 'operated from a mainstream liberal, or to (its left critics) pro-capitalist perspective'.[30] They posited that in developing societies, economic growth would lead to social change conducive to liberal democracy.[31] Advocates of these currents recommended that LDCs pursue development planning, which called for state-engineered economies with resources allocated by governments.

[25] *See* Issa Shivji, *Three Generations of Constitutions and Constitution-Making in Africa: An Overview and Assessment in Social and Economic Context, in,* Constitutionalism in Transition: Africa and Eastern Europe 74, 75 (Mihaela Serban Rosen ed., Helsinki Foundation for Human Rights, 2003).

[26] Id. at 75–76.

[27] Id.

[28] Id. For a similar account offered by Shivji's professor, see Y. Ghai, *A journey around constitutions reflecting on contemporary constitutions*, 122 S. Afr. L. J. 804, 808-809 (2005).

[29] "The Least Developed Countries: Historical Background," http://www.un.org/events/ldc3/prepcom/history.htm

[30] *See* Vicky Randall, *Changing Analytical Approaches to the Study of Politics in the Developing World, in* Politics in the Developing World 14, 14 (Peter Burnell, ed., Oxford University Press, 2014).

[31] Id. at 17.

According to Issa Shivji, these modernization theories had African or 'domestic counterparts': various developmentalist ideologies.[32] Those domestic developmentalist ideologies made the state the key instrument of social change.[33] The instrumentalist law and the developmentalist state, says Shivji, therefore 'became *the* norm' (in Africa) in the 1970s.[34] The new authoritarian party-state constitutions, which the African elites, whether civilian or military-led, scrambled to adopt during the 1970s, reflected that norm.[35] Indeed, Shivji suggests that in so adopting such authoritarian constitutions, African elites were merely embracing the paradigm peddled by the West.[36]

The authoritarian constitutions, which typified many African states during the 1970s, spawned authoritarian regimes, which systematically and routinely violated citizens' rights, using the arms supplied by both the superpowers.[37] Despite their dismal human rights records, these regimes continued to be backed by the West and the BWIs.[38] Whereas, as we saw in the previous chapter, those with socialist leanings, such as Patrice Lumumba in Congo, were deemed radical by Western powers, and for that reason were overthrown. The aforesaid authoritarian regimes pushed Africa's masses, by the end of the 1970s, deeper into poverty and deprived them from adequate water supply, healthcare, and educational facilities.[39]

### *Middle-East*

It helps to note that during 1950–70, Tunisia, Libya, Egypt, Iraq, and Syria unsuccessfully strove to tread their own path, one different from what was dictated by their former colonial powers, the very time when the modernization paradigm was the passport for gaining

32 Shivji, *supra* note 25 at 76.

33 Id.

34 Id. (emphasis in original).

35 Id.

36 Id.

37 Id.

38 Id. at 77–79.

39 Id. at 81.

international legitimacy.[40] Therefore, modernize they did. They modernized their economy and society, but lest mass political mobilization imperil their new found political power, they left their masses disempowered.[41] As a result, authoritarian regimes spawned in the MENA region, which 'pursued a revolution from above', and plunged the masses into poverty.[42]

Regrettably, by the 1970s, both African and MENA states were sucked into the vortex of poverty and debt. For instance, sub-Saharan Africa's debt grew mountainous, from US$7 billion in 1971 to US$84,049 billion in 1981.[43] So too, were swamped in debt (for reasons beyond their control), some non-African LDCs, including Peru, Mexico, and Argentina.[44] All these states were insolvent. Not surprisingly, the BWIs faulted aid recipients for the failures of the very policies they imposed. Meanwhile, by 1982, the IMF, for reasons noted above, stood poised to manage the Mexican debt and subsequent debt crises: to survey Third World states, including regulating broad areas of their domestic policy.[45] This means, LDCs' economic decision-making would be internationalized even during the 1980s, and after 1989, when the Cold War ended.

Indeed, unbeknown to many, a series of UN-hosted conferences, organized thematically around the LDCs starting from 1981, began to prescribe international constitutional assistance in response to LDCs' supposed inadequacy, framed in the context of market reform and democratic consolidation. The first LDC Conference (1981) endorsed market-oriented proposals for debt-relief. I will elaborate on this point in section 5.1.2.2's final paragraph.

[40] Toby Dodge, *From the 'Arab Awakening' to the Arab Spring: Power Shift in the Middle East? the Post-colonial state in the Middle East* 6 (London School of Economics, 2012).

[41] Id.

[42] Id.

[43] *See* M.A.B. Siddique, *The Eternal Debt Problem of sub-Saharan Africa: 1971-1990* 64 S. Afr. J. of Economics 122, 125 (June 1996).

[44] Jolly *supra* note 11 at 206.

[45] Pahuja *supra note* 9 at 781

[46] *See* J. Hobson, *Civilizing the Global Economy – Racism and Anglo-Saxon imperialism, in,* Global standards of Market Civilization 60, 71 (Brett Bowden & Leonarde Seabrook, eds., Routledge, 2006).

### 5.1.2 1983: Structural Adjustment Programmes (SAPs): LDCs Create Western-Style Systems to Secure Debt-Relief

In August 1982, Mexico announced its inability to service its debt, and the US seized this opportunity to politically construct a debt crisis.[46] For powerful states, the least expensive entry point to other states' resources is: via debt.[47] Consequently, backed by the US, the IMF had by 1983, intervened in forty-seven debtor states to impose its SAPs. In this way, Middle Eastern and African LDCs who were sucked into the vortex of debt during 1972-1982, consented in 1983, to implement the BWIs' SAPs: to secure debt-relief.[48] Whereby, they had to liberalize trade, maintain fiscal discipline, protect property rights and foreign direct investment, and promote deregulation, and privatization.[49] To achieve which, they had to:

> restructure their legal and political systems along the lines set out in the American Constitution: that is, create an independent judiciary to ensure that governments cannot interfere with private property rights, .... For, once property rights have been defined and protected in a liberal constitution, they are difficult to change. ... The World Bank has noted this as a key mechanism for reinforcing the new constitutionalist lock in measures discussed above.[50]

(The SAPs served as the spur cum backdrop for the 1985 UN standards for judicial accountability).[51] In fact, the UN and the BWIs co-assisted debtor-states to implement the SAPs and relevant other UN standards[52] (*see e.g.*, UNCA in Angola and El Salvador, Chapter 6). In this way, powerful western states advanced their own economic / own investors' interests in LDCs who thereby lost their battle for PSNR.

[47] Susan George, *A Fate Worse Than Debt* 143, 187 (Penguin, 1988).

[48] *See* World Bank, *supra* note 4.

[49] Id. Stephen Gill, *Globalization, Democracy and the International Financial Institutions, in* KEPA's Reports, *supra* note 4.

at 65; ECA, *supra* note 5.

[50] Gill, *supra* note 49; See World Bank, *supra* note 4.

[51] Those standards were updated in 2002 ("Bangalore Principles"), and are available on the World Bank website.

[52] *See* World Bank, *Legal and Judicial Reform: Strategic Directions* (World Bank, 2003).

Regrettably, SAPs exacerbated rather than alleviated the debt crisis. Indeed, in 1970, the fifteen heavily indebted nations had an external public debt of $17.923 billion—which amounted to 9.8 percent of their GNP.[53] And by 1987, this shot up to US $528 billion.[54] Furthermore, deep cuts in programs like education, health, and social care hurt state functionaries, industrialists, and other members of the middle class.[55] Those cuts disproportionately affected the poorest people who, faced with reduced access to basics such as food and milk, rioted—but only to be violently repressed. As a result, by the early nineties, fourteen African states such as Angola, Burundi, Rwanda, and Côte d'Ivoire, were caught in the vortex of conflict.[56]

Meanwhile, the US and the BWIs, in line with their previous reactions to such development failures, ignored factors such as their policies themselves, or the structure of the international political economy.[57] Accordingly, they continued the SAPs, despite the havoc they caused. And, instead, as Pahuja concludes:

> They sought an explanation grounded in yet another terrain of inadequacy within the Third World. … [T]he IFIs determined that the failure to … reduce poverty derived from inadequacies inherent in the debtor societies. In the variant in question here, after cameo appearances on the human rights … stages, the figure of inadequacy was Third World institutions, most notably legal and regulatory institutions, including the rule of law. … IFIs regarded the wreckage before them and turned to the inadequacy of Third World institutions — state, governance, law — as the cause.[58]

To address this, in 1989, the BWIs commenced their famed "rule of law" movement, prescribing the rule of law framework (as defined by

[53] *See* World Bank International Debt Statistics, 1970-2013 (undated).

[54] *Id.*

[55] Jolly, *supra* note 11 at 137.

[56] Shivji, *supra* note 25 at 182; Javier Couso, *Constructing Privatopia: The Role of Constitutional Law in Chile's Radical Neoliberal Experiment, in* The Politics of Legality in a Neoliberal Age 85 (Ben Golder & Daniel McLoughlin, eds., Routledge, 2018) (revealing that the Constitution's promotion via SAPs triggered conflict and stifled democracy in Chile).

[57] Pahuja, *supra* note 9 at 191.

[58] Id. at 192 [emphasis added].

them—reproduced in Chapter 1, §1.6) as a development strategy.[59] I concur with Pahuja.

### *5.1.2.1 1989–1999: SAPs Internationalize the Western Liberal Constitution, Subsumed under the 'Rule of Law'*

But as I established at the outset, *conceptually*, the Constitution is key to achieving the UN's and the BWIs' ends. Moreover, it underpins the state and enshrines legal institutions. Accordingly, to revamp the Third World's *legal institutions* (*see* Pahuja's quote above)—the BWIs targeted for reform, first the Third World state's *highest law: the Constitution*. And so, from 1989–99, they continued to internationalize the Constitution (via SAPs), but subsumed it under the "rule of law" as evidenced by two definitions, one reproduced in chapter 1, section 1.6 and one here:

> The rule of law requires a set of basic laws that frame the governance of the state and its people. These basic laws include the constitution, civil code and civil procedure and criminal code .... To create a legal framework for investment climate, the following laws are essential: ...property laws (both tangible and intangible), and ....– World Bank.[60]

It is worth noting how in the post-Cold War era, UNCA and rule of law assistance morphed debt-ridden Guinea-Bissau (a former Soviet satellite state – see chapter 6) into a neo-liberal market democracy:

> The Legal Framework for Development
>
> The rule of law's [that subsumes the Constitution] salience is important to the World Bank
>
> Rules are understood here in a broad sense and include legislation, courts' decisions, guidelines and regulations. ....
>
> ... Guinea-Bissua is presently amending its Constitution to transition from a socialist state to a more "capitalist" state. An impediment to developing the private sector is Article 12 of the Constitution, which provides for state ownership of all land (leases are granted to private individuals), minerals, banks, insurance companies and so forth. Article 13

[59] Id.

[60] World Bank, *supra* note 52 at 37 (listing laws in these areas: contracts, commerce, corporations, administration & environment)

> also provides for state control of foreign trade and exchange transactions. One of the objectives of the legal technical assistance provided to Guinea-Bissau is to coordinate the various pieces of legislation financed by external lending so that they can be dovetailed to form a whole.[61]

Before proceeding, four points of which, the first two concern terminology, deserve mention. First, two successive conditionalities, the SAPs and the PRSPs promoted the Constitution under different labels. From 1989 to 1999, the SAPs promoted the "rule of law" as a strategy for (market-oriented) development. And, as section 5.3 will show, from 1999 onwards, the PRSPs promoted "good governance"/"rule of law" as a strategy for development, understood as "market-oriented poverty reduction." Second, and accordingly, the UN and the BWIs co-made the Constitution central to their rule of law, good governance, and poverty reduction definitions.[62] Third, accordingly, the SAPs and the PRSPs promoted the same type of development: market-oriented. Fourth, under SAPs, governance connoted the effective implementation of economic liberalization and allied policies through individual regulatory systems.[63] But, the PRSPs would create a uniform system of global governance, with a view to control Third World states' regulative capacities.[64]

In Chapter 1, I modified and reproduced a peacebuilding figure to indicate in dashes, the missing jigsaw: the Constitution, where it fits in, and to which peace-building goals it relates –see Figure 1. 7. This Chapter presents Figure 5.3 which reproduces the relevant provisions of a widely cited 1999 table (that makes no mention of the Constitution): the BWIs' "two stages [Stages] of economic liberalization."[65] Figure 5.3

[61] World Bank, *Governance and Development - A World Bank publication* 28, 33 (The World Bank, 1992)

[62] *See* Ch. 1, §1.6 (rule of law); IMF, Good Governance Fact Sheet (IMF, 1999), and *infra* section 5.3

[63] *See* Celine Tan, *Governance through Development: Poverty Reduction Strategies, International Law and the Disciplining of Third World States* 113 (Routledge, 2011).

[64] See Kanishka Jayasuriya, *Governance, Post-Washington Consensus and the New Anti-Politics, in* Corruption in Asia: Rethinking the Governance Paradigm 24, 25 (Timothy Lindsey, ed., Federation Press, 2002).

[65] Moises Naiim, "Fads and fashions in economic reforms: Washington consensus or Washington confusion?" Table 1, Foreign Policy Magazine, October 26, 1999.

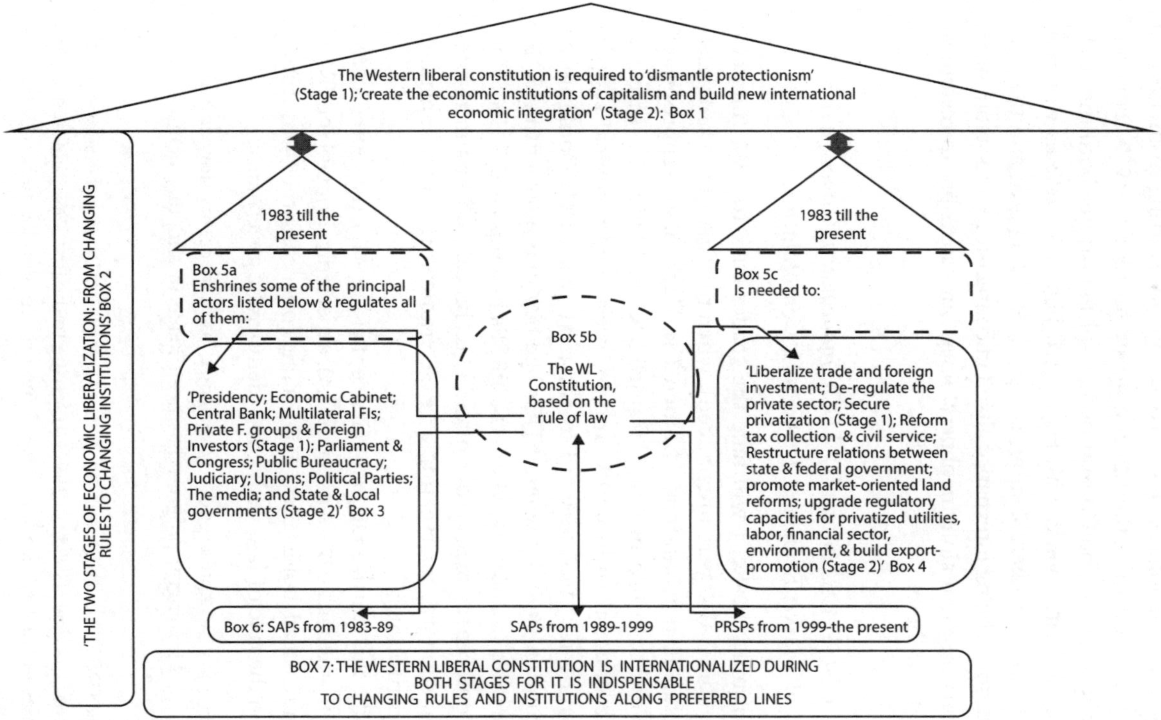


FIGURE 5.3 The Western liberal constitution: The missing jigsaw in the Good Governance Story

*Source*: For words in quotes in Boxes 1, 2, 3, 4 see Moises Naiim, 'Fads and fashions in economic reforms: Washington consensus or Washington confusion?' Table 1, Foreign Policy Magazine, October 26, 1999. All the remainder insights about the Constitution's salience must be ascribed to Sripati, the author.

indicates in dashes, how and why, the Constitution achieves the BWIs' ends, starting from economic liberalization during both stages, and was therefore, internationalized as a conditionality, starting from 1983. In this way, it a) provides the missing jigsaw in the post-1989 economic liberalization story: the Constitution; and b) illustrates both the backdrop for, and intertwines with Figure 1.7. Figure 5.3 reveals why rule of law (economic liberalization) is a peace-building goal and that, the Constitution is being internationalized in conflict-torn and stable states to restructure them along neoliberal lines, but ostensibly, to restore or sustain peace there.

### *5.1.2.2 UNCA (1981 onwards): LDCs' Inadequacy Framed in the Context of Market Reform & Democratic Consolidation*

For continuity's sake, I will take the reader back to 1981 (i.e., two years before SAPs were introduced), when the first LDC conference was held. That Conference framed the "lack of an appropriate" (i.e., Western constitutional) "framework" in LDCs as a threat to the international community, and so, prescribed technical support for creating it.[66] Fast forward to the next two LDCs Conferences, the second in 1990 (by when, LDCs had begun implementing SAPs) and the third in 2001 (by when, the PRSPs had replaced SAPs). Both these conferences expectedly offered "technical and financial international support" for creating a "ROL framework" (that subsumed the Constitution).[67]

Finally, the fourth LDCs conference, held in 2011 (i.e., after UNCA had been outed in 2009 – *see* section 5.5), expectedly dropped the "ROL" term and instead, boldly drew a direct line connecting the Constitution, based on the rule of law, with good/democratic governance:

> LDCs have accepted good governance as a necessity for development.... Meaningful progress has been made in adopting democratic

[66] *See* UNCTAD, *Programme of Action for the Least Developed Countries for the 1990s Paris, 3-14 Sept. 1990* ¶16 (1992) (referring to the first 1981 conference); For "outcomes on LDCs," see http://www.un.org/en/development/devagenda/ldc.shtml.

[67] *See Report of the Third UN Conference on the Least Developed Countries, Belgium, 14-20 May* 2001, U.N. Doc. A/CONF.191/13 20 September 2001

> constitutions, drafting new legislation, and setting up legal frameworks against corruption.[68]

Significantly, this conference lamented the cycle of coups in West African LDCs during 2008–2010, and prescribed good governance (market-oriented measures) as a means of returning them to constitutional order.[69] (For examples see Chapter 6.)

In this way, a Paradigm for LDCs was created by powerful Western developed states, which included a strategy for their development (understood as market-oriented poverty reduction): the Constitution, based on the ROL. But before it could be so conceptualized (i.e., as a ROL/development strategy), it had to be first universalized—a theme that I touched upon in Chapter 1, and will, consider very briefly here.

## 5.2 The Constitution Positioned as a Universal Model

I broadly agree with those who have traced the internationalization of the rule of law (that subsumes the Constitution) to the post–Cold War evangelism of powerful Western states about the universality of liberal (market) democracy, with that conception of democracy centered on the rule of law.[70] Before proceeding, it helps to note that the Constitution registered its triumph on two fronts, the political and scholarly, starting with the former. However, owing to the parallel evolution of international law and constitutional law during the 1990s, which I call point X, the scholarly evangelism of this period focussed only on the universality of liberal human rights and so did those who later questioned that evangelism. Given this, I focus on how the Constitution came to be implicitly universalized, making just three submissions.

First, regarding the political front, the Conference on Security and Cooperation in Europe (CSCE) (September 1990), which drew all members of the European Union and the U.S., affirmed that constitutional market democracy based on free elections is an inherent element of

[68] *See* Report of the UN Secretary-General, *Ten-year Appraisal and Review of the Implementation of the Brussel Programme of Action for the LDC for the Decade 2001–2010*, ¶45 UN Doc. A/66/666-E/2011/78 (7 February 2011).

[69] Id. at ¶36.

[70] Pahuja, *supra note* 9 at 179–185.

the (market-oriented) rule of law.[71] Here is why, post-colonial scholars such as Pahuja have questioned this orientation of rule of law.[72] Un-noticed by many, the CSCE endorsed bilateral and international constitutional assistance for the Constitution's promotion.[73] Second, prominent American international law scholars interpreted the Soviet Union's demise as the triumph of capitalism and against this backdrop, implicitly claimed the universality of those features, and concepts that typify the Constitution: free markets, a market-oriented rule of law, and liberal constitutional market democracy.[74] Third, in this way, scholarly liberal human rights evangelism and liberal peace narratives articulated a particular vision of democracy: liberal market democracy promoted by the Constitution (and as epitomized by the U.S. constitution).[75] More significantly, a process of external legitimation was posited for promoting that vision.[76] Herein lay a public interest for continuing UNCA into sovereign states –in the post-1989 era.[77] Finally, owing to point X and the UN's confusing terms for UNCA (e.g., electoral assistance), scholars recommended electoral assistance for internationalizing Western liberal market democracy.[78]

So universalized, all that remained was for the Constitution to be conceptualized by the BWIs, as a development strategy. Which means that development after 1989, meant the same as when it was first promoted (discussed in Chapters 3-4): opening the Third World for the West's/transnational capitalist class' benefit.

[71] *Para* 3, Document of the Copenhagen meeting of the conference on the human dimension of the CSCE. (*Hereinafter* CSCE Document).

[72] Pahuja, *supra* note 9 at 180.

[73] CSCE Document, *supra* note 71, at ¶26.

[74] See Thomas Franck, *The Emerging Right to Democratic Governance*, 86 (1) AJIL 46, 48 (1992); Francis Fukuyama, *The End of History and the Last Man* 4 (Harper Collins, 2002); Anne-Marie Slaughter, *The Liberal Agenda for Peace: International Relations Theory and the Future of the United Nations* 4 Trans. L. & Contemp. Problems 377, 396 (1994); Louis Henkin, *A post-cold war human rights agenda* 19 Yale J. of Int'l L. 249, 251 (1994).

[75] *See* Slaughter, *supra* note 74 at 416–417.

[76] Id.

[77] See Franck, supra note 74. In fact, Franck favorably cited the (UNCA) project in Cambodia, though he used the term UN electoral assistance.

[78] Id.

## 5.3 1999: The Constitution is Conceptualized as a Rule of Law or Development (Understood as a Market-Oriented Poverty Reduction) Strategy

This brings us to the key milestone on the path to internationalizing economic activity in the Third Word: the PRSPs (the SAPs' successors) [79]: the Constitution's launching pads.[80] (As noted in section 5.1.1.3. during 1989–1999, the Constitution, subsumed under the "rule of law" label was promoted via the SAPs.)

But significantly, the Constitution was now made a strategy for development (understood as market-oriented poverty reduction), and promoted through IMF-supported lending.[81] As previously noted, the Constitution constitutes good governance's constitutional dimension. Therefore governance, symbolized by the Constitution, was made both a condition and a goal of development assistance.[82] So the question is: how was the Constitution purported to reduce poverty? Since I embrace Wilde's "purposive analysis," I concentrate only on the ostensible purposes put forth in this regard.

I therefore start not from 1999, but from 1989, when (in the wake of SAPs' failures), the BWIs first conceptualized the Third World's development problems as a "crisis of governance."[83] The World Bank posited that although its macro-economic policies provided an enabling environment for the productive use of Africa's resources, they were insufficient to achieve development because:

> A root cause of weak economic performance in the past has been the failure of public institutions. Private sector initiative and market mechanisms are important, but they must go hand in hand with good

[79] Frances Stewart and Michael Wang, *Poverty Reduction Strategy Papers in Human Rights Perspective*, *in*, Human rights and development – Towards mutual reinforcement 447, 466–467 (Philip Alston & Mary Robinson, eds., OUP, 2005).

[80] *See* Tan, *supra* note 63 at 165.

[81] Id. *See* Pahuja, *supra* note 9 at 192 (focussing on the rule of law that subsumed the Constitution).

[82] IMF Factsheet, *IMF and Good Governance* (undated) available on the IMF Website.

[83] *See* World Bank, *Sub-Saharan Africa – From Crisis to Sustainable Growth* 60 (November 1989).

> governance, a public service that is efficient, a judicial system that is reliable, and an administration that is accountable to the public.[84]
>
> *Legal and political conditions*
>
> ... All enterprises can benefit from a legal framework that defines contract and property rights clearly, and provides an equitable forum for settling disputes.[85]

In this way, a market-oriented rule of law (symbolized by the Constitution), was invoked as both the cause, and a result of development understood as market-oriented poverty reduction, and as a core element of good governance.[86]

Thereafter, in 1997, the IMF posited that, since "poor governance" "is clearly detrimental to economic activity and welfare," it was adopting a policy on addressing (good) economic governance.[87] Accordingly, the IMF Director, Michael Camdessus, announced that the IMF was moving into its "second generation" of reforms, which aimed at ensuring that the State fulfills its proper role in a market economy and implementing policies that will help to alleviate poverty.[88] The good economic governance/second generation reforms were aimed at: protecting foreign investors and property rights; easier privatization; promoting private sector activity; privatizing natural resources; broadening the tax base; and liberalizing trade and foreign investment. To achieve these goals, the BWIs stipulated good governance reforms under broad themes such as transparency, inclusiveness, and public participation.[89]

First, in an apparent attempt to address the criticism levelled against SAPs, the BWIs made effective public participation in policymaking, a key aspect of good governance.[90] For instance, the World Bank framed

[84] Id. at xii.

[85] Id. at 143.

[86] *See 1997 World Development Report Bank, supra* note 4.

[87] IMF, *supra* note 82 at 1.

[88] Address by Michel Camdessus, Managing Director, IMF, at the 1997 National Banks Convention, Argentina, May 21, 1997. Camdessus clarified that the first-and-second-generation reforms should not be seen as sequential; indeed, the institution building typically associated with the second generation often can, and should occur in parallel with the first generation. Id.

[89] *See* IMF, *supra* note 82.

[90] World Bank, *World Development Report – Attacking poverty, 2000/2001* 129 (2000).

"voicelessness and powerlessness" (e.g., of women), as key dimensions of poverty, and thus, integrated empowerment with market-oriented development.[91] The World Bank claimed that since political freedoms favourably influence the lives and capabilities of citizens, especially poor ones, they have great potential to reduce poverty.[92] On this basis, the Bank called for those institutions:

> that ensure democratic processes function as they should: an independent judiciary empowered to uphold the constitution and rule of law and strong parliamentary institutions with the capacity to monitor the executive.[93]

In the next section, I will show that this effective public participation notion was conceived by the BWIs as a smokescreen to secure public "ownership" of their pre-existing, standard economic policies. What is more, in section 5.4, I will show how this participation notion landed on political shores, masked as a seemingly neutral standard to modernize constitution-making in the Third World. So, as we saw in chapter 3, here too, we have a practice that is essentially fiscally oriented, but held out as modern, or civilized, because it aims ostensibly at advancing Third World women's social plight.

Next, to ensure that states threw open their natural resources to private investment, the Bank urged those with ample resources of oil, minerals, diamonds, and so on, to create "good institutions:" those that are "participatory, credible and accountable."[94] Indeed, the Bank went on to clearly call for constitutional and legal systems and representative political systems that anchor good institutions thereby allowing groups to work out their interests through mechanisms other than violence.[95] However, an economic purpose was put forth for such "good (political) institutions:" they were deemed to be critical to transforming ethnic diversity into a development asset.[96]

Finally, promoting private sector activity lay behind making "transparency and accountability" key good governance criteria.[97]

91 Id. at 15.
92 Id. at 112.
93 Id. at 113
94 Id. at 127, 128
95 Id.
96 Id. at 127.
97 Id.

Accordingly, states were advised to rely on the constitutional "separation of powers"—a principle that the Bank itself concedes has "more recently come to the forefront of development discourse."[98] For only then would they (states) be able to create strong, independent legislatures, executives, and judiciaries anti-corruption commissions, and other regulatory bodies.[99] And only then, would they be able to limit the ability of the government to act arbitrarily in budget deficits, and regulation of financial markets.[100] This thrust to constitutionally crush corruption and/or achieve accountability in the contexts outlined above thus, had a clear economic rationale. However, it was explained as being essential for empowering the poor to hold the government accountable for its actions, and use of resources and improved service delivery.[101]

In these ways, the BWIs prescribed a constitution that enshrined market economy, property rights, the separation of powers principle, an independent judiciary, central bank, and an anti-corruption commission, and permitted privatization of natural resources –as preconditions for economic growth, development, i.e., poverty reduction. And in doing so, the BWIs in effect, prescribed Western liberal market constitutional democracy as a means of promoting such growth or reducing poverty—a point, I will revisit in this section's final paragraph. Which will reveal that, till the present day, the BWIs treat this inherently political issue as non-political.[102] Further, the term "governance" implies not any form of political regime, but one that ensures macro-economic performance. And although political governance was twinned with economic governance, it was treated as being inherently economic. Finally, a normative dimension addressing the quality of governance was introduced in a way that "portrayed development without politics," thus giving governance a "false sense of political neutrality."[103]

[98] World Bank, *Reforming Public Institutions and Strengthening Governance - A World Bank Strategy* 13 (2000).

[99] *See* World Bank, *supra* note 90 at 113.

[100] *Id.* at 102–103.

[101] *See* World Bank, *supra* note 98.

[102] *See* Heather Marquette, *The Creeping Politicization of the World Bank: The Case of Corruption* 52 Pol. Studies 413, 419 (2004).

[103] Carlos Santiso, *Good Governance and Aid Effectiveness: The World Bank and Conditionality*, 7 (1) The Georgetown Public Policy Rev. 1, 4 (2001).

Consequently, reforms on which aid came to be conditional, moved from the economic realm to the political arena. Accordingly, the World Bank's lending policy, which was renamed as "development policy lending," covered considerations of both economic factors and political structures.[104]

So conceptualized, the Constitution was ready to be launched in 1999 as a development understood as a market-oriented poverty reduction strategy. Understandably, but un-noticed by many, prior to launching the PRSPs in 1999, the World Bank devoted its 1997 report to underscoring the Constitution's importance. Conversely, twenty years later, the Bank titles its 2017 report: "Governance *and* the Law:" devoting it to assessing this very Constitution's implementation by debtor-states.[105]

## 5.3.1 The PRSPs (Conditionalities) Launch the Western Liberal Constitution

The launching vehicle arrived, as noted in the previous section, in 1999: PRSPs. PRSPs are policy documents produced by debtor states, outlining the economic and social programmes to reduce poverty, to be implemented over a three-year period. Put simply, they are built on loan agreements with conditions.[106] And each loan supports a specific program of reforms, based on which, the Bank negotiates a policy matrix [Matrix] with the borrower.[107] Of course, the Matrix's governance section spells out a "specific priority action" (conditionality): making the Constitution, which is the ROL Framework's key criterion (*see* Chapter 1, section 1.5). (I will demonstrate this further below regarding Rwanda). Indeed, PRSPs endorse the Constitution, rooted in the rule of law.

[104] World Bank, Operational Manual, OP 8.60—Development Policy Lending, August 8, 2004.

[105] *See* Stephen Gill, *New Constitutionalism, Democratization, and Global Political Economy*, 10 (1) Pacifica Review: Peace, Security, & Global Change 23 (1999); 2017 World Development Report, *supra* note 4.

[106] *See* Poverty Reduction Strategy Papers (PRSPs): A Rough guide 5 (undated) available at the Bretton Woods Project website.

[107] Id. at 4–5.

Meanwhile, other developments reinforced PRSPs' importance. PRSPs were made the basis for the BWIs' lending programmes, and for debt relief for Heavily Indebted Poor Countries (HIPCs). Put simply, all HIPC countries needed to produce a PRSP as a basis for concessional lending. Under the HIPC framework, they have to devise an interim PRSP to reach their decision point and secure partial debt relief.[108] Given this, and other features discussed in the previous paragraph, PRSPs triggered constitution-making in both post-conflict and stable states. Therefore, making the Constitution became a key milestone in HIPCs' PRSP periods.[109]

As a way of showing they had learnt from SAPs' failures, the BWIs stipulated that PRSPs build on existing national plans.[110] They also stipulated that PRSPs be "country-driven, results and partnership-oriented, and based on a long-term perspective of institutional reforms in governance and accountability."[111] But what remains unsaid is this: debtor states are forced to accept the BWIs' pre-determined macro-economic framework—whose implementation requires the Constitution. In fact, the BWIs' Boards approve PRSPs, based on the following two criteria:

> 1) A coherent policy strategy for poverty reduction[112] (i.e., the BWIs' pre-determined macro-economic framework); and
>
> 2) how governance issues are addressed[113] (i.e., whether a commitment to create the Framework/adopt the Constitution, (both, defined in Chapter 1) is expressed.

In this way, the Constitution morphed into a conditionality.

What does the aforesaid reveal? First, that PRSPs are simply "government-led."[114] Indeed, debtor states are barred from devising a poverty reduction strategy as they deem fit. Instead, they are compelled to embrace the macro-economic framework pre-determined by

[108] Id. at 4.

[109] Id. The PRSP period runs for three years from the date of the full PRSP.

[110] Id.

[111] Id. at 2.

[112] Id. at 5.

[113] Id.

[114] Id. at 2.

the BWIs. Second, as I shall show in section 5.4, the "national plans," on which the PRSPs are supposed to build, are scarcely formulated by countries as they see fit. On the contrary, they are simply the "UN's business plans to support the PRSP."[115] In fact, the national plan rule was coined to commence the Constitution's promotion by the UNDP. Meanwhile, since no uniform threshold exists regarding public participation, the degree of participation, the UNDP helps to evoke, is irrelevant.[116] In this way, PRSPs build ownership around pre-existing, BWIs-preferred standard economic policies.[117] They create within poor Third States, a constitutional environment that best suits powerful Western states.

Take Rwanda, a HIPC. Aided by the UNDP, Rwanda formulated and submitted an Interim PRSP in November 2000, wherein it pledged to make a "new," i.e., the Constitution.[118] Its 2002 PRSP (Matrix), listed this commitment as a priority action.[119] In 2003, it adopted a new Constitution with UNCA, and its PRSP progress report accordingly, stated this:

> *10.6. Constitutional Reform & Democratization*
>
> The nation's new Constitution was officially adopted on June 4th 2003. As a result of the new Constitution, several changes have been introduced.[120]

So far, we have seen, how PRSPs operate as conditionality instruments in the sphere of lending. But significantly, their impact extends much further. First, under the Heavily Indebted Poor Countries Initiative, the BWIs made adopting and implementing the PRSPs the key step (at both stages, "decision point" and "completion point"), for states seeking debt-relief.[121] Put simply, to receive interim debt relief, a country

[115] *See infra* note 165.

[116] *See* PRSPs, *supra* note 107 at 6.

[117] *Id.* at 4.

[118] *See Rwanda Interim Poverty Reduction Strategy Paper* ¶17–18 (November 2000).

[119] *See Rwanda Poverty Reduction Strategy Paper* 35 (2002).

[120] *See Rwanda: PRSP Annual Progress Report* 75 (2004).

[121] *See* IMF Fact Sheet: *Debt Relief under the Heavily Indebted Poor Countries (HIPC) Initiative*, 8 March 2018.

must have reached the "decision-point": developed a PRSP: established a track record of reform and sound policies through IMF-and-World-Bank-supported programs. To reach the so-called completion point, i.e., receive the full amount of debt-relief, a country must carry out the structural (governance) reforms agreed upon at the decision point, and satisfactorily implement a PRSP for one year. At the completion point, debt relief becomes irrevocable.[122] According to the IMF, as of March 2018, the total amount of debt relief it has delivered under the HIPC initiative amounts to about $3.4 billion in nominal terms.[123] It helps to see Tables 6.3 and 6.4 in Chapter 6.

Second, PRSPs validate the BWIs-produced knowledge about the Third World.[124] Second, to obtain any type of credit, Third World states need to undergo some kind of a Fund/Bank inspection and demonstrate commitment to their policies.[125] Third, operation-wise, the 2005 Paris Declaration on Aid Effectiveness set common indicators of effective aid. This coupled with the World Bank's "big-footed" role has led to a "functional integration of the three major [the WB, DFID & USAID] and more aid systems" and the standardization of aid.[126] As is evidenced by the manner in which, the UN and non-UN donors took coordinated action in reconstructing conflict-torn Sierra Leone along common lines:

> The Bank was closely involved in developing the key structural reforms, including budget and expenditure management reform, civil service restructuring, debt sustainability analysis, and institutional and governance reform. In addition, successive Fund programs were coordinated with the EU, which provided budget support and TA, Paris Club creditors (debt relief), and DFID (TA and budget support) –IMF.[127]

[122] Id.

[123] *See* IMF, Fact Sheet: The Multilateral Debt Relief Initiative (undated).

[124] *See*, e.g., IMF, Country Report No. 10/336 (2010).

[125] Id.

[126] *See* the Paris Declaration on Aid Effectiveness (2005); Gita-Steiner Khamsi, *For All by All? The World Bank's Global Framework for Education*, in The World bank and education 7 (Steven J. Klees ed., Sense Publishers, 2012).

[127] *See* IMF, Staff guidance note on the Fund's engagement with countries in fragile situations (IMF, 2012).

[Note: TA=technical assistance; Governance reform includes constitutional reform – see Chapter 6].

Fourth, PRSPs function as surveillance mechanisms. They provide an assessment of macroeconomic, structural, and trade policies, and of potential financial risk. And are, thus, increasingly relied upon by other state creditors, commercial lenders, development institutions, and state and multilateral aid agencies.[128] It is telling that, this author found valuable details about constitutional reforms in virtually all UNCA recipients-states, in BWIs' documents: PRSPs and other surveillance mechanisms such as Article IV consultations.

It helps to note that, in 1999, Asia-Pacific's regional powers (e.g., Australia) and the Asian Development Bank (ADB), embraced the UN-and-the-BWIs' good governance definition and Poverty Reduction Strategy (PRS),[129] positing that states can secure good governance through constitutional reform.[130] So too, did the African Development Bank.[131] What is more, in 2011, the U.S. prescribed the UN-BWIs' good governance for MENA states, in order that they may blossom with UNCA, into full-fledged Western liberal (market) democracies.[132]

### *'New Legal Imperialism' = 'New Constitutionalism'*

The Constitution's internationalized making illustrates the "new legal imperialism," i.e., how Third World states—entrapped as they are by "contractual modes of domination—agree to, and enforce, the terms of their own subjection."[133] In fact, this is precisely why I argued in

[128] Id.

[129] *See* ADB, "The Poverty Reduction Strategy of the Asian Development Bank" (2004); AUSAID, "Good governance: Guiding principles for implementation" (Australia, 2000).

[130] Bjorn Dressel, *Strengthening governance through constitutional reform*, 13 ADB-The Governance Brief 1–2 (2005).

[131] *See* AfrDB, "Bank group policy on good governance" (1999).

[132] *See* Fact Sheet: G-8 Action on the Deauville Partnership with Arab Countries in Transition (May 2011).

[133] *See* Peter Fitzpatrick, *Modernism and the Grounds of Law* 212 (Cambridge University Press, 2001).

section 5.0 that the UN's premise that UNCA is offered in response to states' "requests" is misleading, to say the least. Indeed, the BWIs' conditionalities constitutionalized in UNCA-recipients-debtor-states (see next chapter, Table 6.4) illustrates how sovereign politico-economic decision-making authority has slipped from Third World states to the BWIs, thus, perpetuating their economic dependency.

Here comes Professor Stephen Gill whose legitimate lament that students of political economy have missed the constitutional aspects of global restructuring resonated with me. Indeed, this chapter reveals what mechanism is used to 'restructure' Third World states, stable and conflict-torn: UNCA. Next, my findings (Table 6.3) affirm what Gill and other (Constitutional law) scholars (for example, Upendra Baxi, Ran Hirschl and Jim Tully) 1) point to: a post-1989 constitutionalization-of-property-rights-trend (Trend); 2) trace that Trend to: the incestuous relationship amongst hegemonic political leaders and economic elites (e.g., the World Bank)[134]; and opine: (3) such constitutionalization immunizes national economic policy-making from democratic oversight.[135] Based on 1)–3), they conclude that such constitutionalization does not necessarily herald the dawn of social justice.[136] In sum, UNCA promotes what Gill calls 'new constitutionalism'.[137] Finally, my findings unite with prominent post-colonial international law scholar, B. S. Chimni's argument that the UN Family restructures Third World states in tune with the transnational capitalist class' neoliberal standards – see Chapter 8.

## 5.4 The UNDP Internationalizes the Western Liberal Constitution

As noted in section 5.0, to be internationalized, the Constitution was first positioned as a conflict prevention tool, and next fitted into the UN development system. In positioning it as a conflict prevention tool, the

134 *See* Ran Hirschl, *The Political Origins of the New Constitutionalism*, 11 (1) Indiana Journal of Global Law Studies 71–72 (2004).

135 Id.

136 Id. Upendra Baxi, *The Future of Human* Rights (Oxford University Press, 2001).

137 Stephen Gill, *Market Civilization, New Constitutionalism and World Order, in* New Constitutionalism and World Order 29 (Stephen Gill & Claire Cutler, eds., Cambridge University Press, 2012).

UN followed the route laid out by its 'brothers': the BWIs (see Chapter 1). Before proceeding, it helps to note that the Constitution's internationalized making in "post-conflict" states occurs in a relatively straightforward way—via a Security Council mandate—ostensibly to prevent conflict, an international law and policy (*hereinafter* Law and Policy) goal. Knowing this much, will suffice to understand projects so mandated, and discussed in the next chapter: Chapter 6. (Chapter 8 analyzes UNCA's use in the post-conflict context to implement law and Policy.) Whereas UNCA's use in the development context/stable states, by the UNDP is virtually uncharted. Therefore, in this section, I will foreground the UNDP's role, considering for continuity's sake, how it frames its constitutional assistance in terms of implementing Law and Policy.

As previously discussed, by 1992, SAPs' harsh measures had triggered conflict in over fourteen African countries, causing thousands of deaths, and resulting in more than eight million refugees, returnees, and displaced persons (*see* Chapter 1).[138] The UN, having attributed this havoc to the Third World's bad governance, more particularly, its deficient constitutions, called for replacing them with a universal constitution potentially fit to promote sustainable peace: the Constitution.[139] What is more, perceiving third world states to be unable and unwilling to create its preferred constitution, the UN positioned itself to build their capacity to do so. Based on this rationale, in the early 1990s, it harnessed a 'core conflict prevention activity' to the entire peace, security, and development architecture: UNCA.[140]

## 5.4.1 The Constitution's Internationalized Making=Development=Market-Oriented Poverty Reduction Activity

In preventing conflict, the UN says that 'no actor or state acts alone'.[141] Resting its holistic approach on this idea, it defined 'conflict' broadly to

[138] Report of the Secretary-General, *The causes of conflict and the promotion of durable peace and sustainable development in Africa,* ¶ 5 U.N. Doc., A/52/871 – S/1998/318 (13 April 1998).

[139] Id. at ¶ 76–77.

[140] *See Progress Report of the Secretary-General on the prevention of armed conflict,* Annex 32, 38, 40, U.N. Doc. A/60/891 (18 July 2006).

[141] *See* UN *Report, supra* note 2 at 2.

include 'structural causes'.[142] Accordingly, it demarcated three types of prevention strategies: structural, operational, and systemic. Structural prevention required programs aimed at promoting development and remedying governance.[143]

Given this broad way in which conflict was defined (*see* above), in addition to the Security Council, other UN family members were roped in to lend their mighty hands to preventing conflict: the Economic and Social Council, the UNDP, and the BWIs.[144] In this way, development (understood as market-oriented poverty reduction), acquired a preventive hue, and conflict prevention was woven into the work of all the UN agencies such as the UNDP.[145] Accordingly, the market-oriented Constitution came to be equated with development—just as it did, (whether imposed by the colonial power or the PMC), during the Mandates System. In this way, assistance towards making it, which as noted in Chapter 1, was understood as a conflict prevention activity, morphed into a development one, in the post-Cold War era.

Conflict prevention, says the UNDP, begins and ends with the promotion of human development, which is:

> a world where all human beings on earth, —in this and future generations, — can live free from fear, hunger and poverty.[146]

So then, ongoing violence, the immediate political symptom of conflict, does not alone impede development. Rather, government deadlocks may impede development because they block reforms to, for instance, outdated or contradictory legislation affecting free markets and women for instance.[147] It is to remove these challenges, says the UNDP, that it establishes and convenes:

> formal and informal opportunities for dialogue to address specific conflicts, and build consensus around *constitutional* or governance reforms.[148]

142 *Report of the Secretary-General, Prevention of Armed Conflict,* ¶6 U.N. Doc. A/55/985-S/2001/574 (7 June 2001).

143 Id.

144 *See* UN, *supra* note 143 at annex.

145 Id.

146 UNDP, *Sustainable Development: Time for Action* 2 (undated).

147 UNDP, *Changing nature of conflict: Priorities for UNDP response* 1 (July 2013).

148 UNDP Fast Facts, *Conflict Prevention* 1 (February 2013).

This marriage of politics and development politicized the roles of UN Country Teams (UNCTs) and the UN Resident Coordinators (UNRCs) heading them.[149] Which the UN General Assembly endorsed, framing such politicized roles of the UNCTs as a means of strengthening national capacities for conflict prevention.[150]

Accordingly, UNRCs increasingly began to address ethnic tensions, election-related violence, land disputes, and other forms of competition for natural resources.[151] Starting from 1995, UNRCs received support from Peace and Development Advisers (PDAs) in addressing these types of national tensions in many countries including, Fiji, Kenya, Yemen, Maldives and Zimbabwe.[152] Furthermore, in states with peace operations, the UNRCs started to enjoy the status of the Secretary-General's Deputy Special Representatives.[153] Their peace-making tasks included, drawing into the peace process a wide spectrum of political actors, donors, and international financial institutions such as the World Bank.[154] UNRCs can also:

> facilitate participatory forums for national dialogue that allow all actors to have a say in the shaping of ...a constitutional ... framework for good and accountable governance.[155]

For instance, in Sierra Leone, the Secretary-General urged the UNCT to assume the departing peace operation's constitutional assistance, with a view to complete the ongoing constitutional reforms.[156]

[149] *See generally* UNDG, Synthesis of Resident Coordinator Annual Reports 2008 (2009).

[150] *See* UNFPA, *Guidelines on women empowerment for the UN Resident Coordinator System* ¶5 (undated) (Referring to UNGA Res. 49/128).

[151] *See* Chetan Kumar, *Building National "Infrastructures for peace:" UN Assistance for internally negotiated solutions for violent conflict, in* Peacemaking: From Practice to Theory 384, 386 (Susan Allen, ed., ABC-CLIO, 2011).

[152] Id.

[153] Douglas Lindores, "Enhancing the functioning of the UN Resident Coordinator system" 15 (2012) [slides].

[154] *See* UN, *Handbook on UN Multidimensional peacekeeping operations* 202 (UN, 2003).

[155] Id.

[156] *Eleventh report of the Secretary-General on the United Nations Integrated Peacebuilding Office in Sierra Leone*, § VIII, A U.N. Doc., S/2013/547 (12 Sept. 2013).

*Preventing Conflict through Women's Participation*

As we saw in section 5.3, the idea of public participation was conceived by the BWIs, as a smokescreen for securing the public's ownership around their pre-determined macro-economic policies (PRSPs). The Security Council (Council) propelled this idea onto political shores, masked as a neutral constitution-making standard, but intended essentially for the Third World. Indeed, within a few months of the PRSPs' inauguration, the Council passed a resolution widely known as just '1325'.[157] 1325 urged states to prevent conflict by making transparent, inclusive, and participatory not only their constitutional but also their peace, electoral, and developmental processes.[158] 1325 urged states to include women in these processes.[159] And achieving this became the UNDP's ostensible goal for its constitutional assistance.[160]

### 5.4.2 Poverty Reduction Strategy Papers and UN Development Assistance Frameworks (UNDAF): The Two Contexts for Making the Constitution

Constitutional assistance as a development activity brings us to the context for its use, i.e., making the Constitution: the four integrated processes, PRSPs, Common Country Assessments (CCAs), Post-Conflict Needs Assessments (PCNAs), and UNDAFs.

We already know that PRSPs are "strategies," which launch the Constitution and make their appearance in the development context because development equates with poverty reduction. Indeed, UNCTs team up with the BWIs in helping debtor states to prepare PRSPs.[161] In fact, UNCTs are encouraged to do so. In this way, the UNDP uses its constitutional assistance to help states implement the BWIs' conditionalities. Thus, the formulation of PRSPs triggers the Constitution's

[157] *See* S.C. Res. 1325 (2000), SCOR, 4213th mtg., U.N. Doc. S/Res/1325 (Oct. 2000).

[158] Id. at ¶8 (a)-(c).

[159] Id.

[160] UNDP, Constitutional Support Guidance Note 35 (2014).

[161] *See* any PRSP document's cover page.

making, and conversely, PRSPs' implementation equals making the Constitution. Or put differently, a debtor state's PRSP is the first milestone in its constitution-making process.

Again, as I shall show, PRSPs intersect with CCAs, PCNAs, and UNDAFs in this area: constitution-making. CCAs are analytical documents that the UNCTs and other partners develop with the governments.[162] CCAs provide a common comprehensive picture of the development situation in a country, identify gaps in norms, institutions, and constitutions, and describe how they affect the fulfillment of human rights.[163] 'PRSPs can be developed in tandem with the CCA or feed into the CCA process'.[164]

PCNAs are regarded as a 'special type of CCA'.[165] PCNAs are political processes co-launched by the UN, UNCTs, and the World Bank to mobilize development assistance to countries in transition from violent conflict to peace. Therefore, PCNAs cover political issues including peace agreements, creation of a legitimate market economy, and promotion of national dialogue.[166] (PCNAs produce documents against which individual donors make pledges).[167] Herein comes the Constitution, whose making in post-conflict states, typically results from a peace agreement's implementation, which I will demonstrate in the next chapter.

UNDAFs are essentially obligatory documents.[168] They are the 'UN's business plans to support PRSPs' implementation.'[169] In preparing UNDAFs, UNCTs are urged to use the following check-list:

> Are there any new opportunities to get the buy-in of key decision-makers in government or civil society and ally with them to influence national priorities?

162 UNDG, "How to prepare an UNDAF?" 4 (January 2010).

163 Id. at 20–21, 24–27.

164 *See* First UNDG Guidance Note to UNCTs on the PRSP (undated) (Annex 1: "Examples of the linkages between CCA-UNDAF-PRSP").

165 *See* World Bank *et al.*, *Practical Guide to Multilateral Needs Assessments in Post-Conflict Situations* 4 & foreword (World Bank, 2004).

166 Id. at 6.

167 Id. at 4.

168 Since the government is required to sign off on the UNDAF, its content, in effect, also represents the government's views.

169 *See* UNDG, *supra* note 165 at 2.

> Are there any major changes in government expected, *e.g.*, through elections or a new constitution?[170]

And so, UNCTs may – as a long-term conflict-prevention measure, promote good governance in two ways. First, they use the UNDAF process to propose changes to existing constitutions (e.g., enshrine National Human Rights Institutions (NHRIs) and anti-corruption commissions).[171] Next, they help organize "national dialogues" and tutor the participants in a manner that manufactures consent for these conditionalities.[172]

Take the HIPC, Bhutan. Its first PRSP (2004) (prepared with UNDP support) listed making a new constitution as one of the key strategies.[173] Prepared by the UNCT in 2008, its UNDAF listed "outcome four" as follows:

> UNDAF OUTCOME FOUR: ... The country will undergo major political transition with the adoption of the Constitution in 2008. This is expected to bring about fundamental changes in the governance....[174]

This is why and how the CCAs, UNDAFs, PCNAs and the PRSPs came to constitute the context for the making of the Constitution, in post-conflict and more than a dozen stable states. And, where constitution-making in certain post-conflict states has lagged, the UNDP takes over residual constitutional assistance functions from the departing UN peace mission. In these ways, the UN Family slipped UNCA into development assistance, and thus avoided treading the inflammatory path of discounting national sovereignty, and instead supposedly worked in lockstep with it.

170 *See* UNDG, *supra* note 163 at 18.

171 *See* Plan of Action, strengthening human rights-related UN action at country level 13–14, (undated) *at:* http://www.un.org/events/action2/action2plan.pdf; UNDP, *Anti-corruption Practice Note* 5, 13 (February 2004).

172 *See e.g.*, UNDP, Support to the National Dialogue during the transitional period in Yemen, *available at:* http://www.ye.undp.org/content/yemen/en/home/operations/projects/democratic_governance/support-to-the-comprehensive-national-dialogue-during-the-transi.html.

173 IMF Country Report No. 04/246 9 (2004).

174 UN, "United Nations Development Assistance Framework for the Kingdom of Bhutan 2008-2012" 10 (2007).

To conclude, my analysis of the relevant periods (*see* sections 5.1 and 5.3–5.4.) suggests that the activity of internationalized economic decision-making is an "institution" or "established practice." Indeed, FPs sought to use the Third World for its resources, both before and after decolonization. Accordingly, they framed sovereign Third World states' domestic constitutional issues (e.g., NRG and FI) as 'economic' and 'international development' ones that required international regulation, ostensibly to "develop" and modernize them, for despite becoming independent, they had supposedly failed to develop. This internationalization of economic decision-making in the LDCs, reflected, required and resulted in the Constitution's internationalization. Which during 1983-1999 and 1999 till now, occurred through the BWIs' two similar, consecutive but differently named conditionalities: SAPs and PRSPs respectively. The FPs internationalized the Constitution ostensibly to promote free markets, rule of law, good governance and women's rights in the LDCs and thereby develop them. This internationalization of economic decision-making/the Constitution's internationalization created, and was carried out through the 'developed'/'least developed countries' Paradigm.

### 5.4.3 Conflict and Development (Understood as Market-Oriented Poverty Reduction) Constitutionalized

As we can see, the good governance story is not about the internationalization of the rule of law or development, but about the internationalization of the Constitution. I set out a few preliminary conclusions here, (which I will revisit in later chapters).

- The Constitution is being imposed to promote rule of law (economic liberalization) and market-oriented development.
- According to the UN, the Constitution promotes development understood as poverty reduction. Conversely, it is claimed, development so understood, promotes constitutionalism and the rule of law. By extension, in implementing the PRSPs' reforms (i.e., BWIs' conditionalities), states are understood to be promoting respect for the constitution. And where there is a constitutional 'breakdown', the international community prescribes implementing the BWIs' conditionalities (that is, PRSPs' reforms) for restoration.

- Since the Constitution is ostensibly used to curb conflict, the implicit notion is that a free market— the Constitution's salient feature—promotes peace, or at least has the potential to do so.
- As a result, of the above-noted ideas, development and conflict are constitutionalized. (I argue that conflict is 'constitutionalized' when conflict is ended through a peace agreement that mandates the making of the Constitution.)
- We learned from Tony Anghie's seminal work about the 'economization of sovereignty' during, and by the Mandates System.[175] I argue that the aforesaid account about the Constitution's use to curb conflict, results in the constitutionalization, and 'economization' of conflict. As a result, as I will illustrate in the next chapter, the UN interprets the breakdown of constitutional order (in the wake of conflict) in economic terms, and therefore, conceives market-oriented reforms (as prescribed by the PRSPs) for its restoration: the Constitution.

This brings us to the good governance story's final part, where I briefly trace the events that led to UNCA becoming public, after working silently and undetected for almost 16 years.

## 5.5 2009: UNCA Brought Out of the Closet: Theory Follows Practice

A series of key world conferences and summits (hereinafter referred to as Conferences) that took place from 1990 to 2005 endorsed the Constitution's internationalized making (UNCA), ostensibly in response to the Third World's supposed incapacities for creating good governance.

### 5.5.1 UNCA Endorsed by World Conferences: 1990–2005

Those Conferences dealt with women, children, indigenous groups, and environment, and social and sustainable development.[176] They

[175] *See* Anghie, *Colonialism and the Birth of International Institutions: Sovereignty, Economy, and the Mandate System of the League of Nations* 34 NYU J. of Int'l L & P 513, 581 (2002).

[176] *See* UNDESA, Development Agenda: Development for all (2007).

endorsed democracy, rule of law (that is, economic liberalization) and development, and human rights as interdependent and mutually reinforcing. In this way, they articulated a common development agenda.[177]

The aforesaid Conferences (like the LDC conferences) consistently recommended that the Third World states should take full responsibility for their own economic development. However, they made the international community's support conditional on these states creating the Framework (defined in Chapter 1). For instance, the Children's summit, the first in the series, affirmed in 1990, that child protection required the rule of law.[178] As a result, states requiring international support had to fit their child protection strategies within privatization, and other neoliberal policies endorsed in the PRSPs, which by 1999, had become the accepted way of tackling poverty. Similarly, the Conference on women, the fourth of its kind, which was held in Beijing in 1995, firmly urged the UN to strengthen states' capacity to promote the rule of law, to prevent violations against women.[179] However, subsequent UN Reports have shown that rule of law promotion (economic liberalization), caused the feminization of poverty.[180]

The Millennium Assembly (2000) and the World Summit (Summit) (2005), the series' last two global conferences, catapulted UNCA explicitly onto the UN agenda in 2006.[181] The Summit Outcome affirmed that the market-oriented rule of law was the all-important framework for advancing the MDGs. It also reaffirmed commitment to 1325 (2000), which as previously mentioned (see section 5.4), urged states to include women in constitution-making processes, and therefore, peace, electoral, and developmental ones.[182] A summary of some of the main commitments of the Millennium Assembly, such as empowering women and slashing poverty by half by 2015, became two of the

[177] Id.

[178] *See* World Declaration on the survival, protection and development of Children (1990).

[179] *See* Beijing Declaration, 1995.

[180] *Report of the Special Rapporteur on Violence against Women, Its Causes and Consequences*, U.N. Doc. A/HRC/11/6 (May 18, 2009).

[181] *See* UN Millennium Declaration; Summit Outcome, 2005 (Outcome).

[182] *See* Outcome, *supra* note 182 at ¶116.

ten Millennium Development Goals (MDGs).[183] The MDGs were in turn integrated into the UN Development Agenda. From 1990 to 2005, a synthesis was sought in the aforesaid ways between neo-liberal ideas and poverty-reduction strategies. Reflecting that synthesis, the Summit proposed a 'Rule of Law Assistance Unit' (Unit) at the United Nations to ensure that every nation has the capacity to respect the rule of law.[184]

#### *5.5.1.1 UNCA Institutionalized: The UN-Rule of Law Unit*

In this way, 2005 ushered in the right moment for outing UNCA, which had been silently operating for more than a decade. In fact, in 2005 a UN Committee (Committee) was tasked with formulating the UN's 'policy' for internationalizing the Framework (see Chapter 1, section 1.5).[185] The Committee was tasked with rationalizing UNCA's use in *sovereign* states. Toward this end, policy papers and questionnaires were circulated within the UN Secretariat.[186] The Committee's deliberations culminated in the creation of a focal point for UNCA in 2006: the Unit. With a view to promote preferred standards, the Unit released two allied guidance notes on UNCA and the Rule of Law in 2009.[187] The latter note endorses the Framework (see Chapter 1), which subsumes the Constitution under the rule of law.

As mentioned in Chapter 4, guidance notes are the successors of operationally oriented documents that the former UN Secretary-General, the late Dag Hammarskjöld recommended should guide UNCA, –or International Executive Rule (IER) practices as he called it.

#### *5.5.1.2 The Mediation Support Unit: Standard-Setting*

Standard-setting brings us to the body created in 2006 to promote the Constitution in poor, conflict-torn or post-conflict Third World states:

183 For MDGs, see http://www.un.org/en/events/pastevents/millennium_summit.shtml.

184 *See* Outcome, *supra* note 182 at ¶134 (e).

185 *See* Security Council Report, "Special Research Report No. 2," 3 (5 October 2007).

186 Id.

187 Although the UNCA Note was meant for internal circulation, this author gained access to its contents in 2008.

The Mediation Support Unit [MSU]. Understandably, the MSU was nestled in the Department of Political Affairs (DPA), which plays a central role in UN efforts to prevent and resolve deadly conflict around the world. And, it (MSU) comprised a standby team of experts (Experts), fully available at all times (24 hours a day/7 days a week), which was deployed within seventy-two hours of a conflict, erupting in any part of the world, and for up to one month.[188] In what areas might MSU's team possess expertise? The answer is: Those very topics that cover the conditionalities: wealth sharing, fiscal decentralization, and so on.[189] (This triggered a demand for relevant experts who in turn wrote a lot on federalism, NRG and so on.) Expertise in "wealth sharing" and fiscal federalism, as we know, is essential to crafting the Constitution's investor-friendly provisions, and achieving privatization of natural resources, respectively.[190]

However, what I am concerned with, is how UNCA's use to promote these conditionalities was portrayed? For instance, Lynn Pascoe, the UN's Deputy Secretary-General identified peace processes, and constitution-making, as ideal entry points for the Experts to steer negotiations about natural resources along good governance lines, and thereby prevent conflict.[191] Moreover, the UN Secretariat (UN) claimed that the MSU was created in response to a 'growing demand for the formal mediation of disputes, and professional cross-cutting support to "good offices" activities ....'[192] It was created as a 'center of expertise, best practice, and knowledge management on mediation-related activities.'[193]

Within a decade of the MSU's creation, explanations such as those noted above, which frame UNCA in terms of implementing Law and

[188] UN-DPA, "*Mediation Support Unit Programme of Work 2008*" (2 January 2008).

[189] Id.

[190] World Bank, "Decentralization and Subnational regional economies" *at:* http://www1.worldbank.org/publicsector/decentralization/political.htm.

[191] Press release, "Security Council underscores need for peacekeeping mandates to consider helping states prevent illegal exploitation of natural resources from fueling conflict," U.N. Doc. SC/9060 2 (25 June 2007).

[192] *See* DPA, *supra* note 189 at 1.

[193] Id.

Policy, helped normalize its use in sovereign states in the twenty-first century. What is more, in 2009, the UN unhesitatingly and explicitly declared that the Constitution's internationalized constitution-making — and concomitantly, UNCA —is here to stay.[194] This declaration is a fitting end to this story of "good governance."

## 5.6 Conclusion

This chapter has revealed what the good governance story is essentially about: internationalized constitution-making as a conditionality to promote the Constitution (with its property rights). It also reveals that in addition to 'post-conflict', the better known context for internationalized constitution-making, there is a second context: development assistance. And that the UNDP ostensibly offers UNCA to implement Law and Policy. Indeed, this story mirrors the earlier European initiatives of internationalizing economic decision-making in the Third World with a view to bring commerce, civilization, and (market-oriented) 'development' to the Third World. (Chapter 9 will analyze how the Constitution has been internationalized with a view to 'civilize' Third World states). In this way, this chapter sets the context for Chapter 6, which shows how, from 1989–2019, more than forty, poor stable and conflict-torn Third World states, produced the Constitution with UNCA: to secure debt-relief.

194 UN, *supra* note 1 at 2.

6

# United Nations Constitutional Assistance

## An 'Institution'

### 6.0 Introduction

This chapter poses the question: Is UNCA an "institution," that is, an "established practice"? In this way, it addresses the first component of my overarching plan: To conceptualize UNCA as a "Policy Institution," as defined by Ralph Wilde. I began answering this question in Chapter 4, where I traced UNCA's birth in Libya, and Eritrea in 1949, and its revival in 1960 in the newly decolonized Congo. Here, I complete my answer. Based on the periodicity of UNCA projects since 1945, I suggest that the practice they involve—the Constitution's internationalized making—fulfills Wilde's criteria for an "established practice," thus rendering the projects an "institution."[1] In fact, from 1960, 1989–2018, UNCA has operated in 41 sovereign states and 3 territorial units. It has enabled:

- 26 states and 3 territorial units to adopt a new constitution (including new transitional constitutions),
- 3 states, to complete their new constitutions' drafts (Solomon Islands, Guinea-Bissau & Yemen); and
- 6 states to revise their constitutions along good governance lines.

[1] Ralph Wilde, *International Territorial Administration: How Trusteeship and the Civilizing Mission Never Went Away* 36–38 (Oxford University Press, 2008). Note: This chapter will use WB, as a short form for the World Bank.

Currently, UNCA is assisting twelve states in making a new constitution, or revising their existing constitutions along good governance lines.

In fact, UNCA produces that very document, which as the highest law of the land provides the framework for international territorial administration (ITA), as defined by Wilde, and whose projects he has collectively conceptualized as an "institution."[2] Indeed, I assert that UNCA projects collectively constitute a *parent* Policy Institution – and this is why, so do ITA's.

As previously noted, the Structural Adjustment Programs (1983–1999) and Poverty Reduction Strategy Papers (PRSPs) (post-1999) launched the same conditionality: the Constitution (*see* Chapter 5). Tables 6.1–6.2

TABLE 6.1 Connecting the 2 Cs: Implementing the conditionalities = the Western liberal Constitution's internationalized making (1960, 1989–1999)

| **United Nations Constitutional Assistance projects: 1960, 1989–1999** | | | |
|---|---|---|---|
| **No.** | **UNCA-recipients-states** | **Conditionalities** | **Year, new constitution adopted/ Status of constitutional reforms (CR)** |
| ASIA | | | |
| 1. | Cambodia; UNCA-(partial) ITA | SAPs | 1993 |
| AFRICA | | | |
| 1. | Congo | IMF conditionalities | 1964 |
| 2. | Angola | SAPs | CR completed |
| 3. | Mozambique | SAPs | CR completed |
| Central America | | | |
| 1. | El Salvador | SAPs | CR completed |
| 2. | Guatemala | SAPs | CR completed |

*Note*: The Heavily Indebted Poor Countries' debt-relief initiative does not apply to the pre-1999 period.

2 Id. at Ch. 6.

**Table 6.2** Connecting the 2 Cs: Implementing the conditionalities = the Western liberal Constitution's internationalized making (1999–2019)

| UNCA projects: 1999–2019 | | | | |
|---|---|---|---|---|
| **No.** | **PRSP and UNCA-recipients states / Units** | **Interim PRSP/ its equivalent, Year** | **Full PRSP/ its equivalent, Year** | **Year, new constitution adopted/ Status of Constitutional reform (CR)** |
| ASIA | | | | |
| 1. | Afghanistan* | National Dev. Framework (Nov. 2002) | 2008 | 2004 |
| 2. | Bhutan | — | Aug. 2004 | 2008 |
| 3. | Kyrgyzstan | 2001 | 2007; 2010 (IMF's RCF) | 2010 |
| 4. | Nepal | — | Oct. 2003 | 2007 (interim constitution); 2015 |
| THE INDIAN OCEAN REGION | | | | |
| 1. | Madagascar* | Nov. 2000 | Oct. 2003; 2007 | 2010 |
| 2. | Maldives | — | January 2008 | 2008 |
| ASIA-PACIFIC | | | | |
| 1. | East-Timor (territorial unit) UNCA-plenary ITA | National Development Plan, 2001–2002 | 2005 | 2002 |
| 2. | Fiji | — | Strategic Dev. Plan, 2007–11 | 2012 |
| 3. | Nauru | — | National Sustainable Dev. Strategy, 2007–11 | CR completed |
| 4. | Papua New Guinea | IMF Conditionalities | | 2004: Bougainville's independence referendum due in 2019 |

*(Cont'd)*

TABLE 6.2 (*Cont'd*)

| UNCA projects: 1999–2019 | | | | |
|---|---|---|---|---|
| **No.** | **PRSP and UNCA-recipients states / Units** | **Interim PRSP/ its equivalent, Year** | **Full PRSP/ its equivalent, Year** | **Year, new constitution adopted/ Status of Constitutional reform (CR)** |
| 5. | Solomon Islands | National Dev. Strategy, 2013 | — | Only draft constitution (2013) is ready |
| AFRICA | | | | |
| 1. | Angola | 2002 | 2006 | 2010 |
| 2. | Burundi* | Jan. 2004 | Sept. 2005 | 2005 |
| 3. | Central African Republic (CAR)* | Dec. 2000 | Feb. 2007 | 2004 |
| 4. | Côte d'Ivoire* | Jan. 2002 | May 2009 | 2016 |
| 5. | Democratic Republic of Congo* | March 2002 | Sept. 2007 | 2005 |
| 6. | Guinea* | 2000 | 2002; 2007–2010; 2nd PRSP | 2010 |
| 7. | Guinea-Bissau* | Sept. 2000 | Oct. 2007 | 2010 |
| 8. | Kenya | July 2000 | Jan. 2005 | 2010 |
| 9. | Liberia* | Feb. 2007 | July 2008 | CR completed; parliamentary approval awaited |
| 10. | Malawi* | Aug. 2000 | 2007, 2012 | CR ongoing |
| 11. | Mali* | July 2000 | May 2002; April 2008; May 2013 | Constitution-making ongoing |
| 12. | Mozambique* | 2001 | — | 2004 |
| 13. | Rwanda* | June 1991–Dec. 1994; SAPs I-PRSP, Nov. 2000 | June 2002 | 2003 |
| 14. | Sierra Leone* | June 2001 | June 2005 | CR ongoing |

**UNCA projects: 1999–2019**

| **No.** | **PRSP and UNCA-recipients states / Units** | **Interim PRSP/ its equivalent, Year** | **Full PRSP/ its equivalent, Year** | **Year, new constitution adopted/ Status of Constitutional reform (CR)** |
|---|---|---|---|---|
| 15. | Somalia (UNCA-plenary ITA) | LICUS Initiative: Garowe Principles, I & II, Dec. 2011 | | 2012 |
| 16. | Sudan | IMF conditionalities (since 2000); 2004 | Nov. 2013 | INC 2005 New Constitution's making ongoing |
| 17. | South Sudan | *See* Sudan entry | | 2011 (Transitional Constitution); CR Ongoing |
| 18. | Gambia, The* | — | 2007–2011 (2nd PRSP) | Constitution-making began in 2018 |
| 19. | Zambia* | — | July 2002; 2006 (2nd PRSP) | CR Completed |
| 20. | Zimbabwe | Strategy for Arrears Clearance, Debt and Development for Zimbabwe (ZADDS) 2010 | | 2013 |
| MIDDLE EAST & NORTH AFRICA | | | | |
| 1. | Egypt | IMF's conditionalities | | 2014 |
| 2. | Iraq (FTA-UNCA) | IMF's conditionalities | | 2005 |
| 3. | Libya | IMF's conditionalities | | New constitution's making ongoing |
| 4. | Syria | Civil war ongoing | | Peace/ constitutional talks ongoing Oct. 2019: Constitution-making with UNCA has begun |

(*Cont'd*)

TABLE 6.2 (*Cont'd*)

| | | UNCA projects: 1999–2019 | | |
|---|---|---|---|---|
| **No.** | **PRSP and UNCA-recipients states / Units** | **Interim PRSP/ its equivalent, Year** | **Full PRSP/ its equivalent, Year** | **Year, new constitution adopted/ Status of Constitutional reform (CR)** |
| 5. | Tunisia | World Bank, Country Assistance Strategy | | 2014 |
| 6. | Yemen | 2000 | 2003–2005 | Draft constitution (2015) is ready; But conflict has resumed |
| THE CARIBBEAN REGION | | | | |
| 1. | Haiti* | 2006 | 2008 | CR ongoing |
| CENTRAL & SOUTH AMERICA | | | | |
| 1. | Bolivia* | — | | March 2001 |
| 2. | Colombia | National Development Plan (2014–2018) | | CR begins in 2017 |
| EASTERN EUROPE | | | | |
| 1. | Kosovo (UNCA-ITA) | World Bank, Country Assistance Strategy, 1999 | | 2008 |

States marked with an * have received debt-relief under the HIPC Initiative Assistance as of October 2017.
Source: IMF, Debt Relief Under the Heavily Indebted Poor Countries (HIPC) Initiative, 8 March 2018.

illustrates just this: They show how the two Cs: Conditionalities and the Constitution (hereafter "two Cs") connect. This chapter maps out the post-1989 UNCA projects under the same categories, and in the same order, that they appear in Tables 6.1–6.2. Each project's analysis will cover the events that led to UNCA, and the forms it took.[3] UNCA

[3] The processes that cover the Constitution's making, such as post-conflict needs assessment (PCNA), explained in Chapter 5, will be mentioned here, without further explanation.

typically covers: 1) political negotiation, 2) knowledge-based support (provision of drafting assistance, materials, and foreign experts' advice), and 3) public participation and consultation activities (however elementary) (*see* Chapter 1). It helps to note that transparency, anti-corruption, fiscal federalism, and so on fall within the Conditionalities; therefore, activities 1 to 3 typically involve orienting the stakeholders and/or the public about them. To preserve my chapter's analytical nature, I will refer to activities (*see* 1-2) as "UNCA's standard form." In these ways, I offer a comprehensive inventory of UNCA projects, providing details and insights that have never before been offered, let alone put together.

## 6.1 UNCA Projects 1989–1999 [Asia, Africa, and Central America]

### UN Transitional Authority in Cambodia (UNTAC), 15 March (Date of Operation) 1992 to 24 September 1993

From 1970 to 1989, Cambodia convulsed with a multi-layered internationalized civil war, prompted and sustained by repeated and cynical foreign interventions. From 1975 to 1979, a totalitarian regime—widely known as the "Khmer Rouge"—controlled Cambodia, killing more than one million people.[4] From 1979 to 1989, Vietnam occupied 80 percent of Cambodian territory (calling it the People's Republic of Kampuchea (PRK)), and finally withdrew under Soviet pressure.[5] Yet, three resistance groups (Groups), which had opposed the PRK's socialist regime, and in June 1982 formed a government in exile (Democratic Kampuchea – DK), occupied the seat reserved for Cambodia at the United Nations.[6] In 1989, the US sought to make Cambodia, economically ruined by then, constitutionally "safe for its exports."[7] (And to block the Khmer Rouge's return to power, which it had backed until then – despite its abysmal human rights record).[8] This was how prospects for peace were ushered in Cambodia.

[4] *See* UN, *The United Nations and Cambodia, 1991-1995* 5 (UN, 1995).

[5] Id.

[6] Id. at 5–6.

[7] Christopher Brady, United States Foreign Policy towards Cambodia, 1977–92: A Question of Realities 172 (St. Martin's Press, 1999).

[8] Id.

On 28 August 1990, the UN Security Council's five permanent members made a plan[9] for transforming Cambodia into a western liberal market democracy. The Groups and the Phnom Penh government in Cambodia accepted the Plan, and agreed to form the Supreme National Council (SNC) as "the unique legitimate body in which, throughout the transitional period, the national sovereignty … of Cambodia would be enshrined."[10] In October 1991, the SNC signed the Paris Accords (which embodied the Plan), and invited the UN to establish the UNTAC and to provide it with a far-reaching mandate.[11] Importantly, the Security Council specified that the factions supporting the Paris Accords alone would receive international financial assistance for reconstruction.[12]

## The Impending Western Liberal Constitution Governed and Guided (Partial) ITA

The second Paris Accord prescribed a new, that is, the Constitution, and empowered the UN to:

- Organize elections for a Constituent Assembly (CA);
- Assist and supervise the CA's making of the prescribed constitution (UNCA); and
- Control key ministries with a view to cancelling or replacing socialist laws with matching Western liberal laws (partial ITA).[13]

Accordingly, the UNTAC:

- Directed the National Bank of Cambodia to introduce privatization and renew Cambodia's access to the IMF;
- Secured Cambodia's ratification of major human rights treaties;
- Nullified laws that were inconsistent with the (impending) Constitution, and drafted new media, fiscal and electoral laws;

9 *See* UN, *supra* note 4 at 7–8.

10 Id. at 8.

11 Id. at 8, 132-48 (reprinting the Final Act of the Paris Conference).

12 *See* S.C. Res. 766, U.N. SCOR., 3099th mtg., ¶12 U.N. Doc., S/Res/766 (July 21, 1992).

13 *See* UN, *supra* note 4 at 134–136 (§ II Art. 2, 6, 1–17).

- Registered over five million voters;
- Conducted public education programs; and
- Successfully organized the CA elections in May 1993, and;
- Supported the CA via three seminars and drafting assistance.[14]

The new Constitution was adopted in September 1993. In this way, UNCA-ITA ostensibly promoted market democracy and human rights.

## UN Angola Verification Mission (UNAVEM-II), 31 May 1991—February 1995; UN Angola Verification Mission (UNAVEM-III), February 1995—30 June 1997

UNCA first served to amend Angola's 1991 constitution, which was adopted to implement the BWIs' conditionalities—to hold free and fair presidential elections. Eventually, the UN Family assisted Angola adopt a new Constitution, to implement the BWIs' conditionalities.

Angola gained independence in 1975. However, its decolonization was greatly complicated when a civil war broke out that year, between its two rival nationalist movements, the National Union for the Liberation of Angola (UNITA) and the Popular Movement for the Liberation of Angola (MPLA), each backed by the US and Soviet Union respectively.[15] Meanwhile, during the conflict, in return for the IMF's aid, Angola, a one-party state led by the MPLA, introduced a market economy via a Western-style constitution (the Constitutional Act 12/91 of 6 March 1991) (1991 constitution).[16] The prospects for peace brightened with the Soviet Union's demise. Pressured by the United States and Portugal, UNITA and MPLA concluded the Bicesse Accords (Accords) in Bicesse, Portugal on May 31, 1991. Although the U.S. played a key role in designing the Accords, their implementation fell to the UN.[17] By now, the World Bank states, Angola had made "real progress" in reforming

[14] *Sources*: Id. at 15–49; IMF, *Report No. 04/324* 4 (October 2004).

[15] UN-DPA, *Developments in Angola*, II (4.) Decolonization 3 (March 1975).

[16] *See* World Bank, Report No. 25471-ANG ¶20 (March 2003).

[17] *See* Attachment II-IV, & Annex, Peace Accords for Angola; S.C. Res. 747, UN SCOR, 3062nd mtg., ¶ 4, 6 UN Doc. S/Res/747 (24 March 1992) (broadening UNAMIR-II's mandate to include constitutional electoral assistance).

its economy along preferred lines.[18]Aiming at fully transforming Angola into a western liberal democracy, the Accords called for among other things, multi-party elections. The Accords' implementation (for example, undertaking the prescribed electoral reforms) required starting with amending the 1991 constitution. In 1992, mandated by the Security Council, UNAVEM-II:

- Approved constitutional amendments, previously discussed in a multiparty conference, and with M. Ant*see*, the SRSG;
- supervised all stages of the electoral process;
- drafted the electoral code of conduct; and
- Educated the public about elections-related human rights through a seminar and short plays in *khwe* and *Umbundu* languages respectively.[19]

Constitutional amendments enabled the MPLA to switch to a proportional representation system, ease the registration requirements for political parties, (thus, enabling UNITA to morph into a political party), and thereby, hold elections from 29 to 30 September 1992.[20]

Regrettably, because Jonas Sambivini (UNITA) rejected the verdict, war broke out, and was sustained by the outflow of Angolan oil and diamonds, and inflow of foreign weapons. The 1994 Lusaka Protocol (concluded after the electoral violence) stipulated a Transitional Government (Government) formed under UN supervision, in which UNITA members would hold a series of posts, with the remainder positions of patronage going to the government.[21] And so, when President dos Santos proposed creating two posts of vice-president, offering Savimbi one of them, the Secretary-General cautioned that:

> If such posts were to be created, the Constitution of Angola would have to be amended and the prerogatives of the two posts carefully defined.[22]

[18] *See* World Bank, *supra* note 16 at 1 .

[19] *See* Margaret Anstee, *Orphan of the Cold War – The Inside Story of the Collapse of the Angolan Peace Process, 1992–1993*, 87–126, 194 (St. Martin's Press, 1996).

[20] Id.

[21] *See* Sixth Annex, Lusaka Protocol, 15 November 1994.

[22] *Report of the Secretary-General on the United Nations Angola Verification Mission – UNAVEM III* ¶7 U.N. Doc. S/1995/588 (17 July 1995).

In July 1996, UNAVEM-III's constitutional assistance helped Angola do just that.[23]

### *A New Constitution via Development Assistance*

The conflict formally ended in 2002. And, the Government, (in office since April 1997), faced with depleted cash reserves, consented to implementing a BWIs-monitored program, –a prelude to a PRSP: making a new constitution.[24] Accordingly, aided by the UNDP (policy advice), UNICEF, and the BWIs, Angola began work roughly around 2002/2003 on the constitution, which was adopted in 2010.[25] And, expectedly, as early as 2007, the WB expressed relief that Angola's (draft) "Constitution, –and the Private Investment Law, do guarantee the foreign investor the right to compensation…."[26]

## United Nations Operation in Mozambique (ONUMOZ), December 1992-January 1995

The UN first helped Mozambique amend its 1990 constitution and later, adopt a new one in 2004. In both instances, UNCA served to implement conditionalities.

Mozambique gained independence in 1975 and became a one-party socialist state. From 1975 to 1992, it convulsed with an internationalized civil war, in which Resistência Nacional Moçambicana (RENAMO), the principal domestic group (backed by the US and South Africa) opposed the Mozambique Liberation Front (FRELIMO), that is, the Marxist leaning government of Mozambique (GoM).[27] Faced with a devastated economy, FRELIMO adopted a Western liberal constitution in 1990,

[23] *See* Law No. 18/1996 of 14 November 1996.

[24] UNDP-Angola, Economic report on Angola in 2002–2004, 2 (2005) (DRAFT).

[25] *See* UNDP's support to strengthening governance in Angola: an outcome evaluation (January 2010); World Bank, *Angola: Oil, Broad-based Growth, and Equity* 93–94, 127 (2007); UNGEI, Angola: Background 4 (undated) (on file).

[26] World Bank, *supra* note 25 at 94.

[27] *See* UN, *The United Nations and Mozambique, 1992-1995* 7-10 (UN, 1995)

in return for foreign assistance, and to appease the Western powers.[28] (Hence, Mozambique was not fully democratic.)

The UN lent its expertise to the peace talks that the US convened in Rome, in June 1992.[29] On 4th October, President Chissano and Renamo leader Afonso Dhlakama signed a General Peace Agreement (GPA). The GPA tasked the UN with implementing its three interlocking sets of provisions: political, military, and electoral, which in turn, required amending the 1990 constitution.[30] Meanwhile, the GPA was "initially de facto above the Constitution."[31] Therefore, as a first step toward implementing the GPA, in October 1992, the UN helped the GoM to constitutionalize the GPA, and by extension, the democratic principles articulated therein.[32] The ONUMOZ followed up with assisting the GoM sculpt a new electoral law, switch to the proportional electoral system, support RENAMO's transformation into a political party, and complete other steps in the electoral process.[33] ONUMOZ rounded off its assistance by helping organize Mozambique's presidential elections in October 1994 (in tune with the reformed constitution).[34]

Meanwhile, ONUMOZ, having organized a donor's conference in Rome in December 1992, next, assisted GoM officials in implementing the conditionalities: draft clearly defined property rights and strengthen financial markets.[35] This was a second way in which UNCA served to keep Mozambique's peace process on track. According to the European Commission (EC), the UN was clearly mandated to "directly shape

[28] Id. at 11; IMF, 'Republic of Mozambique Enhanced Structural Adjustment Facility Policy Framework Paper for April 1999–March 2002,' ¶1 (1999).

[29] UN, *supra* note 27 at 14, 18.

[30] Id. at 23. *See* S.C. Res. 797, U.N. SCOR., 3149th mtg., ¶6,9 U.N. Doc., S/Res/797 (16 December 1992).

[31] Irae B. Lundin, 'The peace process and the construction of reconciliation post-conflict: The experience of Mozambique' 16 (Maputo, February 2004).

[32] *See* UN, *supra* note 27 at 23–24, 26. To help the parties carry out the actions required of them, and thereby keep the peace process on track, a senior UNDP official, arrived in Maputo on 15th October, as part of the initial token UN presence. Id. at 23–24.

[33] Id. at Ch. IV & VII.

[34] Id. at 55.

[35] Id. at 26. *See* Report of the Secretary-General, *Support by the United Nations System of the Efforts of Governments to Promote and Consolidate New or Restored Democracies*, ¶101 U.N. Doc., A/50/332 (7 Aug. 1995).

(Mozambique's) constitutional and legal set up,"[36] and so, provided "significant legal advice."[37] Indeed:

> The 1994 Presidential Elections, heavily supported by the UN peacekeeping mission (ONUMOZ), marked a successful and peaceful transition… but the national electoral authorities played in practice, a very limited role –EC.[38]

Yet UNCA, laments the EC, remained "less visible."[39] Indeed, I suggest, the UN most shrouded UNCA in its early run, through this bland description: 'technical assistance in the area of jurisprudence.'[40]

### *1999-2004: UNCA Melded With Development Assistance*

Throughout the post-conflict period, Mozambique relied on concessional financing from external donors and held elections in 1999. Aided by the European Union and the UN, the new government as part of implementing the first PRSP (2001-2005)[41] adopted a new constitution in 2004, and created a NHRC in 2010.[42]

## The Mission of the United Nations in El Salvador (ONUSAL), July 1991–April/May 1995

El Salvador erupted in a vicious internationalized civil war from 1989-1992.[43] In this war, The Farabundo Marti National Liberation Front

[36] European Commission, 'EC Methodological guide on Electoral Assistance' 75 (2006).

[37] Id.

[38] Id. at 203 [emphasis added].

[39] Id.

[40] *See* UN, *supra* note 27 at 56

[41] 'Evaluation of the European Commission's support to the Republic of Mozambique, - Final Report 2007' (14th Dec. 2007); UNDP & EU, 'Government of Mozambique, Supporting citizens access to justice' 2-3 (undated) *at:* https://info.undp.org/docs/pdc/Documents/MOZ/Supporting_Citizens-_Prodoc.pdf.

[42] United Nations Country Team in Mozambique, Report for the Universal Periodic Review (undated).

[43] Graciana Castella, *Rebuilding War-Torn States: The Challenge of Post-Conflict Economic Reconstruction* 103 (Oxford University Press, 2010).

(FMLN) fought against the Government of El Salvador (GoES).[44] The FMLN was melded from five weak, poorly organized guerrilla groups that were supplied with arms and financing by the Soviet Union. The FMLN protested the GoES' neoliberal polices (export crop production) which had left them landless and poor.[45]

The then Secretary-General Javier Perez de Cuellar and his special representative, Alvaro de Soto, mediated the peace process.[46] Since the US and the BWIs backed the GoES during and after this civil war, the peace agreements that the GoES concluded with the FMLN channeled the IMF's conditionalities.[47] Indeed, according to the WB, 'to recover and grow,' El Salvador needed 'peace and better economic policies.'[48] Accordingly, from 1991 to 1995, the WB co-organized consultative meetings (the UN attended the 1992 meeting), where it informed potential donors of the peace-making efforts and the financing and technical assistance needs that might be required to conclude the peace process. These meetings garnered grants from the international community that averaged more than three percent of GDP.[49]

Of the seven peace agreements so concluded, three are relevant. The first, the Geneva Agreement, recommended a solution for lasting peace: democratizing El Salvador via those very policies (political and economic liberalization) that had triggered the conflict.[50] And whose implementation entailed revising El Salvador's 1983 constitution, (initially adopted in part, at the US's behest).[51] In this way, the Geneva Agreement placed constitutional reform along neo-liberal lines on the peace agenda. As per the Mexico Agreement and the Chapultepec Agreement, the UN assisted the GoES in:

- Constitutionalizing four new autonomous bodies with a view to bringing the armed forces under civilian control: A National Civil

44 Id.

45 Id. at 104–105.

46 UN, *The United Nations and El Salvador 1990-1995* (UN, 1995).

47 World Bank, El Salvador: Report No. 23626, 1-2 (February 2002).

48 Id. at 1.

49 Castella, *supra* note 43 at 108.

50 Art. 1-2, *The Geneva Agreement*, 4 April 1990.

51 Mary Fran T. Malone, *The Rule of Law in Central America: Citizens' Reactions to Crime and Punishment* 33–34 (Continuum, 2014).

Police, a State Intelligence Agency, a Supreme Electoral Tribunal and a National Counsel for the Defense of Human Rights; and
- Eliminating corruption in the judiciary and armed forces and the national police.[52]

Implementing these agreements required revising the Salvadoran constitution, which ONUSAL helped to achieve.[53]

## United Nations Mission for the Verification of Human Rights in Guatemala (MINUGUA), 21 November 1994–31 December 2004

UNCA served to secure the BWIs' preferred constitutional reforms.

Guatemala convulsed with a 'Cold War civil war' from 1960 to 1996.[54] (Its roots can be traced to the violent coup orchestrated in June 1954, by the United States, which toppled President Jacob Arbenz, ended his agrarian revolution, enabling Guatemala's reactionary agro-export oligarchy to regain power). In this war, the Guatemalan National Revolutionary Unity (URNG, a Leftist guerilla movement), opposed the oligarchy-backed military administration, which had blocked the electoral politics route.[55] Nearly two dozen Mayan, Xinca, and Garifuna indigenous communities, who have historically suffered racism and grave injustices, initially supported the URNG.[56] Exploiting this link between the Maya and the guerillas, 'the government promulgated an ideology that perceived all Maya as natural allies of the insurrection,' and by extension, enemies of the state.[57]

[52] Bertram Spector, *Negotiating Peace and Confronting Corruption: Challenges for Post-conflict Societies* 25–35 (USIP, 2011).

[53] Report of the Secretary-General, *The situation in Central America: Procedures for the establishment of a firm and lasting peace and progress in fashioning a region of peace, freedom, democracy and development,* ¶8–13 UN Doc. A/50/517 (6 October 1995).

[54] Susanne Jonas, *Of Centaurs and Doves – Guatemala's Peace Process* 20 (Westview Press, 2000).

[55] Id.

[56] Id.

[57] The Centre for Justice and Accountability, http://www.cja.org/article.php?list=type&type=294.

Consequently, over 200,000 indigenous peoples were killed or forcibly disappeared.[58]

The peace process ran from 1985 to 1996. Initially, the UN acted as observer, sending Jean Arnault, the Special Representative of the Secretary-General, as a mediator only in 1994.[59] Arnault's efforts led to the participation in the peace talks of one indigenous woman, Luz Mendez.[60] The government and the URGN signed a total of seven peace agreements,[61] of which only the four discussed here, required for their implementation, amending or leaving intact the 1985 (Western style) constitution. The military administration had adopted this constitution only to appease the domestic 'New Right'[62] and the BWIs: liberalize the economy.[63] (Here is why, it had some authoritarian features as well).

## The Land Reform Agreement [Agreement]

Accordingly, the 'the UN Secretariat

- brought in the BWIs in an advisory role, early in the peace process' who 'drafted, in tune with their best practices in economic development, the Agreement.'[64]

This Agreement

- required ignoring the Left's pleas to amend the constitution (articles 39-40) to 'stipulate property's social function,' and instead:
  - Respect the existing inequitable distribution of land,
  - Endorse absolute property rights,

[58] Id.

[59] UN, *The Guatemala Peace Agreements*, 7–8 (UN, 1998).

[60] UN Women, 'Women's Participation in Peace Negotiations: Connections between Presence and Influence' 8 (2012).

[61] *The Agreement on the Implementation, Compliance, and Verification Timetable for the Peace Agreements,* December 1996.

[62] William I. Robinson, *Transnational conflicts – Central America, Social Change, and Globalization* 113 (VERSO, 2003).

[63] Jonas, *supra* note 54 at 26.

[64] William Stanley, *Enabling Peace in Guatemala—The Story of MINUGUA* 39–43 (Lynne Rienner Publishers, 2013) (quote); World Bank, Report No. 18036-GU (1998).

- o Curb corruption, and
- o Make the poor finance its implementation through austerity.[65]

MINUGUA helped to implement this Agreement.

The remainder three agreements concerning human rights, indigenous peoples, –and the security sector (drafted by Jan Perlin, an UN expert)[66] mandated the government to 'modernize' constitutional bodies: the courts, police, and prosecutors;[67] constitutionally re-characterize Guatemala to empower indigenous peoples,[68] and constitutionally subordinate the police to civilian authorities.[69]

In May 1999, MINUGUA helped organize a referendum where a package of 50 constitutional amendments (prepared with its support to implement these agreements) was put to a public vote.[70] Although MINUGUA mounted a nation-wide information campaign to generate public enthusiasm for this referendum, the amendments were rejected because they sought to alter the status quo.[71]

## 6.2 UNCA Projects: 1999-2019 [Asia]

### United Assistance Mission in Afghanistan, (UNAMA), March 2002 – 17 September 2019 (latest renewal in March 2019)

In September 2001, the Al Qaida forces based in Afghanistan perpetrated terrorist attacks in the US.[72] In response, on 7 October 2001, a US-led international coalition [Coalition] mounted a combat operation

[65] Id. Robinson, *supra* note 62 at 113,114 (quote); World Bank, Report No. 16392-GU (1997).

[66] Stanley, *supra* note 64 at 46.

[67] *Comprehensive Agreement on Human Rights,* March 1994.

[68] *Agreement on Identity and Rights of Indigenous Peoples,* March 1995.

[69] *Agreement on the strengthening of civilian power and the role of the armed forces in a democratic society, September 1996.*

[70] Stanley, *supra* note 64 at 184-185.

[71] Id.

[72] Aurora Alambra, *Eighth Anniversary Today of 2001 Afghan Interim Authority*, UNAMA news, 17–24 December 2009.

against Afghanistan.[73] The Taliban, a group of Islamic fundamentalists headed by Mullah Omar, had controlled most of Afghanistan from 1996 to 2001.[74] The Taliban and its key opponent, the US-backed *Mujahidin* (which had opposed the Soviet occupation of Afghanistan–1979–89) abducted girls and women, forcing them into prostitution, and committed many other atrocities. The Taliban even banned education and shuttered hospitals.[75] The Northern Alliance, a coalition of different groups based in Faisabad, Puli Khumri and other north-eastern cities had emerged as the main opposition to the Taliban.[76] On 13 November 2001, Kabul fell to the Northern Alliance forces, which were being supported by the Coalition.[77]

The UN-sponsored peace talks began in Germany in November 2001, just as the International Steering Group (ISG) (including the US, the BWIs, the UNDP, and the ADB) had finalized plans for reconstructing post-conflict Afghanistan along good governance lines (PCNA).[78] Those invited to Bonn included Afghans primarily from the Northern Alliance and other groups trusted by the US. The talks concluded successfully on 5 December with the signing of the Bonn Agreement.[79] The delegates at Bonn, which comprised only certain ethnic groups, also selected members of the Interim Administration (IA).[80] Reflecting the PCNA's goals, the Bonn Agreement urged the Afghan government to create and maintain — until the new constitution was adopted — 'peace, order, and good government.'[81] The IA was specifically tasked with fighting terrorism, drugs, and organized crime.[82]

[73] Id.

[74] Id. However, the UN recognized President B. Rammani's government in exile as the official government.

[75] *See generally* Ahmad Rashid, *Taliban: Militant Islam, Oil and Fundamentalism in Central Asia* (Yale University Press, 2010).

[76] Alambra, *supra* note 72.

[77] Id.

[78] *See* PCNA Review: Phase one Afghanistan Preliminary Needs Assessment (2006).

[79] *See Agreement on Provisional Arrangements in Afghanistan Pending the Re-establishment of Permanent Government Institutions*, December 5, 2001.

[80] Id. at pmbl ¶ 6.

[81] Id. at III, C, 1.

[82] Id. at V, 3.

The Bonn Agreement mandated a new constitution.[83] Toward this end, it tasked the UN with creating the Emergency Loya Jirga, the Transitional Administration, the Constitutional Commission, the NHRC, and the Constitutional Loya Jirga (CLJ).[84] Established in March 2002, to achieve just this, the UNAMA, comprised senior gender and human rights advisers.[85]

In January 2002, UNDP secured funds via a donor's conference (Tokyo, November 2001) for making the Constitution (implementing the PCNA).[86] Soon thereafter, the Afghan government (aided by UNAMA and the IMF) began to 'modernize' the Ministry of Finance and the central bank, and designed monetary policy to transform Afghanistan into a market-oriented economy, where the private sector plays a central role.[87]

Within the next two months, UNAMA had helped to convene the ELJ. By November, the Transitional Administration (with the UNDP's support) had completed the PRSP's equivalent, the Afghan National Development Framework (ANDF), which stated as follows:

> We know that good governance is a precondition for attracting direct foreign investment. .... Our goal is to have a budgetary process that would meet the international standards.[88]

By 2002, the UNAMA had the Constitutional Commission (Commission), a nine-member constitution-drafting body up and working, which reportedly, owing to the UN's tireless efforts comprised two women.[89]

83 Id. at §I.

84 Id.

85 *See* S. C. Res. 1401, U.N. SCOR., 4501$^{st}$ mtg., U.N. Doc., S/Res/1401 (March 2002).

86 PCNA, *supra* note 78.

87 *See* Afghanistan National Development Framework (ANDF) 9 (2002) (DRAFT).

88 Id. *See also* Islamic Republic of Afghanistan: Poverty Reduction Strategy Paper (2008).

89 UNDP, *Support to the Constitution-making Process in Afghanistan, Final Report 2002-2004* 5, 9 (undated).

*UNAMA and UNDP*

- supported the Commission with UNCA's standard form; Mark Halle (UNEP) drafted the environmental constitutional provisions;
- provided the Commission with books and materials, and hired Yash Ghai, Muna Ndulo and other experts to advise it on topics including fiscal federalism and human rights;
- conducted public consultations in all 32 provinces and in refugee camps in Iran and Pakistan to ascertain the Afghan peoples' views about the proposed constitution; elicited the views of more than hundred, mainly illiterate Afghan women, brought safely to the UN compound in Farah;
- channeled the consultation's results to the Commission, which incorporated them into the preliminary draft, which was ready by 24 April 2003;
- distributed more than 5,000 copies of the draft; and
- helped establish the 500-delegate CLJ, ensuring that half of the 50 delegates appointed by President Karzai were women, and drafted procedures as per which, the CLJ deliberated over the draft constitution for ten days.[90]

The new constitution was adopted by the CLJ on 4 January 2004.

## Bhutan

Bhutan, an absolute monarchy, agreed in 1998 to embrace good governance.[91] Accordingly, King, Jigme Singye Wangchuck devolved executive powers to an elected Council of Ministers.[92] Next, it was decided that a Committee chaired by Lyonpo Tobgye, and a democratically elected Parliament would draft and adopt the new Constitution, respectively.[93] In the Drafting Committee (Committee), established in 2001, the government had 13 representatives, the judiciary three, the dratshang two, and 27 were members directly elected by the people.[94]

90 Id. at 5-34. For first point, *see* UNEP, *UNEP in Afghanistan* 28 (2009).

91 UNDP, Bhutan Elections: Fact Sheet 1-2 (Updated 25 March 2008).

92 Id.

93 Lyonpo Sonam Tobgye, Making of the constitution of the Kingdom of Bhutan (undated).

94 Id.

Finally, the UNDP:

- Helped Bhutan formulate and submit its UNDAF and PRSP;
- Offered UNCA's standard form to the Committee;
- Hired the late Prof. Osiatynski as a constitutional advisor
- Deputed an UNICEF official who consulted Bhutanese children for their views;
- Co-audited (with the UNEP, and the OHCHR) the draft constitution,
- Circulated copies of the draft constitution in March 2005, for input from the public, judiciary, civil servants, and Bhutan's chamber of commerce and industry; and
- Held mock polls to educate the public and;
- Assisted in conducting the parliamentary elections on 31 December 2007, and 24 March 2008.[95]

The draft constitution was first discussed by the lower house (47 members elected by direct, popular vote) and then adopted by the full Parliament in May 2008.[96] The King signed it on 2 June.[97]

## Kyrgyzstan

In 2010, the UN helped return Kyrgyzstan (until 1991, a part of the former Soviet Union – FSU) to constitutional order by assisting it to implement the conditionalities.[98]

In February 2010, civilians violently demonstrated in Bishkek (the capital city) against price hikes caused by the privatization of utilities (a conditionality), and President K. Bakiyev's authoritarian and corrupt government.[99] State forces used violence to tamp down the protest, killing 85 people.[100] Meanwhile, the riots spread to the cities of Osh

[95] IMF Country Report No. 04/246 ¶2.14 (2004); UNDP, *supra* note 91; UNDP-Bhutan *Annual Report 2004* 4–5 (2005); Country Progress Report, Plus 5, World Fit for Children, Review for the kingdom of Bhutan, 1 (2006)

[96] UNDP, *supra* note 91

[97] Bhutan formally adopts new constitution, July 21, 2008, *USA Today*.

[98] Kyrgyzstan had previously adopted a new constitution in 2003 as part of implementing its first PRSP. *See* IMF, Kyrgyz Republic: PRSP (July 2007)

[99] Charles T. Call, *Political Missions and Departures from Constitutional Order*, in Review of Political Missions – 2011 12 (United Nations, 2012).

[100] Id.

and Jalalabad (southern Kyrgyz), morphing into a bloody anti-Uzbek ethnic pogrom, killing some 2,000 Uzbeks and displacing 300,000 in just a few days. More broadly, the FSU's nationalist Central Asia policy, and the BWIs' economic liberalization that had long favored the urban Uzbeks but marginalized the southern Kyrgyz, triggered these pogroms.[101]

President Bakiyev who was forced to resign, fled the country in April. The UN neither condemned the coup nor sought the Bakiyev's return to power. However, UN Special Envoy Jan Kubiš, together with the OSCE and the EU, arrived in Bishek to mediate Kyrgyz's return to constitutional order.[102]

### *The IMF Influences the New Constitution's Content*

Roza Otunbayeva was appointed interim President, and on 3 July was officially inaugurated as President. He took up the functions of the President, Government and Parliament and by decree dismissed the Constitutional Court.[103] To appease the public, the Transitional Government partially reversed the large electricity tariff increase (previously introduced by President Bakiyev) that had hurt socially vulnerable citizens (hereinafter Reversal).[104]

According to the IMF, the ethnic violence 'weakened investors' confidence,' creating a 'balance of payments' problem with a 'moderate risk of debt distress.'[105] Therefore, the IMF staff co-led a joint donor economic assessment (DEA) in May 2010 (and another in July 2010), and proposed a Fund-monitored RCF program concerning financial stability and bank restructuring toward which the IMF provided significant legal assistance.[106] The IMF says this assistance 'is expected to continue.'[107] Against this backdrop, the provisional government promised

[101] Boris Petric, *Where Are All Our Sheep? Kyrgyzstan, a Global Political Arena* 154 (Berghahn Books, 2015).

[102] *See* Call, *supra* note 99 at 1.

[103] IBP, *Kyrgyzstan Criminal Laws, Regulations, and Procedures Handbook: Strategic Information, Regulations, Procedures* 31 (2016)

[104] IMF, Kyrgyz Republic: Letter of Intent 11, 13 (June 2, 2011)

[105] IMF, *Kyrgyz Republic: Country Report No. 10/336* ¶29 (October 2010)

[106] Id. at 11.

[107] Id.

that it would implement constitutional reforms within three months, would carry out a referendum on the adoption of a new constitution, and would hold elections within half a year.[108]

Accordingly, the UNDP assisted:

- the 75-member constitutional commission to 'draft' that very new constitution; (so did the Venice Commission); and
- Kyrgyz in holding a referendum on 27$^{th}$ June, where voters approved the new constitution, and chose Ms. Roza Otunbayeva as president for an 18-month period.[109]

Having found the TG's 'fiscal policy response to the economic crisis appropriate,' the IMF noted that the new constitution among other things, reduced the powers of the president, in favor of the prime minister and strengthened Kyrgyz's National Bank.[110] The IMF so concluded:

> RCF-supported policies would restore banking sector stability, … improve governance, … and catalyze lending from other donors by providing reassurance that crisis response is set within a sound overall macroeconomic framework.[111]

This affirms my point that, to obtain any type of credit, Third World states need to demonstrate commitment to the BWIs' policies (*see* Chapter 5).

Meanwhile the results of the May and July DEA were presented at an IMF-staff-attended-donor conference in Bishkek on July 27, 2010, where the donors pledged US$1.1 billion over a 30-month period for Kyrgyzstan's reconstruction.[112] In 2011, Kyrgyzstan assured the IMF of, among other things:

- Setting right the Reversal 'which had … worsened the financial condition of the energy sector'; and
- 'Compiling Kyrgyz's banking laws into a banking code to ensure that only the new constitution will supersede the banking laws.'[113]

108 *See* IBP, *supra* note 103

109 UN News Centre, 'Kyrgyzstan: UN jobs scheme *seeks* to aid recovery in areas hit by unrest,' 22 July 2010.

110 *See* IMF, *supra* note 105 at 16, 8.

111 Id. at 13, 14-15.

112 Id. at cover page.

113 *See* IMF, *supra* note 104 at 11, 13.

And, the Constitution's adoption enabled the UNDP to begin in 2013, rule of law promotion: Strengthen the judiciary, the budget process, and anti-corruption, –thus, affirming UNCA's salience (*see* Figure 1.6).[114]

In conclusion, it should be noted that Charles Call's possibly factually correct statement that Kyrgyz heeded 'only one concern raised by external technical advisers,' (Venice Commission), vis-à-vis the draft constitution,[115] implicitly suggests that Kyrgyz's constitution was free from external influences. However, the IMF's hugely influential role, which Call ignores, disproves that. In fact, as we will *see*, Kyrgyzstan's African, Asian, and Asian-Pacific counterparts will return to constitutional order, either partly on their own or jointly with UNCA, via this very route: adopting the BWIs' preferred Constitution.

## UN Mission in Nepal (UNMIN), 23 January 2007–15 January 2011

Nepal is home to several indigenous groups which have long suffered denial, exclusion, and discrimination.[116] A *Jana Andolan* (People's movement) in 1990 swept away King Birendra's absolute monarchy, leading to a new constitution that year, and the first multi-party democratic elections.[117] But soon, disenchantment set in. From 1996 to 2006, Nepal convulsed with conflict wherein the Maoist Communist Party in Nepal (CPN-M) fought the US-backed Nepali government, protesting the defective 1990 constitution, the continuation of discrimination, and a rise in water prices owing to privatization (a conditionality).[118] In fact, during the conflict, Nepal was well into

114 *See* UNDP-Kyrgyzstan, Enhancing Democratic rule of law and preventing conflict in Kyrgyzstan (undated).

115 Call, *supra* note 99 at 12.

116 UNDP, *Empowered Lives. Resilient Nations* (2010).

117 *See* Tonie Bleie, *The Historical Path to Violent Destabilization in Nepal: Elements of an Exploratory Framework* 8 (1) Hum. Rights in Dev. 371 – 415 (2002); Saubhagya Shah, Policy Studies 48: Civil Society in uncivil places: Soft state and regime change in Nepal (East West Center, Hawai'i, USA, 2008).

118 *See* Bishnu Raj Upreti, *A Decade of Armed Conflict and Livelihood Insecurity in Nepal, in* Livelihood Insecurity and Social Conflict in Nepal 16 (B. Raj Upreti & Ulrike Muller-Boker, eds., The Social Asia Regional Coordination Office, 2010); World Bank, *Interim Strategy for Nepal for the period FY 2010-2011* (2009).

implementing the Conditionalities, having submitted its PRSP with the UNDP's support.[119]

From 2000-2006, the UN deputed advisers including Ian Martin and Tamrat Samuel, a senior political officer, to support the UNDP's peacemaking efforts.[120] The OHCHR-Nepal was established to prevent human rights violations during the peace process.[121]

### *The Comprehensive Peace Agreement Enshrines the Conditionalities*

Before turning to consider the CPA, it helps to recall that by 2006, Nepal's creation of the Framework (defined in Chapter 1) was already underway.[122] Furthermore, having secured two IMF-approved two PRGF loans, one in 2003 and one in 2007, Nepal was compelled to complete the Framework.[123] The UN's mediation led to the warring parties concluding a comprehensive peace treaty (CPA) on 28 November 2006, whereby they agreed to

- Restructure the state along the lines of good governance, through first, an 'interim constitution' (which provided Nepal's framework from 2006-2015);
- Create fiscal federalism and check corruption;
- Establish a NHRC and protect the rights of women and children; and finally
- Adopt a permanent new Constitution adopted (with UNCA), and via an elected Constituent Assembly (CA).[124]

119 *See* UNDP *Review of the Poverty Reduction Strategy Paper* 15, Annex (PRSP).

120 *See* UN, *UN and Nepal's peace process* 5 (2008).

121 Id.

122 *See* World Bank, *Nepal: The Legal and Judicial Environment for Financial Sector Development: A Review* (2005).

123 *See* Nepal: *Letter of Intent* to the IMF, 31 Oct. 2007 ('describing the policies that Nepal intends to implement in the context of its request for financial support from the IMF').

124 *See* §3 & 7, *Comprehensive Peace Agreement between the Government of Nepal and the Communist Party of Nepal (Maoist)*, November 2006; Art. 33 (c), *Interim Constitution of Nepal* (2007).

As per the CPA, and the Security Council,[125] the UNMIN:

- Ran a constitutional unit headed by Yash Ghai; this unit mounted numerous programs, with a view to tapping the voices of children, women, and indigenous groups, and helping increase the political representation of the last two groups and preventing child abuse;
- Assisted in conducting the CA's elections in May 2008;
- Monitored the 575-member CA's proceedings; [126] and
- Joined the OHCHR and UNEP in drafting and auditing the constitution.[127]

The WB, which also assisted the CA, framed its contribution as follows:

> The work of the Constituent Assembly (CA) in drafting a new constitution is expected to lead to dramatic changes to the state as it decentralizes. .... The CA has requested that IDA contribute to the consultative process by providing advice and analytical work on fiscal federalism, building on the work on public financial management and global knowledge.[128]

After long delays caused by various factors, including an earthquake, and over which the UN had no control, Nepal adopted a new constitution in 2015.[129]

Nepal and Mali (discussed further below), indicate that UNCA moves fluidly from the development context to post-conflict, and so, is offered successively or goes through many rounds. Thus, right from the start,

[125] S.C. Res. 1740, U.N. SCOR., 5622nd mtg., U.N. Doc., S/Res/1740 (2007).

[126] *See Report of the Secretary-General, on the Request of Nepal for United Nations Assistance in Support of its Peace Process,* ¶ 37–42 U.N. Doc., S/2008/454 (10 July 2008) .

[127] *See Report of the UN High Commissioner for Human Rights, on the human rights situation and the activities of her office, including technical cooperation, in* Nepal, 12 U.N. Doc. A/HRC/13/73 (5 February 2010); UNEP, Mainstreaming environmental rights and sustainable development principles into the New Constitution of Nepal 1 (undated).

[128] *See* World Bank, *supra* note 118 at ¶36.

[129] Nepal adopts first democratic constitution, *The Hindu*, 30 October 2015.

UNCA works to promote multiple, inter-connected standards – but one standard is constant: good economic governance. And, this is so, because it is a conditionality.

## The Indian Ocean Region

### Madagascar

Madagascar became independent in 1950. UNCA was used to restore constitutional order to this island-state, which has since, enjoyed little politico-economic stability.[130] President Mark Ravalomanana, who had been implementing the PRSP from 2000-2008,[131] was overthrown in a coup in 2008. (Ravalomanana's PRSP, that is, the Madagascar Action Plan (MAP) included, introducing a bold investment law, an effective arbitration system to ensure security of investments and strengthening anti-corruption measures).[132] Andry Rajoelina, the popular thirty-five-year-old mayor of the country's capital, staged that coup, and subsequently formed, and headed a High Transitional Authority (HAT) to govern the country.[133]

#### *UNCA: April 2009-March 2010*

At this juncture, the WB did not suspend assistance.[134] And the UN, failed to condemn the coup. The UN deputed two senior political advisers who provided mediation and drafting assistance. Together with the UN Resident Coordinator, they began negotiations between Ravalomanana and Rajoelina and the opposition: two former presidents, Ratsiraka, and Zafy.[135] These four parties signed a power-sharing

[130] *See generally* Richard Marcus, *Politics of Institutional Failure in Madagascar's Third Republic* (Lexington Books, 2016).

[131] IMF, Republic of Madagascar: Poverty Reduction Strategy Paper (February 2007).

[132] Id. at 016.

[133] Lauren Ploch & Nicolas Cook, 'Madagascar's political crisis' 1 (June 2012).

[134] AfrDB, Madagascar, *Combined Report on the 2014–2016 Interim Country Strategy Paper (I-CSP) and the Country Portfolio Performance Review* (CPPR) §1 (2014).

[135] *See* UN-DPA, Politically Speaking, *Madagascar* 16 (Winter 2009–2010).

agreement (Maputo) in June 2009. But, on December 18$^{th}$, Rajoelina declared Maputo void.[136] Rajoelina also rejected participation in the next round of multilateral mediation.[137] Instead, HAT initiated its own dialogue, and concluded the Ivato agreement (Ivato) with 99 political parties and civic associations. In tune with Ivato, the HAT discussed the new constitution at a national conference, after which it was adopted in a referendum in 2009.[138] Expectedly, the new 2010 constitution upheld Ravalomanana's MAP.[139] And the new constitution enabled the government that assumed power in early 2014, following the elections, to demonstrate its commitment to reduce poverty/pursue the IMF's policies, and so receive its 'rapid credit facility.' For instance, in 2014, the government aided by the IMF began a reform of the Central bank in an effort to increase its independence.[140]

In so returning to constitutional order, Madagascar acted in pursuit, of a locally concluded agreement and not one, brokered by the UN. In this regard, Charles Call is factually correct to state that 'the reforms taken up in the constitution, which passed in the …referendum, were determined by Malagasies rather than by the UN.'[141] However, in so stating, Call implies that those reforms were freely arrived at, and would have been different had the UN's roadmap been accepted. I respectfully disagree, with both these implications. For, as the foregoing analysis suggests, there is only one route to Restoration of Constitutional Order (RECO) in a HIPC, regardless of which actor, spearheads it, local or international: adopting the Constitution, a conditionality.

## Maldives

In the late 1990s, the Bank prescribed UNDP-monitored good governance reforms for Maldives – in return for debt-relief.[142] However,

[136] *Political Handbook of the World 2015* 890 (Tom Lansford, ed., Sage Publications, Inc. 2012).

[137] Id.

[138] Id.

[139] Id. *See infra* Table 6.3.

[140] *See Republic of Madagascar—IMF Country Report No. 15/24* 5 (January 2015).

[141] *See* Charles T. Call, 'UN Mediation and the Politics of Transition after Constitutional Crises' 21 (International Peace Institute, February 2012)

[142] World Bank, Report No. 21301-MAL 23, 25, & ¶60 (2000)

the Bank framed good governance as being critical to 'better manage Maldives' economy, and fragile natural environment, and attract increased investment.'[143] Operationally, this meant replacing Maldives' 1968 constitution with the 'good' one, via the UN Development Assistance Framework (UNDAF) and the PRSP processes. Maldives successfully undertook both, though the PRSP's submission was delayed owing to an intervening tsunami.[144]

Meanwhile, in June 2004, President Gayoom established a Special Majlis (Constitutional Parliament), tasked with drafting a new Constitution.[145] And the UNDP:

- Provided the Special Majlis with the expert guidance of Dr. Hashim Kamali, an expert in Islamic jurisprudence;
- Mounted programs (in English and *Dahiveli*) to spread information about the constitutional review process and invite public input;[146] and;
- Assisted the Majlis in drafting the new constitution, and;
- Helped create the ACC,[147] and the human rights commission.[148]

President Ghayoom signed the new constitution on August 7, 2008.

## UNCA Projects 1999–2019 [Asia-Pacific]

### United Nations Transitional Administration in East-Timor (UNTAET), October 1999–May 2002

In 1975, Indonesia invaded and annexed East-Timor, making it its $27^{th}$ province.[149] The UN refused to recognize this annexation, which

[143] Id. at 13

[144] Maldives, *The Roadmap for the Reform Agenda: A Progress Report* (2007)

[145] Toby Mendel, Assessment of Media Development in the Maldives 1 (2009).

[146] UNDP-Maldives, *Fast Facts* (undated).

[147] UNDP-Maldives, Quarter 1, News in brief 1 (2013).

[148] Written submission by the UNDP to the UN Commission on Human Rights, ¶20 U.N. Doc. E/CN.4/2005/133 (8 March 2005).

[149] Sarah Williams, *Hybrid and Internationalised Criminal Tribunals: Selected Jurisdictional Issues* §VA (Hart Publishers, 2012).

though brutal, was ostensibly undertaken to fight communism. Xanana Gusmao, leader of Falintil (Armed Forces of National Liberation of East Timor), the armed wing of Fretilin, fought for independence into the late 1990s.

### *UNCA-ITA Envisaged Prior to Post-Referendum Violence*

On 5 May 1999, UN-led talks resulted in a set of agreements between Indonesia and Portugal (East Timor's former colonial power), wherein these two states tasked the UN with:

1. Conducting a popular consultation with a view to ascertaining whether the East Timorese people accepted, or rejected a special autonomy for East Timor within the unitary Republic of Indonesia; and/or
2. 'Receiving authority over East-Timor' and 'initiating a process enabling it to begin a transition towards independence' ('were the popular consultation to result in a majority of the East-Timorese people rejecting the proposed special autonomy within Indonesia').[150] Note: As we know, conceptually, adopting a new constitution is a key step toward independence.

On 30 August 1999, following the announcement that 78.5 per cent of Indonesians voted to reject the proposed autonomy, pro-integration militias, at times with the support of elements of the Indonesian security forces, launched a campaign of violence throughout the entire territory. Given this, Indonesia and Portugal, at a meeting with the UN, decided on plan 2.[151]

### *The Impending Constitution Guides Plenary ITA*

Accordingly, established on 25th October 1999, the UNTAET

- was tasked with fully administering East Timor during its transition to independence and 'building Timorese' capacities';

[150] *See* Art. 6, *Agreement between the Republic of Indonesia and the Portuguese Republic on the Question of East Timor* (5 May 1999).

[151] Background, East Timor, UNTAET website.

- *replaced* all pre-existing authorities in the territory, becoming in every respect the formal government of the country; and
- was headed by the SRSG, Sergio De Mello, who in the absence of an elected legislative assembly, enjoyed both legislative and executive powers, including sole authority to issue regulations as national legislation.[152]

The UNDP raised over USD 520 million to implement the WB's decision to reconstruct East Timor along good governance lines.[153] As noted in Chapter 5, the BWIs, having conceptualized the Constitution as a 'development strategy' in 1999, renamed their lending policy as a development policy. Reflecting this trend, the UN Resident Coordinator heading the UNDP Office in Dili in 1999, came to be designated in March 2000 as the 'UN Development Coordinator.'[154]

Accordingly, the UNTAET with a view to laying the foundations for a market economy:

- focused on developing a macroeconomic framework to guide economic decision making and establishing key economic institutions;[155] and
- aided by the IMF
  - established the Central Fiscal Authority, Central Payment Office; and
  - developed an appropriate tax and customs regime, banking and payment system, and rules on accounting policies and procedures.[156]

(It helps to revisit the IMF's quote reproduced in Chapter 1, in connection with my review of Carsten Stahn's ITA analysis.[157]) These

[152] *See* S.C. Res. 1272, U.N. SCOR., 4057th mtg., ¶2 (e) U.N. Doc., S/Res/1272 (October 1999); *See generally* Jarat Chopra, *Building State Failure in East-Timor* 33 Development & Change (2002).

[153] World Bank, The East Timor Reconstruction Program: Successes, problems, and tradeoffs 1,7 (2002).

[154] UNDP, Post-conflict Assistance of the government of Japan through UNDP in Kosovo and East Timor 52 (2002).

[155] IMF, *Establishing the Foundations of Sound Macroeconomic Management* 21, 33 (2000).

[156] Id.

[157] *See* text in Chapter 1 to which footnote 132 refers.

deliberate policy choices were however framed as neutral 'capacity building,' undertaken 'to prevent the squandering of East-Timor's limited natural resources.'[158]

### *Internationalized Constitution-Making Process*

Against this background, the UN decided in March 2001, that a 88-member Constituent Assembly (CA) (constituted through UN-organized elections), would prepare a constitution for a 'democratic' East Timor, within ninety days of the first day of its sitting.[159] Significantly, the CA was to take into consideration such draft regulations as would be referred by the UN.[160] During March 2001-May 2002, UNTAET:

- trained over 5,500 community leaders to strengthen public participation and consultation, particularly of women;
- held 200 Constitutional public hearings in June and July 2001, 'at which 38,000 East Timorese turned out to air their views on what should be considered by the CA when drafting the first constitution.'
- held CA elections on 30th August 2001; and
- organized a seminar to orient the CA members, providing them with materials, a team of experts, and a legal drafter.[161]

In May 2002, the CA adopted a new Constitution and East Timor declared independence.[162]

## Fiji

In December 2006, Bainimarama, an ethnic Fijian, overthrew the government (which was then implementing the ADB's conditionalities),[163] ostensibly to end corruption.[164]

[158] Id. UNTAET Press Office, Fact Sheet 2 (1 April 2002).

[159] UNTAET Regulation No. 2001/2, 16 March 2001

[160] Id.

[161] *See* UNTAET Fact Sheet 1 (April 2002).

[162] *See* 2002 Yearbook of the United Nations 318 (UN, 2003).

[163] ADB, Governance in the Pacific: Focus for action 2005-2009 (2004).

[164] Steven Ratuva, *Politics of Preferential Development: Trans-global Study of Affirmative Action and Ethnic Conflict in Fiji, Malaysia and South Africa* (Australian National University Press, 2013).

From 2006 to 2009, UN officials such as Jehangir Khan offered mediation support to restore constitutional order. So too did the Pacific Forum and Australia.[165] Meanwhile, the 2008 global financial crisis and the floods of January 2009 had strained Fiji's economy still more.[166] At this juncture, Bainimarama changed track. He abrogated the 1997 constitution, which had been adopted to appease the WB.[167] Bainimarama cancelled planned elections, imposed press restrictions, and in September 2009 informed the UN he had decided to make a new constitution.[168]

### *The IMF Recommends Good Governance*

In December 2009, an ADB-IMF Team (Team) visited Fiji.[169] Subsequently, Bainimarama released a Roadmap, which outlined in aspirational terms, the Reforms (that the Team recommended), indicating that his government wished to pursue them.[170] The Roadmap envisaged a new constitution by September 2014.[171]

The UNDP provided the Government-appointed Constitution Review Committee (CRC) with UNCA's standard form.[172] Yash Ghai headed the CRC. The CRC was to produce a draft which would be submitted to a constituent assembly, and to engage in wide consultations. The CRC's draft contained human rights protections and market-

165 *See* UN News Centre, Fiji: UN fact-finding mission on post-coup situation finishes work, 27 April 2007; UN News Centre, 'At UN, Fijian regime asks critics to have patience during reform period, 26 September 2009 [2009 UN Item].

166 J. Bainimarama, 'Strengthening the Foundations of Economic Growth and Prosperity'—2010 Budget Address.

167 *See* for example, Yash Ghai & Jill Cottrell, *The Role of Constitution-building Processes in Democratization* 10 (IDEA, 2004).

168 *See* 2009 UN Item, *supra* note 165.

169 *See* Press Release No. 09/427, Statement of an IMF Mission at the Conclusion of the Article IV Discussions with Fiji, 23 November 2009.

170 Fiji Ministry of Planning, 'A Better Fiji for all: Roadmap for Democracy and Sustainable Socio-Economic Development, 2010-2014' (2009).

171 Id at i. *See* ADB, *Public Financial Management Systems – Key elements from a Financial Management Perspective* June 3–7, 2017 (lucidly explaining the Constitution's centrality to achieving sectoral reforms).

172 UNDP, The Dialogue Fiji Process 1-24 (undated).

oriented land reform provisions (owing to the IMF's prescriptions),[173] and ignored the government's instructions regarding immunity for coup participants.[174] As a result, those who had committed human rights violations were denied immunity, a provision that Bainimarama's government opposed.

In January 2013, Bainimarama therefore, rejected the CRC's proposed constitution in favor of one prepared by his government. (It is telling that ADB provides this detail, namely, that the original idea of having a Constituent Assembly debate over the draft constitution was shelved.)[175] Meanwhile, Fiji's key donor Australia was sympathetic to Bainimarama's rejection of the ICC's draft, because it contained features that 'do not enjoy precedence anywhere else in the constitution of a democratic country.'[176] Fiji's constitution came into force on 6 September 2013.[177] According to the IMF, in adopting this constitution (and holding elections in tune with it), Fiji moved decisively toward democratic governance.[178]

Fiji returned to constitutional order by adopting the Constitution, though this was not mandated by an UN-brokered peace agreement. Indeed, akin to Madagascar, the decision (Decision) of making the Constitution was ostensibly, arrived at locally. Nonetheless, that Decision flowed in part, from Fiji's need for aid and good international credit ratings, and from UNCA provided by the UNDP and the UN-DPA.

## Nauru

Nauru gained independence from Australia in 1968. Although rich in phosphate, a sought-after fertilizer ingredient, two factors pushed

173 *See* Section 9, Draft Constitution Explanatory Report; IMF Country Report No. 10/136 (May 2010).

174 Wadan Narsey, Trashing the Ghai Constitution: The Positives, January 14, 2013 *at:* http:narseyonfiji.wordpress.com/2013/01/14/trashing-the-ghai-constitution-the-positives-14-january-2013/.

175 *See* ADB, Fiji: Update 2 (June 2013).

176 *See* 'Australia adopts softer stance on Fiji's constitution,' *News*, January 14, 2013.

177 *See* IMF, Fiji: Report No. 13/370 ¶1-3 (December 2013).

178 IMF, Fiji: Report No. 14/3213 3 (November 2014).

Nauru deep into debt by the 1990s. First, by 1968, Australia's unconscionable exploitation had eroded two-third of the phosphate. Indeed, Australia, New Zealand and Britain, 'in a final act of exploitation, before bowing out, forced Nauru to borrow against its future earnings from mining to buy out their shared phosphate company.'[179] Second, was the bad investments made by successive unstable, post-independence governments, cheating by unscrupulous foreigners, and a drop in the price of phosphate.[180]

In these circumstances, Nauru agreed (in return for debt-relief) to curb corruption, create investor-friendly and market-driven land laws and land-tenure system, and so on.[181] This required reforming its 1968 constitution that Australia, its former colonial power had imposed.[182] Accordingly, Nauru (aided by the UNDP) submitted its PRSP-equivalent in 2004, and commenced its constitution-review process in 2005.[183] The UNDP supported Nauru's Constitution Review Committee with UNCA's standard form from 2005-2010.[184] The foreign experts included Prof. Katy le Roy. The reform process comprised six steps. The first two (July - August 2006 & October to November 2006) were meant to increase the Nauru people's understanding of the need for constitutional review and receive their written submissions.[185] Expectedly, a number of the amendments were designed to enhance fiscal transparency and so, included constitutionalizing a good governance code.[186] The UNDP organized a referendum on certain proposed constitutional amendments on 27 February 2010.[187]

179 'Nauru, Paradise well and truly lost,' *The Economist*, December 20, 2001.

180 Id. *See also* Tony Anghie, *The Heart of My Home: Colonialism, Environmental Damage, and the 'Nauru Case'* 34 (2) Harv. Int'l. Law. J. 445-506 (Spring 1993) .

181 Nauru, *National Sustainable Development Strategy 2005-2025* 55 (October 2009)

182 Id.

183 UNDP, Nauru Constitutional Reform Project 1, 3 (undated), *at:* https: / /info.undp.org/ docs / pdc / Documents / FJI / 00058097_Nauru%20CRC_Prodoc.pdf.

184 Id. at 2.

185 Id. at 4.

186 Id.

187 Government of the Republic of Nauru, http: / / www.naurugov.nr / parliament-of-nauru / projects / constitutional-review-project.aspx.

## UN Political Office in Bougainville (UNPOB), August 1998–December 2003; UN Observer Mission in Bougainville, (UNOMB), January 2004–June 2005

Bougainville, a province in a debtor island-state Papua New Guinea (PNG), pursued a secessionist rebellion. The UN enabled Bougainville to achieve autonomy via adopting the Constitution.

Bougainville experienced a decade-long violent secessionist civil war from 1989. While the reasons for the conflict are complex, the trigger was Bougainville Copper Limited (BCL), the Australia-owned mining company's unfair practices.[188] The conflict soon became two-layered. At the first level, the secessionist Bougainvilleans (the Bougainville Revolutionary Army (BRA)) fought the PNG Police and Defense Force (PNGDF).[189] The second level sprung from local differences that pitted groups gathered under the Bougainville Resistance Forces (BRF) against the BRA.[190]

### *The BWIs*

Since 1995, the Government of PNG (GoPNG), was undertaking a BWIs'-monitored Structural Reform Programme (SRP).[191] And in 1997 it had, with the UNDP's support, submitted the Medium Term Development Strategy for 1997-2002.[192] Against this backdrop, PNG gathered together with the BRA and BRF in June 1997, in New Zealand, for peace talks, which gave space for further talks.[193] UNPOB entered the peace process in 1999. Its efforts led to the parties signing the

---

[188] Anthony Regan, *Bougainville: Conflict Deferred?* in Diminishing Conflicts in Asia and the Pacific: Why Some Subside and Others Don't 120-123 (Edward Aspinall *et al* eds., Routledge, 2013).

[189] Id.

[190] Id. at 122.

[191] *See* UN, *Papua New Guinea: Common Country Assessment* §1.3 (December 2001).

[192] Id. ('Essentially, the MTDS aims to limit government activity to those areas on which the government must focus to create an environment in which the private sector … can flourish'). Id.

[193] *2002 Yearbook of the UN* 392 (UN, 2003) .

Bougainville Peace Agreement (BPA) on $29^{th}$ August 2001,[194] whereby the GoPGN consented to:

- Constitutionally guarantee autonomy for Bougainville, (which obviously entailed amending the PNG constitution) – and a referendum on Bougainville's independence, deferred for 10 to 15 years, on the condition that its governance met 'internationally accepted standards of good governance.'[195]
- Bougainville adopting a new, that is, Constitution (with UNCA) to transition to autonomy.[196]

As expected, the IMF released its loan to PNG a day after the BPA, which so channeled its conditionalities was signed.[197]

On January 23, 2002, the PNG Parliament unanimously passed the Constitutional amendments, giving more autonomy to the Bougainville Government.[198] The amendment also allowed for a referendum on independence to be held within 10 to 15 years.[199]

Bougainville crafted its new constitution from September 2002-August 2004.

UNPOB:

- helped to establish the Bougainville Constitutional Commission in September 2002;[200] and
- enabled the Commission to begin a process of consulting the people, developing recommendations and considering successive versions of the draft of the constitution.[201]

The Constituent Assembly was established in February 2003. The constitution went through four drafts and was discussed for over two

194 Scott S. Smith, *The role of the UN Observer Mission* 12 Accord 54–55 (2002).

195 *See* §C, Bougainville Peace Agreement, 30 August 2001.

196 Id. at § B, ¶3, 10-26.

197 *See* Papua New Guinea, Letter of Intent (addressed to IMF), 31 August 2001.

198 'Papua New Guinea: Bougainville agreement tabled before parliament,' BBC Monitoring Asia Pacific, October 18, 2001.

199 Id. Scott S. Smith, *The role of the UN Observer Mission* 12 Accord 54–55 (2002).

200 UN-DPA, *Repertoire of the Practice of the Security Council, Supplement 2000-2003*, 533–538 (2011).

201 Id.

weeks, before it was finally reviewed by the National Executive Council (cabinet) in January 2004. On 14$^{th}$ January, the Cabinet handed over the constitution to the Autonomous Bougainville Government in Arawa.[202] As part of promoting good governance nationally and sub-nationally in PNG, the ADB helped establish or strengthen the Independent Commission on Corruption, the Ombudsman, and the offices of the Attorney General and the Auditor General.[203]

A referendum on independence is scheduled to be held in June 2019.[204] Akin to Kosovo, Bougainville's future political status hinges on its governance meeting good governance standards.

## Solomon Islands

UNCA was mandated to amend Solomon Islands' (SI) 1978 constitution, but eventually, it served to help SI make a new Constitution, whose process is reportedly ongoing.[205]

SI gained independence in 1978. Since then, it has experienced chronic instability, with 14 different governments unable to complete their terms.[206] SI comprises a multi-racial population. Honiara (the capital) and Guadalcanal, two of the largest island cities, house most of the multinational corporations. Also housed there, are most of the migrants from Malaita, a neighboring island. The Guadalcanal Islanders are called Guale.

In May 1998, an indigenous Gaudalcanalese militia – the Isatabu Freedom Movement (IFM) – violently evicted the Malaitan settlers

202 Id.

203 *See* ADB, *Country Assistance Program Evaluation – Papua New Guinea* ¶99 (2015).

204 Autonomous Bougainville government, Referendum, Bougainville's vote on its future political status, *available at*: http://www.abg.gov.pg/peace-agreement/referendum.

205 *See* 12 UN-Decolonization, *Solomon Islands* 1-18 (June 1978); UN News Centre, 'UN Development Program to boost constitutional reforms in Solomon Islands,' 5 November 2002; UNDP, National Parliamentary Strengthening Project, Phase 2, 2008-2012 (undated)

206 *See* Shahar Hamieri, *The Trouble with RAMSI: Re-examining the Roots of Conflict in Solomon Islands* 19 (2) Contemp. Pacific 409 (2007) .

(who later grouped themselves as the Malaita Eagle Force – MEF).[207] Overall, the violence killed over 200 people, displaced more than 35,000 Solomon Islanders, and ruined the economy.[208] What might have triggered Gaule resentment? The answer: The harsh effects of the PFM reforms (ADB's conditionalities) that SI began implementing from 1997.[209] So did the decades of inequitable development, inter-island migration, illegal settlement, lack of political autonomy, and the large-scale presence of prosperous Bougainvilleans.[210] This economically driven conflict took a political twist when the MEF, which included large segments of SI's security force, staged a coup, forcing the democratically elected Prime Minister Bartholomew Ulufa'alu to resign at gunpoint.[211]

*From Constitutional Reform to the New Constitution*

In August 2000, SI's key donors including Australia, the ADB, and the BWIs, agreed to rebuild SI along good governance lines.[212] Accordingly, three months later, Australia coaxed the Central Government (SIG) and the provincial governments of Malaita and Gaudalcanal to sign the Townsville Peace Agreement *(TPA)*.[213] The TPA mandated the SIG to:

- rewrite the constitution to provide greater autonomy for Malaita and Guadalcanal provinces (however, the new post-coup government decided to achieve this via a new constitution); and
  *see*k (UN) international support for its implementation.[214]

SI's constitution-making lagged for various reasons, and the UNDP offered constitutional assistance from 2002-2016. As might be expected, rule of law assistance paralleled UNCA from July 2003 to 2013 because

207 Id. at 410.

208 Id.

209 Id. at 426–427.

210 Id.

211 Id. at 430.

212 ADB, Document No: *RRP:SOL 34513* 1-3 (November 2000).

213 Townsville Peace Agreement (October 2000).

214 Id. at Part Four (1) (a) & Part six; UNDP, CCA-Solomon Islands 37 (23 March 2002).

SI was designated as a failed state in 2003.[215] Accordingly, Australian forces and civil servants displaced local officials to train the police, promote the market economy, manage the national debt, and so on.[216] From 2002 to 2016, the UNDP:

- helped relevant governments submit their PRSPs in 2002 and –in 2011 (the most recent constitution-making milestone)[217];
- educated the public and ascertained their views on conditionalities/issues: anti-corruption, decentralization, ombudsman, and women's rights; and,
- prepared guidelines for a new Federal Constitution.[218]

During 2011-2012, the UNDP supervised constitution-drafting (including by parliamentarians).[219] A Draft was ready in 2013 and updated in 2014. From 2013-2016, foreign experts advised stakeholders on issues including anti-corruption and the NHRC, and programs raised public awareness about, and invited the public's (including economic groups') comments on, the 2014 draft constitution.[220] The OHCHR encouraged women's participation, particularly those affected by the violence.[221] As per the SIG Website (visited in July 2018), a thorough and complete review of the 2014 Draft ended on 24 June 2016.[222]

[215] See Jon Fraenkel *et al.*, "The RAMSI Decade: A Review of the Regional Assistance Mission to Solomon Islands, 2003–2013" (2014).

[216] Id.

[217] *See* Solomon Islands, *National Development Strategy 2011–20* 9, 44–45 (2011) (Final Draft); UNDESA, Mapping of Sustainable Development Strategies in Countries Emerging from Conflict: Asia and the Pacific- WORKING DRAFT 88 (August 2009); IMF, Solomon Islands, Report No. 14/12 13 (January 2014) (stating that the authorities submitted the NDS to the IMF Executive Board as an Interim Poverty Reduction Strategy Paper (I-PRSP).

[218] *See* UNDP, Constitutional Reform Project (SOI/02/003) 1, 2-56 (March 2003).

[219] Evaluation of the UNDP: *Parliamentary Strengthening Project: 2012–2015* 31 (undated).

[220] 2013 Draft Federal Constitution of Solomon Islands.

[221] *Report of the Special Rapporteur on violence against women, its causes and consequences*, ¶14 U.N. Doc. A/HRC/23/49/Add.1 (22 February 2013)

[222] *See* Solomon Islands Constitutional reform website.

## Africa

### UN Office in Burundi, 1993–2004; UN Operation in Burundi (ONUB), 1 June 2004 to 31 December 2006; UN Integrated Office in Burundi (BINUB), 1 January 2007 to 31 December 2010; UN Office in Burundi (BNUB), 1 January 2011 to 31 December 2014

A constitutional crisis triggered Burundi's twelve-year civil war (1993-2004) (Civil War) in which the Tutsi dominated army fought the Hutu rebels.[223] The UN Office in Burundi, which was established in 1993 to return Burundi to constitutional order,[224] picked up speed only after 2000, when Nelson Mandela became the key negotiator – and also because Burundi's economy declined.

Therefore, Burundi's peace talks (January–August 2000) overlapped with its negotiations with the IMF (January–March 2000).[225] Small wonder that the Arusha Peace and Reconciliation Agreement (APRA), concluded in August 2000, mirrored the conditionalities attached to the IMF's March 2000 emergency assistance. Indeed, APRA stipulated a new Constitution made with UNCA during the transitional period (that ended on 31 October 2004).[226]

The Security Council welcomed the APRA, although it was concluded only between the government of Burundi and the majority of the Hutu and Tutsi political parties. Indeed, one key Hutu rebel group had stayed out of the negotiations.[227] And so, the civil war continued.[228] As per APRA, an ethnically balanced Government of National Unity

[223] *See* Stephen Jackson, '*ONUB — Political and Strategic Lessons Learned*' 3 (July 2006).

[224] Id. at 5. *See* UN Dept. of Public Information, 'UN Office in Burundi' (Sept. 2000) [document on file].

[225] *See* IMF, 'IMF Concludes Article IV Consultation with Burundi,' April 7, 2000.

[226] *See* Art. 5, Chapter I, *Arusha Peace and Reconciliation Agreement for Burundi*, 28 August 2000 .

[227] Ashild Falch & Megan Becker, 'Power-sharing and Peacebuilding in Burundi' 17-18 (Centre for the study of Civil War PRIO, 2008).

[228] Id.

(GONU) comprising Hutus and Tutsis, governed by the interim (transitional) constitution assumed office in November 2001.[229]

In 2004, ONUB:

- Promoted women's and children's political participation;[230]
- Helped the GONU submit its interim PRSP;[231] and establish the constitution-drafting body;[232]
- Pressured the GONU to finalize the draft constitution by 1 August 2004, failing which it proposed to have 'the constitution drafted by national or international experts.'[233] The stakeholders consented, signing the Pretoria power-sharing agreement, in August 2004, which was subsequently endorsed by a regional initiative;[234] and
- Discussed and audited the draft constitution,[235] once it was revised in tune with the Pretoria Agreement.

The extension of the transitional period until August 2005 was approved.[236] And the draft constitution, which was adopted by Parliament on 28th October 2004, was declared to be the interim constitution until the referendum on 28 February 2005.[237] Meanwhile, when President Ndayizeye decided to amend the interim constitution in a way that would violate the Pretoria Agreement, ONUB coaxed him

[229] *Child Soldiers Global Report 2004* 1 (2005).

[230] 'Burundi and women's participation: the role of ONUB' (UN, 2006).

[231] *See Burundi – ONUB – Background, at:* http://www.un.org/en/peacekeeping/missions/past/onub/background.html.

[232] *Second report of the Secretary-General on the United Nations operation in Burundi*, ¶6, U.N. Doc., S/2004/902 (15 November 2004).

[233] *See* First *report of the Secretary-General on the United Nations Operation in Burundi*, ¶19 U.N. Doc., S/2004/682 (25 August 2004).

[234] *See* S. C. Res. 1577, U.N. SCOR, 5093rd mtg., pmbl ¶5-6, U.N. Doc. S/Res/1577 (2004).

[235] *See Report of the Secretary-General, Children and armed conflict*, ¶9 U.N. Doc. A/59/695-S/2005/72 (9 February 2005).

[236] *Fourth report of the Secretary-General on the United Nations Operation in Burundi*, ¶3 U.N. Doc., S/2005/328 (19 May 2005).

[237] *See 2004 Yearbook of the UN* 153 (2005); Art. 306, Burundi's Constitution, 2005.

to abandon his plans.[238] In this way, conflict was avoided. The interim constitution was endorsed at the referendum held with UNCA.[239] Two consecutive peace missions, after ONUB (BINUB and BNUB), and the OHCHR established a NHRC and created an anti-corruption brigade.[240]

## United Nations Mission in the Central African Republic (MINURCA), 15 April 1998 to 15 February 2000; United Nations Peacebuilding Support Office in the Central African Republic (BONUCA), February 2000 to December 2009; United Nations Integrated Peacebuilding Office in the Central African Republic, BINUCA, January 2010–10 April 2014

BONUCA helped the Central African Republic (CAR) make its new constitution. (Initially MINURCA and BONUCA helped CAR revise its 1995 constitution as part of implementing a 1997 peace agreement's good governance provisions.[241] And, that the UNDP, organized public awareness-raising campaigns in the country in November and December 1997, since a new constitution's making was envisaged).[242]

### *The 2003 Coup and a New Constitution*

In early 2003, Francois Bozize overthrew President Patasse, suspended the 1995 constitution, and dissolved the government. Squished under mountainous debt, aid was key to propping up, and enabling CAR perform core state functions. Accordingly, Bozize established

[238] *Third report of the Secretary-General on the United Nations Operation in Burundi*, ¶6-8, U.N. Doc. S/2005/149 (8 March 2005).

[239] *See* UN, *supra* note 237 at ¶7.

[240] *Report of the Secretary-General on the United Nations Office in Burundi*, §D, F U.N. Doc., S/2013/36 (18 January 2013).

[241] *Report of the Secretary-General pursuant to resolution 1136 (1997) Concerning the situation in Central African Republic*, ¶4-7 U.N. Doc., S/1998/61 (23 January 1998) (describing MINURCA's activities).

[242] Id. at ¶13.

a 28-member Transitional Government (TG), which embarked on making the Constitution on 30 May 2003.[243] Toward this end, the TG established a National Transition Council (NTC) comprising 135 rebels, rival politicians and everyone in between, which prepared a draft based on the 1995 constitution, suspended since the 2003 coup.[244] According to the IMF, 'the transitional government [that is, the TG] worked closely with regional and international partners, who provided significant technical and financial support.'[245] When the TG rejected some of the draft constitution's provisions (relating to the BWIs' conditionalities), General Lamine Cissé, the Secretary-General's Special Representative, intervened pushing the government and the NTC to make 'mutual concessions' and resolve their disputes.[246] In this way, BONUCA restored donor confidence, and consequently, the World Bank approved the first LICUS grant in July 2004.[247]

The draft constitution was endorsed at a referendum, held with UNCA, on December 5, 2004.[248] In 2008, the IMF affirmed that CAR's 'satisfactory implementation' of its conditionalities (anti-corruption provisions constitutionalized in articles 44 and 75) were triggers for securing debt-relief.[249]

In 2010, BINUCA helped to establish the national human rights institution (NHRI).[250]

[243] Polity IV Country Report 2010: Central African Republic 2–5 (undated).

[244] Id. at 2.

[245] IMF, Central African Republic: Report No. 06/42 37 (February 2006).

[246] Sources: *See Report of the Secretary-General on the situation in the Central African Republic and the activities of the United Nations Peace-Building Support Office in the Central African Republic,* ¶ 5 U.N. Doc. S/2004/1012 (23 December 2004); IMF, *supra* note 246 at 35–36.

[247] See sources in *supra note* 247.

[248] *See* Volume 56 *2004 Yearbook of the UN* 161 (2006).

[249] IMF, Central African Republic: Country Report No. 08/14 26 (January 2008); World Bank, Review of World Bank Conditionality vi (2005) ('Triggers are the Bank's conditions and expected prior actions').

[250] *See OHCHR Report 2012* 198 (2013).

### The UN Political Mission in Côte d'Ivoire (MINUCI), May 2003-April 2004, United Nations Operation in Côte d'Ivoire, (UNOCI), April 2004 to the present (as of February 2019)

From 2003 to 2016, UNCA served to: implement a peace agreement that mandated constitutional reform; provide an interim constitution for two years; and finally, help Côte d'Ivoire adopt a new Constitution. To understand UNCA's use in response to a civil war in 2002, requires noting that:

- In the four years leading up to the civil war, three successive presidents, Bedie, Robert Guei (1999–September 2000), and Gbagbo were implementing the BWIs' conditionalities;[251] and
- All of them used a discriminatory concept to fuel ethnic rivalries, scapegoat foreigners who had long contributed to the Ivorian economy, shore up support, and thereby, remain in power: Ivoirité.[252]

In fact, Ivoirité was constitutionalized by Guei who (grabbed power through a coup), and adopted a new constitution in January 2000, (as part of implementing the conditionalities), which stated: 'candidates for the presidency must be of Ivorian origin, born of a father and a mother of Ivorian origin' (Article 35).[253] In this way, 'outsiders'/political rivals were excluded from the political process.

'Amid such divisions, a military rebellion in September 2002 triggered a protracted civil war between northerners, resentful of their exclusion from power, and forces loyal to President Gbagbo (in office since October 2000).'[254] Indeed, Côte d'Ivoire split into a government-controlled economically developed South (predominantly Christian), and a rebel-held North (predominantly Muslim). The rebels demanded an end to corruption and discrimination/Ivoirité. Peace talks convened by France (Côte d'Ivoire's former colonial power) and attended by the

251 Nick Branson, Constitution-making in Côte d'Ivoire 3 (Africa Research Institute, London, October 2016).

252 Id.

253 Id.

254 Id.

UN, ended with the Linas-Marcoussis (peace) Agreement, January 2003 (LMA).[255] The LMA called for:

- Creating a transitional government of national reconciliation and unity (GONUR) (comprising President Gbagbo and the rebels),
- an NHRI; and
- Amending article 35.[256]

The UN and the BWIs were tasked with monitoring LMA's implementation.[257]

### *Efforts to Remove Article 35*

GONUR's creation met with several obstacles. Therefore, so did securing Article 35's removal. Hence, MINUCI and then, UNOCI offered UNCA. (It helps to note that since the Ivorian external debt had, by the end of 2003, become unsustainable, re-establishing state authority, the first benchmark for restoring constitutional order required implementing the BWIs' PFM reforms).[258]

A small breakthrough arrived in April 2005 (the Pretoria Peace Agreement) (hereinafter Pretoria) when, upon suggestion by Thabo Mbeki, the International Mediator, and Kofi Annan's intervention, President Gbagbo used Article 48 (granting him powers in times of crisis) to temporarily suspend the application of the stipulations, in Article 35.[259] (As a result, all party signatories of LMA would be eligible to stand as a candidate in the presidential elections). The modification in nationality requirements so acquired, was subsequently endorsed by the Security Council.[260]

[255] *See Report on the Secretary-General on Côte d'Ivoire*, ¶19-20 U.N. Doc., S/2003/374 (26 March 2003).

[256] Id.

[257] Id.

[258] Id. at 21. *Second Report of the Secretary-General on Côte d'Ivoire*, ¶49 U.N. Doc., S/2003/1069 (4 November 2003).

[259] Email from UN official, Francois Simmard, dated 12 December 2009 [on file with the author].

[260] S.C. Res. 1603, U.N. SCOR., 5194th mtg., U.N. Doc., S/Res/1603 (3 June 2005).

Pretoria underscored UNCA's salience in the organization of the upcoming general elections. It called for a High Representative for the elections (HRE) who would enjoy autonomy from UNOCI and powers over the national Electoral Commission and over the Constitutional Court.[261] (Policymakers recommended the HRE as a remedy to the total lack of confidence between the Ivorian parties). The HRE rendered decisions consistent with the Pretoria Agreement but in conflict with national laws.[262]

### *The Security Council Offers Constitutional Assistance*

Meanwhile, a constitutional vacuum loomed, because no elections could yet be organized but, President Gbagbo's presidency and the National Assembly's term ended on 30$^{th}$ October 2005, and 16$^{th}$ December 2005 respectively. Therefore, in October 2005, the Security Council extended the mandate of President Gbagbo until October 2006, and called for presidential elections before the end of the extended mandate.[263] Again, following violent clashes in July 2006, the Security Council extended the mandate of President Gbagbo and the Prime Minister in November 2006, for another 12 months and postponed Presidential and legislative elections, which were expected to take place before October 2007.[264] In this way, from the end of 2005 to 2007, both the President and Prime Minister of Côte d'Ivoire derived their powers from Security Council resolutions.

### *Making the Western Liberal Constitution*

In 2007, the political parties agreed on UN-assisted presidential elections, but they were delayed until 2010, due to fighting and electoral reform issues. Meanwhile, in August 2007, with a view to become

261 *Thirteenth progress report of the Secretary-General on the United Nations Operation in Côte d'Ivoire*, U.N. Doc., S/2007/275 (14 May 2007).

262 *See* email, *supra* note 260.

263 S.C. Res. 1633, U.N. SCOR., 5288th mtg., ¶3 & 13 U.N. Doc., S/Res/1633 (21 October 2005).

264 *See* S.C. Res. 1721, U.N. SCOR., 5561st mtg., ¶6 U.N. Doc. S/Res/1721 (November 2006).

eligible for debt-relief, the government began implementing an IMF-monitored program.[265]

In the 2010 elections A. Ouattara, former Africa director of the IMF, triumphed. Ouattara also won the elections in 2015, thus, becoming President for two terms. In April 2016, Ouattara proposed making the new Constitution, which would, among other things, abolish Article 35.[266] The Security Council welcomed this.[267] (In fact, Ouattara's administration had taken the first step toward making this constitution in 2011, when aided by the UNDP, it submitted the PRSP. Since then, it had begun creating a new business code and commercial court).[268] In May, a government-appointed Committee (Committee) comprising those who were previously involved in making the 2000 constitution/implementing the BWIs' conditionalities, began work on the new constitution.[269] An IMF visiting Team welcomed this, viewing it as the government's 'commitment to intensifying structural reforms.'[270]

UNOCI worked with the Committee to:

- Constitutionalize the NHRI and child rights; and
- Monitored human rights 'to enhance perceptions of the legitimacy of the proposed constitutional referendum's outcome.'[271]

A draft constitution, based on the consultation of 40 stakeholder groups was approved by Parliament and endorsed at a public referendum in October 2016.[272] The Secretary-General welcomed the new constitution.[273] In November 2016, as a debtor state, Côte d'Ivoire

[265] *See* AfrDB, *Côte d'Ivoire Dialogue paper 2007-2008* iv (October 2007).

[266] *See* AfrDB, *Côte d'Ivoire: Combined Country Strategy Paper (CSP) 2013-2017 Mid-term review* 1 (26 July 2016).

[267] S.C. Res. 2284, U.N. SCOR 7681st mtg., ¶1 U.N. Doc. S/Res/2284 (28 April 2016).

[268] Côte d'Ivoire: Poverty Reduction Strategy Paper 16, 32 (June 2013).

[269] Branson, *supra* note 252 at 3 .

[270] IMF Country Report No. 16/147 3 (June 2016).

[271] *See Special Report of the Secretary-General on the UN Operation in Côte d'Ivoire*, ¶8 U.N. Doc. S/2016/297 (31 March 2016).

[272] *See* Branson, *supra* note 252 at 3.

[273] *Secretary-General Welcomes Adoption of New Constitution in Côte d'Ivoire*, Press release, SG/SM/18249-AFR/3481 (2 November 2016).

informed the IMF of its new constitution and made known its commitment to making its economy attractive for foreign investors. A month later, the IMF approved a US$658 million loan.[274]

## United Nations Organization Mission in the Democratic Republic of Congo (MONUC), 30 November 1999-30 June 2010

UNCA was used to make a new constitution mandated by a post-conflict peace agreement.

The Democratic Republic of Congo convulsed with two successive and complex wars from 1996-2003.[275] The first war began in 1996, when Laurent Kabila overthrew President Mobutu to become the president.[276] The second, a pan-African war, stemmed in part from the greed of mining multinationals who supported the Congolese rebels in the east, in exchange for zinc, gold, silver, and diamonds.[277] Thousands of women were raped. Over 10,000 children were recruited as soldiers.[278]

The 1999 Lusaka Cease-fire Accord (signed by President Laurent Kabila and five regional states) established a political imperative to hold the Inter-Congolese Dialogue (ICD).[279] MONUC was established to implement the Accord, but Kabila prevented its deployment. In January 2001, the DRC went bankrupt, and President Joseph Kabila (Laurent Kabila's son and successor), quickly began to reconstruct ties with the IMF, reactivate the Lusaka accord, and start the ICD in October 2001.[280]

[274] *See* for example, IMF, Republic of Côte d'Ivoire: Letter of Intent 1-2, 4 (21 November 2016); IMF Executive Board approves US$ 658.9 million under the ECF and EFF arrangements for Côte d'Ivoire, December 13, 2016.

[275] *See* UNDP, *Democratic Republic of the Congo—Evaluation of UNDP Assistance to Conflict-Affected Countries* 6 (2013).

[276] Id.

[277] Id.

[278] Id.

[279] *Report of the Secretary-General on the United Nations preliminary deployment in the Democratic Republic of the Congo*, ¶ 2 UN Doc. S/1999/790 (15 July 1999).

[280] *See* Letter of Intent of the government of the Democratic Republic of the Congo, 20 June 2001.

Importantly, in 2001, Kabila liberalized the diamond sector, which the IMF welcomed, and therefore cancelled the DRC's debts, backdating the debt relief to 2000.[281] So did the Security Council, which considered these reforms critical to attaining peace.[282]

Although the peace process lagged for two years, the UN drew in women, Mayi-Mayi (religious groups), traditional chiefs, and the Congolese Diaspora. Finally in April 2003, the UN Special Envoy, Moustapha Niasse, successfully mediated the Global and All-Inclusive Agreement (Global Agreement).[283] The Transitional Constitution (for the 30-month transitional period) anchored in the Global Agreement was promulgated on 4$^{th}$ April 2003.[284] MONUC:

- advised the stakeholders about what the constitution should contain, and helped draft its provisions;[285]
- conducted civic campaigns, prepared questionnaires for inviting public comments on the first draft, which was ready by June 2004[286]; and
- drafted an anti-corruption law in 2005.[287]

At the referendum, held with UNCA on 18 to 19 December 2005, the constitution was accepted.[288]

[281] *Id. See* DRC, Interim PRSP 31-33 (March 2002).

[282] S.C. Res. 1355, U.N. SCOR., 4329$^{th}$ mtg., ¶24 U.N. Doc., S/Res/1355 (2001).

[283] *See Second special report of the Secretary-General on the United Nations Organization Mission in the Democratic Republic of the Congo*, ¶ 4-5 U.N. Doc., S/2003/566 (27 May 2003).

[284] Art. 1, *Inter-Congolese Political Negotiations, The Final Act* (6 March 2003).

[285] Séverine Autessere, *The Trouble with the Congo — Local violence and the failure of international peace-building* 254 (CUP, 2010); UNDP, *First regular session of the UNDP/UNFPA Executive Board 20 to 27 January 2006* 8 (undated); *Seventeenth report of the Secretary-General on the United Nations Organization Mission in the Democratic Republic of the Congo*, ¶76 U.N. Doc., S/2005/167 (15 March 2005).

[286] *Third special report of the Secretary-General on the United Nations Organization Mission in the Democratic Republic of the Congo*, ¶9 U.N. Doc., S/2004/650 (16 August 2004).

[287] Transparency International, *Overview of anti-corruption in the Democratic Republic of Congo* 5 (undated).

[288] UNDP, *supra* note 276 at 4.

## United Nations Office of West Africa, (UNOWA), January 2008–December 2010

In December 2008, a military junta calling itself the National Council for Democracy and Development (CNDD), dissolved Guinea's 1990 constitution and installed Captain K.D. Camara as the interim national president.[289] (When the coup occurred, the government was well into implementing its PRSP-II with the UNDP and the OHCHR.) [290]

To restore constitutional order, an International Contact Group on Guinea (ICG-G) opened talks between the CNDD and the Forces Vives, a collection of civil society and political groups, in Conakry on 16 and 17 February 2009 where, in addition to the Security Council's permanent members,

> the following organizations attended the meeting: the United Nations, ... the European Union ... and *the World Bank*.[291]

Herein began UNOWA's constitutional assistance. The talks ended in February 2009, with Camara (CNDD) agreeing to adopt the Constitution under UN supervision, and to hold elections in which he would not contest the presidency.[292] But on 28$^{th}$ September, the Guinean military opened fire at protestors who had gathered at the national stadium in Conakry when it became clear that Camara might renege on his promise.[293] One hundred and fifty-seven persons were killed. Still more were sexually assaulted.[294]

Therefore, the international community heaped sanctions on Guinea.[295] And the UN pressured President Camara and the Forces Vives to conclude the Ougadougou Agreement, whereby they agreed

[289] *Security Council Report*, Update No. 3 Peace consolidation in West Africa: Guinea (11 January 2010).

[290] IMF, *Guinea Poverty Reduction Strategy Paper* ¶ 118 (2008).

[291] *See* Letter dated 11 March 2009 from the Permanent Representative of Burkina Faso to the United Nations addressed to the President of the Security Council, Annex U.N. Doc. S/2009/140 (12 March 2009).

[292] Id.

[293] Alexis Arieff & Nicolas Cook, *Guinea: Background and Relations with the United States* 12-13 (Congressional Research Service, Washington, DC, March 2010).

[294] Id.

[295] Id.

to form a National Unity Government, adopt a new Constitution (the Constitution), reform laws in the mining, security, and PFM sectors, and organize elections within six months.[296] Welcoming this accord, the Secretary-General Ban Ki-Moon called on Guinea's international partners to provide the necessary support to help this debtor-state through the transition.[297]

Accordingly, the UNOWA and the Meditation Support Unit helped to establish the National Transition Council (NTC), which comprised 150 members from civil society, labor unions, political parties, the private sector, security forces, and other important organizations.[298] The MSU assisted the NTC, which acted as the transitional legislative body, in drafting a new constitution.[299] The new constitution was finally promulgated in May 2010.[300] Two years later, the WB explicitly connected the two Cs, this way:

> Emerging from instability and military rule, Guinea adopted a new constitution, … and fully re-integrated into the international community. …. Macro-economic stability was restored, and debt sustainability dramatically improved with the attainment of the enhanced Highly Indebted Poor Countries (HIPC) completion point in September 2012.[301]

## UN Peace-building Support Office in Guinea Bissau (UNOGBIS), 25/26 June 1999–31 December 2009; The United Nations Integrated Peacebuilding Office in Guinea-Bissau (UNIOGBIS), 1 January 2010–28 February 2020

UNCA was used to return Guinea-Bissau (Bissau) to constitutional order.

[296] UN Peacebuilding Fund, 'Support to the international mediation in Guinea' – Project Document Cover Sheet 1-15 (2010).

[297] UN News Centre, *'Guinea: Ban Welcomes Steps to Restore Constitutional Order,'* 19 January 2010.

[298] *See supra* note 297 at 7.

[299] Id.

[300] *See* Alexis Arieff, *Guinea's New Transitional Government: Emerging Issues for U.S. Policy*, 3–5 (Congressional Research Service, Washington, DC, April 2010).

[301] World Bank, *Guinea: Report No. 76230-GN* 1 (September 2013).

From 1980, Guinea-Bissau experienced a cycle of coups, attempted coups, and counter-coups.[302]

In 2003 Yala, the newly elected president, was deposed in a coup, and the constitution (previously promulgated in 2001, to implement the interim PRSP) was suspended. Against this background, the mandate of UNOGBIS (first established in 1999) was revised in 2004 to 'maintain and restore constitutional order.'[303]

From 2004 to 2014, UNOGBIS and its successor, UNIOGBIS, strengthened the government's capacity to carry out core governmental tasks and implemented good governance – the Security Council's two benchmarks for restoring constitutional order (RECO).[304] These two benchmarks intertwine, for the UN posits that privatization and liberalization allow the state to recover economically;[305] moreover, such 'economic recovery' forms part of any viable strategy to reduce political instability[306] because it enables the state to maintain donor confidence and attract foreign aid. Thus, good governance promotion is a core governmental task, and the Constitution is integral to RECO.

Accordingly, UNOGBIS financially propped up the post-coup administration, thereby ostensibly 'strengthening' its capacity.[307] (UNIOGBIS acted similarly in response to another coup in 2013.)[308] Second, as we know, aid/PRSP equates to the making of the Constitution. Therefore, in 2011, President Sanha announced securing appropriate revisions to the

[302] *See* Guinea-Bissua, Chronology of Events, Security Council Report.

[303] *See* S. C. Res. 1580, U.N. SCOR. 5107$^{th}$ mtg., ¶2(b) U.N. Doc. S/Res/1580 (2004).

[304] Id. at ¶2-3; *Report of the Secretary-General on the restoration of constitutional order in Guinea-Bissau*, ¶53 UN Doc. S/2014/332 (12 May 2014) [2014 UNSG Report].

[305] *See* 2014 UNSG Report, *supra* note 305.

[306] *See* UN News Centre, Security Sector reform vital to stability in Guinea-Bissau, says UN Report, 3 March 2010.

[307] *Report of the Secretary-General on developments in Guinea-Bissau on the activities of the United Nations Peacebuilding Support Office in that country*, ¶ 3 U.N. Doc. S/2005/174 (16 March 2005).

[308] *See* 2014 UNSG Report, *supra* note 305 at ¶48.

(hastily promulgated) 2001 constitution.[309] In turn, Joseph Mutaboba, the Special Representative of the Secretary-General, welcomed Sanha's decision, offering UNCA.[310] Accordingly, the UN:

- Offered drafting assistance,
- Created a national youth platform to promote inter-ethnic dialogue; and
- Conducted 22 'Voice of Peace' conferences throughout Bissau and one each, in Europe and Africa.[311]

In December 2011, the revised constitution which endorsed good governance was ready.[312] UNIOGBIS and UNODOC helped to criminalize human trafficking, to draft the 2012 Anti-Money Laundering Law, and to secure Bissau's ratification of anti-corruption treaties.[313] UNIOGBIS and the OHCHR helped to create Bissau's NHRC.[314] Since 2015 Guinea-Bissau has been experiencing cycles of instability. In its most recent resolution, that is, in 2018, the Security Council has urged the national authorities to expedite the constitutional review process and mandated UNOGBIS to offer UNCA.[315]

[309] *Report of the Secretary-General on Developments in Guinea-Bissau and on the Activities of the United Nations Integrated Peacebuilding Office in That Country*, ¶3-4 U.N. Doc. S/2010/106 (26 February 2010).

[310] UN Dept. of Public Information, Guinea-Bissau entering decisive phase of reform leading to 'sensitive' electoral process in 2012, Security Council hears in briefing by Special Representative -- Speakers echo secretary-general's recommendation to extend United Nations presence in country by one year following expiration of mandate in December, Security Council, SC/10434 (3 November 2011).

[311] *See supra* note 310.

[312] Draft constitution (Portuguese version) sent by UN official, Gabriel Dava [on file].

[313] IMF, Guinea-Bissau: Report No. 13/197 ¶18 (July 2013); UNODOC, *Guinea-Bissau New Hub for Cocaine Trafficking* Issue 5, Perspectives 6 (May 2008).

[314] *See* 'Human rights promotion and the rule of law,' (undated), UNIOGBIS, http://uniogbis.unmissions.org/Default.aspx?tabid=9889&language=en-US.

[315] *See* S.C. Res. 2404, U.N. SCOR., 8194$^{th}$ mtg., ¶3 (c), U.N. Doc. S/Res/2404 (28 February 2018).

## Kenya

Kenya convulsed with post-election violence in December of 2007.[316] The conflict, which shattered the economy, was almost all ethnicity-based, tapping into long-standing grievances over land and resources.[317]

A panel of eminent Africans led by former UN Secretary-General Kofi Annan, supported by the UN Secretariat, mediated between the warring parties to end the crisis.[318] On 29 January 2008, Annan's panel formally launched the Kenyan National Dialogue and Reconciliation Process (KNDR), whose two principals were President Mwai Kibaki and Raila Odinga.[319] Kenya required concessional lending to jumpstart its shattered economy. Only one route lay open for it in this regard: the PRSP process.

Accordingly, on 14 February 2008, the KNDR's principles pledged to tackle the 'root causes of the political crisis through:'[320] 1) 'Comprehensive constitutional reforms' and 2) 'Poverty reduction.'[321] On 4 March 2008, the principals agreed to undertake a participatory constitutional review process, prepare a draft constitution with the assistance of expert advisers, and submit the proposed constitution to a vote at a referendum.[322] The Parties agreed to complete the Review with the 'expertise and support' of the international community.[323]

Meanwhile, the Party of National Unity (led by President Mwai Kibaki) and the Orange Democratic Movement (led by opposition leader and former presidential candidate Raila Odinga) concluded a power-sharing agreement, which led to a Grand Coalition Government

[316] *See* Alfred Anangwe, *Kofi Annan's Conflict Resolution Model and Peacebuilding in Kenya, in* Conflict and Peacebuilding in the African Great Lakes Region 106-109 (Kenneth Omeje *et al* eds., Indiana University Press, 2013).

[317] Id.

[318] *See* Security Council Report, Kenya - Chronology of events.

[319] *See generally* Kenyan National Dialogue and Reconciliation Process.

[320] *Id.* at Agreed Statement on how to resolve political crisis, 4 February 2008.

[321] *Id.* at § III. On 4 March 2008, Annan's Panel supported the establishment of three important commissions and the constitutional review process.

[322] Id. at 23 May 2008 Statement.

[323] Id.

(GCG).[324] And, aided by the UNDP, Kenya submitted a PRPS ('Vision 2030'), pledging to draft a new Constitution to shape Kenya into a modern state with a market-based economy.[325] As expected, the PRSP, prepared in broad consultation with the staff of the WB and the IMF, identified the 'inadequacy' of the 1963 Constitution and the need for a modernized … constitutional order as the reasons for undertaking the (good governance) reforms envisaged therein.[326]

The GCG established a committee of experts (Committee) to draft the constitution.[327] UNDP assisted the Committee with equipment, drafting, and relevant materials; conducted stakeholder meetings; and helped build consensus around contentious issues (fiscal decentralization).[328] UNDP also mounted participatory and consultation programs.[329] In August 2010, at a referendum held with UNCA, 68% of Kenyans accepted the proposed constitution.[330] Which the Bank has since upheld as a model for good governance.

## UN Peacebuilding Support Office in Liberia (UNOL), 1 Nov. 1997 to 30 Sept. 2003; UN Mission in Liberia (UNMIL), 1 Oct. 2003 to 30 March 2018.

In Liberia, UNCA was used to implement a peace agreement that *implicitly called for Western constitutional reforms* because it called for introducing good governance.

From 1987 to 2003, President Charles Taylor's government forces fought with various warring factions, killing about 150,000 civilians, raping hundreds of women and children, and using many of them as combatants.[331] This war was fueled in part by illegal competition for

[324] *See* The National Accord and Reconciliation Act 2008, *at:* peacemaker.un.org/kenya-national-accord-act2008.

[325] *See* IMF, Kenya Poverty Reduction Strategy Paper xi, §6.1.4 (July 2010).

[326] Id. at §6.1.2.

[327] *See* Report of the Committee of Experts on Constitution Review (2010).

[328] *See* UNDP-Kenya, *2010 Annual Report* 3 (2010).

[329] *See* 1 UN Constitutional 3–4 (Winter 2013/2014).

[330] Id.

[331] Liberia's Governance and Economic Management Assistance Programme 1 (May 2006) .

Liberia's resources, especially timber.[332] Pressured in part, by the UN, these parties concluded the comprehensive peace agreement (CPA) in August 2003.[333]

The following three tasks triggered UNCA because they entailed revising the 1986 constitution along the UN's preferred lines:

First, the CPA laid the framework for a power-sharing arrangement during the transitional period: the National Transitional Government of Liberia (NTGL) comprising warlords, rebels, or mutineers.[334] Next, the CPA tasked the NTGL with promoting good governance in the ways discussed below, and the UN with assisting in such implementation.[335] The BWIs' conditionalities thus, shaped the NTGL's power-sharing functions in governance. For instance, the CPA divided power between the NTGL and the Contract and Monopolies Commission (CMC), a five-member body.[336] The latter supervised the NTGL. The CMC oversaw the NTGL's contracting activities to ensure it operated in a transparent fashion, supervised the NTGL's public fiscal and budgetary obligations to ensure it implemented the BWIs'-approved macro-economic policy.[337] In this way, the CMC ensured that the NTGL pursued privatization, liberalization, decentralization, and other standard BWIs' policies.

Second, the BWIs and donor states, having jointly attributed the war to bad governance in the forestry and diamond-mining sectors – and with a view to opening them to foreign investment – prescribed creating property/tenure rights, constitutional guarantees, and excellent

[332] Id.

[333] *See Comprehensive Peace Agreement between the Government of Liberia and the Liberians United for Reconciliation and Democracy (LURD) and the Movement for Democracy in Liberia (MODEL) and Political Parties*, Accra, 18 August 2003 [Hereafter CPA].

[334] *See* Jeremy Levitt, *Illegal Peace in Africa: An Inquiry into the Legality of Power Sharing with Warlords, Rebels and Junta* Ch.4 (Cambridge University Press, 2011).

[335] The Constitution of Liberia was suspended to allow the NTGL to function with executive and legislature branches selected exclusively from the parties to the conflict and civil society rather than through elections. *See* CPA, at pmbl ¶7.

[336] Id. at Art. XXVII.

[337] Id.

market and investment conditions.[338] The Security Council endorsed this (good) governance and economic assistance program (GEMAP) as a conflict-prevention measure.[339]

Third, in 2011, the UN Mission in Liberia (UNMIL) was tasked with assisting Liberia in holding elections in accordance with international standards.[340]

As per the recommendations of the Good Governance Commission (headed by Professor Amos Sawyer), a Constitution Review Commission (CRC) was established in 2012.[341] The UN Secretary-General welcomed constitutional reforms as they would strengthen property rights; privatize the forestry, mining, land, and petroleum sectors; curb corruption; and develop fiscal decentralization.[342] Accordingly, from 2003 to 2014:

- The UNDP helped Liberia to submit its PRPSs (first and second) and strengthen anti-corruption measures
- The OHCHR created a NHRC.[343]

UNMIL:

- Organized a constitutional referendum for three election-related proposed constitutional amendments.
- Provided the CRC with experts including Ekuru Aukot, Louis Aucoin, Jason Gluck, and Hassan Ibrahim, who advised the CRC on drafting and land reform issues, and held public discussions about the review process in Monrovia;[344] and a Child Rights Adviser who drafted protective measures (for example, anti-rape law).[345]

338 *See supra* note 332; The World Bank, *Roots for Good Forest Outcomes: An Analytical Framework for Governance Reforms*, 16 (2009).

339 *See supra* note 332 at 5.

340 S. C. Res. 2008, U.N. SCOR., 5902nd mtg., pmbl ¶ 7 U.N. Doc. S/Res/2008 (Sept. 2011).

341 *Twenty-fourth Progress Report of the Secretary-General on the UN Mission in Liberia*, ¶67 U.N. Doc. S/2012/641 (2012).

342 Id. S.C. Res. 1607, U.N. SCOR., 5208th mtg., ¶4 & 10 U.N. Doc. S/Res/1607 (21 June 2005).

343 *See* OHCHR in Liberia (undated).

344 *See* Liberia: UN Constitutional Experts in Town, 22 April 2013, *at:* allAfrica.com.

345 *See* CPA, Art. XXXI 2a-2c.

- Accepted the Council's directive and strengthened women's political participation through various programs.[346]
- The programmes of Dr. Kamil Kamaludeen, UNDP's Country Director, amplified the voices of youth, refugees, and the Liberian diaspora (in Kenya and Ghana).[347]

In August 2015, President Sirleaf Johnson transmitted to the Legislature 25 proposed amendments emerging from the CRC's review process, along with her recommendations.[348] But as of May 2018, those amendments have been found to be flawed by the Election Coordinating Committee, which recommends making a new constitution.[349] In any event, Liberia cannot forego its compliance with the BWIs' conditionalities.

## Malawi

Malawi had adopted a new Western liberal constitution in 1994 to implement the BWIs' SAPs.[350] Securing continued debt-relief required scrapping laws inherited from the one-party system, and a fuller implementation of good governance: strengthening the constitutional/public financial management-PFM bodies (*for example*, the Auditor-General and the Anti-Corruption Bureau).[351] Accordingly, Malawi submitted its PRSPs (SAPs' successor), with the UNDP's support.[352] As part of implementing the PRSPs, B.W. Mutharika, the newly elected President, tasked the Law Commission (Commission) in 2006 with reviewing the constitution.[353] The UNDP:

346 *See* 4 UN Constitutional 10 (Spring 2015).

347 *See* UNDP, 'UNDP director calls on youth to own constitutional review process,' 10 July 2014.

348 *Liberia Making Progress on Numerous Fronts, UN Peacekeeping Chief Tells Security Council*, UN News Centre, 10 September 2015; *Twenty-Sixth Progress Report of the Secretary-General on the UN Mission in Liberia*, ¶8 U.N. Doc., S/2013/479 (12 August 2013)

349 *See* William Q. Harmon, 'ECC Proposes New Constitution,' Daily Observer, May 10, 2018.

350 *See* Final Draft, Malawi Poverty Reduction Strategy Papers 101 (2002).

351 Janet Chikaya-Banda, *Constitutional and Law Reform*, in Malawi, 1–10 (Africa Research Institute, 2012).

352 *See* PRSP, *supra* note 351.

353 Banda, *supra* note 352 at 4.

- provided the Commission with drafting assistance, expert guidance on fiscal decentralization, PFM, judicial independence; and sent its members on 'study trips' to South Africa, Namibia, and Zambia;
- hosted two consecutive national conferences in March 2006 and April 2007 respectively, each of which was attended by more than two hundred participants representing political parties, tribal groups, the private sector, businesses, and civil society; and
- collected and channeled to the Commission, the public's views on many topics including curbing corruption.[354]

Work on implementing this Commission's report, including the draft Constitution (Amendment) bills finalized in 2007, is ongoing.[355] One of the most recent amendments (February 2017) aims at ending child marriage.[356]

## United Nations Office in Mali (UNOM)/UN Mission in Mali (UNOM), 21 January 2013–24 April 2013; United Nations Multidimensional Integrated Stabilization Mission in Mali (MINUSMA), 25 April 2013–current authorization until 30 June 2019 (latest renewal in June 2018)

In March 2012, Tuareg people in the northern part of Mali rebelled against long-standing discrimination and launched a secessionist rebellion that led to the 1992 constitution's suspension.[357]

The UN set five intertwined benchmarks for returning Mali to constitutional order.[358] Meanwhile, on 1 April 2012, A.H. Sanago (Mali's *de facto* head since the military took control in a coup) reinstated the

[354] Interview by V. Sripati of Fred Mwathengere, Assistant Resident Representative, Governance Cluster, UNDP-Malawi, March 2, 2009 [on file with the applicant]; On these points, *see* also *supra* note 352.

[355] Banda, *supra* note 352 at 7.

[356] 'Malawi: Constitution no longer allows child marriage,' *available at*: Girls not brides https://www.girlsnotbrides.org/malawi-constitution-no-longer-allows-child-marriage [visited in July 2018].

[357] Vicenc Fisas, *2014 Yearbook of Peace Processes* 26 (2014) .

[358] *See, for example, Report of the Secretary-General on the Situation in Mali*, U.N. Doc. S/2013/189 (26 March 2013).

country's constitution.[359] On 6 April 2012, Sanago's junta concluded a Framework Agreement with Economic Community of West African States (ECOWAS) whereby President A.T. Toure resigned, and a transitional 32-member 'government of national unity' was formed.[360]

It helps to note that the coup interrupted Mali's PRSP (constitutional) fiscal reforms.[361] So too was interrupted, the finalization of Mali's 2012 PRSP.[362] Given this, the UN pressured GONU to endorse the 'political roadmap' (outlining the conditionalities). *Only after this* did the BWIs approve aid (2012 PRSP).[363] Next, in February 2013, Helen Clark, the UNDP chief, urged Mali to first adopt a 'time-table for national dialogue, constitutional reform ....'[364] 'Otherwise Mali will fall over again,' she cautioned.[365] Accordingly, in May 2013, to restore donor confidence, the UNDP presented to the donors a revised (2012) PRSP,[366] listing an essential task: constitutional reform.[367] The UNOM and UNDP prioritized reviving Mali's constitutional reforms, to introduce liberalization, privatization, and so on (good governance –benchmark two) because the UN deemed these to be critical to reviving Mali's economy, and thereby, restoring its state authority (benchmark one).

Restoring state authority in turn was deemed key to conducting close and continued dialogue between the rebels (benchmark three).[368] Again, conducting dialogue meant including women – which entailed promoting their political participation and safety, and the safety of their

359 *See* Global Legal Monitor, 'Mali Constitution to be reinstated,' April 9, 2012.

360 *See* ADB, *Republic of Mali: Transition Management Support Strategy 2013-2014*, 1–2 (March 2013).

361 *See* World Bank, Interim Strategy Note for Mali for the period FY2014-2015 ¶7 (May 2013).

362 *See* Isaline Bergamaschi, *Building State Capacities? The case of the Poverty Reduction Unit in Mali, in* States at Work — Dynamics of African Bureaucracies 271, 296 (Thomas Bierschenk & Jean-Pierre Olivier de Sardan, eds., Brill, 2014) .

363 *See* ADB, *supra* note 361 at 2.

364 *See* Harvey Morris, *To Build Lasting Peace in Mali*, N.Y. Times, 12 February 2103.

365 Id.

366 *See* Bergamaschi, *supra* note 363.

367 *See* IMF, Mali Poverty Reduction Strategy Paper 9 (May 2013) .

368 *See Report of the secretary-general on the situation in Mali*, §A U.N. Doc. S/2013/582 (October 2013).

children (benchmarks four and five).[369] MINUSMA monitored schools to stop kidnapping by armed groups (benchmark five).[370] The input of Said Djinnit, Special Representative for West Africa, amplified women's voices in the peace talks. Indeed, the preliminary Ougadougou Agreement, signed in June 2013 by the Tuareg rebels, described sexual violence as a cease-fire violation, and envisaged reforms in politico-economic governance as a means to address grievances.[371] Accordingly, the final peace agreement (2015) channeled the BWIs' conditionalities (for example, decentralization) to implement which, Mali readied a draft constitution in 2017, and aided by the BWIs, also finalized draft laws on decentralization.[372] The Council has mandated MINUSMA to help Mali in holding a constitutional referendum this year.[373]

## UN Assistance Mission for Rwanda (UNAMIR), October 1993-March 1996

Rwanda is made up of two major ethnic groups, the Tutsis and the Hutus. Discrimination practiced first by Belgium, and then from 1962 by successive post-independence regimes, triggered cycles of ethnic violence, culminating in a civil war (War) in 1990. So did the WB's economic programs (conditionalities) which adversely affected the poor, who therefore protested.[374] Indeed, President Major Habyarimana's government (a single-party Hutu-dominated dictatorship) had begun implementing the WB's conditionalities from 1991, which included the adoption of a Constitution in May 1991, and Burundi's consequent

369 Id. at 10.

370 Id.

371 Id. at 1-3 *See* S.C. Res. 2164, U.N. SCOR, 7210 mtg., ¶pmbl U.N. Doc. S/Res/2164 (25 June 2014).

372 *See* Letter dated 22 January 2018 from the Permanent Representative of Mali to the UN addressed to the President of the Security Council, ¶II A, UN Doc., S/2018/58 (31 January 2018); World Bank, Report No. 94005-ML 77 (November 2015); For Peace Agreement's text (French) *see* https://photos.state.gov/libraries/mali/328671/peace-accord-translations/1-accord-paix-et-reconciliation-francais.pdf.

373 *See* S.C. Res. 2423, U.N. SCOR, 8298th mtg., ¶ 38A (iv) U.N. Doc. S/Res/2423 (28 June 2018).

374 The World Bank, Rwandese Republic: Report No. 14873 i (July 19, 1995).

transition to a multi-party system.[375] (This served as a prelude to negotiations on power-sharing.)[376]

But the War continued (albeit with long periods of cease-fire). So did the peace talks and the conditionalities. Accordingly, in 1993 the Arusha Peace Agreement incorporated protocols stipulating:

- Rule of law promotion (for example, anti-corruption);
- A multi-party, broad-based transitional government within 37 days of signing;
- A NHRI and;
- A new Constitution made by a commission, (with UNCA), to be to be presented for a public vote at a referendum. For, the 1991 constitution was not effectively applied.[377]

Rwanda's 1991 Constitution and the 1993 Arusha Agreement formed the national legal framework for, and guided the Transitional Government during, the transitional period.[378] Welcoming Arusha's conclusion, the Security Council tasked the UNAMIR in October 1993 with UNCA.[379]

The War's last phase from April to July 1994 degenerated into genocide, so the UN withdrew its forces in April, leaving a skeletal presence in Kigali. In July 1994, the RPF unilaterally declared a ceasefire, allying with four other political parties to form the Government of National Unity (GONU),[380] created a Transitional National Assembly, and in return for debt-relief, pledged to implement the Arusha accords during the new transition period, 1994 to 2003.

[375] Id.

[376] Id.

[377] Art. 7, 23, 5–6, 24 (b), 41, 15, *Peace Agreement between the Government of the Republic of Rwanda and the Rwandese Patriotic Front, available at:* peacemaker.un.org/rwanda-peaceagreementrpf93.

[378] Id. at Art. 3.

[379] *See* S. C. Res. 872, U.N. SCOR, 3288$^{th}$ mtg., ¶11 & 14 U.N. Doc. S/Res/872 (1993).

[380] *See* W. Gasanegara, *The constitution-making process in Rwanda: Lessons to be learned, Presented to the 7$^{th}$ Global Forum for Reinventing government*, Austria, June 26–28, 2007.

### *UNCA Fused with Development Assistance: 1994-2003*

The UN therefore returned in the summer of 1994.[381] The PRSPs replaced the SAPs in 1999. Accordingly, the UNDP helped Rwanda commence its constitution-making with the I-PRSP's submission in 2000.[382] The UNDP next assisted the Constitutional Commission with UNCA standard form.[383] The UNDP's trilingual campaigns (in French, English, and Kinyarwandan) prepared a wide section of Rwandese for the May 2003 referendum, where 93% of them accepted the constitution.[384]

## UN Observer Mission in Sierra Leone (UNOMSIL), 13 July 1998 to 22 October 1999; UN Mission in Sierra Leone (UNAMSIL), 22 October 1999 to 31 December 2005; UN Integrated Office in Sierra Leone (UNIOSIL), 1 January 2006 to 30 September 2008; UN Integrated Peacebuilding Office in Sierra Leone (UNIPSIL), 1 October 2008 to 24 March 2014

Sierra Leone convulsed with an eleven-year civil war from 1990 to 2002. The Revolutionary United Front (RUF), a rebel group comprising disaffected youth controlling Sierra Leone's diamond mines, and based in Monrovia (Liberia), fought against the government of Sierra Leone (GoSL). The war choked the economy. Within three months of its outbreak, in 1991, the GoSL adopted a new Western-style constitution,[385] in return for the BWIs' aid. It had used this aid intermittently from the 1980s, and was to use it continuously from 1994.[386] Accordingly, the UNOMSIL-brokered Lome Agreement (July 1999), which ended the

381 UN, *The UN in Rwanda: Ten Years on: Helping Rebuild a Nation* 4 (UN, 2004).

382 Id.

383 Id. *See also The Government of Rwanda: PRSP* (June 2002).

384 *See* Final Report, Workshop on civic education for elections in Rwanda, May 15-18, 2002; Rwanda: UN, donors to assist government in 2003 elections, 18 November 2002; Europa publications, *Africa South of the Sahara 2004* 873 (2003).

385 UNDP, 'Support to Sierra Leone Constitutional Review Project,' *available at:* www.sl.undp.org.

386 *See* IMF, Sierra Leone: Ex Post Assessment of longer-term program engagement (2005).

war, channelled the BWIs' conditionalities.[387] (However, peace was only formally declared in 2002.)

The Lome Agreement (Agreement) implicitly and explicitly stipulated constitutional revisions.[388] I will discuss the implicit and explicit stipulations in this, and the next para respectively. The Agreement brought the junta, warlords, and their cohorts fighting over gold and diamonds, onto a legal platform, stipulating that they together form a Government of National Unity (GONU), *i.e.*, exercise power in the politico-economic domains through 'illegal peace.'[389] Creating this GONU required constitutional revisions[390] – which was just what the UNOMSIL accomplished. So, a GONU comprising the GoSL and RUF was formed, which co-managed (and profited) from the privatized natural resources' sector from 1999 to 2007.[391]

The Agreement explicitly called for a Constitution Review Commission (CRC), a call repeated in 2002, by the Truth and Reconciliation Commission.[392] However, a CRC was not established until September 2006, and then only to restore donor confidence.[393] (In July that year, Sierra Leone, crushed by the global financial crisis, had signed the Improved Governance and Accountability Pact in return for further debt relief).[394] Welcoming these developments, the Security Council mandated UNIOSIL to promote women's participation.[395]

A new CRC came up in July 2013.[396] From 2014, the UNDP offered this CRC drafting and knowledge-based support to enable it 'to

[387] *See* pmbl ¶ *Peace Agreement between the Government of Sierra Leone and the Revolutionary United Front of Sierra Leone*, Lomé, (Togo, 7 July 1999).

[388] Id. at VII, art. 14 & Art. X.

[389] *See* Jeremy Levitt, *Illegal Peace in Africa: An Inquiry into the Legality of Power-Sharing With Warlords, Rebels & Junta* 93 (Cambridge University Press, 2011).

[390] Id.

[391] Id. at 94.

[392] UNDP, *supra* note 1.

[393] *See Sixth Report of the Secretary-General on the United Nations Integrated Office in Sierra Leone*, §F U.N. Doc. S/2008/281 (29 April 2008).

[394] *See Second Report of the Secretary-General on the UN Integrated Office in Sierra Leone*, ¶ 38 U.N. Doc. S/2006/695 (29 August 2006).

[395] *See* S.C. Res. 1734, U.N. SCOR, 5608$^{th}$ mtg., ¶8-9, U.N. Doc. S/Res/1734 (2006)

[396] UNDP, *supra* note 386.

more effectively' undertake its responsibilities.[397] By February 2016, the public participation and consultation phases were completed.[398] Next, Sanaullah Baloch, the UNDP's Technical Adviser, introduced discussion on: natural resources, fiscal transparency, and so on (conditionalities).[399] UN-Women reviewed the 1991 Constitution to identify discriminatory provisions to guide the CRC on strengthening gender equality.[400] And, the UN helped to draft a child-protection act and create an anti-corruption commission and a NHRC.[401] A white paper containing the government's official response to the CRC's recommendations was published in November 2017. The next step will be for the government to table a Constitutional Amendment bill before parliament.

## UNCA-ITA

### UN Operation in Somalia, UNOSOM–I, April 1992–March 1993; UN Operation in Somalia, UNOSOM-II, March 1993–July1994; August 1994–March 1995 (downsized); UN Political Office in Somalia, UNPOS, 15 April 1995–3 June 2013

*UNCA-(Plenary) ITA: March–October 1993*

Somalia broke out into a civil war in 1991.[402] According to the UN, by 1991, clan-based guerrilla groups had taken over central Somalia, and the south-central regions had plunged into instability.[403] For these reasons, the UN took over this 'failed state's' governance in ways set out in this paragraph. The UN operation in Somalia (UNOSOM-II) was introduced in March 1993, to secure with the support of the Somali

[397] Id.

[398] Id.

[399] Id.

[400] Id. at 11.

[401] *See* UNSG Report, *supra* note 394 at ¶44, §D, ¶40 .

[402] *See* 'Historical Background,' *at:* United Nations Operation in Somalia I (UNOSOM-I).

[403] The UN in Somalia 2014, New York, United Nations Development Programme, 2014, p. 1 http://www.undp.org/content/dam/unct/somalia/docs/publications/FINAL%20UN%20SOMALIA%20Yearbook%20Layout.pdf.

factions, a political solution to the conflict (an example of UNCA).[404] And, UNOSOM-II simultaneously strove to manage hospitals, distribute food, restore law and order, and demobilize the combatants (an example of plenary ITA).[405]

### *October 1993: American Losses in Somalia Ends Plenary ITA there, and in Other Sovereign States*

However, in October 1993, Somali forces instead of demobilizing, downed two American Black Hawk helicopters. In retaliation, all the major Western powers, including the US, withdrew their forces by 31 March, 1994.[406] For this reason, the UN's plenary ITA ended as well.[407]

### *October 1993–July 2012: Only UNCA Marches on*

However, UNOSOM II continued to offer constitutional assistance until March 1995, for 'one primary ostensible purpose:' 'Political reconciliation.'[408] UNPOS (UNOSOM II's successor) was established a month later, but achieved a breakthrough only in February 2004, when the Somali factions concluded the Transitional Federal Charter (Charter).[409] Given Somalia's utter breakdown, aid was mobilized not through the PRSP, but via the WB's Low-Income Countries under Stress (LICUS) Initiative.[410] As we might expect, the Charter enshrined the market economy, outlawed corruption, and encouraged foreign investment.[411] The Charter, operating simultaneously as a transitional constitution, provided for a Transitional Federal Government (TFG), which

[404] Somalia - UNOSOM-II (undated); S.C. Res. 814, U.N. SCOR., 3188$^{th}$ mtg., ¶4 U.N. Doc. S/Res/814 (26 March 1993). The impending Constitution influenced ITA.

[405] *See* Wilde, ITA *supra* note 1 at 222.

[406] *See* Background, UNOSOM-II website.

[407] Id. In UN jargon, this meant the start of UNOSOM-II's 'downsizing' culminating in its 'liquidation' on 31 March 1995.

[408] Id.

[409] Transnational Federal Charter for the Somali Republic, February 2004.

[410] *See* World Bank, Additional Activities Note on Somalia 1–6 (2005).

[411] Id. at Art. 27, 4 (b), 71 (10).

functioned from 2004 to 2009.[412] The Security Council welcomed the TFG, assuring it of the UN's support.[413]

As per the Charter, an Independent Federal Constitutional Commission (IFCC) comprising men, women, judges, and religious elders, and representing different Somali clans, was established in 2006 to craft a new constitution.[414] Meanwhile, the Djibouti peace process and the resulting Agreement (18 August 2008) led to a new moderate Islamist TFG (new TFG, 2010 to 2012).[415] This in turn, doubled IFC's membership to thirty members, of whom six were women.[416]

Somalia's market-oriented transition was begun by the Charter, and came full circle with the Garowe Principles. The Garowe Principles stipulated that a National Constituent Assembly (NCA), comprising no less than three hundred women, adopt the (federal) constitution through a participatory process.[417] Accordingly, UNPOS:

- sent experts (for example, Hassan Ebrahim & David Cameron) who provided drafting assistance and advised the IFCC's members on fiscal federalism and natural resources governance;[418]
- audited the constitution;[419]
- invited public input on the Draft constitution, which was ready by July 2010;[420] and
- helped establish the NCA.

412 *See* United Nations-INSTRAW, Women, peace and security in Somalia, 14–15 (August 2008).

413 *See* S. C. Res. 1744, U.N. SCOR., 5633rd mtg., ¶3 U.N. Doc. S/Res/1744 (21 February 2007)

414 *See* Sylvia T. Panfil, *Somalia, in,* Constitutional Development with Civil Society — Case Studies from Southern and East Africa 4 (2012) (on file).

415 Id.

416 Id.

417 *See* Statement on Adoption of the Roadmap, Mogadishu, 6 September 2011; *Somali National Constitutional Conference, Garowe, Somalia, 21-23 December 2011.*

418 *Sources: Report of the Secretary-General on the situation in Somalia,* §69, U.N. Doc. S/2008/178 (14 March 2008); Tel. Interview with Alvaro Rodriguez, UNDP official, April 2011.

419 *See* interview, *supra* note 419 .

420 UNPOS, Somali Constitution-Making Support Project 6–9 (undated).

The draft constitution was adopted by the NCA on 1 July 2012, [421] and welcomed by the Security Council.[422]

## UN Mission in Sudan (UNMIS), 24 March 2005–9 July 2011, UN Mission in South Sudan (UNMISS), July 2011–March 2019 [current authorization]

On 9 July 2011 South Sudan became the world's newest country through its secession from the Sudan.[423] To understand UNCA in South Sudan requires starting from UNCA in united Sudan's (Sudan), constitutional past.

### *Sudan's Constitutional Past*

Sudan experienced two civil wars that extended from 1955-1972 and 1983–2005, respectively. At their crux, these civil wars arose because successive regimes (in Khartoum or the north) had left the South undeveloped.[424] The North/'Southern Sudan' divide, also lies in the ethnic and religious cleavages, and the repression of, and resistance to Khartoum's authoritarian rule.[425] For instance, the North's imposition of sharia law in 1983 (as a prelude to an Islamic constitution) over the largely Christian South fueled intense conflict.[426]

As for the second civil war — relevant for this discussion — the UN closely followed and supported the efforts of the Intergovernmental Authority on Drought and Development (IGADD) to end it.[427]

[421] *See* UN News Center, 'UN Officials welcome 'historic' approval of new constitution for Somalia,' 1 August 2012

[422] S. C. Res. 2067, U.N. S.C.O.R. mtg., pmbl ¶4 U.N. Doc. S/Res/2067 (18 Sept. 2012)

[423] UN News Centre, 'Sudan: UN hails South's vote for independence, but cautions on tasks ahead,' 9 July 2011.

[424] *See* Matthew Le Ritchie & Mathew Arnold, *South Sudan: From Revolution to independence* 23–31 (Columbia University Press, 2012)

[425] Id.

[426] Tim Niblock, *The Background to the Change of Government in 1985 in*, Sudan after Nimeiri 34, 39 (Peter Woodward, ed., Taylor & Francis, 1991).

[427] *See* 'UNMIS Background,' United Nations Mission in the Sudan, *available at:* http://www.un.org/en/peacekeeping/missions/past/unmis/background.shtml.

(Importantly, since 2000, Sudan had been receiving 'IMF technical advice,' and 'implementing a series of its Staff Monitored programs').[428] Finally, in January 2005, the Khartoum-based regime of Omar Hassan al-Bashir and his National Congress Party (NCP) and the Sudan People's Liberation Army/Movement (SPLA/M) concluded the Comprehensive Peace Agreement (CPA).[429] Meanwhile, the WB-and-UN-conducted Sudan Joint Assessment Mission (JAM) ran for one year, in parallel to and to support the peace process.[430] As might be expected, the CPA.

- positioned the Constitution—made with UNCA—at Sudan's national and sub-national level: the Interim National Constitution of Sudan (NIC) and the Interim Constitution of Southern Sudan (IC), both endorsed free markets and called for curbing corruption.[431]

And UNMIS' Child Protection Unit and Gender Unit:

- worked to ensure the IC and NIC recognized children's rights;
- strove to strengthen women's rights in the interim constitutions, including securing explicit quotas for their representation in government; and
- monitored the CPA rule, which made sharia inapplicable to non-Muslims throughout Sudan during the Interim Period.[432]

In this way, the CPA:

- allowed the national government and Southern Sudan to maintain separate Constitutions—and armies, budgets, and laws;

[428] *See* IMF, Sudan: Country Report No. 11/86 2 (2011).

[429] *See The Comprehensive Peace Agreement between the Government of the Republic of the Sudan and The Sudan People's Liberation Movement/Sudan People's Liberation Army*, 2005 [CPA].

[430] *See* Taj E. Mahjoub, 'Framework for sustained peace, development, and poverty eradication,' 4, 6 (Nairobi, 2005) [slides]. The JAM report's drafting was completed in January 2005 and was presented to the donors' roundtable in March 2005. Id. S.C. Res. 1574, U.N. SCOR., 5082th mtg., ¶3 U.N. Doc., S/Res/1574 (9 November 2004).

[431] CPA, *supra* note 430 at Machakos Protocol, Ch.1, Part C & II.

[432] Id.

- addressed Southern Sudan's marginalization by setting a six-year Interim Period (9 July 2005–9 July 2011), during which time the seeds of good governance were to be sown;
- and toward this end, allowed Southern Sudan the right to govern affairs in its region according to the IC and to participate equitably in the national government; after which, it would have the right to vote in an UN-monitored referendum either to confirm Sudan's unity or vote for secession; and
- provided for a roughly 50:50 sharing of revenues from oil produced in the Southern Sudan between the two parts of the country.[433]

In this way, (1) the Constitution came to be imposed over a united Sudan, and thus, shaped South Sudan's constitutional future, even after secession; and (2) the BWIs' *conditionalities* guided a united Sudan's constitutional present (which became South Sudan's constitutional past), (and future of both Sudan and South Sudan.

### *Southern Sudan's Constitutional Present and Future: December 2011–18*

On 7 July 2011, Southern Sudan adopted the Transitional Constitution of the Republic of South Sudan (TCSS).[434] Prepared with international assistance, the TCSS provided Southern Sudan (which was then an autonomous region) a framework to transit into, so as to operate as the independent *state of South Sudan*. As one would expect, the TCSS promoted free markets, human rights, and anti-corruption measures.[435]

Meanwhile, officially speaking, a permanent constitution mirroring the South Sudanese's concerns was envisaged. Therefore, the National Constitutional Review Commission (NCRC) began a review of the TCSS in January 2012. At the time of writing in 2016, that review is underway. So too, is the IMF's rule of law assistance in these areas: fiscal, monetary, and exchange rate policies.[436] Established to help the NRC,

[433] Id. at Chapters I–III.

[434] *See The Transitional Constitution of the Republic of South Sudan*, 2011.

[435] Id. Thomas Omestad, 'Just days from independence, South Sudan approves Transitional Constitution,' 7 July 2011, *available at*: https://www.usip.org/events/building-inclusive-stronger-peace-processes-heres-how.

[436] *See* IMF, *supra* note 429 at 10.

the UN Mission in South Sudan's (UNMISS) role includes amplifying the voices of women, and youth in making the permanent constitution.[437] Since 16 December 2016, the Security Council has passed no new resolution regarding UNCA.

### *UNCA in Sudan, 2005-till Date*

On 12 December, 2010, the BWIs hosted a debt workshop in Khartoum, where they provided the CPA's parties with factual information and objective analysis to help them understand issues related to Sudan's unsustainable external debt.[438] This workshop stressed 'the importance of laying out a roadmap for Sudan to normalize its relations with IMF and move swiftly toward debt-relief.'[439] Against this background, and expectedly, the UNMIS and the UNDP offered their 'support to the Government [of Sudan] in preparing the ground for the process of Sudan's constitutional revision' (along good governance lines).[440]

That support (UNCA's standard form) is currently being offered.[441] For instance, in May 2011, UNMIS, UNDP and 5 other UN entities (UN Women, WHO, UNICEF, UNHCR and UNFPA), in collaboration with the Advisory Council for Human Rights, held a forum at the Burj al-Fateh in support of constitution-making processes in Sudan.[442] Next, the UNDP helped Sudan submit its Interim PRSP (2011).[443] And, two years later, as part of implementing it, 'President Omar al-Bashir called for a comprehensive participation in a national dialogue on political reforms, including preparation of a new constitution to replace the Interim Constitution....'[444] The IMF welcomed this decision. It reminded Sudan that 'the preparation of a constitution' 'would provide the opportunity

[437] *See* S.C. Res. 1996, U.N. SCOR., 6576th mtg., ¶12 U.N. Doc., S/Res/1996 (8 July 2011)

[438] *See* IMF, *supra* note 429 at 13.

[439] Id.

[440] UNDP-Sudan, Concept Note: Support to the constitution-making process in Sudan 1(undated).

[441] Id. at 1–3.

[442] *See* Republic of Sudan, Constitution-making Symposium (undated), *available at:* http://unmis.unmissions.org/Default.aspx?tabid=4865.

[443] Sudan: IMF Country Report No. 13/318 2 (October 2013).

[444] Id. at 5.

for strengthening the basis for decentralized and inclusive governance.'[445] We have previously noted how a BWI explicitly connected the two Cs: Conditionalities and the Constitution (*see* Guinea entry). Here is another instance. Another instance will appear in the next entry.

Finally, during 2005-2011, Sudan (aided by the OHCHR and UNMIS) promulgated the Human Rights Commission Act, 2008, (and established family and child protection units) and the Act on combating money laundering and financing terrorism (2011) respectively.[446] David Cameron and Muna Ndulo served as foreign experts.

## The Gambia

UNCA began in The Gambia in 2017, making this smallest country in continental Sub-Saharan Africa, the most recent UNCA-recipient-state. Gambia lacks natural resources and relies heavily on its ties to the global economy.

### *The Gambia Implements the SAPs: Adopts the 1997 Constitution*

From 1983 till the present day, Gambia has consistently relied on the BWIs for aid.[447] According to the IMF, most donors cut off aid and budget support when Yahya Jammeh seized power through a coup in July 1994.[448] Jammeh remained in power for the next 22 years. With a view a view to normalize relations with donors, he took 'corrective measures': he sought to restore macro-economic stability by adopting a new Constitution in 1997.[449] Gambian efforts to reform the legal and regulatory system along Western lines continued through the 1990s and the 2000s under the auspices of the PRSPs.[450] In fact, in December 2016, The Gambia was well into implementing its 2nd PRSP when, in

[445] Id. at 20, –76 (Annex 1: Policy Matrix).

[446] Id at 23, 27.

[447] *Enhanced Structural Adjustment Facility Policy Framework Paper*, 1998-2000, *at:* https://www.imf.org/external/np/pfp/gambia/gam01.htm.

[448] Id.

[449] Id.

[450] *See* IMF Country Report No. 09/75 48-50 (February 2009); IMF Country Report No. 07/38 §6.1.2. (September 2007).

the elections held that month, Jammeh was defeated by a seven-party coalition that supported current President Adam Barrow as a nonpartisan unity candidate.[451]

### *The Constitutional Crisis*

On 1 December, Jammeh, publicly recognized and accepted the Independent Electoral Commission's (IEC) verdict that Mr. Barrow had won.[452] But by the 9th , Jammeh declared that he would not step down. On December 13, 2016, the Gambian armed forces took control of the IEC and on January 18, 2017, the Gambian Parliament attempted to extend his term for three months beyond his current mandate. On 19th January 2017, the Security Council endorsed the African Union's decision that as of that day, President Jammeh will cease to be recognized as legitimate President of the Republic of The Gambia.[453] The Council requested the Secretary-General to offer UNCA (in tandem with ECOWAS) to ensure the Presidential election's outcome is respected.[454]

### *UNCA Works To Build Peace: Ensure Gambia Fulfills Its Conditionalities*

As we know and the World Bank's statement reproduced below evidences, re-establishing state authority, the first benchmark for restoring constitutional order, requires ensuring a continuity in implementing the BWIs' conditionalities. To ensure just this, Mohamed Ibn Chambas, the SRSG and head of the United Nations Office for West Africa and the Sahel (UNOWAS) visited Banjul on a regular basis from February where he engaged with all stakeholders, and guided the efforts of the United Nations Country Team.[455]

451 S.C. Res. 2337, U.N. SCOR., 7866th mtg., ¶pmbl 4 U.N. Doc., S/Res/2337 (19 January 2017).

452 Id. at pmbl ¶ 5.

453 Id. at pmbl ¶ 11.

454 Id. at ¶ 12.

455 UNDPA, 2017 *Annual Report – Multi-Year Appeal* 13 (undated) *at*: https://www.un.org/undpa/sites/www.un.org.undpa/files/MYA_2017_AR_Screen_19MAR18.pdf.

### *The BWIs Call For a New Constitution*

The World Bank and AfDB teams co-conducted a parallel joint Fragility and Resilience Mission in Banjul Dakar between February 24 and March 9, 2017 and co-concluded that:

> The Barrow administration inherited an economy on the verge of crisis. The public debt-to-GDP ratio is estimated at 119.5 percent …. The preliminary results of a 2017 joint World Bank-IMF Debt Sustainability Analysis indicate that The Gambia's risk of external debt distress has risen …to high. The government lacks access to international financial markets and relies on borrowing to finance a large structural fiscal deficit. In this context, the new government must remain firmly committed to … structural reforms ….
>
> The government has stated its commitment to … structural reform…. A failure to engage the support of international financial institutions would threaten the stability of the new government, as the alternative would be a forced fiscal and external adjustment with deeply negative implications for the Gambian economy.
>
> Without robust assistance from the donors, it is unlikely that the new government will be able to accomplish its goal of creating a fully functioning democratic government supported by appropriate checks and balances. …. Both the constitutional separation of powers and the reform of legislative procedures should be included in the policy dialogue that underpins external budget support.[456]

Barrow's party, the United Democratic Party won the majority of seats in the April 2017 Gambian National Assembly (GNA) elections. The Barrow-led GNA followed up in November, by adopting a Law establishing Gambia's Constitutional Reform Commission that will draft the new Constitution (enshrining among other things, a Truth and Reconciliation Commission TRC).[457] The 1997 Constitution lacks a TRC, which the UN considers essential to enabling The Gambia meet the challenges thrown up by the 2016 crisis.[458] On 19 January, 2018, President Barrow was sworn in at his country's embassy in Dakar (capital of Senegal) with which The Gambia shares a single 749-kilometer

[456] A Joint AfDB-WB Report No. 117432-GM (June 9, 2017).

[457] Ozonnia Ojielo, Gambians are ready to rebuild their country, 24 March 2017 *at:* UNDP-Africa website.

[458] Id.

overland border. Ambassadors from countries in the Security Council and key African states were present at the swearing-in ceremony. The UNDP has just begun to offer UNCA's standard form.[459] Thus, both of The Gambia's recent constitutions will result from the BWIs' conditionalities.

## Zambia

The UNDP offered UNCA from 2003 to 2016.[460] This was so because each sitting President initiated his own process to reform Zambia's 1991 constitution,[461] to implement relevant PRSPs from 2000 to 2007.[462] The aim was to introduce privatization, economic liberalization, and so on, which evoked strong public protests because it primarily benefited foreign investors.[463] For example, in 2002 trade unionists demanded that states retain ownership of companies.[464] President Levy initially accepted their demands. However, he turned *volte face* in December 2002, when the IMF publicly warned that rejecting privatization 'would breach Zambia's PRSP, threatening the debt relief possible under the PRSP.'[465]

In November 2011, President Sata appointed the Technical Committee on Drafting the Zambian Constitution (TCDZC), mandating it to produce a constitution that would 'effectively entrench and promote good governance, the rule of law.'[466] Accordingly, the UNDP educated the TCDZC's commissioners on concepts including decentralized governance (a conditionality) by funding foreign experts and trips to Asia and Europe.[467]

459 Id.

460 *See* The UN Constitutional – Issue 5, 17 (2016).

461 *See* Neo Simutayni, *The Politics of Constitutional Reform in Zambia: From Executive Dominance to Public Participation, in* Accountable government in Africa 26–42 (Danwood M. Chirwa and Lia Nijzink, eds, 2012).

462 *See Zambia: Poverty Reduction Strategy Paper Progress Report* 6 (June 2004); UNDP, *Government of the Republic of Zambia (GRZ): Governance Programme (2011-2015)* 1-2 (2012).

463 Miles Larmer, *Mineworkers in Zambia: Labour and Political Change in Post-colonial Africa* 179 (Palgrave Macmillan, 2007).

464 Id.

465 Id.

466 Dimpho Mostamai, Zambia's constitution-making process 5 (2014).

467 UN, *supra* note 461.

UNICEF, UNPFA, and UNHCR audited the Draft Constitution (Draft), 'to ensure it has stronger human rights provisions.'[468]

The Draft was completed in 2013.[469] However, the Minister of Justice, Edgar Lungu held onto it until late 2014, until finally releasing it to the general public.[470] Lungu became President in January 2015, and he resumed the reform process that month.[471] An IMF Team visited Zambia in April, and commented at length on how the Draft met the conditionalities, and how it could be further aligned with the IMF's ongoing rule of law assistance in Zambia.[472] (Here comes the instance of how a BWI explicitly connects not only the two Cs: Conditionalities but also rule of law assistance with its parent: UNCA.) Against this backdrop, president Lungu proposed a 'compromise' in July 2015. He rejected the popular pleas to submit the Draft to a referendum, and presented it to parliament (minus the Bill of Rights and Amendment clauses) for immediate enactment.[473] Moreover, he gave his own assent on 5 January 2016.[474] (Hence, constitutional provisions, supposedly deemed 'non-contentious,' that is, concerning the conditionalities, were not put to a public vote.)[475] Lungu communicated that he opted for this process because it was cost effective.[476] However, the Bill of Rights and the amendment clauses were put to a vote in a referendum, held with UNCA in August 2016.[477]

## Zimbabwe

Zimbabwe experienced post-electoral violence in 2008. The international response to the conduct of the March 2008 elections and

468 Id.

469 M.M. Munalula, The 2016 Constitution of Zambia: elusive search for a people driven process, 2016 *available at:* www.constitutionnet.com.

470 Id.

471 Id.

472 IMF, Zambia: IMF Country Report No. 15/240 1-57(June 2015).

473 Munalula, *supra* note 470.

474 Id.

475 Id.

476 President Lungu ushers in a new constitution, calls for a new approach to politics, *Lusaka Times*, January 5, 2016.

477 *See* Munalula *supra* note 470.

the violence thereafter led to an internationally brokered agreement between the three largest parties: The Global Political Agreement, 2008 (GPA).[478] The GPA was brokered by the Southern African Development Community.[479]

### *The Trigger: BWIs'-Approved Strategy for Debt Relief (in Lieu of a PRSP)*

For a long time, the international community had shunned Zimbabwe, and the IMF had frozen ties with it.[480] The GPA therefore gave Zimbabwe an option to re-enter the international community: by embracing good governance (conditionalities). In return for aid, the parties consented to do just that.[481] Accordingly, they decided to urgently address the issue of poverty,[482] by mobilizing 'the international community to support their economic recovery plans.'[483] The GPA provided the framework for a power-sharing arrangement, later known as the Government of National Unity (GNU).[484] The GNU arrangement installed Robert Mugabe as President and Morgan Tsvangirai as Prime Minister. Together, they governed Zimbabwe - albeit contentiously.[485]

As per the GPA, in 2009 the GNU created and tasked the Constitutional Parliamentary Committee (COPAC) with preparing a new draft of a Constitution through a gendered participatory process, within eighteen

[478] Global Political Agreement (Government of National Unity), 15 September 2008 [GPA]. These three are the largest parties: Zimbabwe African National Union-Patriotic Front (ZANU-PF), led by Robert Mugabe, The Movement for Democratic Change-Tsvagirai, led by Morgan Tsvangirai (MDC-T) and The Movement for Democratic Change-Ncube (MDC-N) led by Welshman Ncube.

[479] pmbl ¶ 13.

[480] *See* OFAC, Zimbabwe sanctions program (2013); IMF, Zimbabwe: Country Report No. 13/193 33 (July 2013) [IMF].

[481] GPA, *supra* note 304 at pmbl ¶8.

[482] Id.

[483] Id. at ¶22.7

[484] Id. at ¶20.1.

[485] Jacob W. Chikuhwa, *Zimbabwe: The End of the first Republic* 200-230 (AuthorHouse™ UK Ltd. 2013). Constitutional Amendment No. 19 provided the legal basis for the formation of the GONU in February 2009. Id. at 201.

months.[486] And by 2010, the BWIs had finalized the Strategy for Arrears Clearance, Debt and Development for Zimbabwe (ZADDS).[487] As a first step toward implementing the ZADDS, Zimbabwe commenced the Constitution's internationalized making.[488]

The UNDP:

- Offered drafting assistance;
- Organized a 'stakeholders conference,' and '4,821 meetings throughout the country (reaching approximately 1.2 million people, and targeting women and children, in particular),'
- and so, enabled COPAC to receive '51 written submissions and 2,397 electronic submissions'.[489]

On March 16, 2013, the draft constitution (finalized by COPAC) was put to a public vote at an UNDP-assisted referendum.[490] The constitution was adopted on 22 May 2013.[491]

## Middle East & North Africa [MENA]

### UN Assistance Mission in Iraq, UNAMI, 14 August 2003–31 May 2019

The US invaded and occupied Iraq in March 2003, ostensibly because it had produced weapons of mass destruction, and so had imperiled world security.[492]

#### *FTA & UNCA: April 2003–28 June 2004*

The US established the Coalition Provisional Administration (CPA), which laid the (constitutional) framework: privatized the Iraqi economy,

486 UNDP, *Country Analysis Report for Zimbabwe* 10–18 (2010).

487 IMF, *supra* note 481 at 1.

488 Id. at 31-41; UNDP, *supra* note 487.

489 UNDP, The Road to a New Constitution (undated), *available at:* www.undp.zw.org.

490 Id.

491 Id.

492 David. E. Sanger, *The Struggle for Iraq*, *N.Y. Times*, January 30, 2004.

promoted anti-corruption, and so on.[493] And the UN Assistance Mission in Iraq (UNAMI) was established to co-create with the Bretton Woods Institutions' (BWIs)[494] the good *legal* framework (for example, rule of law assistance). The conditionalities kicked in from the start of occupation, although Iraq, owing to the massive destruction, submitted a formal PRSP only in 2009.[495]

## *Towards Iraq's New Constitution*

In July 2003, Iraq ostensibly moved towards 'self-rule' when the Iraqi Governing Council (IGC), a CPA-appointed 25-member body comprising Iraqi nationals, met for the first time. The IGC announced that it would hand over power to a transitional government by June 2004. As expected, the IGC modeled Iraq's Transitional Law of Administration (TAL) on the Constitution.[496] Accordingly, UNAMI aided the IGC in restoring 'national and local institutions for representative government.'[497]

TAL mandated that an elected Iraqi Constituent Assembly (CA) would make Iraq's new constitution.[498] This recalls how UNCA was introduced, ostensibly to *democratize* Iraq. For hitherto, Iraq's prominent cleric A.A. Sistani had opposed the US idea of having Iraq's constitution sculpted by a CPA-selected body. Sistani had therefore issued a fatwa, calling for an elected CA.[499] Against this background, David Kay, the UN chief weapons inspector, made a damning revelation in 2003: no significant weapons of mass destruction had been found in Iraq.[500] Having

[493] *See* § 1, ¶ 2, *CPA* Reg. No. 1, Doc. No. CPA/REG/16 May 2003/01 (May 16, 2003); CPA, *An Historic Review of CPA Accomplishments* 4 (June 28, 2004).

[494] *See for example,* S.C. Res. 1483, U.N. SCOR., 4761st mtg., ¶8 U.N. Doc. S/Res/1483 (2003); S.C. Res. 1500, U.N. SCOR., 4808th mtg., U.N. Doc. S/Res/1500 (August 2003); World Bank, Report No. P7615 1–12 (January 2004).

[495] Iraq, National Strategy for poverty reduction (2009).

[496] *Law of Administration for the State of Iraq for the Transitional Period* (8 March 2004) [TAL].

[497] S.C. Res. 1511, U.N. SCOR, 4844th mtg., U.N. Doc. S/Res/1511 (16 October 2003).

[498] Id. at art. 59.

[499] *See* Secretary-General, Letter dated 23 February 2004, ¶11 U.N. Doc. S/2004/10 (23 February 2004).

[500] Sanger, *supra* note 493.

thus, lost face, the US now requested the UN to ascertain Iraqi views about constitution-making, ostensibly to protect the rights of the Sunni minority.[501] (Indeed, then-US-President George Bush had famously remarked: 'I do think it would be helpful to get the United Nations in to help write a constitution. I mean, they're good at that.'[502]) Toward this end, a UN fact-finding mission was sent to Iraq, which after touring the country from 6 to 13 February 2004, recommended a democratic process, based on its findings.[503] This recommendation was accepted by the US, which ended its occupation on 28$^{th}$ June 2004 and transferred sovereignty back to an Interim government.[504]

At this juncture, as per the Security Council, the UNAMI:

- Convened a national conference and mounted several programs to strengthen Sunnis' and women's political participation; and
- Assisted in holding the Transitional National Assembly elections on 30 January 2005, wherein United Iraqi Alliance, a Shi'a coalition, won the majority of the seats and Kurdish parties came in second.[505]

From January to October 2005:
The OHCHR established a NHRC.
The UNAMI helped to:

- Establish an 'inclusive' seventy-member Constitution Drafting Committee, to which it added 15 new (Sunni) members and 10 experts; and to which it provided knowledge-based support, including expert guidance on fiscal federalism, constitutionally sharing oil equitably, (because Iraq was deemed 'a divided country'); Sami Shubber (UNEP) drafted the environmental clauses;
- Invite submissions on the draft constitution; and hold the referendum on October 2005, in which the new constitution for an Islamic federal democracy was approved.[506]

501 *See supra* note 500 at 18–19.
502 *See* France lifts veto threat on Iraq, BBC News, 22 September 2003.
503 Id. at 3–4.
504 US hands over power in Iraq, *The Guardian*, 28 June 2004.
505 *Factsheet*: *UN's Support in Iraq's Constitution-Making Process* 2 (undated).
506 Sources: Id. OHCHR in Iraq; UNAMI Fact Sheet 1–2 (7 August 2007); *Report of the Secretary-General Pursuant to Paragraph 30 of Resolution 1546 (2004)*,

*Preface to UNCA in the Arab Spring Context*

UNCA as we know enables debtor states to produce the Constitution and thereby secure debt relief. To understand UNCA's use in Tunisia, Libya, Yemen, Syria and Egypt (MENA states) requires noting that:

(1) In the wake of the Jasmine Revolution (Revolution) (December 2010), the May 2011 Deauville Partnership (Partnership) prescribed UNCA for MENA states, which
(2) in the years leading up to the Revolution, were implementing, in one way or the other, the BWIs' conditionalities.[507]

This preface describes the Revolution and the Partnership.

On 17 December 2010, Mohamed Bouazizi, a Tunisian street vendor, torched himself in protest against the police confiscating the fruit he had bought on credit to sell. This triggered the Revolution (popular protests) across the MENA region. By the end of January, the Revolution had forced Tunisian President, Ben Ali, to flee to Saudi Arabia after twenty-four years of rule. Within the next month, Cairo's youth spearheaded mass demonstrations that forced out of office President Hosni Mubarak, who had ruled Egypt for thirty years. In February, violence flared up in *Dar'a*, a Southern Syrian city. And by June 2011, the Syrian uprising had become militarized. In Yemen, a mass movement that included diverse elements called for ending President A.A. Saleh's reign. And a ceasefire that had been signed in February 2010 with Houthi Northern rebels, now broke down.[508] (Yemen, which has

---

U.N. Doc., S/2005/141 (7 March 2005); *Report of the Secretary-General Pursuant to Paragraph 30 of Resolution 1546 (2004)*, U.N. Doc., S/2006/137 (3 March 2006); For second environment bullet point, *see* UNEP, UNEP in Iraq 36 (2007).

[507] *See generally* IMF, Toward New Horizons - Arab Economic Transformation amid Political Transitions (2014); *See*, for example, World Bank, *Tunisia's Request for Country of Operations Status, Technical Assessment* 4–19 (21 October 2011); World Bank, *Republic of Yemen: Report No. 35070-RY* 32 (May 16, 2006) (affirming that Yemen's first PRSP was from 2003 to 2005, and the second PRSP was slated for 2006-2010); World Bank, *Arab Republic of Egypt: Report No.: 94554-EG* Boxes 1–2 (November 2015).

[508] UN-DPA, Yemen, available *at:* http://www.un.org/undpa/en/middleeast-westasia/yemen.

a history of tribal, regional, and sectarian violence was in December 2010, implementing its second PRSP.) Finally, Libyans from Zelman, Al Beyda and other cities used Twitter and Facebook to demand an end to M. Qaddafi's forty-year dictatorship.

In May 2011, the G8 countries (led by the US) launched the 'Deauville Partnership with Arab countries in transition' (hereinafter Partnership) to support Arab countries transitioning toward becoming 'free, democratic and tolerant societies.'[509] (The Partnership included among others, the European Union, the UN, the Arab League, the OECD, and IFIs including the BWIs and the AfrDB.)[510] With a view to stabilizing the transition countries' economies and supporting their 'governance,' the Partnership proposed to:

- build their capacities to implement good governance reforms; [511] and
- encourage direct assistance through IFIs, and provide bilateral assistance, for 'country-owned reform plans' that would promote growth and opportunity.[512]

This is why MENA states are implementing the same conditionalities *even after the* Revolution and producing the internationally prescribed-Constitution (with UNCA) *despite the Revolution*.

## Egypt

After the Revolution, Egypt adopted a new constitution in 2012, which was short-lived.[513] Egypt therefore adopted a second constitution, on which I will focus. The Revolution led to a delay in finalizing Egypt's UNDAF, which the UNDP had readied in 2011.[514] Therefore, in November 2011, 'the UN in close collaboration with the Government

509 'Deauville Partnership with Arab Countries in transition' (2012).

510 Id.

511 Id.

512 Id.

513 UN, *Strengthening of the democratic process in Egypt, Project No: 00079914 - Progress report* 1(2013).

514 *See UN Development Assistance Framework (UNDAF) for Egypt 2013-2017* 8 (undated).

of Egypt (GOE) reviewed the draft UNDAF,' determining a 'priority area' for its 'development assistance:' 'democratic governance.'[515]

On July 3, 2013, following several days of mass demonstrations against President Mohamed Morsi (the Muslim Brotherhood's one-year leadership), the Egyptian military unilaterally dissolved Morsi's government, suspended the 2012 constitution, and installed Judge Adli Mansour as interim president, pending a new election.[516] (By now, President Morsi's administration had with the BWIs' assistance begun implementing their reforms, which according to the WB, 'prompted a sovereign rating upgrade by Fitch in December 2014;currently Fitch, ... and Moody have a 'stable' outlook for Egypt.').[517] Meanwhile, in July 2013, UN Secretary-General Ban Ki-moon repeatedly expressed concern about 'military interference' in Egypt and urged a quick return to civilian rule.[518]

On 8$^{th}$ July, interim President Mansour issued a constitutional declaration (CD) that served as the country's legal framework until January 2014.[519] The CD/the 2013 transitional roadmap included the review of the constitution and a constitutional referendum.[520] This was reportedly aimed at ensuring the support of Salafists like the *Nour* party, which played a role in drafting the 2012 constitution.[521] On 19 August, the Secretary-General dispatched a top official to hold wide-ranging talks in Cairo on how the organization could best support peace efforts there.[522]

Meanwhile, according to the UN, its 'impartiality'[523] proved to be particularly important during the political events of July-August 2013.[524]

515 Id.

516 *See* UN, *supra* note 514 at 1.

517 World Bank, *Arab Republic of Egypt: Report No.: 94554-EG* 7 (November 2015).

518 UN News Centre, Egypt: Amid violent protests, Ban says all sides must work for peaceful return to civilian rule, 5 July 2013.

519 *See* UN, *supra* note 514 at 1.

520 Id.

521 Jeremy Sharp, 'Egypt: Background and U.S. relations' 2 (July 2013).

522 UN News Centre, *UN Chief Spotlights Egypt, Syria and Pakistan in First Press Conference since Middle East Visit*, 19 August 2013.

523 *See* UN, *supra* note 514 at 1.

524 Id. at 2.

'Within this context,' the UN says, 'it maintained its long-term capacity-building approach, with its particular emphasis on youth and women empowerment.'[525] During July to December 2013, two successive drafts of the new constitution, the second building on the first, were prepared by a committee of 10 judicial experts (C-10), and a constitutional committee of 50 (C 50) members.[526] Accordingly, during this period, UN Women:

- brought together 68 women and trade union leaders, and civil society representatives to develop and advocate 50 recommendations submitted to Egypt's Constitutional Committee;[527] and
- UNDP provided stakeholders with drafting assistance through a series of roundtables on constitutional issues.[528]

Finally, the draft constitution was submitted to the Interim President on 3 December 2013.[529]

On the eve of the referendum, the Secretary-General called on all Egyptians 'to express their differences without violence.'[530] The constitution was ratified at a referendum held with UNCA on 14–15 January 2014.[531] Subsequently, the IMF noting this, stated that:

> The government has developed a plan centered on structural reforms and investment promotion. Crucially, the authorities have already begun the reforms needed to ... make Egypt a more attractive destination for investment.[532]

## United Nations Support Mission in Libya, (UNSMIL), 16 September 2011–15 September 2019

In March 2011, the Security Council sanctioned military intervention in Libya.[533] The goal, as articulated by the U.S. President, was regime

[525] Id.

[526] Id.

[527] *UN Women Annual Report 2013-2014* 54 (undated).

[528] *See* UN, *supra* note 514 at 1.

[529] Id.

[530] UN News Centre, *As Egyptians Vote on New Constitution, Ban Calls for Peaceful, Inclusive Referendum*, January 4, 2014.

[531] *See* UN, *supra* note 514 at 1.

[532] IMF, *Arab Republic of Egypt: Country Report No. 15/33* 1(January 2015).

[533] S.C. Res. 1973, U.N. SCOR., 6498$^{th}$ mtg., S/C/Res 1973 (2011).

change: 'Qaddafi must go, and go for good.'[534] By September 2011, a self-appointed institution, the Transitional National Council (TNC), came to be recognized by the IMF and the Libya Contact Group as the sole representative of the Libyan people.[535] (The Libya Contact Group comprised among others, the US, the UN, the EU, and the Arab League.)[536]

On 3 August 2011, The NTC adopted a Constitutional Declaration (CD), a brief constitutional document to lead the country during the transitional period.[537] Article 30 of the CD drew a road map for the second transitional period, which envisaged a Constituent Assembly 'Committee of the Sixty' (C60) drafting the new constitution and over-*see*ing the national referendum on the new constitution.[538]

Mandated to offer UNCA, UNSMIL helped draft electoral laws and hold elections to the General National Congress (GNC) on 7 July 2012, and the Constituent Assembly on 20 February 2014.[539] UNSMIL mounted several programs to strengthen public participation, particularly of women and youth.[540] On July 7, 2012, the NTC transferred power to the GNC and dissolved itself. The GNC elected M. Yusuf al-Maqarif as the President of the first democratically constituted national unity government.[541] Forty-seven members were elected to the CA, with the other 13 remaining unfilled due to violence.[542]

As mandated by the Security Council,[543] the BWIs, helped Libya to:

[534] Barrack Obama et al, *Libya's pathway to peace*, N.Y. Times, April 14, 2011.

[535] *See* Libya, Chronology of Events, Security Council Report.

[536] Id.

[537] *See* AfDB, *Libya: Country Re-Engagement Note 2014-2016* 3 (April 2014).

[538] Id.

[539] *See* S.C. Res. 2009, UN. SCOR., 6620th mtg., ¶12 U.N. Doc., S/Res/2009 (16 September 2011); *See* Activities, UN Support Mission in Libya (UNSMIL), *at:* https://unsmil.unmissions.org. *See Report of the Secretary-General on the United Nations Support Mission in Libya*, §A U.N. Doc., S/2012/129 (March 2012).

[540] Id.

[541] *See supra* note 536.

[542] Id.

[543] *See* S.C. Res. 2095, U.N. SCOR., 6934th mtg., ¶7a-b U.N. Doc. S/Res/2095 (March 2013).

- enact a specialized anti-corruption law;
- start dismantling restrictive labour laws; and

  modernize the tax and public financial management systems.[544]

UNSMIL established the National Council of Civil Liberties and Human Rights;[545] and the IMF, given Libya's 'hydrocarbon dependency:'

- showed the CA how to 'institutionalize a fiscal rule in the forthcoming constitution with a view to maintaining macro-economic stability.'[546]

The UNSMIL followed up with UNCA (standard forms).[547] It engaged with the CA to promote consensus on decentralization and local government[548] and to constitutionalize the rights of children, women, and minorities.[549] In this way, two drafts were produced, the second incorporating the input provided on the first.[550] However, as of April 2016, some members of the Assembly continued their boycott of the process.[551] In July 2017, the draft received votes in favor from the committee tasked with drafting it.[552]

## United Nations Supervision Mission in Syria (UNSMIS), 21 April 2012–17 August 2012

As of December 2015, Syria's internationalized and multidimensional civil war (War) is ongoing. The US, Russia, Russia, France, United Kingdom, Iran, Turkey, and Saudi Arabia are involved, with the US

[544] *See* AfrDB, *supra* note 538 at 1–13.

[545] *See* The National Transitional Council, Law No. 5/2011.

[546] *See* IMF, *Libya: Country Report No. 13/50* 17 (May 2013).

[547] *See* UNSMIL, *supra* note 561.

[548] *See Report of the Secretary-General on the United Nations Support Mission in Libya*, §III, U.N. Doc. S/2016/452 (16 May 2016).

[549] *Report of the Secretary-General, Children and armed conflict*, ¶92 U.N. Doc. A/70/836-S/2016/360 (20 April 2016).

[550] *See supra* note 549 at 6.

[551] Id.

[552] Libya Committee Votes in Favor of Constitutional Draft, N.Y. Times, 31 July 2017.

backing more moderate elements among the rebel forces and opposing the government of President Bashar al-Assad, as well as the Islamic State and other Islamic extremist groups. However, Russia backs President Assad.[553] The War is 'partly a war of government against people; partly a religious war pitting Assad's minority Alawite sect, aligned with Shiite fighters from Iran and Hezbollah in Lebanon, against Sunni rebel groups'.[554]

So is peace-making/UN Constitutional Assistance, whose current phase only, I will focus on: May 2014–August 2016.[555] UNCA's previous use produced no lasting outcomes: February 23–2 August 2012 and 17 August 2012–14 May 2014.[556] It helps to note that the UNDP and the BWIs supported the 'national economic vision for new Syria' (Plan), which Syria's Working Group on Economic Recovery and Development released in May 2012, at its first meeting in Abu Dabhi.[557] As would be expected, the Plan 'offers no fundamental changes to the neo-liberal macroeconomic policies that were pursued by the Assad regime.'[558]

Staffan de Mistura, who became the Special Envoy for Syria in October 2015, convened multilateral talks in Vienna, which concluded with a road map.[559] To implement this, the Security Council (*see* resolution 2254) set January 2016 and mid-2107 as the target dates for shepherding the government and opposing sides for talks towards a political transition,

[553] *See* Samer N. Abboud, *Syria* 12 (Polity, 2016).

[554] *See* Kathy Gilsinan, The Confused Person's Guide to the Syrian Civil War: A Brief Primer 1 (2015).

[555] *See Letter dated 17 February 2016 from the Secretary-General Addressed to the President of the Security Council*, U.N. Doc., S/2016/152 (17 February 2016); S.C. Res. 2118, U.N. SCOR., 7038th mtg., U.N. Doc., S/Res/2118 (27 September 2013); S.C. Res. 2268, U.N. SCOR., 7634th mtg., U.N. Doc., S/Res/2268 (26 February 2016).

[556] *See for example, Report of the Secretary-General on the implementation of Security Council resolution* 2043 (2012), U.N. Doc., S/2012/523 (July 6, 2012).

[557] *See Chairmen's Conclusions of the International Meeting of the Working Group on Economic Recovery and Development of the Group of Friends of the Syrian People*, Abu Dhabi, 24 May 2012.

[558] Linda Matar, *The Political Economy of Investment in Syria* 145 (Palgrave Macmillan, 2016) (quote); *See* Jeanne Gobat & Kristina Kostial, Syria's conflict economy – IMF working paper ¶40 (2016).

[559] *Statement of the International Syria Support Group Vienna*, 14 November 2015.

and facilitating the new constitution's adoption respectively.[560] The Council encouraged the meaningful participation of women in this UN-facilitated 'political process.'[561] The UN-convened round of talks that lasted from 29 January to 3 February, was suspended due to continuing violence.[562] 2254 continues to guide the UN's ongoing efforts to bring the parties to the negotiating table and end the war. Meanwhile, it is worth noting that Syrian civil society groups have expressed their fears that this unrealistic deadline 'opens the door for the ready imposition of pre-prepared constitutional drafts on the Syrian people.'[563]

In January 2018, at a Russian-hosted peace conference, an agreement to draft Syria's new constitution was reached. As this book goes to the press, the UN Secretary-General, Antonio Guterres has announced the formation of an "inclusive Constitutional Committee that will be facilitated by the UN in Geneva."[564]

## Tunisia

In March 2011, B.C. Essebsi, a long-time official in Ben Ali's regime who became the interim prime minister, consented to the 'Jasmine Plan'/the Deauville Partnership.[565] Essebsi announced elections for a National Constituent Assembly (NCA) that would be responsible for drafting a new constitution and acting as the transitional government's legislative branch. UNCA was offered to achieve just this.[566] For instance, to educate Tunisia's 'highly-wired' youth, the UN uploaded 'Democra Tweet,' a voter's game

[560] S.C. Res 2254, U.N. SCOR 7588th mtg., ¶4, U.N. Doc., S/Res/2254 (2015).

[561] Id.

[562] U.N. announces start of Syria peace talks as government troops advance, February 1, 2016 at: www.reuters.com.

[563] *See* The International Syria Support Group's letter dated 22 April 2016, addressed to the United Nations Special Envoy Stefan de Mistura and his Team).

[564] UN News Centre, UN's Guterres announces Syria's constitutional committee formation, 23 September 2019.

[565] World Bank, Tunisia's request for Country of Operations Status, Technical Assessment 5 (21 October 2011).

[566] UN News Centre, *Ban Pledges Full UN Help for Tunisia's Transition to Democracy*, 22 March 2011.

on Tunisian Radio Mosaique, FM's Facebook page. The UN-assisted elections to the 217-member NCA were held on 23 October 2011.[567]

In the NCA, 58 members were women and the Ennahda, the once-banned Islamist Party, captured 89 seats.[568] The Ennahda formed a 'troika' coalition with two center-left secular political parties, the Congress for the Republic (CPR) and Ettakatol, the social democratic party.[569] The troika adopted a provisional constitution for the transition period (December 2011-January 2014), which saw two governments, the first headed by Hamadi Jebeli (December 2011 to March 2013), and the second headed by Ali Larayedh (March 2013 to January 2014) (discussed in order). M.B. Jaafar became President of the NCA.[570]

### *Constitution-drafting Period: October 2011-January 2014*

This period was buffeted by rising insecurity and disunity in which political parties split both on religious/secular *and* economic issues.[571] For instance, Ennahda's supporters called for the inclusion of Islamic law in the country's future constitution.[572] Some supported the Partnership's neoliberal agenda; others did not.[573] Meanwhile, the WB, having assisted the NCA/Jebeli administration in drafting the new National Investment Code,[574] emphasized the need for Tunisia's compliance with its conditionalities in this way:

> The drafting of a new constitution provides an opportunity for the government to develop a road map for reforms that emphasize good governance principles.[575]

[567] UNDP *Democratic Governance Practice Network* (28 January 2014).

[568] *See* World Bank, *Tunisia: Report No. 86052-TN* 3 (April 1, 2014).

[569] Id.

[570] Mathieu Rousselin, *Is Religion Truly the Main Source of Cleavage in the Tunisian Party Landscape, in* The Tunisian Constitutional Process: Main Actors and Key Issues 7, 40 (Mathieu Rousselin & Christopher Smith, eds., Centre for Global Cooperation Research, 2015).

[571] Id.

[572] Id.

[573] Id.

[574] World Bank, *supra* note 568 at 23.

[575] World Bank, *Interim Strategy Note for the Republic of Tunisia for the Period FY13–14*, 22 (May 17, 2012) .

Small wonder that the first Constitution draft (Draft), released in August 2012 and prepared with UNCA, enshrined an ACC.[576]

Further, although the 1959 Constitution, which was in force while Ben Ali was in power, provided for gender equality, the Draft 'placed women on *unequal* footing with men, and so provoked widespread demonstrations.'[577] At this juncture, the OHCHR audited the draft constitution, providing suggestions on substantive aspects.[578]

The assassinations of two popular opposition leaders in 2013, led to a new mixed, *non-partisan*, and technocratic government headed by Larayedh replacing Jebali's as a means to end the crisis.[579] The second assassination disrupted the NCA's working,[580] which in turn led to the IMF withholding further assistance.[581]

Against this background, four civil society organizations (the Quartet), successfully pressured Larayedh to accept its 'Roadmap' on September 23, whereby:[582]

The NCA:

- Recommenced work on October 25, 2013;
- Deputed two representatives from each of its political parties to participate in a 'national dialogue process' (NDP) (mediated by the Quartet), starting from October 25,[583] who were co-trained by the UN and WB in topics including financial management and budget analysis;[584]

576 For tangible UNCA details *see* UNDP, *supra* note 567; Art. 7.13, Draft of the Constitution of the Republic of Tunisia, August 14, 2012 (Unofficial translation prepared on behalf of International IDEA).

577 *See* UNDP, *supra* note 567

578 *See OHCHR Report 2013* 348 (2014); *UNICEF 2014 Annual Report regarding social inclusion* 5 (UNICEF, New York).

579 *See* Chris Thornton, *The Rocky Path from Elections to a New Constitution in Tunisia: Mechanisms for Consensus-Building and Inclusive Decision-Making* Oslo Forum, 59, 60 (2014).

580 Id.

581 Id. *See also* World Bank, *supra* note 568.

582 Thornton, *supra* note 579 at 62.

583 Id.

584 *See* World Bank, *Report No: ACS18676* 1–10 (June 7, 2016) .

- Elected on December 14, Mehdi Jomaâ, a non-partisan politician, who enjoyed strong support ('reportedly even from many European governments') as the caretaker PM, responsible for organizing fresh elections, and over*see*ing Tunisia until then;[585] and
- Adopted the new (preferred) constitution on January 14, 2014 only after which, the IMF loan was released.[586]

According to the WB, Tunisia's constitutional 'provisions on access to information, natural resource management, PFM, and decentralization are key areas of progress that will likely provide opportunities for WBG support in Tunisia.'[587]

## The Office of the UN Special Adviser on Yemen, January 2012-June 2012; Special Envoy Yemen, June 2012 – till the Present

In November 2011, pressured by the Gulf Cooperation Council, President Saleh stepped down.[588] Under the Transition Agreement (Agreement) brokered by the UN Special Envoy, Jamal Benomar, feuding politicians formed a 'Government of National Unity' (GONU) on January 2012. The cabinet portfolios were split equally between the former ruling party, the General People's Congress and the opposition bloc, the Joint Meeting Parties (JMP).[589] The GONU was ratified through presidential elections held on 21$^{st}$ February 2012, where A.R.M. Hamdi, came to be elected as acting President.[590]

As might be expected, the Agreement called for:

- Immediate compliance with the rule of law and 'good governance' standards; and
- Ending the transition period in February 2014, through a new constitution made with UNCA through a 'National Dialogue Conference'

585 Thornton, *supra* note 579 at 62.

586 Id.

587 *See* World Bank, *supra* note 568 at 7.

588 Yemen, Chronology of events, *available at:* Security Council Report.

589 Id.

590 Id.

(NDC) and a Constitution Drafting Committee (CDC), and submitted a popular vote at a referendum.[591]

The Security Council welcomed the GONU's implementation of the BWIs' program for the envisaged 'transition period and its immediate aftermath.'[592]

Next, the Office of the UN Special Adviser on Yemen (UN) organized the National Dialogue Conference (NDC) from April 2013 – January 2014, ostensibly to address the grievances of groups such as Houthis in the north and Hirak in the south.[593] The NDC comprised 565 participants, representing a wide spectrum of constituencies, including women, youth, and civil society.[594] The UN's efforts led to including over 170 women and youth.[595] The WB's 'high-caliber international experts' offered the NDC participants with 'just-in-time policy advice,' and also, launched '*Sahemye*' (contribute initiative),' a Facebook website on topics covered by the conditionalities.[596] On conclusion, the NDC proposed a series of governance reforms, including an agreement to transition to a federal system with six regions.[597]

The UNICEF:

- conducted activities in 15 governorates, improving public awareness of agreed key outcomes of the NDC as they related to the rights of women, children and minority groups;'
- engaged approximately 153,219 people through interactive and direct (face-to-face) communication activities including: women,

[591] *Agreement on the Implementation Mechanism for the Transition Process in Yemen in Accordance with the Initiative of the Gulf Cooperation Council* (GCC), November 23, 2011.

[592] World Bank, *Report No. 70943-YE* i (October 1, 2012) (quote); S.C. Res. 2051, U.N. SCOR., 6784th mtg., ¶pmbl U.N. Doc., S/Res/2051 (12 June 2012).

[593] Middle East and North Africa Multi Donor Trust Fund (MENA MDTF), *Results Story on the Yemen Decentralization and Local Governance Initiative: World Bank Support to the National Dialogue in Yemen* 2 (undated).

[594] UNDP, Yemen National Dialogue & Constitutional Reform Trust Fund: Report 2 (undated).

[595] Id.

[596] *See* MENA MDTF, *supra* note 593.

[597] UNDP, *supra* note 594.

youth, and community leaders (including *imams*/sheikhs, clan leaders and government and civil society leaders);[598] and the
- OHCHR worked to establish a NHRI.[599]

In March 2014, the UN helped the GONU nominate a 17-member Constitution Draft Committee to translate the ND recommendations into a draft Constitution, providing it with drafting assistance and the policy advice of over 20 international experts, in addition to OHCHR and UNICEF experts.[600] The advice covered a range of topics, including federalism, finance, rights and freedoms, gender equality, natural resources, and security and defense.[601] Next, in April 2014, the UN helped to establish a National Body (NB), comprising 82 members who were NDC delegates and were responsible for reviewing the draft constitution to ensure all relevant NDC outcomes were accurately reflected.[602] The constitution draft was finalized on 5th January 2015. But since then, the transition government and warring factions, mainly Houthi and al-Qaeda, have been locked in a major armed conflict.[603]

## The Caribbean Region

### United Nations Stabilization Mission in Haiti (MINUSTAH), 1 June 2004–October 2017

In February 2004, an armed rebellion forced the US-backed President Aristide out of office.[604] Therefore, MINUSTAH was established in July to restore constitutional order.[605] MINUSTAH was tasked with

[598] Id. at 1–5.

[599] UNDP, *Support to Human Rights during the Transition Period in Yemen* (2012–2014).

[600] *See* 13 UN Constitutional 14–15 (2014).

[601] Id. at 14.

[602] UNDP, *supra* note 594.

[603] *See supra* note 600 at 2. Note: As regards UNCA in the post-2105 period, the website of the Office of the Special Envoy of the Secretary-General for Yemen provides no new information.

[604] Alex Dupuy, *Haiti: From Revolutionary Slaves to Powerless citizens – Essays on the Politics and Economics of Underdevelopment, 1804-2013* 93–115 (2014).

[605] S. C. Res. 1542, U.N. SCOR, 4961st mtg., ¶2A, U.N. Doc. S/Res. 1542 (2004).

promoting good governance (via the 2006 PRSP), and promoting political dialogue, focusing on women.[606] This required Haiti to amend its 1987 constitution.[607]

MINUSTAH started by helping to set up and strengthen a transitional government's fiscal capacity to hold elections, and deployed experts to promote harmony.[608] Next, the newly elected President Préval (2006-2011) accepted the advice of an UN expert-economist, Professor Paul Collier, and declined to raise the daily minimum wage for workers.[609] Third, MINUSTAH supported the constitutional commission created by President Préval and commenced drafting laws on appropriate topics (such as anti-corruption).[610] As a result, in 2009 the Security Council commended MINUSTAH for 'the adoption of the constitutional reform.'[611] From 2010 to 2011, MINUSTAH actively worked toward liberalizing the mining sector.[612] During this period, it worked with the Interim Haiti Recovery Commission, the supra-national body that had displaced Haiti's dissolved parliament.[613]

The Parliament was reconvened in 2011, only to ratify the constitutional amendments that were finalized a day before Préval's term ended. The amendments thus, became suspect.[614] Nonetheless, goaded by the Security Council,[615] the new President re-published the amendments in 2012, creating:

606 Id.

607 *See* The World Bank, *Haiti: Public Expenditure Management and Financial Accountability Review* xxvii–xxviii (2008).

608 *Report of the Secretary-General on the United Nations Stabilization Mission in Haiti*, ¶9 U.N. Doc., S/2009/129 (March 6, 2009).

609 Id. Mark Schuller, Humanitarian occupation in Haiti, NACLA, July 28, 2015.

610 *See supra* note 608 at ¶ 17; *Haiti: PRSP Progress Report* 10 (2009).

611 S. C. Res. 1892, U.N. SCOR, 6200$^{th}$ mtg., pmbl¶3 U.N. Doc. S/Res. 1892 (2009).

612 Haiti, *supra* note 610 at 10.

613 S.C. Res. 2012, U.N. SCOR, 6631$^{st}$ mtg., pmbl ¶5, U.N. Doc. S/Res. 2012 (2011).

614 *See* Schuller, *supra* note 609; Charlie Hinton, 'Haiti's constitutional horror show,' Counter Punch, October 5, 2012.

615 *See supra* note 613.

- a new constitutional court;
- a supreme court that ensured judicial independence;
- a permanent electoral council empowered to curb corruption;

And establishing:

- a quota of a 30% representation of women in the public sector; and a
- new definition of Haitian nationality that allowed dual citizenship.[616]

As of 2016, the UN family (MINUSTAH, OHCHR, and the UNICEF) became engaged in strengthening the police, the human rights commission, and women's electoral participation.[617] Given UNCA's salience, it continues with these activities.[618] All of this is ostensibly operating to 'modernize' Haiti.[619] Indeed, for this reason, the Security Council has advised Haiti to 'take full advantage' of MINUSTAH's support.[620]

## Central America

### Bolivia

In 2001, Bolivia sold off the city of Cochabamba's public water system to British investors, who tripled the water prices.[621] Therefore, the poor, particularly the indigenous groups, protested violently during 2001 to 2003, demanding constitutional justice.[622] According to the UN, it responded to Bolivia's request to send a UN Special Envoy, José Ocampo, to help defuse the crisis.[623] Ocampo followed up with another

[616] Maureen Taft-Morales, Haiti under President Martelly 5 (2014).

[617] *See Report of the Secretary-General on the United Nations Stabilization Mission in Haiti*, U.N. Doc., S/2016/225 (8 March 2016).

[618] *See* Resolution, *supra* note 611 at ¶15.

[619] Id.

[620] Id.

[621] *See* IMF, Bolivia: Enhanced Structural Adjustment Facility Policy Framework Paper, 1998–2001 (describing the IMF-driven reforms).

[622] Nicole Fabricant, *Mobilizing Bolivia's Displaced: Indigenous Politics & the Struggle over Land* 163 (University of North Carolina Press, 2012).

[623] *See* UN Press release, J.O. Ocampo to serve as UN focal point for Bolivia, SG/SM/9199, 15 March 2004.

visit in March 2004, when he advised the government about introducing good governance among other things, through fresh, UN-assisted presidential and constituent assembly elections.[624]

In the December 2005 elections, Evo Morales, heading the Movement toward socialism (MAS) triumphed to become the first indigenous president.[625] Morales vowed to sculpt a new constitution to 'decolonize' Bolivia.[626] But, meanwhile, in May 2006, an IMF team visited Bolivia, and advised the government:

> The medium term outlook is characterized by ... major uncertainties regarding private investment .... These risks are compounded by the prospect of wide-ranging institutional changes in the context of the forthcoming constituent assembly elections, which could complicate macroeconomic management. The mission noted that, to mitigate these risks, the authorities will need to ... enhance competitiveness. In this context, it is very important to improve governance and maintain a stable legal framework, including in ... property rights.[627]

In July 2006, the National Constituent Assembly (NCA) was elected.[628] However, the MAS failed to secure enough votes to approve a constitutional text on its own.[629]

The NCA faced massive protests from Bolivia's agrarian elites,[630] who feared that the new constitution would curb their property rights.[631] Therefore, the NAC's MAS deputies had to make several concessions: disallow the redistribution of existing agricultural estates and 'sustain the ... highly unequal landholding patterns in the east.'[632] Meanwhile, the UNDP strove to pacify the protestors.[633]Next, having assisted Bolivia

[624] *See* UN Press release, Secretary-general encouraged by agreements on Bolivia elections, says UN committed to assisting process, SG/SM/9989, 8 July 2005.

[625] Fabricant, *supra* note 622 at 162.

[626] Id.

[627] IMF, Bolivia: Report No. 06/270 1, 18–19 (July 2006).

[628] *See* UNDP, *A Story of Dialogue, Conflict and Peacebuilding in Bolivia* 4 (undated).

[629] Id.

[630] *See* UNDP, *supra* note 628 at 30.

[631] Fabricant, *supra* note 622 at 177.

[632] Id. at 173–174.

[633] *See* UNDP, *supra* note 628.

to submit its first PRSP in 2001, the UNDP educated the NCA on how to constitutionalize the commitments made therein: indigenous rights, anti-corruption, and so on.[634] So did other UN agencies: the FAO[635] and the OHCHR, which also helped to establish the NHRI.[636] Finally, on January 25, 2009, in a referendum held with UNCA, the public accepted the constitution.[637] Thus, *powerful (oligarchic) domestic forces and the UN* worked to smother social justice, and to promote the interests of private capital.

## UN Mission in Colombia, 25 June 2016–September 25, 2016; The UN Verification Mission in Colombia, September 26, 2017 till date [Special Political Mission]

UNCA is being used to reform a constitution that was adopted to implement the SAPs.

Colombia witnessed both conflict and peacemaking for over five decades (1964–2016). Since 1989, the BWIs have shaped the peace process and financed 'pro-peace policies.'[638] Accordingly, in 1991, Colombia adopted a new constitution which protects the right to private property and recognizes the country's ethnic, religious, and cultural pluralism. Next, with a view to remove hurdles for foreign investors, Colombia amended this constitution in 1994 and adopted a new (Agrarian) 'Law 160' (drafted by the World Bank).[639] Finally, Colombia's PRSP (National Development Plan, 2014–2018) shaped the 2016 Final Agreement (discussed below)[640] which envisages further constitutional reforms, to implement, which UNCA has been mandated.[641]

[634] Id. at 14-41.

[635] Fabricant, *supra* note 622 at 177.

[636] Report of the Secretary-General, *National Institutions for the promotion and protection of human rights*, ¶10, 79–80 UN Doc. A/HRC/16/76 (February 7, 2011).

[637] *See* UNDP, *supra* note 628 at 31.

[638] World Bank, 'Colombia: Addressing Violence & Conflict in a Country Strategy' (undated) [slides]; World Bank, Colombia: Essays on conflict, peace and development (World Bank, 2001).

[639] Andrei Gomez-Suarez *et al*, *Foreign Investors and the Colombian Peace Process*, 18 Int'l L. Rev. 223, 232 (2016).

[640] The World Bank, Report No. 101552-CO (February 2016).

[641] *See* S.C. Res. 2366, U.N. SCOR., 7997th mtg., ¶2 U.N. Doc., S/Res/2366 (July 2017).

The conflict which comprised successive waves of confrontation among guerrilla, government and paramilitary forces has killed more than 5 million people. Political exclusion, socio-economic inequality, and Colombia's failure to end the unequal distribution of land have been the conflict's key triggers. In fact, the Revolutionary Armed Forces of Colombia (FARC), a signatory to the Final Agreement took up armed struggle in 1964, to end land ownership concentration.[642] Drugs and crime undoubtedly have prolonged Colombia's conflict. Therefore, in some regions of Colombia, Transnational Corporations (TNCs), foreign investors and narco-traffickers who acquired large portions of land and replaced big landowners, allied forces to combat the guerrilla insurgency.[643] Finally, the BWIs-sponsored-neo-extractive-model of development has triggered violent aggressions against the Afro-Colombian populations.[644]

## *United Nations Constitutional Assistance*

On 24 November 2016, the Government of Colombia and FARC-ELN signed the 'Final Agreement for Ending the Conflict and Building a Stable and Lasting Peace' (the Final Agreement) in Bogotá, Colombia. The UNDP-supported fora enabled more than 6,000 people drawn from civil society, indigenous groups, and victims' groups to contribute peace proposals.[645] The peace agreement's provision about the truth commission reflects these peoples' proposals to bring their suffering into the open.[646]

Expectedly, the Final Agreement aims at reducing poverty.[647] It calls for market-oriented land reforms; enabling FARC to transition to civil

[642] FARC and the National Liberation Army (ELN) are the two remaining groups.

[643] Boa Santos, *Colombia between Neoliberal Peace and Democratic Peace*, 11 (2) In Factis Pax 41 (2017).

[644] Id. at 50.

[645] Colombia participates in the peace process, *available at:* http://www.undp.org/content/undp/en/home/ourwork/ourstories/colombia-participates-in-the-peace-process.html.

[646] Id.

[647] The Colombian Peace Agreement, The opportunity to build peace – A publication of the Office of the High Commissioner for Peace (undated).

life; protecting victims of the conflict, electoral reforms with a view strengthen women's political participation; combating illicit drugs, and a comprehensive transitional justice mechanism.[648] With the UN's support, a total of 11 laws, including six constitutional reforms, were approved by Congress.[649] As landowners, TNCs could delay the implementation of those reforms that negatively affects their interests.[650]

## Eastern Europe

### UNCA-ITA: UN Interim Administration in Kosovo (UNMIK), June 1999–June 2008

#### *The UN Fills a Vacuum Created by the International Community*

In 1998, Kosovo was a province of Serbia (with a majority ethnic Albanian population) in the Federal Republic of Yugoslavia (FRY). Kosovar Albanians fought against the Serbs and the rump of FRY (comprising the republics of Serbia and Montenegro) because starting from 1989, their Serbian leader, S. Milosevic began to steadily erode their constitutional autonomy, within the, FRY.[651] The conflict raged from 1998 to 1999. A 78-day air campaign forced Milosevic to accept the Kosovo Peace Plan in June 1999, whereby he had to: a) withdraw Yugoslavian forces from Kosovo, within seven days, and b) allow an UN civilian administration, backed by a peacekeeping force, to fill the vacuum so created.[652]

#### *Internationalizing Kosovo's Future Status*

As per Security Council Resolution 1244 (*hereafter* 1244), in June 1999, the United Nations Interim Administration Mission in Kosovo (UNMIK) was established to:

648 Id. at 1–24.

649 *Report of the Secretary-General on the United Nations Verification Mission in Colombia*, ¶8 UN Doc., S/2017/745 (30 August 2017).

650 Gomez-Saurez, *supra* note 639.

651 *See* Carsten Stahn, *Constitution without a state? Kosovo under the United Nations Constitutional Framework for Self-Government* 14 LJIL 531, 533 (2001).

652 *See* Annex to the letter dated 4 June 1999 from the Permanent Rep of France to the United Nations addressed to the Secretary-General, UN Doc. S/1999/648 (June 7, 1999).

a) Undertake basic civilian administration and 'economic reconstruction'
b) promote substantial autonomy and self-government for the people of Kosovo *within the FRY*;
c) 'facilitate a political process designed to determine Kosovo's future political status;' and protect and promote human rights;
d) work, as expected with the BWIs, to introduce good economic governance.[653]

The WB's Low Income States aid package funded Kosovo's reconstruction.[654]

*The Impending Constitution Guides Plenary ITA*

With a view to administer Kosovo along preferred lines, in July 1999, the UNSG's Special Representative assumed legislative, executive and judicial powers, declaring that his regulations and subsidiary instruments issued thereunder would serve as the applicable law in Kosovo.[655]

For, in July 1999:

> ... the UNMIK had severed virtually all links with the Federal Republic of Yugoslavia in the area of economic policy.[656]

In fact, that very month (July 1999), the IMF's executive Board approved the provision for technical services to Kosovo,[657] and from 1999 onwards,

> Kosovo became a laboratory of economic institution building from the ground up. *At the request of UNMIK*, ... the IMF [began] assisting institution building and economic policy implementation in Kosovo. ...[658]

653 *See* S.C. Res. 1244, U.N. SCOR., 4011$^{th}$ mtg., ¶11 (a)-(k) U.N. Doc. S/Res/1244 (10 June 1999) Note: Determining the legality of this concentration of power lies outside the scope of my enquiry.

654 *See* Dimitri G. Demekas *et al., Kosovo - Institutions and Policies for Reconstruction and Growth* 1-2 (2002).

655 Id. *See* UNMIK Regulations: No. 1999/1 (25 July 1999) & No. 1999/24 (12 December 1999).

656 Id.

657 See Demekas, *supra* note 654, at fn. 1.

658 Id. at 1.

The IMF and the World Bank co-established Kosovo's treasury, the central fiscal authority, the Banking and Payment authority, and functioning tax and customs administrations.[659] The WB's aid package funded Kosovo's reconstruction. In this way, the foundations for a Constitutional market democracy were set.

### *The Constitution Promulgated by UNMIK Provides a Formal Framework for Plenary ITA*

Against this backdrop and accordingly, in May 2001, UNMIK promulgated Kosovo's new, provisional constitution (2001 Constitution) to introduce market democracy, ostensibly to promote 'economic prosperity.'[660] Conceptually, this Constitution enabled UNMIK to administer Kosovo on good governance lines (for example, to draft laws to privatize natural resources) until its final status was resolved.[661] In April 2002, a (Kosovar) self-government, the Provisional Institutions of Self Government (PISG) took office and co-administered Kosovo with UNMIK in tune with the 2001 Constitution. But again, unsurprisingly, the UNSG's Special Representative remained the final legal authority and enjoyed reserved powers for instance, in determining economic policy.[662]

### *'Standards Before Status'*

UNMIK simultaneously set in motion a process for determining Kosovo's status that required its governance to meet eight standards, of which four bear mentioning:

- functioning democratic institutions;
- rule of law;
- freedom of movement;
- market economy;
- property rights.[663]

659 Id. at 1–4. World Bank, Report No. 24275 - KOS (2002) (Annex VI).

660 *See* UNMIK Regulation No. 2001/9 of 15 May 2001.

661 *See* UNMIK, *'Kosovo in June 2008'* 1–15 (undated).

662 *See* 2001 Constitution, *supra* note 660 at § 8.

663 *See* UNMIK, *Standards for Kosovo* (2003).

Marti Ahtisaari, the UN's Special Envoy, led a seventeen-month (November 2005–March 2007), status-determining process, meeting with Kosovars in numerous towns, villages, and hamlets.[664] Ahtisaari also held several rounds of negotiations with Security Council members, officials in Vienna, and political leaders in Kosovo and Europe.[665] Still, what mattered most in determining Kosovo's status were the views of the Contact Group (for example, the US).[666] Finally, in March 2007, Ahtisaari concluded that Kosovo should transition to independence, based on the Constitution made with UNCA.[667] This (Ahtisaari) Plan, neither incorporated in an agreement nor endorsed by the Security Council, was simply submitted to the Secretary-General.[668]

### *Kosovo's Internationalized Constitution-Making Process*

Accordingly, an Assembly elected in November 2007 promulgated a Unilateral Declaration of Independence. UNMIK helped create an ethnically-scrambled 21-member constitution-drafting body, which completed the draft constitution in 2007, aided by foreign experts, including Prof. Louis Aucoin. UNMIK used the Internet and held public hearings to receive comments on the draft constitution. The website received two million hits and 'the Commission changed 30% of the articles of the draft, based on public comment.'[669] UNIFEM's programs drew in women, amplifying their voices. The constitution came into effect after

[664] *See Report of the Special Envoy of the Secretary-General on Kosovo's Future Status*, U.N. Doc. S/2007/168 (26 March 2007); Fact Sheet, Summary of the Comprehensive Proposal for the Kosovo Status Settlement (January 20, 2009).

[665] Id. at ¶2.

[666] Id.

[667] *See Letter dated 26 March 2007 from the Secretary-General addressed to the President of the Security Council, Comprehensive proposal for the Kosovo Status Settlement*, S/2007/168/Add. 1 (March 26, 2007) .

[668] *Report of the Secretary-General on the United Nations Interim Administration Mission in Kosovo*, ¶3 UN Doc., S/2008/354 (June 12, 2008).

[669] *On Constitution Writing: The Case of Kosovo—Interview with professor Louis Aucoin*, Vol. XXIII Praxis, The Fletcher J. of Human Security, 124, 125 (2008). Michael Riegner, *The Two Faces of the Internationalized Pouvoir Constituant: Independence and Constitution-Making under External Influence in Kosovo*, 2 Goettingen J. of Int'l L. 1035–1062 (2010).

Pieter Feith, the International Civilian Representative, certified it met Ahtisaari's guidelines.[670] In this way, UNCA guided ITA and worked symbiotically with it toward common policies and ends in Kosovo. But of course, the Constitution/UNCA given its salience and status as a conditionality was indispensable. Indeed, the UN Family had all along envisaged the Constitution and worked toward creating it for Kosovo. But for political and strategic reasons, its work there was framed in neutral terms such as carrying on 'economic reconstruction,' providing a "civil administration" and/or "legal framework," and so on.

Table 6.2 illustrates relevant UNCA-recipients-states' status under the Heavily Indebted Deft Relief Initiative including those who have received debt-relief. Tables 6.3-6.4 reveal the constitutional commonalities produced by UNCA, and how the UN shrouded UNCA during its early run.

## 6.3 UNCA is *a parent* 'Institution'

I began conceptualizing UNCA as an institution, starting from Chapter 4. I argue that the three UNCA projects discussed in chapter 4, together with all of the above-analysed UNCA projects, fulfill Wilde's following two criteria, and so can be considered collectively as an institution or 'established practice:'

They all:

(1) have taken place periodically, since the birth of the UN; and more importantly, they
(2) involve a distinctive activity.[671]

That distinctive activity is the Constitution's internationalized making (that is, making it anew or reforming an existing constitution along good governance lines), which in turn provides the framework for international territorial administration, as defined, and conceptualized as an 'institution' by Wilde. Indeed, UNCA is a parent institution that sires and enables ITA to achieve its, and UNCA's common ends, and

670 *Kosovo Business Law Handbook: Strategic Information and Laws* 21 (International Business Publications, USA, 2000).

671 Wilde, *supra* note 1 at 196.

TABLE 6.3. United Nations Constitutional Assistance produces constitutional commonalities

| No. | UNCA-Recipient/ SAP/PRSP-State | CS | Jud. Ind. | EC | GE | Safeguards | | NHRI | Fiscal transp./ ACC | C. Bank | Prop. Rights, ME, FI |
|---|---|---|---|---|---|---|---|---|---|---|---|
| | | | | | | Child/ Youth | Environment | | | | |
| 1. | Cambodia | 1, 150 | 128 | L | 31, 45-46 | 73 | 59 | — | — | — | 56 (ME) |
| 2. | Afghanistan | — | 116 | 156 | 6 | 49 | 15 | 58 | 75(3) | 12 | 10, 41 (ME) |
| 3. | Bhutan | 1,(9) | 21 | 23 | 7, 15 | 7, 9 | 5 | L | 8, 26 | — | 7 (P) |
| 4. | Nepal | 1 | Part 11 | 245 | 4(1)-(2) | 39 | 30 | Part 25 | Part 21 | — | 6(P) |
| 5. | Kyrgyzstan | 6 | 94 | 106 | 16(4) | 20(4); 23, 2) | 12(5); 48 | 108 | 108 | L | 12, 42 (P) |
| 6. | Maldives | 8, 268 | 142 | 167 | 20 | 35 | 22 | 189 | 199 | — | 40(P) |
| 7. | Madagascar | 1,5 | 108 | — | 5,6 | — | 95(6) | L | Pmbl | — | 34 (P) 38 (security to FI) |
| 8. | East-Timor | §2x | Ch1, 119 | — | 17 | 18 | 61 | 27 | 161 | 143 | 54 (P), 140 |
| 9. | Fiji | 2(1) | Ch.5, 97(2) | Part C | 26(1) | 41 | 40 | 45 | 115 | 153 | 27 (P) |

*(Cont'd)*

TABLE 6.3 (*Cont'd*)

| No. | UNCA-Recipient/SAP/PRSP-State | CS | Jud. Ind. | EC | GE | Safeguards | | NHRI | Fiscal transp./ACC | C. Bank | Prop. Rights, ME, FI |
|---|---|---|---|---|---|---|---|---|---|---|---|
| | | | | | | Child/Youth | Environment | | | | |
| 10. | Angola | 6,11 | 175 | 107 | 21(k), 23 & 35 | 80-81 | 16, 21 (M) & 39 | 192 | 104 | 93,100 | Preamble & 89 (ME); 14, 37-38, & 92 (P) & 97 (FI) |
| 11. | Burundi | 18, 48 | 209 | 89, 66 | 13, 22 | 44-45 | 35 | 268 | 69 | — | 36 (P) |
| 12. | Central African Republic | 108 | 78 | 73 | 5 | 6-7 | 9 | 104 | Pmbl; L | — | 11 |
| 13. | Côte d'Ivoire | — | 139 | — | 12,14 | 10,16 | — | L | 41 | — | 11 |
| 14. | Democratic Republic of Congo | 220 | 149 | 211 | 8 | 41 | 53-54 | L Ethics & ACC | 165 | 176 | 34 – 35 (FI) |
| 15. | Guinea | 2 | 107 | 2, 132 | 27 | 1 | 16,21 | 146 | L | — | 13(P) |
| 16. | Kenya | 2 | 160 | 88 | 11 (e) | 53 | 42 | 59 | 79 | 231 | 40 |

| No. | UNCA-Recipient/SAP/PRSP-State | CS | Jud. Ind. | EC | GE | Safeguards | | NHRI | Fiscal transp./ACC | C. Bank | Prop. Rights, ME, FI |
|---|---|---|---|---|---|---|---|---|---|---|---|
| | | | | | | Child/Youth | Environment | | | | |
| 17. | Mozambique | 3 | 292 | L | 35-36 | 47 | 117; 90 | Ch. III | L | 132 | 108 (FI), 97 (ME) |
| 18. | Rwanda | 12 | 140 | 180 | 10 | 27 | 49 | 182 | 32 | L | 29(P) |
| 19. | Somalia | 4 | 106 | 111G | 11 | 29 | 25 | 41 | 111C | 123 | 26(P) |
| 20. | Zimbabwe | 2 | 164 | 238 | 56 | 19, 81 | 73 | 242 | 254 | 317 | 71(P) |
| 21. | Egypt | 1 | 94 | §9 | 11 | 80 | 30,32 | 214 | 218 | 220 | 35(P) |
| 22. | Iraq | 2 C, 13 | 19,87 | 102 | 14 | 29 | 33 | 102 | 73 | 103 | 23 (P), 25 |
| 23. | Tunisia | 2 | 102 | 126 | 21 | 47 | 12, 45 | 128 | 130 | — | 41 (P) |
| 24. | Kosovo | 16 | Ch. VII, 102 | 139 | 3 | 50 | 52,7 | 133 | 120 | 140 | 10 (ME); 46 (P), 119 |
| 25. | Bolivia | 410 (II) | Ch. VI, 120 | Title IV | 8 11 | § V | 108 | 218 | 123, 231, 306, 323 | 327 | 300; 320 (FI) |

CS= Constitutional Supremacy; JI= Independent judiciary; GE=Gender Equality; EC=Electoral Commission; NHRI=National Human Rights Institution; CB= Central Bank

TABLE 6.4 UN terminology for United Nations Constitutional Assistance: 1960,1989-2009

| Acronym of Mission Name | Security Council Resolution | Paragraph | Terms used for: | |
|---|---|---|---|---|
| | | | **Constitutions; Constitution-making &/ or constitutional reform** | **UN Constitutional Assistance (UNCA)** |
| ONUC | 143 (1960) | 2 | – | Technical assistance |
| UNAVEM-II | 747 (1992) | 6 | – | Finalize political, legal, and budgetary preparations for free and fair elections |
| ONUSAL | 729 (1992) | 2 | – | Verification and monitoring of the implementation of all the agreements |
| UNTAC | 745 (1992) | pmbl 4; 1 | National reconciliation Process | Contribute to the right to self-determination of the Cambodian people through free and fair elections; implement the mandate envisaged in the agreements on a comprehensive political settlement to the conflict |
| UNOSOM-I | 751 (1992) | 7 | Negotiated political settlement | To promote the process of reconciliation and political settlement |
| ONUMOZ | 782 (1992) | pmbl 3 | – | Monitor and guarantee the implementation of the General Peace Agreement |
| UNAMIR | 872 (1993) | 2 | – | The UN should make its full contribution to the implementation of the Arusha peace agreement |
| MINUGUA | 1094 (1997) | pmbl 3 | – | International verification of peace accords |
| MINURCA | 1159 (1998) | 14(e) | – | To provide advice and technical assistance in the areas of good governance and the rule of law |

| Acronym of Mission Name | Security Council Resolution | Paragraph | Terms used for: | |
|---|---|---|---|---|
| | | | Constitutions; Constitution-making &/ or constitutional reform | UN Constitutional Assistance (UNCA) |
| UNAMSIL | 1270 (1999) | 1, 8 a), h)-i) | – | To cooperate in the implementation of the Lome Agreement; to support the operations of UN human rights officers |
| UNTAET | 1272 (1999) | 2(e) | – | To support capacity-building for self-government |
| UNMIK | 1244 (1999) | 11 (a), (e) & (g) | – | The main responsibilities of the international civil presence will include: Promoting the establishment, … of substantial autonomy and self-government in Kosovo, …; Facilitating a political process designed to determine Kosovo's future status, … and Supporting the reconstruction of key infrastructure and other economic reconstruction |
| MONUC | 1291(2000) | 7(h) | – | To cooperate closely with the Facilitator of the National Dialogue and provide support and technical assistance to him |
| UNMIL | 1509 (2003) | 3 (l), (n), & (q)-(s) | – | Human rights assistance, with particular attention to vulnerable groups, including refugees, women, children, demobilized child soldiers; To assist the transitional government in: ('Support for security sector reform'): in restructuring the police force, consistent with democratic policing; creating a national legal framework; the proper administration of natural resources; and the preparation for national elections |

*(Cont'd)*

Table 6.4 (*Cont'd*)

| Acronym of Mission Name | Security Council Resolution | Paragraph | Terms used for: | |
|---|---|---|---|---|
| | | | Constitutions; Constitution-making &/ or constitutional reform | UN Constitutional Assistance (UNCA) |
| UNOCI | 1528 (2004) | 1) l), n) & p)-r) | — | To support the implementation of the peace process; To assist in the field of human rights; and to assist the government of national reconciliation in re-establishing the authority of the judiciary and the rule of law |
| ONUB | 1545 (2004) | 5 | – | To contribute to the successful completion of the electoral process stipulated in the Arusha Agreement, by ensuring a secure environment for free, transparent and peaceful elections to take place |
| UNMIS | 1590 (2005) | 4 (x) | – | To support implementation of the Comprehensive Peace Agreement by performing the following tasks: To support the preparations for, and conduct of elections and referenda, provided for by the Comprehensive Peace Agreement |
| UNMIN | 1740 (2007) | 1 (d)-(e) | – | To provide technical support for the planning, preparation and conduct of the election of a Constituent Assembly in a free and fair atmosphere, in consultation with the parties. |

purposes (*see* also next chapter). I therefore suggest that UNCA-ITA are parent-child 'institutions'/ 'established practices.'

## 6.4 Conclusion

This chapter has revealed twelve significant aspects about UNCA. First, that it operates in widely divergent scenarios in poor, post-conflict, *and stable states.*

Second, UNCA is salient. For, strengthening budget processes, judicial independence, and electoral commissions (to hold presidential/ parliamentary elections), and securing civilian control of the military, all require first, adopting a Constitution or reforming an existing constitution along preferred lines. Third, UNCA also works to return states to constitutional order. Fourth, UNCA is a UN Family enterprise; the UN Secretariat, the BWIs, the UNDP, other UN agencies, *and the Security Council* all offer it.

Fifth, Chapter 4 revealed that at its birth, UNCA comprised a key element: the IMF's advice. This chapter reveals that it continues to do so. Indeed, the BWIs' staff participate in peace talks and high-level political negotiations; draft peace agreements; provide model legislation (fiscal crime),[672] train or educate stakeholders (constituent assembly members), review draft constitutions; host debt-relief workshops, sanction funds, and make decisions on finance projects in support of good governance. This is so, because, since its birth, and regardless of which UN members have offered it, UNCA serves to create an environment conducive to transnational interests/to implement the BWIs' policies/ conditionalities. This is why, as Table 6.2 evidences, it replicates the same constitutional model everywhere.

Sixth, since UNCA is key to achieving all the peacebuilding goals, it is central to UN Transitional Governance. Which as defined by some scholars, refers to UN peacebuilding from October 1993 till the present day. Accordingly, UN Transitional Governance refers to only UNCA (without ITA) in sovereign states, as illustrated by Figure 1. 4.

Seventh, my findings unite with Paris' arguments (*see* next para) for they provide their missing constitutional dimensions. As per

[672] *See* Model Legislation *at:* UNODC, https://www.unodc.org/unodc/en/money-laundering/Model-Legislation.html.

Roland Paris' international law analysis of peacebuilding (minus the Constitution's making), during 1989-99, the UN promoted economic liberalization and conducted fresh elections (*hereinafter* Goals) to build peace in Cambodia, East-Timor, Angola, Rwanda, Liberia, Mozambique, El Salvador, Guatemala, and Kosovo – *see* chapter 1. My findings reveal that:

- the BWIs made the Constitution a conditionality during 1989-1999 (SAPs) and 1999 – till date (PRSPs),
- *which is why, the UN's Goals in the aforementioned States included economic liberalization*, to achieve which UNCA was used, but remained shrouded under confusing terms – *see* Table 7.1; and
- the Constitution produced by UNCA *enabled* the UN to hold free and fair elections.

Eighth, this Chapter reveals why the UN, far from leaving a 'light-foot print' in Afghanistan (as the former SRSG, Lakhder Brahimi, famously but erroneously stated),[673] instead left the *same* footprint.

Ninth, regarding El Salvador, many commentators faulted the BWIs for prescribing, and the UN for implementing the former's conditionalities (for example, budget discipline), which hindered the disarmament of the combatants, and thus peace itself.[674] As a result, a situation was co-created in El Savador that Professor Castillo aptly described as follows: 'it was as if a patient lay on the operating table, with the left and the right sides of his body separated by a curtain, and unrelated surgery being performed on each side.'[675] I suggest, what the commentators have missed is this: that situation was not a pattern of errors. Indeed, it represents what I previously called the UN Family's constitutionalization of conflict, whose guiding notion is this: fiscal discipline, economic liberalization and so on, achieved through the market-oriented Constitution, supposedly *end and/or prevent conflict* and promote peace (*see* Chapter 5).

[673] Lakhdar Brahimi, Former Special Adviser of the Secretary-General of the United Nations, 'State Building in crisis and post-conflict countries,' June 2007, *available at:* http://unpan1.un.org/intradoc/groups/public/documents/un/unpan026896.pdf.

[674] *See for example,* Francisca Wehinger, Have International Financial Institutions improved? August 2013.

[675] Id. (quoting Castillo).

Tenth, Osin Tansey, neglects to note that state-building-recipients-states are debtor states, and argues (based on a cursory analysis), that their 'national elites are often in a position to engage with, and constrain international actors, thus … frustrating their efforts at political change.'[676] This chapter provides an alternative account, based on more thorough analysis.

Eleventh, my findings both evidence, and reveal *why*, as the UN itself concedes, 'foreign models, foreign experts, and foreign-conceived solutions' have produced broadly speaking, a one-size-fits-all model in UNCA-recipients-states, without addressing their particular contexts.[677] Meanwhile Fiji's experience affirms a point that I have previously asserted in Chapter 1, namely, that the practice of using foreign experts is by itself not colonial. What is relevant is considering, as professors Chinkin and Ratuva have also suggested, the wider conditions under which, and the broader ends for which, foreign experts are brought into the picture. Fiji's experience mirrors that of Chile, –a non-UNCA-recipient-state– where the BWIs controlled and collaborated with national (authoritarian) elites to impose neoliberalism by *constitutionalizing* neoliberal principles.[678]

Twelfth, Chapter 3 revealed that in certain situations, foreign powers relied on peace agreements and engaged in other forms of rudimentary constitution-making to achieve preferred goals. We see this practice continue in modern times (see for example, UNMIK's May 2001 Regulation).

In the next chapter, I ask whether this common practice, that is, the Constitution's internationalized making, is being put to common purposes and ends, thereby rendering UNCA projects collectively a 'Policy Institution.'[679]

[676] Osin Tansey, *Statebuilding and the Limits of Constitutional Design, in* Political Economy and State-Building: Power after peace 72, 75 (Mats Berdal & Dominik Zaum, eds, Routledge, 2013).

[677] The UN quote appears in chapter 1, section 1.0.

[678] Javier Couso, *Constructing 'Privatopia' The Role of Constitutional Law in Chile's Neoliberal Experiment, in*, The Politics of neoliberal legality in a neoliberal age 85 (Ben Golder, ed., Routledge, 2018).

[679] Wilde, *supra* note 1 at 22.

7

# How Does the UN Justify Offering 'Constitutional Assistance' in This Post-Colonial Era?

## A 'Purposive' Analysis

## 7.0 Introduction

1986 Mogadishu, Somalia

> For years Boya had dived daily into the Indian Ocean to catch lobsters. However, with his city's economy gutted by the civil war, he now joins his gang to hijack towering commercial shipping vessels—some stretching to over two hundred yards and weighing thousands of tons—the lifeblood of international trade.
>
> Until the war erupted, his sister Shamso grazed cattle. One night, a gang of militiamen burst into her tin-roofed shack and raped her at gun-point. As a rape victim, she was shunned by her clan, so she fled with her son to a faraway town in the Banaadir region. Suffering from syphilis, she now sells *Khat* (a mildly narcotic plant) to support herself. To fetch water she daily trudges for miles, 'rolling a water barrel across the parched landscape'.[1]

[1] Compiled by the author based on information in Security Council Report No. 2, October 2013; Jay Bahadur, *Pirates of Somalia: Inside Their Hidden World*

2007 Kathmandu, Nepal

> Tek Suhang, an Adivasi (indigenous person) was thrown out by his government from his *Kipats* (traditional forestlands) and denied compensation. Further, the government banned indigenous languages in schools, colleges, and offices, thus forcing Suhang and his family into a life of illiterate darkness. Snared into bonded labour by a high-caste landlord, he now heaves and smashes stones. His wife Srijana, who once earned money by crafting and selling cane and bamboo products, now slaves as a domestic servant. Suhang and his family have no one to speak up for them.[2]

This chapter poses the question, which the American Society of International Law, ASIL 2009 merit prize Committee (*see* Chapter 1), rightly found critical to appraising the legitimacy of International Territorial Administration or ITA (and by extension, its parent, United Nations Constitutional Assistance's [UNCA's]) use in sovereign states: How does the United Nations (UN) justify tutoring Third World peoples in territorial units or sovereign states in the allied activities of sculpting their own constitution and administering their territories? I endeavour to answer this question using Wilde's Method: 'policy institution' – 'purposive analysis',[3] which means first, that my objective is:

> Not to attempt to explain the 'actual' or real reasons for the [UNCA] projects, for example in terms of causation; nor to suggest whether the projects 'succeeded' or 'failed' in serving their stated (or unstated) goals.[4]

Rather, my aim is to establish UNCA projects' 'justificatory framework'.[5] I will reframe my question to ask:

---

(Harper Collins, 2011); Samuel Lowenberg, "The Famine Next Time," *N.Y. Times*, 26 November 2011.

[2] Compiled by the author based on information provided in James Anaya, *Report on the Situation of Indigenous Peoples in Nepal*, ¶ 86-87 U.N. Doc. A/HRC/12/34/Add. 3 (20 July 2009).

[3] *See* Ralph Wilde, *International Territorial Administration: How Trusteeship and the Civilizing Mission Never Went Away* 37 (Oxford University Press, 2008).

[4] Id. [emphasis added]. Wilde's quote refers *only to ITA projects*. For the sake of clarity, I have inserted "UNCA" therein.

[5] Id.

> Is UNCA (that is, the Constitution's internationalized making by the UN), which I previously established as an 'institution' ('established practice'), being put to common purposes and ends, thus rendering its projects collectively a 'Policy Institution'?

Put simply, this chapter does not criticize the UN implicitly or explicitly, for what it does, and does not do. Rather, my aim is only to consider how the UN officially, in its own words, explains displacing local actors from and/or tutoring them in the conduct of, what it admits is inherently a 'sovereign process', and in the creation of what it admits is inherently, a sovereign document. Given this, I will not reiterate on the broader contextual information for each project and instead focus only on policy analysis.

So, how does the UN explain UNCA regarding Shamso and Srijana? Without UNCA, says the UN, local actors would silence Shamso and Srijana's voices; UNCA is what amplifies them.[6] Again, the UN's public consultation and constitution-drafting programs are what constitutionalizes these women's concerns—say, for clean drinking water and access to schooling in indigenous languages.[7] What about UNCA's role regarding Tek Suhang and Boya? UNCA says that the UN restores the rule of law by constitutionalizing strong anti-corruption commissions (ACCs),[8] which secure for Suhang a clerical job (without a bribe), and help revive Boya's life as a lobster diver.

As a response, I will show that, UNCA was conceived, and is being used, with and without ITA, for two common purposes: to address perceived challenges about the conduct of the Constitution-making process by local actors, and the types of constitutional content created by them. (As previously noted, for operational purposes, the UN discusses Constitution-making, a seamless activity, and by extension UNCA, in terms of two artificial categories: process and content—*see* Chapter 1.) UNCA substitutes for the default method a constitution made by national stakeholders (*hereafter* local actors) in terms of both process and content. In so doing, UNCA promotes process, and content-related standards that cover these broad goals: democracy, free and fair elections, women's right to political participation, free markets, the rule

[6] Id.

[7] Id.

[8] Id. at 6.

of law, good governance (including natural resources' exploitation), and gender equality. Based on this 'purposive commonality', I classify UNCA projects collectively as a parent 'Policy Institution'.

I concur with Wilde who has previously conceptualized ITA as a Policy Institution based: the Policy Institution and Purposive Analysis.[9] (This is my chosen method.) I suggest that UNCA sires ITA. This is why ITA is a Policy Institution.

## 7.1 UNCA's Policy Role

Exploring UNCA's policy role requires first noting that the Constitution was internationalized because it was conceptualized as a remedial governance tool.[10] So then, the question is: For which actor is UNCA a substitute? As Chapters 2–3 suggest, traditionally, the answer would be the sovereign because historically it was the sovereign who imposed a constitution. However, the modern concept of 'popular sovereignty' suggests a constitution is born through a process, driven and owned by the people. Interestingly, as underscored in the very first chapter, the UN affirms these views. It suggests that Constitution-making is a 'sovereign national' act, and unless "nationally owned and led," emits a whiff of illegitimacy.[11] A constitution made by local actors, in terms of both process and content, and without international assistance, is the norm.[12]

Why then does the UN displace local actors in Least Developed Countries (LDCs) from the act of constitution-making? Before proceeding to consider the UN's answers, an interesting caveat is due. Wilde asked this very question about ITA by the UN, and answered it in 2008, based on the UN's official explanations (contained in fragmentary sources).[13] My analysis, based on the UN's explicit answers for UNCA, made public in 2009, mirrors that of Wilde. This is so, because Wilde's definition of territorial administration accurately affirms its Western liberal constitutional parentage. Equally solid is Wilde's research method.

[9] Id.
[10] *See* UN, *supra* note 6 at 2.
[11] Id.
[12] Id.
[13] Wilde, *supra* note 3 at Ch. 6.

According to the UN, it conceived the Constitution as a remedial governance tool, in response to a perceived governance Problem, which has two aspects: a) a perceived lack of governance; and b) the perceived absence of good governance.[14] In the first instance, local actors are deemed practically incapable of conducting any governance at all.[15] Therefore, producing the Constitution to "fill a perceived vacuum"[16] forms the policy objective [*hereinafter* Purpose] for UNCA. It is worth noting that fewer UNCA projects (for example, Congo) were ostensibly framed in terms of addressing the Problem's first aspect.[17] Therefore, here I will focus only on Congo. In Congo, the UN refused to recognize Prime Minister Lumumba's government, given its socialist leanings, and rested UNCA's use (to promote free markets) initially to address a supposed governmental vacuum, and next on the Congolese's supposed inadequacies to revive Congo's economy and protect its natural resources.[18]

In the second instance, the UN fears that the locally run administration may violate the principles of democracy or the rule of law, frustrate the operation of free markets, hinder good governance, including the exploitation of natural resources, squelch women's rights, and/or stymie the territorial unit in attaining a certain status.[19] Here, the Constitution is ostensibly produced to promote good governance. The UN explained virtually all, or a majority of UNCA projects, in terms of addressing this aspect. In this way, the Constitution serves to address both aspects of the Problem in the same way. So produced, the Constitution provides ITA's framework. In this way, UNCA – and ITA,[20] which it sires – together substitute for the default method and normal model (governance by local actors) respectively, and work toward common Purposes: democracy, free markets, the rule of law, good governance, women's rights, and achieving Territorial Status. Herein lie their common policy roles and common purposes.

[14] *See* UN, *supra* note 6 at 2, 4–6;

[15] Id.

[16] Wilde, *supra* note 3 at 207.

[17] *See* UNDP, *Governance for Peace: Securing the Social Contract* 14, 68 (2012).

[18] *See* chapter 4; *1964 Yearbook of the UN* 11 (UN, 1965).

[19] *See* UN, *supra* note 6 at 2-6; Wilde, *supra* note 3 at 207.

[20] For ITA only, see Wilde, *supra* note 3 at 203–207.

The following explanations offered by a top UN official and a major UN agency suggest that the default method's deficiencies stem from inadequate knowledge and capacity of local actors. More specifically, they suggest those defects relate to process and content. Let us consider first, former Secretary-General, Ban Ki-Moon's push for UNCA in the 'Arab Spring' context:

> ...[F]rom the beginning of this Arab Spring, whenever I had an opportunity of speaking or meeting with Arab leaders, I made it quite pointedly, this role of women. ... when they were drafting constitutions or regulations, [or to] enact laws, then there must be a clear provision on protecting the human rights as well as providing equal opportunities to women and also youth groups. It is not just lip service.[21]

Consider next, this UNDP advertisement:

> Maldives: UNDP Constitutional Expert (Drafter) Vacancy
>
> ...we urgently seek an international constitutional expert to support the People's Special Majlis to meet the challenges of amending the Constitution. The work of the expert will be to advise and assist the members of the Special Majlis to ensure that the new Constitution meets with international human rights standards and is assist in drafting the constitution by: Advising the Special Majlis to ensure that the constitution *is of a high quality and meets international ... standards.*[22]

How might UNCA serve here? According to the UN, reliance on the default method would shut women out from the process; in such cases, UNCA is the spur that draws them in. In terms of content, in some states reliance on the default method would gut human rights (for example, gender equality) because local actors are steeped in 'male-centered cultures'.[23] In such cases, drafting assistance and/or 'gender audit' (UNCA) is crucial to revive it.[24] Thus, UNCA substitutes for the default method when the operation of the default method would

[21] Press Conference by Secretary-General Ban Ki-moon at United Nations Headquarters, U.N. Doc. SG/SM/14021, 14 December 2011.

[22] *See* UNDP Vacancy "Constitutional Expert (Drafter)" (Closing Date: 21 June 2006) (on file) (emphasis added).

[23] Ajay Chibbar, *"Opening Statement at the Regional Conference on Deepening and Sustaining Democracy in Asia,"* 12 October 2009.

[24] *See* UN, *supra* note 6 at 4.

produce a constitution that falls short of certain standards for 'process' and 'content'.

### 7.1.1 Standard-setting

In fact, the UN's notions of overcoming challenges and setting standards form two sides of the same ideological coin.[25] Standards envision an ideal or at least a direction of change; realizing them necessarily requires overcoming certain challenges. These ideas suggest UNCA's use as a response to process and content-related challenges perceived about the default method. They suggest policymakers understand UNCA's use as a means to interfere in the default method [process and/or content] by controlling the role of local actors.[26]

The UN suggests that its constitutional assistance, or its interference in the default method is legitimate for two reasons. First, as a neutral actor, it is well-suited to intervene between the local actors (or the disputants) involved in Constitution-making, widely considered a peaceful means of dispute resolution.[27] Second, since the default method in some states is deemed defective, UNCA is considered crucial to elevating that method to certain standards.[28] Indeed, policy makers first conceived UNCA (and have been using it) to substitute for the default method.

As already noted, fewer UNCA projects were ostensibly framed in terms of addressing the Problem's first aspect. Whereas, a majority of UNCA projects were ostensibly mounted in terms of addressing the problem's second aspect. Given this, hereinafter, this chapter will reference the remainder of UNCA projects, to consider how their promotion of process-related and content-related standards respectively, can be understood as a response to the Problem's second aspect. Before proceeding, it helps to re-visit the steps in a 'process' (*see* Figure 7.1).

25 Id. at 4.
26 Id. at 2.
27 Id.
28 Id.

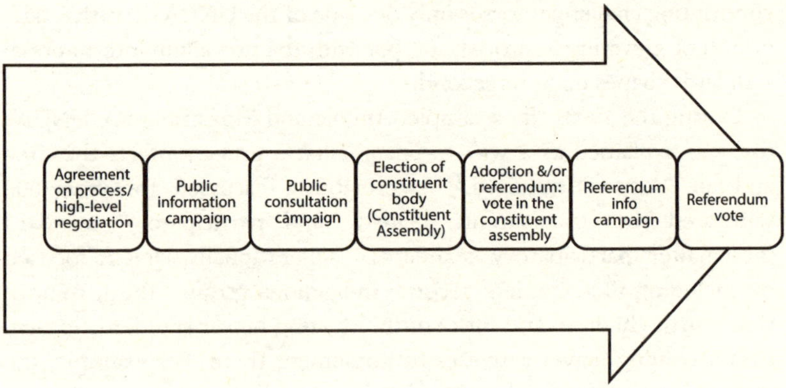


FIGURE 7.1 Steps marking a process
*Source*: Guidance Note of the Secretary- General: United Nations Assistance to Constitution-making Processes Note 9 (2009)

## 7.2 How Does the UN Justify Displacing and/or Tutoring Local Actors in the Conduct of What it Admits is Inherently a 'Sovereign Process'?

According to the UN, local actors lack the necessary experience and knowledge to guarantee 'credible' elections.[29] 'They have virtually no access to the best practices and lessons learned in the field.'[30] The perceived challenge here is the supposed 'knowledge gap'.[31] Second, it considers many locally managed elections typified by fraud, disputes, violence, voters' apathy and low turnout.[32] The notion that a process conducted by local actors locks out youth, women, children, minorities, and indigenous groups produces a related fear. The perceived challenge here is the supposed 'credibility gap'.[33] As I already mentioned,

[29] *See* UNDP, "History and focus on effective electoral assistance," 14 & 16 (1-5 December 2008) [slides] .
[30] Id. at 6.
[31] Id. at 4.
[32] Id. at 6.
[33] Id.

confronting challenges forms only one side of the UNCA narrative. The notion of elevating a 'process' on par with the prevailing international standards shapes up as its second.

During the 1990s (for example, Angola and Mozambique), UNCA's use was explained as a way to ensure that a process meets the 'free and fair' elections standard.[34] As previously discussed, the year 2000 witnessed the 'transparent, inclusive and participatory' standard [hereinafter 'participatory' standard].[35] Operationally, UNCA focused on including first women; second, indigenous groups; third, minorities; fourth children; and fifth youth. Meeting newer standards in turn meant coining newer activities to implement them. For example, the 'participatory standard' produced a new activity: preparing, planning, and carrying out 'public participation and consultations'.[36] In this way, UNCA activities ballooned in number and scope. Indeed, the evolution of UNCA standards paralleled UNCA's expansion.

I now turn to analyse how the UN framed UNCA's use to address perceived 'process-related 'challenges' vis-à-vis these standards.

### 7.2.1 UNCA's First Purpose: Responding to Perceived Process-Related Challenges

Preventing women's exclusion from a process offered UNCA's raison d'être. To best understand this justification requires noting why the UN drafted electoral laws in Namibia—the decolonization context. It did so ostensibly to address challenges associated with the process, conducted by an *external* power (colonizers), once opposed to freeing its colony.[37] Fast forward to 1993, when Cambodian local actors were disallowed from organizing their constituent assembly elections. Why? To address process-related challenges that were now presented as 'internal': Cambodians' authoritarian 'past'.[38]

[34] Guy S. Goodwin-Gill, *Free and Fair Elections – New expanded edition* v (2006).

[35] UN, *Women, Peace, and Security* 167 (2002) .

[36] *See* UN, *supra* note 6 at 6.

[37] *See* S.C. Res. 640, U.N. SCOR., 2882nd mtg., ¶ 5 U.N. Doc. S/Res/640 (1989).

[38] Art. 15 (2) (a), *Agreement on a Comprehensive Political Settlement of the Cambodia Conflict* (23 October 1991).

True, the UN ostensibly conducted participatory programs in Third World states because it considered them lacking in resources and expertise. However, it emphasized the awfulness of 'male-centered cultures', staining certain politico-economic landscapes to justify UNCA's use. Consider:

> In terms of political empowerment women in Asia, struggle with low parliamentary representation, the second worst in the world at 17% after the Arab states – and male-centered political party cultures. ...This trend exists with respect to women's participation and roles even at the local levels.[39]

In fact, this rationale explains why the UN split those more than one hundred, mainly illiterate Afghan women, who had been brought to the UN compound in Farah, from their male relatives.[40] In so doing, the UN was seen as responding to a challenge peculiarly Afghani: 'family-voting' or 'proxy voting by male relatives'.[41] By framing this malpractice as exclusively 'internal', the UN eliminates the idea about external extenuating factors causing it. For instance, Afghan society grew militarized because the United States and the Soviet Union funneled huge amounts of arms into the country (during the Cold War).[42] Militarization as we know, negatively influences men's attitudes towards and treatment of women.

Turning to UNCA's use beyond the post-conflict context, take Bhutan. 'Ask anyone what it will take to make women's equality a reality and "toilets" will probably not be the response,' says the UNDP.[43] How might UNCA fetch toilets for Bhutanese women thereby realizing their right to equality? According to the UNDP, women in poor states like Bhutan and Malawi have more difficulty accessing water supply, sanitation, and education that are critical to development.[44] Herein

[39] *See* Chibbar, *supra* note 23.

[40] *See* Malalai Joya and Derrik O'Keefe, *A Woman among Warlords: Extraordinary Story of an Afghan Who Dared to Raise Her Voice* 62-63 (Scribner, 2009).

[41] UNDP, Online Toolkit for Electoral Assistance (undated).

[42] *See* Norah Niland, *Rights, Rhetoric and Reality: A Snapshot from Afghanistan, in* The UN, human rights and post-conflict situations 322, 346 (Nigel D. White & Dirk Klaasen, eds., Manchester University Press, 2005).

[43] *See* UNDP, Linking poverty reduction and water management 18 (undated).

[44] UNDP, "Fast Facts – Gender equality and democratic governance" 1 (undated)

comes UNCA. Which, by spiking their electoral presence allows them to frame policies benefitting them, and men equitably.[45] This explanation suggests UNCA operates not just in response to local actors' weak capacities, but rather, to address broader, and more ambitious politico-social purposes.

In Nepal, Bolivia, Guatemala, El Salvador, and Colombia UNCA was ostensibly used for promoting indigenous participation.[46] In Bolivia, the UNDP framed its intervention in terms of 'bolstering this state's limited capacity'.[47] Again, in Nepal, the UN paid 'special attention' to Rai, Magar, Limbu, and other Nepali indigenous groups in response to the government's perceived inability to conduct an inclusive process.[48] It explained assuming what is effectively the government's function because it found gaps in the state's support for indigenous participation. Consider:

> As reported previously, these groups – Dalits, *Janajatis*, *Madhesis*, and religious minorities – are represented in the [Constituent] Assembly in greater numbers … than in any other national elected body in Nepal's history.[49]

Finally, most recently, in Colombia, where land rights and distribution have been at the heart of the conflict and more than 2 million indigenous peoples either died or disappeared, the UNDP ran three national fora in order that they contribute to the peace talks, and submit proposals about rural development, political participation, illicit crops, and victims' rights.[50]

Minorities' participation is the participatory standard's third facet. Chapter 4 suggests that policymakers have created a need for UNCA

[45] Id.

[46] *See* UNDP and indigenous peoples: a practice note (undated).

[47] UNDP, "A story of dialogue, conflict and peacebuilding in Bolivia" 18 (undated).

[48] S.C. Res. 1740, SCOR., 5622nd mtg., pmbl ¶ 5 & ¶ 1 (d) & (e) U.N. Doc. S/Res/1740 (23 January 2007).

[49] *Report of the Secretary-General on the Request of Nepal for United Nations Assistance in Support of Its Peace Process*, ¶ 37 U.N. Doc. S/2008/454 (10 July 2008).

[50] UNDP, Colombia participates in the peace process (undated), *available at:* http://www.undp.org/content/undp/en/home/ourwork/ourstories/colombia-participates-in-the-peace-process.html.

in the same way since 1949: by suggesting that local actors, given their disunity, cannot be relied upon to protect their minorities. Indeed, in 1949, Adrian Pelt was entrusted with organizing Libya's process to prevent among other things, the exclusion of minorities. Fast forward to 2003–2005. Now Iraqi Shias, Kurds, and Sunnis are portrayed as divided, and the UN is accordingly, empowered to conduct the Iraqi process to foster a "national dialogue" amongst these antagonistic groups. Next, the UN was tasked with creating Iraq's Constitutional Committee[51] to prevent the Sunnis' exclusion.[52] Minorities' participation touches upon wider sovereignty issues, which according to the UN, its neutrality, renders it particularly suited to tackle.[53] Indeed, this rationale animated UNCA in Kosovo.

Tied to minorities' exclusion, comes yet another perceived challenge: authoritarianism. Indeed, as noted in Chapter 6, although the United States proposed UNCA, essentially as a face-saving altnative, it as framed as critical to democratizing Iraqi constitution-making.[54] As per the UN's underlying view, Iraqi stakeholders cannot be relied upon, given their divisive and authoritarian past, to be united and/or democratic.[55]

Child participation comes next. According to the UN, military leaders and politicians push children to operate roadblocks, impersonate voters, capture polling booths, and hurl stones at opponents or smash their billboards.[56] It is to prevent these forms of child abuse, says the UN, that it managed Nepal's process from start to finish.[57] Again, the UN ostensibly displaced local actors to interview Bhutanese children

[51] Factsheet: UN's support in Iraq's constitution-making process 2 (undated).

[52] Id. S.C. Res.1483, U.N. SCOR, 4761st mtg., ¶ 8 (c) & (g) U.N. Doc. S/Res/1483 (22 May 2003).

[53] B. Lynn Pascoe, Rediscovering Preventive Diplomacy: A View from the United Nations 1–2 (26 July 2010).

[54] *See The Political Transition in Iraq: Report of the fact finding mission, Annex 2,* U.N. Doc. S/2004/10 (2004); *Report of the Secretary-General pursuant to paragraph 30 of resolution 1546* (2004), ¶4 U.N. Doc. S/2005/141 (7 March 2005).

[55] Factsheet, *supra* note 51.

[56] *See* UNMIN, Children in politics 2 (undated).

[57] Id.

to amplify the little ones' voices.[58] In the DRC, Mali, Nepal, Somalia, Afghanistan, Sierra Leone, and Southern Sudan, which share a history of child-soldiers, UNCA was deemed critical to channeling child rights into peace agreements, and thereafter, keeping those commitments alive.[59]

Youth empowerment melds with child participation. This theme appeared on the UN radar screen in December 2010, when popular and youthful protests sparked a powerful wave, toppling long-ruling dictators in the Middle East and North Africa [MENA] region. The UN began promoting youth empowerment from 2011, framing a need for UNCA in these two ways.[60] First, it portrayed the MENA region as 'polarized by tribal communities'.[61] Second, UNCA was deemed essential to address the range of issues concerning youth that were long ignored by MENA's dictators, and so, first brought them to the streets.[62] According to the UN, since Arab governments have long excluded their youth from effective and democratic governance, and denied them proper education and gainful employment,[63] now is the time to bring youth more centrally into the UN's peace, security and development goals. Our future in these areas, says the UN, depends on our respect for their rights.

So, the fear that youth participation shrivels without UNCA, explains why the UNDP uploaded 'Democra Tweet', a voter's game on Tunisian Radio Mosaique,[64] and mounted youth workshops during Yemen's National Dialogue Conference.[65] Commending the UN's role in MENA, Navi Pillay, the Under Secretary-General, stated, '... democratic transi-

[58] *See* "Plus 5 'world fit for children' review for the Kingdom of Bhutan" 2 (2006).

[59] *See* Children's rights and the UN Security Council, *at:* http://www.crin.org/resources/infoDetail.asp?ID=18041&flag=report.

[60] *See* Factsheet, International Year of Youth, 2010–2011.

[61] *See* UNDP, "Voices" 1, 7 (2nd Quarter, 2011).

[62] UN News Center, "Arab nations need to ensure sustainable transition to democracy — UN rights chief," 30 May 2012.

[63] UNDP, Youth Strategy 2014–2017, 5, 19, 29 (2014).

[64] Supporting democratic elections in the new Tunisia, *available at:* http://www.undp.org/content/brussels/en/home/ourwork/democratic-governance-and-peacebuilding/successstories/supporting-democratic-elections-tunisia.html.

[65] UNDP, Yemen National Dialogue & Constitutional Reform Trust Fund: Report (undated).

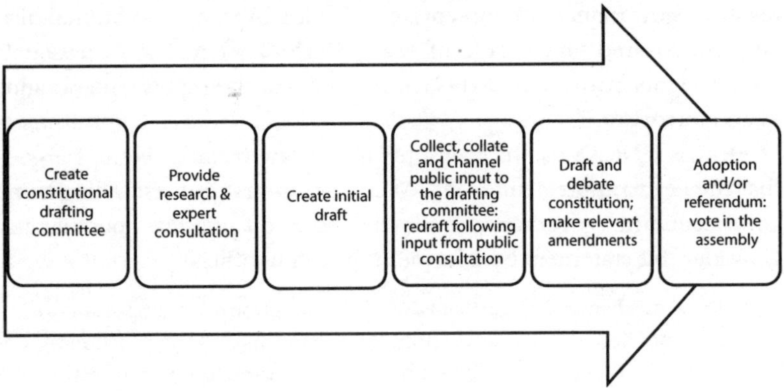


FIGURE 7.2 Steps marking the creation of content
*Source*: Guidance Note of the Secretary- General: United Nations Assistance to Constitution-making Processes Note 9 (2009).

tion is incomplete if it fails to include appropriate … reforms.'[66] Which means, according to the UN, its constitutional assistance is critical to helping revolutions like the Jasmine one (Arab Spring) attain their goals.

Which of the purposes mentioned in section 7.0, might we say, have these UNCA standards met? The UN says: Democracy, rule of law, and good governance and territorial status[67] (*see* section 7.5).

Figure 7.2 illustrates the steps involved in creating content.

## 7.3 How Does the UN Justify Displacing and/or Tutoring Local Actors in the Creation of What It Admits is Inherently a 'Sovereign' Document?

### 7.3.1 UNCA's Second Purpose is Responding to Perceived Content-Related Challenges

UNCA ostensibly promotes many content-related standards,[68] of which seven are key: (1) free markets, (2) judicial independence, (3) natural

66 UN News Centre, Arab nations need to ensure sustainable transition to democracy – UN rights chief, 1 (30 May 2011) (quote).

67 UN, Rule of Law Guidance Note 4–6 (undated).

68 Id.

resource governance, 4) anti-corruption measures, all conditionalities (and so, covered under 'rule of law'), 5) gender equality, 6) national human rights institutions (NHRIs), 7) child/youth empowerment, and 8) anti-terrorism.[69]

How is UNCA's use to promote rule of law framed? Here, I argue that the key to appreciating UNCA's use lies in first understanding how good economic governance is married to good political governance. Consider this statement by a former top UNDP official:

> Political mechanisms of participation and interaction are as important to sustainable development as economic mechanisms and the functioning of markets. Markets must be embedded in legitimate political institutions. ....
>
> There is an overarching need for capacity support efforts by development partners and other non-state actors to bring about lasting change....[70]

So understood, according to the UN and the BWIs, to prosper in this globalized era, the world's Least Developed Countries (LDCs) need to protect property rights, manage modern tax systems, instill fiscal discipline, draw up appropriate budgets, and curb corruption to encourage private investment.[71] LDCs need politically savvy citizens who enjoy the right to, and possess skills to participate in domestic political/constitutional processes and in global forums, and thus, engage, effectively with the World Trade Organization, Financial Action Task Force [FATF], and International Accounting Standards Board. However, LDCs, given their weak capacities, fail to comply with the standards (outlined in this para's opening lines) and so, imperil macroeconomic stability.[72]

Importantly, this rationale has spurred the UN's constitutional assistance right since its inception, and so, animated virtually all its UNCA projects. Take the policy about drawing up appropriate budgets. In 1949, Adrian Pelt brought in International Monetary Fund

[69] Id.

[70] UNDP, *Governance for the Future – Democracy and Development in the Least Developed Countries* 3 (2006).

[71] Id. at 70.

[72] Id. *See also* UNDP, *Making the Law Work for Everyone* (2008) (justifying UNCA's use to protect property rights).

(IMF) experts to make Libyans more 'budget-minded'.[73] So do his successors, now.[74]

Two standards, the first guiding judicial independence ('the Bangalore Principles') and the second, pertaining to natural resource governance (NSG), piggybacked on free markets. According to the UN, in many post-conflict countries, the legal frameworks inadequately address challenges to judicial independence and so, 'advance the rights of dominant social groups while leaving others behind'.[75] It is argued that this is why UN Judicial officers in coordination with the UN Country Teams and the World Bank, draft *constitutions* and 'provide legal analysis and advice' thus, paving the way for UN rule of law assistance (amending or drafting *laws*.)[76]

The UN framed UNCA's need vis-à-vis good NSG in these four ways.[77] First, it suggests that many 'resource rich' states' forests and wetlands disappear, lands become polluted, mineral resources diminish, rivers evaporate, fisheries collapse, species die, and soils erode because they lack the knowledge and capacity to protect the environment.[78] In particular, local actors suffer from 'knowledge-gaps' and weak drafting skills.[79]

Second, ownership (of natural resources) is framed as an 'emotive' issue that pits claims of private ownership against customary rights and state ownership.[80] The perceived challenge here, concerns stakeholders'

[73] Adrian Pelt, *Libyan Independence and the United Nations — A Case of Planned Decolonization* 580 (Yale University Press, 1970).

[74] *See* e.g., MENA MDTF, World Bank support to the Yemen National Dialogue (2014).

[75] *UN Handbook for Judicial Affairs Officers in UN Peacekeeping Operations* 174–175 & 27 (UN, 2013).

[76] Id. at Ch.7; UNDPKO, Justice Components in United Nations Peace Operations §10.8 (2011) (quote); *See e.g., Report of the UN High Commissioner for Human Rights, Technical Assistance for Libya in the Field of Human Rights,* ¶27 UN Doc. A/HRC/25/42 (13 January 2014).

[77] *See generally* UNEP, "Natural resources in conflict and peace-building" (2012); ICJ, Judicial Accountability: A Practitioners' Guide 131-139 (UN, 2016) (reproducing the Bangalore Principles, 2002).

[78] Id.

[79] UN, *supra* note 6 at 3–4.

[80] Nicholas Haysom & Sean Kane, "Negotiating natural resources for peace: Ownership, control, and wealth-sharing" – Briefing Paper 8 (Centre for Humanitarian Dialogue, October 2009).

tendencies to grandstand, whereby they undermine fiscal rationality.[81] At such times, UNCA's benefit supposedly lies in steering constitutional negotiations along technical lines, and basing ownership on 'good governance'.[82]

Third, local actors, particularly from divided societies, supposedly find negotiating 'revenue sharing' 'difficult'.[83] Here, given its neutrality, the UN mediation support supposedly performs a critical service as in Iraq, where it prevented 'identity-based conflicts' over unevenly distributed resources among its often hostile communities.[84]

Fourth, states with muddied laws render ownership rights vague and so, get labelled as 'high-risk locations', and as a result, repel potential investors.[85] All this is said to hurt their economic growth and prosperity. The UN suggests, UNCA enables LDCs to meet the aforesaid 'economic challenges', and thereby promotes macroeconomic stability.

As for anti-corruption, it became one of the UN's fastest growing policy area only after 1989 and more so, after 2000. Yet, here too, the fear that (incapable) local actors create paper tigers for ACCs has spurred the United Nations Office on Drugs and Crime, UNODOC and the IMF to co-draft model anti-corruption laws and help states adopt similar ones.[86]

Fifth comes Gender equality, and an activity ostensibly undertaken to promote this standard: monitoring constituent assembly proceedings. Here too, understanding United Nations Constitutional Assistance's (UNCA) deeper implications requires noting how this activity was explained in the decolonization context. Take Namibia, which South Africa consented to free, only in return for a firm commitment that it would constitutionally guarantee for the settler community, key civil

[81] Id.

[82] Id.

[83] *See* Factsheet, *supra* note 51.

[84] *See* Haysom, *supra* note 80 at 8.

[85] Id. at 12, fn. World Bank, "Angola economic memorandum: Oil, broad-based growth, and equity," (World Bank, 2 October 2006). Id.

[86] *See* e.g., The 2005 UNODC and IMF Model-Legislation on Money-Laundering and Financing of Terrorism *available at:* UNODC, https: / / www.unodc.org/ unodc / en / money-laundering / Model-Legislation.html.

and political rights, including gender equality.[87] Accordingly, the relevant peace agreement contained 'constitutional principles' whose constitutionalization the UN ensured, by monitoring Namibia's Constituent Assembly proceedings (for example, of UNCA).[88] The UN monitored Namibia's constitution-making process ostensibly to save the White settler community from their one-time oppressed groups and Namibians from their one-time oppressors.

Fast forward to Nepal in 2008:

> *Report of the Secretary-General* (2008)
>
> Support for the constituent assembly and its members were provided in a range of areas. It included an initiative to orient women assembly members in parliamentary culture, human rights, gender, and social inclusion.[89]

In so empowering the UN, what challenge did the Security Council perceive? Indeed, now, the problem was protecting Nepali women from their society, widely perceived as patriarchal, and long hostile to their emancipation.[90] This idea also underlay the UN's stepped-up efforts, even outside the Assembly.[91] For instance, the practice of top UN officials orienting assemblies, and gently nudging local (Third World) actors to comply with human rights, including gender equality has become commonplace.[92]

Most recently, the UN gave this monitoring a new twist by adding to its toolbox, the 'Gender Audit' (of draft constitutions).[93] We saw this

[87] *See* Paul Szasz, *Creating the Namibian Constitution, in* The Namibian Peace Process: Implications and Lessons for the Future 241, 245-246 (Heribert Weiland & Matthew Braham, eds., Arnold Bergstraesser Institute, 1994).

[A special thanks to Gregory Fox for pointing me to this book].

[88] Id. In his report to the Security Council dated 16 March 1990, the UN Secretary-General reported that the Constitution, which was annexed, reflected the constitutional principles channeled into the relevant 1982 peace agreement.

[89] *Report of the Secretary-General on the Request of Nepal for United Nations Assistance in Support of Its Peace Process*, ¶ 35 U.N. Doc. S/2008/454 (July 10, 2008).

[90] *See* Chibbar, *supra* note 23.

[91] *See* Richard Bennett, Opening Remarks, 11–12 November, Nepal, 2009, *at:* http:www.nepal.ohchr.org.

[92] Id. *See also* Speech delivered by Ian Martin, the Special Representative of the Secretary-General at Benghazi University, April 10, 2012.

[93] *See*, e.g., UN Women, Sudan-Women's rights 1–2 (undated).

audit's use (melded with drafting assistance) in Sudan, Tunisia, Somalia, Zimbabwe, and so on (*see* Chapter 6). These UNCA activities suggest that UN/international policymakers conceive their roles as protecting Third World women because they need to be saved from their misogynistic societies. This recalls an international policymaker's comment made to a mainstream peacebuilding scholar (who conducted fieldwork in the DRC):

> A European diplomat once explained to me the logic behind his government's approach to the Democratic Republic of Congo: 'It is a bit like with a teenager – someone who is 18 or 20; you want to help them, but you have to mind your manners and build the trust that enables you to do so.' Indeed, the diplomat and his international colleagues – ... UN officials ... –all wanted to help a much-affected population .... However, not only did these foreign interveners regularly forget to 'mind their manners and build trust,' but their perception that Congo was like an adolescent who needed to be manipulated into accepting assistance often precluded them from treating the Congolese people as equal partners in the peace process.[94]

Moving on to the fourth standard, the NHRIs, as we have seen, the Office of the High Commissioner for Human Rights, OHCHR has taken the lead in promoting this standard, in the majority of UNCA-recipients-states (*see* Chapter 6). Why? A task that tops its checklist, answers this question: ensuring that NHRI provisions meet the 'Paris Principles'.[95] According to the OHCHR, '[T]he level of detail that' stakeholders typically use to establish and authorize the functioning of a NHRI 'is not usually appropriate for a constitution'.[96] That local actors create paper tigers for NHRIs is its second fear.[97]

As for child rights, the sixth standard, the UN complains that changes in the political landscape typically roll back gains for children, which leaves them disenfranchised. This is why, it speaks up for them; it audits draft constitutions, and so, stirs those who are

[94] Séverine Autessere, *Paternalism and Peacebuilding,* in Paternalism beyond borders 132, 138 (Michael N. Barnett, ed., Cambridge University Press, 2014).

[95] OHCHR, *National Human Rights Institutions - History, Principles, Roles and Responsibilities* 35 (UN, New York, 2010).

[96] Id. at 32 (quote).

[97] Id.

complacent and/or are unwilling to fulfill their public duties.[98] Again, starting from 2000, Child Advisers were attached to peace operations in order that they may enjoy greater independence, thus enabling them to go where, and do what, others dare not: Spearhead highly political and sensitive activities (constitutional and legal reforms) on the ground.[99]

Since the UN definitions for the term child and youth blur to some extent, the fifth standard has since 2011, come to covers rights for youth as well.[100] In the MENA region, the UN explains drafting constitutions, assuming what is effectively the government's function because it found huge gaps in the state's support for youth, and next, local actors ignorant of 'international best practices'.[101] Indeed, thanks to its drafting assistance, says the UN, the Tunisian constitution underscores 'the state's role to provide the necessary conditions for developing the capacities of youth and realizing their potential'.[102]

The seventh, and last standard, anti-terrorism, emerged in the harrowing aftermath of Al-Qaeda's 2001 terrorist attacks. Therefore, initially UNCA's use (knowledge-based support) to promote this standard, spiked in states with a history of harboring terrorists, ostensibly because they were insufficiently rooted in democratic practices and so, need guidance in thwarting terrorism. Consider:

> But they [Iraqis] are emerging from a long period of dictatorship, they have a dearth of legitimate institutions, and they *do need help* and encouragement.
>
> ...We have a role to play, in the political transition, especially in the constitutional process and in the preparation for elections[103] [emphasis added].

98 UN, *supra* note 6 at 4.

99 UN-DPKO, "Child Protection in UN Peacekeeping" 6, 7, 14, (Spring 2011).

100 UNDP, *supra* note 63 at 47

101 Id. at 5; UNDP, Arab States: Draft Project Document (describing the various forms of UNCA offered).

102 UNDP, *supra* note 63 at 5.

103 Kieran Prendergast, Under Secretary General for Political Affairs at the United Nations, "Challenges to the UN," 1 (February 19, 2004) ("Questions and Answers").

Another related idea animating UNCA is that unless tutored, Islamic states squelch human rights while countering terrorism.[104] So, ridding Libya and Yemen's forthcoming constitutions of such failings explains UNCA's use there.[105] Meanwhile, after 2005, the UN embraced the idea of *globalizing* counter-terror efforts. Accordingly, drafting assistance was ostensibly used to help even stable states (for example, Bhutan) constitutionalize anti-terror provisions.[106]

### *7.3.1.1 Overview of Standards*

The foregoing analysis presents a dimension wholly missing from what little exists about internationalized constitution-making: The UN Family itself, and the broader purposes underpinning its constitutional assistance. First, several purposes attach to UNCA's use, including but going beyond the idea of assisting states reeling from conflict, disease, and destruction. The promotion of free markets, for instance, does not spring from the consequences of conflict. So then, the UN's contention that UNCA was conceived in response to the destruction of, or the absence of local constitution-making capacity does not fully explain UNCA's first use in Congo in 1960, let alone its mushrooming in the post-Cold War era. Rather, what makes UNCA a 'post-conflict' phenomenon is only the UN's portrayal of it as such.

Second, several key allied standards—judicial independence, free markets, anti-corruption commissions, and natural resource governance—stem from the lending conditions imposed on Heavily Indebted Poor Countries (HIPCs) by the BWIs. This means, in LDCs, standards with a social dimension, such as gender equality, stand redefined in the context of market.

Finally, UNCA's standard-setting casts actors into superior and subordinate roles, and positions standards advanced by powerful Western states, as universal and of common benefit.[107] The analysis in Chapters 2 and 3 suggest that this subtext is nothing new.

104 *See* UNDP, *Arab Human Development Report 2009* §1, 5 (2009).

105 *See* S. C. Res. 2051, U.N. SCOR, 6784th mtg., ¶ 3 (d) & 16 UN Doc. S/Res/2051 (12 June 2012).

106 UNDP-Bhutan, Annual Report 4-5 (2004).

107 *See e.g.*, Autesserre, *supra* note 94.

## 7.4 UNCA & ITA Display Common Features

How have policymakers understood UNCA's use to promote the standards discussed in the previous section? Answering this question will help me establish in Chapter 9 that UNCA continues to act as trusteeship. Indeed, as I will show, policymakers have sought to use UNCA in two ways: 'proactively'[108] and reactively. Second, they conceived the Constitution as a governance tool. Accordingly, UNCA adopts a remedial or 'long-term' approach to governance.[109] Third, UNCA fills a need of its own creation. Finally, even as UNCA often interferes with the workings of the default method, it affirms the validity of that method — that is., constitution-making carried out by local actors without international assistance.[110] Wilde's analysis reveals that these features apply to ITA's use, too,[111] which is expected, since UNCA sires ITA. As I will show at all times, UNCA guides and governs ITA's use.

### 7.4.1 UNCA Acts Proactively Only in the Sphere of Process

To maintain continuity, I will analyze policymakers' understanding of UNCA's use in terms of process first and content next. When UNCA responds to process-related challenges, it acts only 'proactively'.[112] Take the former UN Secretary-General, Ban Ki-Moon, who within two months of the Tunisian fruit vendor, M. Bouazizi immolating himself, and triggering the Jasmine revolution, stated thus:

> The United Nations is ready to provide all support to the Tunisian government and people, particularly in the area of electoral process ....[113] [emphasis added]

Again, consider the two following UN statements:

Advance Planning, UNCA Guidance Note (2009)

[108] *See* UN Guidance Note of the Secretary-General on Democracy 3 (undated)

[109] *See* Wilde, *supra* note 3 at 229.

[110] Id.

[111] *Id*. at 229–232.

[112] *See* UN, *supra* note 6 at 6.

[113] *See* UN News Centre, "Ban pledges full UN help for Tunisia's transition to democracy," 22 March 2011.

> Certain elements of a … process require careful *advance planning* to be carried out successfully in an inclusive, participatory and transparent fashion. The UN should advise national actors of these requirements and assist them to begin the process in a timely fashion…[114]
>
> The UN is evaluating its efforts on how best to provide sustainable democracy assistance …. ….
>
> … based on experience to date, the following principles should guide UN democracy efforts: *Proactive approach* to threats to democracy….[115]

What might the aforementioned passages suggest? Indeed, they suggest that policymakers fear the default method walls off youth, women, minorities, indigenous peoples, and other marginalized groups. Accordingly, UNCA serves not to correct violations. Rather, as Ban Ki-Moon alludes, and the above passages explicitly state, UNCA serves to *prevent* them. This is why, the UN initiates at the outset 'best practices', which entail slashing local actors' powers or tutoring them from the outset.

#### *7.4.1.1 UNCA Governs ITA's Proactive Use*

Meanwhile, Wilde suggests that ITA acts proactively.[116] I suggest, since conceptually speaking the Constitution is the state's highest law, and provides ITA's framework, UNCA governs ITA's proactive use.[117] For example, take Cambodia. There, UN officials, as part of preparing for Cambodia's constituent assembly elections, elbowed out local actors to gut socialist laws because they would violate the impending Constitution and enact such electoral law (for example, of ITA) as would be consistent with the (impending) Constitution. In this way, UNCA guides or governs ITA's proactive use.

### 7.4.2 UNCA Acts Reactively in the Sphere of Content

The UN Resident Coordinator, in the wake of auditing Bhutan's constitution, offered this explanation:

114 UN, *supra* note 6 at 6.

115 UN Democracy Guidance Note 3 (undated).

116 Wilde, *supra* note 6 at 228.

117 Id.

....

> It can be seen that the drafters went through great pains to spell out a sound governance framework, providing explicit normative content and stating principles to promote social equality... ...Several features in the draft Constitution are unique to the country, its history, religion, traditions, and culture. The United Nations System fully respects and supports this but would like to raise those aspects of the draft constitution that have a bearing on internationally accepted norms ... with respect to democratic governance, rule of law, and the rights and freedoms of people. From this perspective, important considerations include the compatibility of constitutional provisions with Bhutan's international obligations and the fundamental rights of persons and citizens.[118]

What might this use of UNCA suggest? It shows that the UN exercises power in *ad hoc fashion*. Such exercise of power is deemed essential given the likelihood of local content gutting good practices (the BWIs' conditionalities) such as fiscal decentralization and embedding other practices violating the conditionalities and so, are deemed bad. Consider:

> UNCA Guidance Note (2009)
>
> The UN should consistently promote compliance of constitutions with ... norms and standards. Thus, it should *speak out* when a draft constitution does not comply with these standards, especially as they relate to ... constitutional issues. The UN should be the advocate of the standards it has helped to develop.[119]

So, whereas in its 'proactive' role, the UN takes the lead, here, it puts off intervening until local actors take the first step. The UN thus *reacts*. The message here for local actors is unless they draft content that meets the BWIs' conditionalities: privatization, liberalization, fiscal decentralization, and other standards non-financial for example, gender equality), it will 'speak out' to expose their bad practices. And step in to contain them. Thus, UNCA acts 'reactively' when it deems local actors unwilling or incapable of conforming to preferred standards.

[118] *See* Statement of UN Resident Coordinator, "UN System Statement on Issues of Common Interest," Geneva, 1-4 (15 February 2006).

[119] UN, *supra* note 6 at 4.

#### *7.4.2.1 UNCA guides ITA's reactive use*

Here too, the Constitution guides and governs ITA's reactive use (audit of laws). For instance, in Cambodia, the UN reviewed all laws (including those passed by the Supreme National Council). Why? To veto them, if necessary (for example, of reactive ITA)[120] because it (the UN) perceived them, a threat to ITA's particular objectives, which were simply those of the Constitution: western liberal market democracy. I therefore, concur with Wilde that policymakers explained displacing local actors from law-making (for example, of ITA) to 'step in to correct mistakes'.[121]

To summarize, in UNCA-ITA projects, UNCA and ITA act together, proactively and reactively ostensibly toward common standards and policies, with of course, UNCA guiding its offspring's proactive and reactive uses. Significantly, ideas about local incapacity or unwillingness underpin both forms of UNCA's and ITA's use: proactive and reactive.

### 7.4.3 UNCA Adopts a Remedial Approach

UNCA which produces the Constitution was conceived to remedy governance. With or without, ITA, UNCA adopts a remedial approach. Consider:

> The UN should seek to address … the underlying or structural causes of threats to democracy.
>
> …most threats are internal, such as bad governance, abuses of state power, endemic corruption and entrenched discrimination and inequality, lack of voice of the poor and the marginalized and their right to remedy and justice.[122]

Given this, the UN adopts, not an *ad hoc,* palliative approach to that area, but a more intense 'remedial' one. And indeed, it explains promoting preferred constitutional standards to address these challenges or threats that triggered the need for its use in the first place.

120 *Id. See* Wilde, *supra* note 3 at 228.

121 Id. at 228.

122 *See* UN, Democracy Guidance Note 3 (undated).

#### *7.4.3.1 UNCA Guides ITA's Remedial Role*

As ITA's parent, UNCA enables ITA to remedy governance. Wilde suggests that remedial ITA projects aim at remedying bad local governance which made internationalizing governance essential.[123] I concur with Wilde's suggestion… I suggest that ITA reshapes local governance's structural features in tune with the Constitution. Indeed, in Congo, Cambodia, Kosovo, and East-Timor, UNCA guided ITA's remedial roles. For instance, in Congo, the UN drafted such mining laws as were consistent with the impending Constitution.

### 7.4.4 UNCA Fills a Need of Its Own Creation, and so, Allows ITA to do so

UNCA was co-conceived by the BWIs and the UN to assist poor debtor Third World states meet a conditionality: produce the Constitution. And thereby ensure that these states morphed into western liberal market democracies. To achieve this goal, local actors were portrayed as lacking ability, being divided, and or being otherwise unwilling, to fulfill preferred standards. In this way, UNCA filled and continues to fill a need of its own creation.

UNCA enables ITA to do so. I therefore, concur with Wilde who posits that ITA fills a void of its own making when it works to ensure that governance in a supposed administrative vacuum 'conforms to certain policy objectives' (for example, democracy, the ROL and free markets).[124] Indeed, my previous discussion of UNCA-ITA projects in Congo, Cambodia, Somalia, Kosovo, East-Timor, and Iraq evidences just that (*see* Chapter 6).

To conclude (and as my Chapter 6 shows), regardless of how a vacuum is created, what enables ITA to fill that vacuum is: the Constitution. Again, the Constitution provides a framework for ITA, allowing it to operate/to fill a void, in ways consistent with it. Here is how UNCA enables ITA to fill a need of its own creation.

123 *See Wilde, supra* note 6 at 229.

124 Id at 227.

### 7.4.5 UNCA Pays Homage to That for Which It Is a Substitute; ITA Follows Suit.

What do ideas about UNCA's use, with and without ITA (discussed so far— section 7.4), suggest? Indeed, in operating with and without ITA, UNCA honors in the breach, that which it replaces: the default method. Wilde makes the same point only about ITA.[125] I concur (As I will show in this section, UNCA the parent has to first operate or be envisaged, and so, homage paid to the default method, before ITA can work, and so, homage is paid to the normal model).

So, how does the UN pay lip service to that which it supplants in these two instances:

(1) To fill a perceived vacuum or
(2) To raise governance in a given territorial unit in tune with good governance.

Since UNCA was ostensibly conceived to remedy governance, in the first instance 1), there is deemed to be no constitution/governance at all. Take Congo where, as discussed, in Chapter 4, a void opened up in Congo because Prime Minister Patrice Lumumba's socialist government was deemed inept and clumsy and so, not backed when it was wrongfully dismissed. Accordingly, ONUC officials elbowed out local actors to draft appropriate laws (ITA) in tune with the impending Constitution, to fill a supposed vacuum. In this way, homage was first paid to the default method, (since the Constitution was envisaged), then to the normal model (which ITA substituted).

In the second instance, take Cambodia, Somalia, Kosovo, and East-Timor where UNCA was ostensibly used in response to local unwillingness or local inability to embrace good governance (constitutionalize the market economy, minorities' participation, and so on). These ideas suggest that policymakers consider constitutions made by, and administration conducted by local actors as the default methods. And since, in all four places mentioned in this para, UNCA sired ITA, homage was first paid to the default method, and consequently, next, to the normal model.[126]

[125] *See* Wilde, *supra* note 3 at 232.
[126] Id.

What about UNCA operating on its own? In this case, the UN supports constitution-making by local actors as the method of first resort in three ways. First, it labels all UNCA projects, proactive and reactive, as essentially short-term support, that is, temporary in nature.[127] Second, and furthermore, its reactive projects suggest that content created by local actors is the norm with UNCA's use reserved for correcting mistakes. Third, its remedial approach to governance suggests it prefers constitutions forged without international assistance. Indeed, it explains UNCA as aimed at positively altering local actors' conditions and enhancing their long-term capacities.

To conclude, what triggers UNCA's use are policymakers' judgments about the workings of the default method. Were they to consider it (default method) as flawless, they would never use UNCA.

## 7.5 Summarizing UNCA–ITA's Relationship

I will summarize UNCA–ITA's relationship under these headings:

a) *UNCA and ITA share common features*
First, UNCA sires ITA and so, guides its "proactive" and "reactive" use. Second, since UNCA was born to remedy governance, by producing the Constitution, it adopts a 'remedial' approach to governance. Accordingly, and third, it enables ITA to remedy governance, and so, together, UNCA and ITA fill a need of their own creation. Fourth, if UNCA is not constitution-making by local actors, so is ITA not governance by local actors. In other words, ironically these parent-child 'policy institutions' pay homage to that for which they are substitutes. This is because, their framers have used them to substitute the default method and normal model respectively because they are perceived as defective.[128] Or put another way, in so doing, their framers affirm the idea that a constitution-making carried out by local actors (without international assistance) and administration carried out by local actors is the normal [administration] model or represent the norm.

127 *See* UN, *supra* note 6 at 9.

128 *See* UN, *supra* note 6.

b) *UNCA enables ITA to achieve common ends*
The Constitution remedies governance. UNCA entails displacing local actors, fully or partially, to produce it. The Constitution, so produced provides a framework, based on which, the UN displaces local actors, fully or partially, to administer a territorial unit (for example, make laws): ITA. ITA operates in tune with the Constitution. In these ways, UNCA enables ITA and works with it symbiotically toward achieving common ends: democracy, the rule of law, free market economics, good governance (including the exploitation of natural resources), and modern practices (women's rights).[129] UNCA and ITA are ostensibly used in response to governance-related problems: gap in governance and/or supposed absence of good governance.

c) *UNCA enables ITA to achieve another goal: territorial-status*
In addition to, and as part of remedying governance, the first goal, UNCA fulfills its second goal: territorial status. Here, it enables ITA to do so as well.

Table 7.1 illustrates UNCA and ITA's symbiotic policy-roles.

## 7.6 Establishing UNCA as a Parent 'Policy Institution'

According to Wilde, a Policy Institution is:

1. An institution/established practice that works toward common ostensible purposes and ends.
2. Comprises projects, all of which do not and need not enjoy a 'policy connection'.
   Wilde defines a third criteria: that all the projects manifest 'purposive commonality' at two levels:
   a. *Elemental:* They operate in the same way on a practical level.
   b. *Sophisticated:* They so operate because they follow the same rationale.[130]

I argue that UNCA fulfills all three criteria in these ways.

[129] *See* Wilde, *supra* note 3 at 204–205.
[130] Id. at 233–234.

Table 7.1 United Nations Constitutional Assistance governs and guides International Territorial Administration's policy role.

<table>
<tr><th colspan="7">UNCA AND ITA PLAY COMMON POLICY ROLES</th></tr>
<tr><th colspan="2" rowspan="3">PURPOSE FOR USING UNCA</th><th rowspan="3">UNCA GOVERNANCE POLICIES</th><th rowspan="3">UNCA POLICY ROLE</th><th colspan="2">THE WL Constitution produced by UNCA provides a framework for territorial administration</th><th rowspan="3">ITA POLICY ROLE: PROMOTE UNCA'S / ITS GOVERNANCE POLICIES</th></tr>
<tr><th colspan="2">Purpose for using ITA are same as those for using UNCA</th></tr>
<tr><th>UNCA-ITA Projects</th><th>ITA embraces UNCA's governance policies</th></tr>
<tr><td rowspan="2">'A GOVERNANC PROBLEM'</td><td rowspan="2">SUPPOSED GAP IN GOVERNANCE</td><td rowspan="2">Democracy, ROL, & free markets</td><td>Produce the WL Constitution to fill a perceived vacuum</td><td>Congo</td><td rowspan="2">Democracy, ROL and free markets</td><td>Draft PFM & privatization laws</td></tr>
<tr><td>Organize a process & create content in tune with preferred standards</td><td>Kosovo & East-Timor</td><td>Craft market-oriented laws</td></tr>
</table>

*(Cont'd)*

Table 7.1 (*Cont'd*)

<table>
<tr><th colspan="8">UNCA AND ITA PLAY COMMON POLICY ROLES</th></tr>
<tr><th colspan="2" rowspan="3">PURPOSE FOR USING UNCA</th><th colspan="2" rowspan="3">UNCA GOVERNANCE POLICIES</th><th rowspan="3">UNCA POLICY ROLE</th><th colspan="2">THE WL Constitution produced by UNCA provides a framework for territorial administration</th><th rowspan="3">ITA POLICY ROLE: PROMOTE UNCA'S / ITS GOVERNANCE POLICIES</th></tr>
<tr><th colspan="2">Purpose for using ITA are same as those for using UNCA</th></tr>
<tr><th>UNCA-ITA Projects</th><th>ITA embraces UNCA's governance policies</th></tr>
<tr><td rowspan="2">'A GOVERNANC PROBLEM'</td><td rowspan="2">'SUPPOSED ABSENCE OF GOOD GOVERNANCE'</td><td>Adopt a territorial agenda</td><td>Enact a territorial agenda (e.g., independence)</td><td>Implement the territorial agenda: produce the WL Constitution and thereby promote external self-determination</td><td>East-Timor</td><td>UNCA's territorial agenda</td><td>Implement UNCA's territorial agenda</td></tr>
<tr><td>Adopt a 'status settlement'</td><td>Enact a 'status settlement'</td><td>Implement the 'status settlement': to sculpt the WL Constitution & so promote democracy, free markets, ROL, & human rights</td><td>Kosovo</td><td>The status settlement determined by UNCA</td><td>Implement UNCA's status settlement</td></tr>
</table>

*Note*: The words in quotes are Wilde's

First, each of the 46 UNCA projects (discussed in Chapters 4 and 6) involves this practice: the Constitution's internationalized making and/or constitutional reform along good governance lines. In these ways, they all promote preferred processes and/or content-related standards.

*Common ends*: Second, the Constitution produced by UNCA provides ITA's framework. UNCA sires and guides ITA in this way. Accordingly, ITA projects, for instance, draft electoral laws and privatize natural resources in tune with UNCA's standards regarding process and content respectively. Even where UNCA works to reform an existing constitution along good governance lines, the amended Constitution guides and *governs* the UN's law-making (for example, ITA). In these ways, UNCA and ITA work together toward *common* ends: (1) democracy, free markets, the rule of law, good governance (including national resources' exploitation) and women's rights; and (2) achieve territorial status. In fact, as outlined in the previous section, UNCA enables ITA to achieve its ends. Finally, these ends are essentially the Constitution's, and so attach to *ITA and UNCA*. This is why UNCA promotes these ends, even when it works without ITA.

*Common purposes*:

Third, UNCA, with and without ITA, 'operates in the same way on a practical level':[131] UN officials displace local actors or tutor them in the constitution-making activity. Likewise, they displace local actors to conduct territorial administration or tutor them in the activity of territorial administration. On this elemental level, there is unity across *all* the UNCA and ITA projects.[132]

Fourth, UNCA-ITA and UNCA projects manifest 'policy commonality' on a more sophisticated level: Broadly speaking, they all address a supposed governance problem. In particular, UNCA projects are conceived in response to perceived challenges about the conduct of the constitution-making process by local actors, and the types of constitutional content created by them. On this basis, UNCA projects cluster into two categories.

Fifth, of the 46 UNCA projects (1949–2019), 17 ostensibly operated to address process-related challenges, and so group under the first category. Virtually all 46 UNCA projects operated ostensibly to address content-related challenges, and so cluster in the second category. Within the first category, virtually all projects ostensibly promoted women's politi-

131 Id. at 233.

132 Id.

cal participation or emancipation. However, only four—in Colombia, Guatemala, Bolivia, and Nepal—explicitly promoted indigenous participation. Regarding the second category, virtually all projects have promoted free markets, anti-corruption, private investment, and so on. Only six—in DRC, Iraq, Libya, Bhutan, Yemen, and Afghanistan—shared thwarting terrorism as their ostensible goal. In these ways, and for these reasons, although all projects have not enjoyed a 'policy connection', they have nonetheless manifested 'purposive commonality' on both the required levels (*see* a. and b.).

On this basis, I assert that UNCA, is a *parent* policy institution. In fact, the Constitution produced by UNCA, enshrines and governs the legislature, judiciary, and executive whose activities Wilde collectively calls 'territorial administration'. So, UNCA sires that which Wilde has conceptualized as a 'Policy Institution': ITA by the UN, thus making it (UNCA), and ITA parent-child Policy Institutions. I will complete conceptualizing UNCA as a "Policy Institution" in Chapter 9, where I will consider whether the UN, so promotes the Constitution and its four ends, (that is, by displacing local actors from or tutoring them in the activities of constitution-making) to civilize Third World states/Third World peoples.

## 7.7 Conclusion

This chapter has established that since 1949, the same purposes (remedying Third World's supposed incapacities vis-à-vis a constitution-making process and content), have animated the UN in promoting the Constitution—regardless of the extent to which, it has consequently internationalized constitution-making. The UN has thereby served as a device for promoting distinct policy ends. In this way, this chapter has provided a historical perspective, which I suggest, is critical to understanding how likely the current UNCA *and* its off-spring projects are to succeed, and for what purposes such projects might be used in the future. This chapter has established that the Constitution promotes various purposes, including conferring territorial status, free markets, participatory constitution-making, and so on. Chapter 9 will build on this chapter to establish that UNCA continues to act as international trusteeship in sovereign states. The next chapter will address how the UN fits the Constitution and these purposes into the public international law and policy framework.

8

# United Nations Constitutional Assistance

## A Mechanism to Implement International Law and Policy

### 8.0 Introduction

How does United Nations Constitutional Assistance (UNCA) serve to promote public international law and policy (Law and Policy) goals? This chapter answers this query, based on the United Nations's (UN's) official explanations. In so doing, it reveals the deeper implications of *internationalizing* constitution-making in Third World states to promote the Western liberal Constitution (hereafter Constitution with a capital C) there. This recalls Chapter 7, where we noted that the UN *justifies* displacing local actors from, and/or tutoring them in constitution-making to promote the Constitution, and its four ends: free markets, the rule of law (for example, anti-corruption and so on), good governance, and women's rights.[1] The UN asserts that, in this way, it transforms the lives of assorted people.

So, let us take the example of Shamso, who was raped by militiamen and made a pariah (*see* Chapter 7). The UN suggests that educating and seeking Shamso's views about constitution-making is UNCA par excellence. In this way, UNCA amplifies Shamso's political voice, and

[1] UN, Rule of Law Guidance Notes 1–6 (undated).

thus, promotes her international right to political participation.[2] What about Boya, the Somali lobster diver who lost his livelihood and became a pirate in the 1990s? In curbing corruption, UNCA ostensibly restores the rule of law and Boya's life.[3] It implements a Law and Policy concept: The Responsibility to Protect (R2P).[4] So then, to understand how UNCA fits within the Law and Policy framework requires framing the Constitution's internationalized making by the UN (that is UNCA) *and its symbiotic working* with its child international territorial administration's (ITA),[5] toward common ends in an international dimension. Before proceeding, it helps to keep in mind that territorial administration as defined by Wilde includes law-making.[6]

So, as previously discussed, policymakers internationalized constitution-making (that is, used UNCA) to ensure two objectives about governance. The first objective is to ensure that governance is based on the rule of law, and foster free markets, and the exploitation of natural resources. The second is to ensure that the governance was of sufficient quality to merit a certain status for the territorial unit (*see* Chapter 7). In terms of international law, territorial status relates to statehood and external self-determination, and "State-building',' a public policy doctrine.

From 1960 to 1993, UNCA and ITA, tooled to the UN's dispute prevention and settlement system, worked symbiotically toward common Law and Policy ends.[7] Indeed, I suggest that UNCA enabled ITA to prevent disputes and implement settlements. As previously noted, after 1993, the UN promoted international law objectives by using UNCA without ITA (*see* UNCA statistics—Chapter 1). For, around the same time, the UN shed dispute settlement and embraced the broader goal

[2] Id. at 4.

[3] Id. *See also* UN, UNCA Guidance note (2009).

[4] *See Report of the Secretary-General, Implementing the Responsibility to Protect*, ¶10 (a) U.N. Doc., A/63/677 (12 January 2009).

[5] *See* Ralph Wilde, *International Territorial Administration: How Trusteeship and the Civilizing Mission Never Went away* Ch. 7 (OUP, 2008) (analyzing only ITA's use to implement law and policy).

[6] Id. at 22.

[7] *See Report of the Secretary-General, United Nations Political Missions* ¶8 U.N. Doc. A/68/223 (29 July 2013).

of "conflict prevention'.'[8] Now, UNCA was harnessed as a "conflict preventive activity" to the UN's *entire* peace, security, and development system[9] (hereafter UN System). Accordingly, the Security Council, the Secretary-General, and the United Nations Development Programme (UNDP) ostensibly offered constitutional assistance to extinguish particular "threats to peace'.'[10] (Chapter 5 covers the UNDP's constitutional assistance; therefore, I will focus only on the Security Council's here.)

What might those threats be? According to the UN, they emerge when presidents rig elections, soldiers rape women, police smuggle diamonds, children toil in mines, or wield weapons, ministers trade tusks for arms, governments throw out indigenous groups from their ancestral lands, and misguided youth blow up taxis (cabs), courts, clinics, and classrooms. Emanating from bad governance, these threats denote the immediate political symptoms of conflict. By uprooting them, UNCA supposedly prevents conflict, and achieves its law and policy objectives.[11]

In preventing and settling disputes, implementing particular settlements to disputes, and preventing conflict, UNCA (according to the UN) promotes international policy in yet another area—peace and security.[12]

Thus, UNCA fits within the Law and Policy framework in two ways: 1) Fused with ITA, it formed part of the dispute prevention and settlement system until 1993. 2) Thereafter, separated from ITA, it operated as a "conflict preventive activity'.' In both instances, it is indispensable to achieving these Law and Policy ends: territorial status outcomes, "state-building',' good internal governance, (including the exploitation of natural resources), and peace and security. Why? For, it produces the Constitution, which is conceptually the state's highest law and lends territorial governance political character.[13] Wilde is not wrong to proffer these ends as those met by ITA, since laws may be used to achieve them. But technically and conceptually, a more accurate picture about their

[8] *See* Security Council Report, Conflict prevention, Historical Chronology (undated).

[9] *See* Report of the Secretary-General, *Prevention of Armed Conflict*, Annex, U.N. Doc., A/55/985-S/2001/574 (7 June 2001).

[10] Id. at 2–3.

[11] Id. at ¶7.

[12] *See* UN, *Agenda for Peace* ¶55 (UN, 1992).

[13] *See* UN, *supra* note 2.

promotion requires starting from the Constitution whose salience and attractive features (discussed in Chapter 1, sections 1.1–13) is why, it is being internationalized. Indeed, lying at UNCA's heart (with and without ITA) is the Constitution, around which pivot its and ITA's common, multiple law and policy ends.

## 8.1 UNCA Prods States to Comply with International Law Obligations

So then, UNCA simultaneously fulfills three roles. First, it ensures that states comply with their international obligations. To understand this first role, requires framing its symbiotic process-related and content-related standard-setting (discussed in Chapter 7), in an international dimension. As we know, UNCA is a replacement for constitution-making by local actors, which is the norm or the default method. Similarly, ITA is a substitute for governance by local actors, which is the normal (administration) model. Policymakers substitute ITA for local governance when they deem the latter objectionable in some way.[14] Fears that reliance on the default method in some states might produce a constitution that falls short of relevant process-related and content-related standards animate UNCA's use.[15] An example of a process-related fear is that local actors will lock women and minorities out from the "process" of constitution-making. An example of a content-related fear is that the resulting constitution will chip away gender equality or embed a Potemkin commission.[16]

Promoting gender equality and women's political participation, crushing corruption, and so on, constitute binding international obligations borne by states whose fulfillment according to the UN, requires its involvement.[17] UNCA then serves as a 'neutral" means of pushing states to comply with them.

Next comes peaceful settlement of disputes and conflict prevention that constitute binding international obligations borne by states.[18] Their

14 *See* Wilde, *supra* note 5 at 192.
15 *See* UN, *supra* note 3 at 3.
16 Id.
17 Id.
18 *See* Ch. VI, UN Charter, 1945.

fulfillment, too, according to the UN, requires its involvement of taking prevention of conflict. According to the UN, since it flows from the Charter's mandate to maintain peace and security, comprehensive conflict prevention strategies taken by states offer the greatest potential for promoting lasting peace and security. So, the UN posits, in using UNCA, it supposedly helps build states' preventive capacity thus enforcing their obligation to prevent conflict and promote peace and security.[19]

## 8.2 UNCA Enables the UN to Fulfill Its Charter Obligations

UNCA's second role is to enable the UN to fulfill three Charter obligations: 1) peaceful settlement of disputes and conflict prevention; promotion of 2) human rights; and 3) of peace and security.[20]

To understand the UN's first obligation requires noting that Constitution-making helps resolve disputes in two ways, procedural and substantive. What does UNCA contribute to this activity? According to the UN, given its neutrality, UNCA enables local disputants to conduct a process (that includes elections) and create content without violating their relevant international obligations (mentioned in the previous section). So, UNCA enables constitution-making, a dispute settlement mechanism to function effectively. By using UNCA, the UN fulfills its obligations to settle disputes peacefully.[21]

As for "conflict prevention',' the UN posits that bad governance underlies conflict, and, therefore, it uses UNCA to help build states' preventive capacity thus fulfilling its conflict-prevention obligation.[22]

Moving to its second obligation, human rights promotion, the UN states that by ensuring that a "process" embraces such marginalized groups as minorities, it promotes their international right to political participation. Similarly, by ensuring that local actors constitutionally entrench gender equality and anti-corruption commissions, the UN promotes both law and public policy.[23]

19 *See* UN, *supra* note 3 at 2–3.

20 *See* art. 2 (3) & Ch.VI, UN Charter (1945).

21 Id. at art. 1, & Ch. VI.

22 *See* UN, *supra* note 9 at ¶78.

23 *See* UN, supra note 3 at 4-5.

Finally, UNCA's promotion of peace and security supposedly flows from its previously mentioned roles: preventing and settling disputes, implementing particular settlements to disputes, and preventing conflict. Like the disputes settlement and conflict prevention roles, here too, the UN explains the use of UNCA (with and without ITA) as a way to achieve and maintain peace and security, a central obligation borne by it under the Charter.[24]

## 8.3 UNCA and ITA Pursue Common Roles and Law and Policy Ends

Since UNCA sires ITA, the roles played by UNCA (see sections 8.1–8.2) accrue to ITA as well—a point Wilde affirms.[25]

## 8.4 UNCA Is Indispensable to Achieving Territorial Status and State-Building

UNCA serves to achieve territorial status for entities (*see* Chapter 6). In international law, territorial status can be framed "in terms of a claim based on a right – a claim to statehood ...."[26] Therefore, controlling who can make those claims, and how they might make it, explains why powerful Western states have *internationalized* constitution-making and territorial administration in the Third World.[27]

Let's take the example of Kosovo. As we saw in Chapter 6, UNCA was used in an effort to ensure that powerful Western states determined and implemented Kosovo's status, thereby controlling who could make claims for statehood, and how they might make it. Indeed, UNCA's use ensured that the people of Kosovo did not have the sole view in the process of reaching the status settlement.

Conceptually, UNCA was indispensable because to claim statehood, a territorial unit needs to fulfill four criteria: 1) a permanent

24 *See UN, supra* note 9 at 1-2.

25 *See* Wilde, *supra* note 5 at 239–241.

26 Id. at 245.

27 Id. (commenting only on ITA's use).

28 *See* Art. 1, *Montevideo Convention on the Rights and Duties of States*, Montevideo, 26 December 1933.

population; 2) a defined territory; 3) government; and 4) capacity to enter into relations with others.[28] As for a unit's government, "the legal system is a part of its general system',' and as such relevant to questions of existence, identity, and continuity of statehood.[29] Herein comes the Constitution created with UNCA, which provided a legal order cum framework for Kosovo's government (*see* Chapter 6). Western powers (Powers) displaced Kosovars from and/or tutored them in Constitution-making (and making appropriate laws), to ensure that their sovereignty claims were framed in accordance with the internationally determined settlement, that is that is, protected the Powers' interests.[30] In this way, UNCA enabled Kosovo to meet the key legal criterion for statehood, and enabled ITA to contribute in this regard.

I offer another example: Bosnia and Herzegovina [BoH]. How did the Western powers disallow BoH's break up? Indeed, United States policymakers drafted the Dayton Peace Agreements—and the BoH constitution—that ordained BoH's continued existence.[31] In this way, the United States' (US' constitutional assistance and ITA by the UN (for example, UN electoral assistance) together, prevented those Bosnian Croats who wished to secede from Bosnia and Herzegovina, and form the new state of Herzeg-Bosna from staking their (sovereignty) claim.[32] Here, the constitutional assistance of the US melded with ITA (by the UN) to promote a particular territorial status. For, conceptually, only the Constitution confers territorial status. Which international/US constitutional assistance produced: BoH's constitution.

Policymakers use UNCA with and without ITA towards state-building.[33] However, UNCA is salient here. Indeed, what I termed UNCA's remedial use is just this (*see* Chapter 7): UNCA's state-building role.

[29] James Crawford, *The Criterion for Statehood in International Law*, Br. Y. bk. of Int'l L. 93, 142 (1976-1977).

[30] *See* Wilde, *supra* note 5 at 245–246.

[31] *See* The General Framework Agreement: Annex 4: Constitution, 21 November 1995.

[32] Wilde, *supra* note 5 at 246.

[33] *See* Vijayashri Sripati, *UN Constitutional Assistance in State-building, in* Routledge Handbook of International State-building 143–155 (David Chandler & Timothy Sisk, eds., Routledge, 2013); For ITA's role in state-building, see Wilde, *supra* note 5 at 251.

The right of self-determination offers a second way of approaching territorial status in international law and UNCA–ITA's use to promote it, a theme discussed in Chapter 4. I therefore, turn to analyse UNCA's use to fulfill those policies that concern internal self-determination.

## 8.5 UNCA Promotes Good Internal Governance

Internal self-determination concerns the relationship between a state or government and its people. Policies concerning the political character of territorial governance fall within this dimension of self-determination. Here too, UNCA is salient. For what lends a unit, political character is the Constitution. Thus, in the earlier context, UNCA ostensibly fulfills the state-building objective by fitting a derailed government with a new engine and setting it on track. Here, it powers the government train toward a preferred destination: democracy, free markets, the ROL (anti-corruption, and so on), good governance (including natural resources' governance), and women's rights.

These ends are the Constitution's and therefore, attach to both UNCA and–ITA.[34] These ends pivot around the Constitution, whose role within the Law and Policy framework, I now turn to thematically analyse.

### 8.5.1 Fitting the Western Liberal Constitution into the International Law and Policy Framework

First, the Constitution ostensibly protects international ideals: democracy, the ROL, and free markets. According to the UN:

> *Setting the scene*
>
> *United Nations embraces free markets*
>
> There is a new universal understanding that market forces are essential for sustainable development. The role of the state is changing in most of the developing world: from one that seeks to dominate economic life, to one, which creates the conditions through which sustainable development is possible. .... The organization has a vital role to play in ... preparing the ground for domestic and foreign private investment.[35]

[34] *See* Wilde, *supra* note 5 at 258.

[35] *Report Prepared by the UN Secretariat: Enabling Private Sector Development: Characteristics of the Ideal Policy Environment*, Preface, U.N. Doc. ST/SG/AC.6/1997/L.7 (May 7, 1997).

Therefore, the UN's model constitution anchors key court-policed, political rights, property rights, and an anti-corruption commission [ACC], thereby promoting prosperity.[36] For instance, the freedom of association encourages entrepreneurs. An independent judiciary enforces their contracts, thus creating a stable and predictable legal system. Furthermore, the ACC hardens bribery laws, infuses transparency, and crushes corruption, thus allowing their businesses to expand and investments to grow. Meanwhile, lured by the fair and transparent environment for market transactions, foreign investors pump capital into agriculture and fuel production, thus producing value, which they share with their managers and employees. Sustainable development so achieved ripples outward to promote global macroeconomic stability.[37]

Second, the Constitution integrates human well-being and environmental protection through sustainable development of natural resources. In this regard, consider the praise bestowed by the former Secretary-General, Ban Ki-Moon for UNCA's promotion of these environmental standards:

> From Sierra Leone to Timor Leste, countries have been helped to mitigate the environmental risks to building peace and to harness the economic potential of using their natural resources sustainably. … Strengthening national capacity for transparent, equitable, and sustainable management of natural resources will continue to be an important part of peace-building, as well as our overall development support to Member States. … Given their critical role, United Nations peacekeeping operations are well placed to positively influence how the environment is protected and natural resources are managed.[38]

Third, the Constitution promotes democracy for it is forged through a transparent, inclusive and participatory process. Such a process amplifies the voices of the Mayans and Xincas in Guatemala, the Chiquitanos in Bolivia, and the Magars, Tharus, and Newars in Nepal, helping them to channel their demands, starting from gender equality

[36] UN, *supra* note 1 at 4–7.

[37] *See* Good Governance – the IMF's role, *available at:* http://www.imf.org/external/pubs/ft/exrp/govern/govindex.htm; The IMF and good governance: A Fact sheet (March 2016).

[38] 'Secretary-General's Message,' 6 November 2011, International Day for Preventing the Exploitation of the Environment in War and Armed Conflict.

into the content.[39] UNCA says the UN, ethnically scrambled Kosovo's Constitutional Commission and Iraq's constitution-drafting Committee, with a view to allow minorities enjoy their international rights.[40]

Fourth, the Constitution, proscribes terrorism, and so, forms the first bloc in the UN's global legal foundation for countering terrorism, thus protecting human rights worldwide.[41] Next, it enshrines a human rights commission (NHRI) which tamps down social problems before they boil over into violent tribal, ethnic, and sectarian clashes.[42]

Sixth, the Constitution also protects children and youth.[43] As previously mentioned (ch. 6), in this social media-century, its participatory process mobilizes them through Facebook and Twitter. Furthermore, shielded by electoral laws that ban their use and/or abuse for political purposes, they hurl not stones, or lob grenades during such a process. Rather, they voice their concerns to UN-hired focus groups and/or fill out UN/government-prepared questionnaires.[44] In these ways, they channel their concerns so that the constitution might address them and thereby meet international standards.[45]

According to the UN, in these multiple ways, UNCA promotes international law. Consider:

> The UN should consistently promote compliance of constitutions with international human rights and other norms and standards. The UN should address the rights that have been established under international law for groups that may be subjected to marginalization and discrimination in the country, including women, children, minorities, indigenous peoples, refugees, and stateless and displaced persons.[46]

[39] *See* 'UNDP and Indigenous Peoples: A Practice Note on Engagement' (undated).

[40] *See* Art. 10 & 10.2, Comprehensive Proposal for the Kosovo Status Settlement (2 February 2007) [*Hereafter* Ahtisaari Plan]; Factsheet: UN Support in Iraq's constitution-making process 2–4 (undated).

[41] *See* UN Global Counter Terrorism Strategy, *available at:* https://www.un.org/counterterrorism/ctitf/en/un-global-counter-terrorism-strategy.

[42] *See* UN, *supra* note at 6.

[43] Id. at 4.

[44] Id.

[45] *See* UNDP, 'Youth Strategy 2014-2017' 5(2014).

[46] UN, *supra* note 3 at 2.

The foregoing analysis suggests that in promoting both the existence of the state itself, and its and ITA's goals (good internal governance), UNCA implements 'state-building,' a doctrine that falls within public policy and to a degree within international law. In the next section, I consider how in doing so, it implements three other allied concepts: 1) 'earned sovereignty'[47]; 2) R2P, and 3) serves as a panacea for 'failed states,' under the 'Failed States' thesis.

Figure 8.1 shows UNCA and ITA's common Law and Policy goals.

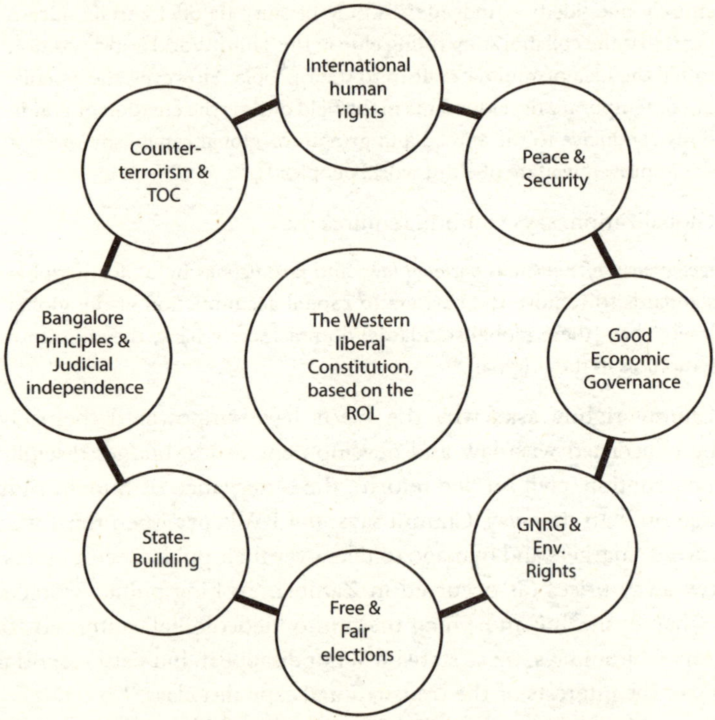


FIGURE 8.1. United Nations Constitutional Assistance & International Territorial Administration's common Law and Policy goals pivot around the Western liberal constitution

[47] *See* Wilde, *supra* note 5 at 261, n. 81 (citing to writings on this theme, all of which ignore UNCA). I discuss UNCA's use to 'strengthen sovereignty' in Chapter 9.

Before proceeding, it is worth considering how the parallel evolution of international law and constitutional law during the 1990s (which I call point X in chapter 1) shaped the discourse about the Constitution's promotion to set global standards. Indeed, as the remainder of this section will reveal, my submissions unite with the arguments of international law scholars who owing to point X, missed the Constitution but acknowledged its standards. For instance, I concur with Professor Chimni who asserts that:

> The developments in the world of international institutions (IIs) are not entirely one-sided; ... Indeed, it is only because IIs offer certain advantages that the collaborating ruling elite in the Third World is in a position to sell the idea of multilateralism to their people. However, the essence of contemporary developments in the field of IIs is the creation of conditions conducive to the spread and growth of global capitalism and not the improved welfare of third world peoples.[48]

Globalization, says Chimni, requires the:

> *replacement of numerous national laws* and *jurisdictions* by uniform global standards to remove the barriers to capital accumulation at the global level. They [these global standards] do not merely bark, they also bite [emphasis in the original].[49]

Chimni rightly asks why the BWIs have empowered themselves to be concerned with law and development issues, budget discipline, anti-corruption, civil service reform, the observance of human rights, and so on.[50] In this way, Chimni says, the BWIs pry open third world countries' markets and manage to take over their public sector assets at throw away prices (as occurred in Zambia, evoking public protects---see Chapter 6), thus morphing them into 'neocolonial' states. For this reason, Chimni says, these states will not disappear, but exist essentially to serve the interests of the transnational capitalist class.[51]

Susan Marks also neglects UNCA. But since she focuses on the BWIs, she reflects on the wider conditions in which their global standards are

48 *See* B. S. Chimni, *International Institutions Today: An Imperial Global State in the Making* 15 EJIL 1, 15–16 (2004).

49 Id. at 16.

50 Id.

51 Id.

conceived, and how they hinder achieving true democratic governance.[52] But again, still more international law scholars have not acknowledged the emerging global standard. For instance, Brett Bowden and Hilary Charlesworth argue that the UN supports (Western liberal) democracy but leaves its content 'vague.'[53]

Turning to Constitutional law scholars including comparatists, a few of these scholars such as Kim Lane Scheppele and Tom Ginsburg who have only begun to notice UNCA,[54] don't focus on the BWIs. Therefore, Scheppele for instance, concludes, after a cursory analysis that the UN says little about constitutional content, contradicting the world body itself.[55]

This recalls Figure 1.8 which illustrates the post-1989 parallel evolution of international law, constitutional law, and international political economy, which I call point X. But there are some hopeful signs that these separate strands are converging into a fuller picture, particularly in the context of the UN Family's standard-setting/ state-restructuring.[56] Two of those signs in Figure 1.8 are two post-2017 books that explore a topic deemed important because it has not yet been analysed: the role of law in the neoliberal project.[57] But as previously noted in chapter 1, still, even where exploring the *law's role* is the explicit goal, the 'supreme law,'

[52] *See* e.g., Susan Marks, *What has become of the emerging right to democratic governance?* 22 Eur. J. Int'l L. 507 (2011).

[53] Hillary Charlesworth & Brett Bowden, *Defining Democracy in International Institutions, in* The Role of International Law in Rebuilding Societies after Conflict – Great Expectations 90, 107 (Brett Bowden *et al* eds., Cambridge University Press, 2009).

[54] Tom Ginsburg, *Constitutional advice and transnational legal order* UC 2 Irvine J. of Int'l, Transnat'l & Compl. L 19 (2017).

[55] Kim Lane Scheppele, '*Worst practices and the transnational legal order (or how to build a constitutional democrator-ship in plain sight*' 35 (Wright Lecture, University of Toronto, Nov. 2016).

[56] *See* e.g., David Singh Grewal & Jedediah Purdy, *Law and Neoliberalism*, 77 Law and Contemp. Problems 14 (2015).

[57] *See* Honor Brabazon, *Neoliberal Legality—Understanding the Role of Law in the Neoliberal Project* 6 (Routledge, 2017) (aiming to: develop 'a holistic and coherent understanding of the relationship between law and neoliberalism' but owing to point X, misses the Constitution); *The Politics of Legality in a Neoliberal Age* (Ben Golder ed., Routledge, 2018).

the Western liberal *Constitution, fails to receive full attention.*[58] Because I am fascinated with the Constitution, my book gives it full attention. And in a nutshell, what mechanism is it that spreads neoliberal standards globally? It is UNCA.

## 8.6 UNCA Implements Public Policy Concepts

The previous analysis shows how the Constitution lays the foundation for a *particular* legal system, economic model, and public sector. In this way, it mirrors the breadth and depth of UNCA and ITA's particular post-Cold War agenda (Agenda). The liberal notions of sovereignty as a graded process, an idea considered in Chapter 3 (see section 3.2.3.2) offers a second way of understanding UNCA's use to achieve the Agenda.

This 'earned sovereignty' policy best explains UNCA's use in two territorial units, Kosovo and Bougainville – *see* Chapter 6. Take Kosovo where the UN's 'standards before status' policy required it to create functioning democratic institutions, to respect the ROL, and to foster free markets before its eventual status would be determined and acquired.[59] The constitution promulgated by the UN introduced those standards.[60] Here is how, UNCA enabled Kosovo to earn its sovereignty.

Analogously, where a state 'earns' sovereignty, can it not lose it as well? Yes, says the UN. Here comes the related notion of R2P that posits sovereignty as responsibility. R2P recognizes states' obligations to protect people from genocide, war crimes, ethnic cleansing, and crimes against humanity.[61] But, if they are unable, the responsibility falls on the broader international community to provide that protection. The same result occurs when they exercise sovereignty *irresponsibly*. That

[58] Only one chapter in Golder's book analyses the Constitution's role in (Chile's) neoliberal project—a topic otherwise missed by both books in *supra* note 57.

[59] *See* Ahtisaari Plan, *supra* note 40 at Art. 1.4 and 9.3.

[60] *See* UNMIK Regulation No. 2001/9 of 15 May 2001.

[61] *See* Daniel Warner & Gilles Giacca, *Responsibility to Protect, in* Peacebuilding: A Lexicon 291, 292 (Vincent Chetail, ed., OUP, 2009); *See* UN, *supra* note 4 at ¶3, 10 (a) (12)

is, when they perpetrate such slaughter themselves.[62] According to the UN, we can see state-irresponsibility in the Ivorian armed forces' attacks on ethnic groups.[63]

How then might we prod states to exercise sovereignty responsibly? We can do so by 'helping states build their capacity to protect:'[64] offering UNCA:

> Experience ... suggests that many of the elements of what is commonly accepted as good governance – the rule of law, a component and independent judiciary, human rights, ... – tend to serve objectives relating to the responsibility to protect as well.[65] [The UN's words]

Indeed, the UN reminds us of how 'its presence' in East-Timor led to the criminalization of gender-based violence – which flows from gender equality, constitutionalized via UNCA.[66]

Two others concepts based on the earned sovereignty idea is that of 'strengthening sovereignty,' –a theme, analysed in-depth in Chapter 9– and failed states. The failed states concept, by definition does not envision 'how,' (to quote Upendra Baxi) 'states *are made* to fail'[67] by any external actors' (e.g., corporations and/or international institution) fault. Rather, it posits that indigenous factors alone contribute to fatally degrading an entity's statehood.[68] In 1992, Gerald Helman and Steven Ratner articulated the 'failed states' paradigm, bemoaning the plight of states utterly incapable of sustaining themselves as the members of the international community.[69] Arguing that, 'something must be done,' they proposed

62 Id. at ¶ 3, § III ¶ 15-21.

63 *See e.g.,* Press conference by Secretary-General's Special Advisers on Responsibility to Protect, 'Genocide in connection with situation in Côte d'Ivoire,' 19 January 2011.

64 *See* UN, *supra* note 4 at ¶139. Indeed, UNCA falls within all three pillars on which the R2P edifice rests. Id at ¶ III.

65 Id. at ¶ 44.

66 Id. at 36.

67 *See* Upendra Baxi, *Remaking Progressive Global Governance: Some Reflections with Reference to the Rule of Law, in* Critical Perspectives on the Crisis of Global Governance: Reimagining the Future 162, 163 (Stephen Gill, ed., Palgrave Macmillan, 2015).

68 *See* Wilde, *supra* note 5 at 252.

69 G. B. Helman & Steven R. Ratner, *Saving Failed States* 6 Foreign Policy 3, 12 (1992)

a solution wherein the UN 'manages' a failed state's affairs,[70] including administering it, in tune with a 'UN-drafted' constitution.[71]

But again, as my analysis in Chapter 4 suggests, Ratner's UNCA-ITA[72] prescription is hardly novel. Indeed, it echoes the UNCA-ITA model (Model) initiated by Dag Hammarskjöld in Congo in 1960. And so, a year after Ratner's proposal, policymakers faced with the so-called 'failed state' of Somalia, recycled that Model, to remedy governance in Somalia. Accordingly, they created the UN Operation in Somalia – UNOSOM II (1993-1995), which distributed food (e.g. of ITA) and offered constitutional assistance.[73] It thus mirrored UNCA's remedial use (discussed in Chapter 7). In recommending UNCA-ITA, the 'failed states' commentators focused on situations of governmental collapse. So too, did the UN, which explained UNCA-(plenary) ITA's use to restore governance in 'situations of fragility and conflict.'[74] Meanwhile, as mentioned in Chapter 7, the UN framed almost all post-1993 UNCA projects as critical to promoting good governance in poor Third World states: conflict-ridden and stable.[75]

As the foregoing analysis suggests, the UN ostensibly and explicitly uses UNCA to implementing R2P and promoting liberal governance in 'failed states.' Meanwhile, UNCA-ITA has been implicated in implementing the concept of 'earned sovereignty', and scholars have recommended its use to restore governance in failed states. The Constitution's role in implementing these concepts brings us to the international context for its birth, which as indicated in the opening section (8.0), materializes in two contexts: 1) When UNCA sires plenary/partial ITA 2) When UNCA works without ITA.

As already, mentioned, UNOSOM-II was the first UNCA-(plenary) ITA project mounted in the wake of Helman and Ratner's proposal. But as noted in Chapter 6, and as Wilde too states, the UN's utter debacle in Somalia, dampened the prospects for using plenary ITA to revive failed states.[76]

[70] Id. at 12.

[71] Id. at 6.

[72] *See* Wilde, *supra* note 5 at 252 (making the same point about ITA).

[73] *See* S.C. Res, U.N. SCOR., 3188th mtg., pmbl¶ 16-19 & 21 U.N. Doc. S/Res/1993 (March 1993).

[74] *See* UNDP, *Governance for Peace: Securing the Social Contract* 14, 68 (2012).

[75] *See* UN, supra note 1 at 1.

[76] Wilde, *supra* note 5 at 254.

I argue that what rolled along, in Somalia and elsewhere, but has regretfully escaped critical attention is the UNCA juggernaut. Indeed, given policymakers' broad, post-Cold War Agenda: promoting western liberal market democracy, the Constitution was indispensable. Here comes UNCA's revival. But, as we saw, now the UN tutored local actors instead of wholly displacing them (see chapters 6 and 7). Furthermore, in dropping plenary ITA, policymakers lost nothing. Rather, they gained much more in using only its parent, for UNCA arguably demanded lesser human and material resources. Above all, since UNCA was widely portrayed as capacity-building, the idea of merely 'assisting' states build their capacity for good governance seemed benign and tranquil.

Thus, liberal ideas, in addition to explaining UNCA–ITA's use in cases of entities aspiring to statehood, and in cases of state-failure, now underlay UNCA's use in existing states, whether 'failed' or not so failed. An existing state's non-conformity to the liberal notions of the state now justified international intervention—UNCA's use: tutoring.

Indeed, consider how after 1993, the landscape morphed into a split screen scenario with plenary ITA projects (using UNCA) being confined to territories, not yet states (*e.g.*, Kosovo and East-Timor) whereas UNCA projects mushroomed in two contexts, 'post-conflict' and development assistance, and in more than thirty-six *sovereign states*, which fell within, and beyond the so-called 'failed states' index (*see* UNCA statistics).

So then, two distinct contexts mark the creation of the Constitution. 1) When UNCA was fused with ITA; and 2) When UNCA worked alone without ITA. Do these contexts matter? Yes. They reveal the two distinct ways that the UN galvanized various actors to use UNCA. In short, they illuminate how it fitted UNCA-ITA and UNCA into the Charter framework.

## 8.7 UNCA Prevents Disputes and Implements Settlements

Democracy, the ROL, free markets and other Law and Policy goals promoted by the Constitution (see section 8.5), bring us to the first context for its birth: dispute prevention and settlement. Here, UNCA and ITA, working together: 1) Prevent disputes; and 2) Settle disputes and implement dispute settlements. Indeed, the story of UNCA-ITA being used as a dispute prevention and settlement mechanism is tantamount to UNCA producing the Constitution as a means of preventing and settling disputes. And therefore, UNCA enabling ITA to do so.

### 8.7.1 UNCA Prevents and Settles Disputes

For instance, writing about itself, the UN states:

> As a new institution, the UN was required to build and refine tools that could help to address emerging issues confronting the international community, from *mediating disputes* … to supporting transition to independence in post-colonial states.[77]

According to the UN, it offers constitutional assistance to fulfill its dispute-prevention and settlements functions in article (1), and article 33 (1) of the UN Charter. Connie Peck, one of the few scholars (barring this author) who recognizes UNCA as a distinct topic, —recommends that the UN strengthens its dispute prevention system by adding it (UNCA) to its toolbox.[78]

The UN suggests UNCA prevents and settles disputes (including their implementation) in four ways. First, as previously noted, UNCA helps to make constitution-making a dispute settlement mechanism function effectively. Here is how its impartial mediation prevents disputes from arising. UNCA creates a neutral electoral environment that is essential for holding free and fair constituent assembly elections. For instance, biased electoral laws, and flawed registration can trigger electoral violence.[79] But, UNCA defuses these situations by helping states adopt the Constitution, which requires fair electoral laws.[80] Second, UN negotiation support enables local actors settle their constitutional disputes in a way that meets international standards.[81] Lynn Pascoe suggests that during conflict national actors are so deeply distrustful of each other

[77] *See* UN, *supra* note 7 at ¶ 8.

[78] Connie Peck, *The United Nations as a Dispute Settlement System* 108 (Kluwer Law International, 1996) (devoting 3 lines to UNCA).

[79] *See* UNDP, 'Elections, Violence and Conflict Prevention Summary Report' 7, 13–29 (June 2011, Barcelona Spain).

[80] Id. at 30-32, 42, 56, 66–68.

[81] B. Lynn Pascoe, 'Rediscovering preventive diplomacy: A View from the United Nations–Remarks at the Brookings Institution' 1 (July 26, 2010).

that they are unable to arrive at necessary compromises without help in the form of international mediation.[82] And so, the UN helps those actors in negotiating contentious issues and drafting clear constitutional prose.

Third, UNCA implements settlements that mandate a new constitution, which equals making the Constitution. So, in this sense, UNCA provides the settlement to the dispute: the Constitution. (And, as I will show in the next sub-section, in this way, it enables ITA to implement settlements' relevant provisions). UNCA-ITA in Cambodia was framed in terms of prevent disputes and implementing a dispute settlement.[83]

### *8.7.1.1 UNCA Enables ITA to Prevent Disputes and Implement Settlements*

*UNCA sires and so, enables ITA* to a) to prevent disputes from arising, b) creates an atmosphere favorable to settling disputes, prevents future disputes and c) provides or enables the functioning of a dispute settlement mechanism.[84] First, many peace agreements mandate the Constitution, which gives rise to and guides ITA.

Second, where UNCA creates a favorable electoral climate, it prevents disputes. Here, the Constitution (whether produced or being made) guides the UN's law-making/ITA activities in that the UN drafts laws in accordance with it and/or cancels those which violate it.[85] In this way, ITA joins UNCA in preventing disputes. Third, by training local actors in negotiating, mediating, and drafting clear constitutional prose, UNCA ensures that they produce the Constitution, and so, prevent future disputes. The Constitution so produced gives rise to ITA; the UN drafts laws (outlawing genital mutilation) consistent with the Constitution and so, for instance, prevents discrimination, and thereby future disputes.

As already mentioned, after 1993, policymakers used UNCA, and dropped out (plenary) ITA, that is, continued promoting preferred standards via UNCA alone. UNCA's use without ITA then brings us to the

[82] Id. at 2.

[83] *See* UN, *UN and Cambodia 1991-1995* 1 (UN, 1995).

[84] Wilde, *supra* note 5 at 241-242.

[85] *See* e.g., UN, *supra* note 83 at 28–29.

second context for the Constitution's creation: Conflict Prevention—(the next section's topic).

## 8.8 UNCA Prevents Conflict

The Security Council (Council) tops the list of actors authorized to maintaining peace and security, and preventing conflict.[86] One way the Council ostensibly prevents the escalation of conflict or a slide back into war is by tasking peace operations with constitutional assistance.

### 8.8.1 UNCA Serves to Forge and Implement Peace Agreements that Mandate Good Governance

UNCA was framed as indispensable to facilitating peace agreements with constitutional implications.[87] As we saw in Chapter 6, sometimes, peace agreements are 'at once political and legal documents, and constitutions,'[88] sometimes they may mandate the Constitution's internationalized making or reforming the existing constitution along good governance lines. In all these various cases, UNCA was cast as essential to ensuring their implementation.

Where transition results not from a peace agreement but, from foreign occupation as occurred in Iraq, the Constitution's internationalized making (UNCA) is explained as a means to promoting democracy, human rights, a market economy, inclusive political processes, and good governance in the environmental and natural resource sectors. (Indeed, these standards flow from the Constitution, as analysed in section 8.5). Finally, in Côte d'Ivoire, the transition President and Prime Minister derived their powers not from the Constitution (as their terms had expired) but from Security Council resolutions. In this way, UNCA enabled the transition government to carry out core governmental tasks, that is, pursue the BWIs' reforms to meet the country's debt service obligations, and so equates with implementing good governance

[86] *See generally* Security Council, 'Threats to International Peace,' Repertoire of the Practice of the Security Council (17th Supplement 2010-2011).

[87] *See* UN, *supra* note 3 at 3.

[88] Christine Bell, *On the Law of Peace—Peace agreements and the Lex Pacificatoria* 199 (Oxford University Press, 2008).

(see Capter 6). Put simply, the Security Council's constitutional assistance enabled Côte d'Ivoire to maintain donor confidence and become eligible for foreign aid.[89] So then, UNCA by the Security Council, a blatantly political body, – with or without a peace agreement – is nothing but the promotion of the Constitution framed as a means of thwarting threats to peace.

What were those threats? They were corruption, natural resources mismanagement, gender discrimination, the political exclusion of women, indigenous discrimination, violations against children, and terrorism.[90] (We have already seen in Chapter 5, how powerful financial tides set in motion by IFIs, floated the participatory standard ostensibly aimed at thwarting gender discrimination, a threat, onto political shores). Therefore, to explore just one example: take corruption. Seen from the BWIs' perspective, what does corruption spook and deter? Private and foreign investors. In fact, as we saw in chapters 1 and 5, the Bretton Woods Institutions' (BWIs) conditionalities triggered a whole host of intertwined standards such as judicial independence, a market economy, anti-corruption, and good natural resource governance.[91] And these standards mirrored the elements of ROL as conceptualized by the BWIs, and before long, the ROL concept as interpreted by the Council as well.[92] So then, this convergence between the ROL definitions of BWIs and the Council that result from BWIs' conditionalities explains how corruption and resource mismanagement came to be labeled by the Council as threats, and found mention in peace agreements, discussed in chapter 6. Finally, this backdrop illuminates why the Bretton Woods Institutions (BWIs) figure in the Council's plans to thwart these threats.[93]

[89] *See* e.g., S.C. Res. 1633, U.N. SCOR., 5288th mtg., ¶3 & 13 U.N. Doc., S/Res/1633 (21 October 2005).

[90] *See e.g.*, UNEP, Greening the Blue Helmets: Environment, Natural Resources and UN Peace-keeping Operations 42, 84 (2012).

[91] IMF Factsheet: The IMF and good governance (2016); UN, *supra* note 1 at 1–6.

[92] *See* Jeremy Farrall, *UN Sanctions and Rule of Law* 32-35 (Cambridge University Press, 2009).

[93] Security Council, *Conflict Prevention & Natural Resources Concept Note 2013* ¶7–10 (b)-(e) (2013).

In these ways, Security Council uses UNCA to disseminate preferred constitutional standards in post-conflict situations, ostensibly to prevent conflict from resuming.

## 8.9 UNCA Promotes International Peace and Security

I now turn to consider the last ostensible law and policy goal: Peace and security. Indeed, promotion of peace and security flows from the three functions, considered in previous sections.

To understand how UNCA ostensibly serves as a means to promote peace and security requires: 1) adopting a working label for peace missions involving constitutional assistance (with, or without ITA) and, 2) knowing the special meaning that the term 'peace process' acquired after 1989. Therefore, I preface my analysis with three caveats. First, in tune with my inventory of UNCA projects, – in Chapter 6, – I adopt 'peace operations' as a working label for peace missions involving UNCA (used with or without ITA), for the purposes of this study. Next, I embrace Boutrous Boutrous-Ghali's classifications of peace operations: Conflict prevention, peacemaking, peacekeeping, and peace building.[94] Finally, I will define 'peace process' as it came to be understood after 1989 at the appropriate place in my analysis, which follows.

In section 8.8, I discussed how UNCA serves to prevent conflict, Boutrous-Ghali's first category. How does it do so with its offspring? Indeed, the Constitution gives rise to ITA (e.g., law-making consistent with the Constitution –privatization of natural resources). In this way, UNCA and ITA ostensibly and simultaneously, serve to uproot bad governance.

To understand the remaining three of Boutrous-Boutrous Ghali's categories requires situating them within the specialized context of a 'peace process' as understood after 1989. Bertrand Ramcharan defines and elaborates on such a process as:

> One that entail efforts of a broad variety, tailored to each situation, to tackle the manifestations and root causes of differences that have led to … conflict and to help re-establish and sustain peace.

[94] *See* UN, *supra* note 12 at ¶ 20–21.

> And, [i]ncludes the peacemaking phase, the phase at which a peace agreement is being pursued, and the implementation phase, the phase at which an agreement is being implemented, as well as the post-conflict peace-building phase.[95]

Similarly, the UN defines peacemaking as '... action to bring hostile parties to agreement, essentially through such peaceful means as those foreseen in Chapter VI of the Charter of the United Nations.'[96]

As previously noted, in the post-Cold War era, UNCA covers peacemaking (see Chapters 1, 6). Indeed, the Constitutions mandated by peace agreements came to be widely regarded as politically negotiated settlements. In fact, those constitutions were deemed capable of promoting peace by resolving identity issues, ending discrimination, allowing rival ethnic groups to share power, and promoting good governance in the natural resource sector.[97] While UNCA operated independently in these states, in Cambodia, as (discussed in section 8.7), it ostensibly fulfilled that role in tandem with ITA.

Turning to Peacekeeping, the next Boutrous-Ghali category, it is a technique that expands the possibilities for both the prevention of conflict and the making of peace. Although peacekeeping was originally a military model of enforcing ceasefires, it evolved into a complex model where '[T]he objective in essence is to assist the parties engaged in conflict to pursue their interests through political channels.'[98] Therefore, today peacekeeping operations comprise military officials and experts in constitutions, elections, and human rights who work together to build peace in the dangerous aftermath of civil wars. So understood, the UN Operation in Congo (ONUC), which drafted Congo's constitution and ran its government, clearly fits within the multidimensional peacekeeping category.

As for Peace-building, the last Boutrous-Ghali category, I have already noted in Chapter 1, how and why it comprises a key activity: the Constitution's making. As for ITA, drafting laws consistent with the

95 *See* Bertrand Ramcharan, *Peace Process, in* Chetail, Peacebuilding: A Lexicon, *supra* note 61 at 231.

96 *See* UN, *supra* note 12 at ¶ 20.

97 *See* UN, *supra* note 9 at ¶78.

98 *See* Kofi Annan, *The Role of the United Nations in the 21st Century at:* http://www.un.org/en/events/pastevents/pdfs/We_The_Peoples.pdf.

Constitution (e.g., to privatize natural resources) is peace-building par excellence.

In sum: UNCA projects fit into the categories of conflict prevention, peacemaking, peacekeeping, and peace-building.

### 8.9.1 UNCA Promotes a Specific Kind of Peace – 'Liberal Peace'

The foregoing analysis suggests that the precise configuration of UN operations (that include UNCA projects) to promote peace and security stems from one root: The Western liberal constitution, which I have so long been referring to as the Constitution, which makes governance 'liberal' in some way. So then, what the above analysis suggests is this: At best, the UN's promotion of preferred constitutional standards leads to liberal peace. Nothing more.

Given this, does not the UN mislead when it asserts as follows?

> The design of a constitution and its process of development can play an important role in peaceful political transitions and peace consolidation. Constitution-making presents moments of great opportunity to create a common vision of the future of a state, the results of which can have profound and lasting impacts on peace and stability.[99]

The above excerpt is antiseptic, simplistic, and overly general. For after all, we know from Chapters 5 and 6, that UNCA serves to producing: the Constitution. And that what is described as a 'common vision' for a state is simply neoliberal market democracy.

Moreover, the UN erroneously suggests that all of the preferred standards promoted by UNCA are concerned with peace. A survey of the standards pursued by all the UNCA projects, including the five UNCA-ITA projects negates that claim. For instance, ONUC hooked Congo to the world markets, promoted federal democracy, and ended Katanga's attempted secession. Indeed, introducing a liberal economic system animated UNCA as much as the 'peaceful' goal of tackling violations resulting from conflict. Likewise, as previously discussed (Ch. 6), in Cambodia, Kosovo and East-Timor, the UN focused not just on ending human rights violations to promote peace (*e.g.* by promoting

[99] *See* UN, *supra* note 3 at 3.

gender equality), but on transforming the economy along neoliberal lines as well.

Similarly consider the standards promoted by an UNCA-only project: free markets and anti-corruption, natural resource governance, and human rights of women and children. From which of these standards may we draw a straight line to peace? In protecting children's rights by banning their use in warfare, one may say the preferred constitution contributes to ending armed conflict. But children's rights consist of far more than just prohibiting their participation in hostilities. And what about free markets? Does their promotion end armed conflict? Not really. Clearly, here, the above UN claim remains untenable.

In the same fashion, Wilde finds the peace labels for UN operations involving ITA to be misleading. For, they pursue ITA goals unconnected to peace, and 'because they are of independent value,' – all the while being shrouded by the peace label.[100] I concur. Indeed, all the ITA purposes are simply those of the Constitution and what bestows 'independent value' on them are: the BWIs' conditionalities. And my previous analysis and Chapter 6 uncover just that.

The foregoing analysis underscores that the Constitution sets a global standard for state governance in a swath of poor and politically weak states. And, what produces its specific blueprint is UNCA.

## 8.10 Conclusion

This chapter, building on Chapters 1 and 5, reveals that the Constitution shapes the UN peace, security, and development system in a constitutional dimension. Indeed, it is indispensable to implementing the broad areas of international law and policy, from the settlement of disputes to conflict prevention, and the protection of human rights and the promotion of international peace and security. In fact, it is precisely because international policymakers have envisaged a highly ambitious, comprehensive, and transformative enterprise that they internationalized the Constitution.

This recalls Chapters 2 to 3, where we saw different actors: states, groups of state representatives, and an inter-war period's IO (the Permanent Mandates Commission) internationalizing the Constitution.

100 *See* Wilde *supra* note 5 at 278.

Indeed, this internationalization was achieved via the same means, and with a view to promoting the same ends as UNCA. On this basis, I reframed Wilde's Family of trusteeship institutions to comprise the Constitution's internationalized making and foreign territorial administration. (In this way, I traced UNCA's origins.)

I began conceptualizing UNCA as a Policy Institution in Chapter 4. In the next chapter, I will complete UNCA's conceptualization: I will consider whether the Constitution has been internationalized to 'civilize' Third World states.

# 9

# United Nations Constitutional Assistance Continues Its Civilizing Role

## 9.0 Introduction

United Nations (UN) Constitutional Assistance (UNCA) was rejected in 1960. In this chapter, I complete my answer to the question I posed in Chapter 1: Why has the UN empowered itself to offer constitutional assistance in *sovereign* Third World states? That is, why has the UN empowered itself to tutor sovereign states in adopting as their highest law, the Constitution? I started building my answer in Chapter 4. Here, I pull the strands together, and conclude my narrative. I will base my answer on the UN's official explanations/ostensible purposes – and on Ralph Wilde's broader definition of trusteeship.[1] I will also draw from Chapters 2–4.

According to the UN Family (which includes the Bretton Woods Institutions, the BWIs), the Constitution is a ROL cum development understood as market-oriented poverty-reduction strategy. Indeed, it symbolizes financial modernity.[2] This is precisely why the UN helps *sovereign* Third World states—in response to their supposed incapacities—to produce this very constitution.[3] In so doing, the UN

[1] *See* Ralph Wilde, *International Territorial Administration: How Trusteeship and the Civilizing Mission Never Went Away* 343–359 (Oxford University Press, 2008).

[2] *See* UN, Guidance Note: UN Approach to Rule of Law Assistance (undated) [UN-ROL Guidance Note].

[3] UN, Constitutional Assistance Guidance Note (2009).

promotes international law and policy (Law and Policy) ends: Free markets, the rule of law, good governance (including natural resources exploitation), women's rights, and territorial status. "It 'modernizes' Third World states, thereby 'strengthening' their sovereignty, which they have supposedly lost or eroded through bad governance.[4]

This means that UNCA continues acting as international trusteeship. For since its birth in 1949, UNCA has:

- produced the same constitution: an eighteenth century 'standard of civilization' (Civilized Standard)[5] that is central to trusteeship: the Constitution,
- in response to the same ostensible purpose: Third World peoples' supposed incapacities, with a view to promoting the same ostensible international law ends:
- free markets, the rule of law, good governance (including natural resources exploitation), and civilized customs, and their modern equivalent: women's rights; and,
- to civilize or 'modernize' Third World peoples, in market-oriented ways, with a view to either manufacture their sovereignty, or strengthen it. (The latter case refers to Third World peoples/states that have supposedly lost their sovereignty through their bad self-governance); and
- has, in so doing, embraced the same notion: graded sovereignty.

All this suggests that, since 1945, UNCA continues to promote the same international law ends toward common allied policies: trusteeship and civilizing/modernizing missions. Indeed, I suggest that UNCA, in so continuing its international trusteeship, has spawned 'Transparent, inclusive, and participatory constitution-making:'[6] a new Civilized Standard.

As noted in Chapter 1, my aim is to conceptualize UNCA as a Policy Institution, which I started doing in Chapter 4. Establishing UNCA and ITA as parent-child 'Policy Institutions'[7] requires showing that UNCA

[4] *See Report of the UN Secretary-General, Prevention of Armed Conflict*, ¶6 U.N. Doc., A/55/985-S/2001/574 (2001); UNDP & UN-OHRLLS, *Governance for the Future - Democracy and Development in the Least Developed Countries* (2006).

[5] *See* Gerrit Gong, *The Standard of Civilization in International Society* 1-20 (Oxford University Press, 1984).

[6] *See* UN, *supra* note 2 at 4.

[7] For criteria, *see* Wilde, *supra* note 1 at 36.

projects, with and without ITA, are 'institutions'/ 'established practices' (*see* Chapters 4, 6), that play common policy roles, and so work towards: Common policies: trusteeship and civilizing mission (*see* this chapter); and Common ostensible purposes and ends (*see* footnote or Chapters 7–8).[8] I am now poised to take the last step toward fully conceptualizing UNCA as a 'Policy Institution:' To establish that UNCA, in promoting the Constitution, and common ends (e.g., free markets and so on, outlined in Chapters 7 to 8), pursues two allied policies: trusteeship and the civilizing mission.

I do just that in the next section, 9.1, where I define trusteeship.

Based on section 9.1's analysis, I will in section 9.2 reframe Wilde's Family of international trusteeship FTA institutions, one last time, to admit a parent Policy Institution: UNCA. Therefore, it is essential, to revisit Wilde's Family listed below, and note what my earlier reframing entailed (*see* Chapter 3). Indeed, there, my reframing entailed starting with FTA/ITA institutions (italicized), and identifying and joining them with their respective parent institution: the Constitution's internationalized making.

1) Post-Renaissance European colonialism (1700–1960)
2) International Territorial Administration (ITA)
   A) 'Protection'—ITA by the League of Nations
   B) ITA by the UN ('ITA projects since 1945')
3) State-conducted administration under the Mandate System of the League of Nations;
4) State-conducted administration under the United Nations Trusteeship System;
5) Representative bodies; and
6) Occupation (including 'belligerent occupation') (conducted by foreign states).[9]

However, reframing in this chapter entails starting with the parent institution, UNCA, which I introduced in Chapter 1 (showing that it

[8] Chapter 7 established that UNCA is a "Policy Institution," based on a purposive commonality between all the UNCA projects, with and without ITA: They worked in response to challenges perceived in the way in which Third World sovereign states make their constitutions, and the content they pour into them; They do so to promote these common ends (Ends): Free markets, the rule of law, good governance, women's rights, and territorial status. Chapter 8 established how UNCA's use in producing the Constitution and these four Ends is explained in terms of promoting public international law and policy.

[9] *See* Wilde, *supra* note 1 at 49–50, 289–311.

sired: ITA). This means that I will in effect, re-open Wilde's Family one last time, to join UNCA with its relevant off-springs: 2B: 'ITA projects since 1945.' Such joining will give us: UNCA-(plenary) ITA projects in Congo, Somalia, Kosovo, and East-Timor, UNCA-(partial) ITA project in Cambodia, and UNCA-FTA and ITA in Iraq.

I will simultaneously admit a new institution: UNCA (without ITA) projects (1993-2018). I will number it 2C. This is because, as noted earlier, in 1993, following the UN's debacle in Somalia, policymakers ended plenary ITA there,[10] but, continued with UNCA. Thereafter, no UNCA-(plenary) ITA project was mounted either in Somalia, or in any other sovereign state. Instead, what ensued from 1993 in sovereign states, was UNCA *(without ITA)* projects (*see* Chapter 6).

As a result, the fully reframed Wilde's Family will comprise:

- The Constitution's internationalized making and FTA and/or ITA (by the League of Nations and the UN respectively) and
- Only the Constitution's internationalized making: UNCA without ITA (1993-2019), that work with, or without, their off-springs toward:
  a) common policies: trusteeship and the civilizing/modernizing mission; and
  b) common ends: i) free markets, ii) rule of law, iii) good governance (including natural resources exploitation), and iv) civilized customs concerning women/women's rights; and v) territorial status.

Indeed, ends i) to iv) flow from the Constitution; thus they were, as civilized standards, integral to international law in the eighteenth century. So too are they now, though as modern international law standards.

In this way, I will show that all of Wilde's reframed institutions 'are of a piece.'[11] In fact, the Constitution's internationalized making – whether by foreign states and/or International Organizations (IOs), including the UN – is the Wilde Family's *Parent* Policy Institution. I will also show that for these reasons, UNCA both, with and without ITA, fulfills Wilde's Policy Institution criteria. To conclude, an eighteenth century Civilized Standard, central to trusteeship heads Wilde's Family: the Constitution. This makes Wilde's Family one of trusteeship institutions.

Table 9.1 illustrates UNCA's salience in Wilde's fully reframed family.

[10] Other forms of "little-noticed" ITA activities such as administering aid programs / "refugee camps" continued however. Id. at 254.

[11] Id. at 312.

TABLE 9.1 Ralph Wilde's Family of International Trusteeship 'Policy Institutions' fully reframed: Admitting UNCA, a parent Policy Institution

| The Western liberal constitution, an $18^{\text{th}}$ century 'standard of civilization' heads Wilde's fully reframed Family of International Trusteeship Policy Institutions | | | | | | | | | | |
|---|---|---|---|---|---|---|---|---|---|---|
| FOREIGN STATES AND/OR INTERNATIONAL ORGANIZATIONS IMPOSE OR PROMOTE THE WL CONSTITUTION TO ESTABLISH JURISDICTION/CREATE FTA/ITA | Wilde's FTA institutions stem from and/or are rooted in the Western liberal constitution (WLC) | | Wilde's Family opened to: admit / identify the parent institution: the Western liberal Constitution's internationalized making | The parent-offspring institutions work toward common policies & ends | | | | | | Wilde's Family FULLY reframed to comprise two international trusteeship 'Policy Institutions': WL Constitution's internationalized making & FTA/ITA |
| | | | | Two common allied policies | | Four allied ends | | | | |
| | | | | T | CM/ MM | 'Standards of civilization' (SOC)/ Public International Law & Policy (PILP) Goals | | | | |
| | | | | T | CM/ MM | FM | GG | ROL | CC/WR | |
| | 1. | European Colonialism 1700-1960 | √ | T | CM | SOC | SOC | SOC | SOC | Internationalized constitution- making & FTA/ITA |
| | 2A. | 'Protection' - ITA by the League of Nations [LON] (interwar period) | √ | T | CM | SOC | SOC | SOC | SOC | Internationalized constitution-making & ITA |
| | 2B. | ITA by the UN (post- 1945 projects) | √ | T | CM &/ or MM | PILP | PILP | PILP | PILP | Internationalized constitution-making & ITA by the UN |

*(Cont'd)*

**Table 9.1** (*Cont'd*)

| | | | | | | | | | | | |
|---|---|---|---|---|---|---|---|---|---|---|---|
| FOREIGN STATES AND/OR INTERNATIONAL ORGANIZATIONS IMPOSE OR PROMOTE THE WL CONSTITUTION TO ESTABLISH JURISDICTION/CREATE FTA/ITA | | | | | The parent institution works on its own toward common policies & ends | | | | | | Internationalized constitution-making by the UN, i.e., UNCA (without ITA) |
| | Post-1993: Plenary ITA's use in sovereign states ends but continues in territorial Units alone | | 2C. | UNCA (without plenary ITA) (1993–2019) | T | CM &/ or MM | PILP | PILP | PILP | PILP | |
| | The parent-offspring institutions work toward common policies & ends | | | | | | | | | | |
| | 3. | State-conducted administration under the League of Nations | | √ | T | CM | SOC | SOC | SOC | SOC | Internationalized constitution-making & FTA |
| | 4. | State-conducted administration under the UN Trusteeship System | | √ | T | CM | SOC | SOC | SOC | SOC | Internationalized constitution-making & FTA |
| | 5. | Representative Bodies | | √ | T | CM | SOC | SOC | SOC | SOC | Internationalized constitution-making & FTA |
| | 6. | Occupation | | √ | T | CM &/ or MM | SOC &/or PILP | SOC &/or PILP | SOC &/or PILP | SOC &/ or PILP | Internationalized constitution-making, FTA & UNCA |

Before proceeding, a few caveats are required. As stated in Chapter 1, since scholars have unwittingly ignored UNCA in some ways, including treating UNCA-ITA projects as only ITA, what ought to have been discussions about UNCA's revival in sovereign states, and hence its trusteeship role there, end up being discussions only about ITA.[12] Given this, I am left with few conversationalists: those who have touched upon UNCA (either implicitly or arrived at it indirectly), and/or who, because they have ignored UNCA, rejected ITA's trusteeship role. Meanwhile, as we will *see*, the insights of Gerrit Gong, David Chandler, and Ralph Wilde, (listed in alphabetical order) are very valuable. I therefore engage with them.

## 9.1 UN Constitutional Assistance Continues as 'International Trusteeship'

*Trusteeship, Broadly Defined*

I suggest, a sophisticated and comprehensive approach to trusteeship, covers and foregrounds its *constitutional* dimension. Therefore, in Chapter 2, I started my discussion with the Constitution, a key civilized standard, showing that it is central to trusteeship. I therefore concurred with Wilde that international trusteeship comprises FTA/ITA[13] – and its parent: the Constitution's internationalized making. Meanwhile, Wilde too, ignores trusteeship's constitutional dimension. Nonetheless, he rightly defines trusteeship, in that he implicitly recognizes FTA/ITA's Western liberal constitutional dimension. Next, he rightly recognizes trusteeship's roots: civilized standards, though he focuses on them in general, arriving at them via this route which is also right:[14] he argues that the:

[12] William Bain, *Between Anarchy and Society: Trusteeship and the Obligations of Power* (OUP, 2003); Henry H. Perritt, *Structures and Standards for Political Trusteeship* 8 UCLA J. Int'l L. & For. Aff. 385 (2003); Michael Bothe and Marauhn Thilo, *UN Administration of Kosovo and East Timor: Concept, Legality and Limitations of Security Council-Mandated Trusteeship Administration, in* Kosovo and the International Community: A Legal Assessment 217–236 (C. Tomuschat, ed., Den Haag, 2002); Ann Orford, *International Trusteeship Administration and the Management of Decolonization* 59 ICLQ 227–240 (January 2010).

[13] *See* Wilde, *supra* note 1 at 312.

[14] Id.

> trusteeship concept is significant in explaining how the internal governance of the territories has been understood, – the basis on which foreign rule was to operate.[15]

And that the racialized concept of a 'standard of civilization' was used to understand the quality of internal governance.[16]

Finally, Wilde states that since trusteeship's colonial era ideas do not define trusteeship 'in its totality,' a broader definition is required.[17] I concur. I therefore, embrace Wilde's broader definition (set out below) wherein trusteeship:

1) has at its heart, civilized standards,[18] particularly the Constitution – a key one;
2) need not be imposed, for some of the seminal articulations of 'trust,' like those of Edmund Burke, do not make it trusteeship's salient feature.[19]
   i. Further, 'the idea of trust itself concerns, only the structure of relations of domination, not also, necessarily, how such structure is introduced;'[20] and,
3) may be present or operate with legal consent,[21] and
4) need not have independence as its goal.[22]

Points 1 to 4 mean that, since the Constitution's internationalized making need not be aimed at independence, trusteeship can operate in a sovereign state. This is so, even if that state has consented to the Constitution's internationalized making. Put simply, trusteeship can be present in a sovereign state, even where the Constitution *is not imposed*. However, domination should typify that state's (internationalized) constitution-making. Finally, I will adopt a broader approach to trusteeship, focusing on how those involved in internationalizing the Constitution's making understand its political character.

15 Id. at 317.
16 Id.
17 Id. at 352.
18 Id. at 317.
19 Id. at 348.
20 Id. at 351.
21 Id.
22 Id. at 360.

*Does UNCA continue as 'international trusteeship'? Yes, it does, in the ways set out below.*

First, UNCA produces that which is central to trusteeship: the Constitution. Henry Perritt is a scholar who affirms my point[23] – even though he is not aware of UNCA's origins, including its rise since 1989. Perritt does so indirectly, in the way he defines political trusteeship: Perritt traces trusteeship to the British common law notion of 'trust,' and in particular, to the British and French colonial policies.[24] He says that trusteeship gains legitimacy because it creates a liberal market democracy.[25] And that the UN acts as a legitimate trustee when it creates liberal market democracy, including appropriate institutions (e.g., anti-corruption institutions).[26] Indeed, as we have seen so far, UNCA promotes these very ends. This is how Perritt, who focuses on the UN's role in Kosovo and East-Timor, arrives indirectly at UNCA. In fact, he recommends trusteeship, so understood.[27]

### 9.1.1 Internationalizing the Constitution to 'Strengthen' Sovereign States' Weakened 'Sovereignty'

*From manufacturing sovereignty for colonies (see Ch. 3) to 'strengthening' their sovereignty as states: The Constitution is indispensable*

Next comes the generalized legal notion that the UN invokes for internationalizing the Constitution's making. That is, displacing local (Third World) actors from, or tutoring them in the activities of, making it. What might that be? The answer is: 'strengthening sovereignty.' This recalls why trusteeship was pursued by the Permanent Mandates Commission (PMC) – an inter-war period IO (and a member of Wilde' Family): ostensibly to manufacture Third World sovereignty (Project)[28] (*see* Chapter 3).

[23] Henry H. Perritt, *Structures and Standards for Political Trusteeship* 8 UCLA J. Int'l L. & For. Aff. 385 (2003).

[24] Id. at 391–393.

[25] Id. at 400–410.

[26] Id. at 441–449

[27] Id. at 386.

[28] *See* Tony Anghie, *Colonialism and the Birth of International Institutions: Sovereignty, Economy, and the Mandate System of the League of Nations* N.Y.U. J. Int'l L. & Pol. 513, 514 (2001–2002).

I will start with the notion of sovereignty, which as we know, equals constitutional independence in its external form. Indeed,

> [Sovereignty] is legal in that, a sovereign state is not subordinate to another sovereign but is necessarily equal to it by international law [....]. Absolute [unconditional] sovereignty is either present or absent.[29]

This definition suggests that the UN has re-conceptualized sovereignty on a par with the PMC. That is, the UN has embraced a graded notion of sovereignty, which implies four things. First, sovereignty is a continuum or a hierarchy where some Third Word states are considered strong (more sovereign) or weak (less sovereign).[30] How might we say these states have weakened their sovereignty? According to the UN, they have acted irresponsibly. That is, when their presidents rig elections and/or practice ethnic discrimination and central banks endorse budget deficits, and so, alarm foreign investors. In sum, bad governance equals exercising one's sovereignty irresponsibly and for that reason, losing it.[31] (Before proceeding, it helps to recall from chapter 8, that the UN ostensibly uses UNCA to implement the R2P). Consider:

> ... the responsibility to protect is an ally of sovereignty, not an adversary. It grows from the positive and affirmative notion of sovereignty as responsibility .... By helping states to meet their core protection responsibilities, the responsibility to protect [R2P] *seeks* to strengthen sovereignty, not weaken. It *seeks* to help States to succeed, not just to react when they fail.[32]

Second, bad governance does not extinguish state sovereignty altogether. Indeed, thanks to the munificence of the international community, Third World states still have a chance of redeeming themselves. In fact, it is their responsibility to rebuild their sovereignty. How might they do that – on their own? No, says the UN. States need to 'partner' with donors or external partners, that is, the BWIs.[33] I argue that, in

[29] *See* David Chandler, *International State-building: The Rise of Post-Liberal Governance* 47 (Routledge, 2010) (quoting Jackson).

[30] Id.

[31] *See* UN, *supra* note 4 at ¶7.

[32] *Report of the Secretary-General, Implementing the Responsibility to Protect*, ¶10 (a) U.N. Doc., A/63/677 (12 January 2009).

[33] *See* UN, *supra* note 4 at ¶105–106.

this way, the UN places the sovereignty discourse on the next dangerous turn.

Third, states rebuild their sovereignty in 'partnership' with BWIs, by re-building their capacity.[34] This means, as David Chandler suggests, that 'sovereignty is associated with a sliding scale of capacities,' instead of rights of equality.[35] In this way, a 'new international hierarchy' of states is created.[36] The hierarchy, so erected, eases the UN's ability to intervene, ostensibly to support sovereignty at the same time as it is undermining states' rights of self-governance.[37]

Fourth, I suggest that the areas in which states need to re-build their capacity is political and economic governance. This means, they are required to adopt through a participatory process, the Constitution, which as we know is a conditionality. In fact, this is why it is central to good governance.[38] This means that states can presumably strengthen or weaken their sovereignty, based on their ability to implement the BWIs' conditionalities. Indeed, for all these reasons, sovereignty no longer connotes a right to self-governance. Rather, it denotes the capacity and willingness of Third World states to create a particular constitutional environment –one that best advances the West's interests. So recast, sovereignty knots Third World states to the tentacles of international regulation, instead of shielding them from its sometimes perilous clutches. In conclusion, where the PMC manufactured third world sovereignty, its successor, the UN, 'strengthens' sovereignty so created, but supposedly eroded subsequently.

Does this argument fully reveal that the UN acts as trusteeship: it promotes the Constitution in Third World states with a view to civilize them, and thereby strengthens their sovereignty? Yes, and no. For, as we saw in Chapters 2 to 3, historically, Third World states had the Constitution imposed over them because they were deemed uncivilized, and so, not fully sovereign. Given this, completing the UNCA-colonial trusteeship jigsaw requires showing that the Constitution 'strengthens'

[34] Id.

[35] Chandler, *supra* note 29 at 50.

[36] Id.

[37] Id.

[38] *See* IMF Factsheet, *The IMF and Good Governance* (2016).

Third World states' sovereignty because it civilizes them. In what follows, I do just that.

*The Constitution: A contemporary 'standard of financial civilization'*

This recalls the International Monetary Fund (IMF) Director, Michael Camdessus' famous argument made in 1999 – the year the PRSPs were introduced/good governance again became a conditionality – that good governance was key to financially 'civilizing' the Third World. Consider:

> *From the Crises of the 1990s to the New Millennium, 27 Nov. 1999*
>
> The topic of your conference, focusing as it does on the challenges of the new millennium, presents a challenge for the head of an institution that, in the popular mind at least, has a strong bias toward the short term, .... ...
>
> Several major factors, with intertwining effects, can explain the recent instability. I will mention just four of them:
>
> - a new breed of national economic crises;
> - a crisis in the world financial system;
> - poverty, as the ultimate systemic threat;
> - a crisis in world governance
>
> These four factors are directly relevant to the activities of the IMF, and indeed each of them calls for large-scale changes, .... ....
>
> The financial foundations of the new structure must be based on five basic principles: transparency, sound financial systems, private sector participation, the orderly liberalization of capital flows, and modernization of the international markets on the basis of universally accepted standards. ...
>
> But, you may say, poverty alleviation is the job of governments .... What can the private sector, with its profit motivation, do to alleviate poverty? In a word, it can invest. ....
>
> Another key result of all our work on the international financial architecture is to improve the framework within which potential investors can assess risk. Greater transparency, ... the spread of internationally recognized principles and standards: all these make the task of risk assessment more straightforward. In brief, what we are *seeing* in many countries, is an improvement in governance, and the establishment of transparent, arm's length relationships among governments, corporations, and financial institutions, as are typical of mature, dare I say, *civilized markets*.[39]

[39] M. Camdessus, *"From the Crisis of the 1990s to the New Millennium,"* 27 November 1999, Graduate School of Management, Madrid (emphasis added).

Which in turn brings us to Professor Gong's valuable insights. For, together, Camdessus and Gong shine the spotlight on the missing jigsaw piece. Gong, who first introduced us to the civilized standards concept in 1984, suggested in 2002 that they had 'returned.'[40] There are, Gong states, 'what might be called 'international standards of civilization today.''[41] And so:

> Especially from a non-European point of view, one cannot speak of 'modernization' or the process of becoming modern in a historical perspective without referring to what an earlier age called civilization.[42]
>
> .... The global financial regime comes with its own evolving institutions and rules, and its own organizing principles. ....
>
> The transactional features of this global financial system may constitute simply a standard of current success, although the interface of financial capital with diverse political, economic, social, and cultural structures clearly impinges on elements of civilization, and may thereby contribute to a contemporary standard of financial civilization. Indeed, today's international system contains criteria for 'financially modern' states.[43]

Meanwhile, David Fidler, who builds on Gong, and though unaware of UNCA, and so ignores it, argues that enabled by international law, international organizations and non-governmental organizations impose a liberal globalized civilization on the world.[44] According to Fidler, the features of the new 'standard of civilization' include protection of key civil and political rights, rule (including right to property, liberalization of markets, anti-corruption measures, and so on) and a state that is able to participate in the processes of globalization.[45]

I concur with Gong and Fidler. Building on the insights I provided in the previous chapters, I will show that according to the UN, the Constitution symbolizes financial modernity, and underpins a

[40] Gerrit Gong, *Standards of Civilization Today*, *in* Globalization and Civilizations 77, 81 (Mehdi Mozzaffari, ed., Routledge, 2002).

[41] Id.

[42] Id.

[43] Id. at 86

[44] David Fidler, *The Return of the 'Standard of Civilization'* 2 (1) Chicago J. of Int'l L. 137, 139 (2001).

[45] Id. at 150.

financially modern cum sovereign state. Here is why, Third World states that have supposedly lost their sovereignty, through their irresponsible actions are required to adopt it. And this is why UNCA was revived.

I remind the reader that the BWIs, having conceptualized the Constitution as a poverty reduction tool, launched it in 1999, via their renamed conditionalities: the PRSPs. With a view to building public ownership for their PRSPs, the BWIs made effective public participation in policymaking, key aspects of good governance.[46] They completed their carefully cultivated smokescreen with this catchy slogan: 'Transparency, inclusiveness, and participation' (TIP), which gained political muscle when the Security Council endorsed it as a standard defining a modern state, including the way its constitution is made, and what it wrote into it.[47] In this way, TIP typified debtor states' *PRSP* cum constitution-making processes that aimed at modernizing them fiscally via a constitution:

- That is, based on the 'rule of law' (co-defined by the UN and BWIs), and enshrines:
- an open economy, an effective system of labor, property, contract, and other elements of a comprehensive legal system that is effectively, impartially, and cleanly administered by a well-functioning judiciary; and independent electoral, anti-corruption, and human rights commissions; and
- Empowers citizens, particularly, children, youth, women, and minorities, with the rights, capacities, and opportunities to participate in forums, both political and economic, and indigenous and global, and thereby, interact with national stakeholders and external development partners.[48]

[46] *See* Poverty Reduction Strategy Papers (PRSPs): A Rough guide 5 (undated).

[47] *See* World Bank Group, Partners in transforming development: New Approaches to developing country-owned poverty reduction strategies (March 2000); UN, *Women, Peace and Security* 1–4, 59, 112, 126, 165–169 (2002).

[48] *Sources*: UNCA Guidance Note (2009); UN-ROL Guidance Note, *supra* note 2; UNDP & UN-OHRLLS, *supra* note 4 at Chapter 2.

Accordingly, UNCA was revived to modernize less sovereign debtor states: adopt just that constitution, and thereby, strengthen their sovereignty. Consider:

> Early action taken nationally to alleviate conditions that could lead to armed conflict, with international assistance, as appropriate, can help to strengthen the sovereignty of states.[49]
>
> ...
>
> The United Nations peace-building support offices can be instrumental in supporting and closely collaborating with the country teams and United Nations agencies/offices, in developing multifaceted programmes .... Examples of this include improving support for ... promoting respect for human rights and providing technical assistance for the constitution and national institutions....[50]

This is how strengthening sovereignty, the UN's trusteeship goal, binds with its civilizing/modernizing mission. Which means that barbarity or backwardness, has economic dimensions – just as it did in the colonial era.[51] And accordingly, as we saw in Chapter 6, so does the restoration of constitutional order.

### 9.1.2 'Transparent, Inclusive and Participatory' Constitution-Making: A New Civilized Standard

In this regard, I make the following submissions, arguing that the UN makes a new addition to the Civilized Standards: 'Transparent, inclusive and participatory' constitution-making (TIP).

- The Constitution tops today's Civilized Standards. It was prescribed with a view to create within the Third World a constitutional environment that best advances the West's interests; It was simultaneously positioned as today's 'standard of financial civilization,' and expectedly enshrines other Civilized Standards (identified by Professor Fidler, e.g., anti-corruption measures, and so on).
- TIP essentially sprung from international economic institutions (the BWIs),

[49] *See* UN, *supra* note 4 at ¶ 6.

[50] Id. at ¶ 78.

[51] *See* Antony Anghie, *Sovereignty, Imperialism, and the Making of International Law* 172, 189 (Cambridge University Press, 2004).

- TIP typifies the process of making a constitution, (which symbolizes financial modernity, and so, lends backwardness, a financial hue);
- Accordingly, its implementation entails displacing or tutoring Third World peoples from the activities of constitution-making, in response to their supposed incapacities, and bad practices (e.g., excluding and/or silencing women, children, youth, minorities and indigenous groups) with a view to strengthening their sovereignty;
- In terms of state practice, UNCA has implemented TIP in an elemental way in more than 40 debtor states/territorial units. In short, UNCA operated in more than 40 states, ostensibly to implement a modern standard: TIP.
- I suggest that the UN and the BWIs have, in this way, co-added TIP to today's Civilized Standards. Indeed, TIP has entered this realm, riding atop a key civilized standard, the Constitution's back.

In this way, I argue, UNCA, which continues the Project (initiated by the PMC), and so, manifests relations of (contractual) domination, fulfills the trusteeship and civilizing mission policies, best represents the 'practices of cultural subordination and economic exploitation' to which Anghie alludes.[52]

But to fully equal trusteeship, the Constitution's internationalized making must result from domination and control, two elements I will next consider.

*Domination and contrived consent typify the Constitution's internationalized making*

William Bain has set out two criteria for trusteeship: 1) relations of domination and 2) absence of consent.[53] Here, I will foreground certain aspects of UNCA, which would qualify criteria 2 in the sense of showing that, there can be trusteeship where there is consent, provided it is contrived.

To start with, for reasons set out in this paragraph, UNCA-recipients states might fulfill Bain's criteria for being considered as 'wards.' As debtor states, they consented to contractual modes of domination, where dominance flows from powerful external actors (the BWIs) who impose their ideas of modernity (*hereafter* Modernity) and backwardness or barbarity. Finally, we also noted that the UN deploys UNCA ostensibly only in those states that have lost their sovereignty. So understood,

[52] *See* Anghie, *supra* note 28 at 518.

[53] Bain, *supra* note 12 at 149–54.

UNCA-recipient debtor states lack sovereignty, and are, thus, incapable of giving consent. So, they might fulfill Bain's criteria for being considered as 'wards.'

Before concluding my analysis of Bain's views on trusteeship, it helps to note why I suggest they are incomplete. First, (as noted in Chapter 4), like most other scholars, Bain has, for no fault of his own, ignored trusteeship's constitutional dimension. Next, in articulating his ideas on trusteeship, although he has referenced the UN's most ambitious UNCA-ITA projects in Kosovo and East-Timor, he treats them as ITA only.[54] (As I mentioned in Chapter 1, scholars can hardly be faulted for doing so.) Third, as a result, he ignores the making, or rather, the 'return' of the Constitution, as today's conditionality, and so, 'standard of financial civilization.' And fourth, he is not yet aware of UNCA, including the UN's argument for reviving it in sovereign states: 'strengthening their sovereignty.' For these reasons, Bain has not yet addressed these points.

Before proceeding, it helps to note that my objective is to consider parallels in their broadest sense, between UNCA and Wilde's other international trusteeship FTA institutions, that I reframed in Chapter 3. I also note Perritt's point that trusteeship can be 'either voluntary or imposed.'[55] I show below how sovereign states' consent to adopting the Constitution has been contrived.

First, having made the Constitution a conditionality, policymakers next framed the causes of conflict so widely, as to lend development and a particular governance model (that is, good governance), a (conflict) preventive hue (*see* Chapters 1 and 5). They then proceeded to prescribe the Constitution as a 'conflict prevention' measure, for all poor Third World (debtor) states – both post-conflict and stable ones.[56] Third, in this way, an 'entry point' opened up for the UN (and the UNDP), to produce the West's preferred constitution, in debtor states, as part of offering development assistance,[57] but ostensibly in response to the Third World's supposed governance incapacities.[58] (I will revisit this point in the next paragraph.) Fourth, as a result, UNCA appears

[54] Id.

[55] Peritt, *supra* note 23 at 390.

[56] *See* UN, *supra* 4 at Annex.

[57] *See* UNDP, Guidance note on constitutional support (2012).

[58] *See* UNCA Guidance Note (2009).

to operate with the debtor states' consent, and in lockstep with their sovereignty, when in fact, their consent has been so contrived, and their sovereignty undermined. These aspects qualify Bain's (trusteeship) second criterion thus making trusteeship in sovereign states possible with their consent, provided such consent has been contrived.

*UNCA's revival rests on powerful western states' ideas about Third World capacities*

How else may we identify UNCA's trusteeship features? It helps to note that trusteeship was conceived in the eighteenth century, ostensibly with a view to providing more humane governance than that which had been provided by the rapacious mercantile companies (e.g., the East India Company).[59] And of course, in response to Third World peoples' supposed incapacities. As previously noted, this proactive approach to remedying governance can be *seen* in the later stages of colonialism, that is, after both the World Wars, when international law institutionalized trusteeship (*see* Chapters 3, 4). Indeed, we saw that these proactive and reactive approaches toward remedying governance underlay UNCA's and ITA's revival (*see* Chapter 7). Here, I will pull the strands together.

Take UNCA's use in Kosovo. There, UNMIK wholly displaced the Kosovars to promulgate the Constitution, with a view to injecting good governance.[60] This approach exemplifies the colonial era's proactive approach. However, in Tunisia, the UN only *tutored* Tunisian stakeholders. For instance, it audited Tunisia's draft constitution in response to challenges perceived with the type of content being drafted, that is, a possible dilution of women's rights.[61] I conceptualized this as UNCA's reactive use (*see* Chapter 7).

Indeed, overall, all of the UNCA projects manifest a combination of these two approaches to remedying governance. In fact, they entail a combination of local actors' displacement from, and their tutoring in, the activities of constitution-making. Importantly, the UN controls local actors, and acts on their behalf, ostensibly for their benefit, even

[59] *See* Leslie William White & W.D. Hussey, *Government in Great Britain: The Empire, and the Commonwealth* 225–226 (Cambridge University Press, 1961).

[60] *See* Constitutional Framework for Provisional Self-Government in Kosovo, May 2001 (December 2002).

[61] *See* UNDP *Democratic Governance Practice Network* (28 January 2014)

if its involvement in all projects does not manifest the scale, scope, and ambition of its Kosovo project. These two approaches—proactive and reactive—in using UNCA (and by extension, ITA,[62] its offspring) are rooted in powerful Western states' ideas about Third World capacities.

*Shrouding the UN's trusteeship: Ignoring the Constitution's internationalized making*

UNCA's working with ITA, brings us to their common trusteeship goals: free markets, the rule of law, good governance (natural resources' exploitation), and women's rights, which fall within these broad rubrics: state-building, democratization, and peace and security.[63] This in turn, brings us to two scholars, Michael Bothe and Marauhn Thilo, *who owing to point X*, failed to recognize these goals as those of trusteeship, and have on that basis, rejected ITA's that is, UN Mission in Kosovo's (UNMIK) and UN Transitional Authority for East-Timor's (UNTAET) trusteeship roles.[64] (Note: Bothe and Thilo treat UNMIK and UNTAET as ITA-only projects).

I will suggest that Bothe and Thilo have shrouded UNMIK and UNTAET's trusteeship roles in a still more powerful way: They overlooked these missions' use to produce the Constitution, which as we know is a key trusteeship activity. As previously discussed in chapter 3, it is indispensable to achieving the goals listed above in this paragraph.

To set the context, I will first set out Bothe and Thilo's argument. Bothe and Thilo, call UNMIK and UNTAET 'Security Council trusteeship administration.'[65] Bothe and Thilo 'essentialize' all the purposes pursued by UNMIK and UNTAET in terms of restoration of international peace and security. Although Bothe and Thilo posit that these two missions involve 'trusteeship,' they conclude that this is not the trusteeship of the UN Trusteeship System,[66] because ITA (in Kosovo and East-Timor) was used to promote peace and security.[67] Wilde sug-

[62] *See* Wilde, *supra* note 1 at Ch.6.

[63] *See* Vijayashri Sripati, *UN Constitutional Assistance in State-building, in* Routledge Handbook of International State-building 143-155 (David Chandler & Timothy Sisk, eds., Routledge, 2013).

[64] Bothe & Marauhn, *supra* note 12 at 217.

[65] Id. at 219.

[66] Id. at 220–221.

[67] Id. at 221.

gests that ITA or UNMIK's and UNTAET's use to promote peace and security objectives, 'marks a continuance with, not a break from, earlier forms of trusteeship.'[68] I concur.

Thilo and Bothe have overlooked UNMIK and UNTAET's trusteeship roles in the following ways. First, Thilo and Marauhn have ignored UNMIK's and UNTAET's making of the Constitution. In this way, they have unwittingly concealed these two missions' use to: 1) democratize Kosovo and East-Timor and 2) rebuild them along the lines of a constitutional market democracy. Second, this means that, when Thilo and Marauhn essentialize UNMIK and UNTAET's policies such as free markets, democratization, and so on, in terms of peace and security, they are basically essentializing a key trusteeship activity: The Constitution's (internationalized) making. Third, in the process, they have failed to note the Constitution's salience to achieving all the trusteeship goals, including peace and security. Moreover, Perritt also identifies peace and security as a trusteeship goal.[69]

Regarding point 3, consider how great power rivalry over Tangier's national waterways was reduced. Again, how was the inter-power rivalry between the United States (US) and the United Kingdom over Iraq's oil wealth minimized? The answer is: In both instances, FPs imposed the Constitution to lend relevant territorial units their preferred political character, and thereby achieve their goals. For instance, the Constitution's open door provision internationalized, that is, opened up, Tangier's inland waterways for use by the US.[70] I suggest that Thilo and Bothe have in the aforesaid ways, more powerfully shrouded ITA's link with earlier forms of trusteeship.

### 9.1.3 UNCA Is Trusteeship, and This Is Why, so Is Its Off-spring ITA

To complete my analysis of UNCA's trusteeship role in sovereign states requires considering that of its offspring, ITA. In this regard, Wilde argues that many of the general areas of policy promoted

[68] *See* Wilde, supra note 1 at 358.

[69] *See* Perritt, *supra* note 23 at 425.

[70] G. Stuart, *The international city of Tangier* 208 (Stanford University Press, 1955)

under state-conducted trusteeship: rule of law, free markets, good governance (natural resources' exploitation) and civilized customs are reflected in the purposes and policies of ITA: free markets, good governance (natural resources' exploitation) and women's rights.[71] I concur.

I suggest this is so, because the Constitution sired Wilde's FTA and/or ITA institutions (considered in Chapter 3) and ITA by the UN. Therefore, each of those FTA/ITA institutions promote the rule of law, free markets and so on – ends that are essentially those of their parent's. It follows from this that UNCA, which produces the Constitution, enables ITA to fulfill its trusteeship goals. Consider how good governance (exploitation of natural resources), a trusteeship goal, was secured in Kosovo. Indeed, a financially modern constitution, promulgated in 2001 by UNMIK, (an example of UNCA), enabled UNMIK to draft laws privatizing natural resources (e.g. of ITA) and, thereby throw them open to foreign investors.[72] In this way, UNCA worked with, and enabled ITA to, 'modernize' Kosovo, and act as trusteeship.[73]

Again, consider what—according to the UN—laws supporting the abandonment of retrograde practices associated with the Third World require. The answer is: The Constitution, because it is the highest law of the land, and so entrenches gender equality. Consider:

> Constitutional measures to uphold the rights of women and girls, such as equality, non-discrimination and protection from violence, are critical and can shape the response of governments to eliminating female genital mutilation.[74]

In conclusion, ITA acts as international trusteeship because so does its parent.

Indeed, UNCA enables ITA to so act.

*'Comprehending the legacies of an imperial political economy in contemporary ITA' requires starting from the Constitution and noting that*

[71] *See* Wilde, *supra* note 1 359.

[72] UN, *Report on the situation in Kosovo*, ¶1-30 U.N. Doc., S/2004/932 (November 2004).

[73] Id. at ¶30.

[74] OHCHR, Eliminating female genital mutilation 18 (undated).

*'inequality in the contemporary global economy' is produced not in overt, but covert ways.*[75]

Before concluding, Ann Orford's three comments (see below) regarding Wilde's book on ITA which she reviewed deserve attention. Her review-article illustrates a work that has wholly missed the Constitution even where its parentage of ITA (internationalized law-making) and its centrality to Colonialism has been conceptually and historically established.

Orford's comments refer to Wilde's argument that ITA is analogous to colonialism, which I have referenced in my book's Chapters ( 2–4 and 7–9). For this reason, I respond to her comments in this Chapter 9's concluding section. She refers to the following five points made by Wilde: [76]

1) The Constitution provides the basis and a blue print for territorial administration: legislative, judicial and executive activities—three functions that ITA logically covers.
2) The Imperial Commercial System comprised commercial laws consistent with the Constitution.
3) FPs imposed laws, ostensibly in response to the natives' supposed incapacities to achieve ends (Ends) / Civilized Standards such as the rule of law (a.k.a. economic liberalization), free markets and good governance (exploitation of natural resources). In this way, they colonized developing states which is what first internationalized the latter's law-making.
4) The internationalization of law-making (and the Constitution's making) was roundly rejected in 1960.
5) Given this, to trace the colonial continuities in contemporary ITA projects, Wilde probes the ostensible ends and purposes for which IOs have internationalized law-making in sovereign states. One quick example will suffice. International officials displaced Bosnians, in response to their supposed incapacities and drafted the Dayton peace agreement (including Bosnia's Constitution); IMF officials sculpted several privatization laws to achieve the same ends

[75] Orford, *supra* note 12 at 233. Words within quotes are Orford's. Her review essay covers three ITA books, one of which is Wilde's.

[76] *See* Wilde, *supra* note 1 at Ch 8.

mentioned in point 3).[77] Wilde shows that ITA has evolved into an "institution," establishing a "purposive commonality" between the ends and purposes of ITA projects, colonial and contemporary. On this basis, he concludes that contemporary ITA is *analogous to colonialism.*

*Orford's three comments*

First, Orford finds Wilde's analysis of the "law and practice of administration," that is, his focus on ITA's *ostensible* purposes and ends, "very abstract and general."[78] She laments that Wilde "provides no detail of practice or law."[79] And therefore, "after 450 pages of text, ... the reader still has no... *basis upon which to respond to Wilde's argument that it is analogous to colonialism.*"[80] (Meanwhile, as we will see, given my revelations until now, Orford's second comment validates Wilde's argument, —and by extension, my book's!)

For Orford next notes that, "colonialism coercively created an 'imperial commercial system' (Imperial System) in which the 'character of [unequal] development' was determined in the metropolis through the imposition of a 'formal framework for economic activity'" and British colonial rule in India is offered as an example.[81] She reminds scholars to however, note while analysing trusteeship, that inequality in the contemporary global economy is produced not in overt, but covert ways. That is, to pay attention to the "force of law" which "operates more indirectly by sustaining the system of economic compulsions, ...the operation of markets."[82] The BWIs' assistance in making laws relating to the privatization of property is offered as an example.[83]

Third, according to Orford, given her first two findings, the key to "comprehending the legacies of an imperial political economy in contemporary ITA," lies in analyzing the "legal and political techniques of administrative rule."[84]

[77] Id. at Ch 7, fn.135.

[78] Orford, Supra note 12 at 232 (emphasis added).

[79] Id.

[80] Id. (emphasis added).

[81] Id. (quoting P. Burroughs).

[82] Id. at 233.

[83] Id.

[84] *See* Orford, *supra* note 76 at 233.

My book reveals what conceptual confusions Orford's comments create and reflect, and how they arose. Figure 1.8 suggests that she reviewed Wilde's book from an international-law-*only* lens. Orford's Constitution-overlooking triggered a domino effect whereby she missed:

- the Constitution's historical and conceptual politico-economic salience (see my Chapter 1) which is why
  - o the Imperial System comprised it (Constitution), and (lower) commercial laws consistent with it, working together toward the former's Ends —see my Chapters 2–4;
  - o its (Constitution) internationalization has globalized administrative law (GAL), including public financial management (PFM) —a typical ITA activity (see Chapter 5 and Figures 1.6 and 1.9).[85]

Consequently, and simultaneously, Orford:

- missed what Wilde established: law-making achieving its and the Constitution's ends;
- missed and/or dismissed his countless examples of internationalized commercial-law-making (ITA) to achieve liberalization, privatization,[86] and so on;

- invalidated his argument in her comment 1, only to unwittingly establish its soundness in comment 2; and,
- finally in comment 3, trained her own and our attention on GAL/PFM that serves to implement the Constitution, and for this reason, is peripheral and falls within Wilde's ITA and so, is already covered by his book.[87]

Given this, in taking Orford's suggestion seriously, we will exalt peripheral activities not knowing what creates the imperial political economy: the Constitution.

[85] My aim is not to minimize GAL's importance but to underscore the Constitution's conceptual salience.

[86] See Wilde *supra* note 1 at Chapters 2, 6–8.

[87] *See* e.g., id. at 588 (Central Bank Entry: Central Bank reform falls within PFM/GAL.).

Fidler's, Bain's, and Orford's non-attention to the Constitution recalls and affirms here, the caveat mentioned in Chapter 1: I have no immediate conversationalist regarding UNCA in the public international law field. My book shows that a proper examination of relevant international law developments requires starting from the Constitution and noting its conceptual and politico-economic significance.

*An important discontinuity*

Before concluding, an important discontinuity from the colonial paradigm merits attention. UNCA with, and without ITA excludes this goal: the direct extraction of human resources in all forms.[88]

## 9.2 Fully Reframing Ralph Wilde's Family of International Trusteeship 'Policy Institutions'

Admitting UN Constitutional Assistance: *a parent* Policy Institution:

Based on the foregoing analysis, I suggest that Wilde's Family must be reframed to admit UNCA with and without ITA, in ways explained in section 9.0. Table 9.1 shows how Wilde's Family, so fully reframed, appears.

I will now turn to show that all of Wilde's reframed institutions and its new entrant, UNCA (without ITA), are 'of a piece.'

First, all of Wilde's six reframed institutions involve the Constitution's internationalized making (*see* Table 9.1). Under each of Wilde's six reframed institutions, the relevant FP is either a foreign state, a group of foreign states, or a collectivity of foreign state representatives and/or an IO. The relevant FP imposes or produces the Constitution, and so creates FTA or ITA.

In UNCA-(plenary) ITA, the UN promulgates the Constitution (e.g., of UNCA) for a territorial unit, based on which it makes laws on a par with the constitution (e.g. of ITA). So, here we have the Constitution's internationalized making by an IO, the UN, creating ITA. This model obtained in Kosovo. In UNCA-(partial) ITA, the UN may have begun crafting appropriate laws (ITA) even before the Constitution was adopted. However, and importantly, the impending Constitution or

88 Wilde also notes this discontinuity. *See supra* note 1 at 359.

UNCA *governs* ITA. This model obtained in Congo, where UN experts drafted such mining laws as would be consistent with the impending Constitution. Finally, the new entrant to Wilde's Family, UNCA (without ITA) is itself the Constitution's internationalized making, even though it does not sire ITA. Again, importantly, here too, UNCA governs territorial administration, even though the sovereign state (and not the UN) carries on self-administration/territorial (*see* Figure 1.4). Here too, laws made by the relevant sovereign state need to comply with the Constitution (made with UNCA).

Second, in Wilde's institutions, (reframed in chapter 3), constitution-making is typified by external domination and control because a Foreign Power (described in point one above) imposes the Constitution. So is it, even in Wilde's institution, reframed in this chapter: UNCA-ITA. Imposition comes about in this way. Powerful external actors (the BWIs) prescribe a conditionality (the Constitution), which sovereign states consent to adopt because they *see*k debt relief. Further, external donors fund the Constitution's internationalized making. Finally, the mode of domination here is of a contractual type. And for reasons already noted, although there is consent, it is contrived.

Third, in each of Wilde's reframed institutions and its new entrant: UNCA projects (2C), Third World peoples are either displaced from, or tutored in, the allied activities of making a constitution and self-administration in response to their supposed governance incapacities. Thus, all the members in Wilde's Family play common or same policy-roles: They substitute for the default constitution-making method and the normal administration model, respectively.

Fourth, the Constitution heads Wilde's Family. It was a key civilized standard in the eighteenth century. During both of colonialism's eras, formal and informal (inter-war period), it was imposed to civilize Third World peoples with a view to make them sovereign. The Constitution has returned as today's civilized standard. Therefore, Third World states are required to adopt it with UNCA, with a view to becoming financially modern, and thereby regain their lost or eroded sovereignty.

Fifth, in all of Wilde's reframed institutions and the Family's new entrant (UNCA without ITA), the Constitution is imposed or produced to promote these Law and Policy ends: free markets, the rule of law, and good governance. The Constitution, and its ends, were integral

to international law in the eighteenth century, since they were then civilized standards. They continue to be integral to international law, though they are not framed as such today. Civilized customs/practices were the Constitution's fourth end in the eighteenth century. From the early twentieth century onwards, this end shaped up as rights prescribed by powerful Western states for Third World women, to save them from Third World retrograde practices and men.

On this basis, I argue that Wilde's reframed institutions 'are of a piece.'

## 9.3 Conclusion

UNCA remains on the UN's agenda; indeed, it has come to stay. In fact, as this book goes to the press, constitutional reform along good governance lines has already begun in two more debtor states: Colombia and Gambia. (This means that we can expect to *see* arising there, UNCA's off-spring projects: UN Parliamentary Support (UNPS), judicial reform, and so on.) To understand why sovereign Third World states have had their constitution-making internationalized again, requires understanding these two aspects about UNCA: its ostensible purposes at the time of its birth, and how it relates to its colonial precursors. This book makes a contribution to precisely this understanding. The next and final chapter considers how the UN revived UNCA in sovereign states and yet, escaped the colonial tag.

10

# United Nations Constitutional Assistance

## Legitimation in the Post-Colonial Era

### 10.0 Introduction

United Nations Constitutional Assistance (UNCA) was born as colonial/international trusteeship. How then has its revival in sovereign states, escaped the colonial tag? This final question is important, for as William Bain and Ralph Wilde commendably remind us, "the argument of self-determination in 1960 achieved something quite different":[1]

- It rejected not just the internationalization of two inter-related activities, constitution-making and territorial administration[2]
- But also, such internationalization on the basis of trusteeship 'in-and-of-itself'
- 'It rendered trusteeship an unsustainable practice by definition.'[3]

[1] William Bain, *Between Anarchy and Society* 132–3 (Oxford University Press, 2006); *See* Ralph Wilde, *International Territorial Administration: How Trusteeship and the Civilizing Mission Never Went Away* 418 (Oxford University Press, 2008) (quoting Bain).

[2] These ideas should be ascribed to V. Sripati and Ralph Wilde, respectively.

[3] *See* Bain, *supra* note 1 at 132–3 (second and third bullets).

This final chapter answers the query as to how the revival of UNCA in sovereign states escaped the colonial tag, based on the UN's explanations. As I will show, the United Nations (UN) has invoked ideas rooted in international law to legitimize UNCA's revival, that is, the continuation of international trusteeship.

First, some caveats. In questioning UNCA's revival, I have only one conversationalist: Steve Ratuva.[4] Next, many scholars have questioned the revival of UNCA's child, International Territorial Administration (ITA) only, and with a view to legitimizing such revival, have invoked ideas that normatively distinguish it (ITA) from that of its colonial antecedents.[5] This leaves me with only the legitimizing arguments put forth by the UN for UNCA, and second, those invoked for ITA, by scholars and/or policymakers. The second category of arguments are relevant for my analysis for, as I will show, they work to essentially legitimize ITA's parent: UNCA.

My objective is to consider how legitimizing arguments, rooted in international law and policy, have made UNCA, (with and without ITA), normatively acceptable. As might be expected, those arguments concern the Constitution, and go like this:

a) It and its ends are universally valid, (which makes the policies pursued by UNCA legitimate);
b) Its internationalized making is not exploitative because the actor producing it, or internationalizing its making, is 'neutral' and rooted in international law: The UN;
c) Its making is lawfully authorized, and so, provides a legitimate basis for UNCA projects; and
d) Its internationalized making is temporary, i.e., UNCA projects are temporary (this is a non-legal idea).

*A few more caveats*

Before proceeding, a few more caveats are in order. As mentioned previously, Wilde and I use the same research method (Wilde's Policy

[4] Steve Ratuva, *The gap between global thinking and local living: Dilemmas of constitutional reform in Nauru* 120 (3) J. of Polynesian Society 241–268 (2011); Osin Tansey, *Statebuilding and the limits of constitutional design, in* Political Economy and State-Building: Power after peace 72 (Mats Berdal & Dominik Zaum, eds., Routledge, 2013) (recognizing international constitutional assistance's colonial origins, but neglecting to question its revival in this post-colonial era).

[5] *See* Wilde, *supra* note 1 at 395–418.

Institution and Purposive Analysis) to analyse ITA (child) and UNCA (parent) respectively (*see* Chapter 1), including the ideas invoked to legitimize their revival.[6] We do so from the same theoretical perspective: *Third world approaches to international law* (TWAIL). As is to be expected, we use overlapping headings to analyse ITA's and UNCA's legitimation respectively. For instance, Wilde discusses ITA's legitimation under these headings:

(1) Legitimate authority;
(2) Legitimate policies;
(3) Legitimate administering actors (international organizations);
(4) ITA projects are temporary.[7]

However, since our subjects vary, so does our analysis in these five ways.

First, and as is to be expected, I begin my analysis with the Constitution's universalization, and all that it promotes, such as the rule of law and human rights under this heading: 'Legitimate Constitution'. Whereas, under a partially same heading, Wilde discusses only the universalization of human rights—ignoring that of the Constitution.[8] Second, as we know, in UNCA–ITA, the same actor or IO internationalizes both constitution-making and territorial administration: the UN. In fact, UNCA gives rise to ITA. Given this, my analysis and that of Wilde's, should necessarily cover the UN. Indeed, that is precisely what we both do, under b) and 3), respectively. However, I confine my analysis to the UN's legitimization as the constitution-producing actor. Whereas, understandably, Wilde ignores this aspect. Instead, he casts his net wider, discussing the UN's legitimization as a territorial administrator, as part of the legitimization of IOs in general.[9]

Third, UNCA projects are temporary. This is why, so are UNCA's off-springs/projects—ITA. Given this, both Wilde[10] and I analyse this non-legal strand of legitimization: temporariness. In fact, I agree with

[6] Id.
[7] Id. at 400–427.
[8] Id. at 408–410.
[9] Id. at 413–418.
[10] Id. at 418–427.

Wilde that temporariness gains purchase when taken together with the previous three legitimating arguments.[11]

Points four and five intertwine. Fourth, as already noted, ideas invoked for legitimizing ITA are relevant for my analysis. And so too are they for Wilde. I will therefore engage both with Wilde and, by extension, with those ITA scholars with whom he engages. However, I will engage with the latter only in the proportion to which they have tangentially dealt with UNCA, or have legitimized ITA because they have ignored the Constitution's internationalized making.[12] I will show that ideas invoked to legitimize ITA implicitly legitimize its parent, UNCA. And some aspects of UNCA, when foregrounded will underscore UNCA's and therefore, ITA's colonial continuities. In this way, I will close on the same theme with which I began this book: UNCA is salient. This is why its revivals entail deeper implications and so merit attention.

## 10.1 Legitimate Constitution

I have previously discussed the first legitimating strategy, the universalization of the Constitution, and the four Civilized Standards it promotes (for example, the rule of law) (*see* Chapter 5). For instance, we saw for reasons noted there, how scholars and policymakers used the Soviet Union's demise to universalize the Constitution. We also noted how the Bretton Woods Institutions (BWIs), which are proscribed from dealing in political matters, adroitly subsumed the Constitution under the "rule of law" label, and universalized the latter.

As I previously argued, prior to 1960 the idea of civilizing non-Western peoples animated the Constitution's internationalization (*see* Chapters 2, 3, and 9). This idea's modern equivalent has underpinned and legitimized UNCA's revival in the post-colonial era: to fiscally 'modernize' Third World peoples. This recalls Professor Gong's valuable insights[13] about the return of the 'standards of civilization' and

[11] Id. at 418.

[12] *See* Henry H. Perritt, *Structures and Standards for Political Trusteeship* 8 UCLA J. Int'l L. & For. Aff. 385 (2003).

[13] *See* Gerrit W. Gong, *Standards of Civilization Today, in* Globalization and Civilizations 77-96 (Mehdi Mozaffari, ed., Routledge, 2003).

the concept of financial modernity (discussed previously in Chapter 9). Indeed, the numerous UN job postings for experts to 'modernize' Third World states' constitutional systems evidence this.[14] Here, I re-assert that the UN legitimizes UNCA on the ground that the Constitution symbolizes financial modernity. So, in enabling Third World states to adopt it, UNCA ostensibly:

- builds their capacities in addressing economic challenges, and in meeting today's standards for financial modernity: rule of law, free markets, good natural resource governance, anti-corruption, and so on; and in so doing, where relevant, it also
- returns them to constitutional order, for constitutional breakdown is interpreted in market-oriented terms; and
- equips them to act as 'fiscally responsible' states and modernizes them in financially oriented ways.

Where the Constitution is universalized, so too are its ends such as good natural resource governance (GNRG) and human rights. In fact, this is the second way in which the UN claims legitimacy for UNCA. The UN portrays GNRG as existing for the Third World's benefit, and excluding the interests of powerful western states. In short, as an end that has 'universal value'.[15] As we saw in Chapter 5, the UN Family morphed the Constitution into a conditionality and promoted it in Third World states, to pry open their economies and throw open their natural resources to foreign investors. Moreover, this is precisely why policymakers demanded good governance in the natural resource sector.[16] And the Security Council framed bad NRG as a threat to world peace. Yet, all this lay shrouded in the portrayal of GNRG as a 'universal' value.

The idea of the universality of human rights (hereafter Idea) strengthened during, and after the Cold War for three reasons. First, during the Cold War human rights treaties cascaded, securing a large number of ratifications not only from former colonies but also from

[14] *See* e.g., UNDP-POGAR, "Modernization of Arab Public Prosecution Offices" (undated).

[15] Security Council, *Conflict Prevention & Natural Resources Concept Note 2013* (2013).

[16] *See generally* World Bank, Governance in the environmental and natural resource sector (June 2006).

former colonial powers.[17] Second, a large number of former colonies constitutionalized international human rights in the late 1980s – though this did not necessarily lead to constitutionalism.[18] Third, as previously argued in Chapter 5, the Soviet Union's demise was widely perceived as the triumph and the universality of the Constitution, and all that it stands for: civil and political rights, economic freedoms, and market democracy. Accordingly, UNCA projects mushroomed in the late 1990s, legitimized as a remedy for these rights' violations.

For instance, gender/child-audit (of draft constitutions) and other recently coined UNCA activities might have been inconceivable during the 1960s and 1970s. Why? It is because decolonization spawned numerous independent governments with both a responsibility to protect human rights and the power to violate them.[19] Indeed, UNCA statistics show only one UNCA project during the 1960–89 period, which as we saw, aimed primarily at linking Congo to the world economy — *see* Chapters 1 and 4, Table 1.1).

UNCA's claims to legitimacy as a remedy for rights violations raises two interesting and allied questions. (I will answer them in order.) As previously noted, Siam, under the threat of losing its sovereignty, and acting on Great Britain's legal advice, scrapped polygamy from its criminal code (*see* Chapter 3.) How is Great Britain's monitoring, imposed to create sovereignty, different from say, the UN's auditing of Tunisia's draft constitution[20] ostensibly to 'strengthen' this independent state's 'sovereignty'? (*see* Chapters 6 and 7.) More specifically, what makes the first intervention—but not the second—'colonial'? Is it the idea about the universality of international human rights? Yes. However, it helps to note that such universality does not necessarily flow from the wide

[17] *See* Bertrand G. Ramcharan, *The Fundamentals of International Human Rights Treaty Law* (Martinus Nijhoff Publishers, 2011); For universality of human rights idea see Wilde, *supra* note 1 at 410.

[18] *See* e.g., Issa Shivji, *Three generations of constitutions and constitution-making in Africa: An overview and assessment in social and economic context, in,* Constitutionalism in transition: Africa and Eastern Europe 74, 80 (Mihaela Rosen ed., Helsinki Foundation of Human Rights, 2003).

[19] *See* Robert H. Jackson, *Quasi-States: Sovereignty, International Relations and the Third World* 146 (Cambridge University Press, 1990).

[20] UN News Centre, "Tunisia must adopt stronger measures to combat gender discrimination – UN experts," 14 January 2013.

ratification of treaties.[21] Indeed, UNCA claims legitimacy as a remedy for rights violations because it claims to promote a constitution that is universally valid.[22]

Meanwhile, the conception of UNCA activities such as gender/child audit makes a broader point. It also recalls the query Professor Chinkin advised I ask: Can any state afford to decline the UN's constitutional assistance offer? The answer is a no. For Third World states are no longer entitled to sculpt their constitutions, free from external intervention. Why? It is for reasons of supposed public interest. The subtext is that, anyone questioning the UN's auditing of sovereign states' draft constitutions must be unsophisticated/anti-West/supporting a misogynistic culture and/or be blind to colonial practices *within* the Third World. (It would require an entire book to document the internal colonialism in Third World states.) The broader concern here is not whether a sovereign state's constitution should, or should not be internationally audited. Rather, it is about how grounds of supposed public interest are invoked to ever widen the scope of international intervention.

Finally, the idea of the universality of human rights renders UNCA legitimate in three more ways. First, it makes UNCA obligatory.[23] The second and third ideas interconnect, the second building on the third. Second is the more general idea, which Wilde too makes, namely that international law is legitimate today, because starting from 1960, former colonies contributed to its making.[24] Third, as previously noted, UNCA is ostensibly used (with and without ITA) to implement certain norms of international law and public policy (*see* Chapter 8). This aspect bolsters its legitimacy.

### 10.1.1 UNCA's Legitimization Gives Rise to ITA's Legitimate Use

ITA's legitimate use hinges on UNCA in these ways. First, the universalization of the Constitution (produced by UNCA) leads first to UNCA's legitimate use, and only then to its child, ITA's. Second,

21 Wilde, *supra* note 1 at 411.
22 *See* UNCA Guidance Note (2009).
23 *See infra* note 39.
24 *See* Wilde *supra* note 1 at 412–413.

UNCA claims legitimacy as a remedy for rights violations. As a result, so does ITA.

Herein comes Wilde's two allied and entirely valid observations (which I respond to, one at a time): First, the idea of using ITA as a remedy for rights violations explains why the number of ITA projects rose during and after the late 1990s.[25] I remind the reader that in 1999, the Bretton Woods Institutions launched the Constitution as a conditionality. Consequently, the new century saw a rise in the Constitution's internationalized making, and by extension, UNCA and ITA projects. Next, ITA claims legitimacy because the ends, which it claims to be promoting (for example, natural resource exploitation), can be, and indeed are portrayed as based, 'not on the superiority of one race over another'.[26] I agree. But again, these ends are simply those of the Constitution, to promote which UNCA was conceived. These ends claim legitimacy only because they belong to a constitution that is deemed legitimate. And so, UNCA requires validation before ITA can be validated.

Third, UNCA claims legitimacy for producing the Constitution, an epitome of financial modernity, and this is why, so does ITA. Fourth, both Wilde and I note that post-1960 international law was deemed to be more legitimate because after 1960 a large number of Third World states became free, and so contributed to its making. Wilde states that that this idea bolstered ITA's legitimacy.[27] However, I remind the reader that as noted earlier, UNCA enables ITA to implement international law (*see* Chapter 8). Accordingly, UNCA's legitimization leads to ITA's.

In conclusion, Western colonial powers (foreign states) have been decried for imposing the Constitution to perpetuate what Jim Tully calls 'constitutional imperialization'.[28] Indeed, Western states did so:

- With a view to exploit Third World states' resources, (for their own benefit and in some instances, the natives as well), and which entailed

[25] Wilde, *supra* note 1 at 411.

[26] Id.

[27] Id.

[28] *See* Jim Tully, *Constitutional Democracy and Imperialism* 46 (3) Osgoode Hall L. School J. 461, 482 (2008).

- De-legitimizing their (indigenous) constitutions and institutions that supposedly imperiled the civilized world;
- Denying Third World peoples the right to sculpt their own constitutions, ostensibly in response to their incapacities; and on grounds of their supposed barbarity and backwardness, where such barbarity was fiscally oriented, and based on racist and Eurocentric standards.[29]

Western powers revived UNCA to produce that very constitution for the same purposes. Yet, they portrayed the Constitution and its ends and standards as universal, and explained its promotion to modernize' Third World states. In this way, they claimed legitimacy for UNCA.

## 10.2 Legitimate Constitution-Producing-or-Mandating Actor

The second way UNCA is legitimized is through ideas that legitimize the constitution-producing actor: the UN. In the previous section, the legitimization involves what UNCA produces (that is, the Constitution). But here, it involves the identity of the actor, which produces the Constitution and conversely, *internationalizes* constitution-making: the UN.

Two factors have caused this legitimization.[30] The first is the way in which IOs have portrayed themselves as neutral actors and their actions as 'public' and multi-lateral.[31] For instance, consider first, how the UNDP positions itself, and explains why it is best-suited to offer constitutional assistance, respectively:

> In supporting constitution-making in a wide range of developing contexts, UNDP is well placed to assist constitution makers … UNDP can offer added value as a neutral provider of assistance … and engage effectively with a wide range of involved stakeholders. This support is most

[29] Id. at Section II; Martii Koskiennemi, *Gentler Civilizer of Nations: The Rise and Fall of International Law 1870-1960* 176 (Cambridge University Press, 2001).

[30] Wilde, *supra* note 1 at 414.

[31] Id.

> effective in country contexts where UNDP is recognized by both government and non-government stakeholders as a trusted neutral partner and "honest broker" of both advice and assistance.[32]

Second, while states are portrayed in dark terms,[33] IOs are shown as their binary opposites: benevolent and selfless.[34] In terms of this portrayal, public or community interests and other exalted values supposedly animate IOs and underpin their actions.[35] Ratuva's field work in Nauru affirms this point. Ratuva faults the UNDP for consistently using its idea about 'universal values' such as human rights and public participation to politically legitimize UNCA,[36] without caring to know how those values play out in the 'local context' in Nauru, that has long been culturally degraded by colonial rule.[37]

Whereas consider how Richard Ponzio (a UN policymaker) who refers to the UN's role in Solomon Islands' peace process (an instance previously discussed in Chapter 6), makes this argument for UNCA to build peace:

> Unlike major powers that take action when and where their national interests are engaged, the UN represents the 'international community' and, therefore, serves as the guardian of 'international interest.' ..... In particular, the UN can bring legitimacy to an external intervention and engage in negotiations ... with local actors that, in particular circumstances might, be more ready to deal with the UN than a regional hegemon.[38]

Conversely, the reification of the international downgrades the local or indigenous. As a result, not only is UNCA rendered legitimate, but also obligatory. For instance, Geraldine Moleketi-Fraser, a top UNDP official, exhorted local actors to internationalize their constitution-making in this way:

[32] *See* UNDP Guidance Note on Constitution-making Support 23 (2014) [emphasis added].

[33] *See* Wilde, *supra* note 1 at 414.

[34] Id. at 414.

[35] Id. at 417.

[36] *See* Ratuva, *supra* note 4 at 247.

[37] Id.

[38] Richard Ponzio, *The Solomon Islands: The UN and intervention by coalition and the willing* 12 (2) Int'l Peacekeeping 173, 183 (2005).

> It is important also to rely on technical expertise, especially from international experiences, to ensure that the Constitution benefits from the lessons learned from other Constitutions-making processes.[39]

So then, in terms of this view, a constitution sculpted without international assistance is bound to be deficient, and therefore, local actors are required to seek out the UN.[40]

### 10.2.1 The Legitimization of the UN as a Constitution-Maker Legitimizes Its Territorial Administrator (Law-Making) Role

As we know, the Constitution provides the framework for ITA. Accordingly, the legitimization of internationalized constitution-making gives rise to legitimized ITA. This recalls the idea about the exalted nature of IOs (considered in the previous section) and raises the question of why constitutional assistance by IOs is deemed un-colonial?

The answers to these questions can be found in the debates carried out during the inter-war period and after the Cold War. (Which means that IOs' reification is not really a post-Cold War phenomenon.) For instance, during the inter-war period, policymakers sought ways in which the civilizing mission could be best carried out, and IOs offered promise in this regard.[41] For instance, foreign-states-driven colonialism was strongly disfavored because it led to inter-state rivalry over overseas colonial resources, and so triggered international tensions.[42] The 'open door policy' (Policy) therefore cropped up as a solution.[43] (This Policy called for keeping each colony's 'door' open to trade for all states and not just the particular administering authority [Foreign Power] involved.)[44] I concur with Wilde. I suggest,

[39] Geraldine Moleketi-Fraser, "Constitutional Values and Rule of Law," Regional Conference on Deepening and Sustaining Democracy Conference in Asia (2009).

[40] UN, *A Strategy for assistance to Iraq, 2004* 21 (2004).

[41] Wilde, *supra* note 1 at 416–417.

[42] Id.

[43] Id. at 417

[44] Penny M. Sonenburg, *Open door policy, in* Colonialism: An International, Social, Cultural, and Political Encyclopedia - Volume 1 440-441 (Melvin E. Page, ed., ABC-CLIO, 2003).

1. We start from the Constitution because conceptually, as the highest law of the land, it provides a framework for territorial administration, and by enshrining the Policy, it *constitutionalizes* it, and so firmly secures its implementation;
2. Given this, policymakers found in the Constitution's internationalization – by an IO instead of a state – the best way to simultaneously remove the state from the picture, and secure the Policy's implementation;
3. The Constitution made by an IO (international constitutional assistance), provided the framework for carrying on ITA (that is, internationalized law-making). In this way, international constitutional assistance and ITA worked together to implement the Policy;
4. Scholars/policymakers do not consider the internationalization of these allied activities—the Constitution's internationalized making and territorial administration by an IO–as colonial. (Here comes Wilde's valid submission (see a.) regarding only ITA, and why it is deemed legitimate (as opposed to Foreign Territorial Administration).[45]) I join Wilde in arguing that scholars so argue because:
   a. Here, the 'other' beneficiary is supposedly the international community (Community) as a whole, where that Community is framed as 'a generalized community interest, rather than the interests of all of the world's states individually'.

## 10.3 Legitimate Basis for Introducing UNCA

So far we have seen that universalizing the Constitution, and legitimizing its internationalized making by an IO, are the two ways in which UNCA has been legitimized. The third idea (discussed in this section), builds on the first and the second, to legitimize UNCA on the ground that a legitimate basis exists for internationalizing a sovereign state's constitution-making. A legitimate basis exists because a legitimate authority mandates such internationalized making of the Constitution: The Security Council (Council). In this way, a valid legal basis is posited for *internationalizing* sovereign states' constitution-making. In this way the 1960 anti-colonial resolution's ban on *internationalizing* constitution-making is overcome.

[45] Wilde *supra* note 1 at 417.

This argument has been invoked in two ways. First, as discussed previously, the UN invokes generalized legal concepts or notions such as saving failed states, 'strengthening sovereignty', and the responsibility to protect (R2P) (*see* Chapters 8 and 9).

Second, two commentators, Henry Perritt and Bertrand Ramcharan, have claimed legitimacy for UNCA, (in the post-conflict context), on the ground that a legitimate authority, the Council, mandates it. These scholars arrive at UNCA indirectly, in two different ways. I start with Perritt. As noted earlier, Perritt arrives at UNCA in the way he defines political trusteeship (*see* Chapter 9). For Perritt, political trusteeship enjoys both internal and international legitimacy. The former stems from obtaining 'appropriate UN approval for the intervention'."[46] The latter arises from what UNCA promotes: liberal market democracy, transparency, and so on.[47] In sum, Perritt legitimizes UNCA when it is lawfully authorized, and because such authorization aims at creating a liberal constitutional democracy.

Next comes Bertrand Ramcharan, who analyses the role of Security-Council-mandated peace missions in conflict prevention, peace-making, and peace-building.[48] In this way, he alludes to UNCA, which as previously discussed, ostensibly serves to prevent conflict, make peace, and build peace (*see* Chapters 1 and 8). (In fact, Ramcharan references to just those Council resolutions that have mandated UNCA in Kosovo, Liberia, Burundi, Guinea-Bissau, Sierra Leone, and Democratic Republic of Congo, and for that reason, are mentioned in Chapter 6).[49] Ramcharan argues that in playing the aforesaid roles, peace missions intervene in areas that hitherto fell within the exclusive domain of states.[50] Nonetheless, he says that the Council is anchored in the UN Charter, and so acts legitimately, lawfully, and respects the principle of 'democratic legitimacy' when it mandates such roles for them.[51]

46 Perritt, *supra* note 12 at 387.

47 Id.

48 *See* Bertrand Ramcharan, *The Security Council and the Protection of Human Rights* 61-119 (Martinus Nijhoff Publishers, 2002).

49 Id. at 124, 126, 94–104.

50 Id. at 35.

51 Id. at 23, 99.

In these ways, Perritt and Ramcharan have implicitly and indirectly legitimized UNCA, respectively. In conclusion, Perritt argues that political trusteeship differs from the imposed nature of colonialism, when it obtains appropriate approval, and because it culminates in creating a liberal constitutional market democracy. On this basis, he recommends its use in sovereign states. Whereas, Ramcharan skips this issue.

### 10.3.1 UNCA's Lawful Authorization Gives Rise to ITA's Legitimate Use

Since ITA flows from the Constitution, it follows from the previous section's discussion that the Constitution, when lawfully authorized, gives rise to ITA's legitimate use. For this reason, in this section I will engage with ideas invoked to legitimize ITA, and in the process, differentiate it (ITA) from colonialism. I will first set out this discourse's key points, and then show how they legitimize UNCA.

First, most ITA scholars have agreed that ITA's lawful use requires the consent of the host state.[52] Second, however, they note the one legitimate means by which such consent could be bypassed: The Security Council's authorization (under Chapter VII of the UN Charter).[53] Third, scholars note that in practice, this legitimate means of bypassing content has been utilized, which makes some ITA projects imposed (for example, Somalia and East-Timor). Fourth, this brings us to the imposed nature of foreign territorial administration under the League of Nations' Mandates System and the UN Trusteeship System. Here it helps to note that although the League of Nations, and the UN respectively, had a say in the allocation of the mandate and trust territories,

[52] Wilde *supra* note 1 at 402. *See e.g.*, Michael Bothe and Marauhn Thilo, *UN Administration of Kosovo and East Timor: Concept, Legality and Limitations of Security Council-Mandated Trusteeship Administration*, *in* Kosovo and the International Community: A Legal Assessment 217-236 (C. Tomuschat ed., Den Haag, 2002); Richard Caplan, *International governance of war-torn territories: Rule and Reconstruction* (OUP, 2005); Henry Richardson, *Failed States, self-determination, and preventive diplomacy: colonialist nostology & democratic expectations* 10 Temple Int'l & Comp. L. J 1 (1996).

[53] Wilde *supra* note 1 at 402.

that allocation eventually endorsed the territorial occupation achieved by the occupying powers after the two world wars.[54]

Fifth, given points 1 to 4, scholars do not consider imposed ITA projects as colonial, for they are authorized by the Security Council, which is a global institution. Further, in so authorizing ITA, the Security Council acts within the bounds of the UN Charter.[55] Put simply, as Wilde notes, under this view, "the Security Council renders legitimate that which would otherwise be illegitimate in the field of intervention." What keeps intact the normative character of these imposed ITA projects is the existence of a global institution, created by the organized international community, which enjoys the authority to make such impositions: the Security Council.[56] I concur with Wilde.

Starting from where Wilde, and other relevant ITA scholars end (*see* aforementioned points 1 to 5), I submit as follows.

UNCA sires ITA, and so, the above argument (*see* points 1 to 5) goes something like this:

- *The Constitution imposed by a foreign state is equal to colonial constitution-making*
  1) The League of Nations' Mandates System and
  2) the UN Trusteeship System mandated the Constitution's imposition or its internationalized making.

  These arrangements are colonial because a foreign state or power was the entity that decided which territories "required" trusteeship, i.e., which peoples deserved to be displaced from the activities of constitution-making and territorial administration.

  *However, the Constitution imposed by an IO or its internationalized making by an IO is not equal to colonial constitution-making.*

  Where the Security Council authorizes the Constitution's making in a sovereign state, constitution-making is internationalized. But such internationalization is not colonial, for the following reasons:
- The Security Council is a global institution;
- Anchored in the UN Charter, it is created by and for 'the organized international community';

54 Id.

55 Id. at 402 (quote) and 453.

56 Id.

- It acts in tune with the UN Charter in mandating a peace mission:
  a) To promulgate the Constitution, which is universal (for example, UNCA in Kosovo), or
  b) To assist the relevant state to adopt the (universal) Constitution, in ways noted in Chapters 5 and 6;
- In so doing, it is deemed to be acting not on behalf of individual states, but on behalf of the international community.
  *Internationalized constitution-making, so legitimized, gives rise to ITA's legitimate use*
- Conceptually, the Constitution, so imposed or produced in a territorial unit/state by UNCA, provides the framework for the UN's administration of that unit, in accordance with the Constitution. In this way, UNCA's lawful authorization *gives rise to ITA, its* child's, legitimate use.

Indeed, these very ideas animated both proposals to use, and the actual use of, UNCA-ITA, in the failed states context (for example, Somalia). In this regard, Henry Richardson (although he ignores UNCA) comments that:

> [t]he proponents of failed states rely heavily on the assumed legitimacy of United Nations organs, such as the Security Council, to mediate such conflicts, and to legitimate actions of intervention that otherwise would be illegal colonialism.[57]

## 10.4 UNCA's Temporary Nature

The final idea, which when taken together with the three previously discussed, legitimizes UNCA is this: it is temporary. The UN invokes this idea in two ways. First, the UN sets out the approximate time it takes to complete each stage of the process of making the (internationalized) Constitution. And indeed, UNCA ends with the Constitution's adoption or the reform of the existing constitution along preferred lines.[58] Second, the UN implicitly portrays the Constitution's (internationalized) making as a temporary phenomenon, carried out in response to

[57] *See* Richardson, *supra* note 52.

[58] *See* UN, UNCA Guidance Note 9 (2009).

the Third World's supposed incapacities. For example, the UN titled its constitutional assistance project in Kosovo as: The United Nations *Interim* Administration Mission in Kosovo. All this renders its making bonafide.

How does the temporariness of UNCA and its child, ITA, enhance their legitimacy? It helps to note here that, scholars invoked the argument about temporariness regarding (and to legitimize) ITA's use in two territorial units: Kosovo and East-Timor. One reason why commentators such as Jarat Chopra have invoked ITA projects' temporary status is to resist the challenge ITA projects pose to the idea of self-determination and independence.[59] For ITA scholars, UN policymakers title their projects 'interim' because they believe they can realize progressive improvement leading to self-administration, and plan to implement it in good faith'.[60] So then, what legitimizes ITA for scholars is the UN's genuine promise cum plan for ensuring eventual self-administration. Whereas in the colonial era, territorial administration was ostensibly internationalized to achieve self-determination, but this goal was endlessly deferred.

I suggest that UNCA's temporary nature acquires purchase when it is coupled with the other legitimating ideas discussed in this chapter in this way:

- The Constitution is a universal model that symbolizes financial modernity, and so provides a legitimate standard according to which governance reforms are judged;
- Next comes the UN, an actor that helps sovereign states produce this universal model: a neutral, global institution;
- And which does so, ostensibly, only in response to challenges perceived with their conduct of the constitution-making process and the types of content created by them, and temporarily, for its assistance ends with their adoption of the Constitution;
- All this means that the UN is acting lawfully, selflessly, respecting 'democratic legitimacy' and temporarily in the interests of the

[59] *See* Wilde, *supra* note 1 at 421, n. 533; Jarat Chopra, '*UN Civil Governance in trust' in* The UN and the Civil Wars 70 (T.G. Weiss, ed., The Centre for Strategic and International Studies, 1995).

[60] *See* Wilde, *supra* note 1 at 421–22.

community, when it internationalizes the constitution-making of sovereign states; consequently, the prospect of remedying governance through international intervention is legitimized;

- All these ideas render UNCA not colonial, and immunize the UN from the following criticism that was hitherto levelled against foreign states/colonial powers: viz. that they:
  - acted on ideas of racial superiority in denying Third World peoples the right to sculpt their own constitution;
  - and imposing the Constitution (thereby internationalizing their constitution-making); and,
  - failed to prepare the natives adequately for self-rule, and to remain true to their promise of granting independence.

### 10.4.1 UNCA is Temporary, and therefore, so is ITA

Conceptually speaking, ITA is temporary only because, so is UNCA. Meanwhile, Wilde argues that state-building (ITA's[61] and UNCA's ostensible goal) does not in, and of itself suggest a short duration. Indeed, that is correct. I suggest, rather, that the state-building goal reveals just the opposite, namely that what international policy-makers have envisaged is long-term and far-reaching in scope, and here is why, they targeted for reform, Third World states' highest laws: their constitutions. Here comes UNCA and its salience. And here lies the key to deciphering that what is being undertaken, is the wholesale transformation of Third World states, along preferred/neoliberal lines.

## 10.5 The Legitimizing Arguments: What is Missing?

### UNCA-Recipients' States' Debtor-States Status

I now set out five aspects of UNCA that the legitimizing discourse ignores. Foregrounding these will serve to show UNCA's colonial continuities.

First, the legal bases for UN peace missions in sovereign states and territorial units (Kosovo and East-Timor, *see* Chapters 4 and 6) com-

[61] Id. at 421.

bined elements of both consent and imposition. These elements related essentially first, to the Constitution's making, –and therefore, next, to ITA.[62] (For, as noted in Chapter 1, conceptually speaking, post-conflict governance reforms in all areas start from, and require the Constitution.)

Second, given this, technically speaking the sovereign authorities in all UNCA-recipient-states, including Liberia, Burundi, Guinea-Bissau, Sierra Leone, and Democratic Republic of Congo (to which Ramcharan refers), consented to adopting the Constitution (via UNCA), and the Council mandated its making via resolutions passed under the Chapter VII.

Third, the Council's resolutions under Chapter VII constitute a 'particular form of imposing authority.'[63] Which means, of the two elements that constitute the legal bases for UNCA projects, the second element (imposition) stems from the Council's authorization.

Fourth, as noted in Chapter 6, given the circumstances in which UNCA–ITA was used in East-Timor and Somalia, legitimacy for UNCA-ITA's use rested exclusively on the Security Council mandate, passed under Chapter VII. (The territorial sovereign or the people of the territory did not consent to UNCA-ITA's use.) Put differently, the Constitution's internationalized making in East-Timor and Somalia secured legitimacy solely from the Security Council resolutions passed under Chapter VII.

Fifth, I suggest that all UNCA recipient-states were, and are groaning under mountains of debt. Their precarious financial conditions pressured them into consenting to implementing a conditionality in return for debt-relief: adopt the Constitution. This situation renders them doubly vulnerable. Herein lies the reason why their consent to UNCA, and so ITA (because it is UNCA's offspring), was utterly compromised. I therefore, concur with Wilde who argues that the states providing consent to ITA were in a particularly vulnerable position, due to internal conflict and external pressure. All of which compromises the significance of their consent.[64]

[62] The question of whether the Security Council does have the powers to intervene in domestic matters or even exercises those powers rightly falls outside the scope of this book.

[63] *See* Wilde, *supra* note 1 at 405.

[64] Id.

## 10.6 Conclusion

This chapter has done two things. First, it has analysed, and established the policy roles of UNCA, and its offspring, ITA, situating these parent-child policy institutions within the broader context cum history of international trusteeship. In this way, it has set the stage for undertaking their normative assessment. Second, it has provided the broader context, essential to contesting the politics of UNCA, and its child, ITA, both on their own terms, and as international law and policy-implementing mechanisms. I thus, join Wilde, whose study has accomplished the same objectives –but regarding ITA.[65]

The Constitution, as we know, is an eighteenth century, international law "standard of civilization." From the $18^{th}$ to early $20^{th}$ century, international law legitimized the Constitution's imposition in Third World states, given its supposed universality, and the supposed backwardness of these states. The foregoing analysis suggests that international law still does, and for the same reasons. Indeed, international law posits that it has sired a supposedly neutral IO, authorizing it to produce a supposedly universal, that is, the Constitution: the UN. Here is why the UN's displacing of sovereign Third World peoples from, and/or tutoring them in, the activity of constitution-making is deemed legitimate.

What about the promise international law had made to the Third World states in 1960? Namely, that henceforth, they would have the freedom to carve their own distinct constitutional futures, and as a result, enjoy control over all matters, including their natural resources. Moreover, that their supposed backwardness or inexperience, would never again be used as a pretext, for denying them these very freedoms. On the contrary, this is the very promise now being snatched back by UNCA: Its underlying notions of graded sovereignty and fiscal modernity, its ostensible goal of the rule of law (which means economic liberalization, and throwing open their natural resources to a transnational capitalist class), and its discourse's patronizing rhetoric cum hegemonic tendencies. (As mentioned in chapter 1, individual peacebuilding case studies are now emerging showing how the UN's neoliberal policies have strengthened foreign investors' interests.) Thus, to not ask this question, or to close our minds to this question, as the

[65] *See* Wilde, *supra* note 1 at Chapter 9.

2016-2019 UNCA projects in debtors-states, The Gambia and Colombia threaten to do, would be to forfeit one of the most significant international promises ever made to the Third World.[66]

[66] I would need two more books to explore how developing states can reclaim their right to self-determination.

# Select Bibliography

## Books


Aharon Barack. *Purposive Interpretation in Law – translated from the Hebrew by Sari Bashi* (Princeton University Press, 2005).

Anstee, Margaret. *Orphan of the Cold War – The Inside Story of the Collapse of the Angolan Peace Process, 1992-1993* (St. Martin's Press, 1996)

Antony Anghie. *Sovereignty, Imperialism, and the Making of International Law* (Cambridge University Press, 2005).

Autessere, Séverine. *The Trouble with the Congo — Local Violence and the Failure of International Peace-Building* (Cambridge University Press, 2010).

Bain, William. *Between Anarchy and Society: Trusteeship and the Obligations of Power* (Oxford University Press, 2003).

Baxi, Upendra. *The Future of Human Rights* (Oxford University Press, 2002).

Brabazon, Honor. *Neoliberal Legality – Understanding the Role of Law in the Neoliberal Project* (Routledge, 2017).

Brady, Christopher. *United States Foreign Policy towards Cambodia, 1977–92: A Question of Realities* (St. Martin's Press, 1999).

Bruce, Ronald, St. John. *Libya and the United States: Two Centuries of Strife* (University of Pennsylvania Press, 2002).

Castella, Graciana. *Rebuilding War-Torn States: The Challenge of Post-Conflict Economic Reconstruction* (Oxford University Press, 2010).

Chandler, David. *International State-Building: The Rise of Post-Liberal Governance.* (Routledge, 2010) .

Chetail, Vincent, ed. *Peace-Building: A Lexicon* (Oxford University Press, 2009).

Dominic, Zaum. *The Sovereignty Paradox* (Oxford University Press, 2007).

Golder, Ben, ed., *The Politics of Legality in a Neoliberal Age* (Routledge, 2018).

Davitti, Daria *Investment and Human Rights in Armed Conflict: Charting an Elusive Intersection* (Hart Publishers, 2019).

Dupuy, Alex. *Haiti: From Revolutionary Slaves to Powerless citizens – Essays on the politics and economics of underdevelopment, 1804-2013* (2014).

Erik-Lane, Jan. *Constitutions and Political Theory* (Manchester University Press, 1996).

Fabricant, Nicole. *Mobilizing Bolivia's Displaced: Indigenous Politics & the Struggle over Land* (University of North Carolina Press, 2012).

Gill, Stephen & Cutler, Claire eds., *New Constitutionalism and World Order* (Cambridge University Press, 2012).

Glenn, Patrick. *Cosmopolitan State* (Oxford University Press, 2012).

Gong, Gerrit. *'Standards of Civilization' in International Society* (Oxford University Press, 1984).

Haack, Kirsten. *The UN Democracy Agenda – A Conceptual History* (Manchester University Press, 2011).

Hayek, F. A. *The Road to Serfdom* (University of Chicago Press, 1995).

Humphreys, Stephen. *Theatre of the Rule of Law – Transnational Legal Intervention in Theory and Practice* (Cambridge University Press, 2010)

Jonas, Susanne. *Of Centaurs and Doves – Guatemala's Peace Process* (Westview Press, 2000).

Koskiennemi, Martii. *Gentler Civilizer of Nations: The Rise and Fall of International Law 1870-1960* (Cambridge University Press, 2001).

Koops, Joachim A. *et al*, eds. *The Oxford Handbook of United Nations Peacekeeping Operations* (Oxford University Press, 2015).

Larmer, Miles. *Mineworkers in Zambia: Labour and Political Change in Post-Colonial Africa* (Palgrave Macmillan, 2007).

Lansford, Tom. *Political Handbook of the World 2015* (Sage Publications, Inc. 2015).

Levitt, Jeremy. *Illegal Peace in Africa: An Inquiry into the Legality of Power Sharing With Warlords, Rebels and Junta* (CUP, 2011).

Malone, Mary Fran T. *The Rule of Law in Central America: Citizens' Reactions to Crime and Punishment* (Continuum, 2014).

Marcus, Richard. *Politics of Institutional Failure in Madagascar's Third Republic* (Lexington Books, 2016).

Matar, Linda. *The Political Economy of Investment in Syria* (Palgrave Macmillan, 2016).

Neuman, Edward & Roland Rich. *The UN Role in Promoting Democracy: Between Ideals and Reality* (UN University, Tokyo, 2004).

Pahuja, Sundhya *Decolonizing International Law: Development, Economic Growth, and the Politics of Universality* (Cambridge University Press, 2011) .

Paris, Roland. *At War's End: Building Peace after Civil Conflict* (Cambridge University Press, 2003).

Pelt, Adrian. *Libyan Independence and the United Nations — A Case of Planned Decolonization* (Yale University Press, 1970).

Petric, Boris. *Where Are All Our Sheep? Kyrgyzstan, a Global Political Arena* (Berghahn books, 2015).

Popovski, Vesselin & Trudy Fraser eds., *The Security Council as Global Legislator* (Routledge, 2014).

Ratuva, Steven. *Politics of Preferential Development: Trans-global study of Affirmative Action and Ethnic Conflict in Fiji, Malaysia and South Africa* (Australian National University Press, 2013).

Rodogno, Davide. *Against Massacre – Humanitarian Interventions in the Ottoman Empire, 1815-1914 – The Emergence of a European Concept and International Practice* (Princeton University Press, 2012).

Ritchie. Matthew Le & Mathew Arnold. *South Sudan: From Revolution to Independence* (Columbia University Press, 2012).

Ramcharan, Bertrand. *The Security Council and the Protection of Human Rights* (Martinus Nijhoff Publishers, 2002).

Robinson, William I. *Transnational Conflicts – Central America, Social Change, and Globalization* (VERSO, 2003).

Santos, Maria Deanna. *Human Rights and Migrant Domestic Work: A Comparative Analysis of the Socio-Legal Status of Filipina Migrant Domestic Workers in Canada and Hong Kong* (Martinus Nijhoff Publishers, 2005).

Sinclair, Guy F. *To Reform the World: International Organizations and the Making of Modern States* (Oxford University Press, 2017).

Spector, Bertram. *Negotiating Peace and Confronting Corruption: Challenges for Post-conflict Societies* (USIP, 2011).

Stahn, Carsten. *The Law and Practice of International Territorial Administration: Versailles to Iraq and Beyond* (Cambridge University Press, 2008).

Stanley, William. *Enabling Peace in Guatemala – the Story of MINUGUA* (Lynne Rienner Publishers, 2013).

Tan, Celine. *Governance through Development: Poverty Reduction Strategies, International Law, and the Disciplining of Third World States* (Routledge, 2011).

United Nations. *The Guatemala Peace Agreements* (UN, 1998).

———, Agenda for Peace (1992).

———, *An Agenda for Democratization* (1996).

———, *The United Nations and Cambodia, 1991-1995* (UN, 1995).

———, *The United Nations and El Salvador 1990-1995* (UN, 1995).

———, *The United Nations and Mozambique, 1992-1995* (UN, 1995).

———. *UN and Nepal's Peace Process* (2008).

## Book Chapters

Baxi, Upendra. *Remaking Progressive Global Governance: Some Reflections with Reference to the Judiciary and the Rule of Law, in* Critical Perspectives on the Crisis of Global Governance: Reimagining the Future 162–180 (Stephen Gill, ed., Palgrave Macmillan, 2015).

Bothe, Michael and Marauhn Thilo. *UN Administration of Kosovo and East Timor: Concept, Legality and Limitations of Security Council-Mandated Trusteeship Administration, in* Kosovo and the International Community: A Legal Assessment 217–236 (C. Tomuschat ed., Den Haag, 2002).

Couso, Javier. *Constructing Privatopia: The Role of Constitutional law in Chile's Radical Neoliberal Experiment, in* The Politics of Legality in a Neoliberal Age 85–96 (Ben Golder & Daniel McLoughlin, eds., Routledge, 2018).

Paul F. Diehl & Druckman, Daniel. *Evaluating Peace Operations, in* The Oxford Handbook of UN Peacekeeping Operations 93–108 (Joachim Koops *et al* eds., OUP, 2016).

Fitzmaurice, Andrew. *The Justification of King Leopold II's Congo Enterprise by Sir Travers Twiss, in* Law and Politics in British Colonial Thought: Transpositions of Empire 109–118 (Shannaugh Dorsett & Ian Hunter, eds., 2010).

Gong, Gerrit. *Standards of Civilization Today, in* Globalization and Civilizations 77–96 (Mehdi Mozzaffari, ed., Routledge, 2002).

Grimm, Dieter. *Types of Constitutions, in* the Oxford Handbook of Comparative Constitutional Law 22-51 (Andras Sajo ed., Oxford University Press, 2012).

Murray, Christina & Wittke, Cindy. *International Institutions, Constitutions and Gender, in,* Constitutions and Gender 107–134 (Helen Irving, ed., Edward Elgar Publishing, 2017).

Schwöbel-Patel, Christine. *The Market and Marketing Culture Of International Criminal Law,* in Critical Approaches to Criminal law 264–281 (C. Schwöbel, ed., Routledge, 2014).

Shivji, Issa. *Three Generations of Constitutions and Constitution-making in Africa: An Overview of Social and Economic Context and Assessment, in,* Constitutionalism in Transition: Africa and Eastern Europe, International Conference on Comparative Constitutionalism, Warsaw, Poland, May 17–20, 2001 74–92 (M.S. Rosen, ed., Helsinki Foundation for Human Rights, 2003).

## Articles

Antony Anghie. *The evolution of international law: Colonial and post-colonial realities* 27 (5) Third World Q. 739–753 (2006).

———. *Colonialism and the Birth of International Institutions: Sovereignty, Economy, and the Mandate System of the League of Nations* 34 NYU J. of Int'l L & P 513–634 (2002).

Baxi, Upendra *Constitutionalism as a site of state formative practices* 21 Cardozo J. of L. 1184–1208 (2000).

Birla, Ritu. *Law as Economy: Convention, Corporation, Currency* 1 UC Irvine L. Rev. 1015–1036 (2011).

Chimni, B. S. *International Institutions today: An imperial global state in the making* 15 EJIL 1–22 (2004).

Fidler, David. *The Return of the 'Standard of Civilization'* 2 (1) Chicago J. of Int'l L. 137-157 (2001).

Gill, Stephen. *New constitutionalism, Democratization, and Global Political Economy*, 10 (1) Pacifica Review: Peace, Security, & Global Change 23–38 (1999).

Ginsburg, Tom. *Constitutional Advice and Transnational Legal Order* UC 2 Irvine J. of Int'l, Transnat'l & Compl. L 5–32 (2017).

Gomez-Suarez, Andre *et al. Foreign Investors and the Colombian Peace Process*, 18 Int'l L. Rev. 222-246 (2016).

Grewal, David Singh & Jedediah Purdy. *Law and Neoliberalism* 77 Law and Contemp. Problems 1–23 (2015) .

Hamieri, Shahar. *The Trouble with RAMSI: Re-examining the Roots of Conflict in Solomon Islands* 19 (2) Contemp. Pacific 409-441 (2007).

Marks, Susan. *What has Become of the Emerging Right to Democratic Governance?* 22 Eur. J. Int'l L. 507-524 (2011).

Mazower, Mark. *The Strange Triumph of Human Rights, 1933-1950* 47 (2) The Historical Journal 379 – 398 (2004).

Paris, Roland. *International Peacebuilding and the 'Mission Civilisatrice'* 28 Rev. of Int'l Studies 637–656 (2002).

Ponzio, Richard. *The Solomon Islands: The UN and Intervention by Coalition and the Willing* 12 (2) Int'l peacekeeping 173–183 (2005).

Ratuva, Steve. *The Gap Between Global Thinking and Local Living: Dilemmas of Constitutional Reform in Nauru* 120 (3) J. of Polynesian Society 241–268 (2011).

Saunders, Cheryl. *Constitution-building in the Pacific in 2015, in* Annual Review of Constitution-Building Processes 31-45 (IDEA, 2016).

Sinclair, Guy Fiti. *The International Civil Servant in Theory and Practice: Law, Morality and Expertise* 26 EJIL 747-766 (OUP, 2015).

Tully, Jim. *Modern Constitutional Democracy and Imperialism* 46 (3) Osgoode Hall L. School J. 461-493 (2008).

## Policy Papers

Call, Charles T. UN Mediation and the Politics of Transition after Constitutional Crises (International Peace Institute, February 2012).

Ghai, Yash & Cottrell, Jill. The role of constitution-building processes in democratization (IDEA, 2004).

Le Roy, Katy . Nauru Constitutional Review: Background and Discussion Paper (UNDP, June 2006).

## International Financial Institutions

### Bretton Woods Institutions


World Bank, *Sub-Saharan Africa – From crisis to Sustainable Growth* (Nov. 1989).

———, *Governance and Development - A World Bank publication* (The World Bank, 1992).

———, *Structural and sectoral adjustment, World Bank experience 1980-1992* (World Bank, 1995).

———, *World Development Report 1997: The State in a Changing World* (World Bank, 1997).

———, Rwandese Republic: Report No. 14873 (July 19, 1995).

———, Report No. 16392-GU (1997).

———, Report No. 18036-GU (1998) .

———, Report No. 21301-MAL (2000).

———, *World Development Report – Attacking poverty, 2000/2001* (2000) .

———, *Reforming Public Institutions and Strengthening Governance - A World Bank Strategy* (2000).

———, Colombia: Essays on conflict, peace and development (World Bank, 2001).

———, *Aid and Reform in Africa - Lessons from Ten Case Studies* (S. Devarajan, *et al* eds., 2001).

———, El Salvador: Report No. 23626 (Feb. 2002).

———, The East Timor Reconstruction Program: Successes, Problems, and Tradeoffs (2002).

———, Report No. 25471-ANG (March 2003).

———, *Legal and judicial reform: strategic directions* (World Bank, 2003)

———, Report No. P7615 1-12 (January 2004).

———, *Practical guide to multilateral needs assessments in post-conflict situations* (World Bank, 2004)

———, *Nepal: The legal and judicial environment for financial sector development: A Review* (2005)

———, Review of World Bank Conditionality (2005)

———, Additional Activities Note on Somalia (2005)

———, *Angola: Oil, Broad-based growth, and Equity* (2007);

———, *Haiti: Public Expenditure Management and Financial Accountability Review* (2008)

———, *Interim Strategy for Nepal for the period FY 2010-2011* (2009).

———, *Roots for Good Forest Outcomes: An Analytical Framework for Governance reforms* (2009).

———, *Tunisia's request for Country of Operations Status, Technical Assessment* (21 October 2011)

———, *Report No. 70943-YE* (October 1, 2012).
———, *Interim Strategy Note for the Republic of Tunisia for the Period FY13-14* (May 17, 2012)
———, *Guinea: Report No. 76230-GN* (September 2013).
———, Interim Strategy Note for Mali for the period FY2014-2105 (May 2013).
———, *Tunisia: Report No. 86052-TN* (April 1, 2014).
———, Report No. 94005-ML (November 2015).
———, *Arab Republic of Egypt: Report No.: 94554-EG* (November 2015).
———, Report No. 101552-CO (February 2016).
———, *Report No: ACS18676* (June 7, 2016).
———, *World Development Report 2017, Governance and the Law* (2017).

## Undated sources

### World Bank

World Bank, "Decentralization and Subnational regional economies" *at:* http://www1.worldbank.org/publicsector/decentralization/political.htm.
———, "Colombia: Addressing Violence & Conflict in a Country Strategy" (undated) [slides].
———International Debt Statistics, 1970-2013 (undated).
Middle East and North Africa Multi Donor Trust Fund (MENA MDTF), *Results Story on the Yemen Decentralization and Local Governance Initiative: World Bank Support to the National Dialogue in Yemen* (undated).

### IMF

IMF, Fact Sheet: The Multilateral Debt Relief Initiative (undated).
———, Good Governance Fact Sheet (IMF, 1999).
———, Good Governance – the IMF's role, *available at:* http://www.imf.org/external/pubs/ft/exrp/govern/govindex.htm.
———, 'Republic of Mozambique Enhanced Structural Adjustment Facility Policy Framework Paper for April 1999-March 2002,' (1999).
———, IMF, "IMF concludes Article IV Consultation with Burundi," April 7, 2000.
———, Establishing the Foundations of Sound Macroeconomic Management (2000).
———, Bolivia: Enhanced Structural Adjustment Facility Policy Framework Paper, 1998–2001, *available at:* https://www.imf.org/external/np/pfp/bolivia/boltab1.pdf.
———, Kosovo - Institutions and Policies for Reconstruction and Growth (2002).

———, Report No. 04/324 (Oct. 2004).
———, Country Report No. 04/246 (2004).
———, Sierra Leone: Ex Post Assessment of longer-term program engagement (2005).
———, Central African Republic: Report No. 06/42 (February 2006).
———, Bolivia: Report No. 06/270 (July 2006)
———, Republic of Madagascar: Poverty Reduction Strategy Paper (Feb. 2007)
———, Kyrgyz Republic: PRSP (July 2007).
———, Country Report No. 07/38 (Sept. 2007).
———, Central African Republic: Country Report No. 08/14 26 (January 2008).
———, *Guinea Poverty Reduction Strategy Paper* (2008) .
———, Country Report No. 09/75 48-50 (February 2009) .
———, Country Report No. 10/136 (May 2010).
———, Kyrgyz Republic: Country Report No. 10/336 (October 2010).
———, Kyrgyz Republic: Letter of Intent (June 2, 2011).
———, Sudan: Country Report No. 11/86 2 (2011).
———, Staff guidance note on the Fund's engagement with countries in fragile situations (IMF, 2012).
———, Libya: Country Report No. 13/50 (May 2013).
———, Guinea-Bissau: Report No. 13/197 (July 2013).
———, Mali Poverty Reduction Strategy Paper 9 (May 2013).
———, Fiji: Report No. 13/370 (December 2013).
———, Fiji: Report No. 14/3213 (November 2014).
———, Solomon Islands, Report No. 14/12 13 (Jan. 2014).
———, Toward New Horizons - Arab Economic Transformation amid political transitions (2014).
———, Zambia: IMF Country Report No. 15/240 (June 2015).
———, Arab Republic of Egypt: Country Report No. 15/33 (January 2015).
———, Republic of Madagascar - Report No. 15/24 (January 2015).
———, Country Report No. 16/147 (June 2016).
———, The IMF and good governance: A Fact sheet (March 2016).
———, Fact Sheet: Debt Relief under the Heavily Indebted Poor Countries (HIPC) Initiative, March 2018.

## Asian Development Bank

ADB, Document No: *RRP:SOL 34513* (November 2000).
———, Governance in the Pacific: Focus for action 2005-2009 (2004).
———, Fiji: Update (June 2013).
———, *Republic of Mali: Transition Management Support Strategy 2013-2014* (March 2013).

———, *Country Assistance Program Evaluation – Papua New Guinea* (2015).
———, *Public Financial Management Systems – Key elements from a Financial Management Perspective* June 2017.
———, The Poverty Reduction Strategy of the Asian Development Bank (2004).
Bjorn Dressel, *Strengthening governance through constitutional reform*, 13 ADB-The Governance Brief 1-2 (2005).

## African Development Bank

AfrDB, "Bank group policy on good governance" (1999).
———, *Côte d'Ivoire Dialogue paper 2007-2008* (October 2007).
———, *Libya: Country Re-Engagement Note 2014-2016* 3 (April 2014).
———, Madagascar, *Combined report on the 2014-2016 interim country strategy paper (I-CSP) .and the country portfolio performance review* (CPPR) (2014).
———, *Côte d'Ivoire: Combined Country Strategy Paper (CSP) 2013-2017 Mid-term review* (26 July 2016).
A Joint AfDB-WB Report No. 117432-GM (June 9, 2017).

### *PRSP-Related Documents*

The Government of Rwanda: PRSP (June 2002).
Haiti: PRSP Progress Report (2009).
IMF, Kenya Poverty Reduction Strategy Paper (July 2010).
Côte d'Ivoire: Poverty Reduction Strategy Paper (June 2013).
DRC, Interim PRSP (March 2002) .
Jeanne Gobat & Kristina Kostial, Syria's conflict economy – IMF working paper (2016).
Islamic Republic of Afghanistan: Poverty Reduction Strategy Paper (2008).
Iraq, National Strategy for poverty reduction (2009).

## United Nations Development Programme

### *Undated*

UNDP, Sustainable development: Time for action, *available at:* http://www.undp.org/content/undp/en/home/sustainable-development-goals.html.
———, The Road to a New Constitution, *available at:* www.undp.zw.org.
———, Yemen National Dialogue & Constitutional Reform Trust Fund: Report, *available at:* file:///Users/vijayashrisripati/Downloads/130201%20YNDCRTF%20One-Pager%20-%20English%20(5).pdf.

——— & EU, "Government of Mozambique, Supporting citizens access to justice" (undated) *at:* https://info.undp.org/docs/pdc/Documents/MOZ/Supporting_Citizens-_Prodoc.pdf.

———, The Dialogue Fiji Process, *available at:* http://www.asia-pacific.undp.org/content/dam/rbap/docs/Research%20&%20Publications/CPR/PC_DialogueFiji.pdf.

———, *A story of dialogue, conflict and peacebuilding in Bolivia, available at:* http://www.undp.org/content/undp/en/home/librarypage/crisis-prevention-and-recovery/bolivia_s_story_ofconflictdialogueandpeacebuilding.html.

———, National Parliamentary Strengthening Project, Phase 2, 2008-2012 *available at:* https://info.undp.org/docs/pdc/Documents/SLB/SOI%20Parliament%20Project%20Phase%203_Final.pdf.

———, *Review of the Poverty Reduction Strategy Paper* (PRSP), *available at:* http://web.undp.org/evaluation/evaluations/documents/PRSP__MainReport.pdf.

UN-DPA, Yemen, available *at:* http://www.un.org/undpa/en/middleeast-westasia/yemen.

———, Nauru Constitutional Reform Project available *at:* https://info.undp.org/docs/pdc/Documents/FJI/00058097_Nauru%20CRC_Prodoc.pdf.

UNDP-Kyrgyzstan, Enhancing Democratic rule of law and preventing conflict in Kyrgyzstan, available at: http://www.kg.undp.org/content/kyrgyzstan/en/home/operations/projects/democratic_governance/enhancing-democratic-rule-of-law-and-preventing-conflict-in-kyrg.html.

UNDP-Maldives, *Fast Facts*, *available at:* http://www.undp.org/content/dam/maldives/docs/UNDP%20Maldives%20Fast%20Facts.pdf.

UNDP and Indigenous Peoples: A Practice Note on Engagement (undated).

## Listed Chronologically

UNDP, Post-conflict Assistance of the government of Japan through UNDP in Kosovo and East Timor (2002).

———, *Support to the Constitution-making process in Afghanistan, Final Report 2002-2004* (10 March 2003).

———, Constitutional Reform Project (SOI/02/003) (March 2003).

*The UN in Rwanda: Ten years on: Helping rebuild a nation* (UN, 2004).

UNDP-Angola, Economic report on Angola in 2002-2004 2 (2005) (DRAFT).

UNDP-Bhutan Annual Report 2004 (2005) .

Written submission by the UNDP to the UN Commission on Human Rights, U.N. Doc. E/CN.4/2005/133 (8 March 2005).

UNDP & UN-OHRLLS, *Governance for the future - Democracy and Development in the Least Developed Countries* (2006).

UNDP, Bhutan Elections: Fact Sheet (Updated 25 March 2008).

———, *Empowered lives. Resilient Nations* (2010).

UNDP's support to strengthening governance in Angola: An outcome evaluation (January 2010).

———, *Country analysis report for Zimbabwe* (2010).

UNDP-Kenya, *2010 Annual Report* (2010).

UNDP, *Support to human rights during the transition period in Yemen* (2012-2014).

———, *Governance for peace: Securing the Social Contract* (2012).

UNDP-Maldives, Quarter 1, News in brief (2013).

UNDP, Changing nature of conflict: priorities for UNDP response (July 2013).

———, Fast Facts, Conflict Prevention (Feb. 2013).

———, *Democratic Republic of the Congo – Evaluation of UNDP Assistance to conflict-affected countries* (2013).

———, *Democratic Governance Practice Network* (28 January 2014).

———, Youth Strategy 2014-2017 (2014).

## United Nations Development Group

First UNDG Guidance Note to UN Country Teams on the PRSPs (undated).

UNDG, Synthesis of Resident Coordinator Annual Reports 2008 (2009).

UNDG, How to prepare an UNDAF? (Jan. 2010).

## Guidance Notes

UNDP Guidance Note on Constitution-Making Support (2015).

Guidance Note of the Secretary-General, United Nations Assistance to Constitution-making Processes (2009).

Guidance Note of the Secretary-General, UN Approach to Rule of Law Assistance (2009).

UN Women, Guidance Note: Women's human rights and National constitutions 5 (New York, 2012).

# Extant Works on UNCA Proper

## Chapters

Sripati, Vijayashri. *Hammarskjöld and international executive rule: A Third world perspective on international law, in* Peace Diplomacy, Global Justice and International Agency: Rethinking Human Security and Ethics in the Spirit of Dag Hammarskjöld 477-507 (Carsten Stahn & Henning Melber, eds., CUP, 2015).

———. *UN Constitutional Assistance in State-building, in* Routledge Handbook of International State-building 143-155 (David Chandler & Timothy Sisk, eds., Routledge, 2013).

## Articles

*Sripati, Vijayashri. To my Karmic Guru-Dev with Gratitude: Prof. Wiktor Osiatyñski, Feb. 1945-April 2017, Obituary* 39 (4) Hum. R. Q. 1033-1035 (Nov. 2017).

———. *UN Constitutional Assistance projects in comprehensive peace missions: an inventory 1989-2011* 19 (1) International peacekeeping 93-113 (2012).

———. *The UN's role in post-conflict constitution-making processes: TWAIL insights* 10 Int'l Community L. Rev. 411-420 (2008).

## Security Council Resolutions

S.C. Res. 747, UN SCOR, 3062nd mtg., UN Doc. S/Res/747 (24 March 1992)

S.C. Res. 766, U.N. SCOR., 3099th mtg., U.N. Doc., S/Res/766 (July 21, 1992)

S.C. Res. 797, U.N. SCOR., 3149th mtg., U.N. Doc., S/Res/797 (16 December 1992)

S.C. Res. 814, U.N. SCOR., 3188th mtg., U.N. Doc. S/Res/814 (26 March 1993)

S. C. Res. 872, U.N. SCOR, 3288th mtg., U.N. Doc. S/Res/872 (1993)

S.C. Res. 1244, U.N. SCOR., 4011th mtg., U.N. Doc. S/Res/1244 (10 June 1999)

S.C. Res. 1272, U.N. SCOR., 4057th mtg., U.N. Doc., S/Res/1272 (October 1999)

S.C. Res. 1355, U.N. SCOR., 4329th mtg., U.N. Doc., S/Res/1355 (2001)

S.C. Res. 1483, U.N. SCOR., 4761st mtg., U.N. Doc. S/Res/1483 (2003);

S.C. Res. 1500, U.N. SCOR., 4808th mtg., U.N. Doc. S/Res/1500 (August 2003);

S.C. Res. 1511, U.N. SCOR, 4844th mtg., U.N. Doc. S/Res/1511 (16 October 2003)

S. C. Res. 1542, U.N. SCOR, 4961st mtg., U.N. Doc. S/Res. 1542 (2004)

S. C. Res. 1577, U.N. SCOR, 5093rd mtg., U.N. Doc. S/Res/1577 (2004)

S. C. Res. 1580, U.N. SCOR. 5107th mtg., U.N. Doc. S/Res/1580 (2004)

S.C. Res. 1607, U.N. SCOR., 5208th mtg., U.N. Doc. S/Res/1607 (21 June 2005)

S.C. Res. 1603, U.N. SCOR., 5194th mtg., U.N. Doc., S/Res/1603 (3 June 2005)

S.C. Res. 1633, U.N. SCOR., 5288th mtg., U.N. Doc., S/Res/1633 (21 October 2005)

S.C. Res. 1721, U.N. SCOR., 5561st mtg., U.N. Doc. S/Res/1721 (November 2006)

S.C. Res. 1734, U.N. SCOR, 5608th mtg., U.N. Doc. S/Res/1734 (2006)

S. C. Res. 1744, U.N. SCOR., 5633rd mtg., U.N. Doc. S/Res/1744 (21 Feb. 2007)

S.C. Res. 1740, U.N. SCOR., 5622nd mtg., U.N. Doc., S/Res/1740 (2007)

S. C. Res. 1892, U.N. SCOR, 6200th mtg., U.N. Doc. S/Res. 1892 (2009)

S.C. Res. 2051, U.N. SCOR., 6784th mtg., U.N. Doc., S/Res/2051 (12 June 2012)

S.C. Res. 1973, U.N. SCOR., 6498th mtg., S/C/Res 1973 (2011)

S.C. Res. 1996, U.N. SCOR., 6576th mtg., U.N. Doc., S/Res/1996 (8 July 2011)

S.C. Res. 2009, UN. SCOR., 6620th mtg., U.N. Doc., S/Res/2009 (16 September 2011)

S.C. Res. 2012, U.N. SCOR, 6631st mtg., U.N. Doc. S/Res. 2012 (2011)

S. C. Res. 2008, U.N. SCOR., 5902nd mtg., U.N. Doc. S/Res/2008 (Sept. 2011)

S. C. Res. 2067, U.N. S.C.O.R. mtg., U.N. Doc. S/Res/2067 (18 Sept. 2012)

S.C. Res. 2095, U.N. SCOR., 6934th mtg., U.N. Doc. S/Res/2095 (March 2013)

S.C. Res. 2164, U.N. SCOR, 7210 mtg., U.N. Doc. S/Res/2164 (25 June 2014)

S.C. Res 2254, U.N. SCOR 7588th mtg., U.N. Doc., S/Res/2254 (2015)

S.C. Res. 2284, U.N. SCOR 7681st mtg., U.N. Doc. S/Res/2284 (28 April 2016)

S.C. Res. 2337, U.N. SCOR., 7866th mtg., U.N. Doc., S/Res/2337 (19 Jan. 2017)

S.C. Res. 2366, U.N. SCOR., 7997th mtg., U.N. Doc., S/Res/2366 (July 2017)

S.C. Res. 2423, U.N. SCOR, 8298th mtg., U.N. Doc. S/Res/2423 (28 June 2018)

S.C. Res. 2404, U.N. SCOR., 8194th mtg., U.N. Doc. S/Res/2404 (28 Feb. 2018)


## Report of the Secretary-General and others


*Report of the Secretary-General pursuant to resolution 1136 (1997) concerning the situation in Central African Republic*, U.N. Doc., S/1998/61 (23 January 1998).

Report of the Secretary-General, *The causes of conflict and the promotion of durable peace and sustainable development in Africa*, U.N. Doc., A/52/871-S/1998/318 (13 April 1998).

*Report of the Secretary-General on the United Nations preliminary deployment in the Democratic Republic of the Congo*, UN Doc. S/1999/790 (15 July 1999).

Report of the Secretary-General, *Prevention of armed conflict*, U.N. Doc., A/55/985-S/2001/574 (7 June 2001).

*Report on the Secretary-General on Côte d'Ivoire*, U.N. Doc., S/2003/374 (26 March 2003).

*Second special report of the Secretary-General on the United Nations Organization Mission in the*

*Second Report of the Secretary-General on Côte d'Ivoire*, U.N. Doc., S/2003/1069 (4 November 2003).

*Democratic Republic of the Congo*, U.N. Doc., S/2003/566 (27 May 2003).

*Third special report of the Secretary-General on the United Nations Organization Mission in the Democratic Republic of the Congo*, U.N. Doc., S/2004/650 (16 August 2004).

Report of the Secretary-General, *The rule of law and transitional justice in conflict and post-conflict societies* UN Doc., S/2004/616 (23 August 2004).

*Second report of the Secretary-General on the United Nations operation in Burundi*, U.N. Doc., S/2004/902 (15 November 2004).

First *report of the Secretary-General on the United Nations Operation in Burundi*, U.N. Doc., S/2004/682 (25 August 2004).

*Report of the Secretary-General on the situation in the Central African Republic and the activities of the United Nations Peace-Building Support Office in the Central African Republic*, U.N. Doc. S/2004/1012 (23 December 2004).

*Report of the Secretary-General on the work of the Organization*, Supplement No. 1, UN Doc. (A/60/1) (2005) .

*Report of the Secretary-General, Children and armed conflict*, U.N. Doc. A/59/695-S/2005/72 (9 Feb. 2005) .

*Fourth report of the Secretary-General on the United Nations Operation in Burundi*, U.N. Doc., S/2005/328 (19 May 2005).

*Third report of the Secretary-General on the United Nations Operation in Burundi*, U.N. Doc. S/2005/149 (8 March 2005).

*Report of the Secretary-General, Progress report on the prevention of armed conflict*, UN Doc. A/60/891 (18 July 2006).

*Second Report of the Secretary-General on the UN Integrated Office in Sierra Leone*, U.N. Doc. S/2006/695 (29 August 2006).

*Report of the Secretary-General on developments in Guinea-Bissau on the activities of the United Nations Peacebuilding Support Office in that country*, U.N. Doc. S/2005/174 (16 March 2005).

*Thirteenth progress report of the Secretary-General on the United Nations Operation in Côte d'Ivoire*, U.N. Doc., S/2007/275 (14 May 2007).

*Report of the Special Envoy of the Secretary-General on Kosovo's future status*, U.N. Doc. S/2007/168 (26 March 2007).

*Report of the Secretary-General on peace-building in the immediate aftermath of conflict*, UN Doc. A/63/881-S/2009/304 (11 June 2009).

*Report of the secretary-general on the situation in Mali*, U.N. Doc. S/2013/582 (October 2013).

*Sixth report of the Secretary-General on the United Nations Integrated office in Sierra Leone*, U.N. Doc. S/2008/281 (29 April 2008).

*Report of the Secretary-General on the United Nations Interim Administration Mission in Kosovo*, UN Doc., S/2008/354 (12 June 2008).

*Report of the Secretary-General, Implementing the Responsibility to Protect*, U.N. Doc., A/63/677 (12 January 2009).

*Report of the Secretary-General on the United Nations Stabilization Mission in Haiti*, U.N. Doc., S/2009/129 (6 March 2009).

Report of the Secretary-General, *National Institutions for the promotion and protection of human rights*, UN Doc. A/HRC/16/76 (7 February 2011).

*Twenty-fourth progress report of the Secretary-General on the UN Mission in Liberia*, U.N. Doc. S/2012/641 (2012).

*Report of the Secretary-General on the United Nations Office in Burundi*, §D, F U.N. Doc., S/2013/36 (18 January 2013).

*Report of the Secretary-General, United Nations Political Missions* U.N. Doc. A/68/223 (29 July 2013).

*Report of the Secretary-General on the restoration of constitutional order in Guinea-Bissau*, UN Doc. S/2014/332 (12 May 2014).

*Report of the Secretary-General on the United Nations Stabilization Mission in Haiti*, U.N. Doc., S/2016/225 (8 March 2016).

*Special report of the Secretary-General on the UN Operation in Côte d'Ivoire*, U.N. Doc. S/2016/297 (31 March 2016).

*Secretary-General welcomes adoption of new constitution in Côte d'Ivoire*, Press release, SG/SM/18249-AFR/3481 (2 November 2016).

*Report of the Secretary-General on the United Nations Verification Mission in Colombia*, UN Doc., S/2017/745 (30 August 2017).

*Report of the Special Rapporteur on violence against women, its causes and consequences*, U.N. Doc. A/HRC/23/49/Add.1 (22 February 2013) .

## Constitutions (Listed Country-Wise and Alphabetically)

The Constitution of the Islamic Republic of Afghanistan, 2004

The Constitution of The Kingdom of Bhutan, 2008

Constitution of the Pluri-National State of Bolivia: January 25, 2009

Burundi's Constitution of 2005

Central African Republic's Constitution of 2004 with Amendments through 2010

The Constitution of the Kingdom of Cambodia, 1993 (as Amended to 1999)

Côte d'Ivoire's Constitution of 2016

*Régime international de la Crète* (Constitution du 16/29 avril 1899).

The Constitution of the Democratic Republic of the Congo, 2005

The Constitution of the Arab Republic of Egypt, 2012

Constitution of the Democratic Republic of East Timor, 2002

Constitution of the Republic of Fiji, 2013

Guinea Constitution of 7 May 2010

Constitution of the Republic of Guinea-Bissau, Adopted in 1984, amended in 1991, 1993, 1996
Draft Constitution of Guinea-Bissau, 2015 (on file) provided by UN official, Gabriel Dava
Haiti's Constitution of 1987 with Amendments through 2012
Iraq's Constitution of 2005
Coalition Provisional Authority, Law of Administration for the State of Iraq fo the Transitional Period, 8 March 2004
The Constitution of Kenya, 2010
UNMIK Regulation No. 2001/9 of 15 May 2001.
Constitution of the Republic of Kosovo, 2010
Kyrgyzstan's Constitution of 2010
Madagascar's Constitution of 2010
Constitution of the Republic of Maldives, 2008
Constitution of the Republic of Mozambique, 2004
The Constitution of the Kingdom of Nepal, 2015
Interim Constitution of Nepal, 2007
2013 Draft Federal Constitution of Solomon Islands
Somali Transitional Charter, Transitional Federal Charter for the Somali Republic, February 2004
The Federal Republic of Somalia Provisional Constitution, August 2012
The Interim National Constitution of the Republic of Sudan, 2005
The Interim Constitution of Southern Sudan, 2005
The Transitional Constitution of the Republic of South Sudan, 2011
Tunisia's Constitution of 2014
Yemen's Draft Constitution, 2015
Constitution of Zambia (Amendment) [No. 2 of 2016]
Zimbabwe's Constitution of 2013

# Index

# About the Author

**Vijayashri Sripati** is a visiting scholar at The University of Toledo, Ohio (2019–20). An expert on United Nations Constitutional Assistance (UNCA), she writes on topics at the intersection of constitutional law and human rights. With an LL.B. from India, she pursued higher studies in law in the US, UK, and Canada. She pursued her doctoral and post-doctoral studies in Canada, at Osgoode Hall Law School and University of Toronto, respectively. As a human rights scholar she has published widely in the fields of public law and human rights and has advised India's National Human Rights Commission. She has served as a visiting scholar at Harvard Law School, USA, and at the Danish Centre for Human Rights, Denmark. Sripati has won many prestigious awards and scholarships including the CN$ 3,500 prize for 'best essay in human rights' (awarded by the Sheldon Chumir Foundation for Ethics in Leadership, Canada). She has lectured on human rights in India, Canada, Denmark, and the US.